Understanding Everyday Life

Sociology and Society

This book is part of a series produced in association with The Open University. The complete list of books in the series is as follows:

Understanding Everyday Life, edited by Tony Bennett and Diane Watson

Social Differences and Divisions, edited by Peter Braham and Linda Janes

Social Change, edited by Tim Jordan and Steve Pile

The Uses of Sociology, edited by Peter Hamilton and Kenneth Thompson

The books form part of the Open University course DD201 *Sociology and Society*. Details of this and other Open University courses can be obtained from the Call Centre, PO Box 724, The Open University, Milton Keynes MK7 6ZS, United Kingdom: tel. +44 (0)1908 653231, e-mail ces-gen@open.ac.uk

For availability of other course components, contact Open University Worldwide Ltd, The Berrill Building, Walton Hall, Milton Keynes MK7 6AA, United Kingdom: tel. +44 (0)1908 858785; fax +44 (0)1908 858787; e-mail ouwenq@open.ac.uk; website http://www.ouw.co.uk

Understanding Everyday Life

edited by Tony Bennett and Diane Watson

First published 2002 by Blackwell; written and produced by The Open University

Blackwell Publishers

108 Cowley Road
Oxford OX4 1JF
UK

238 Main Street
Cambridge, Massachusetts 02142
USA

Index compiled by Isobel McLean

Edited, designed and typeset by The Open University

Printed and bound in the United Kingdom by the Alden Group, Oxford

British Library Cataloguing in Publication Data

A catalogue record for this book is available from The British Library.

Library of Congress Cataloguing in Publication Data

A catalogue record for this book has been requested.

ISBN   0 631 23307 5 (hbk)
        0 631 23308 3 (pbk)

1.1

Contents

The Open University Course Team

Hedley Bashforth, Tutor Panel Member and Author
Melanie Bayley, Editor
Tony Bennett, Joint Course Chair, Author and Book Editor
Peter Braham, Author and Book Editor
Lene Connolly, Print Buying Controller
Margaret Dickens, Print Buying Co-ordinator
Richard Doak, Tutor Panel Member and Author
Molly Freeman, Course Secretary
Richard Golden, Production and Presentation Administrator
Peter Hamilton, Author and Book Editor
Celia Hart, Picture Researcher
Sue Hemmings, Author
David Hesmondhalgh, Media Author
Karen Ho, Course Secretary
Rich Hoyle, Graphic Designer
Jonathan Hunt, Co-publishing Advisor
Denise Janes, Course Secretary
Linda Janes, Author and Book Editor
Yvonne Jewkes, Tutor Panel Member and Author
Tim Jordan, Author and Book Editor
Hugh Mackay, Author
Liz McFall, Author
Margaret McManus, Copyrights Co-ordinator
Gerry Mooney, Author
Karim Murji, Author
Janet Parr, Tutor Panel Member and Author
Steve Pile, Author and Book Editor
Winifred Power, Editor
Peter Redman, Author
Roger Rees, Course Manager
Norma Sherratt, Author
Elizabeth B. Silva, Author
Kenneth Thompson, Joint Course Chair, Author and Book Editor
Diane Watson, Author and Book Editor
Emma Wheeler, Production and Presentation Administrator
Kathryn Woodward, Author

Consultant Authors

Mitchell Dean, Macquarie University
Celia Lury, Goldsmiths College
Jim McGuigan, Loughborough University
Mike Savage, University of Manchester
Merl Storr, University of East London
Bryan S. Turner, University of Cambridge

External Assessor

Rosemary Pringle, University of Southampton

Preface to the series

Sociology and Society is a series of four books designed as an introduction to the sociological study of modern society. The books form the core study materials for The Open University course *Sociology and Society* (DD201), which aims to provide an attractive and up-to-date introduction to the key concerns and debates of contemporary sociology. They also take account of the ways in which sociology has been shaped by dialogue with adjacent disciplines and intellectual movements, such as cultural studies and women's studies.

The first book in the series is *Understanding Everyday Life*, whose aim is to 'defamiliarize' our relations to everyday life by showing how the perspectives of sociology, cultural studies and feminism can throw new light on, and prompt a reflexive attention to, varied aspects of day-to-day social life that are usually taken for granted. The book is designed as a means of illustrating and debating different aspects of everyday life in a number of key sites – the home, the street, the pub, the neighbourhood and community – and in various social activities, such as work and consumption, and teenage romance.

The second book, *Social Differences and Divisions*, in addition to looking at class, which sociologists have treated as one of the central forms of social stratification, also explores social differences and divisions based on gender, 'race' and ethnicity. The book then examines the concepts of citizenship and social justice – concepts that both reflect and influence the perception of social divisions. Finally, the book contains case studies of two key sectors – education and housing – which highlight significant divisions and inequalities; it also looks at the social policies that have been designed to address them.

Social Change, the third book, shows how, from sociology's early concerns with the transition to industrial and democratic social forms to recent debates over the rise of information, networked or global societies, sociology has been centrally concerned with the nature and meaning of social change. However, the book seeks to frame these debates through an explicit examination of the spaces and times of social change. Social transformations are exemplified and questioned by looking at the ways in which societies organize space–time relations. The topics and examples include: urbanism and the rhythms of city life, colonialism and post-colonialism, the alleged transition from industrial to information society, new media and time–space reconfiguration, intimacy and the public sphere, and the regulation of the self. Finally, it examines new perspectives on how sociology itself is implicated in social change.

The last book in the series, *The Uses of Sociology*, discusses the various ways in which sociology is practised and the consequences of sociological activity for public affairs. It explores the main debates in sociology concerning its social purposes. Comparing and contrasting different sociological traditions in sociological thought, it examines a variety of their engagements with 'the social'.

The relevance of sociological knowledge is considered in relation to government, the public sphere (including the media), economic life, social movements, 'race' and ethnicity. The book also considers related questions, such as whether sociology is a science or a cultural endeavour, and whether sociological research and analysis can be detached and unbiased. Finally, it considers different views of what Max Weber called the 'vocation' of sociology, and asks whether sociologists have taken the role of prophets – criticizing present social arrangements and envisaging possible future developments.

Although edited volumes, each of the chapters has been specially commissioned for the series in order to provide a coherent and up-to-the minute introduction to sociology. Each chapter is accompanied by a set of extracts from key, previously published, readings that are relevant to the chapter topic. At the end of each book there is also a set of 'generic' readings selected for their broader relevance to the overall themes of the book. Together these supply a wider view of the subject, with samples of historically important writing as well as of current approaches. Throughout the chapters, key terms and names are highlighted. These can be further studied by consulting a sociological dictionary, such as *The Blackwell Dictionary of Sociology* or *The Penguin Dictionary of Sociology*. The overall approach taken is interactive, and we hope general readers will use the activities and the questions based on the readings in order to engage actively with the texts.

Tony Bennett
Kenneth Thompson
on behalf of The Open University Course Team

Understanding everyday life: introduction

Tony Bennett and Diane Watson

The sociology of everyday life enjoys a distinctive place within sociology as an area of inquiry in which the study of the forms of social behaviour and social interaction that take place within everyday social settings and the analysis of more general social processes and relationships meet and intermesh. This is why the topic of everyday life is an ideal starting-point for a series of books on *Sociology and Society*. For it can serve both to introduce particular aspects of the relations between sociology and society, as well as providing a gateway to the concerns of sociology more generally, by illustrating how the major questions of sociology are caught up in the analysis of the seemingly insignificant routines of everyday life.

Our concerns in this book accordingly have a dual orientation. For they focus, on the one hand, on the particular social sites that are most strongly associated with everyday life – with the home, places of work, the pub, the street, and community, for example. Our aim here is to look at these in close detail in order to bring out their often unnoticed but distinctive social characteristics and dynamics. On the other hand, we are also concerned to see how the routine and familiar aspects of everyday life look when viewed through the lens of broader sociological perspectives. How is what happens in these varied sites of everyday life affected by considerations of class, gender, age and ethnicity, and by the forms of power associated with these? How is everyday life affected by changes in the organization of economic production and the relations between work and leisure that these bring in their wake?

These, then, are the types of question that will be to the forefront of our concerns in this book. However, it will be useful before looking more closely at the issues that such questions involve, to provide two more general settings for our concerns. The first has to do with the historical factors which account for the emergence of everyday life as a significant topic of interest and inquiry, not just in sociology but in contemporary journalistic and documentary practice too, and, indeed, in the affairs of government and business. The second concerns the different ways in which the study of everyday life has been approached within different schools of sociological thought.

The emergence of everyday life

It might seem a little odd to speak of 'the emergence of everyday life'. For if by everyday life we mean the rhythms and routines of daily existence, there is a sense in which everyday life is as old as human society. Yet there is another sense in which everyday life is a relatively recent invention. The concept does not make its first appearance in social thought until the 1920s, while its emergence as a recognized area of inquiry in sociology is limited largely to the period after the Second World War. We need, therefore, to have a more intermediate historical horizon in view – somewhere in-between 'as old as human society' and the post-war period – if we are to understand how and why everyday life first began to come into focus as a matter of interest. For in its current usage, the concept of everyday life does not just refer to whatever might happen in a day, or in each and every day. It also usually brings with it the connotation of ordinariness. When we speak of everyday life, it is usually the daily lives of 'ordinary people' – members of the working and middle classes – that are at issue rather than exclusively the daily lives of the members of powerful social elites or classes. Its focus, to put the point colloquially, is more on the 'poor and nameless' than on the 'rich and famous', though they are also seen as being caught up in the mundane aspects of everyday life pretty much like everyone else.

There is, then, a socially levelling aspect to the concept. Everyday life is also depicted as ordinary in the sense that it is not imbued with any special religious, ritual or magical significance. In this sense, the emergence of the concept of everyday life is closely associated with what Max Weber called the 'disenchantment of the world', the severance of daily life from higher-order systems of meaning or belief. Everyday life is just that: how we get along on a day-to-day basis. As such, the concept of the everyday implies a contrast between some kinds of days and others – between weekdays and weekends, for example, or between the rhythms of regular working life and the occasions when these are punctuated by special events, holidays or celebrations when everyday time is suspended in favour of particular kinds of religious or festive time.

It can be seen even from these brief comments that the concept of everyday life is more specific – socially and historically – than, at first sight, it appears. To speak of the 'emergence of everyday life' is thus a way of recognizing that its perception as everyday depended on the development of a set of distinctions between some kinds of days and others, and on the perception that everyday life was something that all members of a society shared. If, therefore, we want to know why the everyday life of all social classes became a matter of interest, we need to ask first *when* and, second, *why* did the routine aspects of the lives of ordinary people come to seem – in spite of their ordinariness – to be worth knowing and recording? The answer to the first of these questions, at least for Western European countries, their colonies and North America, is: mainly over the course of the late eighteenth and early nineteenth centuries. As to the second question, we can begin to answer this by briefly considering three perspectives, each of which throws a different light on how, why and with what consequences the everyday lives of the members of less powerful social groups and classes have come to be made visible within fields of thought and representation which had hitherto been concerned more-or-less exclusively with the exceptional lives of those who were rich, powerful or famous.

The *first perspective* arises out of Jürgen Habermas's discussion of how the meanings associated with the concept of 'public' have changed in the course of western history (Habermas, 1989). We tend, nowadays, when we think of something as public, to view it as something that is common, ordinary, shared: we think of 'the public' as including everyone, for example. However, in the late medieval and early modern periods, the concept had exactly the opposite meaning. For something to be regarded as worthy of being represented in public – that is, of being written about in a history, or as the subject for a statue or a painting, or for stamping on a coin or medal – it had to be associated with persons of high status. Only kings, queens, lords and princes were regarded as fitting secular subjects for paintings; only members of royalty and of the aristocracy, as well as noted artists and intellectuals, were the fitting subjects for histories; and only kings and queens and great military leaders could have their statues in public places, or have their images imprinted on coins and medals. What was ordinary, shared or common could not become public in this sense.

One part of the story behind the emergence of everyday life as an object of interest, then, consists in the gradual and progressive expansion of what is thought to be worthy of public representation as our understanding of the concept of 'public' has itself been expanded and come to be more democratic. There are many aspects to this process. The expansion of the suffrage to include all adult members of society is obviously crucial in establishing the principle that all the members of a society are of equal worth politically: one person, one vote. But account has also to be taken of developments in the cultural sphere which have vastly expanded the range of what can be judged appropriate subjects for public representation. These developments include, in the seventeenth and eighteenth centuries, the emergence of still life paintings focused on everyday domestic scenes, the extension of portraiture from the gentry and aristocracy to the middle classes, and the rise of the novel, a literary genre which brought the ordinary lives and preoccupations of the middle classes into the purview of literary representation. They would include, in the nineteenth century, the development of photography which vastly expanded the reach of earlier forms of portraiture as it became possible for people from all walks of life to commission individual, family and group photographs. They would include, in the twentieth century, the development of new forms of photo-journalism and documentary film that circulated, to a newly-created mass public, depictions of their own everyday lives and circumstances via new cultural forms (papers like *Picture Post*) and new venues (the cinema). And they would include television which, in both its fictional genres (soap operas) and its documentary forms (fly-on-the wall documentaries of family life), has prepared the ground for the new ways of representing and circulating representations of everyday life associated with 24-hour webcam transmissions of people eating, sleeping, watching television, washing, dressing and working.

There is, however, to come to the *second perspective*, another aspect to the role played by these varied cultural technologies – photography, cinema, television, the internet – in extending the range of what is judged to be worthy of public representation. This concerns their relation to the development of new forms of social discipline and the forms of surveillance these have generated. Michel Foucault's comments on what he calls a reversal in the axis of individualization associated with the development of modern forms of discipline – the prison, the school, the hospital and asylum, the police – take us to the heart of the issues at stake here. Like Habermas, Foucault characterizes feudal and absolutist regimes as ones in which 'individualization is greatest where sovereignty is exercised and in the higher echelons of power' (Foucault, 1977, p.192). This is because these are regimes in which 'power was what was seen, what was shown and what was manifested' (*ibid.*, p.187). The power of the king, for example, depended on images of royal power being put into public circulation and magnified through the spectacles of palaces, tournaments and processions. By contrast, those over whom power was exercised in such regimes – the peasantry and artisans, for example – tended to remain 'in the shade', eclipsed in significance by a power that entirely overshadowed them.

These, then, are regimes in which the source of power is visible and individualized, whereas those over whom power is exercised remain, by and large, invisible and anonymous. In modern forms of discipline, by contrast, these relationships are reversed: the source of power becomes invisible, anonymous and bureaucratized, whereas those over whom power is exercised – the inmates of a prison or of an asylum, the pupils of a school or, more generally, the citizens of a nation-state – are made more visible in new ways in order precisely that they might be better controlled and regulated. This results in what Foucault calls 'descending individualization' (*ibid.*, p.192) as those over whom power is exercised come to be known more and more individually, rather than as parts of an anonymous mass, through an accumulation of records, case histories and visual reproductions relating to each and every prisoner (photographs on entry, probation reports), pupil (examination results and annual reports), patient (medical records) and citizen (passports, driving licences).

It is, then, as part of this more general tendency toward a 'disciplinary society' (a much contested term, but we can let it stand for our purposes) that an interest in knowing more about the everyday lives of ordinary people begins to emerge. This was evident, in the late nineteenth century, in the large number of social surveys – some of them statistical in form, but others depending on first-hand observations and interviews – which aimed, in a telling phrase proposed by Mary Poovey, at the 'ocular penetration' of the lives of the poor (Poovey, 1995, p.35). Examinations of the conditions of housing of the urban poor; studies of their conditions of work; accounts of their pastimes and leisure pursuits: in all of these ways, the late nineteenth century witnesses an accumulating documentation – statistical, photographic and textual – of the everyday lives of the urban poor in order, precisely, to make these sections of the population more visible to, and hence more governable by, new forms of bureaucratic and disciplinary power.

It is worth noting the respects in which these developments connected with the intersecting histories of racism and colonialism. For many of the techniques that were later to be used in making visible the conditions of life and everyday routines of the poor and working classes in Europe were first developed in the context of colonial administrations. Fingerprinting had its origins as a means of differentiating people who, to the colonial eye, 'all looked the same' (Ginzburg, 1980); the classification of populations into ethnic groups so that they might easily be identified was first developed in the colonial administration of India; and the techniques of participant observation – living among a people while observing their customs – and of ethnographic film and photography were first developed by anthropologists in the context of the boom in fieldwork studies that characterized early twentieth-century anthropology (Edwards, 1992). These techniques for knowing and making visible individuals and groups in the context of large populations have all subsequently become a regular part of the ways in which 'western' populations have been surveyed. Ethnographic techniques of participant observation thus had their first wide-scale application in Britain in the context of Mass-Observation, a national network that was established in the 1930s for the purpose of observing and monitoring everyday beliefs, behaviours and customs. As such, it drew explicitly on the model of anthropology as a means of overcoming the class divide that had made the lives of the working classes – especially in the north – seem as remote and impenetrable to educated opinion as the tribal peoples of Borneo.

Clearly, the two perspectives discussed so far see everyday life brought into focus in somewhat contradictory ways: as a part of the democratization of political and cultural life in the one case, and as a part of the emergence of new forms of social discipline in the other. The *third perspective* connects with and cuts across both of these tendencies while also introducing new ones in suggesting how the emergence of the everyday has been linked to the history of social movements. The main points here are best made by focusing on a particular example: the different ways in which feminism, as a social movement, has highlighted the importance of the everyday social relations and practices in which women are particularly likely to be involved. In one line of development, feminist campaigns have aimed to ensure that women's everyday lives, their histories, and cultures have been included in the more general democratic extension of what is judged to be of value and worth representing in the public sphere. In a second line, feminists have often worked in concert with other social organizations – especially health and social welfare agencies – to know more about everyday life within the home in order to regulate it better. This was often true of the relations between the 'first-wave' feminism of the late nineteenth century and various moral hygiene campaigns which aimed to improve the physical and mental fitness of the population through a more rational management of the home environment. In a third line of development, best encapsulated in the slogan 'the personal is political', feminist perspectives have foregrounded the political questions that are posed by the forms of power associated with the relationships of gender that inform and organize the practices of everyday life. And they have done so in order to contest these forms of power as part of an active politics of everyday life.

These, then, are among the more important 'background' social developments that need to be kept in mind when looking at how everyday life has been studied within sociology and adjacent disciplines. For it is only in the light of these long-term historical changes that we can understand why and how everyday life has become a matter of sociological concern. But the ways in which the study of everyday life is approached differ from one school of sociological thought to another and it is to a brief delineation of these, and of the ways in which they have impacted on debates in Britain, that we now turn.

Sociological approaches to the everyday

It is generally agreed that the concept of everyday life makes it first appearance in western social thought in the work of Georg Lukács whose initial use of the term was derived from the accounts of everyday social routines and rituals that had been developed by the German sociologist, Georg Simmel. Everyday life, for Lukács, was characterized by a pre-reflective acceptance of, and immersion in, the social world in its given immediacy. It was a mode of relating to the social world in which existing social relationships were spontaneously reproduced in and through daily routines which are simply taken for granted. As such, this view of everyday life served as a counterpoint to Lukács' definition of tragedy as a literary form portraying a life lived at the limits, transcending the compromises and routines of everyday life to achieve a more authentic form of existence. This aspect of Lukács' thought influenced the German philosopher Martin Heidegger for whom everyday life was defined, essentially, by its banality: that is, as Rob Shields summarizes it, by the run of trivial, repetitive daily cycles of mundane activities through which 'things and living itself became taken for granted' (Shields, 1999, p.14). For Heidegger, too, everyday life was viewed as a lack when looked at from the point of view of what he called 'authentic life' or Being.

In these early philosophical uses, then, the concept of everyday life formed a part of evaluative schema in which the everyday was a devalued term compared with other ways of living which aspired to a higher, more authentic form of existence. This continues to be an aspect of later uses of the term in European sociology. The key figure here is the French sociologist Henri Lefebvre who played a major role in carrying over the debates about everyday life that had characterized the inter-war years through into the post-war period. Developed, initially, in his 1947 study *Critique of Everyday Life* – a title he was to use for a number of subsequent studies – perhaps Lefebvre's most influential account of everyday life is that offered in his 1968 text *Everyday Life in the Modern World* (Reading A)*, a study that was deeply influenced by the student revolts that took place throughout Europe during that year. While owing his interest in the concept of everyday life to the work of Lukács and Heidegger, Lefebvre sought to give this concept a more sociological grounding by relating it to the specific social conditions of daily life under industrial capitalism. His account of everyday life was thus a form of social critique accompanied – after the fashion of his mentors – by the search for more authentic ways of living that would rise above what he viewed as the largely debilitating routines of everyday life. Unlike Heidegger, however, he tried to give such alternative ways of living a definite point of social anchorage in the circumstances of particular social groups and forces.

This aspect of his work owed a considerable debt to the account that Georg Lukács had offered in *History and Class Consciousness* (first published in 1923) of the relationships between capitalism, alienation and everyday life. It was, Lukács argued, because the everyday lives of the working classes in capitalist societies were the most alienated that those classes, in becoming conscious of the need for social change, would be formed into a revolutionary force that would re-organize society along communist lines. This, Lukács argued, would transform everyday life so that – rather than being characterized by dull repetition – it would itself be able to fulfil the need for fuller and more authentic ways of living for everyone. For Lefebvre too, studying the everyday life of the working

* The Readings referred to in this Introduction represent different schools of approach to the study of everyday life. As such, they raise issues which span the concerns of the different chapters rather than being limited to any single chapter. For this reason, these readings are located at the end of the book, arranged in the order indicated here. This Introduction provides a context and setting within which they should be read.

classes made it clear that 'there was a power concealed in everyday life's apparent banality, a depth beneath its triviality, something extraordinary in its very ordinariness' (1971/1968, p.37). But he also argued that, by the 1960s, the working classes had become so integrated into what he characterized as the 'bureaucratic society of controlled consumption' that it was necessary to look elsewhere (to the student movement, for example) for forces capable of bringing about a 'permanent cultural revolution' in everyday life. In this respect his work bore testimony to the influence of the Frankfurt School which, as represented by theorists such as Theodor Adorno and Herbert Marcuse, argued that the cultural and media industries had produced a 'one-dimensional consciousness' from which the possibility of alternative ways of organizing society had been largely erased.

Similar concerns are evident in the work of Jürgen Habermas who, in the opposition he organizes between the world of system (that is, of bureaucratic, political, ideological and economic power) and the lifeworld (the patterns of social relations involved in everyday forms of social solidarity and communication) (Reading B: McGuigan), attributes to the latter an emancipatory potential in relation to the prevailing systems of power (see Habermas, 1987). Related oppositions also inform the perspectives of Alfred Schutz's account of everyday life (Reading C: Schutz; and Reading D: Zimmerman and Pollner). They are also present in the work of Agnes Heller (Reading E) – a student and later research associate of Georg Lukács – whose more positive assessments of the distinctive qualities of everyday life have proved important in recent feminist re-evaluations of the everyday.

Aspects of all these earlier traditions of work can be found in the work of Michel de Certeau whose *The Practice of Everyday Life* (Reading F) helped to shape approaches to the study of everyday life in the 1980s and 1990s. Like Lefebvre and Lukács before him, de Certeau surveyed the contemporary organization of everyday life with a view to discerning within it the seeds of social movements that might lead beyond it. His purpose in doing so was to take issue with Foucault's characterization of modern societies as 'disciplinary societies' in which power was allegedly so ubiquitous and total as to exclude all possibility of opposition or resistance. He did so by contending that it is in the practices of everyday life themselves that power is routinely resisted and contested. For de Certeau, resistance is manifested less in the form of explicit political activity (as in Lukács' conception of a proletarian-led revolution) or exceptional political-cultural events (as in Lefebvre's expectations of demonstrations and festivals) than in the routines of everyday cultural practices themselves. Resistance, for de Certeau, is a matter of 'textual poaching', that is of reading a text (a film, a novel) against the grain, or of subverting the plans of city planners by using city streets or open spaces for purposes other than those for which they are intended. This aspect of de Certeau's work has had an enormous influence on the study of everyday life. It has been especially important in developing the concerns of the 'active audience' approach in media studies in the stress it places on the need to consider the varied ways in which people use, fashion and interpret the mass-mediated cultural forms (film, television, the press) which now play so crucial a role in organizing the rhythms of everyday life (Reading G: Fiske).

The approaches we have considered so far owe their distinctive qualities to the dynamics arising out of the relations between European philosophy and sociology. Early North American contributions to the sociology of everyday life were cast in a different mould. The work of the Chicago School was especially important here. Founded at about the same time that Lukács was writing *History and Class Consciousness*, the Chicago School – so called because it was located at the University of Chicago – comprised a group of sociologists (Robert Park and Louis Wirth are among the key names) who, having been well schooled in European sociology, sought to apply and extend its perspectives by bringing them to bear on the new forms and patterns of social relationship associated with city life in the United States. Whereas Lukács' work tended to be abstract, speculative and revolutionary in its political orientations, the Chicago School aimed to produce an empirically grounded knowledge of cities and their varied social worlds. Its orientations, moreover, were avowedly reformist and pragmatic. If this places it in a line of connection with the late nineteenth-century social surveys discussed earlier, the Chicago School differed from these in its more self-conscious approach to the methodological difficulties associated with studying the ways of life of the urban poor. The result was the production of what remain classical sociological accounts of urban subcultures – that is, of the micro-social worlds of particular social groups within the urban social fabric – in which the everyday social and cultural practices of those groups were accounted for in terms of their relations to the urban environment.

It is this aspect of the influence of the Chicago School that is of most interest to us here. For it generated an ongoing tradition of work based on extensive periods of participant-observation fieldwork – in which the sociologists lived among the groups or communities they were studying – that stretched well into the post-war years. The Chicago School also served as the incubator for another distinctive US contribution to the sociological study of everyday life: the perspective of symbolic interactionism, most notably developed in the work of Erving Goffman (Reading H), which, focusing on the unwritten rules regulating the ways in which people behave and relate to one another in a range of public spaces, threw new light on the public aspects of everyday life in urban settings. This was also an important aspect of Harold Garfinkel's work (Reading I), with the significant rider that Garfinkel's concern was to develop techniques – those of what he called ethnomethodology – for revealing the conventions of everyday life by rupturing and breaking them. The work of Goffman and Garfinkel was also important in drawing attention to the significant social work that is involved in the construction of boundaries of the kind that differentiate the everyday from other spheres of social life. This aspect of their legacy is still active (Reading J: Nippert-Eng).

These, then, are the traditions of US sociology that most influenced the development of sociological approaches to the study of everyday life in post-war Britain. This is attested to by the blossoming, in the 1950s, of detailed accounts – based on extensive periods of participant observation study – of the everyday lives of particular communities. Michael Young and Peter Willmott's 1957 study of the effect of new forms of housing and neighbourhood on the everyday lives of working-class communities in East London is the most famous case in point (Young and Willmott, 1957). There was also a strong tradition of research examining the relations between work and everyday life in the context of particular industries, firms or occupational communities.

The influence of such empirically grounded ethnographic approaches to the study of everyday life was not limited to sociology. It also – in the 1960s and

1970s – began to spill over into the developing trajectories of cultural studies. The legacy of the Chicago School, for example, is clear in *Resistance through Rituals: Youth Subcultures in Post-war Britain* (1976), one of the most influential texts of the Centre for Contemporary Cultural Studies (CCCS) at the University of Birmingham. In this study, Stuart Hall and his co-authors drew on ethnographic techniques to examine the formation of the distinctive array of youth subcultures that dominated the cultural landscapes of the 1950s and 1960s: Teddy boys, mods and rockers, the middle-class counter-culture that was most publicly symbolized by the hippies, and the life of kids on the streets. However, the CCCS was also influenced by those traditions of European social and cultural theory in which – as we have seen from our discussion of Lefebvre and de Certeau – the study of everyday life formed part of an analysis of resistance to the particular forms of power that were held to be tangled up in it. What most distinguished the work of the CCCS, however, was the ways in which it connected these United States and European traditions to the concerns emerging from the earlier intellectual trajectories of British cultural studies as represented by the work of Richard Hoggart and Raymond Williams. Yet the accomplishments of each of these was different. Hoggart's was that of offering, in *The Uses of Literacy* (1957), an evocative account of the post-war pressures that were reconfiguring the everyday lives and cultures of northern, industrial working-class communities (Reading K). While the more general and pervasive nature of Williams' influence makes it more difficult to single out its specific focus, his widening out of the concept of culture to include everyday ways of life provided the basis for a rapprochement between the concerns of the humanities – Williams' own intellectual base – and those of sociology that has had an enduring influence on the development of cultural studies. Culture, as Williams put it in one of his essays (Williams, 1958), is ordinary, integrated into the realm of everyday life rather than – as earlier, more selective and elitist definitions of culture had suggested – a higher realm of 'great art' defined by its opposition to the mundane and ordinary preoccupations of everyday life.

Three other more general approaches to the everyday need to be briefly reviewed in order to complete this rough-and-ready survey of the field. The first concerns the influence of feminist thought in challenging the assumptions of gender underlying many of the approaches to the everyday discussed above. Lukács' account of everyday life never descended beneath the abstract philosophical concept of 'man' to register the significance of questions of gender. Lefebvre, by contrast, did acknowledge the significance of such questions, but often in formulations which – in suggesting that women's mental horizons were so hemmed in and trammelled by the immediacies of everyday life as to make them incapable of critical thought – were profoundly misogynist. There is equally little doubt that the preoccupation with questions of class that characterized the early phases of cultural studies precluded any parity of attention to questions of gender.

It is against this background that the significance of feminist contributions from the 1970s onwards have to be viewed. These have been broadly based and interdisciplinary. The work of feminist historians has been important in the significance it has accorded women's everyday domestic activities in the historical processes of class formation (Davidoff and Hall, 1987). From a different perspective, the work of Dorothy Smith (Reading L) has also been important in stressing the embodied nature of our experience of everyday life. Feminists such as Rita Felski (Reading M) have also challenged the negative values that are often associated with the distinctive temporal rhythms of everyday life in its routine and repetitive aspects, contending that these derive from a masculine preference for linear and progressive constructions of time. In doing so, they have drawn on the more positive interpretation of everyday life developed by Agnes Heller (Reading E). There are also connections between these aspects of feminist accounts of everyday life and Anthony Giddens' assessment of the role that everyday life plays in developing a sense of ontological security – that is, as Roger Silverstone glosses it (Reading N), a known place in a known world – that is necessary for social life to take place at all.

The second more general approach that needs to be considered is characterized by its focus on the role of practices of consumption in the organization of everyday life. New tendencies in anthropology focusing on how people relate to one another through the uses to which they put things and objects have been important here. Pierre Bourdieu's *Distinction* (Reading O) has also stimulated a large number of studies examining how our everyday cultural tastes and preferences organize and symbolize relationships of social distinction which, in their turn, are connected to the social dynamics of class formation. This is matched by the stress that the emerging field of 'cultural economy' studies places on the role which cultural factors play in organizing all aspects of economic life, but especially consumption – through new forms of branding and retailing, for example, and the promotion of distinctive lifestyles as a means of segmenting and organizing markets. There are connections here, too, with the importance that gay and lesbian studies have attached to the development of distinctive lifestyles, raising important political issues concerning the relations between questions of sexual preference and identity and the organization of everyday life.

Account has also to be taken of new approaches to the relations between ethnicity and everyday life. These have been developed in the context of new theoretical approaches to ethnicity which, rather than dividing the population into discrete ethnic groups, each with its own separate culture, sees ethnicity more as a relational phenomenon – as identities which, since they are defined in relation to one another, tend to be fluid and variable in ways that are as true of majority ethnicities as of minority ones. The implications of these developments for the study of everyday life are far-reaching. It is true of most of the approaches to the everyday considered so far that they assume the organization of everyday life to be bounded to particular locations – home, work – or to be embedded in communities with defined spatial locations. A good deal of recent work, by contrast, has focused on the ways in which people of Asian or Afro-Caribbean connection in Britain form part of trans-national networks – or diasporas – in which the horizons and parameters of everyday life are knitted partly into local contexts but also partly into the international flows of peoples and cultures. This presents the challenge as to how best to understand the everyday lives of those whose spatial and temporal horizons are organized by histories of movement.

It is worth noting, finally, that current debates involve a significant reappraisal of the terms in which questions relating to the politics of everyday life are posed. As we have seen, the concept of the everyday has secular connotations because it implies that daily life is mundane and ordinary; it implies a world that is, as Felski puts it, 'leached of transcendence' (Felski, 1999–2000, p.16). This secular aspect of everyday life, however, rarely entirely escapes the expectation that the mundane and banal cycle of everyday life might one day be transcended. This is true of the concern, evident in many of the European theorists discussed above, to distinguish between everyday and authentic life, and to find some social force capable of moving society from the former to the latter. It is not accidental that this politics of transcendence is most notably associated with European schools of thought. For it reflects the extent to which the theories of the everyday initially proposed by European sociologists like Lefebvre were developed in a close association with avant-garde artistic movements which also sought to indict and transcend everyday life. It also reflects the longer-term influence of Christian thought in generating the prospect that everyday life might be exceeded in moments of religious transcendence. The legacy of this politics of transcendence, however, is now being critically sifted in contemporary debates. For some, like Michael Gardiner, it remains important – after the fashion of Lefebvre – to study the everyday to unlock the extraordinary potential that is hidden in its prosaic routines (Gardiner, 2000, p.6). Others are less sure of this. Felski suggests that we should now be wary of the legacy of these earlier approaches to the study of everyday life to the degree that they obscure some of the more prosaic political issues – especially those concerning the relations between men and women – that are caught up in the warp and woof of everyday life.

The sites of everyday life

The above sketch is, of course, a partial and selective one. It has served its purpose, however, in allowing us to 'touch base' with some of the key themes and issues characterizing sociological debate about everyday life. These are developed in the chapters that follow in a number of ways. Each chapter teases out specific aspects of the relationships between everyday practices and the relations of class, gender, age, ethnicity and sexuality. Furthermore, each chapter, through its focus on those particular 'social sites' or 'locations' most strongly associated with the everyday – home, romance, the street, the economy, the pub and community – explores the relationships between the discipline of sociology and the dynamics of society. In so doing each chapter attempts to expose the role such sites play in relationships of power at the level of society. And finally, each chapter assists us in 'de-familiarizing' our understandings of the everyday, by illustrating some of the ways in which the perspectives of sociology, feminism and cultural studies have thrown new light on our taken-for-granted assumptions about everyday practices and everyday situations.

In Chapter 1, *'Home and everyday life'*, Tony Bennett critically examines some of the main approaches to the concepts of the everyday and everyday life and sets the scene for the chapters which follow. The 'home' has often been seen as the archetypal site of everyday life, the scene of habit and repetition and of those cyclical relations of 'everyday time' particularly associated with women and counterpoised to the masculine time of 'modernity'. But these assumptions have been contested, in particular in recent feminist debates, which have argued for a more complex understanding of relations between men and women, between the private and public spheres of life and of the contrasts between the cyclical time of repetition and the linear time of modernity. This chapter engages with these debates by placing the conceptualization of home in its social and cultural context. Bennett illustrates how historical developments have shaped and influenced ideas about the home as an institution in modern societies and how values about the home are not constant but vary according to social position – class, gender and ethnicity – and historical time. Using contemporary research he examines the social factors, which influence attitudes towards the home and activities within the home, concluding that social class, gender and ethnicity are key factors influencing values associated with the home. The home is a key social institution, which plays a role in regularizing social practices and relations and establishing core values. But its place in everyday life has not been settled and there continues to be disagreement about the place of the home in grounding and organizing the rhythms of everyday live and whether the relations between home and everyday life should be evaluated negatively or positively.

Chapter 2, *'Love is in the air: romance and the everyday'*, continues the project of exploring everyday, taken-for-granted aspects of society and approaching them as if they were new, strange and unfamiliar. In this chapter Peter Redman explores the idea of 'romance', inviting us to approach it as a 'social construction'. Romance is a familiar, ubiquitous, everyday phenomenon, which may be seen as both intrinsic to the mundane routines of the everyday, as part of the everyday, and as an alternative to it, providing individuals an escape from habit and routine. This contrast and contradiction is a key focus of this chapter. Being 'in love' may be experienced as something private, emotional and intimate but, as Redman argues, sociologically it may be viewed as a socially constructed social product, which is produced through a repertoire of publicly available cultural practices. Redman explores the genre conventions of the 'classic romance' in contemporary western society which are displayed in novels, films and popular music. He argues that conventional meanings of 'romance' are connected to wider social changes, vary according to historical context and are always in the process of being contested and altered. Links between romance and the everyday are specifically explored through an original case study of sixteen- to eighteen-year-old boys, which was part of a wider ethnographic research project in which Redman was involved. He uses his qualitative interview material to analyse the ways in which these boys talk about being in love and how the terms in which they do so relate to romance as a cultural form that is overwhelmingly coded as feminine. Far from being just an intimate, private and personal experience, romance is a socially constructed experience that is fully located in the social structure of power relations.

With Chapter 3 the focus of this volume moves outwards from the private sphere of home, family and intimate relationships towards the public domain of the street as a key 'locus of everyday life'. In *'The street and everyday life'* Peter Hamilton approaches the idea of the 'street' sociologically, examining different visual and conceptual images and exploring some of the different ways in which the street has been theorized as a locale of the everyday. He outlines two broadly complementary ways of theorizing the street, which he defines as the social and the imaginary. From the social perspective he suggests that the street is seen as a place, a space, a moral locale, where sociability is transacted and social order is displayed. The analytical focus here is on the street as a location for distinctive ways of life and social dynamics. The imaginary perspective, on the other hand, understands the street as an imagined 'state of mind' which is produced and reproduced through the influence of distinctive forms of cultural imagery, generated by writer and poets, composers, songwriters and musicians, painters, film-makers and photographers. From the first perspective Hamilton traces the influence of sociological writing on understanding the social structure of the street, in particular the work of Simmel and the Chicago School of sociology. The Chicago School profoundly influenced the production of rich ethnographies of street life and utilized the method of 'participant observation', which is central to the ethnographic tradition and is explored in the chapter using W.F. Whyte's classic work, *Street Corner Society*. The second perspective, however, is rather more concerned with developing a cultural understanding of relations between the street and everyday life. Hamilton evaluates the influence of writers such as Baudelaire and Benjamin on the imaginary idea of the street as a 'state of mind', on the 'novelty' of modernism, the importance of the artist and the role of the *flâneur* or city-stroller. These interpretations of the experiences of street life are a central theme of modernism and are crucial to the construction of the street as a symbolic space, a domain of dream and intrigue, a narrative of city life and a locale of mystery and poetry.

The relationship between work and leisure is central to the organization of the spatial and temporal rhythms of everyday life in contemporary societies and is the subject of Chapter 4. In **'Everyday life and the economy'** Celia Lury examines this interconnectedness between the economic and everyday life by using two case studies: consumer brand images and new forms of consumer credit. Lury argues that these examples are useful in revealing something about the relations between the economy and everyday life and they also shed light on the idea that the realm of everyday life is increasingly being constituted as a resource for the economy itself. Lury examines changes in the social organization of space associated with the historical separation of work and home, and shows how spatial differentiation, consequent upon this separation, is accompanied also by a shift in the experience of time. Using the work of E.P. Thompson she shows how, in early industrial societies, industrial 'clock time' set the pace of working life and reduced leisure to a residual category, as something left over when work was completed. She explores Castells' argument that we are entering an era of 'timeless time', where such things as the speed of global market transactions, the rise in flexible work practices and changes in the way we experience the life-cycle all affect our experience of temporality. Furthermore, during the course of the nineteenth and twentieth centuries the practices of everyday life have become incorporated into the economy itself, with leisure and consumption providing fruitful new sites for the commodification and rationalization of time and space. Lefebvre's work on the 'consumer society' provides Lury with a basis for exploring modern day 'branding', with McClintock's 1995 study, *Imperial Leather*, showing how economic and cultural interests were at work in the branding of something we take to be ubiquitous and everyday, like soap. These two case studies enable Lury to show how the process of branding uses the objects and routines of everyday life and how the use of extended credit allows consumption to precede production, thus transforming the relationship between effort and reward, and integrating consumption with production in the modern economy.

One site of the everyday, where both work and leisure come together in the same social space, is in the public house. In Chapter 5, **'"Home from home": the pub and everyday life'**, Diane Watson examines the public house as a social institution, as a site of social, political and economic exchange and as an 'icon of the everyday'. She begins by using a piece of 'ethnographic fiction science', to 'do some sociology', and show how we may suspend our everyday, taken-for-granted assumptions about social life and approach so-called 'normal' occurrences as if they are anthropologically strange events. Using the work of the pioneering 1930s' social research organization, Mass-Observation, Watson draws on their fascinating observational map of the everyday to explore the process of constructing what they called 'an anthropology of everyday lives' and evaluate the relevance of 'observation' as a research technique. The observation techniques and descriptive evidence of Mass-Observation are then contrasted with Whitehead's 1970s' ethnographic research in pubs, and the role of participant observation techniques in exposing the routines and habits of customers in a rural pub is evaluated. Placing the pub in its social and historical context enables Watson to highlight the continuities and changes with past and present. She demonstrates how class, gender, family-centrednesss, pub layout and age have all influenced the social and cultural changes taking place in pubs and have had implications for leisure, lifestyles, work and consumption. Pubs are sites of leisure and pleasure but they are also places where people work and experience the stresses and pressures of being engaged in 'emotional labour'. Watson concludes by considering the practical and ethical issues involved in 'doing academic work' as a participant observer in her own research project. She argues that to understand the dynamics of social processes which make up the everyday requires a form of sociological analysis that is able to give insight into processes, meanings and interpretations.

In Chapter 6, *'Community, everyday and space'*, Tim Jordan examines the ways in which communities enclose and frame the everyday, thus allowing community members to identify with each other, to express their own identities and take routine and habitual actions for granted. Jordan argues that communities involve a type of space that helps to form a community's boundaries but that, whilst space is a component of community, communities cannot merely be reduced to physical location or physical characteristics. To illustrate these arguments Jordan explores several case studies of communities: one found in Bethnal Green in the East End of London in the 1950s; one in 1950s' suburban London; one in the 1980s' community of the dance floor; and finally the virtual community of computer hackers. In examining the nature of family and kinship in East London, and the subsequent move of residents to the newly built suburbs, Jordan analyses the ways in which the everyday is played out through repetition, home and habit, though routines and sub-routines. In examining rave culture and the community of hacking Jordan proceeds to question the spatially bounded notion of 'community' by looking at communities which do not at first sight conform to this definition. He shows how the everyday of rave and its community is built out of the re-creation of typical pleasures in a space which is more than just physical, and through which members can identify themselves and others as part of the community of 'ravers'. Hackers, on the other hand, are unlikely ever to have even met each other but Jordan illustrates how they may still be seen to have a sense of community which is marked by common identities, internal everyday structures and boundaries around the community. Jordan concludes by arguing that communities are constructed out of the process of identification through which individuals recognize similarities between one another. Space is clearly an essential element in the definition of community, but the latter cannot be defined only in terms of physical location or physical proximity.

Chapter 7, *'Accounting for the everyday'*, has a theoretical review function in the context of this volume. Each of the six preceding chapters shows that the sociological analysis of the everyday has been informed by a number of different theoretical issues and has had as its focus very different aspects of society and the everyday. This chapter highlights some of the more general theoretical issues implicated in different ways of accounting for the distinctive properties of everyday life. It re-examines the role of time, routine and repetition, exploring those contemporary changes occurring in the way time operates and the ways in which spatial boundaries are reconstituted. What is clear from all the chapters is that the mundane, repetitive and taken-for-granted aspects of everyday life are of considerable significance in the life experiences of specific individuals and groups. Sociological theory and practice have the capacity to make us aware of the taken-for-grantedness of everyday life, its routines, habits and assumptions, and its relationship to the power structures of society. Hemmings, Silva and Thompson use the example of the attempt to re-organize the way in which time was structured in the French Revolution to illustrate how the basic structures of everyday life are organized. Time is integral to all social experience and social relationships such that it is easy to overlook the fact that those diverse cultural definitions of time exist according to historical and social context. Time is a key element in theorizing the everyday but, as the chapters in this volume show, space and the definition of space are equally important. Everyday life is experienced, constructed and reconstructed within a socially produced space where the boundaries are fluid and open to challenge. Hemmings, Silva and Thompson use an analysis of gender to explore further the spatial dimension of the everyday. Theoretically, they conclude that the study of the everyday allows the sociologist to make links between micro-social processes of small-scale interaction and broader macro-level structures and processes of social reproduction and social change. Finally, in their words:

> Everyday life is like the air we breathe or the ground on which we build: it is the foundation of social life. In learning to make strange the taken-for-granted realities within which we live our lives, we take a major step towards adopting a sociological imagination and towards the analysis of the traditional sociological concerns of social order and social change.

References

Bourdieu, P. (1984) *Distinction: A Social Critique of the Judgement of Taste* (trans. R. Nice), London, Routledge and Kegan Paul. First published in France in 1979.

Certeau, M. de (1984) *The Practice of Everyday Life* (trans. S.F. Rendall), Berkeley, CA, University of California Press.

Davidoff, L. and Hall, C. (1987) *Family Fortunes: Men and Women of the English Middle Class, 1780–1850*, London, Routledge.

Edwards, E. (ed.) (1992) *Anthropology and Photography, 1860–1920*, New Haven, CT, and London, Yale University Press in association with the Royal Anthropological Institute.

Felski, R. (1999–2000) 'The invention of everyday life', *New Formations*, no.39, pp.15–31.

Foucault, M. (1977) *Discipline and Punish: The Birth of the Prison*, London, Allen Lane.

Gardiner, M. (2000) *Critiques of Everyday Life*, London, Routledge.

Garfinkel, H. (1967) *Studies in Ethnomethodology*, Englewood Cliffs, NJ, Prentice-Hall.

Ginzburg, C. (1980) 'Morelli, Freud and Sherlock Holmes: clues and scientific method', *History Workshop*, no.9.

Goffman, E. (1971) *The Presentation of Self in Everyday Life*, Harmondsworth, Penguin Books. First published in the USA in 1959.

Habermas, J. (1987) *The Theory of Communicative Action. Volume Two, Lifeworld and System: A Critique of Functionalist Reason*, Boston, MA, Beacon Press.

Habermas, J. (1989) *The Structural Transformation of the Public Sphere: An Inquiry into a Category of Bourgeois Society*, Cambridge, MA, MIT Press.

Hall, S. and Jefferson, T. (eds) (1976) *Resistance through Rituals: Youth Subcultures in Post-war Britain*, London, Hutchinson in association with the Centre for Contemporary Cultural Studies, University of Birmingham (London, HarperCollins, 1991).

Heller, A. (1984) *Everyday Life* (trans. G.L. Campbell), London, Routledge and Kegan Paul. First published in Hungary in 1970.

Hoggart, R. (1957) *The Uses of Literacy: Aspects of Working-Class Life with Special Reference to Publications and Entertainments*, London, Chatto and Windus.

Lefebvre, H. (1971) *Everyday Life in the Modern World* (trans. S. Rabinovitch), London, Allen Lane The Penguin Press. First published in France in 1968.

Lefebvre, H. (1991) *The Critique of Everyday Life, Volume 1* (trans. J. Moore), London, Verso. First published in 1947; 2nd edn, 1958.

Lukács, G. (1977) *History and Class Consciousness*, London, Merlin Press. First published in 1923.

McClintock, A. (1995) *Imperial Leather: Race, Gender and Sexuality in the Colonial Contest*, New York and London, Routledge.

Poovey, M. (1995) *Making a Social Body: British Cultural Formation, 1830–1864*, Chicago, IL, and London, University of Chicago Press.

Schutz, A. (1967) *Collected Papers, Vol. 1: The Problem of Social Reality* (ed. M. Natanson), The Hague, Martin Nijhoff.

Shields, R. (1999) *Lefebvre, Love and Struggle: Spatial Dialectics*, London, Routledge.

Silverstone, R. (1994) *Television and Everyday Life*, London, Routledge.

Simmel, G. (1997) *Simmel on Culture: Selected Writings* (eds D. Frisby and M. Featherstone), London, Sage.

Smith, D.E. (1988) *The Everyday World as Problematic: A Feminist Sociology*, Milton Keynes, Open University Press.

Whitehead, A. (1976) 'Sexual antagonism in Herefordshire' in Barker, D.L. and Allen, S. (eds) *Dependence and Exploitation in Work and Marriage*, London, Longman.

Whyte, W.F. (1943) *Street Corner Society: The Social Structure of an Italian Slum*, Chicago, IL, University of Chicago Press (3rd edn, 1981).

Williams, R. (1958) 'Culture is ordinary' in McKenzie, N. (ed.) *Conviction*, London, MacGibbon and Kee.

Young, M. and Willmott, P. (1957) *Family and Kinship in East London*, London, Routledge and Kegan Paul.

Home and everyday life

Tony Bennett

Contents

1 Introduction

Home is … well, what is it? What does home mean for you? What values – positive or negative – do you associate with home? Do you think these are widely shared? Or do the values that people attach to home differ? As home is a topic that closely concerns us all, it's as well to start with questions of this kind to make explicit some of the assumptions underlying our own particular views about home and its role in everyday life.

ACTIVITY 1

Take a few minutes to think about your own views of home. Think about what home means for you personally, and write two or three sentences summarizing this.

Could you now write one sentence in the form of a definition of home that you might find as a dictionary entry?

These sum up your own feelings and ideas, but can you think of any groups in society who might have different views about home, and why this would be?

There are obviously any number of definitions you could have come up with, any of which would be valid, as it summarizes your own personal experience of home. Listed below are four statements about home which should provide some useful points of comparison for your own definition. They may confirm some of your own ideas, or may present aspects you didn't consider.

1   Home is 'the place where one lives permanently, esp. as a member of a family or household; a fixed place of residence' (*Oxford English Dictionary*).

2   The 'true nature of home' is 'the place of peace; the shelter, not only from all injury, but from all terror, doubt and division … so far as the anxieties of the outer life penetrate into it … it ceases to be a home; it is then only a part of the outer world which you have roofed over and lighted a fire in. And whenever a true wife comes, this home is always round her' (Ruskin, 1868, cited in Morley, 2000, p.281).

3   'Home: Women-headed households, serial monogamy, flight of men, old women alone, technology of domestic work, paid homework, re-emergence of home sweat shops, home-based businesses and telecommuting, electronic cottage, urban homelessness, migration, module architecture, reinforced (simulated) nuclear family, intense domestic violence' (Haraway, 1985, p.194).

4   Home 'may be not so much a singular physical entity fixed in a particular place, but rather a mobile, symbolic habitat, a performative way of life and of doing things in which one makes one's home while in movement' (Morley, 2000, p.47).

What do these different definitions tell us about contemporary understandings of home?

What emerges most clearly for me from these contrasting definitions is how unsettled are current views about, and attitudes toward, the home. In the OED definition, the emphasis falls on the home as an identifiable and fixed place of residence. Yet, for David Morley, writing from a cultural studies perspective, it is precisely this assumption that has to be challenged in order to take account of the new meanings that home has acquired through the increased geographical mobility which has characterized the second half of the twentieth century. Donna Haraway echoes this aspect of Morley's argument while also challenging every aspect of the view of the home as a haven from the outside world that is summarized in the definition of John Ruskin, the influential Victorian art critic. For Haraway, any sense of the home as a domestic idyll is undercut by the economic and technological forces that are currently redefining the home, for many, as a place of work as well as by the exclusions (the elderly) and denials (of domestic violence) which such views of home entail.

But what are the connections between these changing views of home and everyday life?

Take a few minutes to: (a) define what you understand by 'everyday life', and (b) say what the role of 'home' is within it.

Rita Felski (1999–2000) offers a useful perspective on this question when she suggests that everyday life is characterized by three distinctive features. Firstly, she argues, it is characterized by a distinctive sense of time, that of repetition. Everyday time, then, is routine, ordinary time in contrast to the special time of festivals, holidays and celebrations. Secondly, we experience everyday life in a distinctive way, as a matter of habit. Put another way, we just take everyday life for granted. And, thirdly, everyday life is governed by a particular kind of spatial ordering, one that is, as Felski puts it, 'anchored in a sense of home' (*ibid.*, p.18).

Felski is not alone in seeing home as the archetypal setting for everyday life. This is, indeed, a commonplace of popular culture. Think of the role that depictions of home play in soap operas, a genre that is pre-eminently defined by its concern with the everyday lives of ordinary people in everyday settings. Or think of *The Royle Family* (Figure 1.1), an almost perfect illustration of Felski's argument, as, in every episode, the same characters assemble in the same setting – in the living-room, in front of the television – and go through the same routines, caught in an unending daily cycle of repetition and habit which, although interrupted by minor crises and unexpected events, usually reimposes its rhythms by the end of the programme.

This is not to suggest that home and everyday life can simply be equated. A number of other spaces – the workplace and shopping mall, for example – also play a significant role in everyday life and experience. Felski's point is rather that home has a particularly strong connection with everyday life because of the role it plays in anchoring its rhythms, in comprising, for most of us, 'a base,

Figure 1.1 *A scene from* The Royle Family, *a sitcom set exclusively in the home and portraying the repetition and mundanity of everyday life*

a taken-for-granted grounding' (*ibid.*, p.22). It is through home that we connect with other aspects of our everyday lives just as – at the end of the day – it is to home that we return.

It is for these reasons that sociological approaches to everyday life have typically taken the home as their primary point of departure. Yet these have often proceeded from questionable assumptions in the way that the relationships between home and gender have been interpreted. If, one school of thought argues, home most fully represents the routine, habitual, taken-for-granted quality of everyday life, and if home plays a stronger role in the lives of women than it does for men, then there is likely to be a difference in men's and women's attitudes toward time. The horizons of women, so this argument goes, are more likely to be limited to the repetitive, habitual and cyclical rhythms of daily time whereas men's mental clock is more likely to tick to the linear, unrepeatable, eventful time of the world outside the home. This was the view of Henri Lefebvre, the French sociologist who first introduced the concept of everyday life into sociological debates.

Unsurprisingly, these disparaging views of women have been called into question in subsequent feminist accounts of everyday life, and I shall review these in section 4 when we explore Felski's arguments in more detail. First, though, I want to provide a broader context from which to engage with the theoretical and political controversies – briefly reviewed in the foregoing – that now characterize sociological debates about the relations between home and everyday life. I do so by looking at two main sets of issues.

Firstly, in section 2, I place the home – in its dominant western form – in a historical perspective, tracing the development of the separation between place of domicile and place of work that allowed the home to emerge, in the nineteenth century, as a distinctive social and cultural space characterized by specific – but contested – relations of gender and generation. In the course of this history, the home was represented as 'a haven in a heartless world' offering men a respite from their labours in a nurturing culture of domesticity that was women's responsibility. Yet this idealization of the home as a retreat from a threatening outside world was also at marked odds with the tendency for a range of external agencies, both governmental and commercial, to reach into the home, reshaping the practices and interrelationships of its members. In considering this, I shall look most closely at how architectural projects of various kinds have sought to shape social relationships within the home by means of particular spatial arrangements.

Secondly, in section 3, I show how the values that are associated with the home vary in accordance with our social position. What home means to us; the values we associate with it; how, in practical ways, we relate to the home; and what we do within it: these all tend to vary in accordance with our gender, social class, level of education, ethnicity and nationality. I explore these issues by looking at the evidence – some of it statistical, and some of it derived from interviews – provided by a study of the everyday cultural practices of contemporary Australians. I also look at the distinctive role that home plays in the values of people who have migrated from one country to another.

These historical and sociological perspectives will allow us to get a better purchase on current debates concerning gender and the politics of everyday life. For they make it clear why, historically, women have come to be associated with the home and the cyclical relation to time that is associated with the notion of everyday routine or habit, while also providing a basis for challenging that association.

AIMS

In reviewing the issues briefly introduced above, the aims of this chapter are:

1   To introduce those sociological accounts of everyday life which define its distinctiveness in terms of particular relations of time, space and habit.

2   To examine the role that accounts of home play within such approaches to the study of everyday life.

3   To examine the historical development of the home as a distinctively modern social institution.

4   To consider how social practices within, and attitudes toward, the home vary in accordance with considerations of social class, gender and ethnicity.

5   To introduce some of the political controversies which inform sociological debates about everyday life.

2 Home, domesticity and its discontents

Let's go back to the OED definition of home as the place where one lives permanently as a member of a family or household, and look at how this meaning is illustrated through selected quotes from various well-known figures:

'Keep the home-fires burning' *(Ivor Novello)*

'Every family in America deserves a decent home, whether a farmhouse or a city apartment' *(Lyndon B. Johnson)*

'Home is the place we have to leave in order to grow up' *(Michael Ignatieff)*.

A number of values cluster around uses of these kinds: the home as a place for families; its identification as a place of residence rather than of work; the home as a place of retreat or shelter from the harsh realities of the outside world. These are reflected in related terms: as when we call someone a 'homebody' or refer to something as 'home-made'. Other uses carry particular connotations of gender: 'home-maker' is, according to the OED, 'a person, esp. a housewife, who creates a (pleasant) home'. When, by contrast, we say 'An Englishman's home is his castle', particular gendered conceptions of property are clearly entangled with assumptions about the home as a sequestered domain, housing a man's treasured possessions (including wife and children), which he has a right to protect.

Yet it is clear that many of these associations of 'home' are now being called into question. The increase in the number of single-parent families – accounting for 11 per cent of households in 1998 (ONS, 1999, pp.42–3) – and of gay and lesbian households have challenged the strong association of the home with the **nuclear family**: that is, a heterosexual couple and their children. Equally, new communications technologies and the shift – in developed economies – from the industrial to what is often called the 'knowledge economy' are reorganizing the relations between home and work as homeworking becomes increasingly common. If, then, we can now begin to see beyond the rim of the home – begin to see, that is, that it represents a historically particular organization of relationships between family members, and between place of residence and place of work – it is clear, too, that its origins are also relatively recent. While historians are largely agreed that the nuclear family has a much longer history, the development of a close relationship between the home and the nuclear family, the separation of the home from places of work and its organization as a sphere of privacy and intimacy, distinct from the world of public affairs – all of these go back little more than two hundred years. Tamara Hareven offers a useful synoptic perspective on these developments in reviewing a range of factors affecting the development of the home in nineteenth-century England, France and America.

nuclear family

READING 1.1

You should now turn to Reading 1.1 by Tamara Hareven, 'The home and the family in historical perspective' which you will find at the end of this chapter. When you have done so, try to answer the following questions:

1   Hareven argues that the family in pre-industrial society was characterized by '*sociability* rather than *privacy*'. What does she mean by this?

2   What consequences did the emergence of the home as a sphere of privacy have for the organization of spatial relationships within the household?

3   How did the emergence of the conception of the home as a retreat from the world affect the organization of relationships of gender and generation within the home?

4   To what extent was the organization of domestic life subject to the influence of external agencies?

5   What role does Hareven accord considerations of class in differentiating attitudes toward the home? And how was the home envisaged as a means of promoting social reform?

Some aspects of Hareven's discussion need to be qualified. The confidence with which she refers to the existence of 'separate spheres', for example, has been questioned in later feminist writings which have suggested that the relations between the home and the public worlds of work and politics were never quite so unconnected as this term suggests. This literature also casts doubt on the notion that women passively acquiesced in being relegated to the home without struggling to retain aspects of the more public lives they had earlier enjoyed, while also seeking to define new public roles for themselves in the newly developing urban cultures and politics of the period. When all of these qualifications are made, however, Hareven's account usefully brings together four key themes.

Firstly, Hareven shows how the roles of women and men in relation to the home are the outcomes of particular social and historical processes rather than natural attributes rooted in their biological functions.

Secondly, while viewed as 'a haven from a heartless world', the organization of the home was in fact profoundly determined by forces arising out of the very external world it was supposed to be a retreat from.

Thirdly, it is clear that the nature and meaning of home varied in accordance with social class, just as men and women often had different – and sometimes contesting – views about the ideal forms of home and home life.

And fourthly, Hareven highlights the importance of new ways of partitioning space within the household, and of the new kinds of social relationships these made possible.

It will repay our attention to look more closely at each of these themes.

2.1   Women and the culture of domesticity

If domesticity was one of the principal achievements of the bourgeois age, Witold Rybczynski has argued, 'it was, above all, a feminine achievement' (1988, p.75). The case he has in mind is that of seventeenth-century Holland and the role played by Dutch women in enforcing new forms of domesticity on their more reluctant menfolk: new codes of tidiness and cleanliness; the insertion of 'no smoking' clauses into marriage contracts; and, as the primary sphere of women's power within the home, the elevation of the kitchen – previously a space of little account – to a place of major symbolic importance, somewhere between 'a temple and a museum' (*ibid.*, p.73): see Figure 1.2. Yet Hareven's comments on the role of how-to-do-it manuals and etiquette books also make it clear that

Figure 1.2 Pieter de Hooch, Woman peeling Apples, c.1663. De Hooch's paintings depict the home as the woman's domain, defining and upholding the family values of seventeenth-century Dutch society.

women had to be trained for their new domestic responsibilities. Leonore Davidoff and Catherine Hall make the same point in their more detailed study of the development of the English middle-class family over the period 1780–1850. The 'culture of domesticity' which developed over this period involved the cultivation of new qualities for women and the devaluation of older ones:

> Women were mainly responsible for creating and maintaining the house, its contents and its human constituents. To this end, they had first to order

themselves. Those born in the mid eighteenth century had a simpler lifestyle and were cruder in manner and speech. Their children and grandchildren's generations were often shocked by their more relaxed elders ... Not all women made the transition with good grace. Some who had grown up heavily involved in the enterprise refused to move into segregated housing ... Some women chose religious retirement, some more worldly advancement. But whatever the route, the genteel household was becoming the focus of most women's lives.

(Davidoff and Hall, 1987, p.360)

The requirement that men 'must provide a livelihood which made possible a domestic establishment where they and their dependants could live a rational and morally sanctioned life' (*ibid.*, p.227) entailed a similar reformation of the desirable attributes of middle-class masculinity. The cultivation of such a persona required that middle-class men detach themselves from earlier male identities – often defined by their association with extended kin networks, their roles in extra-familial institutions such as the army, and by their participation in exclusively male cultural pursuits (such as blood sports) that were often rough and raucous – and acquire new ones centred on their occupations and domestic responsibilities.

Yet while the culture of domesticity that emerged from these intersecting processes assigned both men and women new roles in relation to the home, there is no doubt that women's roles were, of the two, the most exclusively anchored in the home just as – at least from a moral point of view – they were to serve as the home's anchor. Through a complex set of processes, the nineteenth-century middle-class woman was the heiress of earlier eighteenth-century developments through which women came to be imbued with special moral or improving qualities. Some of these derived from the role that conduct books had played in preparing women for their new role in the culture of domesticity, by encouraging them to look within themselves to find and cultivate a self-developing moral power that might then be used for good within the home by extending its reach to their menfolk and children (Armstrong, 1987). Eighteenth-century conceptions of good taste also centred on women, attributing to them both a greater capacity than men for appreciating the finer qualities of the literary, visual and musical arts while also assigning them a responsibility to use this capacity to promote an atmosphere of refinement and cultivation at home. This continued, into the nineteenth century, in the form of a strong association between women, in their role as consumers, and a new domestic aesthetic which, largely decorative in nature and function, provided a feminine counterpoint to the male-dominated world of public art (Sparke, 1995). The influence of religious evangelism, finally, interacted with these conceptions to promote what Barker-Benfield (1992) calls a 'culture of sensibility' in which women, at home, were supposed to be able to exercise a greater refinement of aesthetic, moral and religious judgement than men.

The organizing centre of the new forces working to forge the new culture of domesticity was thus the woman who functioned as a kind of relay mechanism, passing on these influences to others. Davidoff and Hall again comment on middle-class women:

The minutiae of everyday life, their personal behaviour, dress and language became their arena to judge and be judged in. In 1847, the young daughters of a retired army officer expressed scorn at their prospective sister-in-law. Her menfolk did not 'dress for dinner' and only two weeks after the wedding she allowed her husband entry to her room when she was dressed only in her stays. These young women … were the inheritors of gentility … This canon covered every aspect of an individual's life and its enforcement was central to women, both for themselves and in ordering the behaviour of men. Refusing to countenance dirty finger-nails, coarse speech, or muddy boots sprawling on the new carpets was the material counterpart of influence, particularly effective when wielded by older women over their young male 'family and friends'. Since boy nature was taken to be dirty and rough, it needed the restraining hand and softening influence of a mother or sister.

(Davidoff and Hall, 1987, p.398)

There were, then, a range of forces working to produce the home as a new kind of social and cultural space which provided the primary venue of everyday life, especially for women whose relations to economic life – now located mainly outside the home – became increasingly indirect, mediated through their husbands. However, these forces operated unevenly, bearing more on the middle classes than on the working classes, even though middle-class philanthropists often aspired to refashion the working-class home on the middle-class model as a means of reforming working-class morals and manners. They were aided and abetted in this by retailers – especially the new institution of the department store which, initially in France but in a manner that was quickly imitated in Britain and the United States, served as an important means for spreading middle-class ideals of domestic comfort. The material necessities of working-class life, however, have always remained distinctive in being subject to the requirements of a different organization of the relations between the world of work, home, the couple, and their children.

It is also important to note that these forces have operated with varying pressure at different times. Periods of war have proved important here, resulting – during twentieth-century conflicts – in redefinitions of the codes of femininity that would encourage women to move into industrial or paramilitary roles. However, these redefinitions usually proved to be quite limited in their scope: the ultimate centrality of home and family to women's lives was never really in question. They also tended to be closed down again pretty quickly at the end of the two World Wars when women were once again encouraged to see home and 'domestic duty' as their natural and proper milieu.

2.2 The invaded haven

It will be useful, in considering the respects in which the home was organized as a haven from the outside world, to look briefly at the similarities between the home and the museum. While these might seem strange bedfellows, both function as what Mary Douglas calls 'memory machines' (Douglas, 1993, p.268) – the home as a machine for organizing personal and family memories, and the museum as a machine for organizing public memories, of a nation or of a city, for example. They do so, moreover, in similar ways: through the collection and display of valued objects.

Take a walk around your home and make a list of the kinds of things that you and other members of your household have collected. Then try to identify the roles these play in organizing personal and shared memories among those you live with or, if you live alone, for yourself.

Photographs, souvenirs, mementoes, trophies, pictures, books: these, perhaps, are among the things on your list and you may have noted some differences between the contexts in which different kinds of things are collected and displayed (or hidden): between what's on top of the television in the living-room, for example, and the more personal things that might be in a bedroom drawer.

There is an extensive literature exploring the varied meanings of different kinds of collection. It is, however, Didier Maleuvre who most clearly articulates the role of collecting in transforming a home from being 'simply a house' into 'an image of how we dwell, how we inhabit the world, how we view ourselves in the world' (Maleuvre, 1999, p.120). Viewed in this light, Maleuvre argues, collecting played a crucial role in nineteenth-century French bourgeois (or middle-class) understandings of home, especially for men:

> It is as though the bourgeois individual could only feel at home after assembling a houseful of bibelots [or curios], trinkets, ornaments, and gimcracks, and after surrounding himself with a luxuriance of the priceless, the semiprecious, and the junky. It is as an *owner* of a great many objects that the bourgeois individual inhabits the home. To dwell is to possess … For ownership to shine, the bourgeois dweller must supplement it with collectorship; he therefore needs a display of objects linked to him by sentimental ties. Collecting is a way of taking possession of the world, a way of domesticating the exotic by keeping a tribal mask on the mantelpiece, of securing the distant past through an antique statue, and of enshrining personal memory by means of a souvenir.
>
> (Maleuvre, 1999, p.115)

Maleuvre attributes a special significance to the role that was played by the growing 'taste for things historical' (*ibid.*, p.115) in fashioning the interior of the bourgeois household into an imaginative retreat from the world. By extracting objects from the flow of time, making home a place of personal memory, the increasing popularity of historical collections meant that home became a place 'where things abide, where they stay the same; … an idyllic retreat from the progress of science, social upheaval, and industrialism' (*ibid.*, p.116). If this interest in collecting was originally middle-class, it soon spread to other classes. Alain Corbin notes that, by the end of the century, 'the desire to amass family archives and collections of souvenirs' had spread throughout French society and played a similar function in all classes by organizing the home as a place which, because of its connections with personal memory, was removed from the pressures of the outside world (Corbin, 1990, p.546). The same was true of both the United States and Victorian Britain where, as Asa Briggs notes, collected objects and new items of domestic decoration played a crucial role in transforming a house into a home (Briggs, 1988, p.214). Benjamin Spiers' contemporary painting, *Away from the World and its Toils and its Cares,* illustrates the point neatly: see Figure 1.3.

Figure 1.3 *Benjamin Spiers,* Away from the World and its Toils and its Cares, *1885*

Yet, at the same time that home was being organized as a haven, it was also invaded from without by a range of new agencies which sought to manage and regulate the relations between its members and the conduct of everyday life within the home. Kerreen Reiger (1985) nicely conveys the tension between these two tendencies when she refers to the latter as bringing about a 'disenchantment of the home'. The phrase is one she borrows from the German sociologist **Max Weber** who used it to refer to the declining influence of religious and magical conceptions of the world in the face of the growing influence of rational and scientific forms of calculation and management that were associated with the development of industrial capitalism and bureaucratic forms of government. Her purpose in doing so is to suggest that similar principles were brought to bear on the home through the influence of a new group of experts principally comprising 'members of the medical profession, teachers and kindergarteners, domestic science and child guidance specialists' (Reiger, 1985, p.2). These shared a wish 'to "rationalize" the domestic world: to extend the principles of science and instrumental reason to the operation of the household and to the management of personal relationships' (*ibid.*, p.3). How did they set about doing this? Reiger sees the following as the main ways in which these agents sought to invade the home and reorganize the practices within it:

> The strategies included efforts to introduce technology to the household and to define the housewife as a 'modern', 'efficient' houseworker; to change patterns of reproduction by placing contraception, pregnancy and childbirth under conscious, usually professional, control; to alter childrearing practices in the light of 'hygiene', seen as both physical and mental; and to bring sexuality out from under the veil of prudery and silence.

> (Reiger, 1985, p.2)

Weber, Max

Although these experts were closely related to the bourgeoisie by their own social backgrounds and class position, their activities generated significant contradictions. For they clashed with the bourgeois construction of 'personal life as private, as a refuge of warmth and emotional intimacy' and of 'the realm of home/family/personal life/women' as 'the antithesis of the cold, calculative, rational world of capitalist commerce, industry and the State' (*ibid.*, p.3). The Electricity Commission's advertisement claiming 'Domestic Management is a Science' (Figure 1.4) illustrates the point, and provides a telling counterpoint to Benjamin Spiers' sentimental portrait of the home (in Figure 1.3).

Insights of this kind are not unique to Reiger. Hareven, you might recall, also touches briefly on the role of reformers committed to scientific management in applying the principles of industrial efficiency to the home. This is also the central concern of an earlier study by Barbara Ehrenreich and Deirdre English (1979). With the withdrawal of economic and manufacturing activities from the home and the development of new services for the home (laundries) and labour-saving devices within it (see Figure 1.5), there was a sense, in late nineteenth-century America, of a 'domestic void'. In the attempt to fill this void, the housewife was enlisted for a whole range of new tasks in the pursuit of rational, scientific and hygienic household management and motherhood.

Figure 1.4 *Domestic management and the disenchantment of the home, 1931*

Figure 1.5 *The modernizing role of technology at work in the kitchen, c.1900*

The value of these perspectives from the point of view of our concerns here has to do with the ways in which they complicate our understanding of the relations between men, women, home and the everyday. The association of women with a concept of everyday life grounded in the dull, repetitive cycle of domestic life that Henri Lefebvre proposes is, at best, only half the story. While women were, of course, caught up in these conceptions of the home, they were also subject to appeals which recruited them as the representatives of modernizing scientific and rationalizing forces in their relations to home and their domestic roles. This was not without its consequences. As we shall see, early feminist campaigns for the transformation of domestic life were often fuelled by tensions arising out of the contradictory ways in which women were addressed between the 'culture of domesticity' on the one hand and the 'culture of science' on the other.

2.3 Contested domesticities

The view of the middle-class home as an 'ideal home' that other classes should strive to emulate had its price. This consisted, in part, in the tension between – as Tony Chapman and Jenny Hockey put it – 'the ideal home as it is imagined and as it is lived' (1999, p.1). The exclusion of the elderly; the emotional intensity invested in the relations between husband and wife; the denials and repressions involved in the curtailment of women's aspirations to the home; the pressure-cooker effect of new forms of child-centredness: all of these conspired to turn the ideal home into its opposite – a 'House of Doom', as Jenny Hockey puts it (Hockey, 1999, p.147). This 'other side' of the domestic idyll has been extensively expressed in a rich tradition of literary and filmic representation in which the home becomes an almost palpable destructive force, wreaking havoc in the lives of those who are trapped together within it. The depiction of Rochester Hall in Charlotte Brontë's *Jane Eyre* is a case in point as is, more recently, Virginia Andrews' *Flowers in the Attic* (1979), while *Amityville Horror* (1979) and *Pacific Heights* (1990) are examples of horror films playing on these contradictory attitudes toward the home.

The idealization of the home as an idyll also involved its construction as a fortress and, Mike Hepworth (1999) argues, the demonization of all that fell outside its carefully maintained boundaries (fences, walls, hedges, gates). If the concept of home attains its first full flowering in the nineteenth century, so does the view of homelessness as the direst of all possible conditions. This is the theme of George Smith's 1876 *Into the Cold World* (Figure 1.6), as it is also of a good deal of Victorian fiction – Charles Dickens' *Little Dorrit*, for example. But this demonization also had more specific social characteristics in its depiction of the working-class home – often little more than a room or two affording little space for the forms of privacy essential to middle-class standards of decency – as vicious and demoralizing. Similar issues are raised when the home is considered in the context of the histories of racism and colonialism. If civilizing the working classes meant, among other things, re-organizing their homes along middle-class lines, the history of British colonialism similarly involved attempts to export the concept of home to India as a means of 'civilizing the natives'.

It is, however, equally important to be clear that when white, middle-class home values were relayed across class and racial lines in this way, the results

Figure 1.6 *George Smith,* Into the Cold World, *1876*

were often complex and contradictory. Where they were not actively resisted – although this was sometimes the case – the values of home were, in the very process of being embraced, often given distinctive new twists as they came to form parts of social and political projects quite different from those envisaged by western middle-class reformers. Inderpal Grewal (1996) thus traces the important role that a revised version of western home values played in the strategies of Indian nationalism. Paul Gilroy similarly estimates that the promotion of marriage and domestic values among America's black slave population did a good deal to promote the development of the concept of the 'free self' that was to play such an important role in anti-slavery campaigns (Gilroy, 2000, p.193).

But the ideal of domesticity itself has never been a settled one. It, too, has been contested and often in ways that derive from the contradictory constructions of the home as a haven and as a zone for rational and scientific management. It will be instructive to explore these issues further by looking at the role of architecture in regulating domestic life.

2.4 Architecture and domestic life

It will be best to introduce the issues that concern us here by means of a specific example. As a figure already introduced by Hareven, the first-wave feminist, Charlotte Perkins Gilman, and the campaigns waged by her for feminist motherhood in feminist housing complexes, will suit this purpose nicely.

You should now study Reading 1.2 at the end of the chapter, Dolores Hayden's 'Domestic evolution or domestic revolution?', and answer the following questions:

1   How did Gilman view the role of women in relation to the process of evolution? Why did she see the reform of the home as being essential if women were to fulfil this role?

2   What role did the architecture of the home play in Gilman's conception of feminist motherhood?

3   In what ways did contemporary scientific conceptions inform Gilman's critique of the culture of domesticity?

Hayden's discussion underlines the importance that was attributed to architecture as a means of regulating conduct and social interactions within the home. This reflected the general importance that architecture enjoyed in the nineteenth century as a 'moral science' which was capable – through its partitioning of space and its arrangement of lines of sight and vision – of transforming character and behaviour as well as generating all kinds of new social possibilities. **Michel Foucault** has argued that this was the thinking behind the spate of new designs for prisons and asylums that characterized the period, as it was believed that the organization of their internal space could play a major role, in the former, in reforming the criminal, or, in the latter, curing the insane (see Foucault, 1977). It was also the thinking behind the housing schemes through which reformers aimed to translate the principles of the middle-class home – with its partitioning of space between areas for eating, sleeping and recreation, and its careful regulation of the relations between genders and generations – into a form that would be within the means of the working classes (Guerrand, 1990).

Architecture also played a major role in nineteenth-century utopian, socialist and communitarian movements, promoting the belief that the manipulation of spatial layouts could help to achieve their ideals. Dolores Hayden addresses these questions in an earlier study where she examines the domestic arrangements that were envisaged in the architectural projects of the most influential utopian experiments in nineteenth-century America. My favourite is her account of 'the architecture of complex marriage'. This was designed to help realize, in a practical form, the belief of the Oneida Community that all of its members were married to each other and that, through this group cohesion, they were bonded to Christ. While the rules of this community permitted pair-bonding between couples, these were meant to be temporary in order to avoid 'exclusive personal attachments which might overshadow group feeling' (Hayden, 1976, p.187). This objective was facilitated, architecturally, by arranging the relationships between bedrooms (all designed for single occupancy) and communal sitting and recreational areas such that the latter provided for the easy involvement of all members of the community with each other immediately outside the bedrooms which, in being thus subjected to constant surveillance, could not easily be used for the development of permanent familial or sexual attachments (Figure 1.7a). The scene of the Upper Sitting Room (Figure 1.7b), with bedroom doors leading off both upstairs and downstairs, gives some sense of how effective this mechanism might have proved in inhibiting the development of intimacy.

Foucault, Michel

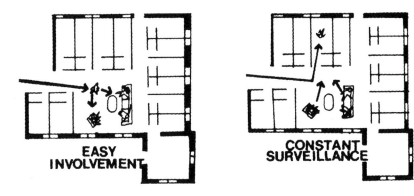

Figure 1.7 *The Oneida Perfectionists built a substantial communal home in central New York, from 1847. The Second Mansion House was built in 1862, with the claim that 'Communism in our society has built itself a house'.*
top (a) The 'architecture of complex marriage': diagram of layouts facilitating 'easy involvement' and 'constant surveillance'
bottom (b) The Upper Sitting Room during the 'Children's Hour', 1870

It is because they ran against the grain that architectural experiments of this kind help us to appreciate the socially and historically distinctive nature of what have proved to be the dominant tendencies in domestic architecture in facilitating the development of intimacy and in ordering and segregating space in specific gendered ways. These architectural strategies are usually particularly evident in the plans for ideal or show homes and the ways of life these are trying to sell. It is therefore worth taking a brief look at a contemporary floor-plan for an ideal home: see Figure 1.8.

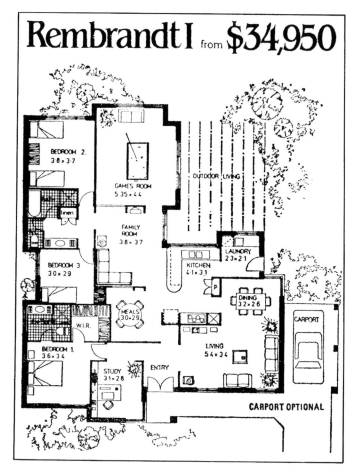

Figure 1.8 *The floor-plan of the 'Rembrandt I' by Artisan homes: a budget-priced bungalow for sale in Australia in the 1980s*

ACTIVITY 5

Take some time to look at Figure 1.8 and answer the following questions:

1 How are the relations between public and private spaces organized in this house?

2 How are the relationships between male and female spaces organized?

3 What are the relationships between public space, family space and the spaces of the couple?

You should also consider how these spatial arrangements compare with those discussed by Hayden in Reading 1.2.

John Fiske, Bob Hodge and Graeme Turner, in discussing this floor-plan, see three main divisions of space within it: the private space of the marital couple on the left of the front door (study and 'master' bedroom), a public area for entertaining visitors to the right (living and dining area) and, straight ahead, the shared generational spaces of the meals area, family and games rooms, with the children's bedrooms off to the left of these. Here is how they see the flow of relationships between different family members and visitors that this organization of space permits:

It expresses social relationships – different categories for family and friends, and for the married couple and their children – yet it also blurs their boundaries. The kitchen is an 'open' kitchen, with no walls dividing it from the rest of the living area; but the structure of benches and cupboards still corrals the mother into the command centre of the house. The opening of the kitchen does not free the mother from the role of cook, but it does signal a change in the meaning of that role in family and social life. The kitchen used to be hidden from the dining room: from it would emerge, almost miraculously, the food for family and guests. This is a residue of the time and class when cooking was seen as a menial task to be performed by servants and then by the mother-as-servant. As she brought the meal to the table, her servant role was left in the kitchen and she became mother-wife or hostess as she sat at the table. Now, however, cooking is seen as less menial, more creative, so not only is the mother-cook not to be excluded from activity and conversation in the living or dining areas of the house, but her role as cook is given a highly visible centrality. The placing of the kitchen between the family meals area and the visitors' dining area, and its openness, establishes the woman as the mediator between the family and the guests, and suggests that children only have access to the visitors and to the 'dining area' through the mother's grace. The laundry, opening off the kitchen, is effectively made invisible to the guest, convenient for the woman in the kitchen, and a long way from the man's private place, the study. Its invisibility suggests that the work performed there is menial, not creative or positive.

Just as the man is excluded (or rather insulated) from the laundry, the children are excluded from the master bathroom – through the interposition of a study on one side and an ensuite bathroom/toilet on the other.

(Fiske, Hodge and Turner, 1987, pp.35–6)

SUMMARY OF SECTION 2

This section has traced some aspects of the historical development of the modern concept of home in order to examine the associated 'culture of domesticity', and to consider the position of women in that culture. It has considered the range of forces bearing on the organization of home and the conduct of activities within it.

Three main points have been made:

1   These forces have pulled in somewhat contradictory directions, constructing the home as a haven, a retreat from the rigours of industry, government and bureaucracy and yet, at the same time, aspiring to subject the home to their rationalizing influence.

2   These contradictions have been productive ones in the sense that women's critical engagement with the 'culture of domesticity' has been partly fuelled by the tensions these forces have generated.

3   We have also seen that attitudes toward the home, and everyday relations to and involvements in it, vary in accordance with considerations of class, gender and ethnicity.

It is to a further amplification of this third point that we now turn.

3 Home values

The most effective way of introducing the focus of this section – the exploration of the variation in values relating to the home – will be by asking you to explore further your own views about home.

Look at these questions about attitudes toward home and home-based leisure activities and take a minute or two to answer them.

Attitudes to home

1 Thinking for a moment about what would be the ideal home for you, choose three terms which come closest to describing your ideal home:

Clean-and-tidy	Uncluttered	Traditional	Elegant
Comfortable	Easy-to-maintain	Distinctive	Lived in
Well-designed	Modern	Imaginative	Spacious

2 Of the activities listed below, which do you do often, which do you do sometimes, which do you hardly ever do, and which do you never do?

	Often	Sometimes	Hardly ever	Never
Home repairs				
Do-it-yourself home improvements				
Gardening				
Drawing or sketching				
Photography				
Creative writing				
Playing a musical instrument				
Craft activity				
Clothes making				
Playing cards or chess				
Computer or video games				
Board games				
Fantasy/role-playing games				
Listening to music				
Reading				
Listening to the radio				

COMMENT

These questions are selected from a study of everyday cultural practices in Australia conducted by myself, Michael Emmison and John Frow. Tables 1.1 and 1.2 summarize the contrasting patterns of women's and men's answers to these questions.

Table 1.1 Ideal home by gender (percentages) $n = 2756$

		Female	Male	Male as % of female
Mainly female	Lived-in	16.1	12.1	75
	Uncluttered	11.4	8.5	75
	Elegant	6.4	5.1	80
	Imaginative	8.2	6.7	82
	Easy-to-maintain	48.6	41.5	85
	Clean-and-tidy	50.6	47.7	94
	Comfortable	59.4	55.6	94
Mainly male	Spacious	24.8	27.1	109
	Traditional	7.7	8.6	112
	Well-designed	31.1	35.9	115
	Modern	8.5	11.9	140
	Distinctive	3.1	6.1	197

Table 1.2 Participation in domestic leisure (often and sometimes) by gender (percentages) $n = 2756$

		Female	Male	Male as % of female
Mainly female	Clothes making	43.4	2.9	7
	Craft activity	61.3	15.1	25
	Creative writing	18.9	9.3	49
	Board games	41.7	32.4	75
	Drawing or sketching	17.2	13.4	78
	Photography	52.1	43.7	84
	Playing cards or chess	45.6	43.9	96
Mainly male	Gardening	77.5	77.8	100
	Fantasy/role-playing games	7.7	9.5	123
	Playing a musical instrument	14.5	20.4	141
	DIY home improvements	39.9	61.6	154
	Home repairs	47.7	77.2	162
	Computer or video games	19.0	32.9	173

■ ■ ■

ACTIVITY 7

This is not the place for a lesson in statistics so, taking the figures in these tables at face value, try to identify what they tell us about how Australian men and women differ in their attitudes and relations to home. Then compare your answers with the ways in which the authors of this study interpret these tables (below). You should also consider how similar or different your own responses are from those reported in the tables.

TABLES 1.1 AND 1.2: AUTHORS' INTERPRETATIONS

Table 1.1 'Women's preferences, when ranked according to how they most differ from men's, reflect an orientation that centres inward on the home and its relationship to its family members. The stress is on practicality ('uncluttered', 'easy-to-maintain', 'clean-and-tidy') and, most importantly, on the home as a place to be lived in. The attributes which men prefer more strongly than women, by contrast, mostly relate to the display functions of the home – its role in presenting an image of the self and of the family to the outside world. At their polarised extremes, if women's most distinctive preference when measured against men's is for a home to have a lived-in feel about it, men differ from women most in their wish that home should be distinctive, that is, that it should make a public statement about the distinguishing style of its owners or occupants' (Bennett, Emmison and Frow, 1999, p.44).

Table 1.2 'While gardening is a more or less equally shared activity, other activities directed towards the maintenance of the home and family are significantly differentiated, with women focusing on family activities (making clothes, craft activities) while men are more engaged in maintaining the physical infrastructure of the home (DIY and home repairs). If this is not surprising, the distribution of other activities is somewhat more notable, with women – except for playing a musical instrument – more likely to engage in creative activities (writing, drawing, photography) than men while also preferring more traditional games (board games, cards, chess) which typically involve the whole family. Men, by contrast, have higher rates of preference for role-playing games and especially for computer and video games which, in pitting one or two players against either the machine or one another, are often less successful in involving the family as a family' (*ibid.*, pp.45–6).

■ ■ ■

variable

Of course, gender is not the only social **variable** influencing our attitudes toward, and activities within, the home. Social class also plays an important role here: in this study, for example, employers were more likely than the members of all other classes to want their homes to be 'distinctive', while manual workers were the most likely to want a home to be clean, uncluttered and modern. However, rather than pursuing this point abstractly, it will prove instructive to look at how considerations of class and gender interact with one another in shaping 'home values'. We do so by looking at how two women interviewed in this study talk about home, and how their 'home values', while sharing some characteristics, reflect their different class backgrounds.

READING 1.3

You should now study Reading 1.3, 'Cultural choice and the home' by Tony Bennett, Michael Emmison and John Frow. While you do so, keep the following questions in mind:

1   What are the main similarities and differences between the 'home values' of Gillian and those of Mary?

2   In what respects do Gillian's and Mary's attitudes toward home reflect (a) shared gendered values, and (b) different class values?

When you have done that, you should think back to Reading 1.1 and consider the similarities between the effects of class differences in this study and those discussed by Hareven.

Although home might be the archetypal site of everyday life, what home is, what it means and what takes place there are clearly not constants. The values that are invested in the home, how the relations between home and other sites of social activity – places of work, holidays – are perceived, and how the home functions as a place for carrying social messages about those who live there: these are all subject to marked social variation. In many respects, these are deeply personal and individual matters. The significance, for Gillian, of her choice of colour scheme clearly relates very much to the specific details of her own personal biography. At the same time, however, these personal and individual choices are never just that. Gillian's personal life story is, at the same time, a social story – a story of upward social mobility – and, as such, her choices are informed by shared social values about the relations between colour schemes and ideas about 'good taste'.

   Mobility of another kind can also significantly affect attitudes toward the home and the values invested in it. The sense of home as a place of refuge from a hostile outside world often assumes new meanings for ethnic minorities caught up in histories of travel. David Morley, for example, records the case of a young Barbadian family growing up in England in the 1960s with a family rule that 'whenever we entered the house we were not English – we were in Barbados and we would behave accordingly' (cited in Morley, 2000, p.52). Here home becomes a crucial place for migrants in retaining a sense of their distinctive cultural identities in the midst of what Paul Gilroy calls their new 'unhomely homelands' (2000, p.247). In other cases, migration can give rise to a sense of rootlessness – of being between homes – so that the concept of home means something different from that of the actual house lived in. David Morley reviews some examples of this phenomenon in the next reading.

READING 1.4

You should now read David Morley's 'The migrant's suitcase' (Reading 1.4 at the end of the chapter) and answer the following question:

■   What are the factors which account for the tendency for migrants to feel that they are always between homes and never fully at home?

Morley's perspective helps us see more clearly the limitations of the OED definition of home as 'the place where one lives permanently' or 'a fixed place of residence' for those whose patterns of mobility mean that they do not see themselves as having a single, fixed abode. For migrants, the values of home often attach more strongly to the place – be it country, region or house – they have left, and to which they wish to return, rather than to where they actually live.

SUMMARY OF SECTION 3

There have been two main arguments in this section:

1   The first is that the values that are associated with home are not constant but vary in accordance with the roles that gender, social class, ethnicity and other social factors play in shaping the general pattern of our value systems and the place of our attitudes toward home within these.

2   It has also been shown that the place of home in everyday life is not a constant either. Its place within the rhythms of daily life, for example, differs depending on whether or not people have been socially mobile, in the sense of rising (or dropping) from one social class to another, or geographically mobile in moving from one country to another.

---

4 Home life, routine and the politics of the everyday

What light do the perspectives explored above, and those developed in section 2, throw on the debates about questions of gender, politics and the everyday that were briefly reviewed at the start of this chapter?

Let us look first a little more closely at what Henri Lefebvre had to say about the relationship of women to everyday life. Owing to their association with home and domesticity, he argued, women are especially likely to be caught up in the habitual, repetitive aspects of everyday life and, therefore, are less likely to develop the broader intellectual horizons that might place everyday life in a critical perspective. Lefebvre argued that,

> Everyday life weighs heaviest on women … Some are bogged down by its peculiar cloying substance, others escape into make-believe, close their eyes to their surroundings, to the bog into which they are sinking and simply ignore it … Because of their ambiguous position in everyday life – which is specifically part of everyday life and modernity – they are incapable of understanding it.
>
> (Lefebvre, 1971, p.73)

ACTIVITY 8

How, drawing on the reading you have done so far, might you take issue with Lefebvre's view?

It is clear, first of all, that Lefebvre's argument is an over-generalization in that it fails to distinguish how women's relationships to the home and everyday life are differentiated by other aspects of their social formation: their class positions and levels of education, for example. Lefebvre's assessment also seems to take little note of the respects in which, while pulled in one direction by the 'culture of domesticity', women's relations to the home have been pulled in other directions by the roles of modern medicine, domestic science and economy, and modernizing forms of domestic technology.

Yet Lefebvre was by no means unaware of the influence of rationalizing and modernizing forces bearing on the organization of everyday life within the home. On the contrary, he was, Rob Shields notes, one of the first social theorists to take seriously the new technological forms that were involved in restructuring domestic life in the post-war period (Shields, 1999, p.96). If Lefebvre had relatively little sense as to how the effects of this might be contradictory in terms of their consequences for the relations between women, everyday life and the home, this was largely because his views on these matters were to a considerable extent predetermined by his perception of men's and women's different relations to the distinctive structure of time that he argued characterizes everyday life.

It is these questions concerning the relations between gender, time and everyday life that concern Rita Felski – who, writing from the perspective of **feminist social theory** – disagrees not only with Lefebvre's suggestion that women, through their relations to home, are unduly immersed in the habit and the repetitive structure of time which characterize everyday life. She is as much concerned by the corollary of this view: that is, that women are excluded from the linear, progressive time of modernity – the time of science, industry and commerce outside the home – which, just as misleadingly, thereby emerges as an essentially masculine time. In engaging with these issues, Felski draws on different approaches to the study of everyday life to question the pejorative assessment of repetition that informs Lefebvre's writings. It is in the light of this – her transformation of repetition from a necessary vice into a possible virtue – that she is able to propose different terms for evaluating the politics of everyday life from those put forward by Lefebvre.

The broader political aspects of Lefebvre's approach to everyday life were shaped by his interest in the Surrealists – an influential avant-garde artistic movement between the two World Wars – and in post-war existentialism. Both of these intellectual and artistic movements were concerned to locate means through which the repetition and banality of everyday life might be transcended in the name of a higher or more authentic set of values: through the shock tactics of new, challenging and disruptive artistic activities in the case of Surrealism, or through defining moments of individual decisions in the case of existentialism. This was echoed, Rob Shields argues (*ibid.*, pp.60–1), by Lefebvre's concern to identify 'moments of presence' – moments of intense emotion or heightened social involvement – that would transcend everyday life as individuals escaped its eviscerating structures to be more truly themselves. Its influence was also evident in his concern to identify new social groups – students or youth – who, supposedly less ensnared by everyday routines, might constitute a social force capable of resisting the 'bureaucratic society of controlled consumption' and of bringing about a 'permanent cultural revolution' in which everyday life would be endlessly disrupted.

feminist social theory

What we now need to clarify is why such views should have led to a low estimation of women's ability either to escape the repetitive rigours of everyday life or to suggest an alternative to it. These are the questions that Rita Felski addresses in the next reading.

READING 1.5

You should now read Rita Felski's 'The invention of everyday life' (Reading 1.5 at the end of the chapter), and then answer the questions below. These are more difficult than the questions asked in earlier activities, so don't be surprised if you find them hard-going – they are!

1   How does Lefebvre view the relations between the cyclical structure of everyday time and the linear time of modern industrial society? Why is the former a drag on the latter?

2   What are the main reasons for women being associated with the cyclical time of repetition?

3   What historical arguments does Felski draw on to question the pejorative assessment of repetition that characterizes Lefebvre's work?

4   On what grounds does Felski question Lefebvre's equation of repetition with domination and of innovation with agency and resistance?

5   Summarize Felski's arguments against the view that modernity should be regarded as being anti-home and the home as anti-modernity.

I want to look more closely at two issues arising from this reading: the first concerns the relations between women, time and modernity; and the second focuses on the role of the media in organizing the 'dailiness' of everyday life.

4.1 Women, time and modernity

There is little space, in Felski's perspective, for any singular view of the relations between women, home and the everyday. As the site for 'an active practising of place' (Reading 5.1, p.49), relations to the home are complexly varied, shaped by the interrelations between gender, class and generational issues just as the nature of repetition in the home and the values to be invested in it are varied. Equally, Felski's perspective affords little space for any singular view of the relations between men, **modernity** and the world – of industry or the streets – outside the home. This is partly because she insists that the 'boundaries between home and non-home are leaky' (*ibid.*) in ways that question any absolute sense of distinction between the home as a private sphere and the public worlds of commerce, organized entertainment and politics such that the values of modernity might be associated exclusively with the latter and denied to the former. Challenging the view that home can – or ever could – be 'seen as existing outside the flux and change of an authentically modern life' (1999–2000, p.26), Felski suggests the need for a theory of everyday life that will explore how the relations between home and everyday life – and the activities of women within these – have themselves been brought into the flow of modernity.

Lesley Johnson's (1996) discussion of the values that Australian women placed on their homemaking activities in the post-war period is an example of

modernity

the kinds of approach Felski has in mind here. Basing her assessments on how women described what homemaking meant to them in letters to women's magazines and varied public authorities, Johnson argues that women did not see their homes as a retreat from the public life of the nation but as a means of contributing to its future development:

> In this scenario, women were active participants in modern social existence; they were central to what they believed to be the project of this new world – ensuring people could be in control of their own lives, to define their futures … Home was not a bounded space, a fortress into which the individual could withdraw and from which all others could be excluded. Their modernity was about actively creating a place called home, securing a future for their children and an everyday life in which personal and intimate bodily relations could be properly looked after.
>
> (Johnson, 1996, p.461)

We have already seen arguments of this kind in our earlier discussion of the role of modernizing views of scientific management, rational hygiene, and domestic science in late nineteenth- and early twentieth-century conceptions of good home management and the distinctive 'spin' that was placed on these arguments by first-wave feminists. Similar concerns are still very much alive in debates surrounding the differing attitudes of men and women towards, and their uses of, new communications and domestic technologies within the home (Livingstone, 1992; Silva, 1999).

It is clear, then, that placing women, home and a repetitive relation to time on one side of a divide and men, the public world, and a progressive relation to time on the other side of that divide will not work. And, even if it did, it is not clear why the first kind of time should be so lowly valued and the second so highly prized. This, indeed, has been questioned in recent debates about the role of the media in everyday life.

4.2 The media and the 'dailiness' of everyday life

In opening his *Television and Everyday Life* Roger Silverstone offers a useful summary of his thesis concerning the extent to which television permeates the structures and routines of everyday life:

> Television accompanies us as we wake up, as we breakfast, as we have our tea and as we drink in bars. It comforts us when we are alone. It helps us sleep. It gives us pleasure, it bores us and sometimes it challenges us. It provides us with opportunities to be both sociable and solitary. Although, of course, it was not always so, and although we have had to learn how to incorporate the medium into our lives, we now take television entirely for granted … in a way similar to how we take everyday life for granted.
>
> (Silverstone, 1994, p.3)

And he is in no doubt about the centrality of the connection between television and the home:

> Television is a domestic medium. It is watched at home. Ignored at home. Discussed at home. Watched in private and with members of family or friends. But it is part of our domestic culture in other ways too, providing in its programming and its schedules models and structures of domestic life … .
>
> (*ibid.*, p.24)

Of course, what is true of television now was earlier true of radio which soon learned to address and construct a world of 'hearth and home', speaking to its audience as a family gathered around the 'radio hearth' (Frith, 1983, p.110). Lesley Johnson tells a similar story in Australia where radio – initially regarded as a scientific marvel appealing mainly to men – had also, by the 1920s, begun to develop what she calls 'an intimate voice' which, in addressing the listener personally and informally, allowed it to become an ordinary part of everyday life in the home (Johnson, 1988). Equally, though, once generalizations like this are made, they immediately need to be qualified. Television may be a primarily home-based media technology in countries such as the United Kingdom, the United States and Australia, but it does not play this role in all societies or cultures. Morley usefully reminds us of societies, such as Paraguay, in which television-viewing takes place mainly outside the home, and of others in which its intrusion into the home is often unwelcome: satellite transmission, in the perspective of an Australian Aboriginal community representative, would be 'like having hundreds of whitefellas visit without permits, every day' (quoted in Morley, 2000, p.151). It is also true that the development of new technologies (video, personal computers, cable, digitization) is reorganizing the place of television in the home and, according to some accounts, weakening its influence.

Be this as it may, there can be no doubting the continuing strength of the relationship that currently exists between home, television and everyday life. Consider, for example, the following statement from a respondent in the British Film Institute's audience-tracking study:

> 'I work. I leave home at 7.30am, return at 4.15pm. My two sons go to school at 10 to 9 and return at 3.30pm. Their mother takes them to and from school. She and the boys have *TV AM* on while getting ready for school and having breakfast, it goes on at about 7am. *This Morning* is usually on while housework and other things are done; and attention is paid to interesting items. *Neighbours* and *Home and Away* are watched by her on their first showing of the day [lunchtime]. *Country Practice* is videoed for her and I to watch in the evening. If she goes shopping in the morning then *This Morning* will be videoed and scanned for interesting items later. Washing and ironing may be done in the evenings, especially if my wife has been shopping, visiting or gardening. So although *Emmerdale* and *Coronation Street* will be on, no great attention need be paid to them. I am an Open University student so I study from 6.30pm to 9pm virtually every evening. Most of my viewing is programmes recorded earlier or from previous days. *Brookside* is about the only "live" transmission I watch during the evening. I watch my recordings from 9pm. I do watch *Neighbours* and *Home and Away*, though at their second showings during the evening meal with the rest of the family. Any videoed programmes will be seen between 9pm and 10.30pm when we go to bed.'
>
> (Gauntlett and Hill, 1999, p.27)

It is this capacity of the media to provide a pattern for the routines of the day that Paddy Scannell has in mind when he speaks about the ability of television to organize the 'dailiness' of everyday life (Scannell, 1996, pp.148–51). For Scannell, moreover, this aspect of the relations between the media and everyday life is something to be positively valued rather than, as in Lefebvre's perspective, a matter for regret. Silverstone offers a similar assessment in his account of the role of television in organizing a sense of 'ontological security' – that is, a confident sense of self-identity – which is both rooted in, and necessary for, everyday life. This ontological security, Silverstone argues, is acquired through, and grounded in, the repetitive aspects of daily life, including – in contemporary societies – the role of the media in organizing and sustaining its rhythms and routines. Here is how he puts the matter:

> Everyday life, it is argued, cannot be sustained without order – and order manifested in our various traditions, rituals, routines and taken for granted activities – in which we, paradoxically, invest so much energy, effort and so many cognitive and emotional resources. In the ordering of daily life we avoid panic, we construct and maintain our identities, we manage our social relationships in time and space, sharing meanings, fulfilling our responsibilities, experiencing pleasure and pain, with greater or lesser degrees of satisfaction and control, but avoiding for the most part the blank and numbing horror of the threat of chaos.
>
> (Silverstone, 1994, p.1)

For Silverstone as for Felski, then, the routines of everyday life emerge in a more positive light than they did for Lefebvre. In this, they both reflect the influence of Agnes Heller (1984) who saw considerable value in the habitual aspects of everyday life as being essential to the formation of a stable, coherent and productive sense of self and identity. But this does not mean that Silverstone sees the relations between media, home and everyday life as working solely to produce a sense of ontological security. To the contrary, he sees the role of the media as also being transformative, especially through their capacity to extend the 'reach' of the home – that is, what can be accessed from home and, thereby, what influences can reach into the home to alter what goes on there.

In order to provide a specific example of what this might mean in practice, it will be useful to consider Lynn Spigel's account of the relations between television and the home in 1950s' USA, a decade in which the ownership of TV sets increased from 10 to 90 per cent and viewing time averaged about five hours a day (Spigel, 1992, p.188). The 1950s also marked a specific moment in the history of the home in the United States owing to the rapid growth of suburbs and, associated with this, worries that those living in the suburbs – uprooted from the urban neighbourhoods of the pre-war period – would feel cut off from any sense of community. The new suburban home was accordingly designed as a more porous space than its predecessors, its interiors flowing into the exteriors of garden and neighbourhood space to allow the home to 'mediate the contradictory impulses for a private haven on the one hand, and community participation on the other' (*ibid.*, p.186). If television, too, was regarded as a means of mediating between the home and the communities – of neighbourhood and nation – outside it, it also helped to fashion the spaces within the home in which it was to perform this role. On the one hand, television shows like *I Love Lucy* – with Lucy and Ricky Ricardo and their landlords, Ethel and Fred Mertz, always in each others' apartments – foregrounded the importance of the connections between home and neighbourliness. On the other, the reorganization of the family sitting-room into a little family theatre, where the family members all faced 'the box' rather than each other, meant that the events of the outside world were relayed into the home as 'a safe and predictable experience' (*ibid.*, p.199) that would not challenge the sequestered peace and harmony of home life.

Television here, in other words, did, as Silverstone suggests, extend the boundaries of the home beyond the front door, but only in a way that simultaneously 'screened out' the unpleasant realities – of urban strife and racial conflict, for example – that did not fit with the idyll of the white family home in the new, white, suburban neighbourhood. But it also brought new tensions into the home in view of the contradictory ways in which it connected with prevailing conceptions about the relations between gender, home and everyday life. On the one hand, contemporary social science surveys found that many women complained that television increased their sense of confinement to the home as it made their husbands more likely to want to stay in and watch the television than to go out and engage in more public forms of socializing and entertainment. On the other hand, this very same tendency was viewed as turning '"real men" into passive homebodies' with the risk that, in being subject to the feminizing influence of certain genres – such as situation comedy and soap operas – that were produced mainly for women at home, they would become emasculated, with dire consequences for the future of the United States.

SUMMARY OF SECTION 4

Our concerns in this section have focused on debates about the relations between gender, time and everyday life, and the place of home within these debates. Two main arguments have been advanced:

1   The supposition that women, through their relations to the home, are caught up in the repetitive, cyclical patterns of everyday time in ways that men are not, has been questioned. So, too, has the assumption that the linear, public time of modernity is essentially masculine. Instead, it has been argued, the ways in which women's activities in the home have been connected to modernity call into question any rigid separation of everyday time within the home from the extra-domestic world of public time.

2   The view that the repetitive aspects of everyday life should be negatively valued has been questioned by examining alternative approaches which value this aspect of everyday time positively for the ontological security it offers.

5 Conclusion

It has been noted at various points in the discussion so far that our relations to everyday life are strongly governed by habit, by a tendency to take its rhythms and routines for granted, almost as if they were natural. Reflecting the strongly anti-naturalizing tendencies which characterize sociology as a whole, sociological approaches to everyday life typically seek to disrupt this natural attitude. They aim to make us look at our everyday practices in a new light, even to make them seem a little strange, by underlining their social and historical peculiarity.

It is, then, worth returning briefly to our starting-point to ask, again: what is home? And what is its place in everyday life?

ACTIVITY 9

Turn back to your initial definitions of home that you noted down for Activity 1. How, now, might you want to revise these? And how would you characterize the relations between home and everyday life?

One approach to the first question of definition is to say that home is an **institution**: that is, that it acts as a means for regularizing both social practices of particular kinds as well as particular kinds of social relations, between genders and generations for example. However, we have also seen that, when viewed as an institution, the home is not a constant. How social relations and practices within the home are organized, and the values that are invested in the home, are matters that vary historically as well as in accordance with the key sociological variables of age, class, ethnicity and gender. A third key point emerging from our discussion has concerned the respects in which the home is organized and regulated from the outside through the activities of a range of external agencies.

institution

Establishing the place of home in everyday life is a somewhat more contentious matter. There is, on the one hand, widespread agreement that home is a key site of everyday life, anchoring and organizing its rhythms, albeit that exactly how it does so can differ from one social group and context to another. On the other hand, however, there are significant disagreements as to how this aspect of the relations between home and everyday life should be assessed: negatively by Henri Lefebvre, but more positively by writers such as Rita Felski and Roger Silverstone. My purpose, in considering these disagreements, has been not to resolve them but to introduce some of the political controversies which characterize sociological debate about everyday life that will be of concern in later chapters.

It is important to add, though, that the **sociology of everyday life** encompasses a broader range of theoretical traditions than we have been able to survey here. Yet the traditions we have reviewed are indicative of this area of sociology more generally in that, rather than being concerned with large-scale social structures and processes, it tends to focus on the smaller-scale, more local and contingent aspects of social life. Equally, however, we have seen that these are not entirely disconnected areas of study, since the questions of power that typically concern such large-scale social structures as class, the state or patriarchy are also very much to the forefront of attention in sociological accounts of the micro-routines of daily life.

sociology of everyday life

References

Armstrong, N. (1987) 'The rise of domestic woman' in Armstrong, N. and Tennenhouse, L. (eds) *The Ideology of Conduct: Essays on Literature and the History of Sexuality*, London and New York, Methuen.

Barker-Benfield, G.J. (1992) *The Culture of Sensibility: Sex and Society in Eighteenth-century Britain*, Chicago, IL, and London, University of Chicago Press.

Bennett, T., Emmison, M. and Frow, J. (1999) *Accounting for Tastes: Australian Everyday Cultures*, Melbourne, Cambridge University Press.

Briggs, A. (1988) *Victorian Things*, Harmondsworth, Penguin Books.

Chapman, T. and Hockey, J. (1999) 'The ideal home as it is imagined and as it is lived' in Chapman, T. and Hockey, J. (eds) *op. cit.*.

Chapman, T. and Hockey, J. (eds) (1999) *Ideal Homes? Social Change and Domestic Life*, London and New York, Routledge.

Corbin, A. (1990) 'The secret of the individual' in Perrot, M. (ed.) *op. cit.*.

Davidoff, L. and Hall, C. (1987) *Family Fortunes: Men and Women of the English Middle Class, 1780–1850*, London, Routledge.

Douglas, M. (1993) 'The idea of home: a kind of space' in Mack, A. (ed.) *op.cit.*.

Ehrenreich, B. and English, D. (1979) *For Her Own Good: 150 Years of the Experts' Advice to Women*, London, Pluto Press.

Felski, R. (1999–2000) 'The invention of everyday life', *New Formations*, no.39, pp.15–31.

Fiske, J., Hodge, B. and Turner, G. (1987) *Myths of Oz: Reading Australian Popular Culture*, Sydney, Allen and Unwin.

Foucault, M. (1977) *Discipline and Punish: The Birth of the Prison*, London, Allen Lane.

Frith, S. (1983) 'The pleasures of the hearth' in *Formations of Pleasure*, London, Routledge and Kegan Paul.

Gauntlett, D. and Hill, A. (1999) *TV Living: Television, Culture and Everyday Life*, London and New York, Routledge in association with the British Film Institute.

Gilroy, P. (2000) *Against Race: Imagining Political Culture Beyond the Colour Line*, Cambridge, MA, The Belknap Press of Harvard University Press.

Grewal, I. (1996) *Home and Harem: Nation, Gender, Empire, and the Cultures of Travel*, Leicester, Leicester University Press.

Guerrand, R.-H. (1990) 'Private spaces' in Perrot, M. (ed.) *op. cit.*.

Haraway, D. (1985) 'Homes for cyborgs' in Weed, E. (ed.) *Coming to Terms: Feminism, Theory, Politics*, New York, Routledge.

Hareven, T.K. (1993) 'The home and the family in historical perspective' in Mack, A. (ed.) *op. cit.*.

Hayden, D. (1976) *Seven American Utopias: The Architecture of Communitarian Socialism, 1790–1975*, Cambridge, MA, MIT Press.

Hayden, D. (1981) *The Grand Domestic Revolution: A History of Feminist Designs for American Homes, Neighborhoods, and Cities*, Cambridge, MA, MIT Press.

Heller, A. (1984) *Everyday Life*, London, Routledge and Kegan Paul.

Hepworth, M. (1999) 'Privacy, security and respectability: the ideal Victorian home' in Chapman, T. and Hockey, J. (eds) *op. cit.*.

Hockey, J. (1999) ' Houses of doom' in Chapman, T. and Hockey, J. (eds) *op. cit.*.

Johnson, L. (1988) *The Unseen Voice: A Cultural Study of Early Australian Radio*, London, Routledge.

Johnson, L. (1996) '"As housewives we are worms": women, modernity and the home question', *Cultural Studies*, vol.10, no.3, pp.449–63.

Lefebvre, H. (1971) *Everyday Life in the Modern World*, London, Allen Lane The Penguin Press. First published in France in 1968.

Livingstone, S. (1992) 'The meaning of domestic technologies: a personal construct analysis of familial gender relations' in Silverstone, R. and Hirsch, E. (eds) *Consuming Technologies: Media and Information in Domestic Spaces*, London, Routledge.

Mack, A. (ed.) (1993) *Home: A Place in the World*, New York, New York University Press.

Maleuvre, D. (1999) *Museum Memories: History, Technology, Art*, Stanford, CA, Stanford University Press.

Morley, D. (2000) *Home Territories: Media, Mobility and Identity*, London, Routledge.

ONS (Office for National Statistics) (1999) *Social Trends*, 1999, no.29, London, The Stationery Office.

Perrot, M. (ed.) (1990) *A History of Private Life: From the Fires of Revolution to the Great War*, Cambridge, MA, The Belknap Press of Harvard University Press.

Reiger, K. M. (1985) *The Disenchantment of the Home: Modernising the Australian Family 1880–1940*, Melbourne, Oxford University Press.

Rybczynski, W. (1988) *Home: A Short History of An Idea*, London, Heinemann.

Scannell, P. (1996) *Radio, Television and Modern Life: A Phenomenological Approach*, Oxford, Blackwell Publishers.

Shields, R. (1999) *Lefebvre, Love and Struggle: Spatial Dialectics*, London, Routledge.

Silva, E.B. (1999) 'Transforming housewifery: dispositions, practices and technologies' in Silva, E.B. and Smart, C. (eds) *The 'New' Family?*, London, Sage.

Silverstone, R. (1994) *Television and Everyday Life*, London, Routledge.

Sparke, P. (1995) *As Long as It's Pink: The Sexual Politics of Taste*, London, Pandora.

Spigel, L. (1992) 'The suburban home companion: television and the neighbourhood ideal in postwar America' in Colomina, B. (ed) *Sexuality and Space*, Princeton, NJ, Princeton Architectural Press.

Readings

 Tamara K. Hareven, 'The home and the family in historical perspective' (1993)

… The concept of the home as the family's haven and domestic retreat emerged only about one hundred fifty years ago, and was, initially, limited to the urban middle classes. In order to understand the development of the home as the family's abode, as a reality and as an ideal, it is necessary to examine the relationship between household, family, and home as they changed over time (Hareven, 1977; Stone, 1977).

…

In preindustrial society there was a significant difference between the family's domicile – the household – and the *home* as it became idealized later in Western European and American society. In addition to serving as the family's place of residence and the focus for the family's various domestic activities such as eating, sleeping, and child rearing, the household was the site of a multiplicity of activities. It served as the site of production, as a welfare agency and correctional institution, as an educational institution, and as a place for religious worship. Rather than catering strictly to the needs of the family, the household served the entire community, by taking in dependent members who were not related to the family and by helping maintain the social order (Demos, 1970, pp.182–5).

Accordingly, household membership was not restricted to individuals related by ties of blood and marriage. The household also contained unrelated individuals such as servants, apprentices, boarders and lodgers, and 'unfortunates' from the community, such as orphans, elderly, the sick and infirm, delinquents, and mentally ill who were placed with families by the local authorities. Even though extended kin were not present in the household as a general pattern, household membership was sufficiently flexible to accommodate extended kin at certain points over the family's cycle, especially when aging parents were too frail to live by themselves and needed to coreside with their children. … Unlike in 'isolated' nuclear families today, apprentices, servants, lodgers, and other unrelated individuals shared household space with the family, worked together, participated in various daily activities, and sometimes slept in the same rooms (Demos, 1970, pp.62–81).

The family in preindustrial society was characterized by *sociability* rather than *privacy*. As Philippe Ariès has emphasized, by contrast to the conception of the home in contemporary society as a private retreat from the outside world, in preindustrial society the family conducted its work and public affairs *inside* the household. Households were teeming with various activities, and family members, even couples, could hardly retreat into privacy within the crowded household space. The head of the household's various business associates and other individuals actively involved in the family's economic or social activities were often present in the household. Ariès (1962) provides a vivid description of life in the 'big house' in preindustrial France and England. As long as family life was characterized by sociability, the household did not serve strictly as the family's private retreat. Rather, the family's public and private activities were inseparable, and the family's domestic life was often conducted with strangers present.

… 'It was the only place where friends, clients, relatives and protégés could meet and talk. … People lived on top of one another, masters and servants, children and adults, in houses open at all hours to the indiscretions of the callers. The density of society left no room for the family. Not that the family did not exist as a concept' (Ariès, 1962, p.404), but its main focus was sociability rather than privacy. As the family gradually emerged as a private entity focused into itself, sociability retreated into the background.

Spaces within the 'big house' were not differentiated into family space and public space. No rooms were specifically designated as bedrooms. Beds stood in public areas of the house, and family members slept behind curtains while social activities including outsiders were going on in other parts of the same room. Similarly, in colonial America bedchambers were not separate or private. Individuals and couples had to share beds with relatives or with unrelated individuals. Colonial American court records, especially those dealing with divorce, abound in various such graphic descriptions, all confirming the lack of privacy that families and unrelated individuals experienced when residing together in the relatively small and crowded houses in the prerevolutionary period, and the exposure of various individuals, including children, to the most intimate activities (Flaherty, 1972; Cott, 1976).

...

The concept of the home as a private retreat first emerged in the lives of bourgeois families in eighteenth-century France and England, and in the United States among urban, middle-class families in the early part of the nineteenth century. Its development was closely linked to the new ideals of domesticity and privacy that were associated with the characteristics of the modern family – a family that was child-centered, private, and in which the roles of husband and wife were segregated into public and domestic spheres, respectively. The husband was expected to be the main breadwinner and worker outside the home, and the wife a full-time housekeeper and mother. This new separation of domestic and public spheres led to the rearrangement of the family's work and living patterns within the home. While earlier all family members, including children, worked together, or participated in various activities, even if they did not work, in the new setting the world of work became separate from family activities (Welter, 1966; Ryan, 1981; Degler, 1980). Family time became restricted primarily to the home, and leisure became an important aspect of domestic life. Reading, embroidering, viewing art, and listening to music had become important pastimes in the home.

Following the removal of the workplace from the home as a result of urbanization and industrialization, the household was recast as the family's private retreat, and home emerged as a new concept and existence. Eventually other agencies took over the functions that had been earlier concentrated in the family. Factories and business places took over the work and production functions of the family, schools took over the family's formal educational functions, and asylums and correctional institutions took over the family's functions of welfare and social control (Demos, 1970; see also Lasch, 1977; Rothman, 1971). The separation of the workplace from the household and the transfer of various other functions and activities of the family to outside institutions resulted in the emergence of the home as a specialized site for the family's consumption, child-rearing, and private life. ...

Among such families 'home' began to assume an enormous symbolic meaning, distinct from the household, from the early nineteenth century on. As Michelle Perrot (1990) put it, 'the house was where the family gathered, the center and the symbol of its success.' In France, Perrot observed, 'The word *"intérieur"* now referred not so much to the heart of man as to the heart of the household, and it was there that one experienced happiness; similarly, well-being was now conditioned on "comfort".' While earlier the family interacted with the community and the house was open to the outside world, now the house was closed off: 'A house was like a private kingdom, whose owners sought to appropriate nature by growing gardens and building greenhouses to abolish the seasons; to appropriate art by amassing collections and staging private concerts; to appropriate time by collecting family souvenirs and memorabilia of journeys; and to appropriate books that described the earth ...'. While earlier the boundaries between the home and the public world had been extremely flexible and, at times, invisible, now there emerged a preference for making the home the center from which the world is viewed and enjoyed.

...

In this new domestic regime it became inappropriate for middle-class women to work outside the home. ... Women's main responsibility and all their energies now had to focus on the home and the family, and especially on children. Homemaking became an occupation in itself, one that demanded physical and material resources, planning, and the persistent following of changing fashions. As one writer in mid-century put it, a house 'is not only the home center, the retreat and shelter for all the family, it is also the workshop for the mother. It is not only where she is to live, to love, but where she is to care and labor. Her hours, days, weeks, months and years are spent within its bounds; until she becomes an enthroned fixture, more indispensable than the house itself.' Homemaking was idealized as part of the cult of domesticity, and was accorded special social status. The complicated tasks of home management required specific advice in how-to-do-it manuals and etiquette books (Welter, 1966; Sklar, 1973).

...

The domestic ideal in American society was strongly linked to an idealization of the home as a utopian retreat from the outside world. Ironically, even though this concept of the ideal home was developed by urban reformers, moralists, and writers, it emphasized the pastoral ideal of rural society. From the early nineteenth century on, a host of popular writers extolled the ideal home in sermons, novels, and advice literature. ... The home began to be viewed as a utopian community, as a retreat from the world – one that had to be consciously designed and perfectly managed. The idealization of the home as a haven was a reaction to the anxiety provoked by rapid urbanization, resulting in the transformation of old neighborhoods and the creation of new ones, the rapid influx of immigrants into urban areas, and the visible concentration of poverty in cities (Jeffrey, 1972, p.24).

...

Since city dwellers could not return to live in the country, they enshrined the home as a rural retreat from the city *within* the city. Hence the garden with its hedges, gates, and walls was of great significance in sheltering the home from the outside world, as well as providing an illusion of serene pastoral settings.

...

The view of the home as the family's private retreat was closely linked to the new definition of woman's separate sphere, which glorified the role of the wife as a homemaker and full-time mother. In American society, the cult of domesticity that characterized this transformation in women's roles placed women on a pedestal as the custodians of the home and segregated them in their domestic sphere, while the public sphere was allotted exclusively to men. ...

... Accompanying the cult of domesticity emerged a large industry that catered to the new consumer styles in the furnishing and appointment of the home by providing various appliances and gadgets. Industrialization had a dual impact on the redefinition of the family's role and on the accompanying emergence of the home as the family's private retreat. First, industrialization led to the separation of the workplace from the home and to the transfer of the welfare, educational, and correctional functions from the family to other institutions and agencies. Second, industrialization contributed to the creation of the necessary technology, communications, and transportation aimed at facilitating the furnishing and running of the new-style home. A variety of new appliances and gadgets made their way into the home from the middle of the nineteenth century on. These inventions became important not only as labor-saving devices but as status symbols of the efficient, well-ordered home. Initially, the most important invention was the cooking stove, which replaced open-hearth cooking. The stove revolutionized cuisine, and opened up a new range of possibilities in the simultaneous preparation of a variety of dishes on the top of the stove, rather than the one-pot meals cooked in the hearth. In addition, a whole slew of

gadgets and implements, such as apple corers and slicers, vacuum cleaners, laundry strainers, and other devices appeared on the market and made their way into the middle-class home. ...

Even if the new appliances did not always result in labor saving for women [Schwartz Cowan, 1983], they were of great symbolic significance in expressing the specialization in the functions of the home, along with those of the family – a specialization that required new codes of behavior, modes of production and management, and, therefore, new roles for women. The home was not just a sentimental entity, as the nineteenth-century cliché ('Home Sweet Home') would suggest. It also became an institution of industrial capitalism, with its characteristic equipment, organization, management, and cast of characters. Accordingly, the wife was cast in the role of a 'home manager', who was judged not only for the making of the home and maintaining its aesthetic and nurturing atmosphere but also for the efficiency and frugality with which she managed this complex enterprise (Hayden, 1981).

It is precisely for this reason that in the late nineteenth century the home, like the office and other institutions, was subjected by reformers to scientific management. As a result, the concepts of industrial efficiency were applied to the home. Housework began to be viewed as a kind of enterprise that was subject to rules of efficiency similar to those of industry. Efficiency in home management had gained extreme significance in its own right, exceeding practical considerations. The first reformer to emphasize and formulate this concept and to popularize it was Catherine Beecher, who defined the role of the housewife as a 'home minister' and 'skilled professional'. In her *Treatise on Domestic Economy for the Use of Young Ladies at Home and at School*, first published in 1841 and reprinted in numerous editions, Beecher extolled the domestic superiority of women. Even though women's work was unpaid and segregated to the home, it was to be considered professional and important in its own right, and had to be provided with the necessary props and equipment in order to be accomplished effectively.

...

The new specialization in the functions of the home and the family also necessitated corresponding architectural designs. Architects joined the trend by busily developing blueprints for new styles of homes that were to accommodate the new domestic life-style. ... Within the home spaces were organized in a manner that separated the family's private activities from the public ones such as receiving guests. The parlor became a central space for the family's social activities and entertainment. The kitchen, which had been previously outside, was brought inside, alas, into the basement or the back of the house. Nevertheless, the kitchen became an important component of the home. The parlor was decorated by the family's heirlooms, portraits, lace and embroidery, shadow boxes, and artwork (Clark, 1976).

The new type of home was intended to serve the specialized activities of various family members. This was reflected in the design of separate rooms for children, for women's activities such as sewing, and for men's activities including libraries and study rooms. Each child was to have a separate bedroom in order to foster the child's attachment to the home. ... Special attention was given to providing young women and young girls with separate rooms, as an encouragement to spend more time at home: 'the young girl that, finding no intrinsic pleasure at home, nor regarding it otherwise than as the sphere of her domestic duties, would seek away from its shelter, and with other companions [find] pleasure and excitements neither so wholesome or refining as a fond parent would wish' ... (Gervase Wheeler, *Rural Homes*, 1851, quoted in Clark, 1976, p.35).

...

While the ideal middle-class domestic home is linked in the contemporary popular image with suburbs, as suggested above, initially the ideals of domesticity were played out in the city. The new middle-class home was designed as a response to urbanization as a retreat from the world of work and from the hustle-bustle of urban life. At the same time it depended on urban services, conveniences, and public activities in order to achieve domestic refinement. Popular writers such as Catherine Sedgwick, who portrayed the newly idealized home life, placed the home firmly in the city. Sedgwick and other writers emphasized the redeeming moral virtue of the home in the urban environment. Despite the corrupting influence of the city, they claimed that the domestic world could transmit its values to the urban environment and maintain purity within it. But as the nineteenth century progressed, the ideals and life-style of domesticity were transferred to the suburbs and became identified with suburban living (Sedgwick, 1835; on the suburban ideal, see Fishman, 1987).

...

... From the 1870s on millions of Americans began to move to the suburbs to fulfill their dream of a tranquil domestic life removed from the city. The movement was pioneered by the wealthy upper class and upper middle class, who moved into elegant 'Victorian' houses in romantic settings. From the 1880s

on, middle-class families who responded to the propaganda for suburban living and to new housing opportunities made possible by the architectural and building professions began to populate the rapidly expanding suburbs around major cities. ... Suburban living held, however, the promise of eventual home ownership. Most importantly, it represented an escape from the city and segregation along class and ethnic lines in 'serene' settings (Wright, 1981; Jackson, 1985).

The development of domesticity as a suburban phenomenon, which flourished in the late nineteenth century, according to Margaret Marsh, was a response to the masculine domestic ideal, which by that point in time emphasized the virtues of a suburban retreat from the pressures of city life: 'The new domestic ideal centered firmly in the suburbs, represented family pride, family identity and togetherness in face of an urban society that promised individual achievement, anonymity and excitement.' By the eve of World War II, she claims, 'a new suburban domestic ideal had materialized – an ideal that both reorganized domesticity to make it independent of the notion of separate masculine and feminine spheres and one which redefined the suburbs to emphasize "place" more than the ownership of property' (Marsh, 1989). As urban life became more bewildering, because of a high concentration of immigrants and poverty, domestic life in the suburbs had become idealized as an escape from the city.

...

The suburban form of domesticity had become entrenched in American society and predominated until the 1960s, despite various challenges by feminist reformers, especially Charlotte Perkins Gilman (1898), who advocated the establishment of urban residential hotels with communal dining rooms for families so that working women would be free of housekeeping chores. Gilman expected that these apartment hotels would enable women to pursue professional careers along with motherhood without being confined to child-rearing and domesticity. ...

...

When discussing these trends, it is important to remember that the separation of the home from the outside world occurred initially in the lives of a small segment of the population, namely, the urban middle classes. In rural families, and in urban working-class families, the home was viewed less as a specialized retreat, and was open to multiplicity of functions and activities as it had been in preindustrial society. Significantly, at the very time when middle-class women were being discouraged from pursuing gainful employment, working-class women and children were being recruited as the primary labor force of the industrial revolution. Even after working-class families began to emulate middle-class domestic life-styles and furnishings, they continued to use the household space in a more diversified and complex way than the middle class. In rural families, the household continued to serve as the site of production in agriculture as well as in domestic industries. Family members worked side by side in related tasks, and there continued to be little separation between domestic life and work life (Hareven, 1982). …

… Even after working-class families adopted the new concepts of domesticity, both home life and attitudes toward the home retained a different character in working-class life than in the middle class. For working-class families the home was not merely a private refuge; it was a *resource* that could be used for generating extra income, for paying debts, for staying out of poverty, and for maintaining autonomy in old age. Accordingly, their household membership continued to be more complex even in the twentieth century. Even though working-class families were also committed to the nuclearity of the household, they frequently took in newly arrived immigrants and, at least temporarily, shared housing with them. Privacy was less important than the flexible use of household space, which could be used to supplement the family's income or could be traded for services. Throughout the nineteenth century and early into the twentieth century a significant proportion of working-class households contained boarders and lodgers (Modell and Hareven, 1988).

…

While homemaking activities and domestic rituals along with child-rearing commanded almost all the waking hours of middle-class women, working-class women could invest only a limited amount of time in the appointment and maintenance of the home and in child-rearing. In addition to spending an entire workday from sunrise to sundown in a factory or in other workplaces, working-class women did not have access to help by servants and to the household equipment that middle-class women controlled. Working-class women often alternated between factory work and home work (taking various jobs such as sewing or laundry into the home), and produced food and various items not only for their family members but for pay or barter as well. Privacy was of less concern to working-class families than solvency, the survival of the family unit, and the improvement of its life-style (Hareven, 1982; Hareven and Langenbach, 1978).

In working-class homes there was little separation between domestic life and work life. The world of work spilled over into the household. In the major cities, 'homework', such as garment finishing, engaged all family members in the household. Under such circumstances, the space in the home was used creatively, and was arranged and rearranged to fit the various functions of the family as they came up. At supper time, bundles of garments or other sewing materials were removed from the table so that family members could eat their supper. Beds for lodgers or boarders, or for children, were opened up in the hallway or in the kitchen in the evening and were folded back again in the morning (Sergeant, 1910; Kleinberg, 1989).

References

Ariès, P. (1962) *Centuries of Childhood: A Social History of Family Life* (trans. R. Baldick), New York, Vintage Books.

Beecher, C.E. (1846) *A Treatise on the Domestic Economy for the Use of Young Ladies at Home and at School* (rev. edn), New York, Harper.

Clark, C.E. Jr (1976) 'Domestic architecture as an index: the romantic revival and the cult of domesticity in America, 1840–1870', *Journal of Interdisciplinary History*, no.7, Summer, pp.33–56.

Cott, N. (1976) 'Eighteenth-century family and social life revealed in Massachusetts divorce records', *Journal of Social History*, vol.10, pp.20–43.

Cowan, R. Schwartz (1983) *More Work for Mother*, New York, Basic Books.

Degler, C. (1980) *At Odds: Women and the Family in America from the Revolution to the Present*, New York, Oxford University Press.

Demos, J. (1970) *A Little Commonwealth: Family Life in Plymouth Colony*, New York, Oxford University Press.

Fishman, R. (1987) *Bourgeois Utopias: The Rise and Fall of Suburbia*, New York, Basic Books.

Flaherty, D. (1972) *Privacy in Colonial America*, Charlottesville, VA, University of Virginia Press.

Gilman, C. Perkins (1898) *Women and Economics: A Study of the Economic Relation between Men and Women as a Factor in Social Evolution* (New York, Harper Torchbooks, 1966).

Hareven, T.K. (1977) 'Family time and historical time', *Daedalus*, no.106, pp.57–70.

Hareven, T.K. (1982) *Family Time and Industrial Time: The Relationship Between the Family and Work in a New England Industrial Community*, New York, Cambridge University Press.

Hareven, T.K. and Langenbach, R. (1978) *Amoskeag: Life and Work in an American Factory City*, New York, Pantheon.

Hayden, D. (1981) *The Great Domestic Revolution: A History of Feminist Designs for American Homes, Neighborhoods and Cities*, Cambridge, MA, The MIT Press.

Jackson, K. (1985) *The Crabgrass Frontier*, New York, Columbia University.

Jeffrey, K. (1972) 'The family as a utopian retreat from the city: the nineteenth century contribution', *Soundings: An Interdisciplinary Journal*, no.55, Spring.

Kleinberg, S.J. (1989) *The Shadow of the Mills: Working Class Families in Pittsburgh 1870–1907*, Pittsburgh, PA, University of Pittsburgh Press.

Lasch, C. (1977) *Haven in a Heartless World: The Family Besieged*, New York, Basic Books.

Marsh, M. (1989) 'From separation to togetherness: the social construction of domestic space in American suburbs, 1840–1915', *Journal of American History*, vol.76, pp. 506–27.

Modell, J. and Hareven, T.K. (1988) 'Urbanization and the malleable household', *Journal of Marriage and the Family*, vol.35, August, pp.467–79.

Perrot, M. (ed.) (1990) *A History of Private Life*, vol. 4: *From the Fires of the Revolution to the Great War* (trans. A. Goldhammer), Cambridge, MA, Harvard University Press.

Rothman, D. (1971) *Discovery of the Asylum: Social Order and Disorder in the New Republic*, Boston, MA, Little, Brown.

Ryan, M. (1981) *Cradle of the Middle Class: The Family in Oneida County, New York, 1790–1865*, New York, Cambridge University Press.

Sedgwick, C. (1835) *Home*, New York.

Sergeant, E. Shepley (1910) 'Toilers of tenements: where the beautiful things of the great shops are made', *McClure's Magazine*, no.35, July, pp.231–2.

Sklar, K. Kish (1973) *Catherine Beecher: A Study of Domesticity*, New Haven, CT, Yale University Press.

Stone, L. (1977) *The Family, Sex and Marriage in England 1500–1800*, New York, Harper & Row.

Welter, B. (1966) 'The cult of true womanhood, 1820–1860', *American Quarterly*, vol.18, pp.151–74.

Wright, G. (1981) *Building the Dream: A Social History of Housing in America*, New York, Pantheon.

Source: Hareven, 1993, pp.228–50

Dolores Hayden, 'Domestic evolution or domestic revolution?' (1981)

Gilman stood out among all of the feminists and the futurists of her time as the charismatic person who synthesized the thinking of suffragists, home economists, and utopian novelists on the question of the home, and produced a program for collective domesticity which made her a leading figure in feminist circles in the United States and Europe. In her first book, *Women and Economics*, published in 1898, and in many subsequent books and articles, she prophesied a world where women enjoyed the economic independence of work outside the home for wages and savored the social benefits of life with their families in private kitchenless houses or apartments connected to central kitchens, dining rooms, and day care centers.

  …

In the 1880s and 1890s, both home economists and authors of futurist fiction tended to argue that human evolution would gradually bring about a society where technology lightened all labor and encouraged the socialization of domestic work. They wrote about the late twentieth century or the year 2000; they prophesied co-operative housekeeping in some future time when human relations were perfected. Gilman took this idea, turned it around, and gave the idea of collective domestic life new urgency. Rather

than arguing that evolution would help to free women, she contended that free women could help to speed up evolution. In *Women and Economics* she stated that women were holding back human evolution because of their confinement to household work and motherhood. The evolution of the human race, she believed, would be hastened by removing domestic work and child care from the home, allowing women to undertake both motherhood and paid employment, making it possible for all women to be economically independent of men. Thus, she argued that the development of socialized domestic work and new domestic environments should be seen as promoting the evolution of socialism, rather than following it. …

  …

Feminist motherhood in a feminist housing complex

In *Women and Economics* Gilman criticized society for confining women to the house and to motherhood: 'Woman has been checked, starved, aborted in human growth; and the swelling forces of race-development have been driven back in each generation to work in her through sex-functions alone' (1898, p.75). For her 'sex functions' meant motherhood. She wrote: 'The more absolutely woman is segregated to sex-functions only, cut off from all economic use and made wholly dependent on the sex-relation as a means of livelihood, the more pathological does her motherhood become' (*ibid.*, p.182). In other words, the more women attempted to look pretty and to behave coquettishly in order to find husbands to support them economically as wives and mothers, the more they held back the strength and intelligence of the human race. Yet motherhood was, according to Gilman, 'the common duty and the common glory of womanhood.' In a world where women were economically independent, she believed that motherhood would be voluntary. Although women might limit the number of their children she felt sure that 'women as economic producers will naturally choose those professions which are compatible with motherhood', that is, roles in new, collectively organized household industries (*ibid.*, p.246).

... The spatial setting for feminist motherhood, according to Gilman, was the feminist apartment hotel, with private suites without kitchens and complete cooking, dining, and childcare facilities for all residents which permitted them to combine jobs and motherhood. She urged entrepreneurs to consider developing such an institution:

> If there should be built and opened in any of our large cities today a commodious and well-served apartment house for professional women with families, it would be filled at once. The apartments would be without kitchens; but there would be a kitchen belonging to the house from which meals could be served to the families in their rooms or in a common dining-room, as preferred. It would be a home where the cleaning was done by efficient workers, not hired separately by the families, but engaged by the manager of the establishment; and a roof-garden, day nursery, and kindergarten, under well-trained professional nurses and teachers, would ensure proper care of the children. ... (*ibid.*, p.242)

She also offered schemes for suburban residences without kitchens:

> In suburban homes this purpose could be accomplished much better by a grouping of adjacent houses, each distinct and having its own yard, but all kitchenless, and connected by covered ways with the eating-house. ... Meals could of course be served in the house as long as desired; but when people become accustomed to pure, clean homes where no steaming industry is carried on, they will gradually prefer to go to their food instead of having it brought to them. (*ibid.*, pp.243–4)

These eating-houses were to be both workplaces and neighborhood social centers. Her vision of collective meeting places for 'free association among us, on lines of common interests', included 'great common libraries and parlors, baths and gymnasia, work-room and play-rooms, to which both sexes have the same access for the same needs' (*ibid.*, p.314). ...

Her proposals for feminist apartment hotels echoed much of the architectural determinism of earlier Fourierists and free love advocates as well as the Nationalists led by Bellamy. In 1890, the year Gilman had first joined the Nationalists, several designers had published proposals for the renovation of row house blocks for co-operative housekeeping and the construction of new urban row house blocks and apartment hotels with collective housekeeping facilities. John Pickering Putnam, in 1890, in *Architecture Under Nationalism,* promised that apartment hotels would not only spare women domestic drudgery, but would also reduce poverty by their efficient use of resources. As Putnam asserted, 'The selfish and narrowing isolation of the separate dwelling will give way to the cooperative apartment-house as surely as the isolated hut of the savage yield to the cities and villages of advancing civilization' (Putnam, 1890, p.13).

...

His actual plans emphasized the flexible design of living spaces, with three types of units: private apartments fully equipped with kitchens and dining rooms; apartments without kitchens but with dining rooms served by the public kitchen; and apartments without either kitchens or dining rooms, whose residents used the collective facilities. Among the shared facilities in his building were a kitchen, laundry, café, and small dining rooms, as well as central steam heating, electric light, elevators, and fireproof stairways. True to the Victorian conventions of gender, respected by Edward Bellamy (but not by Gilman), Putnam added a gentlemen's smoking room and a ladies' parlor, where residents of each sex could gather for conversation.

Gilman's advocacy of the apartment hotel echoed Putnam's and opposed conservatives who believed that such places were bad for women. In 1903 the editors of *Architectural Record* ... conceded that ... 'while the apartment hotel is the consummate flower of domestic cooperation, it is also, unfortunately, the consummate flower of domestic irresponsibility. It means the sacrifice of everything implied by the word "home". No one could apply the word to two rooms and a bath.' They called the apartment hotel 'a big, bold, twentieth century boarding house,' and, they added, 'the apartment hotel is the boarding house at its best and worst. It is the most dangerous enemy American domesticity has yet had to encounter' (pp.89–91).

Noting their concern that American women often chose to live in boarding-houses after marriage and were already all too likely 'to consider the care of the household a burden', the editors expressed concern that many women found industrial, charitable, social, or intellectual pursuits more interesting than domestic life. …

…

… Gilman repeatedly challenged … pious appeals for married women to avoid apartment hotel life. In 1903, in *The Home*, she criticized private houses as 'bloated buildings, filled with a thousand superfluities' (p.121). In 1904 she wrote about urban evolution and women's liberation: '… we hear a cry of complaint and warning about the passing of the American home. Everything else has passed, and without wailing; passed, as must all rising life, "from the less to the greater, from the simple to the complex".' She explained that 'this very apartment-house, with its inevitable dismissal of the kitchen, with its facility for all skilled specialist labor, has freed the woman from her ancient service. …' Calling for feminist apartment hotels equipped with child-gardens, play-rooms, and nurseries, she exhorted, 'let us then study, understand, and help to hasten this passing onward to better things of our beloved American Home. Let us not be afraid, but lead the world in larger living' (Gilman, 1904).

References

Architectural Record (1903) 'Over the draughting board, opinions official and unofficial', no.13, January, pp.89–91.

Gilman, C. Perkins (1898) *Women and Economics: A Study of the Economic Relation between Men and Women as a Factor in Social Evolution* (New York, Harper Torchbooks, 1966).

Gilman, C. Perkins (1903) *The Home: Its work and Influence* (Urbana, IL, University of Illlinois, 1972).

Gilman, C. Perkins (1904) 'The passing of the home in Great American Cities', *The Cosmopolitan*, no.38, December, pp.137–47.

Putnam, J. Pickering (1890) *Architecture Under Nationalism*, Boston, MA, Educational Association.

Source: Hayden, 1981, pp.183, 184, 188–95

1.3 Tony Bennett, Michael Emmison and John Frow, 'Cultural choice and the home' (1999)

What does it mean to prefer one colour scheme to another? What values and significance are attached to the paintings that people choose for their homes? How do people spend their time at home? What kind of home would they most like to have? In what style do people like to entertain their friends and visitors? What food do they like to serve, and in what setting?

In this chapter we concern ourselves with such questions in order to identify some of the social logics which underlie the cultural choices that are involved in the day-to-day decisions we make involving judgements of taste. …

…

Home improvements

Let us go back to our opening question concerning what might be involved in the choice of a colour scheme. The answer, in the case of Gillian, is: quite a lot. Indeed, the colours Gillian wants for her new home are a way of both stating and resolving some of the tensions – personal, familial and social – that she has worked her way through in defining her own social trajectory as a young woman (29 years old) holding a senior and responsible position in health management. Like her husband, also in a management position (giving them an annual household income of between A$80,000 and A$90,000), Gillian's work involves significant supervisory responsibilities. She sees these as distinguishing her own position and its obligations (long hours and a responsibility to make sure that what needs to be done is done) from those of award workers. The influence of her professional responsibilities is also evident in her strongly negative views of trade unions which she regards as impeding her ability, as a manager, to organise productive patterns of team-work while also diminishing individual workers' sense of responsibility for determining their own futures.

For her own part, Gillian is clear that her future – and her children's future – is very much in her own hands. She sees education as having a crucial role to play here. Having arrived at her present station in life by virtue of the mobility conferred through education – her parents had only varying degrees of secondary education but, on a shop assistant's salary, had supported her through university – she has clear views about her children's education. Although their first child was only 7 months old when Gillian answered the questionnaire, she and her husband had already decided to send her children to a private school, seeing this as the key to future generational mobility, and preferably to one that placed a strong emphasis on art and music. This reflects Gillian's own cultural interests. She owns a number of original artworks and has a considerable ceramics collection, while also owning art books, classical literary texts, works of poetry, biographies and historical books. Her artistic interests, however, while broad ranging, are mostly of a conventional kind: she prefers realistic art but is open to abstract art if she can find the right place for it.

Describing herself as middle class, Gillian's main concern is 'getting on in life', and she is keen to pass these values on to her children (she had had a second child by the time we interviewed her):

> 'I guess, (that's) the culture that we've instilled in our kids – to strive for the best.'

How does this manifest itself in the cultural choices she makes in and about the home? That these choices are hers is something that Gillian is very clear about. Although there are some areas in which decisions are shared – her husband, Malcolm, has more contemporary tastes than Gillian, but would sometimes compromise in reaching joint decisions about what furniture to buy – her views prevail when it comes to choosing colour schemes:

INTERVIEWER: And your husband is happy for you just to have the house exactly the way you want it.

GILLIAN: Yeh. Yeh. Doesn't mind at all. Been very good that way.

This proves to be important to the significance that Gillian invests in the colour scheme she plans for her new home as a means of establishing an appropriate distance between her present social status and aspirations, and her social and family origins. Having recently moved to a provincial Queensland city and set up home in a relatively new house, Gillian sees her new home as – for the moment – the co-ordinating centre of her life. *Home Beautiful* and *Home and Garden* are her favourite magazines. Although going out occasionally to the cinema, to musical performances or to art galleries and museums, most of her leisure activities are centred on the home. Eating out only rarely and then mainly for practical purposes (a weekly trip to KFC or McDonald's on the night they shop), Gillian and her husband prefer to do their own entertaining:

> '… we prefer to entertain at home or to go to friends' homes, and I guess it's more relaxing in that sense. Nicer atmosphere. You're not being rushed through a meal, or noise and "carry-on" all around you.'

Most of this entertaining involves work colleagues. Since they have recently moved interstate away from their families of origin, entertaining is no longer a family-centred activity. For this reason, Gillian prefers that her guests not bring their children with them, just as, when eating out, she prefers child-free restaurants.

Although she says she likes to serve an informal buffet-style meal, this seems less and less informal the more she describes it. Serving, always, entrées, a main course and dessert, Gillian's pride and joy is to do so in a dining-room setting with a 14-seater table which functions as a crucial *mise-en-scène* for the display of her persona to the social and professional peers she invites to dinner.

INTERVIEWER: You go to such an effort to do the menu when you do have your dinner parties, (do) you set the table out formally?

GILLIAN: Love doing that … Love collecting china. Eight dinner sets … I've got two antique dinner sets – one was my grandmother's, it was her wedding present and I've got that now. And the rest tends to be very 'everyday' Johnson & Johnson type stuff … Most of it is Royal Albert … That kind of thing. And I love that sort of stuff. I like crystals. I just like nice things. Nice cutlery … Love placemats. That's another quirk. I love placemats and I love clocks …

When choosing the three terms from the survey which come closest to describing her ideal home, Gillian opts, in order of preference, for 'well-designed', 'spacious' and 'easy-to-maintain'. Her three least preferred qualities for a home are, again in order, that it should be 'traditional', 'lived-in' or 'imaginative'. The significance that she invests in the contrast between these two sets of values becomes clear when Gillian talks about her preferred colour scheme in view of the role this plays in establishing a social distance between the traditional, lived-in and imaginative décor of the parental home she has left and the kind of home she aspires eventually to live in. When asked to describe her new home, Gillian talks about little else but the colours: 'the whole theme of the house, to me anyway, tends to be pinkish which I find a little bit hot'. She wants something completely different:

GILLIAN: If I were to choose a colour scheme, I tend more towards the cool, towards blues and green and that sort of thing …

INTERVIEWER: Right. So, why would you choose cool colours?

GILLIAN: I simply have a preference for them. And apart from the fact that even in weather such as this, the temperature hits up to 37, 38 and you feel cool. Definitely the colours that I prefer. So, where I've been able to in rooms where I could have an influence, then I'll put curtains that have got blues and greens in them and that sort of thing. Mostly tapestries, that sort of thing. And, certainly the curtains in the formal area, the creams, the sage. When I had them made they said: 'Oh goodness, I really would advise against it'. And I said: 'Look, truly, I know what I want'.

Gillian does indeed know her own tastes: too well, in fact, for us to believe her account that she just happens to like cool colours or likes them solely for practical reasons. Later in the interview, she draws a sharp distinction between her tastes in colour and Malcolm's in terms which make clear the social and familial issues at stake for Gillian in her preference for cool colours. It also becomes clear why it is so important to her that her husband should let her have the pick of colours in the home. Malcolm's preferences are for reds and blacks, for sharp and bright colours. So were his mother's:

GILLIAN: His mother loved black, red and chrome and red, red and bright things! Everything's very dominant. If she was going to put a tablecloth on the table, it would be red. If she was going to go and choose a suit, it would probably be either red or bright pink … Everything's bright. Nothing wrong with bright colours. I like some bright colours but I couldn't live with that heavy colour all the time.

Malcolm's parents, like Gillian's, were working class. As the conversation unfolds, it becomes clear that Gillian is unable to live with strong and sharply contrasting colours because she associates them with her husband's background and her own in a 'two-bedroom, fibro [prefab] Housing Commission house' that she describes as 'disgusting by anybody's standards'. The gaudy veneer and laminex surfaces of a 1970s working-class décor are something she wants 'to get away from'. Nor is this just a matter of escaping her parental past: Gillian accounts for her colour preferences in terms which suggest that these also serve as a means of measuring her distance from a present that might have been her own but for the route out that her education has given her. Gillian's sister did not go to university but had chosen, like their mother, to be a 'stay-at-home mum' supplementing her husband's salary with bits of part-time work as a shop assistant or as a casual worker with the local council. Unlike Gillian, however, her sister still likes reds, blacks, and chrome, tastes which, in Gillian's mind, reflect her sister's subservience to her husband who, like both Malcolm and Gillian's father, likes bold and strongly contrasting colours. Still trapped in her class background, Gillian's sister also embodies a pattern of gender relations that Gillian associates with the familial and class origins she has herself escaped – and yet is still always escaping. Being able to make the choices about how to decorate her home is, for Gillian, a way of marking her distance from a background of domestic violence in which her father's abuse of her mother is strongly connected, in her recollection, to her mother's subservience to him in all matters of domestic cultural choice – a pattern which she sees being repeated in her sister's choice of partner and, symbolically, of colours.

As we can see, then, a good deal is invested in Gillian's colour-scheme preferences. Her passion for light, cool, subdued colours is an elaborate statement which helps her to organize a clear distinction between where she has come from and where, in both class and familial terms, she is headed. It is not surprising, then, that her tastes in clothes rest on the same principles, particularly since, when dressing for work, these help her in fashioning the kind of professional self she wants to 'wear' in her work settings. Expressing her preference for 'a nice cut with clothes rather than frilly, tizzy things', Gillian, echoing her colour scheme for the home, likes 'light blues and greens', neutral rather than pastel colours, recalling her dislike for red, black and chrome in her rejection of 'very bright things'.

…

Home sweet home

Mary … [is] in her late forties and, having recently retired from a job-share position as a meals-on-wheels co-ordinator, is unambiguously working class in terms of her own occupational location. She and her husband own their own home and enjoy a comfortable joint income of between A\$50,000 and

A\$60,000 a year. Although she did not complete her Catholic secondary education – she was orphaned at an early age and spent much of her adolescence being moved from home to home – Mary and her husband have supported their two sons through university and into safely middle-class occupations: one is a lawyer and the other a health instructor. ... Her husband's class position – as a spare-parts salesman in a two-person business in which he is the employee – is also clearly working class and she has a strong identification with that class position and the values most typically associated with it. ... Mary ... both sees herself as working class and holds strongly to a collectivist set of values: she believes that governments have significant responsibilities in the provision of health, welfare and educational opportunities, for example, and votes Labor.

Although she is clearly proud of her children and pleased that they have done well, Mary shows no signs of being dissatisfied with her own class position or of wanting to follow the middle-class trajectories of her sons. While she admits that their children have introduced her to new tastes (she never had smoked salmon until given some by her daughter-in-law but it now forms a part of her weekly shopping list), there is no sense that she is at all at odds with her class destiny. This is reflected in her attitude to home. In marked contrast to the home improvement projects of Gillian ..., home, for Mary, is a place for a family to be in and, as such, its paramount value is that of comfort:

> 'Some people just have an in-built knack of what looks nice and what goes with something to make it look nice. Me, I just buy what I like. If it matches something, it's good luck more than good management, but I do try to make it a house, so when you come into it you feel comfortable and at home. ... And you know it's not a house that's starchy, that you think, I won't sit there, I'll crush the cushion or I should take my shoes off because everyone's shoes are at the front door, you know. Yeah, it's never been that sort of a home, that's what I like ... And homey, I'm a Cancerian and we like our home and we like our family to like our home. My family are very comfortable coming here. They visit very often and they come in the door and they don't mind helping themselves to whatever's in the fridge or the cupboard. They feel at ease, they feel like it is still their home, they can just make themselves comfortable.'

When asked why she doesn't like a house to be 'distinctive' and 'modern', and why she likes clutter, Mary articulates her refusal to be modernized in terms which express her commitment to a set of working-class family and communal values:

MARY: No, because I'm a bugger for bits and pieces. If you look in there on the piano and that I've got – all the family gives me photos because they know I like to sit the photos around and lots of the family give me frogs because I'm a frog fanatic and everywhere you look in the house there's little frogs ... My china I really love but I use it all the time. My husband started it off years ago, bought me a cup, saucer and plate and I've sort of built it right up and then, when we had our china wedding, we ended up buying the dinner plates and things so that in the Royal Albert we've got our complete dinner service and inside we've got lots of bits and pieces for it. So they're my treasures, but we use them all the time, even with my little grandson. I put them out for him as well.

INTERVIEWER: ... So what do you particularly like about that type of china, why do you think you like that rather than your Ikea plain white plates?

MARY: I think that's because I'm old-fashioned, I'm an old type of person that likes those type of things, straight modern lines are not my thing.

INTERVIEWER: One of the other things you mentioned that were least important to you was distinctive style in housing, what does that mean?

MARY: Well way-out, I class distinctive as way-out.

INTERVIEWER: And I suppose also in this area you'd really stand out if your house was different because they are quite similar.

MARY: Yes, they were all built by one builder basically. They were all project homes, they were cheap at the time. They've stood the test of time, they're quite good, now you see people are adding tops and doing things to them and they look nice. But they're still in keeping with the neighbourhood, like nobody's got any really way-out type houses around here.

Source: Bennett *et al.*, 1999, pp.24, 25–9, 35–7

1.4 David Morley, 'The migrant's suitcase'(2000)

Sometimes a particular symbolic object – such as the key to the house from which the refugee has been expelled – is taken on the exile's journey and comes to function as a synecdoche for the unreachable lost home, and to act as a focus for memories of the exile's past life (cf. Seed, 1999). According to George Bisharat, many Palestinian refugee families 'retained the keys to their [original] homes, prominently displaying them in their camp shelters as symbols of their determination to return' (Bisharat, 1997, p.214). On some occasions, for the migrant home may perhaps come to be symbolized not by a key but by the suitcase containing their most talismanic possessions. ... Thus, in his analysis of the conditions of life of migrant workers in Europe in the 1970s, John Berger reported that when, in some places, the *Gastarbeiter* [guestworkers] were forbidden to keep their suitcases in their dormitories (because these things made their rooms untidy) they went on strike precisely because:

> in these suitcases, they keep their personal possessions, not the clothes they put in the wardrobes, not the photographs they pin to the wall, but articles which, for one reason or another, are their talismans. Each suitcase, locked or tied round with card, is like a man's memory. They defend the right to keep their suitcases.
>
> (Berger and Mohr, 1975, p.179)

Hannah Arendt, having escaped from the Nazis to arrive in New York, is said to have stayed for the rest of her life without unpacking her suitcases.[1] Perhaps the most poignant form of the symbolism of the migrant's suitcase appears in Charlotte Salomon's autobiographical paintings of her life as a Jewish refugee, hiding from the Germans in Vichy France. In one of the paintings, her fictional alter ego 'Lotte' is shown sitting dejectedly on the edge of her bed preparing for exile, staring at the debris of her previously cultured life, which she is forlornly failing to pack into the suitcase she will take with her on her flight. ... In a recent interview, Edward Said expressed exactly this anxiety when he said that 'like all Palestinians' he has a tendency to overpack for any journey, because he is always plagued by a 'panic about not coming back' (Said, quoted in Jaggi, 1999).

Even when the migrant arrives at their destination, the suitcase often remains a potent symbol both of the journey they have made, and of the unstable potential for further movement. In her autobiographical novel, describing growing up in the UK of Indian parents, Meera Syal gives a compelling account of the symbolic significance of the large suitcases which had sat on the top of her mother's bedroom wardrobe for as long as she could remember. She explained that as a child she had

> always assumed this was some kind of ancient Punjabi custom, this need to display several dusty, bulging cases, overflowing with old Indian suits, photographs and yellowing official papers, as all my Uncles' and Aunties' wardrobes were similarly crowned with this impressive array of luggage.
>
> (Syal, 1997, p.267)

Her mother tried to brush off her questions about the significance of the suitcases with the practical observation that they were just a good place to keep 'all the things ... that do not fit into these small English wardrobes'. However, her daughter was not convinced that matters were so simple, as she had

> already noticed that everything in those cases had something to do with India – the clothes, the albums, the letters from various cousins – and wondered why they were kept apart from the rest of the household jumble, allotted their own place and prominence, the nearest thing in our house that we had to a shrine.
>
> (Syal, 1997, p.267)

...

It is not only the suitcase he carries with him that performs this talismanic function for the migrant. If the suitcase is usually full of things brought from home, for many migrants there is often also another crucial physical container, standing empty in their homeland. Thus Lofgren notes that these days, all around the world one can find hundreds and thousands of empty houses, paid for or built by migrants,

> investing a lot of their dreams, ambitions and resources in building and furnishing houses 'back home' [which] may be briefly visited now and then, but really stand as a

materialized utopia of returning home …
[which] in all their emptiness … are full of
longing, nostalgia and dreams.

(Lofgren, 1995, p.10)

In a similar vein, Russell King observes that in many
places, migrants have transformed their districts of
origin by the building of houses in the style of the
countries to which they emigrated. As he observes,

> in Southern Italy, in the early twentieth
> century many towns and villages had
> whole streets of 'American houses' – new
> houses built by the *americani*, the local
> emigrants who went to America; in Hong
> Kong houses built with money earnt in
> England are called 'sterling houses'; in the
> Punjab … *pukka* houses stand out above
> the local dwellings as testimony to a certain
> level of success abroad on the part of their
> owners.

(King, 1995, p.10)

Similarly, there is a strong tendency for Turkish
migrants to Germany to buy apartments in middle-
class areas, furnish them and spend their annual
holidays there, and to endlessly prepare them for an
eventual return which is, in fact, unlikely to ever occur
(Caglar, 1995).

Notes

1 Papastergiadis (1998) – although he notes that this
   possibly apocryphal story is contradicted by Arendt's
   biographer.

References

Berger, J. and Mohr, J. (1975) *The Seventh Man*,
Harmondsworth, Penguin Books.

Bisharat, G. (1997) 'Exile to compatriot: transformations in
the social identity of Palestinian refugees in the West Bank'
in Gupta, A. and Ferguson, J. (eds) *Culture, Power, Place*,
Durham, NC, Duke University Press.

Caglar, A.S. (1995) 'German Turks in Berlin: social exclusion
and strategies for social mobility', *New Community*, vol.21,
no. 3.

Jaggi, M. (1999) 'Out of the shadows', *The Guardian*, 11
September.

King, R. (1995) 'Migrants, globalization and place' in Massey,
D. and Jess, P. (eds) *A Place in the World?*, Oxford, Oxford
University Press/The Open University.

Lofgren, O. (1995) 'The nation as home or motel?',
unpublished paper, Department of European Ethnology,
University of Lund.

Papastergiadis, N. (1998) *Dialogues in the Diasporas*,
London, Rivers Oram Press.

Seed, P. (1999) 'The key to the house' in Naficy, H. (ed.)
Home, Homeland, Exile, London, Routledge.

Syal, M. (1997) *Anita and Me*, London, Flamingo.

Source: Morley, 2000, pp.44–46

1.5 Rita Felski, 'The invention of everyday life' (1999–2000)

Repetition

Everyday life is above all a temporal term. As such, it
conveys the fact of repetition; it refers not to the
singular or unique but to that which happens 'day
after day'. The activities of sleeping, eating and
working conform to regular diurnal rhythms that are
in turn embedded within larger cycles of repetition:
the weekend, the annual holiday, the start of a new
semester. For Lefebvre (1987, p.10), this cyclical
structure of everyday life is its quintessential feature,
a source of both fascination and puzzlement. …
Repetition is a problem or, as he says elsewhere, a
riddle, because it is fundamentally at odds with the
modern drive towards progress and accumulation.

Lefebvre returns repeatedly to this apparent
contradiction between linear and cyclical time. Linear
time is the forward-moving, abstract time of modern
industrial society; everyday life is, on the other hand,
characterised by natural, circadian rhythms which,
according to Lefebvre (1961, p.54), have changed little
over the centuries. These daily rhythms complicate
the self-understanding of modernity as permanent
progress. If everyday life is not completely outside
history, it nevertheless serves as a retardation device,
slowing down the dynamic of historical change. …
Because of its reliance upon cyclical time, everyday
life is *belated*; it lags behind the historical possibilities
of modernity.

… Conventionally, the distinction between 'time's
arrow' and 'time's cycle' is also a distinction between

masculine and feminine. Indeed, all models of historical transformation – whether linear or cataclysmic, evolutionary or revolutionary – have been conventionally coded as masculine. Conversely, woman's affinity with repetition and cyclical time is noted by numerous writers. Simone de Beauvoir, for example, claims that 'woman clings to routine; time has for her no element of novelty, it is not a creative flow; because she is doomed to repetition, she sees in the future only a duplication of the past' (1988, p.610). Here, repetition is a sign of women's enslavement in the ordinary, her association with immanence rather than transcendence. Unable to create or invent, she remains imprisoned within the remorseless routine of cyclical time. Lefebvre's perspective is less censorious: women's association with recurrence is also a sign of their connection to nature, emotion and sensuality, their lesser degree of estrangement from biological cosmic rhythms. …

Why are women so persistently linked to repetition? Several possibilities come to mind. First of all, women are almost always seen as embodied subjects, their biological nature never far from view. Biorhythmic cycles affect various aspects of male and female behaviour, yet menstruation and pregnancy become the pre-eminent, indeed the only, examples of human subordination to natural time and a certain feminine resistance to the project of civilisation. Second, women are primarily responsible for the repetitive tasks of social reproduction: cleaning, preparing meals, caring for children. While much paid work is equally repetitive, only the domestic sphere is deemed to exist outside the dynamic of history and change. …

Finally, women are identified with repetition via consumption. For Marxist scholars of the everyday, commodification is its paramount feature, evident in ever greater standardisation and sameness. As the primary symbols and victims of consumer culture, women take on the repetitive features of the objects that they buy. …

The different aspects of women's association with repetitive time are captured in a suggestive passage that is quoted by Lefebvre, from a novel by the popular American writer, Irwin Shaw. As the hero of Shaw's novel walks down Fifth Avenue looking at women shopping, he idly imagines a museum exhibit devoted to the theme of modern femininity. Like the tableaux at the Museum of Natural History, with their stuffed bears opening honeycombs against a background of caves, this diorama would display modern American women in their natural habitat and engaged in their most typical activities. What would such an exhibition consist of? It would display to the curious viewer 'a set of stuffed women, slender, high-heeled, rouged, waved, hot-eyed, buying a cocktail dress in a department store'. While these women engaged in democratic acts of mass consumption, 'in the background, behind the salesgirls and the racks and shelves, there would be bombs bursting, cities crumbling, scientists measuring the half-life of tritium and cobalt' (Lefebvre, 1991, p.28).

This image eloquently crystallizes the gendering of time. In the background, dwarfing the indifferent shoppers, is the technological sublime of science and war. This is cataclysmic time: the catastrophe of nuclear explosion, mass destruction, monumental history. But the female customers remain caught within the repetitive time of everyday life; passionate yet compliant consumers, they continue to buy dresses, oblivious to the possibility of catastrophe. They are governed by a law of repetition that is both social and natural. Creatures of artifice, they embrace the capitalist imperative to 'shop until you drop'. Yet they also embody the inexorable rhythms of nature. Like the stuffed animals at the museum, their behaviour is framed as the inevitable result of natural instinct combined with appropriate environment. …

Such visions of the horror of repetition, we need to recognise, are distinctively modern. For most of human history, activities have gained value precisely because they repeat what has gone before. Repetition, understood as ritual, provides a connection to ancestry and tradition; it situates the individual in an imagined community that spans historical time. It is thus not opposed to transcendence, but is the means of transcending one's historically limited existence. In the modern era, by contrast, to repeat without questioning or transforming is often regarded as laziness, conservatism, or bad faith. This disdain for repetition fuels existentialism's critique of the unthinking routines of everyday life, its insistence on the importance of creating oneself anew at each moment. It is behind the shock of the new in modern art that is intended to liberate us from our habitual, entrenched, perceptions. …

Yet the attempt to escape repetition is a Sisyphean project, for, as Lefebvre rightly insists, it pervades the everyday. He further argues that daily life is situated at the intersection of two modes of repetition: the cyclical, which dominates in nature, and the linear, which dominates in processes known as 'rational' (Lefebvre, 1987, p.10). Here, as elsewhere, Lefebvre conceives of repetition as taking one of two forms: natural bodily rhythms or the regimented cycles of industrial capitalism. Yet many everyday routines cannot easily be fitted into either of these categories. They are neither unmediated expressions of biological drives nor mere reflexes of capitalist domination but a much more complex blend of the social and the psychic. Continuity and routine are crucial to early child development and remain important in adult life. Repetition is one of the ways in which we organize the world, make sense of our environment and stave off the threat of chaos. It is a key factor in the gradual formation of identity as a social and intersubjective process. Quite simply, we become who we are through acts of repetition. …

Furthermore, there is a tendency, clearly visible in the work of Lefebvre, to equate repetition with domination, and innovation with agency and resistance. Yet this is to remain trapped within a mindset which assumes the superior value of the new. In our own era, however, the reverse is just as likely to be true. Within the maelstrom of contemporary life, change is often imposed on individuals against their will; conversely, everyday rituals may help to safeguard a sense of personal autonomy and dignity, or to preserve the distinctive equalities of a threatened way of life. …

Finally, Lefebvre's often illuminating discussion of the quotidian is weakened by his persistent opposition of cyclical and linear time, the everyday and the modern, the feminine and the masculine. Yet the passing of time surely cannot be grasped in such rigidly dualistic terms. Thus acts of innovation and creativity are not opposed to, but rather made possible by the mundane cycles of the quotidian. Conversely, even the most repetitive of lives bears witness to the irreversible direction of time: the experience of ageing, the regret of past actions or inactions, the premonition of death. The temporality of everyday life is internally complex: it combines repetition and linearity with forward movement. The everyday cannot be opposed to the realm of history, but is rather the very means by which history is actualised and made real (Osborne, 1995, p.198). … Rather than being the sign of a uniquely feminine relationship to time, it permeates the lives of men as well as women.

Home

While everyday life expresses a specific sense of time, it does not convey a particular sense of space. In fact, everyday life is usually distinguished by an absence of boundaries, and thus a lack of clear spatial differentiation. It includes a variety of different spaces (the workplace, the home, the mall) as well as diverse forms of movement through space (walking, driving, flying). Moreover, our everyday experience of space is now powerfully affected by technology; thanks to television, telephones and computers we can have virtual knowledge of places and cultures quite remote from our own.

In spite of these varied locations, several philosophers of everyday life focus on the home as its privileged symbol. Agnes Heller writes: 'Integral to the average everyday life is awareness of a fixed point in space, a firm position from which we "proceed" (whether every day or over larger periods of time) and to which we return in due course. This firm position is what we call "home"' (Heller, 1984, p.239). Like everyday life itself, home constitutes a base, a taken-for-granted grounding, which allows us to make forays into other worlds. … According to Heller, familiarity is an everyday need, and familiarity combines with the promise of protection and warmth to create the positive everyday associations of home.

Home is also important to Lefebvre's discussion of everyday life, but his attitude is more ambivalent. Home becomes an occasion for meditating on his own discomfort with the everyday lives of others. Describing a suburban development at the outskirts of Paris, he is unable to suppress his own sense of irritation. 'The owners' superficiality oozes forth in an abundance of ridiculous details: china animals on the roofs, glass globes and well-pruned shrubs along the miniature paths, plaques adorned with mottos, self-important pediments' (Lefebvre, 1991, p.43). Home is a symbol of complacency, pretentiousness and petit-bourgeois bad taste. Yet Lefebvre is also critical of his own reaction. He admits that going into one of these suburban houses would probably seem like entering heaven to the migrant workers at Renault. 'Why should I say anything against these people who – like me – come home from work everyday? They seem to be decent folk who live with their families, who love their children. Can we blame them for not wanting the world in which they live reasonably at home to be transformed?' (*ibid.*, p.43).

This is surely a key citation in understanding the spatial dimensions of theories of everyday life. Home is not just a geographical designation, but a resonant metaphysical symbol. Lefebvre perceives the petit-bourgeois individual to be reasonably at home in the world. Being at home in the world is an implicit affront to the existential homelessness and anguish of the modern intellectual. … The vocabulary of modernity is a vocabulary of anti-home. It celebrates mobility, movement, exile, boundary crossing. It speaks enthusiastically about movement out into the world, but is silent about the return home. Its preferred location is the city street, the site of random encounters, unexpected events, multiplicity and difference. … This chaotic ferment is in tune with the spirit of the critic, described as a restless analyst, constantly on the move. Home, by contrast, is the space of familiarity, dullness, stasis. …

Home is, of course, a highly gendered space. Women have often been seen as the personification of home and even as its literal embodiment. Houses are often imagined as quasi-uterine spaces: conversely, the female body, notes Freud, is the 'former home of all human beings' (1985, p.368). As a result, feminists have often been eager to demystify the ideal of home as haven. One nineteenth-century female novelist, for example, imagined a utopian future in which the word 'home' would no longer exist (Hayden, 1981, p.137). Modern feminism, from Betty Friedan onwards, has repeatedly had recourse to a rhetoric of leaving home. Home is a prison, a trap, a straitjacket. In recent years, this critique of home has intensified: the discourse of contemporary feminism speaks enthusiastically of migrations, boundary crossings, nomadic subjects. Much of the same language pervades cultural studies. De Certeau dedicates *The Practice of Everyday Life* to 'a common hero, an ubiquitous character, walking in countless thousands on the streets'. His image of the agile pedestrian, adeptly weaving a distinctive textual path across the grid of city streets, has become a resonant symbol of the contemporary subject. Freedom and agency are traditionally symbolised by movement through public space. …

In response, Janet Wolff (1995) has suggested that such metaphors are masculine and hence problematic for feminism. She notes the persistent association of maleness with travel and femininity with stasis. But, as she also acknowledges, women have always travelled, and they now do so in vast numbers, as tourists, researchers, aid workers, guest workers, refugees. To describe metaphors of travel as inherently alienating women seems too simple. …

Still, it is true that such metaphors are partial, casting light upon particular aspects of experience only to relegate other parts of daily life to the shadows. In spite of the hyperbole in postmodern theory about nomadism, hyperspace and time–space compression, writes Doreen Massey, 'much of life for many people, even in the heart of the first world, still consists of waiting in a bus-shelter with your shopping for a bus that never comes' (1992, p.8). Similarly, Massey questions the assumption that postmodern global space has done away with the need for home and has left us placeless and disoriented. She notes the continuing importance of place and locality in everyday life, while questioning the belief that a desire for home is inauthentic or reactionary. …

The everyday significance of home clearly needs to be imagined differently. First of all, home is, in de Certeau's terms, an active practising of place. Even if home is synonymous with familiarity and routine, that familiarity is actively produced over time, above all through the effort and labour of women. Furthermore, while home may sometimes seem static, both the reality and the ideology of home change dramatically over time. Second, the boundaries between home and non-home are leaky. The home is not a private enclave cut off from the outside world, but is powerfully shaped by broader social currents, attitudes, and desires. …

Finally, home, like any other space, is shaped by conflicts and power struggles. It is often the site of intergenerational conflicts, such that an adolescent sense of identity can be predicated upon a burning desire to leave home. It can be a place of female subordination as well as an arena where women can show competence in the exercise of domestic skills. Home is often a place for displaying commodities and hence saturated by class distinctions; a recent ethnography of working-class women notes their embarrassment at the perceived insufficiency of their home (Skeggs, 1997). Home also acquires particularly poignant meanings for migrants and their descendents. In *Zami*, for example, Audre Lorde shapes the meaning of a life story around changing definitions of home. As a child, Lorde absorbs her mother's nostalgic yearning for her Caribbean homeland, as a young adult she must leave her mother's house in order to help create a 'house of difference' in the New York lesbian community, and finally she arrives at a vision of home informed by both her American lesbian identity and her Caribbean heritage (Lorde, 1982).

As this example suggests, the idea of home is complex and temporally fluid. Home should not be confused with a fantasy of origin; any individual life story will contain different and changing visions of home. My definition is intentionally minimal; it includes any often visited place that is the object of cathexis, that in its very familiarity becomes a symbolic extension and confirmation of the self. As Roger Silverstone argues, home is 'an investment of meaning in space' (1994, p.28). Such a familiar location fulfils both affective and pragmatic needs. It is a storage place, both literally and symbolically: home often contains many of the objects that have helped to shape a life-history, and the meanings and memories with which these objects are encrypted. Home is, in Mary Douglas's phrase, a 'memory machine' (1993, p.268). In this regard, Heller's focus on home as central to the spatial organisation of everyday life provides a useful corrective to the current infatuation with mobility and travel.

A number of feminist scholars, while not explicitly concerned with everyday life, are developing alternative visions of the symbolism and politics of home. bell hooks, for example, suggests that the history of home has very different meanings for African-American women as well as for men. 'Historically, African-American people believed that the construction of a homeplace, however fragile and tenuous (the slave hut, the wooden shack) had a radical political dimension. Despite the brutal reality of racial apartheid, of domination, one's homeplace was the one site where one could freely confront the issue of humanisation, where one could resist' (1990, p.42). ...

In a recent essay, Iris Marion Young (1997) also makes a thoughtful case for rethinking feminist attitudes to house and home. Questioning the nostalgic longing for home as a place of stable identities predicated on female self-sacrifice, she nevertheless wants to recognise the symbolic richness and cultural complexity of 'home-making' (which is not just housework). Home, she argues, is a specific materialisation of the body and the self; things and spaces become layered with meaning, value and memory. This materialisation does not fix identity but anchors it in a physical space that creates certain continuities between past and present (Young, 1997, p.153).

References

Beauvoir, S. de (1988) *The Second Sex*, London, Picador (first published in France in 1949).

Douglas, M. (1993) 'The idea of a home: a kind of space' in Mack, A. (ed.) *Home: A Place in the World*, New York, New York University Press.

Freud, S. (1985) *The Uncanny* in *Sigmund Freud, vol. 14: Art and Literature*, Harmondsworth, Penguin Books.

Hayden, D. (1981) *The Grand Domestic Revolution: A History of Feminist Designs for American Homes, Neighborhoods, and Cities*, Cambridge, MA, The MIT Press.

Heller, A. (1984) *Everyday Life*, London, Routledge and Kegan Paul.

hooks, b. (1990) 'Homeplace: a site of resistance' in *Yearning: Race, Gender and Cultural Politics*, Boston, MA, South End Press.

Lefebvre, H. (1961) *Critique de la Vie Quotidienne*, vol. 2, Paris, L'Arche.

Lefebvre, H. (1987) 'The everyday and everydayness', *Yale French Studies*, no.73.

Lefebvre, H. (1991) *Critique of Everday Life*, vol. 1, London, Verso.

Lorde, A. (1982) *Zami: A New Spelling of My Name*, London, Sheba Feminist Publishers.

Massey, D. (1992) 'A place called home?', *New Formations 17*, London, Lawrence and Wishart.

Osborne, P. (1995) *The Politics of Time: Modernity and Avant-garde*, London, Verso.

Silverstone, R. (1994) *Television and Everyday Life*, London, Routledge.

Skeggs, B. (1997) *Formations of Class and Gender*, London, Sage.

Wolff, J. (1995) 'On the road again: metaphors of travel in cultural criticism', *Resident Alien: Feminist Cultural Criticism*, New Haven, CT, Yale University Press.

Young, I.M. (1997) 'House and home: feminist variations on a theme', *Intersecting Voices: Dilemmas of Gender, Political Philosophy and Policy*, Princeton, NJ, Princeton University Press.

Source: Felski, 1999–2000, pp.18–25

'Love is in the air': romance and the everyday

Peter Redman

Contents

I can't explain it very well. 'Just went in the sequence' is probably the best word to describe it.

(Dan, 17-year-old)

There was one day I spent the whole day with her ... I got over to her house, and it was a really warm sunny day, and because [of where she lived], there was loads of fields around so we went off for a walk in the woods and up into a field – a sort of weed field [laughs] – a corn field or something like that. And we just lay down in the grass and just messed about, you know, having a kiss and just lying there talking to each other and stuff and it was really, really great. A really great feeling. I've never experienced anything quite like it, you know? It was almost like I say, 'Mills and Boon'. It was like 'running through fields of corn' sort of thing, you know, it was like that. But ... I mean, that day was just really, really special. It was really good.

(Nick, 16-year-old)

1 Introduction

qualitative research

These two quotations come from **qualitative research** interviews that I conducted with 16- to 18-year-old young men – or, as they tended to refer to themselves, 'boys' or 'lads'. As the quotations suggest, a number of the boys were strongly invested in heterosexual romance and, in the course of the interviews, they told – often in great detail and quite movingly – stories of love found and lost, of love unobtainable or unrequited, and of love as a state of imagined future happiness.

This chapter explores these stories for what they can tell us about the 'everyday'. In particular, it asks:

1   In what ways and to what extent can romance be considered part of the everyday?

2   Is romance socially constructed? If so, how?

3   What does an exploration of romance add to our understanding of the everyday as an object of sociological enquiry?

4   To what extent is qualitative interviewing a useful research method in exploring these issues?

There is, of course, a good reason for exploring romance in the wake of Chapter 1's investigation of the home and the everyday. Romance was itself deeply implicated in the development of the 'ideal' (white, middle-class) home. Most obviously, marriage and the domestic 'happy ever after' provide the culmination of the classic domestic romance story, a genre which developed hand-in-hand with the new domestic ideology of the eighteenth and nineteenth centuries. 'Reader, I married him', Jane Eyre famously tells us in the final chapter of Charlotte Brontë's great nineteenth-century romantic novel. According to this new domestic ideology, the 'ideal' home was, then, the ultimate reward for romance as an ideal love. Equally, romance as an everyday practice is bound up with the home as a central site of intimacy and privacy in contemporary western societies. The practices of romance, and the social identities they entail, are among the most significant forms through which emotional and sexual intimacy are organized in these societies. The home is, of course, one of the primary sites in which these intimacies are lived, a fact given material expression in the architectural separation of the marital bedroom. Similarly, the practices of romance are among the most significant means by which privacy is demarcated in contemporary western societies. They signal a private arena in which the loving couple is separated off from the rest of the world, a fact that is once again reinforced and given material expression in suburban architecture (discussed in Chapter 7) with its characteristic separation between the worlds of paid work and the home. In short, romance and the home are closely entwined.

Your reading of the Introduction and Chapter 1 of this volume will have alerted you to the fact that, in sociology, the concept of the everyday is frequently used as a way of thinking about those features of social life that can be considered commonplace, taken for granted and routine. As Felski (1999–2000) argues, the everyday is characterized by habit and repetition and is to be found in the 'private' dimensions of social life – perhaps paradigmatically in the daily rhythms of the home, but also in, for example, the journey to work or the supermarket, and in the small talk and routines of the workplace and the pub (see Chapters 4 and 5 in this volume). You may also have begun to realize that the forms and practices that make up the everyday are **socially constructed**, despite their familiarity and 'taken for grantedness'.

social constructionism

The two quotations that open this chapter begin to indicate how romance might be considered in the same light as these arguments: that is, how romance might be understood as a repertoire of socially produced forms and practices that help shape the contours and experiences of the everyday. For instance, in the first of the quotations, 'Dan' (all the interviewees' names have been changed to preserve anonymity) appears to acknowledge what we might call the 'textual' dimension of being in love – that is, its reliance on a pre-scripted set of genre conventions and practices. Dan is describing how, at the age of 15, he fell in love with a girl while on a family holiday. In fact, Dan even got engaged to this girl although, perhaps predictably, the relationship did not survive very long after their return home. What is startling about this account is that Dan describes his experience of falling in love as just going 'in the sequence'. It is almost as if he was a character in a romantic story in which the events of the narrative unfolded in a familiar pattern from the moment that he met the eyes of his future girlfriend 'across a crowded room' (or, in Dan's case, on a staircase). This textual dimension of being in love is even more explicitly articulated in the second of the quotations in which Nick relates an event from the previous summer, a day out with a girl, Helen, with whom he was, at the time, intensely in love. This perfect day was, he says, like something out of 'Mills and Boon', that is, like something in a popular romantic novel. Both of these quotations suggest that the experience of being in love may be inextricably bound up with a repertoire of culturally available forms and practices. From this standpoint, then, we might argue that romantic love should not be seen as a universal phenomenon or part of an unchanging natural order but as a *social product*.

If the quotations that open the chapter begin to suggest the ways in which the experience of romantic love may be socially constructed, they also serve to highlight our everyday familiarity with the conventions of romance. Indeed, it is possible to argue that romantic themes and conventions so thoroughly saturate both popular and high culture that they are familiar to us even if we are not active readers or viewers of romantic texts. One important reason for this is that romance conventions tend to leach out of their recognizable homes in films, novels, songs and magazines and permeate wider genres such as soap opera, advertising and news-reportage. In consequence, we all tend to come into contact with the conventions of the romance genre in our daily patterns of viewing, reading and listening.

Stop for a moment and spend a couple of minutes jotting down as many examples as you can come up with of the following:

■ films, novels, songs or other texts which have an explicitly romantic theme or storyline ('text' is used to refer to any representational form – auditory, visual, verbal – not just written forms as is more common in everyday speech);

■ texts that, although not explicitly identifiable as romances, nevertheless contain elements of romantic story-lines (for instance, can you think of any advertisements, soap-opera plots or news stories that appear to recycle romance conventions?).

My guess is that it was very easy to come up with a long list of explicitly romantic films, songs, novels and other texts but that answering the second question was slightly more difficult. Nevertheless, you may have found that, after a bit of thought, you were able to identify examples where romance conventions have appeared in other genres. Soap opera is a good example of this. For instance, you might be familiar with the Australian soap, *Neighbours*, in which there have been a number of celebrated romances such as that between Scott (played by Jason Donovan) and Charlene (played by Kylie Minogue) (see Figure 2.1a). Equally, romance conventions are often recycled in advertising and news-reportage. For example, during the 1990s, there was a highly successful sequence of advertisements for Gold Blend instant coffee on British television that promoted the brand via a 'will-they-won't-they' romantic storyline (see Figure 2.1b). Similarly, the wedding of the Prince of Wales and Lady Diana Spencer in 1981 was, at the time, widely reported as a fairy-tale romance (see Figure 2.1c).

These examples suggest the ways in which romance permeates everyday cultural texts and therefore the background noise of our everyday lives. However, it is also possible to argue that romance informs and shapes a wide range of everyday social practices and interactions. For instance, Sasha Weitman invites us to consider the character of everyday interactions in the workplace:

> Consider … the workplace, regardless of what severe measures are used to suppress socioerotics at work, employees always manage to find locations (in corridors, by the water cooler, at the john, in the snack bar, on the phone) and times (coffee time, lunchtime, commuting time) in order to socialize (to gossip, flirt, exchange niceties, make dates).
>
> (Weitman, 1999, p.99)

For Weitman, 'socioerotics' (that is, romantic and other forms of sexual and erotic meaning and practice) are part of the routine of the everyday. In fact, a wide range of mundane practices and interactions can be seen to be shaped and informed by romance. Casual flirting in the workplace, passing daydreams, everyday conversations about who is going out with whom, and many of the small rituals of coupledom (the kiss goodbye, the cup of tea in bed) – all of these can be informed by romantic themes and conventions, even though they may be casual, habitual or lack the passionate intensity we might sometimes associate with romance.

Figure 2.1 *Romance themes and conventions saturate everyday life*

(a)

(b)

(c)

Think back over the last couple of days. Can you identify any ways in which recognizably romantic themes or conventions may have informed your own everyday activities – particularly those that are mundane, routine and 'private' – or those of anyone you know?

Even if romance does not inform your own life to any great degree (and there is no reason why it should), my guess is that your observation of the world around you means that you will still recognize the extent to which romance is a feature of the everyday. However, if romance may be understood as an inextricable part of everyday life, there is also an important sense in which it may be *opposed* to the everyday. As you may have noticed, the second of the opening quotations – Nick's account of a 'perfect day' – is less a description of the routine and mundane qualities that are generally taken to characterize everyday life than a portrayal of a 'magical moment', something that was precisely out of the ordinary.

Equally, you may also have noticed that the quotation from Dan relates to a *holiday* romance, to a 'time out of life'. Indeed, it is surely significant that, once back home, immersed in everyday routines, the relationship withered and died. These transcendent, utopian or oppositional qualities to romance are something often commented on in sociological accounts (see, for example, Beck and Beck-Gernsheim, 1995; Goodison, 1983). For instance, in Reading 2.3, which you will explore later in the chapter, the German sociologist Ulrich Beck (Beck and Beck-Gernsheim, 1995, pp.175, 178) describes loving as a 'kind of rebellion', which offers 'a way of escaping from the daily grind'. It would, then, appear that we are in the presence of a curious paradox. Romantic love is at once ubiquitous, deeply familiar and inextricable from the everyday and yet also in opposition to it. As such, it points to the existence of particular features of everyday life – among them religious ceremonies, sporting fixtures and other ritualized social occasions such as 'raves' (see Chapter 6 in this volume) that, although routinized, also seek to puncture and escape the more mundane qualities of the everyday.

In the course of this chapter we will be exploring these themes in greater depth. The chapter begins by examining the genre conventions of romance and then moves on to explore the ways in which these informed the boys' relationships. On the basis of this, the following sections then open up the debate over the extent to which the experience of romantic love can be understood as socially constructed and then analyses the complex relationship between romance and the everyday.

AIMS

The aims of this chapter are:

1   To explore the links between romance and the everyday using a case study of 16- to 18-year-old boys.

2   To show how romance adds to our understanding of the everyday as a sociological concept.

3   To consider the extent to which romance seeks to transcend the everyday.

4   To explore the social construction of romance.

5   To show through the case study how qualitative interviewing can be an effective research method for exploring romance and the everyday.

2 What do we mean by romance?

In the introductory section we have talked about romance without defining it formally. In consequence, before exploring the extent to which the boys organized their relationships in romantic terms, we need to be more precise about what we mean by the term. To do this we are going to explore the genre conventions of the 'classic romance' – that version of idealizing love with which, in the western world at least, we are most familiar from novels, films and popular music.

You should now read 'The heart of the matter: feminists revisit romance' by Jackie Stacey and Lynne Pearce (Reading 2.1 at the end of this chapter).

Make notes as you read, then answer the following questions:

1 What are the main conventions of the 'classic romance'?

2 In Activity 1 you were asked to identify examples of films and novels that are identifiably romantic. To what extent do these conform to the conventions of the 'classic romance' as defined in Reading 2.1?

Stacey and Pearce's overview highlights some of the main conventions of the classic romance as it has been constructed as a genre in narrative fiction. What, precisely, are these conventions? Studies of genre frequently draw attention to characteristic features that help distinguish one genre from another (see, for example, Gledhill, 1997). Key among these are: subject matter, medium, narrative pattern, character types, plots, setting and location. Applying these categories to the classic romance, we might come up with a list that looks something like the following:

- *Subject matter*: a heterosexual union revolving round a form of idealizing love.

- *Medium*: appears in diverse media but particularly novels, magazine fiction, films, plays, television drama and popular songs.

- *Narrative pattern*: involves a linear narrative progressing, via a series of 'hurdles' or 'setbacks', towards love's attainment and/or loss.

- *Character types*: the heterosexual couple (generally young to middle-aged, generally white) constructed as opposites: active, powerful, worldly and rational (in the case of the man) and pure, emotional and passive (in the case of the woman). A standard subsidiary character is the 'foil', who either offers competition to the protagonist by threatening to 'steal' the object of her/his desire, or who offers an alternative but ultimately inappropriate relationship.

- *Plot*: a quest, typically revolving round the overcoming of various obstacles that stand in the way of love's fulfilment and/or loss, a fulfilment that is experienced as a profound and life-changing transfiguration.

- *Setting and location*: variable, although may include typical locations (the candle-lit dinner, the moonlit night or sea, the countryside), milieu (such as the worlds of the aristocracy or the rich) and historical periods (such as Regency England).

This analysis of the classic romance is useful in that it will allow us in the next section to explore the extent to which the boys' relationships were shaped and informed by classically romantic themes and conventions. However, in conducting this exploration, there are a number of issues to which we will need to be alert. The first and perhaps most obvious of these is the possibility that the classic romance is now somewhat out of date and so stereotypical that it can no longer be said to inform actual relationships. Indeed, when listing the conventions of the classic romance above (while answering the questions that followed Reading 2.1), it may be that you found these rather hackneyed or even

Figures 2.2 and 2.3 *'Are the conventions of the "classic" romance becoming increasingly subverted?'*

amusing. It is also quite possible that, in response to the second of these questions, you chose a text that played with or sought to subvert the conventions of the classic romance rather than one that simply reproduces them. For instance, when doing the exercise myself, I couldn't decide whether to apply the conventions to David Lean's (1945) classic story of love lost, *Brief Encounter* (Figure 2.2), which is one of my favourite films, or another more recent favourite, Hettie MacDonald's (1996) *Beautiful Thing* (Figure 2.3) which, if not subverting, at least plays with romance conventions by transposing them on to the burgeoning love affair between two adolescent boys.

The facts that romance conventions may appear hackneyed and that we can, furthermore, play with or subvert them, indicate the extent to which the classic romance is, in Stacey and Pearce's term, 'under pressure' from wider social changes. Prominent among these changes are, of course, the challenges that gay and lesbian and feminist politics and theory have posed to conventional heterosexual relations. As a genre, romance cannot remain immune to such changes. Thus, in exploring concrete relationships, we will need to ask to what extent romance conventions are being reproduced and to what extent they are being contested.

The second issue to which we will need to be alert in exploring the boys' use of romantic themes and conventions concerns the 'femininity' of the classic romance genre. In examining the classic romance, it might have occurred to you that romantic texts are routinely, although not exclusively (think of the popular love song), constructed as 'feminine'. This is to say that the classic romance makes available a conventional 'feminine' point of view on the proceedings: it constructs events through the female protagonist's eyes, and explores themes socially constructed as essentially 'female' (for example, getting and holding a man; passion versus virtue; emotion versus rationality; love versus public affairs). We also know from statistical and other surveys that romance has a predominantly female readership. For instance, the study of Australian everyday cultural practices by Bennett, Emmison and Frow (aspects of which you explored in Chapter 1) found that 26.2 per cent of the women in its sample expressed a preference for reading romances while only 1.8 per cent of the men did so (Bennett *et al.*, 1999, p.150; see also Radway, 1984). Of course, the 'femininity' of the genre raises interesting questions about boys' and men's use of and investments in romance. Do boys 'do' romance and if they do, how?

The final matter to which we should be alert in exploring the boys' possible use of classic romance themes and conventions in their relationships concerns the issue of power. You have probably noticed that, in its classic form, the romance tends to assume a heterosexual resolution to its storyline, namely the establishment of a conventional heterosexual-couple relationship traditionally – though not now exclusively – signified by marriage (as I have indicated, such conventions are increasingly under pressure). In addition, the genre is also frequently keen to polarize masculinity and femininity into distinct and opposing entities: the powerful, rational man; the passive, emotional woman. As we shall see later in the chapter, it can be argued that, if reproduced in real relationships, such conventions can serve to reproduce and reinforce conventional relations of power surrounding gender and sexuality.

SUMMARY OF SECTION 2

1   The 'classic' romance genre as it appears in, for example, literary fiction and film provides a useful basis for defining what we mean by 'romance' in contemporary western societies.

2   In using the classic romance as the basis for defining what we mean by romance we need to remember that the meanings of romance may be changing in response to wider social changes; as a literary genre, romance tends to be associated with femininity, although this may not be the case in actual relationships; and that romance may well involve relations of power, particularly as these relate to gender and sexuality.

3   Boys in love: stories of everyday romance

In this section we will be exploring material from qualitative interviews that I conducted in the early 1990s with a group of ten 16- to 18-year-old boys. Qualitative interviewing is generally small in scale and attempts to 'get inside' the social worlds of interviewees in order to gain an insight into the meanings they give to them. Thus, the interview material discussed here does not claim to be representative of a wider population (you may or may not recognize your own experience in it). What it aims to show is how the respondents lived, talked and felt about their heterosexual relationships in the very specific context of their sixth-form college.

We do not have space here for a detailed discussion of the strengths and weaknesses of qualitative interviewing as a research method. However, if we are to be able to assess the plausibility of qualitative research, it is important to have at least some background information about it. As a result, before going on to explore the interview material, we will pause for a moment to reflect on the context of the research and the method by which the material was gathered.

The interview material was collected as part of a wider ethnographic research project (conducted with Debbie Epstein and Gurjit Minhas and funded by East Birmingham Health Authority) that explored the sexual cultures of 11- to 14-year-old young people in secondary schools (see Epstein and Johnson, 1998). My primary aim in interviewing the older group of boys was to get them to reflect on their experiences at a younger age. However, in the course of the interviews, the boys tended to talk about current or more recent relationships as well as their experiences in the earlier years of secondary school, and I rapidly became interested in hearing about these. It is this material that forms the basis of the discussion in this section.

The boys interviewed all self-identified as white, English and heterosexual and, with one exception, came from what can be termed professional and managerial family backgrounds. The biological parents of three of the ten were divorced or separated. All the boys were studying for 'A' levels at a suburban sixth-form college and all expected to go on to higher education. The interviews lasted between 45 and 120 minutes and were taped and transcribed. All but one of the interviews was conducted in a private room at the college during the boys' free time. Eight of the boys chose to be interviewed individually, two chose to be interviewed in a pair. Five follow-up interviews were conducted with four of the boys. The purpose of the research was explained to the boys and they volunteered to be interviewed in the light of this. Their confidentiality was assured and, in conducting the interviews, I took care to distinguish myself from adults teaching in the college by dressing informally.

As previously indicated, in the course of the interviews, I was somewhat surprised to find that a number of the boys talked about their relationships with girls in profoundly romantic terms. This is apparent in the extract below, taken from one of the two interviews I conducted with Dan, the 18-year-old introduced at the start of this chapter. As you will see from the extract, I push Dan to discover whether some of his 'relationships' are purely about physical attraction or are simply attempts to have sex. Because Dan says that some of his relationships have not involved 'any of the feelings stuff', I assume that he is telling me that he had at least some relationships based purely on sex or the promise of it. However, as Dan makes clear, this is not what he means. Rather, he is saying that relationships that do not involve 'the feelings stuff' are simply ones where, although the potential seems to be there, he does not actually fall in love.

PR: … Are all [your relationships] of this kind? They're about
             emotions, about love? Or are some of them more like one-night
             stand kind of things?

DAN: Yeah, like one-night stands but actually like two-week stands, if
             you see what I mean. … And not any of the feelings stuff.

PR: Can you tell me about those, what are they like?

DAN: Yeah, okay. … I met this girl on the biology field trip … and we
             just got on really well, just talking, laughing. … And we went out
             and then like we started getting a bit, a little bit deep, like going
             round to her house – I met her parents. … And, erm, but it wasn't
             any, no feeling came into it at all really. I mean, I say no feeling
             but you know, not 'I love you' and all that, it was just, … just
             good to be with her and she was like really easy-going and easy
             to get on with.

PR: The reason I keep cracking on about this is that, erm, there are some men who just have relationships where they, like, see a girl in the pub and they think, yeah, you know, I want to have sex with her, and they pick her up and have sex. … Maybe they have other kinds of relationships too, but this is more to do with that they want to have sex.

DAN: I've never done that. … There's only been the two [relationships where there's been] something deep. … The others were just [sighs] I don't know, just 'want' I suppose.

PR: Just want? What is the 'want'?

DAN: Just want to have a girlfriend.

Thus, far from expressing an interest in uncommitted sex as I had assumed, Dan seems to be saying that his investments lie in the search for love, or as he puts it, 'something deep'. To my surprise then, in conducting the interviews, I found what appeared to be strong investments in what Nick (also introduced at the start of the chapter) called 'the caring and sharing and actual emotion' of being in love. Not surprisingly, some of the boys spoke of their relationships in more obviously romantic terms than did others. Nick had what were perhaps the most obvious investments in romance though five of the other boys – Dan, Chris, Oliver, Matt and, in particular, Ed – all used the vocabulary of romance to a greater or lesser extent (the remaining four boys in the group had less personal experience of relationships whether of a romantic kind or not). However, despite these variations and contradictions, for the boys interviewed, romance was clearly part of the taken-for-granted repertoire through which relationships were talked about, formed and lived.

One of the most obvious ways in which the boys drew on romance conventions in talking about their relationships was to be found in the stories they told about how they met and fell in love with particular girls. In the introduction to this chapter we noted one such story in which Dan described the process of falling in love as 'going in the sequence', an apparent allusion to the narrative sequence of the romance genre. Another boy, Ed, who had a long-standing relationship with a girl whom he expected one day to marry, told a story of a *coup de foudre*, or 'love at first sight'. However, in the extract that follows, we will examine a story that is particularly explicit in its use of romance conventions. It is the story that Nick told about how he met Helen, the girl with whom he was subsequently to fall deeply in love.

NICK: I never thought she'd go out with me at the beginning.

PR: Why was that?

NICK: Because I thought she was well out of my league. Because her friend at the time, Mandy, was reckoned to be a lot prettier than she was. And she was a very nice girl, you know, she fancied me. And she made a lot of hints towards me, but I couldn't sense the hints because I was fixed on Helen. I actually asked her out because I thought she was a nice girl.

PR: Who? You asked Mandy out?

NICK: No, Helen, and Mandy was very upset about it. But Helen wasn't … She fancied me but she never made it known. She didn't think

I'd go out with her because I was above her station you see. So I thought she was better than me; and she thought I was better than her.

PR: Oh right, and what was it about her that made you think she was out of your league, what in particular?

NICK: Because she wasn't like Mandy. Mandy was, you know, she'd be touching me all the time, you know, like, you know. And you can sense, you know, blatant hints like that, you know? Helen was very reserved and she was very pure, almost. But she didn't make her feelings known towards me because she thought I fancied Mandy. Which wasn't the case.

PR: When you say she was 'pure' was that part of the attraction?

NICK: Yeah, she was so innocent to an extent. She'd had experience, like, with other lads but not a full relationship sort of experience. And that posed a challenge almost. But like I was saying before, I only asked her out because I thought she was a nice girl, I thought she was nice. Sex wasn't on my mind at all. It just didn't play a part. I didn't even think it would last that long but it really did. I really hit the nail on the head, I got it, what I wanted, bang on, you know. But I wasn't out for it, if you know what I mean. … [I]t was just one day she was there. She was really nice, I wasn't really friends, I didn't speak to her and say, okay we're friends, I'd like to go out with you. I run up to her. I was in chemistry – I was talking to my friend John – I run up to her after the lesson. I was frantic, I was trying to find her because I'd really worked myself up to ask her out. So I really was expecting a rejection. And I ran outside and she was just walking along and I skidded on my knees and got on one knee and said 'Will you go out with me?' And she was like really taken aback. And loads of people were watching. And she went red and said, 'Oh I don't know. I'll have to think about it.' I was like, 'Damn' you know. ... And erh … She thought I was actually taking the mickey. She thought I was joking. And she rang me that night, she said she'd speak to me tomorrow, but she rang me that night after speaking to her friend, Sara, and ... [Sara] said, 'Yeh, it's true'. And she rang me back, and she said, 'As long as you're not joking' and I said, 'No, I'm not, and that was it' [laughs].

ACTIVITY 3

What romance conventions can you identify in this story? It may help to refer back to your notes on the conventions of the 'classic romance' as described in Reading 2.1 by Stacey and Pearce.

Perhaps the most obvious way in which Nick's story draws on romance conventions is to be found in the moment he skids to his knees to ask Helen out. However, reading the story carefully, it is apparent that it is shaped by a number of other conventions drawn from the classic romance. One of these is its use of a quest structure. The story is organized round a series of obstacles

(Helen is out of Nick's league, Mandy fancies Nick, Nick has to screw up the courage to ask Helen out, Helen thinks he is joking) that must be overcome before Helen finally agrees to go out with him. This, of course, echoes Stacey and Pearce's point in Reading 2.1 that, 'At the most general level, … romance might be described as a *quest* … [that] requires the … conquest of barriers in the name of love' (see Reading 2.1).

Perhaps even more striking about Nick's story, however, is the way in which character traits are used. Helen, for instance, is constructed as 'pure', a quality that is central to her attraction, and she is contrasted to Mandy who is characterized as sexually more knowing and forward. As such, Mandy appears to pose a threat to the 'proper' union of Nick and Helen, but is quickly dispatched from the narrative because Nick, as the hero, is in reality 'fixed on Helen'. This use of character traits echoes any number of popular romances, and has obvious antecedents in more canonical texts such as *Jane Eyre*. If you know this novel, then you may recognize Helen as the Jane character (at least to the extent that she is 'pure'), Nick as Rochester, and Mandy as Blanche Ingram, the 'base foil' whose deficiencies serve to emphasize Jane's qualities and whose rejection demonstrates Rochester's essential but previously doubted goodness and sound judgement.

If 'falling in love' stories provide one example of the boys' use of romance conventions in talking about their relationships, many others were to be found scattered through the interviews. For example, two of the boys, Chris and Oliver, told stories of 'doomed love' or 'loving from afar'. Oliver, for instance, was strongly attracted to a girl already in a relationship. He explained:

OLIVER: I was attracted to her because, one, she's very good looking and, two, there's just something insecure and, sort of, I don't know, just sort of something about her … she just like looks as though she needs looking after, and I just find that sort of really sort of attractive.

As with the Nick's 'falling in love' story, this appears to draw on conventional romantic character traits: the girl is beautiful but vulnerable and shy; Oliver is strong and capable. Similarly, several of the boys talked of love as a force of nature, echoing popular romance conventions where falling in love is routinely described in terms of tidal waves, lightning strikes and so on. For instance, Nick, eloquent as ever, commented:

NICK: [Falling in love] is a natural process, yeah, it clicks. It's not something you can achieve. It's something that falls into place. One day you wake up and think, 'Wow!' You know, you can work at it but it can't be the same as real, natural love. It just comes naturally … It just happens … it comes from inside you definitely. It's just a magnetism.

This notion of love as a 'force of nature' would also appear to echo the common romantic theme of love as a transcendental experience, something graphically captured in the second of the quotations that began this chapter, Nick's story of a 'perfect day', one in which his love for Helen was so intense that it almost seemed that they were caught up in a romantic novel or film (in Nick's phrase, 'like "Mills and Boon"').

Four of the boys also talked about love as a transformative force, something through which they had found their true or better selves. Ed, for example, clearly experienced his relationship in these terms:

ED: I dunno, when I met Louise it sort of triggered a few things off. I became more interested in me as a person, rather than, you know, as opposed to me trying to please everyone else, sort of thing. … I mean, when I met Louise it was like it cleared a few things up for me. It helped me think better about a few things. Whereas before I hadn't really thought through anything, I suddenly started thinking things. Not because she'd been saying anything. It's not as though she ever tried to put her opinions on to me because she's not like that, but, I don't know, it just opened a few doorways. … I mean, I feel more comfortable with myself these days than ever. There's no, sort of, uncertainty about things.

This theme was echoed by Chris and Nick. Chris (speaking about his current girlfriend, Jess) said:

CHRIS: But she's made a real change to my life, I've changed so badly due to her.

PR: Do you mean a lot or you've changed for the worst?

CHRIS: Well, to my friends, they think I've turned into a real swot and I hardly go out with them now and it's all because of her really. I think I've changed for the better, but they don't seem to think so.

Similarly, Nick commented:

NICK: I mean with [Helen] that helped me to grow up so much more, because it was a serious relationship and it matured me a lot more. … But it helped me to bring, bring out a personality in a way. You know, it helped me to find myself and become somebody.

Likewise, Dan described changing as a result of going out with his current girlfriend:

DAN: I suppose going out with my girlfriend at the moment has like changed my outlook to friends. Instead of treating them like shit, you treat them rightly. … I just used to expect them to listen to me, but whenever they had a problem I'd just go [affects an uninterested look], 'Yeah, yeah'.

None of these comments was given in response to direct questions, suggesting that they are aspects of how the boys themselves experience being in love. They, of course, echo a common theme of the romance genre, that romantic love is healing and transfiguring. Particularly for the hero, this process involves a certain amount of domestication or even feminization (think of the blinded and partially dependent Rochester at the end of Charlotte Brontë's *Jane Eyre*). The romantic hero finds his true, gentler self only in the love of the right woman and a commitment to a shared domestic life, figured conventionally by marriage. It is, then, interesting that three of the boys quoted articulated this sense of being 'transformed' by love in terms that are culturally coded as feminine: Chris became a 'swot' (that is, invested in schoolwork) to the disgust of his more 'laddish' male friends; Dan became more careful and nurturing of other people's feelings; and Ed, as he went on to explain, turned his back on what he came to perceive as the vulgar sexism of his mates:

ED: … after I had been going out with [Louise] for a while – you know, I mean it's not like she sort of expressed an opinion or anything like that – but it just made me realize what a bunch of sexist, chauvinist idiots they all were.

The final area in which romantic themes seemed particularly strong was in relation to what Duncombe and Marsden (1995) have called the 'staging of romance', that is the 'citing' of romance conventions in the practices through which romantic relationships are constructed and lived (examples of such 'citing' might include candle-lit dinners, romantic walks in the countryside, giving Valentines and so on). The most dramatic example of such 'citing' in the interview material was provided, once again, by Nick, who related the following story of a nocturnal visit to Helen's bedroom.

NICK: The most stupid thing I did for her was I rode over to her house about two or three o'clock in the morning and scaled the front of her bedroom – front wall of her house – on to the bay window. And hopped through her window to go and see her [both laugh]. Just silly things like that. It really does make you do silly things, but …

PR: … And this wasn't because you weren't allowed in the house? This was because …

NICK: … Oh no. This was like two o'clock in the morning [laughs]. Her parents wouldn't have been too pleased to see me at that time …

PR: … If you'd kind of rung on the doorbell, and said, 'I want to come in'!

NICK: So she actually fell asleep, I was throwing stones at the window, because she was supposed to wait up for me. And in the end I ended up climbing up [laughs] and then trying to get in the window. And her parents were in the next room, next door. So I had to be really quiet.

PR: Did you succeed in getting in?

NICK: Oh yeah, yeah. I did. Gave her a kiss and she woke up. She just went, 'What the hell are you doing here?' [laughs]. And then she remembered why I was there, 'cause she told me to. But I'd, I'd literally do anything for her, I would have done. I did.

Needless to say, in its use of genre conventions, this episode could come from any number of fictional romances, from Chrétien de Troyes' twelfth-century account of the love of Lancelot and Guenevere, *Le Chevalier de la charette,* to Shakespeare's *Romeo and Juliet.*

All of the above suggest that romantic conventions were influential in informing and shaping the heterosexual relationships of the boys in the study. Of course, the fact that the boys were, to varying degrees, invested in romance did not preclude investments in other, sometimes contradictory, ways of 'doing' heterosexuality. For example, Nick, the arch-romantic of the group, had also had relationships that were primarily organized round sex, or its pursuit. Equally, a number of the other boys talked about 'copping off' with girls at parties and nightclubs – a term that appeared to cover anything from kissing to penetrative sex but which did not necessarily imply a romantic dimension to the encounter. Evidence such as this suggests that, whatever its importance to boys such as Dan, Ed and Nick, romance existed as a part of a wider repertoire of heterosexual practices in the boys' 'little cultural world'.

Moreover, at various places in the interviews, several of the boys expressed scepticism about, or resistance to, romance. For instance, when I asked him whether he thought his relationships were 'romantic', Dan replied:

DAN: No, I wouldn't say that. Definitely not …

PR: So tell me why you disagree.

DAN: Because [in romantic stories] it's always so perfect isn't it? And it's never – you don't get along one hundred per cent all the time. You argue and you fight. And you know the strength of the relationship by how you work those things out. I'm a firm believer in that.

Equally, Ed expressed an opposition to romance on the apparent grounds that it was both unreal and unequal. He commented:

ED: Oh sort of, you know … beautiful princess and a charming hero sort of thing, which I guess does happen but, you know, there's a certain amount of passiveness in one or the other … it's not coming from both sides. … I mean, one of the things I like about Louise [his long-term girlfriend] is, you know, she doesn't take shit off anybody. She's a very, sort of, knows what she wants and will get it.

In moments such as this, the boys could be seen to be describing their relationships via an alternative 'realist' repertoire of meanings and practices (Illouz, 1999). This alternative repertoire clearly prioritizes pragmatism and 'working at' relationships over the emotional intensity of romance and it is possible that, at least for some social groups, it is gaining ground as a preferred way to organize and make sense of relationships (see in particular Illouz, 1997, 1999). As Dan's and Ed's responses suggest, it also appears that this realist repertoire may, to some extent, democratize gender relationships in contrast to the rather polarized version of masculinity and femininity promoted by the classic romance (see, also, Giddens (1992) and Weeks (1995) for a discussion of the putative democratization of relationships in contemporary social life).

Counter-evidence of this kind should inject an element of caution into our interpretation of the boys' investments in romance. The boys clearly 'did' romance but their investments in it were not all-encompassing nor without contradiction. Having said this, we also need to avoid devaluing what, for the boys concerned, were clearly genuine feelings. Ed firmly believed that he would one day marry his girlfriend; Nick longed for the intensity of the love with Helen that he had lost; and Dan tried to avoid thinking about the future because he knew that his relationship was unlikely to survive in the long term. In short, though perhaps 'under pressure' and though most certainly located within a wider and contradictory repertoire of relationship meanings and practices, the conventions of the classic romance appeared alive and well in this particular group of boys.

SUMMARY OF SECTION 3

1 Qualitative interviewing does not aim to be representative of a wider population but to provide rich, detailed and local material that 'gets inside' the social worlds of respondents.

2 The ways in which the boys talked about their relationships suggest that they used recognizably romantic conventions to organize, make sense of and live their heterosexual relationships.

3 The boys had investments in other forms of relationship practice, suggesting that their use of romance was not uniform nor without contradiction. Scepticism expressed about romance by two of the boys suggests that romance may be 'under pressure' as a plausible way to live relationships. Nevertheless, it is more than possible to argue that a number of the boys interviewed had real and personally significant investments in being in love.

---

4 Is romance socially constructed?

In the preceding discussion, we have characterized romance as a social 'repertoire' implying that it constitutes a repository of socially available meanings and practices that were then 'taken up', 'inhabited' or 'cited' in the boys' heterosexual relationships. The assumption here is that romance is in some sense 'pre-scripted': that when we fall in love we do so through the forms available to us in the historical time and social location in which we live. The relevance of this argument to the everyday lives, as we saw in the introduction to the chapter, in the sociological claim that the everyday, while taken for granted and apparently natural, is in reality socially constructed.

In section 4, we explore this social constructionist argument in some detail. We will do this by asking two central questions:

1 Is romance a biological phenomenon common to all human societies?

2 If romance is in some sense 'pre-scripted', how do we come to 'inhabit' it, to speak this script as if it were our own?

In order to help answer the first of these questions, we are now going to turn to an extract from the article 'Love and structure' by the anthropologist, Charles Lindholm.

READING 2.2

You should now read 'Love and structure' by Charles Lindholm (Reading 2.2 at the end of this chapter).

Take notes as you read, then try to answer the following questions:

1 What is the 'sociological' account of romantic love?

2 What is the 'sociobiological' account?

3 How does Lindholm define 'being in love'?

4   In what ways does this differ from the definition of the 'classic romance' offered in Reading 2.1 by Jackie Stacey and Lynne Pearce?

5   Do anthropological accounts suggest that romance is a universal and natural phenomenon? Do you agree?

biological reductionism

risk society

You will probably have gathered from your reading that Lindholm is critical of both sociobiological and sociological accounts of romance. The former he sees as **biologically reductive** and therefore unable to address cultural variation in the types of idealizing love. On the other hand, Lindholm is critical of sociological accounts for their tendency to assume that romance is almost exclusively a western phenomenon emerging only in the modern period and tied to the development of an increasingly individualized **risk society**. These sociological arguments are most often related to the work of the German sociologists, Ulrich Beck and Elisabeth Beck-Gernsheim (see Beck and Beck-Gernsheim, 1995; see also Reading 2.3 below) and the British sociologist, Anthony Giddens (see in particular Giddens, 1991, 1992). Inevitably, there are important differences between the work of these writers. However, they share a common analysis in that they argue that, from the eighteenth century onwards, capitalist relations have spread ever further into all aspects of social life with the result that traditional ties of class, family, nation and religion have been remorselessly dissolved. Beck and Beck-Gernsheim, in particular, argue that romantic love has emerged as a 'secular religion' to replace these traditional ties. As a 'trivialized' form of nineteenth-century Bohemian Romanticism, this 'secular religion' is said to celebrate romance as the 'ultimate form of self-revelation' or personal fulfilment (Beck and Beck-Gernsheim, 1995, pp.170, 180).

Lindholm does not so much disagree with this analysis as reject its implicit claim that what he terms 'idealizing love' is the specific product of (and therefore restricted to) forces of individualization and 'risk' characteristic of advanced capitalist societies. As you have seen, in the main bulk of his article, Lindholm explores the ethnographic record and identifies a range of different societies in different historical periods in which idealizing love is to be found and in which, in each case, it can be said to address or negotiate specific 'structural tensions' within that society. In the light of this survey, Lindholm argues that idealizing love is certainly common across many human societies, though not necessarily universal. However, he argues that it is configured in different ways. Idealizing love among the Marri Baluch is not configured along the same cultural lines as idealizing love among the Ojibway Indians of the Northern Great Lakes or, for that matter, as the idealizing love to be found in contemporary western societies. Thus, Lindholm would argue that 'romance', as we understand it in the 'classical' form identified by Stacey and Pearce in Reading 2.1, should be understood as a specific configuration of a wider phenomenon: 'idealizing love'. Moreover, he goes on to argue that, while the way idealizing love is configured in contemporary western societies may well be a response to and a means to negotiate the individualizing forces of contemporary capitalism, the same configuration might also negotiate a different set of structural relations in a separate society (as with the Ojibway Indians). Similarly, he suggests that different structural relations may result in idealizing love being configured in forms with which we, in the contemporary west, are wholly unfamiliar (as with, for example, the Marri Baluch).

Lindholm's arguments certainly suggest that romance as we understand it in the contemporary west cannot be easily understood as the simple expression of an innate biological capacity or drive. Something more complex than this is evidently going on. However, while this tends to support the social constructionist position, it does not on its own explain how we come to 'inhabit' or 'speak' the 'scripts' of romance. This issue is particularly pertinent to our discussion of boys' investments in romance since, as we noted earlier in the chapter, romance as a textual genre is frequently associated with femininity. It is women who tend to read romance and the classic romance itself tends to presume a feminine 'point of view'. How, then, do boys learn to 'do' romance?

One way to understand how we come to 'inhabit' the social scripts of romance (and how they come to 'inhabit' us) is via the concept of **'discourse'**. The French theorist and historian, Michel Foucault, used the term 'discourse' to refer to the social rules, practices and forms of knowledge that govern what is knowable, sayable and doable in any given context (see, in particular, Foucault, 1977, 1988). In this light, romance can be understood as a discourse consisting of a range of socially available meanings, rules and practices which, although not exclusively, govern how we think about, feel about and (perhaps most significantly) enact intimate and sexual relationships. The feminist sociologist, Stevi Jackson, puts this argument very well when she writes:

> We create for ourselves a sense of what ... being 'in love' is. We do this by participating in sets of meanings constructed, interpreted, propagated and deployed throughout our culture, through learning scripts, positioning ourselves within discourses, constructing narratives of self. We make sense of feelings and relationships in terms of love because a set of discourses around love pre-exists us as individuals and through these we have learnt what love means.
>
> (Jackson, 1993, p.12)

From this perspective, the classic romance as a textual genre provides only one dimension (albeit one that is highly influential) of romance as a wider discourse. As was suggested earlier in the chapter, it may well be true that boys and men do not read or view romance in its classic form to the same extent as girls and women. Equally, as we saw towards the end of the last section, individual boys and men may refuse to identify their relationships in terms of romance. Nevertheless, on the evidence of the respondents in the study, boys and men have access to and deploy romantic meanings, conventions and practices in their everyday lives. This is because romantic meanings, conventions and practices are not restricted to the textual genre of the classic romance but are widely dispersed across social sites and are deeply sedimented in to the fabric of everyday life. Thus, when John Paul Young sang 'love is in the air' in the 1978 hit of the same name, he was – perhaps unintentionally – pointing to a wider sociological truth: namely, that romance conventions form part of the taken-for-granted **'commonsense'** of our culture. Like the air we breathe, they are just 'there'. Of course, this does not mean that all men in all social contexts will invest in romance. In fact, there is quite a bit of research evidence to suggest that many heterosexual men do not 'do' romance (see, for example, Burns, 2000; Duncombe and Marsden, 1995). However, it does seem likely that for particular men, and in particular 'little cultural worlds' like that of the college where I conducted the interviews, romance has continuing salience. Indeed, it may even be that romance has a particular salience in the cultural worlds of adolescence.

discourse

Foucault,
Michel

commonsense
knowledge

Look back over the interview material with the boys cited earlier in this chapter. What are the *practices* through which romance is enacted in these relationships? What does it mean to describe these practices as being informed by a 'discourse' of romance?

Now think back to Activity 2 earlier in the chapter. This asked you to list any ways that romantic meanings and conventions have appeared in your own everyday life in the recent past. In what ways can these romantic meanings and conventions be thought of as 'discursive practices'?

You will doubtless have identified a range of practices. These include the practices of asking someone out on a date (in Nick's story of how he met Helen); romantic 'set pieces' (such as Nick's nocturnal visit to Helen's house); days in the countryside (as in the second of the quotations that begins the chapter); and the practice of telling stories about our relationships – something many of us do both to ourselves and to others. These practices can be understood as part of a wider 'discourse' of romance because they constitute a widely dispersed collective repertoire through which we organize and experience 'being in love' in contemporary western cultures.

1   Lindholm's review of the ethnographic record suggests that, although forms of idealizing love are common in different times and different cultural locations, they are configured in different ways and respond to different 'social tensions'. This suggests, in turn, that the meanings and practices of romance as we understand it in the contemporary west are, like other aspects of the everyday, socially constructed.

2   Following Foucault, romance can be understood as a 'discourse', which precedes individual social actors and 'speaks' them even as they 'speak it'. Boys and men may not read the romance as a textual genre to the same extent as do girls and women but romantic meanings and practices are so widely dispersed in everyday life that they do have access to these and are able to deploy them in their relationships.

5 Romance and the everyday

At the end of the last section it was suggested that romance is produced, reproduced and lived through widely dispersed discursive practices that form part of the 'taken-for-granted' background of contemporary social life. This argument returns us to the issue right at the heart of the concerns of this chapter – namely, the question of what the boys' investments in romance might tell us about the 'everyday'. It seems to me that romance does indeed raise some very interesting issues capable of advancing our understanding of the everyday as a sociological concept. In this penultimate section of the chapter, I want to focus on three of these in particular:

1 Should romance be considered as primarily *part* of the everyday or primarily in *opposition* to the everyday?

2 Should romance – and by extension – the everyday be seen as a significant social site in which relations of power are produced and contested?

3 What are the social forces that might be said to shape the everyday? In particular, how do everyday meanings and practices 'negotiate', or provide a 'subjective orientation' to, the social 'tensions' and the social environments in which we live?

In introducing the subject at the start of this chapter, I argued that romance is a profoundly everyday phenomenon. Its sheer ubiquity in both popular and high culture, its almost hackneyed familiarity, its centrality in defining an intimate and private sphere in contemporary social life, and its widespread influence in shaping everyday interactions (what Weitman referred to as 'socioerotics') make this argument difficult to deny. However, in the course of this discussion, we also noted that romance is frequently associated with moments of particular emotional intensity and with 'times out of life' such as holidays and romantic interludes in the countryside. This begins to suggest that, if the everyday is concerned with routine, habit, repetition and the mundane, romantic love is concerned with the dramatic, the intense and the extraordinary. In the activity that follows we will explore one of the most celebrated expressions of this analysis of romantic love as a 'kind of rebellion': Ulrich Beck's description of contemporary romance as a 'secular religion'. You will also notice that, in this reading, Beck outlines his argument that the contemporary configuration of romance is a response to the individualizing forces reshaping western societies (see the discussion in Reading 2.2 in the previous section).

READING 2.3

You should now read 'Love as a latter-day religion' by Ulrich Beck (Reading 2.3 at the end of this chapter). Although this reading is taken from a chapter Beck wrote himself, the book in which it originally appeared, *The Normal Chaos of Love*, was co-authored with Elisabeth Beck-Gernsheim.

Take notes as you read, then attempt the following questions:

1 In what ways does love offer an escape from the 'daily grind'?

2 Why might love be considered a 'latter-day religion'?

3 What do you understand by the term 'individualization' and why might love be 'the best ideology to counteract its perils'?

4 How might Charles Lindholm (see Reading 2.2) critique this argument?

As suggested, this reading is important in part because it outlines the argument, discussed in the previous section, that the contemporary emphasis on romantic love in western societies is a response to the erosion of previously stable social categories – in particular, the family, religion, class and gender – and the traditional roles and worldviews these categories supported. However, our immediate interest in the reading is to be found in the fact that it provides a frequently cited articulation of the sociological argument that romantic love is a 'kind of rebellion'.

As you have seen, Beck views romantic love as providing a means through which individuals can connect to other people and to an 'authentic' sense of personal experience in the face of an increasingly anonymous and commercialized culture. This offers a very particular 'take' on romance as a utopian project. From this perspective, romance is said to provide us with an inclusive, secure and 'authentic' space to which we can retreat in the face of the everyday 'violences' perpetrated by the 'risk' society: the erosion of community and social bonds; the commercialization of pleasure and intimacy; the promotion of economic and social insecurity and so on. If you think back to the Introduction and to Chapter 1 of this volume, you may realize that this analysis connects Beck's argument to a wider sociological understanding of the everyday (in particular, to the work of Lukács, 1971/1923; Lefebvre, 1971/1968; and de Certeau, 1984) as well as to the Marxist theory of the **Frankfurt School**, in particular **Herbert Marcuse**. For Lukács and Lefebvre in particular, the everyday is a site of dull, unreflecting banality that the individual must transcend if he or she (but usually 'he') is to grasp an authentic and meaningful existence. The specifically Marxist variant of this argument, as developed by Lukács (1971) and in Lefebvre's (1971) *Everyday Life in the Modern World*, views capitalism as the prime cause of the supposedly 'alienating' qualities of the everyday. Beck's argument fits into this tradition but also seeks to update it. For Beck, our contemporary faith in romantic love is both a product of the individualizing forces of advanced capitalism, which have eroded previous collective attachments (to class, religion and so on) and – in its search for human connection – is also a site of resistance to these forces.

While Beck's argument gives us a very clear example of an analysis that sees romance as a potential site of resistance, this analysis is also tied to some very specific historical circumstances. As we have seen, for Beck, the contemporary emphasis on romantic love in the west is a response to the increasing 'individualization' and 'detraditionalization' of these societies. However, it is also possible to view the potentially oppositional qualities of romance in somewhat more prosaic terms than this. For example, Eva Illouz (1997, 1999) draws on Lyman and Scott's (1975) classic study of social performance to argue that romance should be considered as part of a wider category, 'social adventure'. She writes:

> Lyman and Scott identify 'adventure' as a particular type of experience that is isolated from the flow of daily events precisely because of its highly dramatic and tightly knit narrative structure.
>
> Adventures start and end with staccato notes. In contrast, routine life … falls into a context of continuities; adventures are cut off from the entanglements of and connections to everyday life. (Lyman and Scott, 1975, p.149)
>
> (Illouz, 1999, p.174)

From this perspective, romance can be understood as one of a number of strategies through which we inject meaning, emotional intensity and drama into the otherwise highly structured routine flow of the everyday. Other examples might include religious experiences, following football teams, going to 'raves' (see Chapter 6 in this volume) and various kinds of 'life projects' such as studying for an Open University degree.

Frankfurt School
Marcuse, Herbert

What do Beck's and Illouz's arguments tell us about romance and the everyday? Should we see romance as *opposed to* the everyday or *part of* it? If we look for evidence in the interview material reviewed earlier in this chapter it is certainly possible to find examples that suggest that romance falls on the side of 'social adventure' or can be understood as mobilizing what Lefebvre referred to as 'moments of presence' – those moments of intense experience that transcend everyday routines (see Chapter 1). For example, the second quotation to begin the chapter – Nick's account of a 'perfect day' with Helen – would seem to fit perfectly Lefebvre's notion of a 'moment of presence'. Equally, Nick's description of the time he scaled the walls of Helen's house would seem an excellent example of 'social adventure' – a 'highly dramatic' and 'tightly knit' story that contrasts strongly with the routinized qualities of everyday life. The point here is that Nick's relationship with Helen would, in reality, have existed in the realm of the everyday and would, therefore, have been subject to the forms characteristic of everyday life: habit and repetition, and so on. It is therefore possible to argue that Nick's 'staging' of romance and his story-telling reconstruction of the relationship via the genre conventions of romance combined to transform this everyday experience into something more intense, more coherent, more dramatic. As such, it is possible to argue that romance was, for Nick, a way of 'vaulting over the apparently firm boundaries of everyday reality' (Reading 2.3, p.87).

Such arguments would suggest that romance is, in fact, opposed to the everyday and that its utility to us lies in demonstrating what the everyday is *not*. Thus, whereas romance is dramatic, intense, out of the ordinary and characterized by discrete, tightly knit episodes, the everyday can be taken to refer to those aspects of social life that are undramatic, bland and ordinary. However, we may need to inject a note of caution here for it is possible to argue that the boundary between romance and the everyday is more blurred than such an analysis would imply. While aspects of romance clearly do seek to transcend the everyday (understood as the banal and repetitious), other aspects of romance are, as we have seen, very much part of it. For example, when we watch a romantic storyline in a television soap opera or listen to a popular love song, we don't necessarily get profoundly caught up in the emotion of it or experience, in Lefevbre's terms, a 'moment of presence'. Indeed, it is inevitable that much of romance takes place on the terrain of everyday life. With the exception of Dan's holiday romance, the boys I interviewed tended to meet their girlfriends at school or college, at parties or – in Ed's case – while hanging around in a park. There was nothing desperately exciting about these meetings. Similarly, the relationships themselves developed and took place in college common rooms and suburban pubs, clubs and bedrooms. This suggests that, even where romance seeks to over-leap the boundaries of the ordinary it is insistently being pulled back towards them. Indeed, as we noted earlier in the chapter, it may even be the case that the 'everyday' aspects of romance (its associations with the derivative, the mundane and the routine) may be steadily reclaiming and reigning in its 'oppositional' or utopian dimensions, making of it a cliché or a joke.

Perhaps more importantly still, it is also possible to argue that there is something problematic or ambiguous about the way in which both Beck and Illouz use the everyday as a category to which romance is apparently opposed. In Beck's case, you may have noticed a tension in the fact that he sees romance as something that is opposed to the 'everyday' of the 'risk' society (what he describes as the increasingly 'intangible', 'unintelligible' and 'impersonal' aspects of the social world) while simultaneously holding on to a notion that romance is characteristic of a (separate?) everyday sphere of 'authentic' human relations that is somehow prior to and capable of resisting the 'encroachments' of an increasingly individualized and commercialized social world. It is arguable that this ambiguity is inherent in much of the commentary on the everyday from Lukács and Lefevbre onwards. In this work, the everyday is – in a potentially contradictory fashion – characterized as both the site of an 'authentic' human culture or experience (an 'organic' or 'spontaneous' **life-world**) *and* as being 'colonized' or 'alienated' by the forces of capitalism (Crook, 1998). Equally, in the case of Illouz you may have wondered whether 'social adventure' might itself be reasonably considered to be an everyday activity. Is it not possible that the category of the everyday should be widened beyond that which is merely dull and banal and should also embrace all those common, relatively 'private' activities – daydreaming, listening to music, friendships, hobbies, exercise and so on – by which we inject meaning, excitement and emotional depth into our lives (Crook, 1998; Featherstone, 1992)? Such arguments alert us to the fact that the 'everyday' is a contested term within sociology and that its precise boundaries are subject to debate. Ultimately, whether romance is seen as *opposed* to the everyday or *part* of it is not a question that is answerable in objective terms – it depends where you draw the conceptual boundaries of the 'everyday' as a category.

margin: **life-world**

If the topic of romance alerts us to some of the complexities involved in defining the boundaries of the everyday, it is also the case that romance has much to tell us about the everyday as a significant social site in which relations of power are produced and contested. You may remember that, in discussing the conventions of the classic romance, I suggested that the genre was very keen to naturalize a heterosexual resolution to its stories (boy gets girl) and to polarize men and women as opposite character types with men being constructed as strong, active, rational and worldly and women as weak, passive, emotional and in need of protection and guidance. As we have seen via the interview material, conventions of this kind shape and inform the meanings and practices through which boys actually live their relationships. Nick, for instance, sought to position Helen, the object of his desire, as 'pure' and 'nice', rejecting her friend, Mandy, in part because she was 'blatant' in her pursuit of him. This is important because it suggests that the construction of relationships in romantic terms has a real and negative impact on girls' ability to define and negotiate the contours and meanings of their heterosexual relationships. The social 'scripts' of romance require girls to be 'nice' and 'pure'. They are 'prizes to be won' by questing boys rather than active agents making their own sexual choices. Equally, it seems likely that the promotion of heterosexuality as the 'natural' outcome of romance will have real consequences for boys who do not conform to the boundaries of what is deemed an 'appropriate' masculinity. For instance, I asked Dan what it meant if you did not have a girlfriend and he replied that it meant you were 'a bit of geek … a queer'.

Such responses suggest that the meanings and practices of romance were deeply implicated in the construction of elaborate gender and sexual hierarchies in the pupils' culture of the college. Within these hierarchies, particular girls and boys (for instance, girls who were 'too assertive' or boys without girlfriends) were actively disparaged. Of course, these meanings and practices did not necessarily go uncontested by the young men and women who were subordinated by them. We should also remember that romance may contain elements that are positive and affirmatory as well as elements that are potentially oppressive or which lead to inequalities (for example, the boys' relationships appeared to involve real elements of mutuality and respect). Nevertheless, the important point is that the everyday meanings and practices through which the young people were constructing and living their relationships were inevitably involved in the reproduction and negotiation of gender and sexual power relations and inequalities. Power was not something 'imposed' on them from the outside. It was actively produced within such everyday practices as 'fancying someone', 'going out' and 'being in love'. This underlines the extent to which the everyday can be seen as a significant site in which power relations are produced and reproduced.

Questions of power also bring us to the final point that I wish to explore in our discussion of the links between romance and the everyday, namely the issue of the social forces by which the everyday can be said to be constituted. Power is important here because, as we saw in the general introduction to this volume, there is a particularly rich tradition within studies of the everyday which has sought to use ethnographic and other qualitative research methods to study the ways in which everyday cultures (like adolescent cultures of romance) can be said to 'handle', 'negotiate' or 'make imaginative sense' of the social environment of a particular group and thus the wider social relations of power in which the group is located. This tradition stretches back to the inter-war work of the Chicago School through to the famous subcultural studies conducted at the Centre for Contemporary Cultural Studies in Birmingham in the 1970s (discussed in the introduction to this volume) and on to more recent work such as Mac an Ghaill's (1994) study of the making of masculinities within the new vocational curriculum of secondary schooling. It also echoes Lande's argument (in Reading 2.2) that romance negotiates social 'tensions' such as an extreme 'competitive individualism'. As a result, I would argue that a micro-social analysis is likely to be particularly instructive in helping us to understand the interview material on boys and romance.

Several of the boys interviewed gave explicit accounts of the way in which the transition from compulsory education at a secondary school to voluntarily studying for 'A' levels at sixth-form college demanded that they develop new forms of identity. The pupils' culture at the college, they suggested, was 'more mature' compared with secondary school, and far less rigid. In particular, it promoted a more 'individualistic' approach to taste in music, clothing, politics and so on, one that echoed the youth cultural and Bohemian aspects of British undergraduate student life. In the light of this, it is possible to argue that romance was itself part of this wider shift towards a more 'individualized' culture. Indeed, it was noticeable that 'serious' romantic relationships (judged in terms of their duration, intensity and level of commitment) were far more prevalent in the college compared with those reported earlier in the boys' schooling and that these were understood to contribute towards both a greater maturity on the part of the boys and to less involvement with a male friendship group (see, for instance, Chris's claim that he had 'turned into a swot' who hardly went out with his mates any more, as we saw in section 3 above).

It is possible to read evidence of this kind as suggesting that romance, along with other forms of everyday cultural practice such as taste in fashion, was deployed in the pupils' culture of the college as a means to produce a subjective orientation towards, and to take ownership of, the transition from compulsory secondary schooling. In the process, the boys could be seen to be 'working themselves into' forms of masculine identity that sought to address a new range of 'individualizing' demands: the newly acquired status of 'young adult' conferred by entry to post-16 education; the need to choose academic disciplines in which to specialize at 'A' level and, subsequently, higher education; and the need to orientate oneself to the promise of a high-income, high-status future premised on individual academic success at 'A' and degree level. In short, romance can be seen as part and parcel of the means by which the boys sought to negotiate a typically middle-class educational and employment trajectory. Of course, this does not mean that romance is only ever deployed by middle-class boys following middle-class educational career paths. Working-class boys are equally capable of investing in romance (see, for example, Wight, 1996). Middle-class boys are (as we have seen in the chapter) also equally capable of investing in other forms of heterosexual practice. Furthermore, romance can be deployed in many other contexts with many other meanings. The point is not that a particular social environment or set of conditions will produce a uniform set of everyday practices. Rather, the point is that everyday practices can be understood as, at least in part, negotiating the micro-social environments in which we live.

SUMMARY OF SECTION 5

1   Romance appears to contain elements that are both part of and in opposition to the everyday (understood as the sphere of the mundane, the habitual and the repetitious). However, we need to be careful how we define the 'everyday'. The everyday is not an objective category and what we include within it is ultimately a matter of perspective.

2   There may be grounds for expanding the concept of the everyday to include practices that might otherwise be defined as 'social adventure'. There may also be a tension in the way in which the everyday is sometimes used to refer to both a site of 'alienation' and a site of 'spontaneous' resistance.

3   Power relations inherent in the practices of romance underline the fact that the everyday is a significant social site in which power and inequality are produced and contested.

4   The boys' use of romance can be understood as providing them with the means to negotiate or make imaginative sense of a middle-class educational trajectory. This underlines the possibility that everyday practices 'handle' or provide a 'subjective orientation' towards the social environments in which we live.

6 Conclusion

In the course of this chapter we have explored romance as a discursive formation whose meanings and practices are widely dispersed through everyday life. Via the work of Charles Lindholm and an analysis of the classic romance genre, it has been suggested that romance as we understand it in the contemporary west can be best understood as a particular configuration of idealizing love – a more common though not necessarily universal phenomenon. This configuration of idealizing love exists in a number of forms and through a number of practices. For instance, romance conventions are to found in a variety of genres (such as soap opera and news-reportage) as well as in literary, musical and filmic texts that are more explicitly romantic. However, they are also to be found in the practices through which intimate and erotic relationships are actively organized and lived as well as in the wider 'socioerotics' of everyday life – in daydreams, casual flirtations, the more formalized practices of Valentine-giving, white weddings and so on. Although romance as a textual genre is most often associated with femininity, the chapter has used qualitative interview material to explore some of the ways in which a group of 16- to 18-year-old boys actively deployed romance in their heterosexual relationships. Although the boys' use of romance was not without contradiction, it certainly seemed possible to argue that the boys concerned had real investments in 'being in love' and that, in important ways, their relationships were lived *in* and *through* romantic meanings and conventions.

Our purpose in all of this was, of course, to explore the relationship between romance and the everyday and I certainly hope this has been an enjoyable as well as a useful journey. What are we to conclude from our discussions? First, I think we need to conclude that romance is indeed an important part of the everyday and that, although increasingly mutating and 'under pressure', it remains incredibly potent both as a 'system of meaning' within the cultural formations of western societies and as a repertoire of practices that inform our everyday lives – in particular, those that define the intimate and the private. Indeed, following commentators such as Beck and Beck-Gernsheim (1995), it may well be possible to argue that romance has increased in salience since the nineteenth century in response to the increasing uncertainties that have accompanied the 'detraditionalization' of society.

Second, however, I think we need to conclude that, like all sociological concepts, the 'everyday' is not and can never be a purely objective category. It certainly refers to something that is real in our social lives but the boundaries we draw around it are inevitably open to debate. Romance (like other topics explored in this volume such as dance music in Chapter 6) provides a particularly good illustration of this, not least because of its associations with 'social adventure', those practices through which we attempt to inject meaning and excitement into the more mundane aspects of everyday life.

Finally, I think we need to conclude that – like the rest of the everyday – romance is a profoundly social phenomenon. Not only is it configured differently in different societies, it is also an important means through which power relations surrounding gender and sexuality are produced and reproduced in the micro-social interactions of everyday life. Furthermore, our investigation of the relationship between romance and boys' transition from compulsory education suggested that romance can be understood as 'negotiating' (in different ways, in different contexts) aspects of the social environment, a possibility that indicates ways in which wider everyday meanings and practices might also be understood.

References

Beck, U. and Beck-Gernsheim, E. (1995) *The Normal Chaos of Love* (trans. M. Ritter and J. Wiebel), Cambridge, Polity Press.

Bennett, T., Emmison, E. and Frow, J. (1999) *Accounting for Tastes: Australian Everyday Cultures*, Cambridge, Cambridge University Press.

Burns, A. (2000) 'Looking for love in intimate heterosexual relationships', *Feminism and Psychology*, vol.10, no.4, pp.481–5.

Crook, S. (1998) 'Minotaurs and other monsters: "everyday life" in recent social theory', *Sociology*, vol.32, no.3, pp.523–40.

de Certeau, M. (1984) *The Practice of Everyday Life,* Berkeley, CA, University of California Press.

Duncombe, J. and Marsden, D. (1995) 'Can men love?: "reading", "staging" and "resisting" the romance' in Pearce, L. and Stacey, J. (eds) *Romance Revisited*, London, Lawrence and Wishart.

Epstein, D. and Johnson, R. (1998) *Schooling Sexualities*, Buckingham, Open University Press.

Featherstone, M. (1992) 'The heroic life and everyday life', *Theory, Culture and Society*, vol.9, no.1, pp.159–82.

Featherstone, M. (ed.) (1999) *Love and Eroticism*, London, Sage.

Felski, R. (1999–2000) 'The invention of everyday life', *New Formations,* no.39, pp.15–31.

Foucault, M. (1977) *Discipline and Punish: The Birth of the Prison,* London, Allen Lane.

Foucault, M. (1988) 'Technologies of the self' in Martin, L., Gutman, H. and Hutton, P. (eds) *Technologies of the Self: A Seminar with Michel Foucault*, London, Tavistock.

Giddens, A. (1991) *Modernity and Self-Identity: Self and Society in the Late Modern Age*, Cambridge, Polity.

Giddens, A. (1992) *The Transformation of Intimacy*, Cambridge, Polity Press.

Gledhill, C. (1997) 'Genre and gender: the case of soap opera' in Hall, S. (ed.) *Representation: Cultural Representations and Signifying Practices*, London, Sage/The Open University.

Goodison, L. (1983) 'Really being in love means wanting to live in a different world' in Cartledge, S. and Ryan, C. (eds) *Sex and Love: New Thoughts on Old Contradictions*, London, Women's Press.

Illouz, E. (1997) *Consuming the Romantic Utopia: Love and the Cultural Contradictions of Capitalism*, Berkeley, CA, University of California Press.

Illouz, E. (1999) 'The lost innocence of love: romance as a postmodern condition' in Featherstone, M. (ed.) *op. cit.*

Jackson, S. (1993) 'Even sociologists fall in love: an exploration in the sociology of emotions', *Sociology*, vol.27, no.2, pp.201–20.

Lefevbre, H. (1971) *Everyday Life in the Modern World*, London, Allen Lane. First published in 1968.

Lindholm, C. (1999) 'Love and structure' in Featherstone, M. (ed.) *op. cit.*

Lukács, G. (1971) *History and Class Consciousness*, London, Merlin Press. First published in 1923.

Lyman, S. and Scott, M. (1975) *Drama of Social Reality*, Oxford, Oxford University Press.

Mac an Ghaill, M. (1994) *The Making of Men: Masculinities, Sexualities and Schooling*, Buckingham, Open University Press.

Pearce, L. and Stacey, J. (eds) (1955) *Romance Revisited*, London, Lawrence and Wishart.

Radway, J. (1984) *Reading the Romance: Women, Patriarchy and Popular Literature*, Chapel Hill, NC, University of North Carolina Press.

Stacey, J. and Pearce, L. (1995) 'The heart of the matter: feminists revisit romance' in Pearce, L. and Stacey, J. *op. cit.*

Weeks, J. (1995) *Invented Moralities: Sexual Values in an Age of Uncertainty*, Cambridge, Polity Press.

Weitman, S. (1999) 'On the elementary forms of the socioerotic life' in Featherstone, M. (ed.) *op. cit.*

Wight, D. (1996) 'Beyond the predatory male: the diversity of young Glaswegian men's discourses to describe heterosexual relationships' in Adkins, L. and Merchant, L. (eds) *Sexualizing the Social: Power and the Organization of Sexuality*, Basingstoke, Macmillan.

Readings

2.1 Jackie Stacey and Lynne Pearce, 'The heart of the matter: feminists revisit romance' (1995)

The narratives of romance

The dictionary definition of romance as a 'love affair viewed as resembling ... a tale of romance' ... confirms that, in life as well as art, it is first and foremost a *narrative*. ... [I]t is the narrativity of romance which crosses the common-sense boundaries of 'fact and fiction', 'representations and lived experience' and 'fantasy and reality'. In our relationships, as well as in our reading or viewing, romantic scenarios accord to cultural codes and conventions. ... The typical trajectories outlined below extend beyond the Hollywood screen or the supermarket paperback and into the stories we tell ourselves (however much reformulated) about our past, present and future romantic relationships, or lack of them. ... [F]eminist analyses of romance have taken issue with the ways in which the classic romance narrative has constituted gender, power and sexual desire; but first we want to address the question: what characterises this classic romance narrative which has received such critical disclaim?

Typically, the story offers the potential of a heterosexual love union whose fulfilment is threatened by a series of barriers or problems. At the most general level, then, romance might be described as a *quest* for love; a quest for another about whom the subject has very definite fantasies, investments and beliefs. This quest involves a staging of desire whose fulfilment may be realised with attainment, or, just as likely, with its loss. To whichever closure the narrative tends, however, like all quests its structure requires the overcoming of obstacles: in the case of romance this means the conquest of barriers in the name of love, and perhaps, by extension, also in the name of truth, knowledge, justice or freedom.

In its fictional forms, which have produced such a never-ending source of romantic narratives, the classic trajectory might be typified in the following way (see Stacey, 1990). A 'first sighting' ignites the necessary 'chemistry' between two protagonists. A series of obstacles usually function as a barrier to their union:

for example, geographical distance as in the films *Out of Africa* (1985) and *Sleepless in Seattle* (1993); class, national or racial difference, deeming the relationship unsuitable as in Charlotte Brontë's *Jane Eyre* (1847) or, more recently, the film *Mississippi Masala* (1991); inhibition or stubbornness of temperament as in Jane Austen's *Persuasion* (1818); a murky past as in du Maurier's *Rebecca* (1938, film adaptation 1940); the existence of another lover or spouse, as in David Lean's celebrated *Brief Encounter* (1945). Alternatively, an initial clash of personalities may itself be the narrative problem; indeed, mutual dislike with sufficient spark often prefigures the inevitable union of the couple, despite, or rather because of, protestations along the way. One standard Mills and Boon formula, for example, is precisely the taming of the male 'boor' and the heroine's eventual love for the civilised beast (Radway, 1984, p.134). The 'romantic comedies' of Hollywood have repeatedly reused the power of antipathy as a foil for the power of love: Doris Day and Rock Hudson's battle of the sexes in *Pillow Talk* (1959), for example, ends with recognition of their mutual attraction, as does Kenneth Branagh's adaptation of Shakespeare's *Much Ado About Nothing* (1993).

Whatever the barrier to the romantic union, the narrative question is 'will they or won't they', or, rather, *how* will they...? Pleasure in the 'progress of romance' lies in the solution to the narrative problems, and the affirmation of the desire to see 'love conquering all', thus confirming its transcendental power. In popular romantic fiction the underlying pattern, despite more superficial variations, very often moves from the heroine's initial loss of social identity (through force of external necessity) and an initial unpleasant encounter with an aristocratic or otherwise powerful man (whose behaviour is misunderstood) through a series of stages including 'hostility' and 'separation' towards 'reconciliation', and the transformation of the man into an emotional being with a heart who declares his love for the heroine, whose new social identity is in turn restored (Radway, 1984, p.134).

One final favourite variant of the classic formula worth mentioning is the tragic one in which illness or death threatens the loss of the loved one, and in doing so intensifies the desire. From *Romeo and Juliet* (1594) to *Love Story* (1970) and *Shadowlands* (1994), love's connection to loss and death has a long history. In these tragic scenarios, the pleasure lies in the heightened value of love in the light of its loss. Indeed many classic romances (for example, *Wuthering Heights* (1847) and Puccini's opera *La Bohème* (1895)) tell the story of lost loves: of sacrifice and of suffering.

This raises the interesting question of whether 'true romance' is most often affiliated with comedy (in the generic sense of a narrative with a 'happy ending') or tragedy. … The fate of romantic heroes and heroines has been of particular interest to feminists who have baulked at the frequent sacrifice of the heroines for the benefit of heroic status of male characters (as in *Love Story, Rebecca, La Bohème*). Indeed, this 'sexual division of suffering' is investigated in Sally Potter's experimental film *Thriller* (1979) in which the heroine of *La Bohème* returns to life and asks: why is it that the romantic heroines must suffer, if not die, for the tragic heroes to achieve their aspirations to universal transcendence? Furthermore, in many representations, it is taboo for women to try to usurp such heroic status: the majority of heroines in 'non-standard' sexual relationships (i.e. not white or heterosexual) have been similarly doomed. In the majority of lesbian romances in Hollywood cinema, for example, the heroines end up dead, depressed, or lonely and rejected: whatever their punishment, it is usually connected to their 'deviant desires'.

The attainment of 'heroic status' on the part of the male characters relates to another key ingredient common to all these romantic trajectories: that is their power of *transformation* vis-à-vis both male *and* female characters. This process of transformation may take several forms: the bringing to light of something already present (Rochester's love and tenderness for Jane in *Jane Eyre*, for example); the emergence of something entirely new (*Calamity Jane* (1953)) in which the protagonist becomes a lady instead of a tomboy; or the taking on of a characteristic of the new partner (as in *Strictly Ballroom* (1992)). The possibility of becoming 'someone else' through a romantic relationship is most certainly one of the most interesting and positive aspects of the process, and a powerful ingredient in its appeal. This transformative promise holds out possibilities of change, progress and escape, which the romance facilitates through its power to make anything seem possible and to enable us to feel we can overcome all adversities. Such possibilities are often figured through both a literal and a metaphorical journey (to a new self); hence travel, relocation and movement have been central to such romantic trajectories: in the film *Now Voyager* (1942), for example, Charlotte's journey has this dual function, and furthermore, locates the 'union' of the couple in 'another culture' (in this case, Brazil), typically one which is associated with a more 'passionate' temperament. Similarly, in E.M. Forster's 'Italian novels', the protagonists' journey to the exotic 'South' initiates a romantic and sexual awakening. In this way, romance offers its subjects the possibility of a new 'becoming': through the encounter/fusion of self and other, a new self might be imagined … .

References

Stacey, J. (1990) 'Romance' in Kuhn, A. with Radstone, S. (eds) *The Women's Companion to International Film*, London, Virago.

Radway, J. (1984) *Reading the Romance: Women, Patriarchy and Popular Literature*, Chapel Hill, NC, University of North Carolina Press, p.134.

Source: Stacey and Pearce, 1995, pp.14–18

 ## 2.2 Charles Lindholm, 'Love and structure' (1999)

Theory and love

In this article I intend to consider a question that has been little discussed by sociologists; that is, how culturally and historically specific is the experience of romantic love? …

Whatever the moral perspective taken … romantic love has usually been perceived by social theorists to be a relatively modern and particularly Western phenomenon; a direct consequence of the evolution of an uncertain 'risk society' which has liberated individuals from the moorings of kinship, social status and religion without offering any alternative points of attachment and security (Beck, 1995). As Robert Solomon writes, 'We should expect to find romantic love arise in precisely those epochs and cultures where self-identity is in question, when traditional roles and relationships fail to tell a person "Who I am"' (1981, p.57). The appearance of romantic love is also thought to coincide with the advent of a leisure culture, where self-cultivation is possible; it has been linked with the modern 'invention of motherhood'; smaller family size, and a greater emphasis on the emotional tie between husband and wife that occurred in response to the industrial revolution.

In this context, the romantic dream of an erotic bonding to an idealized and unique beloved is understood to serve as a substitute for outmoded loci for identity, offering an experience of self-transformation, personal choice, a meaningful future and sensual expansion. It also simultaneously buttresses some of the central premises of modern culture, including individualism, autonomy, and the hope of personal salvation through the 'meeting of souls'. As the basis of marriage and the family, romantic love, the most intimate of relationships, is at the heart of the mechanism by which contemporary society reproduces itself.

According to Giddens, this new ideal reached its pinnacle in 19th-century Europe, as 'notions of romantic love, first of all having their main hold over bourgeois groups, were diffused through much of the social order' – a diffusion indicated and promoted by the hugely popular literature that provided a new 'narrative form' for love relationships (1992, pp.26, 40) A number of historians, the most famous being Stone (1997, 1988, 1992), Flandrin (1979) and Shorter (1975), have validated this depiction of the history of romantic love through their influential portraits of the origin of the modern family in the social and spatial mobility and the disruption of kin networks that marked the beginnings of the industrial age.

For these writers, romantic love is essentially a kind of culturally constructed eroticism remarkable for its idealization and etherealization of the desired other. As Giddens writes: 'Romantic love made of *amour passion* a specific cluster of beliefs and ideals geared to transcendence' (1992, p.45); while Stone, in blunt fashion, defines falling in love quite simply as 'an urgent desire for sexual intercourse with a particular individual' (1988, p.16).

...

The assumed sexual nature of romance has provided the basis for the most radical challenge to modern social theory about romantic love, which has been offered not by sociologists but by sociobiologists. Taking their cue from contemporary evolutionary theory on inclusive fitness, they have argued that romantic attraction to an idealized other is a mechanism genetically encoded in human beings as a consequence of the inexorable efforts of nature to optimize reproduction and the nurturing of offspring.

From this point of view, romantic attraction is an adaptation serving to negate the human male's innate predisposition to maximize his genetic potential by engaging in sexual promiscuity. Instead, romantic idealization keeps him tied to his beloved, where his labor and protection are required for the necessary task of childraising. Unlike social scientists, sociobiologists understand romantic attraction as a universal phenomenon, though most would admit that cultural and historical factors may intensify or lessen the idealizing impulse.

In general, neither sociologists nor sociobiologists make significant recourse to ethnographic case studies or cross-cultural material that could help to validate or refute their basic assumptions. Instead, Western history is invoked to verify the uniqueness and modernity of romantic love, or else reference is made to the sex lives of simians. Unfortunately, the absence of cross-cultural material is not simply due to the researcher's unwillingness to make use of ethnography (though that may indeed be the case). It is also a result of the widespread lack of interest of anthropologists in the topic.

...

The nature of romance

... [D]oes anything analogous to romantic love exist in societies that are non-Western, and even 'primitive'? Is romantic love, in fact, universal, as the sociobiologists claim? In the following pages, I want to argue for the first proposition, against the second. But to begin to make this case we first need to distinguish sexual attraction, which is more or less omnipresent (though sexual desire, too, is more culturally constructed than is generally admitted), from romantic love, which is, as Giddens writes, 'much more culturally specific' (1992, p.38).

A basic error of sociobiologists has been to assume that romantic love is simply a mechanism for directing sexuality in order to maximize the production and nurturing of children. However, in cross-cultural examples, the beloved is very rarely the person one marries, and reproduction and romantic attraction usually do not coincide. ...

Social theorists and historians similarly understand romantic idealization as a veneer over eroticism, though they believe this veneer to be a particularly modern social phenomenon coinciding with the breakdown of traditional society. However, this link is also challenged when we consider material from other cultures where romantic idealization is elaborated yet chastity is enjoined between the lovers. For example, consider the southern European expressions of courtly love in the medieval period. Here, in a transformation of the cult of the Virgin Mary, the courtier explicitly denied any carnal feelings for his beloved, who was worshipped as an angel above the realm of earthly lust, not be sullied in thought or deed. …

If romantic love is not to be understood as a kind of gloss over sexual desire, what is it?

…

…To define romantic love, … we ought to begin by listening to the words and examining the actions of people who believe and experience romantic relationships to be of ultimate importance to their lives. …

And, in fact, within our own culture, what the words and deeds of lovers tell us is that romantic love is not necessarily sexual, though it is thought to lead to sexual involvement. Rather, it is more akin to a religious experience – a vision of the beloved other as a unique, transcendent, transformative being who can 'complete' one's own life. From this alternative perspective, love is not motivated by the desire to reproduce, or by sexual desire, or by an ideal of beauty; rather, the beloved other is adulated *in themselves* as the fountainhead of all that is beautiful, good and desirable. …

…

Romance and structure

Having established the idealizing nature of love, we are now in a position to consider whether some of the assumptions made about it are accurate. For instance, although most social theorists believe romance to be a modern Western phenomenon, this is clearly not the case. Ample literary evidence indicates that an ideal of romantic love was well developed, at least among the literate elite, in several large-scale non-Western state systems of the past. For example, the love suicide plays of Japan's Tokugawa period give powerful dramatic evidence of a pervasive and irresolvable conflict between the desire for an idealized other and social obligations. …

But romance does not require a cultivated leisure class, nor, as we have already noted, was it necessarily associated with erotic relationships – as we discover in the literary tradition that inspired the troubadours, that is, the poetry of the Middle East, which always stresses the sexual purity of the lovers. According to Ibn al-Jawzi (d.1200), who was the most prolific medieval writer on romantic love , the convention of

chastity derived from the early Bedouin, who 'loved passionately but spurned physical union, believing that it destroys love. As for the pleasure resulting from union, it is the affair of animals, not of man' (quoted in Bell, 1979, pp.33–4). …

…

What sort of society is likely to favor this kind of idealizing and chaste relationship? We know very little about the ancient Bedouin, but we do have the ethnography of a group who live in an analogous environment and who have a similar stated belief in chaste love: these are the nomadic Marri Baluch of the rugged southeastern deserts of Iran, as described in a classic work by Robert Pehrson (1966).

The Marri inhabit a harsh, isolated and unforgiving world. They are highly individualistic, self-interested and competitive, and expect opportunism and manipulation from all social transactions. Their personal lives are dominated by fear, mistrust and hostility; secrecy and social masking are at a premium, while collective action and cooperation are minimal. Yet among these people, as Pehrson writes, romantic relationships are idealized, and a love affair 'is a thing of surpassing beauty and value' (1966, p.65), implying absolute trust, mutuality and loyalty; such a love is to be pursued at all costs. Romance is both the stuff of dreams, and of life. Frustrated lovers among the Marri may commit suicide, and become celebrated in the romantic poems and songs which are the mainstay of Marri art. As one Marri woman tells Pehrson 'it is very great, very hard, to be a lover for us Marri' (1966, p.62).

Unlike Western love relationships, romance among the Marri stands absolutely opposed to marriage, which is never for love. It is, in fact, shameful even to show affection for one's spouse. True romance has to be secret, and with a married woman of a distant camp. This a dangerous matter, since other camps are hostile, and adultery is punishable by death. The striking contrast to the West is a consequence of the social organization of the Marri, who live in small patrilineal, patrilocal campsites ruled lightly by a religiously sanctioned central authority, called the Sardar.

Although political domination does occur, the local units, permeable and shifting as they are, nonetheless have considerable solidity and autonomy, judging their own disputes and controlling their own means of production within a framework of traditional knowledge and local consent. The patrilineal patrilocal ideology means that members of the camp site have absolute rights and duties to one another that are legitimated by close blood ties and co-residence. Participation in blood feuds, payment of fines, rights to pasturage and the punishment of adultery all are incumbent on the minimal lineage group.

However, this minimal group is not one of co-operation and friendship. The camp members, despite their ties, work separately, have their own tents and property, cooperate as little as possible, and are mutually suspicious and rivalrous. If they could, they would separate, but the need for defence and a varied labour pool keeps the camps together; a need validated by the rights and duties of kinship. Within this inimical but constraining structure, Marri men continually manipulate to get a share of power and status that derive from the center. By gaining a loyal following among his cohorts, the poor herdsman can make a claim for becoming the local factotum of the Sardar, thereby gaining points over one's nearest, and most disliked, lineage mates and rivals.[1] Marriage in this context is not a matter of personal choice and attraction. Instead, Marri men use marriage in an instrumental fashion to establish relationships which will help them to pursue their political interests, while women are treated as chattels, to be controlled and dominated for the honor and benefit of the patriarch. As one woman says: 'You know what rights a woman has among us Marris. She has the right to eat crap – that's all' (Pehrson, 1966, p.59).

In this context, romantic involvement, with all its risk, is the only human relationship in the whole of Marri culture felt to be of value in and for itself, and not simply as a means to the instrumental ends of personal power and prestige. It is understood by the Marri Baluch to be opposed to marriage in every way. Marriage is a public and sanctioned relationship between superior men and inferior women, often within the camp and the lineage, and always among allies; it is pre-eminently politically motivated, and it is expected to be cold and hostile at best. Romance on the contrary is secretive, private, and conducted with strangers who are actually potential enemies. Its only possible political consequences are disastrous enmity and feud. Romantic love has the potential for dividing groups while it unites the lovers, while marriage aims to solidify groups, while permitting no attraction within the asymmetrical couple. In marriage, the woman is inferior and despised, while in romance she is honored and revered.

Like the ancient Bedouin, the Marri also claim that a true romantic relationship, in contrast to marriage, is not sexual. Theoretically, at least, the male lover worships his beloved as a pure being and is worshipped in return; forgoing the connotations of female inferiority and degradation that the Marri (like many patrilineal peoples) believe to be implicit in the sexual act, the romantic couple immerse themselves in mutual gazing, spontaneous recitations of poetry and the reciprocal exchange of confidences and love tokens.[2] For the Marri then, romance is with a distant other, and it is consciously perceived as negating the rivalries of power, the inferiority of women and the constraints of the marriage tie. It is chaste and highly idealistic. This romantic complex occurs within a relatively rigidly structured, but characteristically competitive, social formation. Far from providing the basis for reproducing the dominant social configuration, romance in this instance opposes it in every way.

…

Romance in fluid societies

However, all instances of romantic love in the non-Western context are not so markedly different from the Western model. In fact, it is precisely in some of the most 'primitive' of social formations, where people do not have complex kinship structures or central authority, and live by means of hunting and gathering, that we find romantic idealization taking a form remarkably similar to that characteristic of the West. This is because the fluid, competitive, insecure and risky social formation of the modern world resembles, in essential ways, the lifestyles of hunting and gathering societies operating under especially harsh ecological conditions.

…Perhaps the clearest example of a romantic love complex resembling that of the modern West to be found in the ethnographic record is among the hunting and gathering Ojibway Indians of the Northern Great Lakes region.[3] As the ethnographer Ruth Landes writes, for the Ojibway:

> … lovers have a completely romantic attitude that counts the world well lost for love.
>
> (1969, p.56)

> Sentimental and romantic love are valued tremendously and marriage is supposed to be the fulfillment of this attraction.
>
> (1937, p.104)

> What is essential is to have a loved person who can be idealized: and often this is realized in unions that are externally drab.
>
> (1969, p.120)

Love is described by the Ojibway themselves as an experience of great intensity, valued in itself, focused on one idealized and beloved other, and worth the ultimate self-sacrifice. Nor is this simply an ideal. The life histories recorded in Landes's *Ojibwa Woman* show that romantic love was a central event in people's lives; one which often went against their rational best interests and exposed them to great suffering and peril, and even led to suicide should their lover be unapproachable. The similarity of their concept of love to that of the West was recognized by the Ojibway themselves, who quickly adapted American love stories and songs into their own language.

Along with their belief in love, the Ojibway are like modern Western society in other crucial ways. Their society was characterized by extremes of competitive individualism, coupled with a highly developed concept of personal property, which was held even within the nuclear family. According to Landes, 'individuals may grumble, especially close relatives, and there is a weak notion of fair play; but these are as nothing compared with the valuation placed on ruthless individualism' (1937, p.87). There were also few, if any, primordial groups or ties among the Ojibway providing a sense of solidarity and identity. There were no ascribed positions of authority, no stable structures of hierarchy. Even the social roles of men and women were not highly articulated, and each could do the work of the other. Clans, though perhaps cohesive in the past, had long since ceased to have any importance, and the only significant kinship structure was a vague division between parallel cousins and marriageable cross-cousins. Easy divorce made the family itself insecure.

Nor did residence provide coherence, since families lived in isolation during the harsh winters, and shifted residence regularly in the summer. Constant mobility was partly an effort to find better hunting grounds, but also partly as a result of a pervasive distrust of those nearby, combined with a readiness to take insult at minor slights, and a deep fear of treachery from neighbors. This fear was not unrealistic. As Hallowell notes, quoting an Ojibway: 'When I meet [my enemy] face to face I will give no evidence of my hostility by gesture, word or deed' (1940, p.400). Aggressive sorcery was also commonly practiced in secret, destroying the health of an unsuspecting enemy. In Ojibway society then, a smiling face could not be trusted, as it might easily be masking rankling hatred.

The Ojibway social world was evidently quite like the modern 'risk society' of possessive individualists, with its blurring of differentiating ascribed boundaries, its mobility, its competitiveness, and its pervasive sense of mistrust and insecurity. The Ojibway also lived in an extremely harsh physical environment; one in which starvation was a very real possibility, leading to an intensification of pressure on individuals in a way analogous to the pressure caused by adaptation to the constant technological change in the modern world.[4]

…

Sexual freedom and romance

There is, finally, another very different type of social formation I can mention only in passing which seems to favor romantic love. These societies are neither centralized and rigid, nor are they atomistic, or under any extreme social or ecological pressure. Rather, they are group-oriented, non-individualistic cultures that strictly control marriage, but that offer compensation to their youth by means of an institutionalized premarital sexual freedom; a freedom that often leads to powerful romantic attachments and idealizations.

Examples of this type are found in tribal India, Southeast Asia and in the Oceanic cultures where romantic love seems to occur. In these cultures, the young people live together in clubhouses, which offer a private and separate enclave away from the responsible world of adulthood. Here they can pursue sexual encounters, but only with those partners whom they can never actually marry. Within the clubhouse there is a free and easy atmosphere of equality and reciprocity between the sexes. But eventually couples form and are faithful to each other. Sometimes this relationship develops into one of deep involvement that is felt to be the most powerful emotional tie in a person's life. This doomed romance is also regarded as the highest possible cultural and aesthetic value, and is celebrated in song and story.

The clubhouse, with its equality and dyadic love, is considered to be a kind of paradise that everyone experiences in adolescence, and which the rest of life cannot match, for in adulthood men and women are unequal and unloving, and life is a series of responsibilities and obligations, revolving around duties to one's extended lineage. Romantic attachment stands in radical contrast to adult husband and wife relations, and in each of these societies stories are common of lovers committing suicide out of despair at the inevitable separation that is entailed by marriage.

…

We then have three sorts of social configuration in which an elaboration and idealization of romantic love occurs; the West appears to be a subtype of fluid social organization, having evolved from a more hierarchical and rigid system in the past.[5] Because of the paucity of data, it is impossible to 'fill in the boxes' as to what kinds of societies will *not* have an elaborated belief in romantic love, although, from the ethnographic record, it appears that such beliefs are rare indeed (we discovered only 21 possibilities out of 248 cases); but this may well be a fault of the record-keepers. It does seem likely that relatively stable societies with solidified extended families, age-sets and other encompassing social networks that offer alternative forms of belonging and experiences of personal transcendence through participation in group rituals are not prone to valuing romantic involvement. …

Conclusion

Western expectations and beliefs about romantic love clearly develop out of our unique historical trajectory and cultural background. But this obvious truth should not blind us to deeper correspondences between our emotional lives and the emotional lives of people in cultures different from our own, who report the same sort of intense idealization of a beloved other, the same feelings of exaltation in their presence and suicidal despair in their absence. Though sparse, ethnographic material demonstrates that romantic love is not necessarily the prerogative of a leisured class; it does not require a complex society; it is not solely heterosexual, nor does it always lead to marriage; it is not intrinsically linked to capitalism, small families, sexual oppression, a cult of motherhood or a quest for identity; it is neither a disguise for lust nor evidence of evolution at work. Rather, romantic attraction is an attempt to escape from certain types of social contradictions and structural tensions through the transcendental love of another person. As such, it is experientially akin to the experience of religious ecstasy.

Notes

I would like to thank Owen Lynch, William Jankowiak, Laurie Hart-McGrath, Cherry Lindholm, Mike Featherstone and the anonymous reviewers of *Theory, Culture & Society* for their suggestions, which have improved this article immeasurably. I especially want to express my deep gratitude to Andrew Buckser and Susan Buckser (née Rofman) for their invaluable help in the original research and analysis.

1   The potential for minimal social movement is of crucial importance, not the degree of movement possible. An absolutely rigid structure would not evolve the love complex noted here because social pressure would be absent.

2   As in the case of the troubadours, whether all (or any) love affairs are chaste is irrelevant; what is important is that this is the cultural ideal of romantic love the Marri respect, and attempt to enact in their own lives.

3   Andrew Buckser's undergraduate thesis on love among the Ojibway (1986) deserves recognition here as the inspiration for this section.

4   It is significant that the Ojibways' greatest terror is of possession by a cannibal spirit, the windigo, which will drive them to devour their fellows.

5   Though see MacFarlane (1986) on the fluidity of early English and northern European society, which he sees as conducive to a romantic love complex among the poor quite different from that later elaborated among the elite.

References

Beck, U. (1995) *Ecological Enlightenment: Essays on the Politics of the Risk Society*, Atlantic Highlands, NJ, Humanities Press.

Bell, J. (1979) *Love Theory in Later Hanbalite Islam*, Albany, NY, State University of New York Press.

Buckser, A. (1986) 'Love in a cold climate: romantic love and social structure among the Canadian Ojibway', undergraduate honours thesis, Department of Anthropology, Cambridge, MA, Harvard University.

Flandrin, J.L. (1979) *Families in Former Times: Kinship, Household and Sexuality*, Cambridge, Cambridge University Press.

Giddens, A. (1992) *The Transformation of Intimacy: Sexuality, Love and Intimacy in Modern Societies*, Stanford, CA, University of California Press.

Hallowell, A.I. (1940) 'Aggression in the Salteau society', *Psychiatry*, no.3, pp.395–407.

Landes, R. (1937) *Ojibwa Sociology*, New York, AMS.

Landes, R. (1969) *Ojibwa Woman*, New York, AMS.

MacFarlane, A. (1986) *Marriage and Love in England: 1300–1840*, Oxford, Blackwell.

Pehrson, R. (1966) *The Social Organization of the Marri Baluch*, Chicago, IL, Aldine.

Shorter, E. (1975) *The Making of the Modern Family*, New York, Basic Books.

Solomon, R. (1981) *Love, Emotion, Myth and Metaphor*, Garden City, NJ, Anchor Books.

Stone, L. (1977) *The Family, Sex and Marriage in England, 1500–1800*, New York, Harper and Row.

Stone, L (1988) 'Passionate attachments in the West in historical perspective' in Gaylin, W. and Person, E. (eds) *Passionate Attachments*, New York, Free Press.

Stone, L. (1992) *Uncertain Unions: Marriage in England, 1660–1753*, Oxford, Oxford University Press.

Source: Lindholm, 1999, pp.243–63

Ulrich Beck and Elisabeth Beck-Gernsheim, 'The normal chaos of love' (1995)

Love as a latter-day religion

The essence of our faith in love can best be shown by comparing it with religion. Both hold out the promise of perfect happiness, to be achieved along similar lines. Each offers itself as a way of escaping from the daily grind, giving normality a new aura; stale old attitudes are tossed aside and the world seems suffused with new significance. In the case of religion all energy is directed towards another infinite reality, understood as the only true one and encompassing all finite life. In love this opening up of normal boundaries takes place both sensually, personally, in sexual passion and also in new perceptions of oneself and the world. Lovers see differently and therefore are and become different, opening up new realities for one another. In revealing their histories they re-create themselves and give their future a new shape. Love is 'a revolution for two' (Alberoni, 1983); in overcoming antagonisms and moral laws which stand in their way they really prove their love. Inspired by their feelings, lovers find themselves in a new world, an earthly one but a realm of its own.

Love 'as an archetypal act of defiance' (Alberoni): that is what modern love seems to promise, a chance of being authentic in a world which otherwise runs on pragmatic solutions and convenient lies. Love is a search for oneself, a craving to really get in contact with me and you, sharing bodies, sharing thoughts, encountering one another with nothing held back, making confessions and being forgiven, understanding, confirming and supporting what was and what is, longing for a home and trust to counteract the doubts and anxieties modern life generates. If nothing seems certain or safe, if even breathing is risky in a polluted world, then people chase after the misleading dreams of love until they suddenly turn into nightmares.

We are always vaulting over the apparently firm boundaries of everyday reality. Memory takes me back to myself when I was young. I wonder about the clouds and imagine a story behind them. I read a book and find myself in a different epoch; my head is full of scenes from someone's life who is now dead and I have never met; voices I have never heard are conversing in my inner ear. Among the extraordinary experiences in life love has a special status. Unlike illness and death it is sought for and not repressed, at least at this moment in our culture; it is immune to conscious or practical manipulation and cannot be produced on order. Those who hope to find it are looking for salvation here and now, and the 'hereafter' is in this world, with a voice, a body and a will of its own. Religion tells us there is a life after death; love says there is a life before death.

…

Love is communism within capitalism; misers give their all and this makes them blissful:

> Falling in love means opening oneself to a new form of existence without any guarantee of achieving it. It is a rhapsody to happiness without any certainty that there will be a response … And if the answer does come from the person we love, then it seems something undeserved, a miraculous gift one never counted on getting … Theologians have their own term for this gift: grace. And if the other person, our beloved, says he or she loves us too and each is engrossed in the other, this a blissful moment in which time stands still.
>
> (Alberoni, 1983, pp.39–40)

Love is a utopia which is not ordained or even planned from above, from cultural traditions or sermons, but grows from below, from the power and persistence of sexual drives and from deep personal wishes. In this sense love is a religion unhampered by external meanings and traditions, its values lying in the depth of the lovers' attraction to one another and their subjective mutual commitment. No one has to become a member, and no one needs to be converted.

So our faith in love is linked to its lack of tradition; it comes after all the disappointing credos, and needs neither organizing committees nor party membership to be an effective subjective and cultural force. It is the outcome of sex being partially freed of taboos and wide disillusionment with other prescribed beliefs passed down to us. As befits modern social structures, there is no external moral agency responsible for love, but just the way lovers feel for one another.

While a religion which lacks firm teaching usually vanishes, love is a religion without churches and without priests, and its continued existence is as certain as the tremendous force of sexual needs now freed of social disapproval. It cannot be organized, which also means it is independent, and its only place, despite all its cultural offshoots, is in the hearts of those involved; this makes it a non-traditional, post-traditional religion which we are hardly aware of because we ourselves are its temples and our wishes are its prayers.

Now that the old law-givers, the church, the state and traditional morality are on the retreat, even love can shed its old standard patterns and established codes. The result is a kind of positivism making norms out of individual preferences and values. This does not however reduce love's status as a force giving life purpose and meaning; on the contrary it confirms it. Here church and bible, parliament and government are merged into one – a matter of conscience guiding each person how to shape and structure his/her life. This is at least the ideal we share, this is how we would like it to be, even though in practical terms the solutions are often standard ones.

...

... One has to look ... into ... fields, like education, scientific advances, world markets and technical risks if one wants to grasp why so many people plunge into a frenzy of love as if they were slightly insane. The outside world confronts us with a barrage of abstractions: statistics, figures, formulas, all indicating how imperilled we are, and almost all of them elude our comprehension. Loving is a kind of rebellion, a way of getting in touch with forces to counteract the intangible and unintelligible existence we find ourselves in.

Its value lies in the special intense experiences it offers – specific, emotional, engrossing, unavoidable. Where other kinds of social contact are losing their hold, politics seem irrelevant, classes have faded into statistics, and even colleagues at work rarely find time for one another because their shifts and flexible working hours forbid it. Love, and especially the clashes it induces – from the 'eternal issue of the dishes' to 'what kind of sex', from parenting to tormenting each other with self-revelations – has a monopoly: it is the only place where you can really get in touch with yourself and someone else. The more impersonal life around you seems, the more attractive love becomes. Love can be a divine immersion in all kinds of sensations. It offers the same relief to a number-cruncher as jogging through the woods does to an office-worker – it makes you feel alive again.

A society short on traditions has produced a whole range of idols: television, beer, football, motorcycles, cordon bleu meals – something for every phase of life. You can join clubs or peace initiatives or keep up long-distance friendships to guarantee you still share some common ground with someone. You can hark back to old gods, or discover new ones, polish relics or read the stars. You can even insist on continuing the class struggle and sing about being free, although you know that such golden days, if they ever existed, are over.

What distinguishes love from these other escape routes is that it is tangible and specific, personal and now; the emotional upheavals cannot be postponed or handed on, and both sexes find themselves forced to react whether they want to or not. No one can decide to fall into or out of love, but might at any moment find themselves falling through the trap door into a new dimension.

Love is therefore not a substitute or a lightning conductor, nor is it a politically desirable export article or just a television advertisement. The boom in love reflects current living conditions and the anonymous, prefabricated pattern forced on people by the market relegating their private needs right to the end of the list.

Taking over from old categories like class and poverty, religion, family and patriotism there is a new theme, sometimes disguised as uncertainty, anxiety, unfulfilled and unfulfillable longings, sometimes sharply outlined and standardized in pornography, feminism and therapy, but gradually developing its own radiance, its own rhythms, opening up prospects much more alluring than the ups and downs of being promoted, having the latest computer or feeling underpaid.

'Being loved means being told "you do not have to die"' (Gabriel Marcel).[1] This glowing hope seems more delightful and irresistible the more we realize how finite, lonely and fragile our existence is. Illness and death, personal disasters and crises are the moments when the vows prove true or merely lies, and in this respect the secular religion of love can claim like other religions to give life sense and meaning. Or put the other way round, the idea of dying shatters normal life, making it seem highly suspect; in moments of pain and fear love acquires a new dimension. The brittle, carefully constructed shell cracks open – at least momentarily – and lets in questions like Why? and What for?, fed on memories of desperately missed togetherness.

As religion loses its hold, people seek solace in private sanctuaries. Loving is bound up with a hope which goes beyond basking in intimacy and sex. Making love in bed is one way, caring for one another in a sick-bed is another.

...

For all the similarities between love and religion, there are also enormous differences; love is a private cosmos, whereas religion is in alliance with the powers-that-be. Lovers are their own church, their own priests, their own holy scriptures, even if they sometimes resort to therapists to decipher these. They have to create their own rules and taboos; there is an infinite number of private systems of love, and they lose their magic power and disintegrate as soon as the couple ceases to act as priests worshipping their belief in each other.

Love builds its nest out of the symbols lovers use to overcome their unfamiliarity with one another and to provide their relationship with a past. The nest is decorated as the focus of their togetherness, and turns into a flying carpet bearing their shared dreams. In this way the fetishes, the sacrifices, the ceremonies, the incense and the daily rites constitute the visible context within which we love. Instead of being officially sanctified and administered, this private faith is individually styled, invented and adorned: snuggling in Mickey Mouse and teddy symbols, agreeing everything yellow means love, inventing nicknames to use in our secret world, all these are efforts to counteract the nagging fear that it might end and all could be lost and forgotten.

Religion's horizon takes in this world and the next, the beginning and the end, time and eternity, the living and the dead, and is therefore often celebrated as immutable, untouched by time. Love's horizon, by contrast, is narrow and specific, consisting of a small world of you and me and nothing more, exclusive, apparently selfish, somewhere between unjust and cruel in its logic, arbitrary and outside the range of the law. Its imperatives cut across other wishes and its principles withstand any attempt to standardize them.

For these very reasons, however, love is the best ideology to counteract the perils of individualization. It lays stress on being different, yet promises togetherness to all those lone individuals; it does not rely on outdated status symbols or money or legal considerations, but solely on true and immediate feelings, on faith in their validity and on the person they are directed towards. The law-givers are the lovers themselves, phrasing their statutes with their delight in each other.

Notes

1   I am indebted to Christoph Lsu for this quotation.

References

Alberoni, F. (1983) *Verliebsten und lieben: Revoluton zu zweit,* Stuttgart (*Falling in Love*, New York).

Source: Beck and Beck-Gernsheim, 1995, pp.175–81

The street and everyday life

Peter Hamilton

Contents

1 Introduction

How can we look at the street sociologically? Let us start to answer this question by actually looking at two very different images.

Look at the two photographs in Figures 3.1 and 3.2. What seem to you to be the main differences between these two images? Think about who is doing the looking and why.

Figure 3.1

Figure 3.2

COMMENT

There is no 'correct' answer but my thoughts about the two pictures were as follows. Firstly, I would say that both pictures are about the 'street', but that they appear to be separated by place and time. The first is of a city street (perhaps in the 1950s), while the second looks far more recent. In the first, there is one image, of three girls, sitting on the kerb; in front of them is chalk drawing on the road. In the second, there are several apparently sequential images, assembled from a closed-circuit television directed at the street.

Who is looking? In the first, you may have noted, it is us: or seemingly us. For we are looking through the camera lens onto a real scene, as it was photographed some time ago. In the second, we are also looking, but the image carries with it date, time and location information – elements which suggest this is a 'surveillance' camera, so we are not *on* the street but are viewing it from some removed location.

Why are we looking? I would want to argue that – at least initially – we could imagine that two social conceptions of the street are behind the choice and framing of the images. In the first, children play in and on the street by drawing on it. We see a street in which a child is safe to play, but in a way which it would be rare to see today. In the second group of CCTV pictures we see a series of images in which a woman is tracked through a town's streets. Is her behaviour suspicious? Perhaps. Is she being tracked because she has committed a crime – or is in danger? The looking is being done because, it seems, the place itself – 'the street' – is a dangerous place.

■ ■ ■

The first photograph is by Roger Mayne and was made in 1956 in Southam Street, Holland Park, London. It might as easily have been taken a lot earlier (in, say, the 1930s) or rather more recently, yet perhaps not in the last couple of decades. It shows what I would term the *communal street*, a place where children play, where the life of the community is transacted, where it is safe to walk, where much of life has its public aspect. Mayne was fascinated with the 'life of the streets', like many of his contemporaries, and saw it as worth documenting as well as capturing it for artistic reasons. He knew that certain sorts of streets – ordinary, working-class, urban or suburban ones – are where you are likely to find ordinary people going about their business in a sociable manner and children playing. We might even call these images part of a 'humanist' conception of the street which implies that these are images which display the universal humanity of the people involved, their communality, their sociability, their general similarity, their sharing of a common life. They are all part of the great 'family of humanity'.

The CCTV images by contrast offer us perhaps another street, one which seems *less* human: threatening, mechanical, isolating, monolithic. In some ways it is the antithesis of the humanist street, and for that reason it might be appropriate to call it something constructed out of the *post-modern* conception of the street, a locale defined as much by the fact of constant surveillance via a TV camera as by its other features, which indicate a place designed for the individual (as consumer, citizen or whatever) but not perhaps for the community. Under post-modern conditions, many writers would argue, there is great stress on difference, on the absence of universal or common interests, on the mediated nature of experience, on consumerism and individuality. These are streets in

Figure 3.3 Women and prams, Stepney, 1934. *Humphrey Spender's photographs of working-class areas of London and Bolton are typical of the humanist approach to the photography of everyday life which emerged in the 1930s, highly influenced by socialist ideas about the dignity of labour.*

which we would not go looking for community or sociability, although we
might go to them to shop, on our way to work, or for leisure. Or more probably
we would travel through them in a car. Our engagement with the street would
be fleeting, tangential, specific. Only those condemned to live on them – a fact
which demonstrates their social exclusion – experience the street nowadays as
a community, or perhaps, we might say, a negative or marginal community.
Indeed, we might be more likely to experience the sense of being part of a
community via something like the internet than by going into the street – or at
least some would argue that (see Chapter 6).

Pushing these conceptions to their limits we might say that in the *'humanist'*
street we might feel *safe* because of its positively communal nature. In the *'post-
modern'* street we might feel in *danger* because of its individuality, the war of
all against all that might be found there. Now these are not objective differences
between streets now and streets then. They are images which have social
meaning, in the sense that they envisage the street as characteristic of the wider
society. Another image, Figure 3.4, shows a street in Wallasey, photographed in
the 1980s. How effectively does this convey the different social aspects of the
street (in this case in a shopping centre) within a post-modern society?

The street, then, is an idea or conception perhaps as much as it is a real
place. Clearly, streets themselves have changed enormously in the last fifty years
in most western societies. The car has seen to that, but car use is only part of a
wider trend towards greater individualism. When we talk about 'the street', as
opposed to actual streets, we are using the term to describe something
sociological, something beyond us as individuals but which has the power to
make us think and act in certain ways.

Figure 3.4 Wallasey, 1985, by Martin Parr. Parr's photography is seen as a particularly incisive
perspective on the consumer society emergent in the 1980s.

AIMS

The aims of this chapter are:

1   To introduce the concept of 'the street' as a key theme of sociology, concerned with social life in public space, modernity, the city and urban life.

2   To examine the intellectual links between the concept or 'domain' of everyday life and those of the street.

3   To explore and contrast the street as both a social construct and as an imaginary locale.

4   To explore how looking at the street opens up a series of sociological issues and theories about sociability, community, social structure, the public and the private, and social order.

5   To discuss how the street has become a metaphor for modernity, and how sociology has increasingly embraced 'cultural' concepts to explain its centrality in modern life.

2 Defining the street

Although we are going to use 'the street' as a focus of the everyday, it is not a central sociological concept, like community or family. If you look in a sociological dictionary you won't, I'm afraid, find an entry under that term. The street appears in sociological thinking as a type of place and as a type of social relationship, as well as a metaphor for thinking about life in urban settings – something we will look at in more detail later in this chapter.

But even if we can't find it in the sociological dictionaries, we all know what we mean by 'the street', don't we?

ACTIVITY 2

Make a list of what comes to mind when you think of 'the street'.

COMMENT

Everyone would probably come up with a slightly different list, depending on their own experiences of the street. Some may be positive, about your own street and neighbours, possibly street parties for the Jubilee, about shopping and going out with friends, street decorations at Christmas such as Oxford Street in London, and street markets. Others may be more negative, either personal experiences of being mugged or pickpocketed, or the dangers for pedestrians in streets congested by traffic, and homeless people sleeping rough in shop doorways, kids hanging around at night, or of prostitutes and kerb-crawlers.

Or you may have thought first about streets depicted on television and the people whose lives you 'know about' who reside there – in Coronation Street, Ramsey Street, Brookside Close, Albert Square, even Sesame Street!

Or you may have thought about streets as territory – street gangs such as those in southern LA where moving into another gang's area can be punished by drive-by shootings; or the areas in Northern Ireland, such as the Shankill Road, which 'belong' to one section of the community, and the symbolic use of Orange Order marches to assert a presence on certain streets such as the Garvaghy Road in Portadown.

And you may have thought how your experience of the street will depend on who you are, how vulnerable you feel to danger, whether you are a child, or old, or a woman, or a young man, or from a minority ethnic group; and on the time of day, whether the street is experienced at night or during the day, and how 'the street' may conjure up different feelings depending on all these factors.

■   ■   ■

Although there is a variety of ideas about what the street is, if you think about all the ideas listed above and your own ideas, apart from descriptions of *a place*, they are probably about what people *do* there, and the social actions that take place in the context of the street; they are also a mixture of real experiences and images from the media of streets we may not have experienced but which are real to us.

It also suggests that confining our attention to 'streets in themselves' won't be sufficient, that we need to think about the social context of 'the street' and what it means in terms of social space more generally. In order to understand and know what the street is as a feature of everyday life, we have to look at wider ideas and concepts: about the city, about social groups and structures, about the imagery of the street.

The street is, or might seem to be, an important 'locus of everyday life'. Yet compared to even twenty-five years ago, we are now more likely to encounter it in a car than by walking or using public transport. An increasing number of city centres have been pedestrianized, and the out-of-town shopping mall is now a common feature of urban areas not merely in the UK but in Europe and the USA too. Is 'the street' still the same place if encountered in a car? And what about shopping centres and shopping malls? Are they streets in another form? Such issues suggest that 'the street' is not a simple or socially homogeneous entity, but a bundle of disparate things.

If you think back to the discussion of the origins of the concept of 'everyday life' in the Introduction to this book, you will remember that it is linked it to the emergence of concepts about 'ordinary people' and in particular to an interest in their *way of life*, as well as their observation, surveillance and control. As was made clear, some writing about everyday life and ordinary people that has been influential in sociology has at its centre the Marxist notion that 'the everyday' – particularly where it denotes repetition and 'dull routine' – is little more than a synonym for the alienation and oppression of the working class in a capitalist society. We find this view well-expressed at certain points in the writings of the Hungarian literary critic and philosopher Georg Lukács, the French existentialist (and later Marxist) philosopher Jean-Paul Sartre and Henri Lefebvre, for instance, who identified the everyday as the separation of work, household and leisure. Indeed there has been a tendency to view the everyday in negative terms on both left and right, to see the apparent banality and routine of everyday life as oppressive, a symptom of the alienated nature of the life of the working class under capitalism.

It is important, then, to realize that the concept of 'the everyday' may often be used pejoratively. But this is not the only way in which it enters social thought, and especially not in relation to 'the street'. Others – sociologists, writers and artists – have taken a converse view of everyday life. They have tended to be open to, and to promote, value or romanticize the everyday existence of ordinary people, and in particular to look upon 'the street' as a place where a sort of theatre or *spectacle* of everyday life can be seen. A plethora of examples abound in the visual arts, from the Flemish painters of genre scenes of everyday life in the sixteenth century (such as Brueghel), the caricatures of Hogarth in the eighteenth century, to the surrealist movement of the 1920s and 1930s and documentary photographers and film-makers from the 1930s to the 1960s. The presence of ordinary people and their everyday life, especially on the street, seems to have been a major and constant element of European culture since at least the 1500s.

Figure 3.5 Avenue Simon Bolivar, Belleville (Paris), Willy Ronis, 1950 (Rapho/Network). *This photograph is part of a series by a key figure in the French humanist movement, whose detailed study of the Parisian area of Belleville Menilmontant characterizes the key features of everyday life in this working-class area. Humanist photographs are often termed 'poetic' because they celebrate the life of the streets in a positive manner. In this image, many features of the 'humanist' conception of the street as a key locale of everyday life are in evidence: with allusions to family, manual work and sociability.*

2.1 De-familiarizing the street

Here is not the place to inquire too closely as to why some traditions of social thought have placed a low value on ordinary life and everyday existence within capitalist societies. But it indicates that in beginning to think sociologically about this apparently key locale of everyday life, 'the street', we immediately come up against some interesting problems concerning how sociologists 'think' about the domain of the everyday. One way is to take familiar situations, experiences and events and attempt to 'de-familiarize' them in order to understand their dynamics.

For an example of one way of doing this, Box 3.1 describes an imaginary activity which is designed to elucidate the everyday nature of social relations in the street.

BOX 3.1

Choose a local street, preferably one with lots of people in it. Take one shoe off and hold it in your hand. Carrying your shoe fairly prominently, walk down the street from one end to the other, and try to engage passers-by in eye contact. Note their reaction to you, and if possible, any verbal response they might make to you. At the end of what might prove a discomforting but revealing trip into the social unknown, try to note down the variety of responses you encountered, and in particular what they suggest to you about how other people seemed to be reacting to what you were doing. Try to write down something, too, about what you think the 'social rules' were that you might have been breaking: indeed if your experience of this behaviour and its effect on others was something felt more intensely by you or them.

You may need to do the experiment more than once, and to vary the way in which you are disrupting expectations of 'appropriate behaviour' in public locales. As a 'test' you could walk the same route 'normally', to observe the differences in how other people react to you (or not). You could try doing the same experiment in several different streets.

ACTIVITY 3

If you were to carry out this experiment (and we don't recommend that you do!), what reactions do you think you might get from other people in the street? Would it make a difference if you were young or old? Male or female?

Do you think it would be successful in revealing the taken-for-granted nature of social interaction?

This is an example of what is termed a 'breaching' experiment designed by the American sociologist Harold Garfinkel (1967) to disrupt the conventions of normality, and in this way display the 'rules' which underpin taken-for-granted situations. The actual results of this 'breaching' experiment would probably be embarrassing if we were to carry it out ourselves and might well meet with hostility. The whole point of his method was to start with familiar scenes and 'ask what can be done to make trouble', a method that was sometimes difficult for those carrying out the experiment.

Breaching conventional rules in such a manner may help to make more 'real' what it is we are doing when we look *sociologically* at 'the street'. One point is to note how social values, and social structures, can be made visible. Garfinkel's experiment is part of what he called a 'documentary method', a way in which we can use the evidence of experiences gained from disrupting social expectations (as in this case) to show or demonstrate the existence of an underlying social pattern. This experiment begins to show how the street is a place but, more importantly, a *social structure*, which is present in the particular and observable activities of members of society:

> ... the possibility of common understanding doesn't consist in demonstrated measures of shared knowledge of social structure, but consists instead and entirely in the enforceable character of actions in compliance with the expectancies of everyday life as a morality. Common sense knowledge of the facts of social life for the members of the society is institutionalized knowledge of the real world.
>
> (Garfinkel, 1967, p.53)

Sociologically, the street is primarily a space where a complex set of social relationships occur. We walk through it, negotiating our passage with the other people on the street, stopping to enter a shop or to visit a market stall. We encounter others there. We shop. We show off our clothes. We wear the appropriate sort of clothes – *street fashion*. Some might even play 'street-games' there. There may be street-crime. There are often street-traders. Amongst this evident diversity something in common is happening: we all know (or think we 'know') the where and what and how of the street. It is on the one hand a type of social relationship with others in public spaces – with social rules about how we should behave with those others which we don't need to think about but are nonetheless, once we start to think about them or bring them into the open via one of Garfinkel's 'breaching' experiments, still there quite clearly in our minds. In this context, the street is, as a place and as a metaphor, a *moral* locale, a place where social order is displayed, where *sociability* is transacted.

On the other hand the street is also, for our purposes, an *idea* or *image*, an *imaginary* place which we invest with different sorts of meanings via the particularistic imagery of culture. At the same time, the actual streets of our everyday lives are spaces we can only visualize through the memories, pictures, films or descriptions of actual, particular streets. Some of these images might be positive: the well-stocked fruit stalls of a street-market, for instance. Others might be negative: a street-fight, for example. But each of these images contributes to how we 'imagine' the street as a social space.

This chapter, then, is concerned with two (complementary) ways of understanding the street and everyday life that have moulded sociological writing. One is concerned with social order and sociability, while the other is focused on how images of the street have influenced thinking about it.

The first way in which sociologists have thought about the street can be termed the *social*. This sees it as one of the key locations of social relations between people. In the public sphere of the street and the places which surround it, people of all ages, classes and genders encounter each other. It thus becomes a socially defined locale in which everyday life takes place, a theatre in which social interactions occur, and a stage on which social roles are played. In this broad tradition of social thought, the street is thought of as *a central element of the urban way of life.* Indeed, it is assumed that the typical social relations found on the street and in other public spaces of towns and cities are indeed those of a distinctive 'way of life'. In this view, the *social* perspective on the street is concerned with the *distinctive* nature of the *social dynamics* which it denotes.

The second way in which sociologists have discussed the street is in terms of its role in how we *imagine* key aspects of modern life. The street, and all that people imagine takes place there, may thus be seen as a metaphor for **modernity**   modernity
itself. This perspective is concerned with the *imaginary*, with perceptual aspects of 'the street' and its interpretation by artists – writers, painters, photographers and film-makers – since much theoretical writing about modernity and the street involves discussion of the role of images. In one sense, the dominant 'image' of the street is a largely visual concept, and so we will be concerned with the interplay between representation and reality. The *imaginary* perspective can thus be said to be concerned with the street as a *'state of mind'.*

SUMMARY OF SECTION 2

In this section we have:

1   explored the idea that 'the street' may not be a simple or socially homogeneous entity, but a bundle of disparate things;

2   looked at an imaginary experiment designed to reveal the structure of social rules underpinning 'taken-for-granted' everyday life situations, such as the street;

3   introduced two ways of understanding the street and everyday life in sociological writing – the *social* and the *imaginary*.

---

3 The street and modern life

In what follows, we are going to be using the concept of 'the street' as an idea that connects directly with the wider and more encompassing idea of 'the city' – in both its empirical, social dimensions and as an imagined entity. By concentrating on the street we can both limit the range of what is discussed and examine some central ideas of sociology as it has developed in tandem with the rise of urbanism.

With the extension of a successful and powerful capitalist economic system of industrialization and commercial expansion, Europe and North America experienced a massive expansion of their towns and cities in the latter half of the nineteenth century. The great concentrations of population within these rapidly emergent metropolises created new social conditions which had not been seen before. New housing and other forms of urban development created, often within a few decades, massive conurbations of 500,000 persons and more. Urbanization, then suburbanization, followed the development of new transport infrastructures such as the railways – and by the beginning of the twentieth century the emergence of motor transport – which began to extend the limits of the modern city far beyond its medieval confines. Where hitherto cities had been small, often compact, entities constructed on a relatively narrow social base, they now had to contain an increasingly diverse range of social groups:

an urban proletariat of wage labourers; a new and burgeoning middle class of commercial and industrial entrepreneurs; between them in the social hierarchy the small shopkeepers, traders and artisans on the one hand and professionals and administrators on the other; and still powerful but of declining social importance, the remnants of the old landed aristocracy and gentry which maintained its presence in the cities, in the opulent mansions that had been their bases of urban power in pre-industrial society.

It is against the backdrop of such a fundamental set of transitions in the patterning and ordering of everyday life that sociology itself, as a distinctive intellectual discipline, began to emerge. Among the most significant features of early sociology are its concerns with understanding the impact and consequences of urban-industrial social change. In particular, many writers wanted to know why city life seemed to be so different from life in the country. Although not the only writer to direct attention to these shifts, the German sociologist **Ferdinand Toennies** is widely recognized as giving them a conceptual shape when he described them as the change from **Gemeinschaft (community)** to **Gesellschaft** (association). For Toennies, the characteristic feature of urban, industrialized societies was their increasing reliance on a new, rational and contractual type of relationship between individuals and a new mode of social organization, rather than the closer ties and shared values that existed previously.

Toennies, Ferdinand

Gemeinschaft community Gesellschaft

Toennies was to argue that the motives people have for acting together, for relating to each other in social relationships, collectives and social organizations or corporate bodies, depend upon whether they are based on what he termed 'natural will' or on 'rational will'. He saw that 'natural will' (by which he meant the more habitual and emotionally based types of relationships to be found in traditional village and small town communities) tended to give way to 'rational will' in urban settings, where contractual relationships founded on a rational calculation of their outcomes tend to predominate (Toennies, 1887/1955).

The idea that new forms of economic relationships are bound up with the emergence of a distinctive way of life for people in the modern city seems obvious to us now, yet we must also be aware of the context in which sociologists such as Toennies were writing towards the end of the nineteenth century, when other types of explanation might have commanded more attention. For the creation of the vast new modern city seemed also to have brought with it everywhere, in Europe as much as in the New World, a myriad of modern ills: disease, crime, prostitution, civil unrest. Conservative and progressive writers alike viewed the city as a dysfunctional, oppressive entity. Here is Marx's colleague and friend, **Friedrich Engels**, writing about London in his *The Condition of the Working Class in England* (1845):

Engels, Friedrich

> Only when one has tramped the pavements of the main streets for a few days does one notice that these Londoners have had to sacrifice what is best in human nature in order to create all the wonders of civilization with which their city teems, that a hundred creative faculties that lay dormant in them remained inactive and were suppressed ... There is something distasteful about the very bustle of the streets, something that is abhorrent to human nature itself. Hundreds of thousands of people of all classes and ranks of society jostle past one another; are they not all human beings with the same characteristics and potentialities, equally interested in the pursuit of happiness? ... And yet they rush past one another as if they had nothing in common or were in no way associated with one another.

(Engels, 1999/1845, pp.92–3)

The fascination with new forms of social relationship which are consequent upon changes in the economics, technology, demographics and settlement patterns of their societies, thus produced a common interest in identifying how and why people had begun to think and interact in different ways. The city, and the new patterns of life which it imposed on its denizens, especially in their interactions on the street, thus appeared symptomatic of an emergent modern society.

3.1 Simmel and the metropolitan way of life

As this discussion suggests, sociological thinking about the street as a distinctive locale of modern life does not get into its stride until the latter part of the nineteenth century and the early years of the twentieth century. **Georg Simmel** was one of the first to attempt to analyse the social dynamics of street life as typifying modernity. Simmel's work may seem distant from us, but it underpins much contemporary thinking about everyday life on the street, and has had a major influence on post-modern conceptions of the city.

Simmel, Georg

Georg Simmel spent most of his academic life in Berlin, which by the end of the nineteenth century was regarded as one of the leading cities of the modern era. In 1896 he wrote a brief essay on 'The Berlin Trade Exhibition' of that year, an event widely held to have marked the beginning of Berlin's status as a 'world city' (Frisby, 1984, pp.119). In this essay, Simmel uses metaphors for the street, and concentrates on the ways in which the spectator, walking through the exhibition's aisles, is constantly shown commodities arranged so as to give them 'new aesthetic significance'. The aisles of the exhibition are akin to the streets of the new 'world city', a place where department stores, shops and arcades offer a constantly changing 'exhibition', in which the modern life of 'exchange' and 'social distance' predominates.

Although Simmel wrote very widely on philosophy, sociology, psychology, art and aesthetics, it is in his analysis of city life, and especially the characteristic behaviour of people in the street, the 'quality' of its nervous energy ('neurasthenia'), that a sociology of modernity begins to emerge for the first time. Simmel himself was urbane and cultured, yet also, as a Jew, manifestly a marginal stranger in the society in which he lived, and thus ideally placed to sense the fleeting and momentary nature of relationships, the ways in which the life of the streets typifies a new and modern form of social existence. One of Simmel's interpreters describes him as 'a modern urban man … an alien in his native land. Like the stranger he described in one of his most brilliant essays, he was near and far at the same time, a "potential wanderer"' (Coser, 1965, p.1).

Prefiguring what has become almost a cliché of modern urban sociology, Simmel emphasized that the city is not something that emerges independently of social relationships, but is something that is consequent upon changes in their very nature: the City is 'not a spatial entity with sociological consequences, but a sociological entity that is formed spatially' (Frisby, 1984, p.131). In one of his key essays, 'The metropolis and mental life', Simmel develops his analysis of the mechanisms whereby the personality of the individual accommodates to the external requirements of the new urban social structures.

━━━━━━━━━━━━━━━━━━━━━━━━━━━ **READING 3.1** ━━━━━━━━━━━━━━━━━━━━━━━━━━━

Now read Reading 3.1, 'The metropolis and mental life' by Georg Simmel (1903). While reading the essay, please consider the following questions:

1   How does Simmel characterize the personality of the metropolitan individual?

2   Why is the city different from the country?

3   What is the relationship between the economy and the metropolitan attitude?

Simmel emphasizes the 'neurasthenia' characteristic of city existence, the 'vibe' of street-life as we might now call it. He describes the almost neurotic sense of anxiety and stress which surrounds the urban way of life. Simmel argued that 'the deepest problems of modern life derive from the claim of the individual to preserve the autonomy and individuality of his existence in the face of overwhelming social forces' that are to be found in the metropolis.

At the same time as Simmel insists on the social construction of the modern way of life of the metropolis, he also makes clear that the city itself, as a large-scale social organism, does have major consequences for individuals within it. Their reactions to the metropolitan way of life, to the 'modernity' of the city, require that individuals have to 'resist being levelled down and worn out' by this 'social-technological mechanism'. One characteristic form of this resistance is to be found in the search for ways of emphasizing social difference (what we might now term *identity*). This concern with distinctiveness, a need for separation from the social mass, is a key feature of modernity, and may even take the form of 'the most tendentious peculiarities, that is, the specifically metropolitan extravagances of mannerism, caprice, and fastidiousness. Now the meaning of these extravagances does not at all lie in the contents of such behaviour, but rather in its form of "being different", of standing out in a striking manner and thereby attracting attention' (Simmel, 1950/1903, p.421). In this prediction of the importance of street-fashion, it is hard not to see in Simmel's analysis a cogent explanation of why metropolitan cities all have a vibrant and aesthetically dominant fashion culture. Simmel came up with an interesting explanation for the considerable attention paid to fashion in modern cities, with his argument that attracting attention on the street and in public places is essential because 'the brevity and infrequency of meetings' necessitates coming to the point as quickly as possible and making a striking impression in the briefest possible time.

Simmel's ideas about the city, and in particular the everyday life to be found in the streets, thus operate with very similar notions about fundamental shifts in the way of life of modern, urban people as appear in Toennies' famous distinction between Gemeinschaft and Gesellschaft:

> The trend of modern history appears to Simmel as a progressive liberation of the individual from the bonds of exclusive attachment and personal dependencies in spite of the increasing domination of man by cultural products of his own creation. …

> The principle of organization in the modern world is fundamentally different: an individual is a member of many well-defined circles, no one of which involves and controls his total personality.

(Coser, 1977, pp.189–91)

3.2 The Chicago School

Many of Simmel's ideas that bear upon issues about sociability, social distance and social interaction, about the nature of the street, the modern city and its characteristic way of life, were taken over by the **Chicago School** of sociologists, and applied in interesting and instructive ways to the smaller-scale analysis of often unregarded features of everyday life.

Chicago School

Simmel had published a number of articles in American sociological journals which began to appear around the turn of the century (the *American Journal of Sociology* was founded in 1895), so his work was in some ways already established in the USA when the Chicago School began to develop a distinctive body of social research founded on analyses of the city of Chicago in the 1920s. A leading member of the Sociology Department at the University of Chicago, **Robert E. Park** was briefly one of Simmel's students in Germany in the early 1900s, and his writings on the new field of urban sociology owed a great deal to Simmel. His doctoral thesis was on the subject of 'the mass and the crowd', a popular theme of late nineteenth-century social thought, and one particularly related to the behaviour of people in the city streets.

Park, Robert E.

A characteristic feature of the Chicago School was its concern with treating the city itself as a sort of 'social experiment' (at the time the University was founded, the city had only existed as an urban settlement, let alone a metropolis, for barely 60 years). In 'The city: suggestions for the investigation of human behaviour in the urban environment', a seminal essay written in 1916, Park argues strongly for the idea that sociology must 'take to the streets' to study urban problems and social processes:

> The city, in short, shows the good and evil in human nature in excess. It is this fact, more than any other, which justifies the view that would make of the city a laboratory or clinic in which human nature and social processes may be most conveniently and profitably studied.
>
> (Park, 1916)

What, then, was distinctive about the sociology developing at Chicago in the 1920s and 1930s? Like the emergent patterns of life on the streets of the modern city of Chicago itself, it was concerned with those aspects of life we find most contingent, particular and fugitive in social interaction. It was greatly influenced by the philosophy of 'pragmatism' developed in North America in the second half of the nineteenth century. The main thrusts of pragmatism are:

(a) that it is important to deal with the concrete and particular rather than the abstract and universal;

(b) that there is no absolute truth, but that the search for meanings and truths is both necessary and possible; and, finally,

(c) that it is anti-dualistic in the sense that it does not separate 'the knower from the known, the subject from the object, or the creative from the determined' (Plummer, 1996, p.229).

Pragmatist thought was perhaps most clearly expressed in the Chicago School sociologist W.I. Thomas's famous aphorism, 'when people define a situation as real, it becomes real in its consequences for them'.

symbolic interactionism

What pragmatism brings to sociological thinking is precisely the concern with looking closely at the particular and the everyday as ways of understanding social processes, rather than attempting to understand what people really do by deducing their behaviour from large-scale processes or the standpoint of a grand and abstract theory such as Marxism or Social Darwinism. A later commentator on this work suggests that it emerged in an 'attempt to create a unique philosophic rationale for the finer aspects of American society … characterized as it is by respect for the individual and a belief in gradual change to meet society's fluctuating needs' (Plummer, 1996, p.230). What the Chicago sociologists were concerned with was **'symbolic interaction'** in all its forms. Symbolic interactionism developed out of the work of the Chicago School and especially that of the social psychologist G.H. Mead. He argued that social behaviour depended on a complex system of agreed meanings that are learned through the process of symbolic interaction, that is of seeing yourself as others see you. This involves role-playing, and the play-acting of children is a way of learning how to live in society and to use appropriate actions and words to be understood and to behave appropriately in particular roles and situations.

The Chicago School sociologists used this approach to understand the everyday relations of people in modern urban settings. They were concerned with the way in which understanding social interaction requires sensitivity to its 'fluidity and its accent … on flexible interpersonal relationships as a basis for an understanding of the working of society' (Plummer, 1996, p.23). Because of this concern with the pragmatic nature of life in the US city, great attention was paid to the life of the streets themselves. Robert Park told his students researching in the city of Chicago to look for their subjects on the street corners, in the dance-halls and bars, in the immigrant ghettos, among the flop-houses (cheap hotels), and in the 'hobo' (homeless persons) areas which had become a feature of the city.

The Chicago School generated an enormous range of social studies of everyday life, producing a rich and highly detailed analysis of the minutiae of everyday life, much of it conducted in the public and semi-private spaces of the street and its locales. A classic example is Nels Andersen's study of *The Hobo* (1923), which was based on a year he spent living and studying in the areas of homeless migratory men. Andersen's work focuses on the street culture of the homeless, on the symbolic aspects of their interactions within their community. Studies such as this prepared the groundwork for the emergence of a distinctive tradition of sociological research on everyday life. As the symbolic interactionist approach emerged in the 1930s and 1940s it became clear that it understood the urban street as a primary site of, and even in some senses a synonym for, the social life of the street.

For symbolic interactionist approaches, then, the city streets lead to a distinctive type of social relationship. People behave and think differently. Chicago sociologists argued that by observing the ways in which 'normality' is constructed in public spaces, we can begin to understand how deviant behaviour can occur. Indeed, normality itself becomes something to be explained. The emphasis on the symbolic meaning to the individual of his/her actions that was introduced by the Chicago School sociologists led directly to studies of groups and their deviation from this 'norm'.

A classic of this tradition is William F. Whyte's *Street Corner Society* (first published in 1943), a study of an Italian immigrant community in a 'slum' district of Chicago. Whyte lived in the area between 1937 and 1940, getting to know his subjects and participating in their lives. He used what has now come to be known as participant observation. This is a technique taken from social anthropology, but ideally suited to the detailed analysis of a community where the sociologist needs to immerse her/himself in the life of those being studied.

Whyte wrote his study as if it were a novel, concealing the precise location of 'Cornerville' and the identities of his protagonists (a strategy normal at the time and since for protecting the interests of informants), men who were members of a street-corner 'gang', involved in minor ways in racketeering and gambling. Whyte's written interpretation of his research offers the reader a hero, 'Doc' and an anti-hero, 'Chick Morelli', and his study explores the dynamics of small group formation among a group of men who spend their lives 'hanging out' in gangs – a term that might imply they were criminals but also means something quite specifically non-criminal in this context: a group of young men who tended to congregate together, forming a cohesive group, and sharing their social lives, a sort of street-based clique.

READING 3.2

Now read Reading 3.2, 'The gang and the individual', by William Foote Whyte. While reading this extract, consider the following questions:

1   How does life on the street limit or control the social interactions of the gang members?

2   How does the gang create a cohesive social group for its members?

Whyte's study focuses on how individual, community, and family life interact on the streets. The men whom Whyte befriended in the 'gangs' spent much of their time as 'corner-men', hanging around the specific street-corners that defined their membership of particular gangs. The network of relationships between them, the social roles each took and the obligations of each member to the others, and to their 'leader' (that sometimes involved participating in the illegal activities of the 'numbers game', taking small bets and running errands for 'racketeers'), can be seen as stabilizing their community. By looking in detail at the life of the gangs and their members, Whyte was able to show the dynamics of small-group formation and how this 'normalized' deviance, or in certain cases reinforced resistance to it (Whyte, 1981/1943).

3.3 Negotiating the street

Racial, class and gender divisions are features of the social order of 'the street' as experienced by people in most societies, from the *Street Corner* society of Chicago in the late 1930s to Britain and the United States in the 1990s and 2000s. This may be more acutely felt by young people, because of their more intensive use of 'the street' as a locale for leisure activity, and as a geographical space defining identity. The study by Watt and Stenson (1988) of a town in south-east England examines young people's uses and perceptions of public space in relation to issues of safety and danger. Following on from Whyte's 'Cornerville', this study calls two of the areas studied 'Streetville and 'Workville'. It compares the views of urban and suburban youth, reflecting the typical spatial division of working and middle classes, and also introduces the different experience that young women have of public space.

READING 3.3

Now read Reading 3.3, 'The street: "It's a bit dodgy around there"', by Paul Watt and Kevin Stenson. While you are reading it, keep the following issues in mind:

1   What are the main findings of this study on how areas are stereotyped by different groups?

2   What are the differences that class, 'race' and gender make to the way in which the relative safety and danger of the urban scene in Thamestown are perceived?

Watt and Stenson emphasize the basic similarities in the ways in which people from different social, gender and ethnic groups negotiate the public space of the town which they studied. As their work shows, a complex set of interactions emerge that enable residents and visitors to negotiate the threats and dangers posed by the street. In short, they become 'streetwise', because the street itself is perceived as dangerous – and racial or ethnic labelling of an area is often enough to reinforce this perception.

Elijah Anderson's *Streetwise: Race, Class, and Change in an Urban Community* is a study of an ethnically mixed, city district. The next reading is an extract from this book and takes further the ambivalence that residents may feel about their neighbourhood, often based on a fear of the 'Other' in terms of ethnicity, and the strategies that they employ to contain and handle a situation that is perceived as potentially dangerous. Anderson describes a specific situation where 'race' is the key factor:

> … the central strategy in maintaining safety on the streets is to avoid strange black males. The public awareness is color-coded: white skin denotes civility, lawabidingness, and trustworthiness, while black skin is strongly associated with poverty, crime, incivility, and distrust. Thus an unknown young black male is readily deferred to. If he asks for anything, he must be handled quickly and summarily. If he is persistent, help must be summoned.

> … Not only do the perpetrators of crime often view anonymous whites as invaders but, perhaps more important, they see them as 'people who got something' and who are inexperienced in the 'ways of the streets.'
>
> (Anderson, 1990, pp.210–11)

The best adaptation for successfully negotiating street encounters appears to be, argues Anderson, to develop 'street wisdom', to become, in other words, street-wise. It would be possible to see this *street wisdom* as a key feature of modern life in the city, and indeed Simmel's analysis of the effects of the city in 'The metropolis and mental life' is an early suggestion of some of its components. To be 'street-wise' is to possess a particular knowledge of social relationships in order to survive in the social environment of the street, to negotiate its dangers and present social identity in a non-threatening manner, to 'normalize' the situation. How, then, can being 'street-wise' help in a space in which the construction of sociability is problematic and fragile?

Now read Reading 3.4, 'Street etiquette and street wisdom', taken from Elijah Anderson's book. As you read this short extract, try to compare it with the British study in Reading 3.3.

1   Make a note of any differences you find between Anderson's discussion of his US case and the British example of Watt and Stenson.

2   In what ways does being 'street-wise' help to 'normalize' social interactions in the street?

As both Anderson's and Watt and Stenson's work make clear (and as Whyte's much earlier research also indicates), the street may be seen by many people as a space in which the construction of sociability is problematic and fragile, ready at any moment to break down under the threat of social disorder. Only by creating communal structures, or though systems of surveillance and control, can social order be maintained. The 'normality' of street life, its potential for social cohesion, can thus become a problem requiring external agencies such as the police.

SUMMARY OF SECTION 3

In this section we have:

1   explored in greater detail the *social* approach to understanding the street and its role as a locus for sociability and normal social relationships;

2   examined the ideas of the key theorists, Toennies and Simmel, who first identified the qualitative shift in society brought by the new scale and intensity of urbanization;

3   looked at the development of the Chicago School of sociology and its close study of everyday life in its diverse forms;

4   introduced the idea of symbolic interactionism in explaining how people learn the complexities of social behaviour and role-playing;

5   looked in greater detail at recent sociological studies of the street, from Britain and the United States, to explore how people learn to negotiate interactions on the street, especially where they are perceived as potentially dangerous.

4 Normalizing street life

Figure 3.6 Park Avenue, New York, *Garry Winogrand, 1959.*
Winogrand's work demonstrates the ways in which photography was increasingly used to explore the unusual aspects of everyday life. Here, it is the apparent banality of the street which is under inspection. The street can be seen as a theatre, from which only a medium as instantaneous as photography can express the flow and spontaneity of real life. Winogrand's work has many affinities with that of Erving Goffman, in its concern with how role-play can 'normalize' what might otherwise seem to be deviant or bizarre behaviour.

'Normality' is not really a problem for classical social theory: the 'everyday' or quotidian is simply subsumed within a totalizing picture of how society operates, and is not assumed to require any special attention. Yet as we have seen, to be 'street-wise' is to normalize relationships in a deviant setting, and there surely must be a way in which we can relate such seemingly random and personal encounters to a sociological understanding of the street. The social construction of 'normality' thus becomes something to be explained.

If 'normality' is indeed something that has to be explained, then one of the most interesting approaches is that of the Canadian sociologist, Erving Goffman. Goffman was a central figure of the 'second Chicago School' trained in the decade after the Second World War, and his writings represent the more radical approach to the mechanics of everyday life – and in particular the construction of normality – that is characteristic of this new phase of symbolic interactionism (Fine, 1995). His 'dramaturgical' perspective is a highly influential interpretation of the ways in which social interaction occurs in public places. Goffman paid particular attention in his work to what goes on in public spaces between individuals, and to what marks off strangers from those who have some prior acquaintance with each other. For Goffman, as for symbolic interactionism generally, people are social actors who construct appearances to perform the roles they must play in everyday life (Goffman, 1959).

As the term 'dramaturgical' implies, Goffman's perspective is one which uses the metaphors of play-acting on the stage to describe how meaning is constructed in any social situation. Performance, impression-management, role-playing and so on are terms which describe the 'artifice' with which the routine of everyday life is maintained. The simple activity of walking down the street to visit a local shop becomes a complex set of staged performances which require us to behave appropriately towards the other people we encounter, and even to manage the interactions involved in queuing to buy our bread. For what is queuing but a complex set of social rules about how to take turns?

A classic example of Goffman's approach is his analysis of how couples demonstrate, publicly, their 'couple-dom': by what Goffman calls 'couple tie-signs' such as hand-holding, and the social 'norms' or rules which dictate when and how these tie-signs can or cannot be displayed:

> There is a rule in formal etiquette that it is improper for couples to walk down the fashionable shopping streets of a city holding hands. There is another rule that married couples at social parties are supposed to 'mix', that is, to lay aside their excluding relationship temporarily so that they can be active simply in their capacity as members of the party. A corollary of this rule is that they are not supposed to hold hands. (They may hold hands on the way to the party and back from the party but not during the party.) It is also the case that although college students can walk on the campus holding hands – in fact that seems to be one of the special places for this sort of activity – they ought not to listen to lectures thusly encumbered. Furthermore, in some social establishments holding hands even outdoors is forbidden.

> ... The significance of this discipline will be emphasized if we look at situations where hand-holding seems to be approved and even idealized. In our pictorial world of advertising and movies – if not in the real world – vacationing couples are featured walking down crooked little streets in foreign places holding hands. At issue here is the fact that tourists often feel they do not owe the business streets of foreign societies the deference these places often demand from locals;

tourists can therefore withdraw, just as they can wear informal clothing. Further, the very foreignness of the place suggests a slight exposure, if not fear, and, for the woman at least, holding the hand of the one she is paired with is a pictured source of support.

(Goffman, 1971, pp.228–9)

Goffman's work attracted very considerable attention in both the sociological world and the wider media, for it seemed to capture the very essence of existence in modern societies. He focused on the type of social behaviour that can be observed in public locations such as the street, and many of his theories relate to the maintenance of social order in such settings. Being 'street-wise', for instance, involves what Goffman called 'successfully staging a character', or in other words normalizing the way in which people present themselves to others.

There are many connections which link Goffman's dramaturgical approach to the study of everyday life with the 'impressionistic' sociology of Georg Simmel. In both, the emphasis is very much upon the contingent and 'emergent' nature of social relations, the idea that normality has to be continually 'made' by symbolic interaction, and that the everyday life of the streets is something that allows us to observe universal characteristics of social behaviour from small-scale, particular 'snapshots'. But unlike many of their contemporaries who were concerned with creating abstract theory, neither Simmel nor Goffman sought to build a theoretical system from their 'snapshot-like' observations (Smith, 1989, p.19).

Both avoided large-scale theorizing about the social organization of everyday life. In that sense, their work concentrates on the individual's *experience* of life, on the street and in the modern city, and in modern society generally, to the exclusion of generalized assumptions about how society organizes those experiences. And, in large part, both Simmel and Goffman refer to the 'symbolic' construction of everyday life, to the ways in which the 'interaction order' is made meaningful to individuals. And perhaps this idea that everyday life is itself a sort of mental construct, a set of rules about social performance which all of us have to carry around in our heads, in other words a form of new 'imagination', connects us to the second way of understanding the street.

SUMMARY OF SECTION 4

In this section we have:

1   introduced the writings of Erving Goffman and his 'dramaturgical' approach;

2   begun to suggest some links between the *social* and *imaginary* perspectives through the idea of symbolic interaction that Simmel, the Chicago School writers and Goffman employ.

5 The imaginary city and its streets

The street is … the only valid field of experience.

(André Breton, *Nadja*, 1922)

Georg Simmel taught Robert Park that 'The city is a state of mind'. The city is more than a physical presence, a mass of people and buildings; it is, as Simmel suggested, also an experience. The way in which individuals negotiate the city and its streets requires it also to be seen as 'an abstraction from the material' (Donald, 1999, p.8), the imagined environment where we actually live:

> It is true that what we experience is never the city, 'the thing itself'. It is also true that the everyday reality of the city is always a space already constituted and structured by symbolic mechanisms. But representation does not quite get the measure of the relationship between the two realities, for it implies that one reality must be the model for the other, or a copy of it … If it is not quite a representation, maybe … it would be more accurate to think of the city as an imagined environment. This environment embraces not just the cities created by the 'wagging tongues' of architects, planners and builders, sociologists and novelists, poets and politicians, but also the translation of the places they have made into the imaginary reality of our mental life. …
>
> > The city in our actual experience is at the same time an actually existing physical environment, and a city in a novel, a film, a photograph, a city seen on television, a city in a comic strip, a city in a pie chart, and so on [Burgin, 1996, p.48].
>
> (Donald, 1999, pp.7,8)

Charles Baudelaire has come to be seen as a seminal figure for the way in which his ideas express a critical shift in how the city and its streets are imagined. Just as Simmel saw something distinct in the modern city and its effects on the mentality and behaviour of its occupants, Baudelaire is seen as expressing one of the first definitions of modernity, writing in about 1859–60:

> By 'modernity', I mean the ephemeral, the fugitive, the contingent, the half of art whose other half is the eternal and the immutable.
>
> (Baudelaire, 1964/1863, p.13)

As the quote makes clear, Baudelaire was commenting on 'modern' *art* rather than modern *society* – or at least about the modern art of his time. The quote comes from an essay on Constantin Guys, whom Baudelaire idolized as 'The Painter of Modern Life', but who is now not considered as significant. However, Baudelaire has come to be seen as a seminal figure for a number of reasons, and these are tied up with the way in which his ideas have come to express a critical shift in how the city and its streets were *imagined*. This might be best understood as the imagination producing *images* of the street and its life. Put in another way, ideas drawn from the modernist aesthetic influence the way in which social relations in the modern city have increasingly come to be conceptualized, and to be understood as *sights*. Baudelaire was known as a (rather minor) writer until the 1930s, but as the genealogy of modernity itself began to be conceptualized he emerged as a source of key ideas about modernity and its images.

5.1 Baudelaire, Benjamin and the *flâneur*

Modernity was 'both a "quality" of modern life as well as a new object of artistic endeavour. For the painter of modern life, this quality is associated with the notion of newness, with *nouveauté*' (Frisby, 1985, p.15). Thus it is the very *novelty* of the present, its tawdry fascination with the here and now, rather than the ideals of classical beauty which had so marked earlier conceptions of art, that Baudelaire prizes. He wants us to glory in the juxtaposition of ancient and modern, the setting of timeless ideas of value against the ephemerality of the present: 'The true painter will be the man [*sic*] who extracts from present day life its epic aspects and teaches us in lines and colours to understand how great and poetic we are in our patent-leather shoes and our neckties' (*ibid.*, p.16). Beauty itself is to be defined henceforth, as not merely 'made up of an eternal, invariable element' but also 'a relative, circumstantial element, which will be … the age, its fashions, its morals, its emotions' (*ibid.*).

And where is the place where all this novelty will be seen? Where best to observe 'the age, its fashions, its morals, its emotions'? Why, *the street*, of course. And who is to observe it? Baudelaire's 'painter of modern life' whose task thus becomes to capture 'the ephemeral, contingent newness of the present'. In a passage which suggests what photography was then still almost half a century from doing, Baudelaire

> … poses a particular problem of method since 'in trivial life, in the daily metamorphosis of external things, there is a rapid movement which calls for an equal speed of execution from the artist'. It requires a special skill, even a new kind of artistic function: 'Observer, philosopher, *flâneur* – call him what you will; but … you will certainly be led to bestow upon him some adjective which you could not apply to the painter of eternal, or at least more lasting things' since 'he is *the painter of the passing moment and of all the suggestions of eternity that it contains*'.
>
> (Frisby, 1985, pp.16–17, quoting from Baudelaire, 1863; Frisby's emphasis)

This new individual must mill in the crowds which flock onto the boulevards of Paris:

> The crowd is his element … His passion and his profession are to become one flesh with the crowd. For the perfect *flâneur,* for the passionate spectator, it is an immense joy to set up house in the heart of the multitude, amid the ebb and flow of movement, in the midst of the fugitive and the infinite. To be away from home and yet to feel oneself everywhere at home; to see the world, to be at the centre of the world, and yet to remain hidden from the world … The spectator is a *prince* who everywhere rejoices in his incognito.
>
> (Baudelaire, 1964/1863, p.90)

It is in the great cities that the *flâneur* (the saunterer or uncommitted observer of the spectacle of the street) and the artist of modern life find their nurturing environment, and their chief subject matter: fashion:

> 'if a fashion or the cut of a garment has been slightly modified … his eagle eye will have already spotted it from however great a distance'. Yet on the other hand, the artist of modern life 'marvels at the eternal beauty and the amazing harmony of life in the capital cities, a harmony so providentially maintained amid the turmoil of human freedom. He gazes upon the landscapes of the great city – landscapes of stone, caressed by the mist or buffeted by the sun'.
>
> (Frisby, 1985, p.18, quoting from Baudelaire, 1863)

It is evident that Baudelaire sees affinities between the *flâneur* and his artist of modern life. The *flâneur* is a bystander, a person (a man, in point of fact) who has the liberty and means to enjoy the urban crowd, to stroll in the city and partake of its sights and its pleasures. However, Baudelaire's artist

> 'has an aim loftier than that of a mere *flâneur*', namely the systematic search for modernity. His task is that of 'seeking out and expounding the beauty of *modernity*'. The artist must grasp 'this transitory, fugitive element, whose metamorphoses are so rapid'. Only the artist of modern life can release this beauty from its most trivial externalities since, 'for most of us … for whom nature has no existence save by reference to utility, the fantastic reality of life has become singularly diluted'. The artist, on the other hand, concerned with 'the *outward show of life,* such as it is to be seen in the capitals of the civilized world', is able 'to express at once the attitude and the gesture of human beings … and their luminous *explosion* in space'.
>
> (Frisby, 1985, p.18; quoting Baudelaire, 1964/1863, pp.15,18)

It will be clear that Baudelaire's ideas are concerned with how an artist might *imagine* and translate into images the modern city and the life of its streets: what he terms a 'phantasmagoria' of modern life. It is something produced by

Figure 3.7 *Gustave Caillebotte,* Paris, A Rainy Day (rue de Rennes), *1877 (Art Institute of Chicago). The 'Impressionist' painters were part of a wider movement in French art during the mid to late nineteenth century which wanted to show everyday life in a realistic manner, in contrast to the emphasis on historical scenes and genre subjects which had characterized French painting up until that time. Caillebotte's paintings show us the world in which Baudelaire's flâneur watched the spectacle of the streets, but they also seem to presage the photography of everyday life that only became possible at the end of the century. This image offers a 'snapshot' of street life in the 1870s, and the couple – the flâneur and flâneuse – who feature in it appear to be enjoying the visual pleasures afforded by the new street layout of Haussmann's re-designed boulevards.*

'a perceptiveness acute and magical by reason of its innocence' (Baudelaire, 1964/1863. p.11). This is clearly not intended as, nor should it be seen as, an *objective* description of a city or of the modern way of life to be found in it. Baudelaire is above all interested in establishing a basis for his *aesthetic* theories. (They have been widely influential in inspiring some cultural historians to investigate modern ways of seeing as concerned with the spectacle of the city and its way of life: see Clark, 1985.)

The ideas about modernity which Baudelaire developed were taken up again in the 1920s and 1930s by Walter Benjamin, a German intellectual working in Paris, who found in them a fruitful source for thinking about the nature of the modern city. For Benjamin, as a Marxist writer, was concerned to link the emergence of modernity with the advance of commodity capitalism and the 'commodity fetishism' (the investment of value in objects) that drives it. Baudelaire's ideas offered the key to the essential motor driving capitalism: as Benjamin notes, he saw the modern as not merely an epoch, but an *energy* (Buck-Morss, 1989, p.178). Benjamin projected (but never completed) a vast work about modernity itself; it was later reconstructed from the fragments left after his death in 1940 and published as *Die Passagen-Werk* (The Arcades Project). Benjamin finds Baudelaire's theory of the *flâneur* to be one of the keys to understanding how modern capitalism developed through the emergence of the fascination with novelty.

Benjamin's uses of Baudelaire in his writings – despite being often fragmentary and incomplete – have become highly influential in understanding how we can imagine the modern city and in particular the dynamic driving the life of its streets. They also symbolize an increasing fascination with the cultural dimension of everyday life, as viewed through the output of artists, writers, film-makers, photographers and so on, that has come to be known as the 'cultural turn' in sociology. A much greater attention is increasingly given to the cultural products themselves as *indicators* of modernity, and the open interpretation which might be accorded to the unfinished nature of Benjamin's work has helped that process to develop (cf. Buck-Morss, 1989).

Let us now take a closer look at Benjamin's highly influential use of Baudelaire to express this *imaginary* perspective on the street as a *'state of mind'*. This reading looks at the transformation of the centre of Paris by Baron von Haussmann, who created wide boulevards in place of the small medieval streets, and the unexpected effect of this on the imagined city.

READING 3.5

Now read Reading 3.5, James Donald's 'Rationality and enchantment: Paris' from his book, *Imagining the Modern City*. When you have read this extract, consider the following questions:

1   What are the key affinities between Baudelaire's and Benjamin's approaches to the city?

2   What do Baudelaire and Benjamin have to say about the sexual or gender organization of street life?

As Donald observes, 'the *flâneur* is unavoidable'. Yet who is this person? As '*flâneur* theory' has developed as a key approach to understanding the cultural experience of modern life, there have been increasing concerns that the approach is flawed by its emphasis on this essentially male figure, who goes, in Benjamin's redolent phrase, 'botanizing on the asphalt'.

However, as Donald acknowledges, the experience of space is gender-differentiated and, though he plays down the importance of this, there has been much criticism of the dominance of the masculine viewpoint. As Janet Wolff (1985) has argued in a seminal article, we must also consider the 'invisible *flâneuse*'. She identifies the reasons for this absence as relating to the nature of sociological explanation, the consequently partial conception of modernity, and the reality of women's place in society, rather than to any misogyny on the part of the commentators, though Baudelaire's view of women displays 'the classic misogynist duality, of woman as idealized-but-vapid/real-and-sensual-but-detested', according to Wolff (*ibid.*, p.150). In her view, the literature of modernity ignores the private sphere by concentrating only on what is happening in the public domain: 'the particular experience of "modernity" was, for the most part, equated with experience in the public arena':

> This silence is not only detrimental to any understanding of the lives of the female sex; it obscures a crucial part of the lives of men, too, by abstracting one part of their experience and failing to explore the interrelation of the public and private spheres. For men inhabited both of these. Moreover, the public could only be constituted as a particular set of institutions and practices on the basis of the removal of other areas of social life to the invisible arena of the private. The literature of modernity, like most sociology of its period, suffers from what has been called the 'oversocialization' of the public sphere. The skewed vision of its authors explains why women only appear in this literature through their relationships with men in the public sphere, and via their illegitimate or eccentric routes into this male arena – that is, in the role of whore, widow or murder victim.
>
> (Wolff, 1985, p.152)

5.2 Imagining the modern street

Walter Benjamin's fascination with the dynamic of modern capitalism as expressed through the life of the streets was not unique in the 1920s and 1930s. Across Europe, young artists and intellectuals were fascinated by the city, by the new spaces and forms created by modern architecture, by the 'machine age' which promised to transform the world of work, and create new products that would answer every conceivable need. Following the First World War there was a widespread desire to look forward. Nowhere was this clearer than in the 'new media' such as film and, especially, photography:

> Dizzying views up to skyscraper peaks, close-ups of gleaming machine parts, anonymous split-second dramas glimpsed on city streets, landforms revealed as near-abstractions from far aloft – such images suggested the impressions that might have been collected by a mobile eye nervously scanning the surfaces of contemporary life.
>
> (Phillips, 1989, p.95)

In France, however, the machine-age optimism of the 'new vision' was tempered by another movement which also gave considerable attention to images of the streets of the modern city: surrealism. The surrealists, in part inspired by the

Figure 3.8 Mystery of the Street, Umbo (Otto Umbehr), 1928.
The modernist view of the street that emerged within the artistic movement of the 1920s emphasized new ways of looking at the street. In this image by the German photographer, Umbo, the new perspectives and unsettling perspectives are well-expressed.

persuasive character of Freudian pyschoanalytic theory, did not rely on reasoned analysis or sober calculation; on the contrary, they saw the forces of reason blocking the access routes to the imagination.

For the surrealists, the street became the place where the imagination, the unconscious, was constantly lurking – ready to jump out at any moment from the seemingly ordinary. Photographs, in particular, were able to convey this radical coupling of the unconscious and the 'quotidian' – the everyday. Surrealism thus celebrated the intoxicating, disruptive forces that the image might unleash. Louis Aragon, in his 1925 novel *Paysan de Paris* (an extended ramble through the streets of the city, in which Aragon visits the very *galéries* that will later figure in Benjamin's Arcades Project), remarked: 'The vice called surrealism is … the uncontrolled provocation of the image for its own sake, and for the element of unpredictable perturbation and metamorphosis which it introduces into the domain of representation. [For] each man there awaits … a particular image capable of annihilating the entire universe' (Aragon, 1925, p.79). As a result, the surrealists searched among the most ordinary and 'documentary' of images to discover the dynamics of urban life and in particular its key imaginary elements. They discovered the street images made by Eugene Atget (1857–1927). In his photographs of the deserted streets of old Paris, of shop windows haunted by elegant mannequins, of the gaze of a young prostitute, the surrealists recognized their own vision of the city as a 'dream capital', an urban labyrinth of memory and desire (Phillips, 1989, p.99).

Walter Benjamin, too, writes about Atget's Parisian work (in his 'A short history of photography' of 1931): for it deals with the new spaces of modernity in a fashion that allows him an insight into the motors of commodity capitalism. But Benjamin's purposes are different from those of Aragon and Breton, whose fascination with the 'intoxicating reveries about a sort of secret life of the city' are in distinct contrast with his desire to 'waken the world from its dream' or in other words the fantasy life of commodity fetishism (Benjamin, 1970).

Especially for those beginning to explore the world outside the studio with unobtrusive handheld cameras, the surrealist model of an urban *flâneur*, a wanderer open to chance encounters, was crucial. Aragon believed that if one were attuned to the fleeting gestures, enigmatic objects, and veiled eroticism glimpsed in the street, an unsuspected pattern of affinities – a new kind of poetic knowledge – might be revealed. In the late 1920s and early 1930s the belief that the camera could snare and fix these moments of instantaneous,

Figure 3.9 Shop-front, Paris, Eugene Atget, n.d.
Eugene Atget produced large numbers of photographs of the streets of Paris from about 1897 until the mid-1920s, documenting their principal features – architectural as well as social. As a result, they illustrate the scenes of Parisian street life that Baudelaire's flâneur would have encountered. Atget's images document the 'imagined city' of modernism in a particularly clear manner, but they often contain bizarre elements (as in the striking appearance of the woman outside the shop selling wine from Burgundy) which the surrealists picked out as especially indicative of the strange elements lurking just beneath the surface of everyday existence.

lyrical perception had many important adherents among young photographers in Europe. Their images, which found scenes of great interest and beauty in the theatre of everyday life to be found in the streets of great cities such as Berlin, Paris and London, were widely distributed to new mass audiences via the media of the popular illustrated magazine, which emerged in Germany in the 1920s and was to be taken up in the rest of Europe and the USA in the 1930s (Hamilton, 1996). They helped in the process by which the everyday life of the streets came to be thought of as important and celebrated as part of popular culture – i.e. the culture of the mass of ordinary people.

In the late 1920s the French poet and novelist Pierre Mac Orlan proposed that the camera could open a window onto the realm of another aspect of the everyday, what he termed the 'social fantastic'. Mac Orlan was no surrealist; nor was he a comprehensive theorist of photography. He was, however, perhaps the most perceptive French photographic critic during this period, and he developed what amounted to a modern poetics of the medium. Taking his cue from the painter Fernand Léger, who had noted the 'shock of contrast' provided by a modern billboard set in the countryside, Mac Orlan reflected at length on the collision between technological civilization and the remnants of a popular

Figure 3.10 Young woman hailing a taxi, New York, *Willy Ronis, 1981.*
A take on the post-modern street from a key representative of the humanist tradition in French photography. A central theme of humanism was the sociability of the street, and in this image the individual is seemingly placed in a confrontational attitude to the cars and lorries that threaten her.

culture rooted in the past. His notion of the 'social fantastic' referred to the frequently bizarre juxtapositions of the archaic and the modern, the human and the inanimate, glancingly encountered each day in the streets of the modern city – as, for example, in André Kertész's perception of the uncanny correspondence between anonymous passers-by and the cut-out figures of an advertising display. This mysterious new dimension of social reality could, according to Mac Orlan, be best explored by photographers, the most 'lyrical, meticulous witnesses' of the present (Phillips, 1989, p.101). Mac Orlan too recognized Eugène Atget as the precursor of a new photographic sensibility which is rooted in the life of the streets. Such imagery has fed into the public subconscious and influenced how 'the street' is perceived.

It will be evident that the 'imagined city' that emerges from the minds of Benjamin, the surrealists and Mac Orlan in the 1920s and 1930s is increasingly a place of poetic or dramatic images, rather than of an apparently 'objective' social observation.

SUMMARY OF SECTION 5

In this section we have:

1   explored the 'imaginary' perspective in greater detail through the ideas of Baudelaire and his identification of modernity and the role of the *flâneur*;

2   seen how Benjamin used the ideas of Baudelaire to imagine the modern city and understand the forces creating it;

3   outlined other views of the modern city – those of the Surrealists and Pierre Mac Orlan who inspired new ways of looking that included the 'social fantastic';

4   investigated some examples of ways in which the street has been imagined and represented in art and photography.

6 Conclusion

In this chapter we have looked at two perspectives – the social and the imaginary – that sociologists have employed in understanding the street and everyday life. Each of these has moulded sociological writing in particular ways. In both, however, the meaning of 'street' floats between describing a place and what people do there. Within sociology, 'the street' is often a metaphor for the way in which people behave in public places, a locale where social structures become visible through the interactions of those we find in them.

Robert Park may well have suggested that 'the city is a state of mind' but it is also a social and economic organism, a huge collectivity of individuals and groups whose interactions produce and reproduce the everyday life of its inhabitants. These two perspectives on the city offer different but complementary ways of focusing on how the everyday life of the street has entered social thought, from the nineteenth century until the present day. The social city has its own ineluctable reality, and this has been influential in ways of thinking about the street that stress how it is a place where sociability is transacted.

At the same time, Park's dictum has become a distinctive feature of sociological understandings of urban life, and in particular of the nature of the images (what is *imagined*) that express the life of the streets as everyday experience, part of the urban way of life, integral to the texture and feel of the modern city. As we have seen, once we enter into the notion of the street as a 'state of mind' it becomes essential to pay attention to how modernity has been visualized, of the role of images taken from painting, photography and the cinema. These indicate that a sociological understanding and explanation of the role of the street in everyday life must take on board, not just the social dynamics of actors, but the ways in which their visualizations of the city are constructed.

References

Anderson, E. (1990) *Streetwise: Race, Class, and Change in an Urban Community*, Chicago, IL, University of Chicago Press.

Andersen, N. (1923) *The Hobo*, Chicago, IL, University of Chicago Press.

Aragon, L. (1925) *Paysan du Paris*, Paris, Gallimard.

Baudelaire, C. (1964) *The Painter of Modern Life and Other Essays* (trans. and ed. J. Mayne), London, Oxford University Press. First published in 1863.

Benjamin, A. (ed.) (1991) *The Problems of Modernity: Adorno and Benjamin*, London, Routledge.

Benjamin, W. (1970) *Illuminations* (trans. H. Zohn), London, Cape.

Benjamin, W. (1980) 'A short history of photography' in Trachtenberg, A. (ed.) *Classic Essays in Photography*, New Haven, CT, Leete's Island Books.

Benjamin, W. (1999) *The Arcades Project* (trans. H. Eiland and K. McLaughlin), Cambridge, MA, The Belknap Press of Harvard University.

Breton, A. (1963) *Nadja*, Paris, Gallimard (trans. R. Howard, New York, Grove Press, 1960). First published in 1922.

Buck-Morss, S. (1989) *The Dialectics of Seeing: Walter Benjamin and the Arcades Project*, Cambridge, MA, MIT Press.

Burgin, V. (1996) *Some Cities*, London, Reaktion Books.

Clark, T.J. (1985) *The Painting of Modern Life*, London, Thames and Hudson.

Coser, L. (1977) *Masters of Sociological Thought*, New York, Harcourt Brace Jovanovich.

Coser, L. (ed.) (1965) *Georg Simmel*, Englewood Cliffs, NJ, Prentice-Hall.

Donald, J. (1999) *Imagining the Modern City*, London, The Athlone Press.

Engels, F. (1999) *The Condition of the Working Class in England*, Oxford, Oxford University Press. First published in 1845.

Fine, G.A. (ed.) (1995) *A Second Chicago School? The Development of a Postwar American Sociology*, Chicago, IL, The University of Chicago Press.

Frisby, D. (1984) *Georg Simmel*, London/Chichester, Tavistock/Ellis Horwood.

Frisby, D. (1985) *Fragments of Modernity*, Cambridge, Polity Press.

Garfinkel, H. (1967) *Studies in Ethnomethodology*, Englewood Cliffs, NJ, Prentice-Hall.

Goffman, E. (1959) *The Presentation of Self in Everyday Life*, New York, Anchor Books.

Goffman, E. (1971) *Relations in Public*, London, Allen Lane The Penguin Press.

Hamilton, P. (1996) 'Representing the social: France and Frenchness in post-war humanist photography' in Hall, S. (ed.) *Representation*, London, Sage/The Open University.

Park, R. (1916) 'The city: suggestions for the investigation of human behaviour in the urban environment', *American Journal of Sociology*, vol.20, pp.577–612.

Phillips, C. (1989) *The New Vision: Photography Between The World Wars*, New York, Abrams.

Plummer, K. (1996) 'Symbolic interactionism in the twentieth century: the rise of empirical social theory' in Turner, B.S. (ed.) *The Blackwell Companion to Social Theory*, Oxford, Blackwell.

Simmel, G. (1950) 'The metropolis and mental life' in *The Sociology of Georg Simmel* (trans. and ed. K.H. Wolff), New York, The Free Press, pp.409–24. Essay first published in 1903.

Smith, G.W.H. (1989) 'Snapshots 'sub specie aeternitatis': Simmel, Goffman and formal sociology', *Human Studies*, vol.12, pp.19–57.

Toennies, F. (1957) *Community and Society* (trans. and ed. C. Loomis), New York, Harper and Row by agreement with The Michigan State University Press of East Lansing, MI. Published as *Gemeinschaft und Gesellschaft* in Germany in 1887.

Watt, P. and Stenson, K. (1998) 'The street: "It's a bit dodgy around there"' – safety, danger, ethnicity and young people's use of public space' in Skelton, T. and Valentine, G. (eds) *Cool Places: Geographies of Youth Cultures*, London, Routledge, pp.249–65.

Whyte, W.F. (1981) 'The gang and the individual' in *Street Corner Society: The Social Structure of an Italian Slum*, Chicago, IL, University of Chicago Press (3rd edn). First published in 1943.

Wolff, J. (1985) The invisible *flâneuse :* women and the literature of modernity', *Theory, Culture and Society*, vol.2, no.3. (Reprinted in her *Feminine Sentences*, Cambridge, Polity Press, 1990.)

Readings

 3.1 Georg Simmel, 'The metropolis and mental life' (1903)

The deepest problems of modern life derive from the claim of the individual to preserve the autonomy and individuality of his existence in the face of overwhelming social forces, ... the person resists to being leveled down and worn out by a social-technological mechanism. An inquiry into the inner meaning of specifically modern life and its products, into the soul of the cultural body, so to speak, must seek to solve the equation which structures like the metropolis set up between the individual and the super-individual contents of life. Such an inquiry must answer the question of how the personality accommodates itself in the adjustments to external forces. This will be my task today.

The psychological basis of the metropolitan type of individuality consists in the *intensification of nervous stimulation* which results from the swift and uninterrupted change of outer and inner stimuli. Man is a differentiating creature. His mind is stimulated by the difference between a momentary impression and the one which preceded it. Lasting impressions, impressions which differ only slightly from one another, impressions which take a regular and habitual course and show regular and habitual contrasts – all these use up, so to speak, less consciousness than does the rapid crowding of changing images, the sharp discontinuity in the grasp of a single glance, and the unexpectedness of onrushing impressions. These are the psychological conditions which the metropolis creates. With each crossing of the street, with the tempo and multiplicity of economic, occupational and social life, the city sets up a deep contrast with small town and rural life with reference to the sensory foundations of psychic life. The metropolis exacts from man as a discriminating creature a different amount of consciousness than does rural life. Here the rhythm of life and sensory mental imagery flows more slowly, more habitually, and more evenly. Precisely in this connection the sophisticated character of metropolitan psychic life becomes understandable – as over against small town life which rests more upon deeply felt and emotional relationships. These latter are rooted in the more unconscious layers of the psyche and grow most readily in the steady rhythm of uninterrupted habituations. The intellect, however, has its locus in the transparent, conscious, higher layers of the psyche; it is the most adaptable of our inner forces. In order to accommodate to change and to the contrast of phenomena, the intellect does not require any shocks and inner upheavals; it is only through such upheavals that the more conservative mind could accommodate to the metropolitan rhythm of events. Thus the metropolitan type of man – which, of course, exists, in a thousand individual variants – develops an organ protecting him against the threatening currents and discrepancies of his external environment which would uproot him. He reacts with his head instead of his heart. In this an increased awareness assumes the psychic prerogative. Metropolitan life, thus, underlies a heightened awareness and a predominance of intelligence in metropolitan man. The reaction to metropolitan phenomena is shifted to that organ which is least sensitive and quite remote from the depth of the personality. Intellectuality is thus seen to preserve subjective life against the overwhelming power of metropolitan life, and intellectuality branches out in many directions and is integrated with numerous discrete phenomena.

The metropolis has always been the seat of the money economy. Here the multiplicity and concentration of economic exchange gives an importance to the means of exchange which the scantiness of rural commerce would not have allowed. Money economy and the dominance of the intellect are intrinsically connected. They share a matter-of-fact attitude in dealing with men and with things; and, in this attitude, a formal justice is often coupled with an inconsiderate hardness. The intellectually sophisticated person is indifferent to all genuine individuality, because relationships and reactions result from it which cannot be exhausted with logical operations. In the same manner, the individuality of phenomena is not commensurate with the pecuniary principle. Money is concerned only with what is common to all: it asks for the exchange value, it reduces all quality and individuality to the question: How much? All intimate emotional relations between persons are founded in their individuality, whereas in rational relations man is reckoned with like a number, like an element which is in itself indifferent. Only the objective measurable achievement is of interest. Thus metropolitan man reckons with his merchants and customers, his domestic servants and often even with persons with whom he is obliged to have social intercourse. These features of intellectuality contrast with the nature of the small circle in which the inevitable knowledge of individuality as inevitably produces a warmer tone of behavior, a behavior which is beyond a mere objective balancing of service and return. In the sphere of the economic psychology of the small group it is of importance that under primitive conditions production serves the customer who orders the good, so that the producer and the consumer are acquainted. The modern metropolis, however, is supplied almost entirely by production for the market, that is, for entirely unknown purchasers who never personally enter the producer's actual field of vision. Through this anonymity the interests of each party acquire an unmerciful matter-of-factness; and the intellectually calculating economic egoisms of both parties need not fear any deflection because of the imponderables of personal relationships. The money economy dominates the metropolis; it has displaced the last survivals of domestic production and the direct barter of goods; it minimizes, from day to day, the amount of work ordered by customers. The matter-of-fact attitude is obviously so intimately interrelated with the money economy, which is dominant in the metropolis, that nobody can say whether the intellectualistic mentality first promoted the money economy or whether the latter determined the former. The metropolitan way of life is certainly the most fertile soil for this reciprocity, a point which I shall document merely by citing the dictum of the most eminent English constitutional historian: throughout the whole course of English history, London has never acted as England's heart but often as England's intellect and always as her moneybag!

In certain seemingly insignificant traits, which lie upon the surface of life, the same psychic currents characteristically unite. Modern mind has become more and more calculating. ... The relationships and affairs of the typical metropolitan usually are so varied and complex that without the strictest punctuality in promises and services the whole structure would break down into an inextricable chaos. Above all, this necessity is brought about by the aggregation of so many people with such differentiated interests, who must integrate their relations and activities into a highly complex organism. If all clocks and watches in Berlin would suddenly go wrong in different ways, even if only by one hour, all economic life and communication of the city would be disrupted for a long time. In addition an apparently mere external factor: long distances, would make all waiting and broken appointments result in an ill-afforded waste of time. Thus, the technique of metropolitan life is unimaginable without the most punctual integration of all activities and mutual relations into a stable and impersonal time schedule. Here again the general conclusions of this entire task of reflection become obvious, namely, that from each point on the surface of existence – however closely attached to the surface alone – one may drop a sounding into the depth of the psyche so that all the most banal externalities of life finally are connected with the ultimate decisions concerning the meaning and style of life. Punctuality, calculability, exactness are forced upon life by the complexity and extension of metropolitan existence and are not only most intimately connected with its money economy and intellectualistic character. These traits must also color the contents of life and favor the exclusion of those irrational, instinctive, sovereign traits and impulses which aim at determining the mode of life from within, instead of receiving the general and precisely schematized form of life from without. Even though sovereign types of personality, characterized by irrational impulses, are by no means impossible in the city, they are, nevertheless, opposed to typical city life. ...

The same factors which have thus coalesced into the exactness and minute precision of the form of life have coalesced into a structure of the highest impersonality; on the other hand, they have promoted a highly personal subjectivity. There is perhaps no psychic phenomenon which has been so unconditionally reserved to the metropolis as has the blasé attitude. The blasé attitude results first from the rapidly changing and closely compressed contrasting stimulations of the nerves. From this, the enhancement of metropolitan intellectuality, also, seems originally to stem. Therefore, stupid people who are not intellectually alive in the first place usually are not exactly blasé. A life in boundless pursuit of pleasure makes one blasé because it agitates the nerves to their strongest reactivity for such a long time that they finally cease to react at all. In the same way, through the rapidity and contradictoriness of their changes, more harmless impressions force such violent responses, tearing the nerves so brutally hither and thither that their last reserves of strength are spent; and if one remains in the same milieu they have no time to gather new strength. An incapacity thus emerges to react to new sensations with the appropriate energy. This constitutes that blasé attitude which, in fact, every metropolitan child shows when compared with children of quieter and less changeable milieus.

This physiological source of the metropolitan blasé attitude is joined by another source which flows from the money economy. The essence of the blasé attitude consists in the blunting of discrimination. This does not mean that the objects are not perceived, as is the case with the half-wit, but rather that the meaning and differing values of things, and thereby the things

themselves, are experienced as insubstantial. They appear to the blasé person in an evenly flat and gray tone; no one object deserves preference over any other. This mood is the faithful subjective reflection of the completely internalized money economy. By being the equivalent to all the manifold things in one and the same way, money becomes the most frightful leveler. For money expresses all qualitative differences of things in terms of 'how much?' Money, with all its colorlessness and indifference, becomes the common denominator of all values; irreparably it hollows out the core of things, their individuality, their specific value, and their incomparability. All things float with equal specific gravity in the constantly moving stream of money.

Source: Simmel, 1950/1903, pp.409–12, 412–13, 413–14

3.2 William Foote Whyte, 'The gang and the individual' (1943)

The corner-gang structure arises out of the habitual association of the members over a long period of time. The nuclei of most gangs can be traced back to early boyhood, when living close together provided the first opportunities for social contacts. School years modified the original pattern somewhat, but I know of no corner gangs which arose through classroom or school-playground association. The gangs grew up on the corner and remained there with remarkable persistence from early boyhood until the members reached their late twenties or early thirties. In the course of years some groups were broken up by the movement of families away from Cornerville, and the remaining members merged with gangs on near-by corners; but frequently movement out of the district does not take the corner boy away from his corner. On any evening on almost any corner one finds corner boys who have come in from other parts of the city or from suburbs to be with their old friends. The residence of the corner boy may also change within the district, but nearly always he retains his allegiance to his original corner.

Home plays a very small role in the group activities of the corner boy. Except when he eats, sleeps, or is sick, he is rarely at home, and his friends always go to his corner first when they want to find him. Even the corner boy's name indicates the dominant importance of the gang in his activities. It is possible to associate with a group of men for months and never discover the family names of more than a few of them.

Most are known by nicknames attached to them by the group. Furthermore, it is easy to overlook the distinction between married and single men. The married man regularly sets aside one evening a week to take out his wife. There are other occasions when they go out together and entertain together, and some corner boys devote more attention to their wives than others, but, married or single, the corner boy can be found on his corner almost every night of the week.

His social activities away from the corner are organized with similar regularity. Many corner gangs set aside the same night each week for some special activity, such as bowling. With the Nortons this habit was so strong that it persisted for some of the members long after the original group had broken up.

Most groups have a regular evening meeting-place aside from the corner. Nearly every night at about the same time the gang gathers for 'coffee-and' in its favorite cafeteria or for beer in the corner tavern. When some other activity occupies the evening, the boys meet at the cafeteria or tavern before returning to the corner or going home. Positions at the tables are fixed by custom. Night after night each group gathers around the same tables. The right to these positions is recognized by other Cornerville groups. When strangers are found at the accustomed places, the necessity of finding other chairs is a matter of some annoyance, especially if no near-by location is available. However, most groups gather after nine in the evening when few are present except the regular customers who are familiar with the established procedure.

The life of the corner boy proceeds along regular and narrowly circumscribed channels. As Doc said to me:

> Fellows around here don't know what to do except within a radius of about three hundred yards. That's the truth, Bill. They come home from work, hang on the corner, go up to eat, back on the corner, up a show, and they come back to hang on the corner. If they're not on the corner, it's likely the boys there will know where you can find them. Most of them stick to one corner. It's only rarely that a fellow will change his corner.

The stable composition of the group and the lack of social assurance on the part of its members contribute toward producing a very high rate of social interaction within the group. The group structure is a product of these interactions.

Out of such interaction there arises a system of mutual obligations which is fundamental to group cohesion. If the men are to carry on their activities as a unit, there are many occasions when they must do favors for one another. The code of the corner boy requires him to help his friends when he can and to refrain from doing anything to harm them. When life in the group runs smoothly, the obligations binding members to one another are not explicitly recognized. Once Doc asked me to do something for him, and I said that he had done so much for me that I welcomed the chance to reciprocate. He objected: 'I don't want it that way. I want you to do this for me because you're my friend. That's all.'

It is only when the relationship breaks down that the underlying obligations are brought to light. ...

Not all the corner boys live up to their obligations equally well, and this factor partly accounts for the differentiation in status among them. The man with a low status may violate his obligations without much change in his position. His fellows know that he has failed to discharge certain obligations in the past, and his position reflects his past performances. On the other hand, the leader is depended upon by all the members to meet his personal obligations. He cannot fail to do so without causing confusion and endangering his position.

The relationship of status to the system of mutual obligations is most clearly revealed when one observes the use of money. During the time that I knew a corner gang called the Millers, Sam Franco, the leader, was out of work except for an occasional

odd job; yet, whenever he had a little money, he spent it on Joe and Chichi, his closest friends, who were next to him in the structure of the group. When Joe or Chichi had money, which was less frequent, they reciprocated. Sam frequently paid for two members who stood close to the bottom of his group and occasionally for others. The two men who held positions immediately below Joe and Chichi were considered very well off according to Cornerville standards. Sam said that he occasionally borrowed money from them, but never more than fifty cents at a time. Such loans he repaid at the earliest possible moment. There were four other members with lower positions in the group, who nearly always had more money than Sam. He did not recall ever having borrowed from them. He said that the only time he had obtained a substantial sum from anyone around his corner was when he borrowed eleven dollars from a friend who was the *leader* of another corner gang.

The situation was the same among the Nortons. Doc did not hesitate to accept money from Danny, but he avoided taking any from the followers.

The leader spends more money on his followers than they on him. The farther down in the structure one looks, the fewer are the financial relations which tend to obligate the leader to a follower. This does not mean that the leader has more money than others or even that he necessarily spends more – though he must always be a free spender. It means that the financial relations must be explained in social terms. Unconsciously, and in some cases consciously, the leader refrains from putting himself under obligations to those with low status in the group.

The leader is the focal point for the organization of his group. In his absence, the members of the gang are divided into a number of small groups. There is no common activity or general conversation. When the leader appears, the situation changes strikingly. The small units form into one large group. The conversation becomes general, and unified action frequently follows. The leader becomes the central point in the discussion. A follower starts to say something, pauses when he notices that the leader is not listening, and begins again when he has the leader's attention. When the leader leaves the group, unity gives way to the divisions that existed before his appearance.

The members do not feel that the gang is really gathered until the leader appears. They recognize an obligation to wait for him before beginning any group activity, and when he is present they expect him to make their decisions. One night when the Nortons had a bowling match, Long John had no money to put up as his side bet, and he agreed that Chick Morelli should bowl in his place. After the match Danny said to Doc, 'You should never have put Chick in there.'

Doc replied with some annoyance, 'Listen, Danny, you yourself suggested that Chick should bowl instead of Long John.'

Danny said, 'I know, but you shouldn't have let it go.'

The leader is the man who acts when the situation requires action. He is more resourceful than his followers. Past events have shown that his ideas were right. In this sense 'right' simply means satisfactory to the members. He is the most independent in judgment. While his followers are undecided as to a course of action or upon the character of a newcomer, the leader makes up his mind.

When he gives his word to one of his boys, he keeps it. The followers look to him for advice and encouragement, and he receives more of their confidences than any other man. Consequently, he knows more about what is going on in the group than anyone else. Whenever there is a quarrel among the boys, he hears of it almost as soon as it happens. Each party to the quarrel may appeal to him to work out a solution; and, even when the men do not want to compose their differences, each one takes his side of the story to the leader at the first opportunity. A man's standing depends partly upon the leader's belief that he has been conducting himself properly.

Source: Whyte, 1981/1943, pp.255–9

3.3 Paul Watt and Kevin Stenson, 'The street: "It's a bit dodgy around there"' (1998)

'Streetville … it's where all the black and Asian people live. I don't think I'd feel safe there at night.'[1]

'Well I know a lot of people around the area, around Thamestown, so I'd be able so go somewhere and say see somebody I know and say "what's happening[?]", so I feel safe … I don't really need safety, I know everybody, I know all the Asians and the blacks and all the whites, so I know I'm alright.'

This chapter is concerned to investigate young people's uses and perceptions of public space and issues of safety and danger. It is based upon a study of South Asian, Afro-Caribbean and white youth who live in a medium-sized town in the south-east of England which we have called 'Thamestown'.[2] The chapter explores the question of how an ethnically mixed group of young people negotiate public space as part and parcel of their everyday lives when moving about the town. …

The resilience of place: but 'is it safe?'

Despite the postmodernist claims about the declining significance of local neighbourhoods as important for young people's identities and lifestyles (Featherstone, 1991), empirical studies of youth have demonstrated the ways in which young people continue to identify with local places (Hendry *et al.*, 1993; Pearce, 1996; Taylor *et al.*, 1996). By 'place' we mean a space which people in a given locality understand as having a particular history and as arousing emotional identifications, and which is associated with particular groups and activities. Sometimes identification with places can be somewhat confining and 'localist' in the sense of people having restricted spatial horizons, and studies in Belfast (Jenkins, 1983) and Sunderland (Callaghan, 1992) have shown the importance of localism for understanding young white working-class people's spatial orientations; this can include a strong identification and pride in place.

In relation to non-white youth, studies in an inner city Midlands area (Westwood, 1990) and in Manchester and Sheffield (Taylor *et al.*, 1996) have found that young Afro-Caribbean and Asian people tend to lead a localist existence in the sense that they rarely leave the part of the city where they live, partly because of local ties in the area and restricted transport access, but also because of feelings of danger moving outside the 'safe space' of their own neighbourhood. In this sense, the 'localism' of ethnic minority youth partly arises from the fear of racial harassment, as well as from positive attachments to local areas. This fear of racial harassment can be regarded as resulting from 'white territorialism' (Hesse *et al.*, 1992, p.171) which refers to the way in which some white people, mainly males, use various forms of violence to defend 'their' areas against non-white people. …

…

Safety and danger for ethnic minority youth

Whilst we uncovered evidence for inter-ethnic friendships amongst some of our respondents living in ethnically mixed neighbourhoods, this must nevertheless be set against views which indicated that those same places could also be sites of racial harassment against other black and Asian young people if they didn't live there or didn't personally 'know anyone' there. Safety was by no means guaranteed for black and Asian youth and a survey commissioned by the Thamestown local authority showed that 14 per cent of a sample of Asians and Afro-Caribbeans had been victims of racial attacks in a single year. Given such levels of racial attacks on blacks and Asians in Thamestown, one important issue is whether or not non-white youth restricted their movements to their local neighbourhoods and adopted survival strategies in order to traverse public space, as other research has found in large cities (Taylor *et al.,* 1996; Westwood, 1990).

Some of the young Afro-Caribbean people in Thamestown did admit to feeling unsafe in particular areas. One young man mentioned being threatened by white youths in one particular housing estate on the outskirts of the town, also mentioned by several Asians as a dangerous place, and one 18-year-old black female indicated that her feelings of safety were in fact predicated upon not venturing very far out of home territory. Nevertheless, surprisingly the majority of Afro-Caribbean males said that they did not feel unsafe in the town and as individuals felt they could go anywhere. The second quotation at the beginning of the chapter illustrates how the spatial confidence of these black males was based upon their personal knowledge of people in different parts of the town. This in turn arguably reflects life in a town small enough so that many people know each other on the basis of shared schooling, neighbours, use of sports and entertainment facilities, and so on, a situation likely to differ from that found in the large cities in which people are more familiar with particular locales, but not others.[3]

On the other hand, more of our Asian respondents, both males and females, identified areas of the town where they personally, or their friends, had been the victims of racist abuse or physical attacks, and which consequently they avoided. For example, one Asian male respondent, aged 16, said of 'Workville' …:

> 'We used to go up Workville. There are all white people up there, you're just going to get into a fight, you're going to get yourself beaten up bad. No-one's going to go up Workville, especially, you know, Asians. They are racist there.'

Such views might well imply that the Asians in the town led a localist existence, corralled by the fear of racial attacks into particular safe 'Asian neighbourhoods'. To some extent the Streetville area of the town did in fact have this function; it was referred to by many of the Asian respondents as an 'Asian area'. For example, one young Asian male said of Streetville: 'it's always filled with Asians there, it's like no-one messes around with you, we just hang around with each other'. The reputation of Streetville as an Asian area also had benefits for some of the young Asian women:

> 'Where I feel really at home is the Streetville area 'cos there's a lot of Asians in Streetville … I feel safer when there's more Asians and when I know them.'
> (Asian female, aged 18)

Streetville was an area which in many ways represented the clearest expression of local place identity and pride amongst all of the young people we spoke to. This aspect of localism, however, co-existed with a group oriented masculine street strategy which allowed the young Asian males to move into other, potentially hostile, parts of the town. Around half of the Asian males said that they felt safe anywhere in the town in relation to perceived threats from both white and black males, and much of this seemed connected with safety in numbers and going around in large all male groups, as witnessed in the town's main shopping mall; one young Asian man said he felt safe anywhere, 'because I've got too many people to back me up'.

…

Despite clear attachments to their local neighbourhoods expressed by many black, and especially Asian youths, coupled with the very real threats of racial attacks in certain parts of the town if they didn't personally 'know anyone' there, surprisingly we did not find ethnic minority youth to live a *solely* localist existence, contrary to research in inner city areas (Taylor *et al.,* 1996; Westwood, 1990). Many of the non-white respondents, although by no means all, seemed to frequently visit a number of out of town places for leisure activities, with London as a popular destination (Watt, 1998).

In from the sticks: suburban youth

The young white middle-class people who lived in the suburban owner occupied housing estates or the up-market commuter villages several miles from the town centre constituted a distinctive group in several ways. Unlike many of our working-class respondents, both white and non-white, there was little allegiance to their areas of residence; most of the suburban youths found the places where they lived 'boring'. Instead, when asked about where they felt at home, many of them mentioned various places in the town centre, including the park, certain pubs and fast food outlets, and the main churchyard. The latter … was regarded as a common hang-out for the 'Goths' and 'Indie' young people, both males and females, identifiable by their long hair, dark clothes, big boots and a preference for independent, alternative bands, such as The Levellers:

> 'the churchyard … is quite a good place because you've got lots of people there, sort of into my kind of music and everyone knows each other, 'cos it's like a small little, almost kind of community … people sit and talk.'
>
> (White male, aged 17)

However, by no means all of the young people from the suburbs liked either 'Indie' music or the 'churchyard scene', and some of the females felt wary about the latter:

> 'I wouldn't go there … 'cos people are a bit intimidating to be honest. I'd kind of go through there as quickly as humanly possible … there's like groups of leather jacketed types. I mean they're not all, but just the general impression, you just think I don't want to be here. And there's people taking drugs quite a lot.'
>
> (White female, aged 17)

…

Several of the female and male young middle-class people told 'cautionary tales' (Anderson et al., 1994) about the Streetville area as a place of 'danger':

> 'The Streetville area … it's a bit dodgy around there to be honest … I mean some of my friends go round there and well occasionally because they mix with other groups and they say this happened and this happened and you think "I'm not going there" then.'
>
> (White male, aged 18)

The reliance on racialised stereotypes about the Streetville area as a dangerous 'black ghetto' echoes some of the findings of Taylor et al. (1996) on Moss Side in Manchester. As in Moss Side, such stereotypes seemed to be most common amongst those with little personal knowledge of the area; most of the young white people in Thamestown had very little personal contact with the Streetville neighbourhood.

Given the relatively separate social and spatial worlds in which the young middle-class people from the suburbs lived, it is unsurprising that they often felt wary about moving around the town. Such anxieties, ultimately arising from class and racial differentiation, were overlaid in the case of the young women with more gender specific concerns about the town at night.

Young women and public space

In relation to perceptions of safety and danger, there were certain continuities between the young women, irrespective of ethnicity or class background.[4] There was, as other researchers have noted (Stanko 1990; Valentine, 1989), a common emphasis on the need to take precautions to avoid danger, especially when moving around public space in the evening. For some, this constituted a generalised apprehension about the town at night:

> 'I don't think its specific places [where I don't feel safe], but I wouldn't go down, sort of, late at night into Thamestown at all, I mean I just wouldn't be there, especially if I was just with my girlfriends. I mean if there was a couple of blokes with us, or something, then maybe, but the chance is I wouldn't go down. It's nowhere in particular, it's just the whole idea of going down to town in the evening.'
>
> (White female, aged 17)

Young women from all ethnic groups frequented the town centre shopping malls and burger and pizza restaurants during the daytime, whilst the fast food outlets were also popular in the evenings, as were the town centre pubs for some of the young white females from the suburbs. In comparison with the streets, especially in the evenings, these places offered a more secure environment to meet other young people, minimising the risk of unwanted or threatening male attention.

In the context of research on young people in the very different urban environment of the East End of London, Pearce (1996, p.7) says that, as well as window shopping, young women go to shops in order 'to see friends, to hang around and, in their words, to have somewhere safe to be'. The same can be said for the young women of Thamestown in relation to the popularity of the town centre shopping malls as daytime meeting places.

Conclusion

We have argued that there are some similarities in the uses of public space among young people in Thamestown and in larger urban areas elsewhere, not least in relation to the ways in which young women take precautions in pursuing their leisure activities when moving about the town. There is also evidence, through white racist attacks, of the attempt to exclude ethnic minority groups from certain parts of the town, and of defensive organisation by young Asian males in the Streetville neighbourhood. The town centre is itself a contested space for many of the young people, and tensions can be said to exist between the different ethnic groups, notably the males, at various times.

...

For youth in this superficially affluent town, the rigidities of socio-spatial inequality co-exist uneasily with postmodern fluidity. We found a complex pattern of ethnic, racial and class rivalries, as well as the crossing of social and spatial borderlines. That the borders were crossed does not mean that they were removed.

Notes

1 We use the term 'black' in this chapter to refer to people with either an African or Caribbean ('Afro-Caribbean') ethnic origin, and 'Asian' to refer to people with a South Asian ethnic origin based in the Indian sub-continent. This was the dominant nomenclature used by the young informants in our research, although we recognise that the term 'Asian' is itself a generalisation for a number of minority groups differentiated by religion and place of origin (see Modood *et al.*, 1994).

2 The research used a variety of methods, including semi-structured interviews, carried out between June 1994 and July 1995, with 70 young men and women (35 of each) aged between 15 and 21 about their leisure time and use of public space. The respondents were drawn fairly evenly from the three main ethnic groups in the town and included South Asians (mainly Muslims of Pakistani origin), Afro-Caribbeans and whites. As far as possible, we tried to match interviewers and interviewees by ethnic group, although not by gender since only one of our interviewers was male. Our respondents were drawn from those who tended to regularly 'go out' and use public space, so they cannot be taken to be representative of all young people in the town. As well as the interviews

with the young people, we also carried out observations of patterns of youth group organisation in the shopping malls and on the streets, interviewed local government, commercial and voluntary agency officials, and analysed official documents.

3 It is possible that some of the male respondents exaggerated various aspects of their streetwise confidence in the interviews with the female interviewers.

4 We intend to analyse the issues of space, safety and identity for the young women in greater detail in another paper.

References

Anderson, S., Kinsey, R., Loader, I. and Smith, C. (1994) *Cautionary Tales: Young People, Crime and Policing in Edinburgh,* Aldershot, Avebury.

Callaghan, G. (1992) 'Locality and localism: the spatial orientation of young adults in Sunderland', *Youth & Policy*, vol.39, pp.23–33.

Featherstone, M. (1991) *Consumer Culture and Postmodernism,* London, Sage.

Hendry, L., Shucksmith, J., Love, J.G. and Glendinning, A. (1993) *Young People's Leisure and Lifestyles,* London, Routledge.

Hesse, B., Rai, D.K., Bennett, C. and McGilchrist, P. (1992) *Beneath the Surface: Racial Harassment,* Aldershot, Avebury.

Jenkins, R. (1983) *Lads, Citizens and Ordinary Kids: Working-class Youth Lifestyles in Belfast,* London, Routledge and Kegan Paul.

Modood, T., Beishon, S. and Virdee, S. (1994) *Changing Ethnic Identities,* London, Policy Studies Institute.

Pearce, J. (1996) 'Urban youth cultures: gender and spatial forms', *Youth & Policy,* vol.52, pp.1–11.

Stanko, E. (1990) *Everyday Violence: How Women and Men Experience Everyday Sexual and Physical Danger,* London, Pandora.

Taylor, I., Evans, K. and Fraser, P. (1996) *A Tale of Two Cities: A Study in Manchester and Sheffield,* London, Routledge.

Valentine, G. (1989) 'The geography of women's fear', *Area,* vol.21, pp.385–90.

Watt, P. (1998) ' "Going out-of-town": youth, "race" and place in the South East of England', *Environment and Planning: Society and Space* (forthcoming).

Westwood, S. (1990) 'Racism, black masculinity and the politics of space' in Hearn, J. and Morgan, D. (eds) *Men, Masculinities and Social Theory,* London, Unwin Hyman.

Source: Watt and Stenson, 1998, pp.249, 252–3, 256–7, 259, 260–2

3.4 Elijah Anderson, 'Street etiquette and street wisdom' (1990)

The streets have a peculiar definition in the Village community. Usually pedestrians can walk there undisturbed. Often they seem peaceful. Always they have an elegant air, with mature trees, wrought-iron fences, and solid architecture reminiscent of pre-war comfort and ease. But in the minds of current residents the streets are dangerous and volatile. Lives may be lost there. Muggings occur with some regularity. Cars are broken into for tape decks and other valuables. Occasionally people suffer seemingly meaningless verbal or even physical assaults. For these reasons residents develop a certain ambivalence toward their neighborhood. On the one hand, they know they should distrust it, and they do. But on the other hand, distrusting the area and the people who use it requires tremendous energy. To resolve this problem, they tentatively come to terms with the public areas through trial and error, using them cautiously at first and only slowly developing a measure of trust.

...

Those who rely on a simplistic etiquette of the streets are likely to continue to be ill at ease, because they tend not to pay close attention to the characteristics that identify a suspect as harmless. Rather, they envelop themselves in a protective shell that wards off both attackers and potential black allies, allowing the master status of male gender and black skin to rule. Such people often display tunnel vision with regard to all strangers except those who appear superficially most like themselves in skin color and dress.

This is a narrow and often unsatisfying way to live and to operate in public, and many of those who cannot get beyond stiff rules of etiquette decide in the end to move to safer, less 'tricky' areas. But most people come to realize that street etiquette is only a guide for assessing behavior in public. It is still necessary to develop some strategy for using the etiquette based on one's understanding of the situation.

Once the basic rules of etiquette are mastered and internalized, people can use their observations and experiences to gain insight. In effect, they engage in 'field research'. In achieving the wisdom that every public trial is unique, they become aware that individuals, not types, define specific events. Street wisdom and street etiquette are comparable to a scalpel and a hatchet. One is capable of cutting extremely fine lines between vitally different organs; the other can only make broader, more brutal strokes.

A person who has found some system for categorizing the denizens of the streets and other public spaces must then learn how to distinguish among them, which requires a continuing set of assessments of, or even guesses about, fellow users. The streetwise individual thus becomes interested in a host of signs, emblems, and symbols that others exhibit in everyday life. Besides learning the 'safety signals' a person might display – conservative clothing, a tie, books, a newspaper – he also absorbs the vocabulary and expressions of the street. If he is white, he may learn for the first time to make distinctions among different kinds of black people. He may learn the meaning of certain styles of hats, sweaters, jackets, shoes, and other emblems of the subculture, thus rendering the local environment 'safer' and more manageable.

The accuracy of the reading is less important than the sense of security one derives from feeling that one's interpretation is correct. Through the interpretive process, the person contributes to his working conception of the streets. In becoming a self-conscious and sensitive observer, he becomes the author of his own public actions and begins to act rather than simply to react to situations. For instance, one young white woman had on occasion been confronted and asked for 'loans' by black girls who appeared to 'guard the street' in front of the local high school. One day she decided to turn the tables. Seeing the request coming, she confidently walked up to one of the girls and said, 'I'm out of money. Could you spare me fifty cents?' The young blacks were caught off balance and befuddled. The woman went on, feeling victorious. Occasionally she will gratuitously greet strange men, with similar effect.

A primary motivation for acquiring street wisdom is the desire to have the upper hand. It is generally believed that this will ensure safe passage, allowing one to outwit a potential assailant. In this regard a social game may be discerned. Yet it is a serious game, for failing could mean loss of property, injury, or even death. To prevail means simply to get safely to one's destination, and the ones who are most successful are those who are 'streetwise'. Street wisdom is really street etiquette wisely enacted.

Among the streetwise, there is a common perspective toward street criminals, those who are 'out there' and intent on violating law-abiding citizens. The street criminal is assumed to 'pick his people', knowing who is vulnerable and who is not, causing some people to think that victimization is far from inevitable. This belief gives them confidence on the streets and allows them to feel a measure of control over their own fate. Indeed, avoiding trouble is often, though not always, within the control of the victim. Thus the victim may be blamed, and the streets may be viewed as yielding and negotiable. Consistent with this working conception of street life and crime, the task is to carry oneself in such a way as to ward off danger and be left alone. A chief resource is one's own person – what one displays about oneself. Most important, one must be careful.

Typically, those generally regarded as streetwise are veterans of the public spaces. They know how to get along with strangers, and they understand how to negotiate the streets. They know whom to trust, whom not to trust, what to say through body language or words. They have learned how to behave effectively in public. Probably the most important consideration is the experience they have gained through encounters with 'every kind of stranger.' Although one may know about situations through the reports of friends or relatives, this pales in comparison with actual experience. It is often sheer proximity to the dangerous streets that allows a person to gain street wisdom and formulate some effective theory of the public spaces. As one navigates there is a certain

edge to one's demeanor, for the streetwise person is both wary of others and sensitive to the subtleties that could salvage safety out of danger.

The longer people live in this locale, having to confront problems on the streets and public spaces every day, the greater chance they have to develop a sense of what to do without seriously compromising themselves. Further, the longer they are in the area, the more likely they are to develop contacts who might come to their aid, allowing them to move more boldly.

This self-consciousness makes people likely to be alert and sensitive to the nuances of the environment. More important, they will project their ease and self-assurance to those they meet, giving them the chance to affect the interaction positively. For example, the person who is 'streetdumb,' relying for guidance on the most superficial signs, may pay too much attention to skin color and become needlessly tense just because the person approaching is black. A streetwise white who meets a black person will probably just go about his or her business. In both cases the black person will pick up the 'vibe' being projected – in the first instance fear and hostility, in the second case comfort and a sense of commonality. There are obviously times when the 'vibe' itself could tip the balance in creating the subsequent interaction.

Source: Anderson, 1990, pp.207, 230–33

3.5 James Donald, 'Rationality and enchantment: Paris' (1999)

We find ourselves in the Paris of the second half of the nineteenth century. Or, rather, we find ourselves in the shadowy, textual Paris whose foundations were laid by Walter Benjamin in the researches he undertook in the Bibliothéque Nationale for his Arcades project (*Die Passagen-Werk*) (Benjamin, 1980, p.209). This aspired to offer nothing less than a pre-history of modernity through the imaginative recreation of nineteenth-century Paris. It was an attempt to conjure forth Baudelaire's mythical Paris in order to understand the logic (if that is the right word) of the poetic experience of everyday life in the modern metropolis … Benjamin's ruse was to show that the transformation of the city into spectacle and phantasmagoria was as closely linked to the logic of capitalism as either the concept city of urban reformers or planners like Haussmann, or the hidden misery and squalor uncovered by Engels in industrial

Manchester. His touchstone for understanding the consequences of capitalism for both the fabric and the experience of the metropolis was therefore not the slums, but the arcades: glass-covered, gas-lit 'fairy grottoes' of consumerism that prefigured today's shopping malls. These Benjamin saw as 'the original temple of commodity capitalism'. Their shop windows displayed luxurious commodities like icons in niches. Food, drink, roulette and vaudeville shows were abundantly on offer, and, in the first-floor galleries, sexual pleasures could be bought: 'The windows in the upper floor of the Passages are galleries in which angels are nesting; they are called swallows' (quoted in Buck-Morss, 1989, p.83).

Although never completed, and perhaps too sprawling in its ambition ever to be so, the project's sketches, fragments and ruins have in recent decades become the site of a creative if sometimes frenetic archaeology and architecture. A shanty town of conceptual structures has sprung up among them. In the ramshackle laboratory of *modernity*, the historical consequences of processes of social reconstruction (*modernisation*) are studied: not just new economic practices and political arrangements, but the new techniques of government and even the notion of 'the social' itself … Close by, and possibly linked, stands the sleek playhouse of *modernism*. Here are staged both artistic practices and new forms of social commentary which stand in some critical relation to that modernity (see Tagg, 1992, pp.135–6). Milling around these edifices is a noisy throng of social historians, cultural geographers, sociologists, literary theorists, art historians, feminist critics, and other assorted academic tourists like myself.

Inescapably, we come to this Paris through texts. But Paris also comes to us as already a text. That is not least because its representative figures – and maybe this is one of the things that makes the modern – had themselves already begun to think about the city in that way. Some of these new urbanites and urbanists self-consciously *read* the city to decipher its enigmatic meanings; others attempted to reshape the city to the text of their plans. These figures are social types – the *flâneur*, the administrator, the planner, the artist, the photographer, the detective – but we also ascribe their own names to them: Baudelaire, Haussmann, Manet (see Clark, 1984), Atget, and by now also Benjamin himself.

It is difficult not to be overwhelmed by the ever-growing heaps of text. To pick my way through them, I shall hold onto two threads in my story. One is the question of how the planned modernisation of Paris was conceptualised, and what often unintended consequences the rebuilding of the city has actually had. The other is more methodological: how is it possible to grasp these complex processes?

In attempting to answer either question, the *flâneur* is unavoidable. Even if the figure risks becoming a cliché – sometimes, it seems, little more than a way of claiming a frisson of outlaw glamour for the pedestrian tasks of the sociologist of urban culture – the *flâneur* remains a pivotal term in Benjamin's unfolding project and in his emerging perspective.

In part, the *flâneur* represents one of Benjamin's defining topics; or rather, the figure condenses a number of themes. It stands for a certain historical moment, a social type associated with the period from the Revolution of 1839 to the creation of Haussmann's boulevards and the opening of the first great department stores. It thus also denotes a certain relationship to an intensifying process of commodification. The *flâneur* is a creature first of the arcades themselves, but later, in his twilight, of the stores and the Great Exhibitions which were the commodity's first great cathedrals. But, as an author or journalist, as the writer of *feuilletons* and physiologies, the *flâneur* is himself also locked into an especially insecure form of commodity production; and one that, in selling the urban crowd to a bourgeois audience as a repertoire of vignettes, characters, and caricatures, colludes in the domestication of its dangers. The *flâneur* thus occupies an uncertain social position: sometimes a dandy, an aristocrat or gentleman stylishly on the slide, sometimes a bohemian (here following Frisby, 1985, pp.85–6).

Above all, the *flâneur* embodies a certain perspective on, or experience of, urban space and the metropolitan crowd. In the anonymous ebb and flow of the urban crowd, Baudelaire as *flâneur* felt himself able:

> To be away from home and yet to feel oneself everywhere at home; to see the world, to be at the centre of the world, and yet to remain hidden from the world. The spectator is a *prince* who everywhere rejoices in his incognito.
>
> (quoted in Frisby, 1985, pp.18–19)

The *flâneur* thus combined the passionate wonder of childhood with the analytic sophistication of the man of the world as he read the signs and impressions of 'the outward show of life'. He has to be something of a detective. Otherwise, *flânerie* is no more than gawping.

> In the *flâneur*, the joy of watching is triumphant. It can concentrate on observation; the result is the amateur detective. Or it can stagnate in the gaper; then the *flâneur* has turned into a *badaud*.
>
> (Benjamin, 1973, p.69)

Like other nineteenth-century detectives, Baudelaire adopted other perspectives – or guises – in order to get the correct distance from, and closeness to, the city. Among them were those of the dandy, the whore, and the rag-picker. In these marginal, despised figures, living on their wits and for whom reading the signs of the city right could be a matter of life or death, Baudelaire saw an image of the modern poet's social location and role.

This is where the *flâneur* as a historical figure shades into *flânerie* as critical method. As his researches progressed, Benjamin increasingly narrowed his focus specifically to Baudelaire – that is, a self-conscious theorist of *flânerie* when *flânerie* had already become history – and to the *flâneur* as detective. This is only in part because, as David Frisby argues, the *flâneur*/detective, together with the archaeologist/critical allegorist and the collector/refuse collector, illuminates what Baudelaire was doing when he was botanising on the asphalt of Paris. Above all, these figures are methodological metaphors for Benjamin's own way of working in the Arcades Project. Both Baudelaire and Benjamin watched and interpreted the city: crowds moving through space, architectural and human configurations, signs and images, the sounds and tempi of everyday life. Both also transformed those styles of imagining into distinctive types of texts: Baudelaire's lyrical and prose poetry, Benjamin's poetic journalism and (for all his disavowals) his sociology of urban experience (Frisby, 1994, pp.82–3).

What Benjamin shares with Baudelaire above all is not just a way of seeing the city or a way of experiencing its newness, but a concern with the possibility of representing the space and the temporality of (to use Baudelaire's coinage) *modernité*. This the poet perceived not in grand schemes or epochal changes, but in representational spaces characterised by *le transitoire, le fugitif, le contingent* – what is transitory, fleeting, and contingent. His task as a modern artist was, he believed, to capture 'the ephemeral, contingent newness of the present'. What was new was not the figure of the *flâneur*. It was almost because he knew that the *flâneur* was already an anachronism, because the figure was slightly out of synch with the new city, that it enabled Baudelaire to make sense of the traumatic moment of modernisation he was living through. As the Paris he had known was blasted apart and recreated by Baron Haussmann, he was less interested in predicting the future than in capturing the unintended and unexpected imaginative consequences of the changes.

Haussmann represents, in part at least, a new conception of the city. In the second half of the nineteenth century onwards, the modernisation of the great Western metropolises was characterised, physically, by the spectacular redesign of city centres and the growth of residential suburbs. An early embodiment of de Certeau's planner as *dieu voyeur*, Haussmann saw Paris largely as a space for economic exploitation – his projects fuelled a boom in property speculation on the grand scale – and a space that needed to be opened up for effective circulation and communication.

What impact did this way of seeing the city have on the physical fabric of Paris? Haussmann was appointed as Napoleon III's prefect of the Seine in 1853. By 1870, when he was dismissed for dodgy wheeling and dealing to finance his projects, he had got rid of the medieval walls that had surrounded the city, one-fifth of the streets in central Paris were his creation, and the acreage of the city had been doubled by annexation. At the height of the reconstruction, one in five Parisian workers was employed in the building trade. In the name of slum clearance, some 350,000 people (on Haussmann's own estimation) were displaced from the *quartiers* of old Paris to make way for his new boulevards, parks and 'pleasure grounds'. The boulevards, lined by the uniform facades of new apartment blocks, created unprecedented urban vistas which had in part a pedagogic purpose. They were interspersed by national monuments, which Haussmann had studiously excised from their original context and functions and placed strategically as ornamental fragments and focal points in the new landscape. Equally important was the creation of the physical infrastructure to sustain the new developments. A hundred miles from Paris, aqueducts were laid to improve the city's tap-water supply. New lenses were fitted on the gas lamps. The great collector sewer and a new morgue were opened. An outer circle of railways surrounded the city, and a ring of stations acted as city gates. Haussmann broke the monopoly of the cab company in 1866, and promoted that of the makers of street lamps in 1856 (Clark, 1984, pp.37–8; Buck-Morss, 1989, pp.89–90; Boyer, 1994, p.195).

The purpose of Haussmannisation were, naturally, complex and sometimes contradictory. There was certainly an element of Saint-Simonian utopianism in the 'concept city' of Haussmann and Napoleon III. They wanted to create a clean, light and airy city protected by policemen and night patrols. They wanted to provide trees, schools, hospitals, cemeteries, bus shelters, and public urinals (for men at least). As I have suggested, though, the needs of commerce and social control were probably more powerful motives. What Haussmann understood by a modern city was one designed to allow the most efficient circulation of goods, people, money, and troops. Famously, the boulevards provided the shortest routes between the barracks and working-class districts.

What, then, were the social consequences of Haussmannisation? Insofar as Haussmann's schemes reflected the logic of the stock market and commerce rather than that of the factory and its disciplines, they were based on a static conception of both urban space and the social relations of the city. In that sense, they represented an already archaic reading of the city (Rabinow, 1989, p.77). Although he could understand the political, economic and technological problems of Paris, Haussmann did not think in the emerging social terms of technocratic and administrative rationality. He did not understand the social logic of the concern with the welfare, morality and efficiency of an urban population which reforming administrators like Kay-Shuttleworth and Chadwick were already putting into practice in England.

One result was to intensify the misery of the population displaced by his schemes. However egalitarian the new public spaces of boulevards and parks may have appeared, the practical effect was to raze working-class neighbourhoods and shift the eyesores and health hazards of poverty to the suburbs. In Paris, Engels saw the division between bourgeois show and working-class squalor that he had observed in Manchester being repeated. In Manchester the split had been a by-product of capitalist industrialisation. Here it had become a matter of policy. He commented on 'the method called "Haussmann"' in his 1872 pamphlet, *The Housing Question*.

> I mean the practice, which has now become general, of making breaches in working-class quarters of our big cities, especially in those that are centrally situated. ... The result is everywhere the same: the most scandalous alleys and lanes disappear, to the accompaniment of lavish self-glorification by the bourgeoisie on account of this tremendous success – but they appear at once somewhere else, and often in the immediate neighbourhood.
>
> (Engels, 1955, pp.559,606–9; cited in
> Berman, 1983, p.153)

Even for more bourgeois Parisians, the benefits of Haussmann's carefully planned upheavals were ambivalent. Many complained that he had created an artificial city in which they no longer felt at home. The boulevards, parks, and other new public spaces created a backdrop against which the worlds of rich and poor – supposedly cordoned off from each other – now became more visible to each other, if no more legible. Even his 'strategic beautification' proved of limited value when barricades appeared across his boulevards in the Paris Commune of 1870.

What fascinated Benjamin in this new city – and this is what he was trying to get at by adopting Baudelaire as his surrogate – was the way that the displacements brought about by Haussmannisation lent a fantastic and elusive quality to life in the city. The arcades may have been waning in popularity as the Second Empire progressed, but it was during this period that the urban phantasmagoria they represented burst out of these confines and spread

across Paris. Giant advertising hoardings began to appear, creating a new layer of visual textuality in the city. Commodity displays became ever more grandiose and impossible to ignore.

This ostentation reached its public peak in a series of world expositions inspired by London's Crystal Palace in 1851. The Paris expositions were staged in 1855, 1867, 1889 and 1900. Industrial products and machine technologies were displayed like artworks. They were set off against ornamental gardens, statues, and fountains. Military canons were juxtaposed with fashion costumes in a dazzling fantasy world. The fairs also left permanent traces on the city landscape: the Grand Palais, Trocadero, and the Eiffel Tower were built for them.

In these international fairs Benjamin saw the origins of a pleasure industry which developed advertising techniques skilfully calibrating spectacle and fantasy to the tastes and dreams of a mass audience. In a magnified version of the *flâneur's* window shopping, their message was: 'Look, but don't touch.' The crowds were taught to derive pleasure from the spectacle alone. At these fairs, buying and selling were less significant than their function as fantastic metropolitan folk festivals of capitalism. Here mass entertainment itself became big business (Buck-Morss, 1989, pp.83–6).

A more enduring legacy of this realignment of urbanity as commodity fetishism was the department store. This has been presented as both the culmination and the final undoing of *flânerie*. One of the characteristics of the *flâneur's* ambiguous relationship with streets and crowds, and one of the reasons for his affinity with the arcades, was that both entailed a blurring of boundaries between outside and inside. 'The appearance of the street as an *intérieur* in which the phantasmagoria of the *flâneur* is concentrated is hard to separate from the gaslight', writes Benjamin (Buck-Morss, 1989, p.50).

> The crowd was the veil from behind which the familiar city as phantasmagoria beckoned to the *flâneur*. In it, the city was now landscape, now a room.
>
> (Benjamin, 1973, p.170)

The glass coverings and gas lamps of the arcades reclaimed for artifice a space which was nonetheless *outside* in the sense of being *public*. With the coming of the department store, however, the ambivalence between landscape and room, between exterior and interior that had defined *flânerie* in its pure form – which translates, although Benjamin does not confront this, as its masculine form – is resolved on the side of room, interior, commodity, the feminine.

If the arcade is the classical form of the *intérieur,* which is how the *flâneur* sees the street, the department store is the form of the *intérieur's* decay. The bazaar is the last hang-out of the *flâneur.* If in the beginning the street had become an *intérieur* for him, now this *intérieur* turned into a street, and he roamed through the labyrinth of merchandise as he had once roamed through the labyrinth of the city.

(Benjamin, 1973, p.54)

The department store was undoubtedly a symptom of the decline of the *flâneur.* No great cause for mourning there. But what if the stronger argument is right: that the department store was an institution created to invent the *flâneuse?* Does this make it possible to rescue a female version of the type from invisibility? Or does it confirm that the *flâneur* as historical figure was both empirically and axiomatically male, at least until new public spaces like the department store and the cinema enabled women to appear safely and respectably in public by reconfiguring the boundaries of outside/inside and public/private (see Friedberg, 1993; Hansen, 1991)? Put like that, it may not seem terribly important. What matters more, perhaps, is that the remapping of urban modernity around the spatialisation of sexual difference undercuts any easy equation between public, outside and masculine and then the opposition of this chain of equivalencies to domestic/inside/feminine. That, in turn, does not mean that men and women have been able to move through urban landscapes and to occupy rooms in the same way. But it is less a question of barred spaces and sexually inflected repertoires of public, private, or intimate behaviour and performance.[1]

What does the question of the sexually differentiated experience of space have to do with Haussmann's grand designs? My argument has been that, whatever their economic and social purposes, the effect of Haussmann's metropolis on the mental life of Parisians was to produce (as just one retrospectively comprehensible but unpredictable example) Baudelaire's spleen. Parisians did not necessarily grasp or accept the pedagogy of the boulevards. More significant, perhaps, were the exacerbated divisions between centre and suburb, and so between public and home. New means of transport, new modes of communication, and new forms of entertainment engendered perceptual and psychological changes through their reconfigurations of time and space. In such ways, the landscape,

rhythms and dynamism of the city became internalised. Modern consciousness became urban consciousness (Sharpe and Wallock, 1987, p.13; Williams, 1973, p.235). Inner space cannot be securely separated from the space of the streets. And vice versa. That is why the experience of ourselves as sexual beings, supposedly our most intimate sense of ourselves, both inflects and absorbs the way we walk the streets.

This modernist conception of the self helps to explain the impossibility of governmentalist attempts to manage the conduct and welfare of potentially insurrectionary urban populations by reorganising and regulating space. Whenever modernisers have sought to impose the rationality of the 'concept city' on urban life, *flâneurs*, artists and the rest of us have systematically re-enchanted their creations: as comic parade, as sexual display, as hellish dream-world, or simply as home. This is one of the key lessons from Benjamin. He perceived enchantment not only in the spectacular or mysterious aspects of Paris. Myth even whispered its presence to him in the most rationalised urban plans that, 'with their uniform streets and endless rows of buildings, have realised the dreamed-of architecture of the ancients: the labyrinth' (Buck-Morss, 1989, pp.253–4).

Notes

1 The literature on this topic is now extensive. See, for example, Janet Wolff (1985, 1994); Griselda Pollock (1988); Elizabeth Wilson (1991); Anne Friedberg (1993); Rachel Bowlby (1985); Mica Nava (1996); Anke Gleber (1997), pp.67–88.

References

Benjamin, W. (1973) *Charles Baudelaire: A Lyric Poet in the Era of High Capitalism,* London, New Left Books.

Benjamin, W. (1980) 'A short history of photography' in Trachtenberg, A. (ed.) *Classic Essays in Photography*, New Haven, CT, Leete's Island Books.

Berman, M. (1983) *All That Is Solid Melts into Air: The Experience of Modernity,* London, Verso.

Bowlby, R. (1985) *Just Looking: Consumer Culture in Dreiser, Gissing and Zola,* London, Methuen.

Boyer, M.C. (1994) *The City of Collective Memory: Its Historical Imaginary and Architectural Entertainments,* Cambridge, MA, MIT Press.

Buck-Morss, S. (1989) *The Dialectics Seeing: Walter Benjamin and the Arcades Project,* Cambridge, MA, MIT Press.

Clark, T.J. (1984) *The Painting of Modern Life: Paris in the Art of Manet and his Followers*, London, Thames and Hudson.

Engels, F. (1955) *Marx-Engels Selected Works*, 2 vols, Moscow.

Friedberg, A. (1993) *Window Shopping: Cinema and the Postmodern*, Berkeley, CA, University of California Press.

Frisby, D. (1985) *Fragments of Modernity*, Cambridge, Polity Press.

Frisby, D. (1994) 'The *flâneur* in social theory' in Tester, K. (ed.) *op. cit.*.

Gleber, A. (1997) 'Female flânerie and the *Symphony of the City* ' in von Ankum, K. (ed.) *Women in the Metropolis: Gender and Modernity in Weimar Culture*, Berkeley, CA, University of California Press.

Hansen, M. (1991) *Babel and Babylon: Spectatorship in American Silent Film,* Cambridge, MA, Harvard University Press.

Nava, M. (1996) 'Modernity's disavowal' in Nava, M. and O'Shea, A. (eds) *Modern Times: Reflections on a Century of English Modernity,* London, Routledge.

Pollock, G. (1988) 'Modernity and the spaces of femininity' in *Vision and Difference: Femininity, Feminism and Histories of Art*, London, Routledge.

Rabinow, P. (1989) *French Modern: Norms and Forms of Social Environment,* Cambridge, MA, MIT Press.

Sharpe, W. and Wallock, L. (eds) (1987) *Vision of the Modern City*, Baltimore, MD, Johns Hopkins University Press.

Tagg, J. (1992) *Grounds of Dispute: Art History, Cultural Politics and the Discursive Field*, Minneapolis, MN, University of Minnesota Press.

Tester. J. (ed.) (1994) *Flâneur*, London, Routledge.

Williams, R. (1973) *The Country and the City,* London, Chatto and Windus.

Wilson, E. (1991) *The Sphinx in the City,* London, Virago.

Wolff, J. (1985) 'The invisible *flâneuse*: women and the literature of modernity', *Theory, Culture and Society*, vol. 2, no. 3. (Reprinted in her *Feminine Sentences*, Cambridge, Polity Press, 1990).

Wolff, J. (1994) 'The artist and the *flâneur*' in Tester, J. (ed.) *op. cit.*.

Source: Donald, 1999, pp.42–51

Everyday life and the economy

Celia Lury

Contents

1 Introduction

In opening her book on *Home and Work*, Christena Nippert-Eng asks the reader to 'consider your keys; calendars; purse and/or wallet contents; commuting, drinking, and reading habits; your lunchtime and vacation plans; the photographs in your living room and work space; and the people with whom you socialize' (1996, p.xi). These everyday items, she suggests, have one thing in common. They are dimensions through which each of us draws the line between home and work: 'Often practical yet eminently symbolic, publicly visible yet intimately revealing, these are the kinds of things with which each of us places a mental, physical, and behavioral boundary between these two realms' (*ibid.*). Boundary drawing – what Nippert-Eng describes as the 'never-ending, hands-on, largely invisible process through which boundaries are negotiated, placed, maintained, and transformed by individuals over time' – is fundamental to the process of creating classifications. And as Nippert-Eng's examples show, while boundaries may be purely conceptual, they often also reflect and result in physical forms, in objects and everyday practices and rituals that reinforce and make visible the categories they create. In other words, by shaping the very ways we think about and act toward each other and things, classificatory boundaries are an essential element of social life. This is because placing lines here or there has definite implications for how we treat each other and the world around us. In drawing boundaries, we perpetuate a particular way of thinking, and enact our membership of distinctive social groups.

This chapter will consider how *boundary work* shapes our participation in, and understanding of, the economy. Historically, this participation has involved a complex set of relationships between work, leisure, consumption, property, and money (among other things!). In considering these changing relationships, particular attention will be paid to the boundaries we draw in **time** space and, especially, **time**. We will explore how boundaries in space and time – drawn through practices, rituals and objects – enable us to bridge and divide everyday life and the economy. Of course, it is not possible to consider all these boundaries here. So the second half of the chapter will explore the boundaries that are drawn by the consumer brand (the name and symbolic associations given to a specific product or service by a company to differentiate it from others), and the increasing availability of credit. These examples have been chosen both for what they reveal in general about the interrelationship between the economy and everyday life, and because they shed some light on a particular thesis we will explore: namely, that everyday life is increasingly being made into a resource for the economy.

But first, to give you some idea of how this attention to boundary work might be revealing, let us consider the example of 'the break' as described by Nippert-Eng:

> Whether for coffee, lunch or vacation, any formal break in the workday or work year provides an opportunity to demarcate public and private time. In fact, it actually encourages us to do so. However, just because an organizational break policy entitles or even encourages a worker to make this distinction does not mean he or she must. The choices individuals make on how to spend their breaks tell a great deal about if and where they draw the line between their 'work' and 'personal' lives.

Historically, segmentist assumptions underlie the very idea of 'taking a break' in today's workplace. Marx describes the temporal dynamics of the segmentist contract, which hinges on the exchange of labor for a specific amount of time and money. The time encompassed by the workday is sold by the laborer to the employer and transformed into more 'public' time for the duration. The workday thus becomes time during which we are officially accountable to the people we work for. During 'breaks', however, we temporarily repossess that time. When we 'take a break' (i.e., take our time back from an employer), time becomes personal or 'private' (Zerubavel, 1985) again for a short, predetermined period of relative unaccountability.

C. Wright Mills describes a historical alternative to this segmentist view of a work 'break' (1956, pp.215–38). The 'craftsman' neither distinguishes between the realms of private and public interests nor the time in which they are pursued in the way of the modern, segmenting wage worker. The integrative life of the 'craftsman' thus manifests in a more integrative view of work 'breaks', where neither this pocket of time nor that which surrounds it are so distinct. Rather than seeing breaks as a qualitatively, diametrically opposite kind of time, the 'craftsman' sees a break only as a temporary reprieve from a specific task. The craftsperson seeks a refreshing, relaxing opportunity away from the work at hand in order to return to it with renewed vigor and insight and do it right, which might even be achieved by turning to another work task for a while.

(Nippert-Eng, 1996, p.91)

Nippert-Eng points here to the ways in which breaks may not only mark a distinction in time, but do so in ways that help structure the experience of what they divide. The craftsman, she suggests, takes a break that is integrally linked to the nature of the task in which he or she is engaged; it may not even be a break from work as such, but rather a change of task, a shift in orientation, an interlude in which the worker is refreshed. In what she calls a segmentist orientation, in contrast, the worker draws a sharp distinction between work and non-work, seeing the two as irreconcilable. Non-work is viewed as an escape, perhaps an entrée into an alternative, private realm, or perhaps nothing more than the dregs of the day, as residual or left-over time.

Nippert-Eng suggests that how we take breaks is a matter of choice, and explicitly says that she does not 'mean to equate more "segmented" home-work juxtapositions with [the] alienated worker and meaningless work' (1996, p.92). So, for example, in the place of work she studied, a research laboratory in the north-east United States (what she calls the Lab), she found a number of individuals who were able to exercise considerable autonomy at work, but nevertheless chose to make clear distinctions between home and work. However, the ability to choose how to draw boundaries between home and work is not always equally available to everyone. Instead, as we shall see, the terms of existence of formally recognized breaks are closely tied to historical shifts in the economy and for most people are a matter of constraint as much as choice.

ACTIVITY 1

Do you personally draw a boundary (or boundaries) between work and home?

In thinking about this question, you may need to reflect on who it is that is most able to draw a distinction between home and work. Many women, for example, find it hard to draw a clear-cut distinction between work and home since they typically do most, if not all, of the housework and/or look after children in the home – either as well as or instead of paid work. In these circumstances it is very hard to draw any boundaries between work and home at all; instead it may be important to draw a boundary between such activities and time out, time for oneself, even if the resulting breaks are few and far between.

Taking the examples that Nippert-Eng mentions – 'your keys; calendars; purse and/ or wallet contents; commuting, drinking, and reading habits; your lunchtime and vacation plans; the photographs in your living room and work space; and the people with whom you socialize' – ask yourself how each item/practice marks a boundary between work and home (or work and non-work).

For example:

- Do you keep all your keys on one key-ring?

- Do you have more than one diary or calendar? Where is it/are they kept? What events do you record on it/them? Do you share a calendar with others? Who?

- What do you keep in your purse/wallet?

- Do you travel to work? If so, how? Do you have any rituals connected to your journey? Are they different on the way home from work than on the way in?

Note that your boundary work may involve both dividing and bridging strategies. It is also very likely that you will draw the boundary between work and home (if you do so at all) in a number of different ways and at a number of different points during the day.

- What does the way in which you draw these boundaries say about your experience of work and home?

- Are these boundaries the result of your choices?

Of course, much of the discussion above presumes that there *is* a separation between work and home. And certainly the presumption of such a separation has been fundamental to many understandings of the economy since the industrial revolution, with the economy seen to be restricted to the activities carried out in dedicated workplaces. However, while empirical studies suggest that such a separation does exist for many people, it is not absolute, and only ever applies to a greater or lesser extent. Nevertheless, as Chapter 1 describes, it is a separation that has had enormous significance for the characteristics of everyday life which are often defined in opposition to work. The separation between work and home is in part marked by the social organization of space, with the historical emergence of a clear spatial differentiation between places of work and the household occurring as agricultural workers were drawn into cities to become wage labourers. However, even this separation was only ever clear-cut for some social groups, since for many people the household continued to be a place of work. Many working-class women, for example, were employed in the homes of the middle classes as well as working in their own home in the nineteenth and early twentieth centuries, and the household still continues today to be a place of (paid and unpaid) work for many women, both working and middle class, for most of their lives.

In addition to this spatial distinction, the separation between home and work is also marked by boundaries drawn in time. Indeed, the changing terms of the temporal boundaries drawn between work and non-work have helped form our understandings of the economy and the everyday as much as the spatial boundaries just mentioned. Consider, for example, what Henri Lefebvre has to say about temporality in relation to the everyday:

> Everyday life is made of recurrences: gestures of labour and leisure, mechanical movements both human and properly mechanic, hours, days, weeks, months, years, linear and cyclical repetitions, natural and rational time, etc.; the study of creative activity (of *production*, in its widest sense) leads to the study of re-production or the conditions in which actions producing objects and labour are re-produced, re-commenced, and re-assume their component proportions or, on the contrary, undergo gradual or sudden modifications.
>
> (Lefebvre, 1971, p.18; emphasis in original)

Here Lefebvre points to what he considers a central, defining characteristic of modern everyday life: the inevitability of recurrence. He does so in such a way as to highlight the dependence of modern industrial production on re-production. This is important to Lefebvre since he believes that this dependence is often obscured in many understandings of the economic, which focus exclusively on production. In contrast to these views, Lefebvre insists upon the importance of reproduction (not only the reproduction of the next generation of workers but also the reproduction of workers on a daily basis) and the recurrences of everyday life for the economy. However, this emphasis on recurrence does not prevent Lefebvre from acknowledging the profound transformations in temporality associated with the changing boundaries between home and work. Instead it allows him to highlight the complex interrelationship between the rhythms of the everyday and the temporality of the economy, and to recognize that each is dependent on the other. In the following section, this interrelationship will be explored historically.

AIMS

The aims of this chapter are:

1　To place the relationships between everyday life and the economy in a historical perspective.

2　To consider the role which changes in the organization of boundary relationships of space and time play in the context of broader transformations in the relationships between everyday life and the economy.

3　To examine how contemporary forms of consumer branding and contemporary forms of credit effect a distinctive organization of the relations betweeen the time of everyday life and that of the economy.

4　To review the extent to which, as a consequence of these developments, everyday life is increasingly being made into a resource for the economy.

2 The economy, time and everyday life

In a pioneering article entitled 'Time, work-discipline, and industrial capitalism', the social historian E.P. Thompson provides a powerful analysis of the importance of the boundaries drawn in time for the early stages of the emergence of modern capitalism. He shows that as a consequence of a variety of factors – 'the division of labour; the supervision of labour; fines; bells and clocks; money incentives; preachings and schoolings; the suppression of fairs and sports – new labour habits were formed, and a new time-discipline was imposed' during the eighteenth and nineteenth centuries (1967, p.90). He notes that time *sense* and time *keeping* developed in tandem. 'There was', he says, 'a general diffusion of clocks and watches occurring at the exact moment when the industrial revolution demanded a greater synchronization of labour'. Additionally, time-clocks and punch-cards were used to facilitate workers' growing awareness of the duration and exchange value of time (the **'labour theory of value'**). Thompson's concern is to show that the real novelty of the industrial revolution is not so much a strengthening of external compulsion, as the elimination of the pattern of work and leisure that obtained before industrialism. He argues that the disciplines of the industrial workplace created needs for the self-regimentation of labour through a prior restructuring of time itself. In short, he suggests that the emergence of new forms of boundary work led to a new understanding of temporality, what he calls *clock time*.

labour theory of value

More particularly, Thompson shows that agricultural-turned-manufacturing workers had to abandon what he called a 'task' orientation to work. This orientation is similar to the approach described above by Nippert-Eng as that of the craftsman. It is an independent, autonomous approach to work in which tasks are tended to in their own time, within the demands of the day and the constraints of the season. In its place, early manufacturing workers were required to adopt a 'time' orientation to work, in which the arbitrary divisions of clock time mandated the way workers approached and scheduled work tasks. Simultaneously, workers were required to subordinate the routines of the home and the community to the demands of the workplace (although it is in this regard that Thompson has been criticized for his failure to acknowledge the ways in which clock time was experienced differently by men and women (Glucksmann, 2000)).

ACTIVITY 2

Summarize what you see as the main differences between task and time orientations.

For Thompson, 'task' versus 'time' orientation is one of the most profound points of distinction between pre- and post-manufacturing everyday lives. It extends the transformation of labour into a commodity, as time becomes the medium through which labour is translated into an abstract exchange value, something that may be exchanged on the market for other commodities. Clock time is thus fundamental to the exchange between work and money, and to the development of a capitalist economy. Its logic leads to later ideas about the body, motion and productivity, encapsulated by the time and motion management practices devised most famously by Frederick Winslow Taylor, and that gave rise to the

scientific management movement of the early twentieth century. These practices were intended to transform the administration of the workplace on a more scientific basis so as to increase efficiency and profitability.

Inevitably, the transformation Thompson describes involved a profound shift in values. Puritanism, or more specifically, the **Protestant ethic**, is seen by many to be of fundamental importance in this respect. As Thompson puts it,

> Puritanism, in its marriage of convenience with industrial capitalism, was the agent which converted men to new valuations of time; which taught children even in their infancy to improve each shining hour; and which saturated men's minds with the equation, time is money.
>
> (Thompson, 1967, p.95)

As theorized by the sociologist **Max Weber** (1904–05/1930), Protestants were subject to a 'salvational anxiety', since their salvation was not tied to the institutionalized means of grace found in the Catholic Church. However, this anxiety could be alleviated by self-control, deferred gratification and hard work as such qualities were believed to be a sign of election for salvation. In this changing religious and cultural context, the idleness of the workforce came to be identified as a major problem, and Thompson gives numerous examples of moral tracts produced during the early stages of the industrial revolution that exhorted the worker to make productive use of every waking hour. What is at issue here, from our point of view, however, is how the redrawing of boundaries in time and space had significant effects for the interrelationship of the economy and everyday life. With the rise of clock time, a temporal grid began to settle on activities in the workplace, requiring paid workers to manage their own time in relation to the abstract divisions of clock time.

But by the nineteenth and twentieth centuries, it is fatigue, rather than idleness, that comes to be the problem for industrialists. There was a complex set of reasons for this shift, involving as it did a shift in belief of 'the infirmity of the spirit to the infirmity of the body' (Rabinbach, 1992, p.290), as the role played by religious belief in the new work ethic gradually came to be overlain by the principles of scientific management. In contrast to traditional liberalism that had promoted unstinting effort and efficiency as the preferred solution to poverty (the view that initially underpinned the work ethic), the new social liberalism of the nineteenth century substituted a *calculus of energetics*. This was a set of beliefs focused on the body in which workers were encouraged not only to expend their energies, but also to conserve and replenish them according to a complex set of calculations. It assumed a view of the body as a human motor and required the rational deployment of the body's forces in the interest of productivity. Importantly, in this calculus, the economies of motion and the conservation of the energies of the working body held the key not only to greater productivity, but also to progress and social justice, for they would lead to the physical and moral improvement of the economy and the workforce. Thus, the nineteenth and twentieth centuries saw the increasing expansion and rationalization of leisure activities and the growing institutionalization of the right to holidays alongside the organization of the workplace. In other words, the time of non-work was also coming to be more and more directly regulated by the requirements of production.

What has been suggested so far, then, is that the drawing of boundaries in time and space have enormous implications for the interrelationship between everyday life and the economy. In early industrial societies, industrial time set the rhythm of the work cycle, and leisure was rendered residual. As such, it was recognized as the marker of time left over from work, as an activity produced by work, and justified by work. However, leisure and consumption increasingly became the site for the commodification and rationalization of time and space in their own right during the nineteenth and twentieth centuries. And it is the result of the new kinds of boundary work involved in these processes that will be explored in the next sections. The thesis to be considered is whether the practices of everyday life are increasingly incorporated into the economy. A detailed discussion of two examples will be presented to explore this suggestion. First, we will look at the development of the brand as one example of how the contemporary economy draws upon the objects, routines and recurrences of everyday life. Second, we will consider how the extension of credit associated with the huge increase in the number and range of goods available for purchase may be transforming the temporality of both the economy and everyday life. In both cases, what is of interest to us are the particular ways in which the contemporary economy and everyday life are interdependent, and whether and how everyday life is constituted as a resource for the economy.

SUMMARY OF SECTION 2

This section has:

1   outlined the importance of boundaries in time and space for the interrelationship between everyday life and the economy;

2   introduced the concept of 'clock time' and illustrated its significance in the emergence of industrial capitalism;

3   outlined the historical links between the Protestant ethic and understandings of the relationship between work and reward.

3 The objectification of everyday life

In a discussion of everyday life in the second half of the twentieth century, Henri Lefebvre comments,

> ... the most remarkable aspect of the transition we are living through is not so much the passage from want to affluence as the passage from labour to leisure. We are undergoing the uneasy mutation of our major 'values', the mutation of an epoch.

> Who can deny that leisure is acquiring an ever increasing importance in France and in all so-called industrial societies? The stress of 'modern life' makes amusements, distractions and relaxation a necessity, as the theoreticians of leisure with their following of journalists and popularizers never tire of repeating.
>
> (Lefebvre, 1971, pp.52–3)

He goes on to argue that what has changed is that leisure is no longer simply marked by being that which is not work; instead leisure has become an organized display, a site of rationalization and commodification in its own right. This, he believes, is one of the important transformations of the second half of the twentieth century. Lefebvre suggests that if people were to produce timetables of their activities, three categories of time would emerge: pledged time (work), free time (leisure) and compulsive time (demands other than work), and that the latter increasingly encroaches on both the other two, especially the second.

READING 4.1

Now read the extract from Henri Lefebvre's *Everyday Life in the Modern World*, which you will find reproduced as Reading 4.1 at the end of the chapter.

When you have done so, consider the following questions:

1 Why does Lefebvre argue that the term 'consumer society' is not adequate to describe modern society?

2 What does Lefebvre suggest is involved in the 'objectification' of everyday life?

In this provocative, polemical extract, Lefebvre argues that the relationship between work and leisure has undergone a profound transformation. In the reconfiguration of the calculus of energetics that emerged in the nineteenth century, leisure is no longer a reward for work done, but neither is it a freely chosen activity. Instead, Lefebvre suggests that leisure itself is increasingly rationalized, and that this rationalization requires a greater penetration of everyday life. So, for example, he notes that the boundary between work and home becomes ever more permeable, and the practices of everyday life are reflexively incorporated into an organized **consumer society** in the activities of compulsive time (of which even holidays may be seen as an example). As Lefebvre sees it, the impetus for this process of the colonization of everyday life is the capitalist imperative for profit. He concludes that everyday life, rather than work, has become the key site for the reproduction of capitalism and is thus a kind of internal colony.

consumer society

Of special concern to Lefebvre, here, are the ways in which the practices of everyday life are recorded, classified and used as the basis of further product development in the practices of market research. In this process, Lefebvre believes, the practices of everyday life are dis-embedded and acquire an objectivity, that is, a fixed and abstract character, that obscures their subjective meaning. Many of you will have participated in market research yourself, whether knowingly, by participating in focus groups or answering survey questions in the street, or unknowingly, as when you provide details of your occupation, family and ownership of other products on guarantee forms. Indeed, providing such information is now a common feature of many routine activities. Moreover, as the article below indicates, market researchers do not only rely upon information collected through surveys, but also conduct research within the sites of everyday life. For Lefebvre the collection and use of such information in market research does not enhance the heterogeneity or inventiveness of everyday life; instead, it standardizes, regulates and fixes it.

Read the account in Box 4.1 of the research conducted in Culture Lab, an experimental consumer research department run by Siamack Salari in the UK advertising agency BMP DDB. One of the interesting issues that it raises is the relationship between social science and market research.

1   How is 'the everyday' understood here? How does this understanding compare with those to which you have been introduced so far?

2   What research methods are described here? What similarities and differences can you identify in the methods described here and those adopted in qualitative social science studies of consumption and everyday life? Perhaps some of the differences are to do with how the everyday is already defined in relation to consumption and the brand? Are there also differences in the uses of the knowledge gained?

BOX 4.1

Culture Lab is a context-based observation research unit. Our premise is that no action or occasion can be understood in isolation or as a discrete event. Context is the unexplored frontier in marketing services. Consumers are increasingly unpredictable and less likely to be persuaded by advertisers' messages. Their responses to brands are more likely to be based on how they relate to family and friends, and the contexts in which they encounter goods. By gathering this data, we can tell our clients how their brands fit into people's lives and how their brand values are interpreted.

Our method is to set up relationships with individuals and households, documenting the random and inconsequential instances of their daily lives, to build up a picture of them as consumers. Subjects are also given cameras and encouraged to film themselves. Because we do not describe our findings as objective, they are made as transparent as possible to both client and subject. Households are actively involved in the research process, and the researcher becomes a participant in the process of discovery. The emphasis with observational research is to keep the subjects as animated and comfortable as possible. Their behaviour is affected by the presence of the observers, but the way we explore decision-making processes is by telling households, at opportune moments, about their own habits and traits.

The home is where most happens. We cook, write shopping lists, save vouchers sent by post, plan our finances, read magazines, watch television and discuss the near and distant future with our families and friends. The home, therefore, is a decision-making backdrop against which most buying choices can be understood. It is impossible to explain a mode of behaviour without understanding its context.

A tired parent may choose a frozen or ready meal to prepare for the family after a hard day. Only, before she places it in the oven, she adds her own grated cheese, some extra pepper, onion or tomato. By the time the pizza is ready, the preparation time is the same as it would have been to make it from scratch. The reality of the scenario is that her choice took her less thinking time, but her actions personalised the family meal.

Home is also where we organise our relationship with brands, and each household has a nerve centre for the management of this – by the phone, on a pin board, where the bills and money-off vouchers are kept. It is where we choose to read or throw away junk mail. Whatever the location, it is here we can discover an individual's brand preferences and observe decisions being made that the buyer may not be conscious of when acting on them.

Sometimes the most insightful data comes in the form of stories that we are told concerning a particular subject. These can be sad, funny, angry ones or even lies. They reveal an enormous amount about an individual and his or her realities; the way we perceive the world around us. We observe activities and naturally occurring conversations in order to decode everyday behaviour and understand how brands fit into people's lives. Brands are like chess pieces – the moves we make with them are an indication of our relationship to others.

Source: Salari in Pavitt, 2000, pp.106–7

In making his argument about the objectification of everyday life, Lefebvre develops the view that industrial production is increasingly controlled by consumer demand. In using this term he does not mean to imply that production is user-led. (It is precisely because he does not that he refuses to accept the description 'consumer society'.) Instead he is at pains to point out that what is involved in the increasing emphasis placed on 'demand' (a construct of modern economic practices) is the management of everyday life. He identifies the importance of market research in this regard, arguing that this research is concerned only with the identification of problems to which consumer goods and services can be developed as solutions. Such a process, he suggests, is entirely inadequate to identify the social needs peculiar to modern existence. And he also argues that a further effect of the processes of market research is their impact back on the needs and desires that they are supposedly intended to describe: freezing behaviours, itemizing lifestyles and reifying identities. This reaction contributes to a 'flattening out' of the qualitative distinctions previously existing in everyday life:

Everyday life has become an object of consideration and is the province of organization; the space–time of voluntary programmed self-regulation, because when properly organized it provides a closed circuit (production–consumption–production), where demands are foreseen because they are induced and desires are run to earth; this method replaces the spontaneous self-regulation of the competitive era.

(Lefebvre, 1971, p.72)

In what follows, we will consider this thesis of the objectification of everyday life in more detail and focus, in particular, on whether objects are increasingly being 'emptied out' of broader meaning. The case we will consider is that of the brand.

SUMMARY OF SECTION 3

This section has:

1   outlined the argument that leisure has become the site of commodification and rationalization, so changing the relationship between everyday life and the economy;

2   explored the importance of the construct of 'consumer demand' as part of this process of commodification by looking at the practices of market research.

4 The brand and the objectification of everyday life

In the introduction to a recent book on brands, the editor claims:

> From cornflakes to cars, our daily lives are increasingly dominated by branded goods and brand names; the brand is the prefix, the qualifier of character. The symbolic associations of the brand name are often used in preference to the pragmatic description of a useful object. We speak of 'the old Hoover', 'my new Audi' or 'my favourite Levi's' – not needing to qualify them with an object description. The brand is at the heart of this process for many of the goods we buy and sell. The concept of the brand is central to our society.
>
> (Pavitt, 2000, p.16)

The suggestion here is that the brand dominates our everyday lives in unnoticed ways, inserting itself into mundane activities, even replacing previous relations with objects based on use with its own set of symbolic associations. But is this so?

ACTIVITY 4

Taking one of your kitchen, bathroom or bedroom, itemize all (or up to 10 of) the branded objects in the room.

In relation to each item, ask yourself, as was done in an old advertisement for a soap powder, would you be willing to exchange it for that of a leading rival? If not, why not?

Simmel, Georg

To try to understand the centrality of the brand today, it is helpful to look at the work of the early twentieth-century sociologist **Georg Simmel**, in which he addresses the ever more rapid circulation of subjects and objects in the increasingly abstract space of the market. For Simmel, all societies may be characterized in terms of what he calls an *objective culture* and a *subjective culture*, the first of which refers to the systematic relations between objects while the second refers to the cultivation of subjects. In Simmel's eyes, these two cultures are neither symmetrical nor analogous. In modern industrial societies objective culture is in some sense autonomous from, and more developed than, subjective culture:

> Particularly in periods of social complexity and an extensive division of labour, the accomplishments of [objective] culture come to constitute an autonomous realm, so to speak. Things become more perfected, more intellectual, and to some degree more controlled by an internal, objective logic tied to their instrumentality; but the supreme cultivation, that of subjects, does not increase proportionately.
>
> (Simmel, 1971/1908, p.234)

Simmel identifies a number of tendencies to explain how a partially independent objective culture might arise in modern industrial societies. The first of these is that the *sheer number of objects increases* to such an extent that no single individual is capable of comprehending the system of objects as an ensemble or totality. One demonstration of this impossibility is the never-realized attempts of international exhibitions during the late nineteenth and early twentieth centuries to bring the totality of objects together. Secondly, with the *intensification of the division of labour*, exchange relations become increasingly complicated with the result that the economy necessarily establishes more and more relationships and obligations that are not directly reciprocal. The producer and the consumer lose sight of each other, with the consequence that both are unable to comprehend the many stages and processes that are involved in the production, promotion, distribution and use of objects. The third tendency identified by Simmel is that *the specialization of objects themselves* contributes to the process of their estrangement from human subjects. This appears as an independence of the object, as the individual's inability to subject the object to his or her own daily rhythms. Simmel offers the example of furniture here, a case which he uses to demonstrate a growing estrangement between the subject and its products that ultimately invades even the more intimate aspects of everyday life: 'During the first decades of the nineteenth century, furniture and the objects that surrounded us for use and pleasure were of relative simplicity and durability ... The differentiation of objects has broken down this situation' (Simmel,1990/1900, pp.459–60). The number of very specifically formed objects makes a close and, as it were, personal relationship to each of them more difficult. Here Simmel points not only to the rapidity of their consecutive differentiation (a differentiation which he famously analyses in terms of fashion), but also to their concurrent differentiation, as objects become more and more specialized.

The brand may be seen as a response to all of these processes: the increase in numbers of products, the intensification of the division of labour and the specialization of products. It provides a means by which the gap between objective and subjective culture can be bridged. Anne McClintock's study of soap (1994, 1995) provides a useful example here, giving bite to the rather dry analysis that Simmel presents. McClintock shows that towards the end of the nineteenth century, economic competition between nations had created a climate within which the aggressive promotion of products was becoming ever more intense. This competition contributed to the first real innovations in advertising and thus to the development of modern consumer culture. In 1884, for example, wrapped soap was sold for the first time under a brand name. This small event signalled a major transformation in the economy: items formerly indistinguishable from one another – soap sold simply as soap – came to be marketed as distinctive through the use of corporate signatures. Notable examples of these at the time included Pears' and Monkey Brand. In Victorian culture, the monkey was an icon of metamorphosis, and therefore an apt choice to represent soap, with its alleged powers to transform nature (dirt, waste and disorder) into culture (cleanliness, rationality, industry).

McClintock suggests that while the production of many other commodities also underwent this shift, soap had a special place in this economic transformation. This is because, she argues, branded soap was credited not only with bringing moral and economic salvation to the lives of Britain's great unwashed, but also with magically embodying the spiritual ingredient of the imperial mission itself. In other words, both economic and cultural interests were at work in the branding of soap; it hygienically cleansed not just the white body but also the white race. McClintock writes,

> Soap did not flourish when imperial ebullience was at its peak. It emerged
> commercially during an era of impending crisis and social calamity, serving to
> preserve, through fetish ritual, the uncertain boundaries of class, gender and
> race identity in a world felt to be threatened by the fetid effluvia of slums, the
> belching smoke of industry, social agitation, economic upheaval, imperial
> competition and anti-colonial resistance. Soap offered the promise of spiritual
> salvation and regeneration through commodity consumption, a regime of
> domestic hygiene that could restore the threatened potency of the imperial
> body politic and the race.
>
> (McClintock, 1995, p.211)

In the terms of our analysis here, two interlinked processes are especially
important. The first of these – the domestication of imperial space (see Figure
4.1) – involves the insertion of domestic items into the imperial project, while
the second – the racialization of domestic space (see Figure 4.2) – makes use of
racialized figures to promote everyday consumer goods. Together these
processes suggest that branding involved transformations in the ways in which
boundaries between the economy and everyday life were drawn in time and
space, leading to an increasingly close interrelationship between the two. They
also explicitly show that it is not only the hierarchies of class and paid labour
that are involved in the drawing of boundaries between the economy and
everyday life, but also those of gender, family, 'race' and nation.

In general terms, the rise of the brand is linked simultaneously to the
stretching out of the market over first national and then international space and
the occupation of specific places, including especially the home. In the last
twenty years or so, this paradoxical movement has been developed as a part of
flexible   the **flexible specialization** of the economy, a set of developments in which
specialization   short production runs, increasing design intensity and **specialization** of
products enable the targeting of niche markets (Lash and Urry, 1994). This
involves a changing relationship between production and consumption, in which
a new importance is given to information (such as age, gender, family size and
composition, income and shopping habits) about the consumer as interpreted
by the discipline of marketing and its use of socio-economic, cultural and psycho-
graphic data. As the President of the J. Walter Thompson advertising agency
puts it, 'The difference between products and brands is fundamental. A product
is something that is made in a factory; a brand is something that is bought by a
consumer' (quoted in Klein, 2000). Alternatively, as a designer at the electronic
goods company Philips notes:

> Technologies are increasingly shared among companies, so that the real
> differentiating factor is the way technology is shaped. This is more than a
> question of styling. To design is to shape the future. The Italian for design is
> *progetto*, or *architectturra* – project, or architecture. These expressions clearly
> convey how design gives physical shape to ideas that will affect people's lives.
> Viewed in this way, design is a continuous attempt to create future civilisation
> – no small undertaking.
>
> (Marzano, 2000, p.59)

In seeking to develop this *Vision of the Future* (Philips Corporate Design, 1996),
the company makes use of practices of modelling or simulating everyday life.

Figure 4.1 *Pears advertisement, 'The White Man's Burden'*

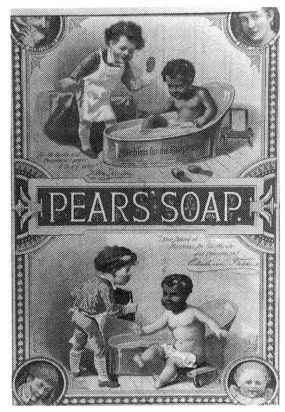

Figure 4.2 *Pears advertisement,*
'Race and the cult of domesticity'

Multidisciplinary teams are brought together to develop 'scenarios', that is, 'short stories describing a product concept and its use'. Such scenarios are then evaluated in relation to four 'domains' that 'represent all aspects of everyday life': 'personal', 'domestic', 'public' and 'mobile'. New products are then proposed for production in the form of 'tangible models, simulations of interfaces and short films'.

More widely, the information about consumers collected in market research becomes increasingly important insofar as it can be related to product purchase, a relationship that is identified in a further market research sub-discipline, 'relationship', 'integrated' or database management, in which one set of object choices may be statistically related with others. At the same time, details collected in the recording of a transaction or the transmission of information – including the Universal Product Code that each good has (contained in the bar code), and the names, addresses, phone numbers of consumers – are correlated with demographic and lifestyle data to provide the basis of new systems of objects. Even the individual consumer's use of many objects and spaces is now dependent on the use of codes, whether these be telephone numbers, keyboard layouts, security entry codes, the menu of video recorders and mobile telephones, the PIN code required to access bank accounts, or the secret codes required by banks for recognition through telephone and internet access. The use of such codes alongside credit cards, smart cards, loyalty programmes and the internet – all activities adding to what Lefebvre calls *compulsive time* – increasingly ensure that the individual leaves an information trail. This information is recorded, interpreted and then, crucially, anticipated in the product development and promotion practices of the new economy.

READING 4.2

Now turn to 'Chucked out your chintz?', which is an account, originally published in *The Independent Magazine*, of a study of interiors commissioned by the furnishing company Ikea and carried out by the advertising agency, St Luke's. The study includes a survey of 1000 households, focus groups and specially commissioned photographs by Jim Naughten.

When you have looked at Reading 4.2, try to answer these questions:

1   What is the value of this research for Ikea?

2   What role do photographs play in this study? You may also remember that in the study conducted by the agency St Luke's described in Reading 4.2, participants were encouraged to film themselves. Perhaps the use of visual methods in both these cases is a result of the importance of tacit knowledge in everyday practice. Such knowledge is difficult to put into words, but may be captured in an image.

3   What is the significance of the reproduction of these commercial findings in a newspaper? How does it transform the relationship between the private and the public? Does it contribute to the reification of the everyday described by Lefebvre?

What are the implications of the developments in the use of information in the objectification of everyday life described by Lefebvre and further illustrated here? During the eighteenth century, Simmel argues, objective culture was developed in relation to the ideal of *the individual*, by which he means an internal, personal value. By the nineteenth century, he suggests, objective culture is assimilated via *education* in the sense of a body of objective knowledge and behavioural patterns. But, at the beginning of the twenty-first century, *information* may be said to have replaced education as the medium in which objective culture is

information society organized. In other words, we are living in an **information society** where it is information that increasingly determines where and how we draw the boundaries in our lives through the objectification of everyday life in brands. The contemporary sociologist Manuel Castells (1996) describes this in terms of the rise of what he calls 'informationalism', that is, a mode of development in which not only is information the raw material of the economy, but information technologies provide enormously enhanced information processing capacity. And in this respect it does indeed seem that both Simmel's and Lefebvre's

reflexivity anxieties may be found to have a basis. The market **reflexivity** of the contemporary economy that is facilitated by informationalism increasingly enables the incorporation of the disparate activities of everyday life into the production of the object. In this way, the closed circuit of production–consumption–production that Lefebvre describes does indeed seem possible.

Yet, so other commentators suggest, everyday life is not so easily objectified or incorporated into the economy. As Agnes Heller (1984) notes, the overriding characteristic of everyday life is that it is heterogeneous, tied to an assortment of operations that are often irrelevant or antagonistic to one another. So, for example, the pragmatic character of everyday thought means not only that it is a step towards the realization of some practical purpose, but also that this thought process does not become detached from the task to be performed. It is meaningful in relation to the proposed aim and to nothing else. Hence, for Heller, everyday knowledge is an embedded, heterogeneous amalgam, and as such will always resist representation as information. Similarly, in their description of 'ordinary culture' Michel de Certeau, Luce Giard and Pierre Mayol argue that everyday life 'hides a fundamental diversity of situations, interests, and contexts under the apparent repetition of objects that it uses' (1998, p.256). In order to consider whether and how this is so, let us turn now, in the final reading in this section, to their description of cooking as an everyday set of knowledges, or what they call an empirical *savoir-faire* or know-how.

READING 4.3

Turn to Reading 4.3, 'Gesture sequences', which is an extract from *The Practice of Everyday Life* by Michel de Certeau, Luce Giard and Pierre Mayol. When you have read it, try the next Activity.

ACTIVITY 5

Now describe your own relation to cooking, and the shopping involved in cooking. Is it a personal relation? How is it mediated, either by others or by the media?

One of the things that may strike you in thinking about these questions is that routine shopping and cooking is still done mainly by women. However, while, as is the case with the piece by Salari you read above in Box 4.1, the gender of the person who is most likely to be doing the cooking is acknowledged by the use of 'she', no explanation of this likelihood is given here. It is not even seen to be in need of explanation. This is a serious omission of the importance of gender to understandings of everyday life discussed by Felski. But, as we have noted all along, many analyses of everyday life only indirectly reflect this importance.

- Are you able to recall specific gestures involved in your cooking or shopping activities?

- What are the elements of your empirical *savoir-faire* ? How is it different to that described here?

- How do you choose ingredients? Where do you buy them from?

- Is the food you buy pre-prepared? Does this save you time? To do what?

- When do you cook? And who for? Are you doing anything else – such as looking after children – when you cook?

- Is there a nerve-centre for the management of your relationship to brands in your household?

While this account may seem somewhat idealistic, it is a compelling discussion of both the sensuous and the practical elements of everyday life. In this respect, it provides an important rejoinder to the thesis that everyday life is increasingly being objectified, represented as information, and incorporated into the economy as a resource. The authors conclude:

> By itself, culture is not information, but its treatment … of objectives and social relations. The first aspect of these operations is *aesthetic*: an everyday practice opens up a unique space within an imposed order, as does the poetic gesture that bends the use of common language to its own desire in a transforming sense. The second aspect is *polemical*: the everyday practice is relative to the power relations that structure the social field as well as the field of knowledge. To appropriate information for oneself, to put it in a series and to bend its montage to one's own taste is to take power over a certain knowledge and thereby overturn the imposing power of the ready-made and preorganized. It is, with barely visible or nameable operations, to trace one's own path through the resisting social system. The last aspect is *ethical*: everyday practice patiently and tenaciously restores a space for play, an interval for freedom, a resistance to what is imposed (from a model, a system, or an order). To be able to do something is to establish distance, to defend the autonomy of what comes from one's own personality.
>
> (de Certeau *et al.*, 1998, pp.254–5)

To further explore the thesis of the incorporation of everyday life into the economy let us now turn to our second example, that of credit. This example both testifies to the increasing importance of consumption to the economy (as suggested by Lefebvre) and also to the ways in which the drawing of boundaries in time both bridges and divides the economy and the everyday.

SUMMARY OF SECTION 4

This section has:

1   outlined the thinking of Georg Simmel on the relationship between objective and subjective culture;

2   introduced a historical account of the brand to illustrate the argument that objective culture is becoming increasingly independent of subjective culture;

3   outlined the growing importance of information, rather than education, in the patterning of consumption and subjective culture.

5 Timeless time?: debt, credit and the future

In a development of his ideas about the rise of an information economy, Manuel Castells suggests that we are witnessing the rise of what he calls a **network society**. He argues that this shift from information economy to network society has come about as a consequence of the ways in which information and information processing are transforming our understandings of space and time (the effect on social action of '**time–space distantiation**'). So, for example, while space has traditionally been understood in terms of the space of places – of home, of neighbourhood, locality and nation, this, he suggests, is no longer the case. Rather, it is now the space of global flows – described by Castells in terms of the movements of people, products and ideas between nodes in a network. Furthermore, according to Castells, while the social organization of time in agrarian societies was dominated by the rhythms of nature, and that of industrial society by clock time, the time of the network society is *timeless*. By this, he means that it is without socially meaningful sequencing, subject only to random disturbances:

> The transformation is … profound: it is the mixing of tenses to create a forever universe, not self-expanding but self-maintaining, not cyclical but random, not recursive but incursive: timeless time, using technology to escape the contexts of its existence, and to appropriate selectively any value each context could offer to the ever-present.
>
> (Castells, 1996, p.433)

network/social network

time–space distantiation

Castells gives a fascinating set of social examples to make the case that we are entering the era of 'timeless time'. Among others these include: split-second capital transactions in global markets; the practices of flexi-time enterprises; variable life working times; the blurring of the life-cycle (such as the increasing ability to control reproduction, the prevalence of re-marriage and increasing longevity among populations in developed countries); the search for eternity through the denial of death; instant wars; and the emerging culture of the internet.

As one example of the rise of timeless time, Castells discusses the flexibilization of the workforce, including a flexibilization of working time. The growth of part-time and shift work as well as weekend and evening work are all examples of working patterns associated with this change. As a number of commentators have noted, the flexibilization of working time brings with it far-reaching changes to many people's lives:

> The decoupling of work time from the time of the organisation and from the collective rhythms of public and familial activities erodes communal activities in both the public and private realm. For workers, flexi-time can have a number of different, even conflicting consequences: it can mean that workers are able to achieve greater control over the allocation of their own time on the one hand, while it may be used by their employers as a tool for improving efficiency on the other.
>
> … Elchardus designates the difference as one of flexibility for the worker on the one hand and flexibility of the worker on the other. While the former allows

workers a greater degree of control over their time, the latter entails an increase
in the unpredictability of working time. Rarely, however, are these two analytic
categories neatly separated; instead, they interpenetrate and constitute
simultaneous, multiple complexities.

(Adam, 1995, p.103)

ACTIVITY 6

Consider, once again, the boundaries you draw between home and work.

- Is your work time flexible? If so, is it a flexibility designed *for* the worker, that is, for you, or is it a flexibility *of* you, requiring you to continuously adjust yourself to the demands of work? Or is it both?

- Is this flexibility so intense that you consider you live in timeless time?

- What other aspects of your life contribute to an experience of timeless time? Here you might think of examples relating to the time of 'non-work' such as the impact of 24-hour television, the internet, the rise of weekend shopping, and the use of mobile phones.

On the whole, Castells seems to have a pessimistic view of the consequences of
the contemporary transformations in temporality. The effects of timeless time,
he suggests, will increasingly be felt in economies and daily lives around the
world in terms of:

- recurrent monetary crises, ushering in an era of financial instability;

- the wrecking of companies and of the jobs they provide, regardless of performance, because of sudden, unpredictable changes in the financial environment in which they operate;

- growing risks for pension funds and private insurance liabilities, so introducing uncertainty into the long-term security of working people around the world;

- the destruction of a shared ethos of the necessity of sacrifice and deferred gratification in favour of an orientation towards immediate reward, emphasizing individual gambling with life and the economy; and

- fundamental damage to the social perception of the correspondence between effort and reward, work and meaning, ethics and wealth.

Indeed, referring to the scandal following the revelation of gross financial
impropriety by a key employee of a highly reputable bank, Castells' conclusion
is that, 'Puritanism seems to have been buried in Singapore in 1995 along with
the venerable Barings Bank' (1996, p.436). In what follows, we will consider
some accounts of individual debt, credit and our relation to the future as a
means of evaluating whether or not we are witnessing the demise of the
Protestant ethic and whether and how the practices of everyday life might be
involved in this demise. This might seem a strange example through which to
explore this issue but, as the following discussion shows, the extension of credit
has been seen both to transform our understandings of effort and reward as a
consequence of the ways in which it reconfigures our relationship to the future.

READING 4.4

Now turn to Reading 4.4, 'Credit' by Jean Baudrillard. While you read it, keep in mind the following questions:

1   What arguments does Baudrillard put forward to suggest that we are witnessing the demise of the Protestant ethic?

2   What implications of this shift does he identify for the workings of the household, the family and for how we understand property?

In this extract, Baudrillard argues that, until the end of the nineteenth century, for most people the acquisition of objects was seen as the material expression of work done. Put simply, they were a reward for all the effort expended. But, as he puts it, today objects are with us before they are earned: they steal a march on the effort, the labour, that they embody. In a sense their consumption precedes their production. Reward precedes effort. This reversal is, of course, one of the reasons for the traditional moral disapproval of the extension of credit or, rather, debt. However, Baudrillard believes that this disapproval has largely disappeared; instead, he says, we are now encouraged to borrow money as part of the rise of a new ethic. Indeed, we take it for granted that it is our right as what he calls consumer-citizens to be extended credit.

However, Baudrillard seems to believe that the economic duties of the consumer-citizen outweigh his or her rights. Thus, although he recognizes that people are learning how 'to make use of objects [acquired through the extension of credit] in complete freedom as if they were already theirs', his emphasis is on the obligations and costs incurred once the individual takes up the offer of credit. His concern is to challenge the purported freedom offered by the contemporary extension of credit. He notes that the length of time of repayment often coincides with the length of time over which an object will lose its value. This ensures that the consumer is never free of debt since as soon as the loan is paid off, he or she will need to make use of further credit to replace the item. One example here are car credit repayment deals, many of which now build in the opportunity for consumers to sell their cars back to the original dealer after two or three years and purchase a new one. While this means, on the one hand, that the consumer will always be driving a nearly new car, it also ensures a new sale and brand loyalty for the car manufacturer on the other. Baudrillard further points out that the speed of 'using up' may outpace the speed of 'paying up' objects. In relation to the illustration overleaf, for example, it is difficult, as a potential purchaser of a sofa, to imagine what the payments involved in this 'free choice' might involve. As a consequence of this kind of uncertainty, Baudrillard argues, credit cannot be integrated into everyday life without producing anxiety, the anxiety of meeting ongoing, periodic payments for something that may no longer be of economic value.

In assessing this anxiety, Baudrillard suggests that the management of finance has become an obligation. As such it can be seen as an example of Lefebvre's compulsive time, requiring training in the new disciplines of purchase and involving complex temporal skills. Indeed, one US bank has decided that its consumers need educating in this respect. In 2001, Citibank launched a series of comic strips as part of its student financial education programme, in which the names of the characters indicate something about the revised relation to the

Figure 4.3 *Credit is widely available and a big selling-point, as at this furniture store*

future which the banks' customers are being encouraged to consider as part of their financial training:

> The six-episode saga charts the progress of the rakish Les Foresight as he embarks on his college career. From the outset he tumbles into all the classic traps, spending money like water, paying for restaurants to impress his friends, and running up vast debts.
>
> 'You see,' he explains to a friend. 'With a credit card you can buy anything you want, even if you have no cash at all. It's like you're rich.'
>
> 'Dude, that's cool,' remarks the crony.
>
> In a later frame, Les's spree is brought to an abrupt halt when a shop attendant informs him that the card has reached its limit.
>
> 'Dude, that's not cool,' moans the same pal.
>
> But Les's antics are not mirrored by the ever-sensible Anita Future – a careful cardholder who tracks her account on the internet and limits her Christmas spending allowance. Her penny-wide self-restraint becomes the envy of the other students.
>
> (Lewis, 2001, p.2)

Despite the humorous tones of this description, the obligations of financial management are seen by Baudrillard to impose a discipline equivalent to Thompson's clock time. However, this discipline pervades not only the sphere of production, but also consumption. Moreover, the periodicities of financial discipline are so many, so uneven, and so complex as to be less transparent than those of production. The consumer has to negotiate an open-ended temporal horizon within which the prediction of future is an extremely tricky business.

The temporal disruption to everyday life caused by the systematic intrusion of credit is further explored by Baudrillard in relation to a shift in the terms of economic valuation in the household. Importantly, he points here to the different ways in which a sense of ownership of objects may be legitimated, or not, in the terms of their possession as property. He suggests that the ownership of goods is no longer understood by the individual in a relationship to effort, that is, work done, or, through inheritance, to the lineage of a family. The ownership of things is thus no longer understood in terms of a set of property values linked to the social relationships of patrimony and secured by the apparent fixity of domestic capital. Instead of a sense of ownership linked to the values of effort, the household and the inheritance of a shared past, the consumer system of objects now imposes a disjointed rhythm on the recurrences of everyday life. As a consequence of their availability on credit, consumer goods come to act as accelerators and multipliers of tasks, propelling us in a tendency to forward flight, disembedding us from familial ties and cutting us off from our relationship to the past. As a consequence of the precariousness and disequilibrium credit introduces into our everyday lives, Baudrillard argues, objects no longer represent payment from the past and security for the future; rather we are disconnected from our past and alienated from our future.

Baudrillard's argument is important, then, insofar as it shows how the increasing availability of credit has implications for our relationship to the past, present and future. It also proposes an argument about changes in the relationships between effort and reward, production and consumption, and between private and public, the household and family. But from some points of view Baudrillard may be seen to be constructing an idealized view of the past. So, for example, he does not stop to acknowledge that the individual who acquired ownership of possessions in a patrimonial regime was more likely to be male than female. Strictly speaking, as the word patrimony indicates, **patrimonialism** refers to a regime in which property is passed on within a family from father to son. And while it has become common practice for all the children of a family to inherit whatever possessions remain on their parents' death, there are still often class and gender differences in inheritance and family economies, both in terms of access to and control of money, transfer of possessions across generations and on the break-up of families as a consequence of divorce (Pahl, 2001). Moreover, Baudrillard also ignores the ways in which possessions often require continual upkeep if they are to facilitate a sense of security and duration, an upkeep that requires ongoing work. Possessions were never just an expression of work done; they were, and are, also signs of work to do.

Baudrillard is perhaps also a little too quick to equate this, as he sees it, displaced form of patrimonialism with some essential notion of everyday life. In this respect, he seems to hold a view of everyday life as naturally dominated by 'an economy of the proper place'. In this understanding, as described by Michel de Certeau, there are two principal dynamics. The first is the accumulation of capital, of material and symbolic wealth, through the expenditure of effort, and the second is the care and development of the individual and collective body (through reproduction and inheritance) (de Certeau, 1984, pp.52–6). As implied by Baudrillard, the economy of the proper place works to reproduce and enhance these two dynamics in a productive and harmonious way. In this economy, property and propriety are brought together in the proper place. However, as

patrimonialism

de Certeau points out, this proper place is not the same as everyday life, for everyday life is more heterogeneous, less proper and less legitimate. It is not tied to *any* particular, organized regime of accumulation.

To consider some empirical evidence on how people actually do conduct their financial arrangements, let us now turn to a study of people and their money conducted in the UK by social psychologists, Peter Lunt and Sonia Livingstone. They used a variety of methods, including a detailed survey questionnaire completed by 279 people who varied in gender, age, social class, income and family status, a series of personal interviews covering financial life histories, and a number of paper-and-pencil tasks, all intended to elicit people's experiences of money and possessions in their everyday lives. They ask:

> … what money means to people and what role it plays in their everyday lives. We consider how people spend or save their money, what they buy and why, whether they talk about money and to whom, what they think of consumerism, credit cards, shopping and people's feelings about changes in consumption.
>
> (Lunt and Livingstone, 1992, p.1)

One of the most striking things that emerges is how central money is to everyday life for most people.

ACTIVITY 7

What becomes clear in Lunt and Livingstone's study is that the opposition between credit and debt, saving and borrowing, is neither simple nor straightforward in most people's lives. While, as a general pattern, saving and borrowing are opposed activities – the more you do of one, the less you do of the other – it is also clear that they are not homogeneous categories. Ask yourself, for example, which of the following counts as being in debt?

- Using credit cards and not paying the overdraft each month

- Having an overdraft

- Owing money to your family

- Buying furniture on HP

- Having a bank loan for a car

- Having a mortgage

- Using credit cards and paying the total each month

1 What stops you borrowing more (or any) money?

2 Do you try to economize? If so, in what ways?

In their study, Lunt and Livingstone found that recurrent savings may be explained differently from total savings, being in debt is explained differently from getting further into debt, and repaying debts is not simply the reversal of this process. And they found distinct patterns of income management amongst their sample, even though the resulting groups did not differ significantly in disposable income level. Even the variety of perceptions of what counts as credit and what counts as debt indicates that the distinction between the two is not as clear-cut as Lunt and Livingstone's analysis of the answers given to the first question you addressed above indicates (see Table 4.1). Moreover, in respect to the demands of everyday life, borrowing and saving may serve a similar purpose – both may be used to even out varying incomes or varying needs over the life course, for example. Both borrowing and saving are also similar, of course, in that they involve participation in consumer society, making choices as a modern citizen, acting on beliefs, and contributing to economic trends.

Table 4.1 Response to 'Which of the following counts as being in debt?'

Using credit cards and not paying the overdraft each month	97%
Having an overdraft	94%
Owing money to your family	92%
Buying furniture on HP	89%
Having a bank loan for a car	83%
Having a mortgage	52%
Using credit cards and paying the total each month	25%

Source: Lunt and Livingstone, 1992, p.38

READING 4.5

Now read 'Saving and borrowing' by Peter Lunt and Sonia Livingstone, which is reproduced as Reading 4.5. While you are reading it, keep in mind the following question:

■ How do Lunt and Livingstone evaluate the extent and meaning of debt in contemporary society?

Lunt and Livingstone locate their study in relation to a number of changes in the economic, cultural and moral context in which people make financial decisions in the UK. They highlight both the rapid increase in consumer credit since the late 1970s and the overall decline in household saving. However, they are wary of drawing any conclusions from this fact alone, pointing out that it is unclear how present levels of consumer debt compare with levels of indebtedness over the twentieth century. Nevertheless, they do point out that forms of credit have been increasingly subject to government regulation, although, of course, this does not mean that there is not considerable public debate about the legitimacy of both the extent and the terms of credit currently available. Indeed, in an interview in 2000, Kim Howells, the Minister for Consumer Affairs, described what he saw as 'a fundamental cultural shift':

> People seem to have evolved a different attitude and they are not as worried about being in debt.

> There has also been a change in the way that banks and other lenders market their products. People seem to be inundated with offers of credit cards now. The upside of this marketing is that it offers lots of financial products to people, but the downside is if they do not get it right then it can lead to trouble.
>
> (quoted in Carter, 2000, p.10)

Even since Lunt and Livingstone completed the study, consumer credit has increased substantially – by 60 per cent during the period 1996–2000 according to the Office of Fair Trading and running at £159 billion a year in 2000. By December 1999, the average debt per credit card was £717, a rise of 50 per cent in four years. Additionally, an even wider range of financial services and products has become available to many people, suggesting that financial management does indeed have the potential to become a burdensome obligation.

In general terms, Lunt and Livingstone's findings show that there is still considerable support for the Protestant ethic. There is, for example, much concern expressed about the morality of borrowing, with a significant proportion of the respondents giving this concern as the reason they do not borrow more, or any, money. However, there is also evidence to suggest that its future is uncertain, with respondents giving three other kinds of reasons for not borrowing more: the experience of bad debt; the costs of borrowing; and the sense that the need for goods does not warrant borrowing. And the detail of the interviews indicates some of the complexity of people's relation to the future as it is mediated by credit:

'For women I think that buying clothes is much more in terms of our personality, so you are buying something to save something. I suspect that that is not so true of men. But of course the amount of time that you keep clothes has changed an awful lot, I mean there were only, when I was young, every man had to own at least one suit and you would expect that to last him most of his life. So you spent an awful long time choosing that. It did cost a lot. It was a thing you saved up for. It was a costly thing to save up for.'

(Lunt and Livingstone, 1992, pp.51–2)

'We would have very lavish trips abroad and everything would go on Visa card, the idea being that we could then pay it off, even with the interest rates it would be cheaper to have it on credit and have it that year than save up for it when the prices have gone up the following year, and we worked out it would probably be about the same. And, occasionally, I would have bank loans, personal bank loans to go abroad, but it was in the days when you could actually ask for a bank loan and say it was for house improvements and you'd get tax relief, which I'm sure everybody does, you'd say it was the damp proof course, this has to be done and that has to be done, but really it was for America ...'

(Lunt and Livingstone, 1992, pp.51–2)

What is apparent here and in the other interviews is the way in which the extension of credit has transformed notions of money, of need and the consumer durable. Indeed it has recently been suggested that money is becoming not only a means of consumption but also an object of consumption in its own right as people are increasingly forced to choose between financial products and services (Pahl, 2001). And while consumer goods may continue to give substance to a sense of time, it does seem that the time is not the predictable, irreversible temporality of industrial clock time, rather it is the unpredictable, discontinuous time of consumer credit, of fashion and nostalgia. The case of credit thus gives some credence to Castells' argument for the emergence of timeless time at the intersection between the economy and everyday life. It also shows the ways in which while timeless time might appear to imply a loosening of social obligations it is actually an example of the disciplines of compulsive time. In this respect, the example of credit, like that of the brand, suggests that the interrelationship of the economy and everyday life has become so close that the latter is often little more than a resource for the former.

SUMMARY OF SECTION 5

This section has:

1   outlined the thesis that we are entering into an era of timeless time in which the boundaries between everyday life and the economy are drawn more and more flexibly;

2   introduced a number of accounts which explore the significance of credit in transforming everyday understandings of time, and in particular our relation to the future;

3   outlined the view that the obligation to acquire skills of consumption – including those of financial management – has a disciplining effect in contemporary society.

6 Conclusion

In this chapter, we have considered some of the ways in which economic life and the everyday are interconnected. In doing so, we have focused on the effects of the boundaries we draw – conceptual and physical – for our understanding of production and reproduction, of home and work, of effort and reward. The arguments put forward here, although by no means similar in many other respects, all suggest that there is an interrelationship between the economy and everyday life. Moreover, many of the studies discussed here are also critical of recent developments in this interrelationship, arguing that it is not simply one of co-dependence, but one in which the practices of everyday life are increasingly constituted as resources for production. They suggest that there has been a tightening of the circle of production–consumption–production through the drawing of new temporal and spatial boundaries.

This shift in the interrelationship is further linked by many of the commentators to the decline of the Protestant work ethic and the new terms under which consumption is integrated with production in the contemporary economy. Indeed, most of the arguments presented here suggest that while effort may still dominate the recurrences of everyday life described by Lefebvre, it is no longer primarily managed in terms of an economy of 'the proper place' or the rational calculus of energetics that dominated much of the twentieth century. Rather, they suggest that effort is increasingly understood in relation to an open-ended future mediated by information and is part of an economy of temporal uncertainty, flexibility and networks. These arguments thus do not suggest that people are no longer motivated to work in the contemporary economy, but rather map a series of transformations in the relationship between effort and reward, in which the subjective links between the two have become more and more attenuated. The example of credit may be seen as an example of this. At the same time, the objective links between production and consumption have become stronger and stronger, as the case of the brand would seem to indicate. This double movement – in which subjective links are weakened, while objective ones are strengthened – would be seen by some as both an indication of the increasing autonomy of objective culture in the contemporary economy and the incorporation of everyday life. But for others, the recurrences of everyday life cannot be contained:

> Each of us has the power to seize power over one part of oneself. This is why gestures, objects and words that live in the ordinary nature of a simple kitchen have so much importance.
>
> (de Certeau, Giard and Mayol, 1998, p.213)

References

Adam, B. (1995) *Timewatch: The Social Analysis of Time*, Cambridge, Polity Press.

Baudrillard, J. (1996) *The System of Objects* (trans. J. Benedict), London, Verso. First published in France in 1968.

Carter, H. (2000) 'Credit card frenzy leads to debt society', *The Guardian*, 19 December.

Castells, M. (1996) *The Rise of the Network Society*, Cambridge, Polity Press.

Certeau, M. de (1984) *The Practice of Everyday Life* (trans. S.F. Rendall), Berkeley, CA, University of California Press.

Certeau, M. de, Giard, L. and Mayol, P. (1998) *The Practice of Everyday Life, Volume 2: Living and Cooking*, Minneapolis, MN, University of Minnesota Press.

Glucksmann, M. (2000) *Cottons and Casuals: The Gendered Organisation of Labour in Time and Space*, Durham, The Sociology Press.

Heller, A. (1984) *Everyday Life* (trans. G.L.Campbell), London and New York, Routledge. First published in 1970.

Klein, N. (2000) *No Logo*, London, Flamingo.

Lash, S. and Urry, J. (1994) *Economies of Signs and Spaces*, London, Sage.

Lefebvre, H. (1971) *Everyday Life in the Modern World* (trans. S. Rabinovitch), London, Allen Lane The Penguin Press. First published in France in 1968.

Lewis, L. (2001) 'Citibank dudes back comic turn', *Independent on Sunday, Business*, 28 January, p.2.

Lunt, P. and Livingstone, S. (1992) *Mass Consumption and Personal Identity: Everyday Economic Experience*, Buckingham, Open University Press.

Marzano, S. (2000) 'Branding=distinctive identity' in Pavitt, J. (ed.) *op. cit.*, pp.58–9.

McClintock, A. (1994) 'Soft-soaping empire: commodity racism and imperial advertising' in Robertson,G., Mash, M., Tickner, L., Bird, J., Curtis, B. and Putnam, T. (eds) *Travellers' Tales: Narratives of Home and Displacement*, London and New York, Routledge, pp.131–54.

McClintock, A. (1995) *Imperial Leather: Race, Gender and Sexuality in the Colonial Contest*, New York and London, Routledge.

Mills, C. Wright (1956) *White Collar*, New York, Oxford University Press.

Nippert-Eng, C. (1996) *Home and Work: Negotiating Boundaries through Everyday Life*, Chicago, IL, and London, University of Chicago Press.

Pahl, J. (2001) 'Couples and their money: theory and practice in personal finances' in Bochel, C., Ellison, N. and Sykes, R., *Social Policy Review*, no.13, London, Social Policy Association.

Pavitt, J. (2000) 'At home with the Joneses' in Pavitt, J. (ed.) *op. cit.*, pp.106–7.

Pavitt, J. (ed.) (2000) *Brand.new*, London, Victoria and Albert Museum.

Philips Corporate Design (1996) *Vision of the Future*, Eindhoven, Philips Corporate Design.

Rabinbach. A. (1992) *The Human Motor: Energy, Fatigue and the Origins of Modernity*, Berkeley, CA, University of California Press.

Simmel, G. (1971) 'Subjective culture' in Levine, D.N. (ed.) *Georg Simmel: On Individuality and Social Forms, Selected Writings*, Chicago, IL, and London, University of Chicago Press, pp.227–34. First published in 1908.

Simmel, G. (1990) *The Philosophy of Money* (ed. D. Frisby, trans. T. Bottomore and D. Frisby), London and New York, Routledge. First published in 1900.

Sweet, M. and Naughten, J. (2000) 'Chucked out your chintz?', *The Independent Magazine*, 2 September, pp.11, 13–15.

Thompson, E.P. (1967) 'Time, work-discipline, and industrial capitalism', *Past and Present*, no.38, pp.56–97.

Weber, M. (1930) *The Protestant Ethic and the Spirit of Capitalism*, London, Allen and Unwin. Written in 1904–05.

Zerubavel, E. (1985) *Hidden Rhythms*, Berkeley, CA, University of California Press.

Readings

 4.1 Henri Lefebvre, 'Everyday life in the modern world: an inquiry, and some discoveries' (1971)

The term *consumer society* has increased in popularity since the period under consideration (1950–60). It has been proved by convincing statistics that in highly industrialized countries the consumption of material and cultural goods is on the increase and that so-called 'durable' goods (cars, television sets, etc.) are acquiring a new and ever greater significance. These observations are correct but trivial. The theoreticians of the 'consumer society' mean or imply something more by this term; they assert that once upon a time in the pre-history of modern society, when capitalist economy and industrial production were still in their infancy, production was not controlled by demand, and that contractors were ignorant of market and consumer alike and their haphazard production was launched to await the expected and desired consumer. Nowadays, we are told, the organizers of production are aware of the market, not only of solvent demands but of the desires and needs of the consumer; thus consumer activity would have made its momentous debut in organized rationality; everyday life, in so far as it exists, would be taken into consideration and (integrated as such with scientific rationality) embodied in the experience of a highly organized society; there would no longer be any reason to consider it as a level of reality.

Our answer is first that in France we have not noticed any serious attempts at social and cultural 'market research' but only at research into *specific* needs, and therefore into solvent demands. It would indeed be too easy to show how badly and belatedly the *social* needs peculiar to *urban* existence have been studied.

Moreover, even specific needs are not submitted to unbiased research; the manner of the inquiry reacts on the needs and becomes a part of social practice that freezes them. There exist, besides, other more powerful methods of directing needs than market and motivation research. What, for instance, is the role of advertising? Is the advertiser the magician of modern times working out spells to entrap and subjugate desire, or is he merely a modest, honest intermediary investigating public requirements and broadcasting the discovery of new, exciting products to be launched shortly on the market in answer to such requirements? No doubt the truth lies between these two extremes. Does advertising create the need, does it, in the pay of capitalist producers, shape desire? Be this as it may, advertising is unquestionably a powerful instrument; is it not the first of consumer goods and does it not provide consumption with all its paraphernalia of signs, images and patter? Is it not the rhetoric of our society, permeating social language, literature and imagination with its ceaseless intrusions upon our daily experience and our more intimate aspirations? Is it not on the way to becoming the main *ideology* of our time, and is not this fact confirmed by the importance and efficiency of propaganda modelled on advertising methods? Has not institutionalized advertising replaced former modes of communication, including art, and is it not in fact the sole and vital mediator between producer and consumer, theory and practice, social existence and political power? But what does this ideology disguise and shape, if not that specific level of social reality we call everyday life, with all its 'objects' – clothing, food, furnishing?

The term we have just examined is not entirely satisfactory. The transition from penury to affluence is a fact; in this society of a modified capitalism we have seen the transition from a state of inadequate production to one of boundless, sometimes even prodigal, consumption (waste, luxury, ostentation, etc.), from privation to possession, from the man of few and modest needs to the man whose needs are many and fertile (in potential energy and enjoyment); but like all transitions it is not easily accomplished, dominated as it is by inexplicable compulsions and trailing shreds of a past age in its wake. It is the transition from a culture based on the curbing of desires, thriftiness and the necessity of eking out goods in short supply to a new culture resulting from production and consumption at their highest ebb, but against a background of general crisis. Such is the predicament in which the ideology of production and the significance of creative activity have become an *ideology of consumption*, an ideology that has bereft the working classes of their former ideals and values while maintaining the status and the initiative of the bourgeoisie. It has substituted for the image of active man that of the consumer as the possessor of happiness and of perfect rationality, as the ideal become reality ('me', the individual, living, active subject become 'objective'). Not the consumer nor even that which is consumed is important in this image, but the vision of consumer and consuming as art of consumption. In this process of ideological substitutions and displacements man's awareness of his own alienation is repressed, or even suppressed, by the addition of a new alienation to the old.

...

In Western neo-capitalist countries there has been no overt programming of production, no total rationalization of industry; yet a kind of programming, a sort of total organization has sneaked in unobtrusively; offices, public organizations and subsidiary institutions operate on this basis, and though the structure lacks coherence, grates and jolts, none the less it works, its shortcomings hidden behind an obsessive coherence and its incapacity for creative integration disguised as participation and communality. And what do these organizations organize, if not everyday life?

Around 1960 the situation became clearer, everyday life was no longer the no-man's-land, the poor relation of specialized activities. In France and elsewhere neo-capitalist leaders had become aware of the fact that colonies were more trouble than they were worth and there was a change of strategy; new vistas opened out such as investments in national territories and the organization of home trade (which did not exclude the exploitation of 'underdeveloped countries' for manpower and raw material and as sites for investments – only they were no longer the main preoccupation). What did the leaders do? All areas outside the centres of political decision and economic concentration of capital were considered as semi-colonies and exploited as such; these included the suburbs of cities, the countryside, zones of agricultural production and all outlying districts inhabited, needless to say, by employees, technicians and manual labourers; thus the status of the proletarian became generalized, leading to a blurring of class distinctions and of ideological 'values'. This well-organized exploitation of society involved consumption and was no longer restricted to the productive classes only; capitalism, while requiring that people 'adapt' to modern circumstances, had

adapted too. Formerly the leaders of industry produced haphazardly for a problematic market; limited family business concerns predominated adding their bourgeois treble to the chorus praising the wonders of trade, of quality, of dearly beloved labour. In Europe after the war a few gifted and intelligent men (who they were is not our concern) saw the possibility of exploiting consumption to organize everyday life. Everyday life was cut up and laid out on the site to be put together again like the pieces of a puzzle, each piece depending on a number of organizations and institutions, each one – working life, private life, leisure – rationally exploited (including the latest commercial and semi-programmed organization of leisure). ...

The following inferences may be drawn from what precedes:

(a) In France as in other neo-capitalist countries the changes in social practice had not eliminated the notion of *everyday life*; we were not confronted with a choice between modernity and everyday life. But the concept of the quotidian had undergone a metamorphosis by which it acquired a greater not a lesser significance; it had lost some of its implications, the striking contrast between want and affluence, between the ordinary and the extraordinary for instance, but otherwise it was unchanged, even consolidated.[1] In the modern world everyday life had ceased to be a 'subject' rich in potential subjectivity; it had become an 'object' of social organization. Far from disappearing as subject of reflection, however (which it could not have failed to do if the revolutionary movement had prevailed), it was more firmly entrenched than ever.

(b) All the suggested definitions of our society have proved unacceptable. How can the distinctive features that have emerged during this inquiry be summarized and formulated? We propose the following term: *Bureaucratic Society of Controlled Consumption* whereby this society's rational character is defined as well as the limits set to its rationality (bureaucratic), the object of its organization (consumption instead of production) and the *level* at which it operates and upon which it is based: everyday life. This definition has the advantage of being *scientific* and more *precisely* formulated than any of the others[2]; moreover it owes nothing either to literature or to a 'social philosophy' extraneous to social reality.

Notes

1 The author admits that he hesitated for some years before reaching such conclusions. More than once between 1950 and 1960 he considered abandoning both concept and inquiry, and this explains the time-lapse between the first volume (*Introduction à la critique de la vie quotidienne*, 1946) and the second (1962).

2 This definition is not incompatible with certain others such as 'monopolistic capitalism of State', for instance; but in our opinion it allows for a more thorough analysis of the society's functions and structure and it goes further into actualities and potentialities than the latter, which appears to stress the economic aspect and denotes a certain partiality for *economism*, ideology and 'values' in the society it defines.

Source: Lefebvre, 1971, pp.54–6, 57–9, 59–60

4.2 Matthew Sweet, 'Chucked out your chintz?' (2000)

Photographs by Jim Naughten

Whether your style is wrought-iron and calico, or ornaments and fringed lamps, you're sure to fit into one of the categories unearthed in Ikea's interiors survey.

Here's something to get the net curtains twitching: Mitchell Bates, a bright-eyed strategic planner at the St Luke's advertising agency, has spent a year generating a taxonomy of English taste on behalf of their Swedish client Ikea. Using focus groups and a survey of 1,000 households, his team has completed the most thorough investigation ever undertaken into the stippling and pelmets and polished floorboards of England. The result: six 'style groups' reflecting a spectrum of attitudes to home decoration, and a stack of evidence collected by photographer Jim Naughten. For some, a paint roller was a necessary evil, for others, an essential tool of self-expression. 'We've attempted to record how taste is changing,' Bates explains. 'If the survey is repeated in five years, we can map these trends further.'

The survey exposes the gap between images of Llewellyn-Bowenisation that fill interiors magazines, and the real state of the nation's dadoes. It suggests that *Wallpaper* is no bible for modernist living, just the *Razzle* of the urban middle classes; that ranks of polished whimsies are infinitely more common than Charles Eames ottomans; that much of our chintz remains unchucked; that making do is far more prevalent than making over. 'It's been something of a reality check,' says Bates.

Redecorating, he explains, 'has a viral structure. If you buy a new piece of furniture – say, a modern sofa – it makes you reassess other things. It doesn't go with the floral curtains, so you replace them with a blind. Then the blind looks silly with the patterned carpet, so you get laminate flooring.'

There's very little snobbery in these images. 'It's very easy to ridicule people's taste from a middle-class, metropolitan perspective,' says Bates. 'I didn't want images that were cynical.' But Bates and Naughten were unable to suppress the narratives offered by these spaces – tales told by the grubby cruet set parked on the mantelpiece, the portrait of a dead husband, immortalised as a laughing cavalier. There is an inescapable element of melancholy in these pictures, a whisper of what Larkin, in 'Home is so Sad', characterised as 'A joyous shot of how things ought to be,/Long fallen wide.' Unoccupied armchairs bear the impression of a pair of buttocks. Ornaments sit rowed like figures in an ancient Egyptian tomb. Remote controls wait patiently on coffee tables, as if their owners had been suddenly evacuated or abducted. The music on the piano stool. That vase.

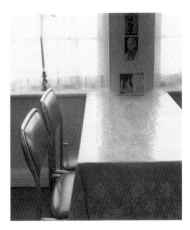

'Not really interested' This is the group that would like to dunk Carol Smillie's head in a tin of Jocasta Innes hot paprika paint. They're not interested in DIY, restoration or decoration, and believe that repainting their homes is a necessary evil. 'I decorate through necessity,' says Mr H. 'This [room] needs redoing – I'll do it the same, only perhaps slightly darker. I never look forward to doing it.' Sociodemographically, they include many people on low incomes (20 per cent of them earn less than £7,500 per year), they prefer reading the classics to cinema, theatre or – horror of horrors – recreational shopping. 'Our style's all different, really,' say Mr and Mrs C. 'It's dark wood in here, but we've got pine in the dining room. Nothing matches.'

'Self-expressive' This group sees the home as a canvas upon which they can express their inner thingummies. Anything goes, as long as it's energetic, individual, and not what the neighbours would do. So it's yes to feng shui, the restoration of crenellated architraves, imaginative use of MDF, and no to net curtains, velour and Axminster carpets. Bates's number-crunching reveals that they're the most likely to speak a foreign language or have an original artwork on their wall. 'My style is *colourful*', enthuses Mrs L. 'Happy, cheerful, quite way out. Some people say, "How do you have the nerve to have it like this?" But it's just me.'

'Modern and co-ordinated' For some in this category, modernisation extends to the erasure of history. 'I talked to one woman who had moved house, and the only object that came with her was a punchbowl,' recalls Bates. They tend to be younger, female, in full-time work, and better-educated than subjects in other groups. They plump for calico over Dralon, and wouldn't be seen dead at an antiques auction. But they are not acolytes of Le Corbusier – the odd floral border was placed happily next to a sleek sofa. 'I went to the Ideal Home Exhibition [and] this shelf unit caught my eye,' says Mrs B. 'So I followed the theme through to the tables and chairs, and it just took off.'

'Child-bound' Jammy fingerprints on the wallpaper, tricycle tyre-bumps in the wainscot, PlayStation games and copies of *The Lion King* all over the living room – this group has to accept that there are financial and practical limits on how elaborate their decoration can be. So they fantasise instead. 'I do watch *Changing Rooms*,' admits Mrs S, 'But I'd never attempt anything they do. They always show couples without kids.' The research reveals that this group favours traditional attitudes to discipline and morality, and rarely pays for anything with a credit card. 'Everything has to be high,' says Mrs G. 'The kids wreck everything. I've got darker carpets for practical considerations.'

'Just normal' This is the largest group of subjects – but that's something of a statistical aberration, as, unlike the other groups, they are united by indifference, not the pursuit of a particular aesthetic. 'Decorating is a bit of a chore,' says Mr T, one of Bates's interviewees. 'I probably do the living room every seven years.' This group is more fond of going out than staying in, is more likely to live in local authority housing, has a weakness for velour and Dralon, and – beyond home furnishings – they are very conscious of keeping up with trends. 'To me,' says Mrs L, 'a carpet makes a room. The idea of floorboards horrifies me. I would never, never have wooden floors.'

'Home is my castle' The most conservative – both socially and aesthetically – of all Bates's categories, this group includes many retired people and a disproportionate number of dog-owners. These people hoard ornaments, they are very keen to express their lineage with photographs of living and dead family members, they are pessimistic about the future, and comparatively well read. 'A couple we know have just spent a fortune redoing their house,' says Mrs D. 'They've completely thrown everything out and brought new in. I couldn't do that. I was adopted, so I've got no family history other than that I've created myself. I think you have security in things because you have none from people. The things that are most important to me are things which have memories.'

Source: Sweet and Naughten, 2000, pp.11,13,14,15

4.3 Michel de Certeau, Luce Giard and Pierre Mayol, 'Gesture sequences' (1998)

How can one find the right words, words that are rather simple, ordinary, and precise, to recount these sequences of gestures, bound together over and over again, that weave the indeterminate cloth of culinary practices within the intimacy of kitchens? How can one choose words that are true, natural, and vibrant enough to make felt the weight of the body, the joyfulness or weariness, the tenderness or irritation that takes hold of you in the face of this continually repeated task where the better the result (a stuffed chicken, a pear tart), the faster it is devoured, so that before the meal is completely over, one already has to think about the next.

A succession of gestures and steps, repeated and required. *Inside* : to the kitchen to prepare; from the kitchen to the dining room to serve and eat, getting up constantly to run and check the things on the grill or to fetch the mustard missing from the table; from the dining room to the kitchen to clear away the dishes; once again in the kitchen to wash and put things away. *Outside* : from the house to the market, to the grocery store, the bakery, the butcher shop, the wine shop; then back to the house, arms full of shopping bags. On the way, you pass a young woman even more heavily laden than you and who mumbles to no one in particular: 'I'm just the family packhorse. All I do is carry, carry, carry'. *Inside*: to the kitchen to empty the bags; put away the groceries; wrap up the things to be put in the refrigerator; note down the expenses, check the change and the receipts. Sit down, finally. Today, tomorrow, and the day after, repeat the same chain of events, engage in the same litany of questions: What's left for tonight? How many people will there be? And what about lunch tomorrow?

> The hardest thing for me is *knowing what to do* ! It's not so much in the execution … In fact, the big problem for me is always having to know what to eat. And that just kills me! It's something that Paul, for example, does not understand, the need to *always think about it*. All you can do is think about it. I would like to be able to not think about this place, you know, to be able to do something else. As dinnertime approaches – what are we gonna eat? It's traditionally that way, every day.
>
> (Colette)

But the word *gesture* here is misleading; one would have to find a term that could include the movements of the body as well as those of the mind. 'Cooking is not complicated – you have to know how to organize yourself and to have a good memory and a little taste. Quite simply, I learned to cook by doing' … Yes, in cooking the activity is just as *mental* as it is manual; all the resources of intelligence and memory are thus mobilized. One has to organize, decide, and anticipate. One must memorize, adapt, modify, invent, combine, and take into consideration Aunt Germaine's likes and little François's dislikes, satisfy the prescriptions for Catherine's temporary diet, and vary the menus at the risk of having the whole family cry out in indignation with the ease of those who benefit from the fruit of other people's labor: '"Cauliflower *again*! We just had it on Monday and on the Friday before, too! I don't want anymore! I don't like it!" Me neither, but how can one make them understand that it is the only affordable fresh vegetable available right now? They will arrogantly respond: "You'll just have to figure somethin' out!"'

In cooking, one always has to *calculate*, both time and money, not go beyond the budget, not overestimate one's own work speed, not make the schoolboy late. One has to *evaluate* in the twinkling of an eye what will be the most cost-effective in terms of price, preparation, and flavor. One has to know how to *improvise* with panache, know what to do when fresh milk 'turns' on the stove, when meat, taken out of the package and trimmed of fat, reveals itself to be not enough to feed four guests, or when Mathieu brings a little friend to dinner unannounced and one has to make the leftover stew 'go a little farther'. One has to *remember* that the Guys already had cabbage *à la saucisse de Morteau* the last time they came to visit and that Béatrice cannot stand chocolate cake, or that the fishmonger, the only one in the neighborhood, will be closed all week, even though he is usually open. With all these details quickly reviewed, the game of exclusion, impossibilities (from lack of time, money, or supplies), and preferences must end in the proposal of a solution to be quickly realized because one has to come up with a menu for tonight, for example, roast beef with oven-baked potatoes. But one also has to choose a wine to *match* and not plan on a dessert made with cream if the proposed appetizer is *cornets* with béchamel or if one of the guests cannot stand dairy products.

Doing-cooking thus rests atop a complex montage of circumstances and objective data, where necessities and liberties overlap, a confused and constantly changing mixture through which tactics are invented, trajectories are carved out, and ways of operating are individualized. Every cook has her repertoire, her grand operatic arias for extraordinary circumstances and her little ditties for a more familial public, her prejudices and limits, preferences and routine, dreams and phobias. To the extent that experience is acquired, style affirms itself, taste distinguishes itself, imagination frees itself, and the recipe itself loses significance, becoming little more than an occasion for a free invention by analogy or association of ideas, through a subtle game of substitutions, abandonments, additions, and borrowings. By carefully following the same recipe, two experienced cooks will obtain different results because other elements intervene in the preparation: a personal touch, the knowledge or ignorance of tiny secret practices (flouring a pie pan after greasing it so that the bottom of the crust will remain crispy after baking), and entire *relationship to things* that the recipe does not codify and hardly clarifies, and whose manner differs from one individual to another because it is often rooted in a family or regional oral tradition.

Source: de Certeau *et al.*, 1998, pp.199–201

 # 4.4 Jean Baudrillard, 'Credit' (1968)

Rights and duties of the consumer-citizen

Today, then, objects appear under the sign of differentiation and choice – but they also appear (or at least, all key objects do) under the sign of *credit*. When you buy something you certainly have to pay for it, but the *choice* is yours 'free', and by the same token credit terms are proposed as a free gift, as a kind of bonus from the world of production. The unstated assumption is that credit is the consumer's right, and ultimately an economic right of the citizen. Restriction of any kind on the possibility of buying on credit is felt to be a retaliatory measure on the part of the State; to do away with such arrangements – which is in any case unthinkable – would be experienced by society at large as the abolition of a freedom. ...

...

... Once property had priority over use; now the reverse is true, and the extension of credit, among other phenomena defined by David Riesman, marks the gradual transition from an 'acquisitive' civilization to a practical one. Credit customers are gradually learning how to make use of objects in complete freedom as though they were already 'theirs'. The difference, of course, is that while such objects are being paid for they are simultaneously wearing out: the final payment-due date is not unrelated to the 'replacement-due' date – indeed, as we know, some American firms strive to make the two intervening periods coincide exactly. There is always the risk, therefore, as in the event of defectiveness or loss, that an object will be, so to speak, used up before it is paid up. Even when credit seems to have been perfectly integrated into everyday life, this danger is the basis of an insecurity that was never experienced in connection with the 'patrimonial' object. Such an object was mine: I owed nothing. An object bought on credit will be mine when I have paid for it: it is conjugated, as it were, in the future perfect.

The anxiety that attaches to periodic payments is very specific. It eventually sets in train a parallel process which weighs down on us day after day even though we never become conscious of the objective relationship involved. It haunts the human project, not immediate practice. An object that is mortgaged escapes us in time, and has in fact escaped us from the outset. ...

In the end the credit system merely exemplifies what is a very general way of relating to objects in the modern context ... *We are forever behindhand relative to our objects.* They are here before us, yet they are already a year away, located either in that final payment or else in the next model by which they are bound to be replaced. So credit simply transfers a basic psychological situation onto the economic plane; the obligation to follow a sequence is the same at both levels, whether it is economic, as with successive hire-purchase payments, or psycho-sociological, as in the systematic and ever-accelerating succession of series and models. In any event, we experience our objects in a predefined, mortgaged temporal mode. If there are now barely any restrictions on the use of credit, perhaps the reason is that *all* our objects today are apprehended as if they were obtained on credit, as debts incurred to society as a whole – debts that are always susceptible of adjustment, always fluctuating, always prey to chronic inflation and devaluation. … [C]redit must be viewed as far more than a financial arrangement, for it is nothing less than a fundamental dimension of our society and in effect a new ethical system.

The precedence of consumption: a new ethic

A single generation has witnessed the eclipse of the notions of patrimony and of fixed capital. Until our parents' generation, objects once acquired were owned in the full sense, for they were the material expression of work done. It is still not very long since buying a dining-table and chairs, or a car, represented the end-point of a sustained exercise of thrift. People worked dreaming of what they might later acquire; life was lived in accordance with the puritan notion of effort and its reward – and objects finally won represented repayment for the past and security for the future. They were, in short, a capital. Today objects are with us before they are earned, they steal a march on the sum total of effort, of labour, that they embody, so that in a sense *their consumption precedes their production*. True, these objects, which I merely make use of, no longer impose any patrimonial responsibility on me; they are bequeathed to me by nobody and I, in turn, shall bequeath them to nobody. They do, however, exert another kind of constraint for they hang over me as debts as yet unsettled. If they no longer locate me in a relationship to a family or customary group, I am nevertheless brought into relation through them with society at large and its agencies (the economic and financial order, the fluctuations of fashion, and so forth). And I must pay for them over and over again, month by month, or replace them every year. This means that everything has changed: the significance these objects have for me, the projects they embody, their objective future, and mine. It is worth pondering the fact that for centuries generations of people succeeded one another in an unchanging décor of objects which were longer-lived than they, whereas now many generations of objects will follow upon one another at an ever-accelerating pace during a single human lifetime. Where once man imposed his rhythm upon objects, now objects impose their disjointed rhythm – their unpredictable and sudden manner of being

present, of breaking down or replacing with one another without ever aging – upon human beings. Thus the status of a whole civilization changes along with the way in which its everyday objects make themselves present and the way in which they are enjoyed. In a patriarchal domestic economy founded on inheritance and stable rents, consumption could never conceivably precede production. In accordance with good Cartesian and moral logic, work preceded its fruit as cause precedes effect. The ascetic mode of accumulation, rooted in forethought, in sacrifice, and in a resorption of needs that created great tension within the individual, was the foundation of a whole civilization of thrift which enjoyed its own heroic period before expiring in the anachronistic figure of the *rentier* – indeed, of the ruined *rentier*, who in this century has perforce learnt the historical lesson of the vanity of traditional morality and traditional economic calculation. By dint of living within their means, whole generations have ended up living far below their means. Work, merit, accumulation – all the virtues of an era whose pinnacle was the concept of property are still discernible in the objects that stand as witness to that time, objects whose lost generations continue to haunt the petty-bourgeois interior.

The obligation to buy

Today a new morality has been born. Precedence of consumption over accumulation, forward flight, forced investment, speeded-up consumption, chronic inflation (implying the absurdity of saving) – these are the motors of our whole present system of buying first and paying off later in labour. Credit has thus brought us back to a situation that is in fact feudal in character, reminiscent as it is of the arrangement under which a portion of labour would be allocated in advance, as serf labour, to the feudal lord. There is a difference, however, for our system, unlike feudalism, reposes on complicity: modern consumers spontaneously embrace and accept the unending constraint that is imposed on them. They buy so that society can continue to produce, this so that they can continue to work, and this in turn so that they can pay for what they have bought. Witness the following American advertising slogans, noted by Vance Packard, which make the point very well: 'Buy days mean pay days – and pay days mean better days!'; 'Buy now – the job you save may be your own!'; 'Buy your way to prosperity!'.

The illusionism is truly remarkable: society appears to extend credit to you in exchange for a formal freedom, but in reality it is you who are giving credit to society, alienating your future in the process. Of course the system of production still depends fundamentally on the exploitation of labour-power, but today it is strongly reinforced by the circular consensus or collusion whereby subjection itself is experienced as freedom, and is thus transformed into an independent and durable system. In every individual the consumer colludes with the production system while having no relationship to the producer – the victim of the system – that he also is. Paradoxically, this split between producer and consumer is the mainstay of social integration, because everything is done so that it can never take the living and critical form of a contradiction.

...

The ambiguity of the domestic object

In sum, credit pretends to promote a civilization of modern consumers at last freed from the constraints of property, but in reality it institutes a whole system of integration which combines social mythology with brutal economic pressure. Credit is an ethic, but it is also a politics. The tactic of credit works in tandem with that of personalization to give objects a socio-political function they never used to have. We no longer live in the age of serfdom or in the age of usury, but both these constraints have been incorporated in abstract and amplified form into the realm of credit. Credit is a social realm, a temporal realm, a realm of things by virtue of which, and by virtue of the strategy that imposes it, objects are able to fulfil their function as accelerators and multipliers of tasks, satisfactions

and expenditures. They thus become a kind of trampoline, their very inertia serving as a centrifugal force which lends everyday life its rhythm – its tendency to forward flight, its precariousness and disequilibrium.

At the same time, objects, on which domesticity once depended as a means of escape from the pressures of society, now on the contrary serve to shackle the domestic universe to the circuits and constraints of the social one. By means of credit – which is a free gift and a formal freedom but also a social sanction, a form of subjection and a fatality at the very heart of things – domesticity is directly colonized: it acquires a kind of social dimension, but in the very worst sense. The most extreme and absurd effects of credit are eloquent: for example, when car payments are so pressing that the buyer cannot afford petrol for his vehicle, we have reached the point where the human project, filtered and fragmented by economic pressures, begins to feed upon itself. A fundamental truth about the present system emerges here too: *objects now are by no means meant to be owned and used but solely to be produced and bought.* In other words, they are structured as a function neither of needs nor of a more rational organization of the world, but instead constitute a system determined entirely by an ideological regime of production and social integration. Indeed, private objects properly so called no longer exist: thanks to their multiple use, it is the social order of production, with its own particular complicities, which now haunts the intimate world of the consumer and his consciousness. This penetration also marks the fading of any prospect of effectively contesting or transcending that social order.

Source: Baudrillard, 1996, pp.156, 157–61, 162–3

 ## Peter Lunt and Sonia Livingstone 'Saving and borrowing' (1992)

Developments in consumer credit, debt and saving

Recent rapid growth in consumer credit and in personal debt problems has received widespread popular attention in the media and in everyday conversation over the last decade and has been documented through a range of economic indicators (see, for example, Hartropp *et al.*, 1987; Parker, 1988; Leigh-Pemberton, 1989; Berthoud and Kempson, 1990). Consumer credit has been growing in Britain

by at least 10 per cent in real terms nearly every year since 1977 (Hartropp *et al.*, 1987). In 1988, 15.3 million people had a Visa card and 12.2 million had an Access card, figures which have increased over four-fold since the mid-1970s. Two-thirds of all adults now possess some kind of plastic money card (*Social Trends*, 1991).

The amount of outstanding personal debt

(excluding mortgages) reached £48.2 billion in December 1989, three and a half times the amount outstanding in March 1982 (*Social Trends*, 1991). This represents some 14 per cent of annual household disposable income (compared to 8 per cent in 1981: *Social Trends*, 1989). In 1989, household expenditure exceeded household income for the fourth successive year (*Social Trends*, 1991).

In 1990, 76,300 households were in mortgage arrears of 6–12 months, with 18,800 in arrears of more than 1 year (*Social Trends*, 1991). In 1987, 22,900 properties were repossessed by building societies (compared to 4200 in 1981) and there has been a substantial increase in the number of people using the Citizens Advice Bureaux (*Social Trends*, 1989). The situation has been worsening consistently over the 1980s and 1990s. There have been public calls for tightening up lending agreements, shop practices and advertising restrictions, and for increasing debt advice provision.

In recent years, household saving, expressed as a percentage of household disposable income, has fallen from around 4 per cent in the 1970s to a negative 2 per cent by the late 1980s (*Social Trends*, 1991). In other words, household expenditure is exceeding income: 'consumers have recently not merely spent the whole of their PDI [personal disposable income], but borrowed in order to finance yet further consumption' (Curwen, 1990, p.43). However, the proportion of adults with a building society account rose from 15 per cent in 1968 to 64 per cent in 1986, albeit with a fall in National Savings accounts (*Social Trends*, 1989), suggesting that many are also saving money. Further, 'there was every sign in the booming house market of 1988 that saving for asset accumulation was as popular as ever' (Curwen, 1990, p.43).

It is unclear how far present levels of consumer debt, with their attendant problems, compare with or exceed levels of indebtedness over the twentieth century as a whole. Most discussions of debt chart its growth over the last decade or so, and comparisons with earlier times are extremely difficult to make, given the changing forms of credit, the widespread practice of informal or unregulated forms of credit, the paucity of records, and the many other social and economic changes which have occurred in the same period.

Certainly, over this century, the forms of consumer debt have altered. A general pattern can be observed in which a particular form of credit becomes available, then widespread, then problematic, and finally it is regulated by governments, who are generally reluctant to intervene, in order to meet public concern over the need to protect both consumers and creditors (who must themselves avoid becoming debtors). Thus, at the turn of the century, most credit was offered by money lenders, who charged high prices and proved difficult to regulate, and by pawnbrokers, a major source of credit for the working class – with licensed pawnbroking for the artisan class and illegal 'pop' shops for the very poor (Parker, 1990). Between the wars, pawnbroking declined as a result of increased prosperity, the slum clearance programmes and the beginnings of state provision and welfare (Parker, 1990). Thus the building society movement grew and local authorities began to advance money for house purchase, as did the Public Works Loan Board (Barty-King, 1991). More 'respectable' forms of credit became available to take the place of pawnbroking. Hire purchase in particular grew rapidly hand in hand with the rise in mass-produced consumer durables (Galbraith, 1970), gradually losing its association with 'buying on tick' (Roebuck, 1973).

After the Second World War, finance houses offered increasing numbers of personal loans, which were more appropriate than hire purchase for the services now demanded (home improvements, central heating, etc., goods which cannot be 'snatched back'). While money lending, pawnbroking and check trading (or trading in shop vouchers) all continued throughout the [twentieth] century, mail order buying and shop credit at the point of sale grew rapidly after the war (Parker, 1990). Home ownership increased in the 1950s as building societies advanced ever larger proportions of the price, encouraged by the then Prime Minister, Macmillan (Barty-King, 1991). Traditional banking attitudes began to change in the mid-1960s, with banks diversifying particularly by making links with or taking over finance houses and credit card companies (Drury and Ferrier, 1984). Bank credit was not regulated until the Consumer Credit Act 1974.

Over the [twentieth] century, there has been a continuing public debate over the responsibilities and obligations of lenders, of the rights of consumers to credit and of the need to protect consumers from themselves, while also maintaining that for 'a free society … people themselves must be the judge of what contributed to their material welfare' (Barty-King, 1991, p.175). The debate culminated in the Crowther Committee Report of 1971, which 'resulted in sweeping criticism of the existing framework of law and suggested a radical recasting of the whole of credit legislation' (Drury and Ferrier, 1984, p.146). As a result, we have seen both increasing government intervention and regulation and the increasing institutionalization of credit organizations themselves, with codes of practice, trade associations, etc. (Barty-King, 1991). In 1974, the Consumer Credit Act reorganized and integrated the regulations regarding many different forms of credit. It focused on three main areas: '(a) The control of credit-granting and hiring institutions. (b) The supply of information to debtors and hirers. (c) Protection of the consumer debtor and hirer' (Drury and Ferrier, 1984, p.148).

Responses to consumer pressures

> Today I had a Marks & Spencers account, I don't owe them anything so it was a nil account, but at the bottom it said do you want to start saving with us, and also they offer loans as well. Everyone is trying to make a little bit of money somehow from us, aren't they? It strikes me that it doesn't matter how they do it, I thought that Marks & Spencer sold clothes. They are now offering to lend me money.

> I am not saying that there shouldn't be any credit at all, there was credit in our days when a man used to knock on the door every week, you paid him a shilling or something a week for the children's clothes, you know. I am not against credit as such, but when there are full-page newspaper adverts, on the television, everywhere, Dixons, all these shops, £1000 credit, NOW, you know. I think that it is wrong.

A common topic in our discussion groups was the pressure to consume, a pressure which people felt was recent and growing and to which certain groups, for example the young, were especially vulnerable: 'Some young people would say that credit is a normal thing nowadays. They would say that it is a normal part of life nowadays, that you are in debt.'

In our questionnaire, we began to explore people's responses to this perceived pressure by asking respondents how they resist consumer pressures (or how they best manage to respond to those pressures given their means). First, we asked people what stops them borrowing more money than they have already borrowed, if any (Table 1). There appear to be four categories of reasons why people constrain their borrowing: some don't borrow because they have moral objections to borrowing, believing that it is better to save up for things; some don't borrow because they are afraid of debt, possibly based on previous experiences of debt; others more pragmatically don't borrow because they think they can't afford to repay or because they resent the costs of borrowing; and lastly, some don't borrow because they don't feel strongly enough that they need anything which they cannot afford outright:

> Nowadays you are encouraged to borrow money for, say, holidays, borrow for a holiday, which isn't a necessity. In my days you would have saved up before you went on a holiday. But now you are encouraged to borrow £500 or whatever and pay it back later, but of course you get into debt.

Table 1 What stops you borrowing more (or any) money?

	%*
Morality	
Dislike/hate being in debt	17
Against borrowing in principle	8
Prefer to save up to get money to buy	4
Foolish to borrow	2
Experience of debt	
Fear of borrowing/repayments could get out of hand	8
Debts are source of worry	5
Too much in debt already	4
Bad past experience of debt	1

Table 1 continued

Costs of borrowing	
Can't afford to repay	19
High interest rates/high cost of repayments	12
Dislike paying interest/waste of money	9
Need for goods	
Don't need to borrow/have enough money	16
Prefer to live within means/try and do without	10
Don't want to commit to future repayments	10
Goods aren't worth it	1

Note: *Percentage of people mentioning each reason (275 respondents in total).

It seems that only one of these groups would borrow more if their economic situations improved, namely those who cite financial reasons against borrowing. Those against borrowing in principle and those who have had their fingers burnt previously are not unmoved by the pressure to have new goods, but would avoid borrowing as the means of obtaining them. Those who want nothing they cannot afford appear to formulate their desires according to their means, rather than allow their means to constrain their performed desires. These people may be equivalent in incomes and possessions, it is a matter of how they define necessities and luxuries, how they balance the pleasure and costs of acquisition, and of the moral and economic considerations which they consider relevant. People also interpret the similar financial situations differently. For example, one claims that 'while I am training I don't mind being a little in debt, but once I am no longer a student I will no longer allow myself debts', while another does not borrow because of 'being a student and therefore having no chance of paying it back'.

We also asked people how they economize, when necessary, revealing the variable ways in which people respond to an equivalent situation (Table 2).

This question reveals people's general priorities, their common and particular concerns, and the intricate linking of psychological values and attitudes with specific economic practices. People would clearly rather cut back on their spending to economize, reducing expenditure on particular, usually luxury or unessential items, rather than calculate a detailed budget and stick to it in a systematic way, as generally advocated by financial advisers. Planning spending is more work and more constraining, although possibly also more successful, than the simpler principle of cutting out certain goods from one's lifestyle.

Many people would reduce spending on their social life first, suggesting that the need to economize reduces participation in social life. This may have many hidden consequences for those who regularly economize in this way: loss of social support, loneliness, a more introverted lifestyle, loss of connection with the world, and so forth. A second form of social participation is also lost when economizing, that of participation in consumption itself – a common and socially shared means of occupying leisure time: people recognize that going shopping is by no means a simple matter of deciding to buy a particular good, selecting an appropriate shop and going there to purchase that good. Rather, they recognize the dangers in going shopping, seeing shopping as a persuasive, pleasurable and tempting situation in which they may lose control.

When people economize, their means of payment changes, as a preference for cash over credit or cheques emerges: this makes clear a popular belief that one has more control over cash, and so it is easier to limit spending by limiting one's means of payment; people are aware that with credit cards and cheques the pressures of the moment of consumption may override previously elaborated budgeting plans, and rather than always battling with themselves at the shop counter they would make it impossible to purchase without building in the time to go away and think it over: 'If one is going to live within one's means, in a situation where one is with friends and

Table 2 How do you economize?

	%[*]
Reduce spending	
Stay at home instead of social activities/eating out	22
Cut out luxuries/treats	20
Spend less on food	16
Spend less on clothes	16
Limit spending to essentials/necessities	13
Cut down on bills (phone, heating, hot water, etc.)	9
Spend less on alcohol	6
Cut down on spending generally	6
Save on petrol/travel by cycling or walking	6
Spend less on convenience foods/takeaways	4
Spend less on books/records	3
Spend less on cigarettes/stop smoking	2
Spend less on things for the house	1
Budgeting	
Watch where money goes, keep records of spending	6
Buy cheaper alternatives (e.g. own brand)	5
Stick to planned budget with clear spending limits	3
Make specific food lists	1
Look for waste and cut it out	1
Try to save regularly	1
Refuse requests for money	1
Draw out set amount from bank each week and manage	1
Shopping habits	
Visit shops less/no window shopping/avoid temptation	7
Shop around to compare prices for best buy or bargain	6
Before buying, ask oneself if it is really necessary	1
Cut down on impulse buying	1
Buy food in bulk	1
Strategies	
Postpone spending, defer major purchases	4
Make do and mend	3
Buy second-hand clothes	2
Avoid carrying spare cash	2
Don't carry credit card	2
Plan meals to make cheap food pleasurable	1
Don't carry cheque book	1
Eat at parents'/friends' house	1
Make extra money	
Work harder/do overtime	1
Sell unwanted/extra possessions	1

Note: [*]Percentage of people mentioning each way of economizing (272 respondents in total).

family and things all making demands, you have got to be able to say no, sometimes. And with credit cards it is that much more difficult to say no.'

Many principles of economizing – spending less on luxuries, treating only necessities as essential – raise more general issues about how we, as a culture and as individuals, identify needs and wants and the necessary and luxury goods which satisfy them. Strategies of economizing which people do not mention are often as interesting as those they do mention; notably, few people consider the second-hand market, rather doing without altogether than doing without things new and up-to-date. Similarly, few see their general financial situation as flexible, thinking of making extra money or doing more work; rather, they see the financial constraints as fixed, and try to manoeuvre within these. The focus on necessities and luxuries is constructed within an expectation of having the best, having things new, having things when they first appear, and such a focus itself directs attention towards personal needs and wants, an inward assessment, rather than towards examining the parameters of one's financial situation and attempting to alter these.

Finally, we note the variety of strategies which people adopt, many of which are tried and tested for them individually, though often not shared by others. These included the following: hiding or stashing a few pounds away each day or week; more do-it-yourself; think of simple ways to enjoy life; socialize at home; don't spend savings; avoid the sales; buy food in season; look for better interest rate on savings; remind self of financial situation when tempted to spend; use public buildings in winter; dodge fares; discuss finances with partner; don't take children shopping.

References

Barty-King, H. (1991) *The Worst Poverty: A History of Debt and Debtors*, Stroud, Sutton.

Berthoud, R. and Kempson, E. (1990) *Credit and Debt in Britain*, Report of first findings from the PSI Survey, London, Policy Studies Institute.

Curwen, P. (1990) *Understanding the UK Economy*, London, Macmillan.

Drury, A.C. and Ferrier, C.W. (1984) *Credit Cards*, London, Butterworth.

Galbraith, J.K. (1970) *The Affluent Society*, 2nd edn, Harmondsworth, Pelican.

Hartropp, A., Hanna, R., Jones, S., Lang, R., Mills, P. and Schluter, M. (1987) *Families in Debt: The Nature, Causes and Effects of Debt Problems and Policy Proposals for their Alleviation*, Jubilee Centre Research Paper no.7, Cambridge, Jubilee Centre Publications.

Leigh-Pemberton, R. (1989) 'Personal credit problems', *Bank of England Quarterly Bulletin*, vol.29, no.2, pp.243–5.

Parker, G. (1988) 'Credit' in Walker, R. and Parker, G. (eds) *Money Matters: Income, Wealth and Financial Welfare*, London, Sage.

Parker, G. (1990) *Getting and Spending: Credit and Debt in Britain*, Aldershot, Avebury.

Roebuck, J. (1973) *The Making of Modern English Society*, London, Routledge and Kegan Paul.

Social Trends (1989) Vol.19, Government Statistical Service Publication, London, HMSO.

Social Trends (1991) Vol.21, Government Statistical Service Publication, London, HMSO.

Source: Lunt and Livingstone, 1992, pp.27–33

'Home from home': the pub and everyday life

Diane Watson

Contents

1 Introducing the 'pub'

In this chapter we are going to examine the public house as a 'site' of everyday life and experience. But, before we do this, let us imagine for a moment that we have walked into the following everyday scene in a pub and are observing the interactions taking place between the various participants.

BOX 5.1

'Pint of bitter, please Thomas. And a glass of red wine, if you've got anything half decent.'

'My pleasure, young Sam. And if the wine is for Sandra, then nothing but the best.'

Tom, the landlord of The Hare and Hounds, waves across to Sandra who has sat down in a corner seat while Sam has gone up to the bar: 'Nice to see you Sandra, and so early in the evening. To what do we owe this great honour?'

Sandra starts to explain to Tom that Sam has persuaded her to call in with him on the way home from work because he has had a bad day in an over-heated office and is desperate for a drink. But before she has got very far into her explanation she notices that the only other two people in the bar are staring at her. She feels that they might be displaying disapproval of her being in 'their pub'. And they look as if they are anxious to hear every word of her explanation for her rare visit to this pub where her boyfriend, Sam, is a regular client. Sandra therefore leaves her seat and joins Sam at the bar to complete her account of her arrival at the pub with Sam shortly after 6pm on a Monday evening.

'Here, have a bar stool, Sandra', offers Sam, as he eases himself onto the other of the two tall stools which the pub provides for customers who want to position themselves at the bar rather than sit themselves on one of the upholstered benches fitted around the walls of the bar or at one of the tables which fill about half of the floor space of the room. Sandra scowls at him, trying to signal her reluctance to take up such a position – one that might imply to anyone coming in to the pub that she was some sort of regular drinker in the pub, or someone who wanted to be seen as a 'friend' of the landlord. However, she feels she had better be polite to Tom. Last time she reluctantly visited the pub with Sam she had been very rude to Tom about what she had called the 'very, very stale and very, very poor quality' red wine which he had served.

'Yes, I thought I'd better come in with Sam and just say sorry about what I said to you at New Year,' she says, as she pulls herself up onto the tall seat. 'He told me you were quite upset.'

'Well, I was pretty tired and emotional that day, I must admit. Joan and I had been working flat out over Christmas and New Year and we were both exhausted. I broke my rule about not drinking whilst working and, frankly, we were both getting close to deciding to leave the pub trade altogether. I admit I didn't like the way you spoke to me. But I shouldn't have been snappy with you about the wine. I'm always telling the staff here that the customer is always right, within reason. It's part of the job to smile at the punters, whatever you might actually think of them or what they are saying. And you weren't any old customer either. You were the girlfriend of one of our best regulars, making a rare visit to your bloke's local.'

'But I was right about the wine, Tom. It was awful.'

'I know. I know. That's actually what really upset me. And it's why I am so pleased to see you here again. Here, sip that and tell me what you think.'

Tom passes the red wine to Sandra. He has filled the glass right up to the brim. She carefully tastes the wine, anxious not to spill it, perched as she is on the barstool. This is a rather awkward form of seating for someone who has rarely stood at a pub bar, let alone sat at one, chatting to the publican like a well-seasoned local.

'Yes, that's really quite good', she reports to the obviously delighted Tom.

'Excellent. Now I'm really happy. You see I was not just upset with you at New Year. That awful wine was all that the brewery would supply me with. They said that there wouldn't be a call for a decent wine in this area. "Just because your pub has a country name, you shouldn't get above yourself", they told me when I complained. But I pointed out to them that the wine was so poor that people avoided it. The result of that was that any bottle I opened tended to hang about and to get stale. I did get through a few bottles over the holiday but when you came in I must have been down to a bottle which had been opened a week or two earlier. Not good enough, OK?'

'Sure. But how stupid of the brewery. That's a good example of a self-fulfilling prophecy if ever I heard one.'

'Well, Sandra, I don't know what one of them is – a self-filling whatsit. But what you're saying sort of makes my point anyway. We are getting and more people like you coming in – you know, teachers like you – and office people. You are more discriminating. And the brewery needs to wise up to how the clientele is changing in this area. This has been happening since the factory up the road closed and the new shops and offices opened, as I pointed out to the idiots in the brewery.'

'That's really interesting, Tom. We are doing a project at school about how the area is changing.'

'This pub has actually seen a lot of changes. Look, if you are staying for another drink, you'll probably catch Jack Fisher. He is the most regular of all our regulars. And he knows the history of this place better than anyone does. In, let me see, ten minutes' time he'll come through that door on his way home from work. I will have his pint ready for him and a packet of salted peanuts when he arrives. I'll get him to fill you in on this place.'

At this point, Sam decided it was time he came back onto the scene, 'That's nice of you, Tom. Give us the same again and have one yourself. We might even get Sandra, the great pub hater, to treat the Hare as much as her home-from-home as I do. She was just saying the other night that she envies me my "local". Although I am not sure if you'd want her in here falling asleep over piles of kids' homework.'

'Oh, so you're a bit like me then, Sandra', Tom speculated, 'always working and beginning to wonder whether your home is really your home, or just another work place? As Joan always says, managing a pub is more a way of life than a job.'

At that point Jack Fisher arrives at the bar. He picks up his glass of beer and with a 'Cheers everyone' swallows nearly half of its contents. Sandra, who is now herself more than half-way down her second glass of wine, introduces herself to Jack. She winces at his reference to her as 'Sam's other half' but is nevertheless feeling well disposed towards everyone around her as the wine takes its effect.

'So what's this that Tom's telling you then?', he asks, 'Was he giving you the line that the pub is a way of life? I like that. What I always say is …'

'We were hoping to get you to play your role as pub historian, actually,' Sam interjected, 'not the pub philosopher this early in the evening'. He handed some more money to Tom, indicating that this was for a second pint for Jack.

'Thanks young man,' said Jack, as he struggled to open his packet of peanuts. 'It's the same thing really. Pubs are part of history and part of the way of life of this country. And they change over time as the country changes. As you probably realized, this pub was here when this was a rural area – and the only real record of that part of the history of these parts is our Hare and Hounds pub sign.'

'Well pubs have not been part of my life,' Sandra reflected, 'And the area of Glasgow where I grew up didn't have pubs, just a lot of foul "bars" where only the roughest members of the community ever ventured. And I'm not sure what you mean by "this country" anyway. It's very different things to different people, and not just whether they are English, Scottish, or whatever. I mean there are a lot of black people in this town, but I've never seen any in here.'

'Fair point, Sandra,' came back Jack. 'And I'd be pleased if that changed. I can remember, for example, when women simply weren't allowed in this pub. That's changed. The pub changes with the world around it. Ordinary people who would never dream of going into a restaurant nowadays find they can go down to their pub and get quite a good meal. There are places that define themselves as family pubs – a big change that. And nowadays we have a gay pub in the town. That would have been unthinkable in this town ten years ago. If you like Irish music you can go to the Irish pub down the road. And you like Country and Western music this is the place on Friday nights. And you get jazz on a Sunday night.'

'So what is a pub then?', ventured Sam. 'When does a pub become an eating place rather than a pub, or an entertainment place, or a picking up place?'

'Well indeed,' followed up Tom, 'When is a wine bar a wine bar, a bistro a bistro, a drinking factory a drinking factory, a pub a pub? This is getting too complicated, folks. I've got to go down the cellar and change a barrel. There's no peace for the wicked. Anyway Sandra, it's jolly nice to have you with us tonight. I hope we'll see you again soon. It would be nice if the Hare was to become part of your everyday life, like it is for Jack, and Sam, and me.'

'Uhm, pubs and everyday life,' Sandra responded, 'I don't know about that.'

This account is not a 'record' of a particular event which actually took place but more a 'story' or 'scenario'. It is a distillation of a number of such events, which I observed and experienced in the course of a research project, one that though 'made up' is also 'true'. It is at one and the same time a piece of fiction and a piece of social science writing, which 'uses the imagination but is also theoretically informed and draws upon fieldwork research' (Watson, 2000). We want to use it here to 'do some sociology', to explore some of the connections between everyday life and the 'pub'.

1.1 The pub and everyday life

ACTIVITY 1

Sandra is not too sure about what connections can be made, or should be made, between pubs and 'everyday life'. But she has not had the advantage of reading what has been said in earlier chapters about the sociological concept of 'everyday life'. Looking back to what has been said so far about the concept, note down some of the ways in which you think we might use the concept of 'everyday life' to analyse what is going on in this scenario.

One of the ways in which we try to understand **everyday life** is to try, temporarily, to suspend our taken-for-granted acceptance of it as something which is utterly 'normal' and is therefore not consciously perceived. The above story of Sam, Sandra, Tom and Jack has been constructed from a variety of observational 'materials' gathered as part of an '**ethnography**' of public houses. And, in the story, Sandra helps us to suspend our taken-for-granted notion of the 'everyday'. This notion might be summarized with regard to pubs in terms of, 'Well, a pub is a pub is a pub, so what?' Sandra has prompted us to treat this as more than a rhetorical question and to respond to it. Her arrival in the pub has to some extent subverted the taken-for-grantedness of a normal early evening in The Hare and Hounds. And in her disrupting of the normality of the 'everyday', we are encouraged to ask questions that we might not otherwise ask. We are

sociology of everyday life

ethnography

sensitized to matters, which are worthy of sociological reflection but which, without her presence, we might simply pass by.

Public houses are one of the most frequently visited of leisure venues, with 69 per cent of the entitled population stating that they visit pubs at some time as part of their leisure activity (Mintel, 2000). However, as Sandra in the scene above reminds us, pubs may not be part of the immediate everyday life of all of us. There are many people who are not 'regulars' like Sam and Jack; there are plenty of others who would be unable to point to any particular public house as their personal 'local'; and there are those who have never entered a public house at all. Nevertheless, it is possible to see the public house as somehow playing the role of an 'icon of the everyday' within the culture, to which a majority of us can relate. A popular alternative to the rather archaic representation of the 'ordinary' or average person as the 'man or woman on the Clapham omnibus' is the 'man or woman in the pub'. What do television writers and producers do when they want to give soap opera viewers a regular stage in which their everyday characters can be seen going about their everyday business? They set a 'Rovers Return' in the middle of their Coronation Street or a 'Queen Victoria' at the heart of life in their Albert Square. When a man storms out of the house, in one situation comedy after another, he shouts that he's 'going down the pub' as he crashes out of the door. If the entertainment is a police story then the chances are that a criminal caught with stolen goods will tell the police that they 'bought them off this bloke in the pub'. And where do the police officers retire to when they finish their shift, so that we can hear them reflecting on their day of keeping the peace, and even observe them relaxing the rules and behaving badly? Yes, we see them in their local pub.

ACTIVITY 2

Take a few minutes to think back to Chapter 1, where the ideas of Rita Felski were introduced (section 4). Elsewhere, Felski argues that,

> Everyday life is the most self-evident, yet the most puzzling of ideas … everyday life simply *is*, indisputably: the essential taken-for-granted continuum of mundane activities that frames our forays into the more esoteric and exotic worlds. It is the ultimate, non-negotiable reality, the unavoidable basis for all other forms of human endeavour. … At first glance everyday life seems to be everywhere, yet nowhere. Because it has no clear boundaries it is difficult to identify. … Everyday life is synonymous with the habitual, the ordinary, the mundane …
>
> (Felski, 1999–2000, p.15)

In the light of this definition of 'everyday life', what connections can we make between the scene in the 'pub' and the sociology of 'everyday life'?

As you discovered earlier, everyday life is about 'repetition', about 'home' and about 'habit' (Felski, 1999–2000, pp.15–31). As we examine our scene more closely, it is clear that these three elements are central to what is 'going on' in this 'pub' as a 'site' of everyday life and experience and, as concepts, they help us make better sense of it. For Sam and for Jack, visiting the 'local' is, in part, about regularity and repetition. One aspect of their personal and social identities is as a 'regular' in the 'local', as a 'friend of the landlord', or as 'the most regular of all our regulars' in this complex activity space. Repetition is one of the strategies through which they, as individuals, organize and make sense of the world; it is also central to the formation and maintenance of their identities. Whilst this particular 'pub' may have seen many significant changes over time, it is still able to provide for Sam and Jack a sense of continuity, regularity and ordering of experience which is fundamental to their sense of place, of time and of security.

For Sam the pub serves as a 'home from home'. It is something of value to him and something he has that Sandra is, to a degree, envious of. Essential to the very idea of the notion of a 'public house' is the idea of a 'home' with a 'host'. It is a 'house' which is open to the public but which has formal and unspoken rules of behaviour and which welcomes some types of customer more than it welcomes others. It may be 'public' but it is still under the control and direction of the 'landlord'/'landlady' who has the legal right to bar entrance or refuse to serve a person, without being required to give an explanation. There are norms of behaviour and codes of conduct that must be learnt if the visitor is to feel welcome and at ease in this semi-public social space.

Finally, everyday life is about habit. Whilst visiting a pub is not a regular habit for Sandra, for Sam it is a habitual leisure activity which is pretty predictable from the perspective of those who know him. This is even more so the case with Jack. Habit is fundamentally a part of the relationship between Jack and Tom, the landlord. Tom knows at exactly what time Jack will arrive, what he will want to drink and what he will eat with it. And Tom is habitual in his responses. He pours the pint at the same time and in the same way, secure in the knowledge that it will be welcomed and not wasted. These elements of everyday life allow us to bring order, control and predictability into our daily lives and social relationships. Everyday life is precisely about these habitual, routine, self-evident, ordinary and mundane aspects of life, which we generally take for granted and do not ask critical questions about. By suspending our everyday assumptions about the world, as Sandra does by virtue of her more marginal role in the scene, we can approach everyday events with a fresh eye, as if they were 'anthropologically strange' to us. In adopting this approach, we are better able to suspend the 'natural attitude' (Schutz and Luckmann, 1974) and gain new insights into these everyday processes and experiences.

AIMS

By exploring the connections between everyday life and the pub, this chapter provides a sociological analysis of the public house as a 'site' of everyday experience. The aims of the chapter are:

1   To place the public house in its social and historical context and explore continuities and changes with the past and present.

2   To examine the role of ethnography, observation and participant observation in sociological research. It will demonstrate how sociology, as a set of academic practices, can provide the 'tools' to distance the individual from taken-for-granted aspects of everyday life, such that everyday experiences may be approached as 'anthropologically strange' events to be understood in a new light.

3   To explore some of the social processes and cultural practices which take place in this particular site of the everyday. It will pay particular attention to: gender and social class; rural and urban contexts; work and employment

relationships; modern lifestyles and consumption patterns; and the 'Englishness' of the pub as an institution.

4   To focus on the public house as a semi-public 'activity space' where public and private worlds meet, where the distinction between work and leisure is sometimes hard to define, and where individual identities and lifestyles are expressed. Public houses are sites of leisure, pleasure and work, which are located between the 'private' world of home and family and the 'public' world of work and neighbourhood.

2 Historical contexts and sociological continuities

Public drinking 'houses' of one kind or another have been important sites of social, political and economic exchange in almost every type of society. In his history of the 'English alehouse' Clark argues that,

> ... drinking houses are both ubiquitous and indispensable social agencies, their importance extending well beyond the provision of alcohol and other forms of refreshment to their role as the centre for a host of economic, social, political and other activities.

(Clark, 1983, p.2)

The particular form that these drinking houses have taken has varied according to history and place and it is important to recognize the peculiarities of the 'English' public house as a particularly nineteenth- and twentieth-century social phenomenon. This is not to suggest that the pub is the only significant type of drinking place in modern cultures. Clearly it is not. In Australia, America and Scotland, for example, traditionally there have been 'bars' rather than 'pubs' and in Europe there have been bistros, beerkellers and licensed cafés. In England, too, as in the rest of the UK, there is a proliferation of hotels, restaurants, bars, cafés and clubs, all in competition with pubs for customers, and all manifesting social and cultural variation. However, the 'typically English pub' is sociologically interesting for its particular place in 'English' culture and for its symbolic role as, what we have called earlier, 'an icon of the everyday'.

Historically in Britain, public houses have served as the social focus for geographical and occupational communities. The public house has taken different forms over time and has its origins in the 'inns', 'taverns' and 'alehouses' of the pre-industrial era. In that period alehouses were more numerous then than any other type of public meeting-place and were the focus for a huge range of social and economic activity. Ordinary people went there to 'buy and sell goods, to borrow money, to obtain lodging and work, to find sexual partners, to play folk games and gamble, in addition to the usual eating, dancing, smoking and carousing' (Clark, 1983). However, it was not until the early 1800s that the purpose-built public house as we know it began to be built in large numbers and the 'alehouse' gave way to the 'public house'. By the beginning of the nineteenth century the term 'alehouse' had all but disappeared and by 1865, according to the *Oxford English Dictionary*, the word 'pub' had entered the language in what was termed colloquial or 'low' usage.

The rise of the Victorian public drinking place has been associated with both industrialization and urbanization where:

> Public houses and the like have been portrayed as refuges for men escaping the monotonous toll of factory work, from the misery of unemployment and big-city alienation; or alternatively, as places to spend high industrial wages at a time when men had few outlets for conspicuous expenditure. In recent years, however, a number of historians have stressed some of the important traditional aspects of nineteenth century drinking houses, not least as venues for old-style games and other communal recreations and activities.
>
> (Clark, 1983, p.2)

By the end of the nineteenth century, public houses were such an established feature of the English cultural landscape that the social reformer and early statistician, **Charles Booth**, observed that public houses were then more important in the lives of people than clubs or friendly societies, churches or missions, and possibly all of those institutions put together (*ibid.*, p.1). **Booth, Charles**

At the start of the twenty-first century, public houses are still an established feature of the British cultural landscape. However, they have undergone many changes in themselves and in the role they occupy in culture and society. By placing the public house in this wider historical context we are able to trace some of the ways in which this institution has both changed and developed over time. As Jennings has observed,

> In some ways the public house might seem unchanging: people go there in the late twentieth century to drink, talk, play games and enjoy music just as they did in the late eighteenth century, deriving, no doubt the same basic satisfactions of stimulation, relaxation, company or escape. This fact has, of course, helped to ensure the long-term survival of the pub, together with its accessibility – wherever you lived or whatever your means – and adaptability – to village or city life and to many and varied purposes. But that world has also changed in innumerable ways; from what and how much was drunk and its significance in people's lives, to the physical surroundings in which that drinking took place and to the overall importance of the pub in the life of the community.
>
> (Jennings, 1995, p.13)

Jennings and Clark are not sociologists but social historians. And it is interesting that, for such an important social institution, there has been surprisingly little sociological analysis of the public house and, consequently, little written about public houses in the academic literature of sociology. Hey, for example, has commented on the

> … dearth of work by men on this prime site of 'male enjoyment'. Given that 'popping out for a quick one'/'taking the dog for a walk'/'wetting the whistle' is one of the most popular male recreational activities, what is it that has prevented men from taking this institution seriously?
>
> (Hey, 1986, p.8)

By way of explanation Hey suggests that this is possibly because, in a **patriarchal** society, 'male standards become generalized as generically human standards. Consequently, the maleness of men has been hidden from sociological enquiry' and the 'political relations of men and women acted out inside the pub' have been obscured (*ibid.*). For the purposes of our discussion this is a useful illustration of the way in which our 'taken-for-grantedness' of everyday life may **patriarchy** serve to obscure our understanding of this key institution. The nature of the institution and its social and cultural role is so 'taken for granted' that it has not struck sociologists to be worthy of sociological study.

2.1 Mass-Observation: *The Pub and the People*

mass
observation

One of the earliest published social scientific studies of the public house, *The Pub and the People* (1987/1943), is available to us, however. This work was one of the products of the pioneering social research organization, **Mass-Observation**, set up in the late 1930s by Tom Harrisson and Charles Madge. Madge was at that time a newspaper reporter and Harrisson, who had been educated at Harrow public school, had spent time during the early 1930s exploring what he referred to as 'some of the most primitive and uncivilized parts of the world'. Describing how he gradually became aware that what he was 'doing at great expense in these difficult jungles had not been done in the wilds of Lancashire and East Anglia', he determined to devote the rest of his life to studying the 'so-called civilized peoples of the world'. Using the research tools of the concealed notebook and camera, their aim was to observe and record the thoughts and behaviour of ordinary people in their everyday surroundings, with a view to producing an 'anthropological survey of ourselves' (Harrisson, 1942, p.xiv). To achieve this,

> ... fifty people in different parts of the country agreed to co-operate in making observations on how they and other people spend their daily lives. These fifty Observers were the vanguard of a developing movement, aiming to apply the methods of science to the complexity of modern culture. ... One aim of Mass-Observation is to see how, and how far, the individual is linked up with society and its institutions.
>
> (Jennings and Madge, 1937/1987, pp.iii–v)

The development of Mass-Observation took two main strands. First, there was the countrywide network of observers. This was organized by Madge and took as the starting-point the individual Observers, working 'outwards from them to their social surroundings' (Jennings and Madge, 1987, p.iv). Secondly, there was the 'intensive survey of a local town'. This was organized by Harrisson and took, as its starting-point, the 'whole-time research workers studying a place from the outside and working inwards, getting into the society and so coming to the individual' (*ibid.*). Thus it was that, in 1937, Harrisson, along with a 'heterogeneous group of leftish middle-class intellectuals' (Gurney, 1988, p.1), established a base for Mass-Observation in Bolton. For two years they collected empirical material relating to all aspects of everyday life in 'Worktown', their fictional name for Bolton and Blackpool, and published their detailed findings in *The Pub and the People*.

Mass-Observation ultimately grew to use a team of countrywide, paid observers and volunteer recruits to observe all aspects of everyday life in Britain between the years of 1937 and the early 1950s. The Mass-Observation archive (now housed in the University of Sussex Library) is made up of hundreds of observation reports and surveys, produced by paid fieldworkers, and a collection of diaries and self-observations, which were submitted regularly by members of the volunteer panel.

Figure 5.1 *The Grapes Hotel, Water Street, Bolton, 1937*

Mass-Observation was, therefore, an ambitious, long-term, comprehensive research project, which produced a wealth of countrywide information about the everyday lives and experiences of ordinary people during the 1930s, 1940s and 1950s. More specifically *The Pub and the People* gives us local survey material, and fine-detail observations, which create for us a picture of everyday life in public houses in Bolton and Blackpool in the late 1930s (see Figure 5.1). This material ranges from a description of geographical location to physical layout; from a description of the landlord to a discussion of 'drink servers'; from the drink and drinkers to drinking a pint and getting drunk; from other leisure activities taking place in the pub to non-drinking and the temperance movement. This fascinating observational map of 'the everyday' is a significant starting-point for any present-day sociologist wishing to understand the pub in its social and cultural context. And much can be learned from this project, both positively and negatively, about the methods and processes involved in conducting social scientific research into the everyday lives and experiences of ordinary people.

READING 5.1

Turn to Reading 5.1, which is part of the Preface to *The Pub and the People*, written by Tom Harrisson in 1942. As you read it, consider the following questions:

1   What was the 'aim' of the Mass-Observation study of 'Worktown'?

2   What method and research techniques did the observers use?

3   What difficulties did these observers face in conducting their observations?

4   Are there any ethical issues raised by this research?

From this extract the members of Mass-Observation appear to have strong convictions concerning the value of their project and what it would deliver in terms of an 'anthropology of everyday lives'. According to Harrisson, their aim was to 'observe objectively' with a view to making an 'objective, unbiased appraisal of the pub'. As observers, they asserted that they were not intent on making value judgements or criticisms about life in 'Worktown' because 'Mass-Observation has no interest either in proving pubs are good or pubs are bad'. They didn't use interviews with people but reported conversations with key informants. And they – and, in particular, Humphrey Spender, a professional photojournalist working with Mass-Observation from 1937–8 – took photographs: see, for example, Figure 5.2. The research project followed a programme of stages: reconnaissance; description; covert observation; overt observation; and the use of documentary materials and statistics.

reflexivity

The problems and difficulties facing this team of observers are broadly the same as those confronting any contemporary researcher undertaking observation. However, the extract you have just read suggests a belief in objectivity and value neutrality, which would be questioned by many researchers today. The extract appears to display a certain lack of **reflexivity** about these problems. This was a team of middle-class observers operating in a largely working-class environment. And, as Gurney (1988) suggests, their reports were 'invariably written by middle-class people and this undoubtedly coloured the representation of Bolton work-people'. There would inevitably be bias in selection and in the writing of the reports and it is important to recognize this. Attempting covert observation must also raise ethical issues but again this does not appear to have featured as a major concern. Apparently Humphrey Spender often used to work with a 'small camera concealed beneath his raincoat; only

Figure 5.2 *The vaults in an unidentified Bolton pub, photographed by Humphrey Spender for the Mass-Observation study*

the lens protruded and the camera operated through the holes in the pockets. Working-class Boltonians who noticed this intrusion were frequently angered' (Gurney, 1988, p.3).

These problems are graphically illustrated, according to Hey (1986), by the following extract from the 'drink servers' section of *The Pub and the People*, called 'Beautiful Barmaids':

> Two young men play quoits with the barmaid, who is, thinks observer, attractive in a coarse way. She is good at quoits anyway, and wins. One player leaves. She plays again with the other, winning again. This chap, young, red faced, blond, healthy looking, unshaved, cap on one side of his head, face washed but hands dirty, is apparently on fumbling relations with the barmaid.
>
> (Mass-Observation, 1987/1943, p.56)

Hey argues that this description 'typifies the complex class and gender patronage underlying Mass-Observation's operational ideologies'. It perfectly characterizes 'bourgeois masculinity' in the way that it articulates 'a complex perspective in which class is both counted and discounted … she might be a daughter of the "workers" but she is after all a women! "Attractive in a coarse way"' (Hey, 1986, p.41). Hey also suggests that *The Pub and the People* manifests a 'sociological voyeurism' which she sees as 'endemic in the methodology of Mass-Observation and of qualitative sociology generally'. This has the effect of reducing the observed, both male and female, to 'the status of objects' and the 'objectification of women is also secured by the ability of the male observers to both share and collude in the male chauvinism of pub cultures that cuts across social class'. She suggests that 'the relations *between* men of various classes is the substance of patriarchal male practices which find expression in the discourse of the middle-class editor and his middle-class and working-class respondents' (*ibid.*, p.42; emphasis in original).

These, then, are some of the limitations of the Mass-Observation project and it is inevitable that the contemporary sociologist will feel uncomfortable with some aspects of its ideology and methodology. However, with these qualifications in mind it should also be acknowledged that Mass-Observation has provided the academic community with an enormous amount of descriptive material about the lives of ordinary people, at a particular point in history. *The Pub and the People* has, in particular, given us a wealth of information about the lives of working-class men in Bolton, even if it neglected to give us a female perspective on events.

READING 5.2

To give a flavour of the results of Mass-Observation as published in *The Pub and the People*, turn to Reading 5.2. Bearing in mind our interest in the 'everyday', this extract gives us an insight into the sort of material that was produced by the Mass-Observation observers. It illustrates how they described the taken-for-granted aspects of everyday life in a pub in Bolton and what they, as observers, inferred about the 'function of the pub in all English industrial communities' (Mass-Observation, 1987, p.19).

■ What can you infer from this extract about gender relationships, about social class and about the 'geography' of the physical space?

This is a fascinating description of the 'things that people do in pubs' in Blackpool in the 1930s. The observer's inference is that this is a typical or 'characteristic record' of an evening in the pub which, whilst particular to 'Worktown', can also tell us something about the role of the pub more generally in English industrial communities. What further can we infer about the 'Worktown' everyday from this extract? First, note that, with the exception of Molly, the 'barmaid', the 'people' are all males and their behaviour and conversation is, to the observer, both repetitive, routine and mundane. Conversation is reported in the vernacular. We learn something about the 'geography' of the social space because we discover that there is the 'vault' bar and a 'back parlour' and that different activities are taking place in these different rooms. It is possible that there are women in the back parlour but this is not made explicit here. The only reference to women, apart from the barmaid, is a drinker's comment that 'Wife's always asking what I do wi' me overtime' (Reading 5.2, p.220). We know that the pub is very much a 'local' because the drinkers' houses are 'seldom more than three minutes walk away'. The observer, is most certainly male (he wouldn't be in the 'vault' otherwise), and very likely to be middle class (because he is a Mass-Observation paid observer), and this probably colours what he regards as important to comment upon. Note that one of the things that they observe happens in pubs is that 'prejudices gather'. Men wear caps and clogs and have gaps in their front teeth. Their clothes are 'different' from each other yet also appear to the observer to be all 'alike'. The drinkers' clothes are made of 'shapeless, greasy grey-blue cloth' whilst the landlord 'wears a clean dark-grey suit' and a 'clean white shirt'. This is 'essentially a social group around widespread and commonplace social activities', which are 'bound together by the bond of beer habits' (1942, p.25). Note their conclusion that there are 'few things that are peculiar to the pub in Worktown' and that they can reach some generalized conclusions about what is typical in a pub of this type in this sort of neighbourhood.

The Pub and the People is a valuable reference point for sociologists who wish to learn more about the pub as a social institution and its role as a 'site' of the everyday. Hey argues that Mass-Observation took a radical approach in pursuing the goal of showing the pub as a 'living social organism' and that, 'It is Mass-Observation's serious commitment to seeing pubs as venues for the expression of social relations that provides a fascinating opportunity to eavesdrop on gender/class ideologies of the 1930s and 1940s' (Hey, 1986, p.39). Through this process of 'eavesdropping', in this short extract alone we have learned something about gender and gender relationships; about the spatial layout of the pub and the male monopoly of the social space; about the social class of the participants in the scene (and possibly of the observers too); about aspects of working in a pub; and about the role of the commonplace in creating social bonds in the local community. As we discovered in Reading 5.1, the methods of Mass-Observation were, by their very nature, based on observation and direct acquaintance with 'the mass of people who left school before they were 15'. The observers used both covert and overt observation, reported conversations, the study of individuals' letters, diaries and documents, 'data from important people' and published sources and statistics. We also learnt that the Mass-Observation team were concerned about what they saw as the British 'obsession for the typical', 'the representative' and the 'statistical sample'. They formed the view that social issues could not be properly understood using only quantitative methods, such as 'statistical interviewing, the formal questionnaire and the compilation of data on the library level' (Mass-Observation, 1987/1943, p.xiv). On the other hand, they were not participants in the scenes they were observing and they did not use the technique of direct interviewing. Ultimately, the material produced by Mass-Observation was largely descriptive in nature.

SUMMARY OF SECTION 2

In this section we have placed the public house in its social and historical context and explored the role of observation in sociological research. We have:

1   examined the public house as a social institution, as a site of social, political and economic exchange and as a site of 'everyday life';

2   used an example of 'fiction science' to 'do some sociology' and explore how, in suspending our everyday, taken-for-granted assumptions about social life, we are better able to approach 'normal' occurrences as if they are anthropologically strange events and gain new insights into everyday social interactions;

3   identified historical continuities in the role of the pub which in part accounts for its continued relevance as an 'icon of the everyday' and a site of everyday social life;

4   explored the value and relevance of observation as a research technique, examining some of the strengths and weaknesses of this approach and evaluating some of the descriptive evidence provided by Mass-Observation research;

5   gained some insight into how, in a patriarchal society, the 'maleness of men' has been hidden from sociological enquiry, leading to a lack of sociological research on the pub and the dynamics of social relations within it.

3 'Doing' ethnographic research

What might other types of sociological study be able to tell us about the 'everyday life' of pubs in the twenty-first century? In his preface to *The Pub and the People* Harrisson acknowledges Mass-Observation's indebtedness to the academics of the **Chicago School** of sociology, which dominated US sociology between the two World Wars. Most of the studies undertaken by the Chicago School were ethnographies, and were particularly concerned with the social construction of identities, achieved through processes of social interaction and the meanings attributed to situations by the actors involved. In recent years there has been a growing interest in **qualitative research** approaches in social science, and ethnography has become far more widely used in academic research. This has been partly because of disillusionment with the traditional, dominant quantitative approaches in social science and partly because it is an approach which is particularly suited to the study of everyday life. In ethnography,

Chicago School

qualitative research

> The ethnographer participates, overtly or covertly, in people's daily lives for
> an extended period of time, watching what happens, listening to what is said,
> asking questions; in fact collecting whatever data are available to throw light
> on the issues with which he or she is concerned.
>
> (Hammersley and Atkinson, 1990, p.2)

**participant
observation**

Ethnographic researchers use the research technique of **participant
observation** to undertake their 'fieldwork'. You will be introduced to an example
of participant observation later on in this chapter. However, for now it is important
to emphasize that participant observation involves a researcher taking part in
the lives of the people who are being studied, but demands an ability to maintain
a professional distance from the scene, to allow observation and data gathering.
This approach tends to produce qualitative research material. In ethnographic
settings the researcher may take on one or more research roles, which will vary
according to the type of setting in which they find themselves and the particular
stage in their research. Junker (1960) has suggested that these roles may range
from the extremes of 'complete participant' and 'complete observer', to a position
somewhere along the continuum in the role of 'participant as observer' or
'observer as participant' (Hammersley and Atkinson, 1990, p.93). Mass-
Observation probably comes closest to the 'complete observer' end of the
continuum.

3.1 The pub and community life: gender and social relations

Ethnography is particularly suited to the study of everyday life and social
interactions and was the research approach used by Ann Whitehead (1976) in
her study of a Herefordshire parish. Whitehead uses the concept of patriarchy
to help understand and explain gender relations in this community. She interprets
pub culture in this small rural parish as expressive of wider patriarchal marital
relations, where the local pub is part of the broader social context in which
marital roles are set and where 'drinking in pubs was both ideally and in practice
a man's privilege' (1976, p.175). She concludes that 'what happens to men and
women in pubs is explicable in terms of patriarchal social relations'. Whitehead,
who lived in this Herefordshire community for a number of years, found that
she encountered difficulties in gaining entry to this particular pub as a research
site until an 'insider' from the parish assisted her entry:

> The only unmarried woman who drank regularly at The Wagonner was the
> anthropologist. My class and stranger position, and my general eccentricity (by
> Herefordshire standards), made my first visits tolerable, but my access to the
> pub was only finally gained after one young married lorry driver whom I knew
> well pronounced the facilitating formula: 'Ann and me, we're like brother and
> sister. She's like a sister to me.'
>
> (Whitehead, 1976, p.176)

Once she had gained access, Whitehead – as both participant and observer –
used the concepts of patriarchy and the 'joking relationship' to analyse the
patterns of gender and class underlying the taken-for-granted patterns of
everyday social interaction, and the routines and habits of the local population.

For an example of Ann Whitehead's findings, now turn to Reading 5.3, 'Sexual antagonism in Herefordshire'. As you read:

1   Note how Whitehead 'suspends her taken for granted assumptions' about what is going on in the pub and the parish in order to approach the activities in the pub as 'strange' events and question what she thinks is 'self-evident' about what she sees.

2   What can you discover about the role of The Wagonner in parish life?

3   What is distinctive about the geography of the pub?

4   What can you learn about gender relations in this community?

5   What is the role of 'joking' and teasing in this particular pub?

By observing everyday pub conversations and social exchanges taking place over time, Whitehead builds up a picture about the role of The Wagonner in community life and the nature of social and relationships taking place within it. The Wagonner is a very small pub, drawing its working-class customers from the immediate vicinity. Activity is based in the 'bottom bar', which is largely a male preserve, friendly for the regulars, and where people come to have a good time.

What we learn from this brief extract is that men and women do not have equal access to this pub as a source of leisure and pleasure: men are dominant and women are socially disenfranchised. Gender stereotyping is clearly at work, with most of the talk and banter being focused on wives, marriages or sexual relationships. The pub is a bone of contention between husbands and wives and – for the women – a bitterly resented intrusion into their family lives. Only when men are segregated from the women are they fully able to participate in the verbal banter of pub life. Many women respond by avoiding the pub altogether and by taking a hostile attitude to the husband's involvement there.

Whitehead pays particular attention to the reciprocal drinking between men and to the nature of the joking, which takes place between them. A whole range of other leisure activities take place in the pub but it is as a 'major locale for verbal games' in particular in which the male dominance and women's domination is played out. Whitehead observes that conversation frequently 'developed into a highly characteristic set of exchanges in which joking and humour were uppermost' and on these occasions the pub became 'an unparalleled situation of social drama'. This humour, however, is not generic and universal but depends on matters internal to the group, involves their finding a point of vulnerability in another customer and often uses women as 'counters in joking currency'. Women are central to the exchanges. Most jokes are about sex and sexual relations and about the degree of control a man has over his wife, her sexuality and how much freedom she should have. The drinking situation is 'an arena of public confrontation in which men can come together and engage in verbal competition'.

Clearly, according to Whitehead's interpretation, what goes on in the pub is not separated from other areas of life but inextricably involved in it. Social relationships in the pub are intimately linked to social relationships outside and play a key role in reinforcing men's position of control and dominance in relation

Figure 5.3 *A rural pub – at the centre of village social life?*

to wives and girlfriends. This is what Whitehead has deduced from her ethnography. As Brake has suggested, she

> ... shows how in a rural setting, the pub is used to reinforce the cult of masculinity, women are used to maintain solidarity and ambivalent rivalry between men: jokes were used to stereotype women as contemptible and as sex objects to be controlled, prestige was related to an ability to control one's wife, and that these invariably influence marital relations.
>
> (Brake, 1980, p.150)

Although Whitehead's research was conducted by a woman, in a rural environment, thirty years after Mass-Observation, one can't help but be struck by the strong resonances between both works. The pubs studied were predominately male domains where woman were only invited at certain times and then only to inhabit their own, largely segregated space. Men were hostile to women's presence and bonded with each other at their expense. For men the pub was a retreat and refuge from the pressures and constraints of work, home and family. The 'proper place' for women was seen to be the private sphere of home and family. They were merely tolerated or, on occasion, 'invited' by their men to join them in the pub.

Thus far we might be tempted to stress those continuities we have observed over historical periods and, more specifically, between the public house culture of the 1930s and 1970s. We might be justified in our impression of pubs as almost entirely male domains, offering men solace and refuge from the pressures of work and family and we might readily concur with Hey that 'public' houses have 'never really been "public" for women'. For her, history suggests that the public house is 'a political institution expressive of deeply held gender ideologies' where 'women alone, or together, are still likely to attract collective hostility from men' (1986, p.72).

3.2 Regulation and social control

It is certainly true that the history of the public house suggests that the role of the pub, and the activities taking place within it, have been viewed with fear, suspicion and concern by many. Mass-Observation noted that the public house,

> … is the only kind of public building used by large numbers of ordinary people where their thoughts and actions are not being in some way arranged for them; in the other kinds of public buildings they are the audiences, watchers of political, religious, dramatic, cinematic, instructional or athletic spectacles. But within the four walls of the pub, once a man has bought or been bought his glass of beer, he has entered an environment in which he is participator rather than spectator.
>
> (Mass-Observation,1987/1943, p.1)

But you will also remember from Reading 5.2 that Mass-Observation also suggested, perhaps more negatively, that pubs were places where 'prejudices gather'. This very freedom to 'participate' rather than 'spectate' could, it was feared, bring with it the dangers of social unrest and upheaval, licentiousness, drunkenness and disaffection, particularly in what were viewed as the 'lower social classes'. The social histories of Clark (1983) and Jennings (1995) are full of centuries of evidence of concern about drink, drunkenness and the role of the public house in fostering these undesirable behaviours. Over time, drinking became a highly legislated, controlled and regulated area, with landlords requiring licences not only for drink but also to allow activities such as singing and dancing, and where drinking became restricted to certain times of the day and certain days of the week and year (Jennings, 1995, pp.201–10).

This interest of state institutions in curbing and regulating the spontaneity of social activity associated with public houses and drinking, and the fear of the influence of drink and drunkenness, was not confined to the UK either. Whilst Britain had its Temperance Societies, and the United States experimented with prohibition, Australia introduced the six o'clock closing time, in the context of a five o'clock end to the working day, and created the 'six o'clock swill' (Fiske, Hodge and Turner, 1987, p.4). One unintended consequence of this regulation was to focus and intensify drinking in the hour after work and create functional and utilitarian public bars, given over entirely to men and designed for hard drinking. In Australia 'the pub was a male preserve matching male preserves in other cultures' (*ibid.*, p.3). Where women were present, unless they were working in the bar as 'wife' or 'barmaid', they were, as in Britain, generally confined to the 'best rooms' (Mass-Observation, 1987/1943, p.92), rooms such as the 'ladies' lounge', the 'parlour' or the 'snug'.

Whilst pubs and drinking were licensed, controlled and regulated in this legal sense, for men the pub also provided 'regulation' of quite a different kind. The pub served as a refuge or safe retreat from the rest of their lives. For them in particular it appears to serve as a 'home from home' or a 'home away from home', in which they have 'license' to behave in ways not necessarily appropriate and acceptable at home, at work or in other social contexts. In an earlier context this is what Whitehead calls the 'licensed familiarity of the pub' (1976, p.175). As Fiske *et al.* argue, 'the pub is a building, but more importantly it is a category of place … a social space, organized by a set of rules which specify who can be in it and what they can do' (1987, p.5). As we suggested earlier, the pub is a semi-public activity space which occupies the boundaries between the public and private spheres of life. It is both a 'home away from home' and a 'place away from work'. In exploring the pub-world of the 'Birdwatcher's Bar' in the 1980s Fiske *et al.* suggest that the social space of the public bar is 'a kind of anti-world, a bracketed space where the normative relationships of the real world were suspended or inverted, though only temporarily. Its cultural function was to achieve that status and to control it; to limit it in place … and time' (*ibid.*, p.3).

The pubs of Bolton and Herefordshire, which we have explored in some detail, are features of particular times and places. They may persist in a similar form in some areas today but, as Jennings (1995) has suggested, the pub as an institution has survived in large part because of its flexibility and adaptability in new times and changed circumstances. The pub has both retained its fundamentals as a 'site' of everyday leisure and adapted to new times and new expectations. We would anticipate therefore that, at the beginning of the twenty-first century, pubs will have seen many significant changes, providing different kinds of leisure activity and making them more accessible to wider groups of people, particularly families, children and women.

SUMMARY OF SECTION 3

In this section we have examined the role of ethnography and participant observation in sociological research, exploring in more depth social relationships taking place within the pub as a social institution. We have:

1   analysed an example of ethnographic research to evaluate the role of participant observation in exposing the routines and habits of customers in a rural pub;

2   used this research to place a particular pub in its social and cultural context, utilizing the concepts of patriarchy and the joking relationship to examine the social and cultural processes and practices which take place in the pub, paying particular attention to gender, social class and the rural environment;

3   examined the place of gender stereotyping in the dynamics of social relations in the pub, making connections between the social relationships within the pub and connections with social relationships in the wider community of which it is a part;

4   analysed the role of the pub in reinforcing men's position of dominance in relation to women, noting the continuities between the work of Mass-Observation and research in the 1960s;

5   identified the role of the state in regulating social activity associated with the pub and the role of the pub itself as an institution of social regulation, providing a refuge and retreat in which customers have license to behave in ways not necessarily acceptable in the public sphere.

4 Leisure, lifestyle, work and consumption

If we return to the pub scene with which we started this chapter, we see that Tom and Jack argue that The Hare and Hounds has itself seen many changes. There were times when women weren't even allowed in the pub but now it is accepted and commonplace. People who in the past wouldn't have dreamt of going to a restaurant are happy to go down to the pub for a meal. There are places which define themselves as family pubs or gay pubs, and pubs where you can go to listen to Irish music, country and western or jazz. Sandra is worried about the whole notion of the typical 'English pub'. She recognizes that, not only have there been different types of pub serving different types of clientèle in different localities, but also a proliferation of bars, clubs and cafés targeting different socio-cultural groups. And Sam, in thinking about his taken-for-granted assumptions about what a pub *is*, is not even sure that he now knows what a 'pub' is at all!

4.1 Leisure

ACTIVITY 3

Pause for a moment and make a list of factors you think may have influenced the changes that have taken place in drinking habits and patterns of pub usage since the Mass-Observation era. You may be able to categorize the factors on your list under some of the following headings.

- geographical
- architectural
- economic
- demographic
- social
- cultural

- legal
- industrial restructuring
- consumption patterns
- marketing patterns
- health issues

So, what might some of these factors for change be? Mass-Observation concluded that, in Bolton, the pub was a key social institution in which 'more people spend more time than they do in any other buildings except private houses and workplaces' (1987/1943, p.17). However, they also noted that it was beginning to play a smaller part in the life of the town than it had done previously because of a cultural shift from active and communal forms of leisure to more individual and passive forms. In *Brewing for Victory* Glover has argued that the Second World War began a whole chain of events which were to break down 'old social conventions' and 'open up' the pub to a 'much wider range of customers' (1995, pp.25–8). In 'class-ridden' Britain, landlords were even accustomed to refusing to serve 'other ranks' if officers were in the bar and it was common knowledge that 'respectable' woman never went into a pub. The War was instrumental in breaking down these **taboos** with the result that the pub became a 'home from home' and a place of 'rest and recreation' for new and unexpected groups of people.

taboos

Figure 5.4 *Salford, 1971: an urban pub in a declining area*

Jennings (1995) has identified a number of trends that began to affect the pub from the early 1950s onwards. Amongst them was the decline of traditional working-class neighbourhoods, communities and extended families and a trend towards a more geographically mobile, individualistic society, where the nuclear family became the key consumer unit. (You will meet an example of this in Chapter 6, which explores the shift of population from Bethnal Green in East London out into the suburbs.) There was a proliferation of new consumer goods on which to spend a rising disposable income. Although there was a decline in the total number of public houses, new pubs were permitted on the proliferating new housing estates whilst old ones disappeared through the process of urban redevelopment (see Figure 5.4). The physical stock of pubs was also changing. The traditional layout, with combinations of separate bar, vault, tap room, music room, back parlour, lounge and snug, was being opened up to more spacious and open-plan designs, with consequences for the social use of space.

Ownership of pubs became increasingly concentrated in the hands of a few brewery conglomerates with a virtual monopoly over what drinks could be sold. Over time pub licensing laws relaxed and became more flexible. But the introduction of the breathalyser and drink-driving laws had a significant and continuing impact on drinking habits, as well on the viability of many – particularly the rural – pubs (at the time of writing closing at the rate of six a week (*The Guardian*, 6 December 1999)). There were many more places where people could drink, particularly in the home with alcohol bought more cheaply in off-licences and (later on) in supermarkets, as well as a proliferation of alternatives to the pub such as clubs and wine bars. More recently, tastes have shifted from beer to lager, wine and a range of other mixer-type or 'alcopop' bottled drinks, although pressure groups such as CAMRA (the Campaign for Real Ale) have organized to try to reverse the trend to lager and keg beer back to good quality, real ale.

Industrial structures and work patterns were also changing. The traditional, male-dominated heavy industry declined as the service sector grew. Women entered paid employment in large numbers and work patterns changed. Flexible working and part-time jobs have increased in number as society has become more attuned to a pattern of twenty-four-hours-a-day, seven-days-a-week work and leisure. There has been a large increase in the population of young drinkers looking for new leisure and entertainment opportunities and an increase in the 45–64 and over 75 age groups (Preece *et al.*, 1999, pp.13–16).

Whilst these environmental trends (which we can categorize by the factors identified in Activity 3) may have precipitated changes in the nature and role of the traditional pub in the second half of the twentieth century, it could also be argued that, over several decades,

> ... the image of the British pub was steadily deteriorating. It was widely regarded as a malodorous den of iniquity, a strictly male domain, with dirty lavatories, dilapidated furnishings, substandard selection of drinks and paltry provision of life-threatening snacks ... the stomping ground for thugs and hooligans, the dregs of society, a place where outbreaks of violence were part of the floorshow. By 1986, unsurprisingly, the pub's share of UK beer sales had slumped ... and it was deemed terminally ill, done for by colour television, video recorders, wine bars and the Thatcherite decimation of heavy industry with its beer quaffing, fag smoking, turf accounting ethic.
>
> (Brown and Patterson, 2000, p.653)

Figure 5.5 *Changes in a market town in Lincolnshire*
(left) A street-corner pub (right) A 'new-style' pub on a 1950s' housing estate

Pubs were certainly declining in popularity in the face of competition from home entertainment, the revitalization of cinema with the introduction of multiplexes, the growth of shopping for leisure, eating out in restaurants (especially the upsurge in Chinese and Indian restaurants), gambling, foreign holidays and sport and leisure activities. In the last decade of the twentieth century these forms of leisure were growing at roughly 10 per cent per annum with the only declining sectors being the consumption of alcoholic drinks in retail premises and bingo, which retreated as the National Lottery took hold (Preece *et al.*, 1999, p.14). With the combination of poor image and attractive alternatives the tradition of the pub as a key social institution must certainly have looked in doubt.

So how was the pub as a site of everyday life and leisure to adapt in the face of such change and competition? It is generally accepted that the Monopolies and Mergers Commission investigation into the pub retailing sector, resulting in the 1989 legislation known as 'Beer Orders', had far-reaching effects on the

Figure 5.6 *Modern pubs and new markets. As tastes and markets change, old pubs are re-invented or re-branded as part of a chain*

place of the pub in modern leisure and consumption patterns. The established link between brewing and retailing was broken down, the big brewers were forced to divest of large numbers of their pubs, and opportunities were presented for smaller regional brewers and non-brewing leisure groups to enter the pub sector in a significant way. This presented a new opportunity for public houses to be refurbished, remodelled and revitalized in an attempt to make them attractive to wider groups of consumers, especially women, families and youth. And from the perspective of the sociology of everyday life it has presented us with an opportunity to explore the pub as a site of new patterns of work and consumption, which are expressive of individual lifestyles and identities.

4.2 Lifestyle and consumption

One of the values of suspending our taken-for-granted assumptions about institutions such as the 'traditional' English pub is that we are able to approach them sociologically as if they are new and 'strange' to us. We try to observe what is going on with fresh eyes. But because we are concerned with understanding everyday life we are not just interested in observing what people *do*. We are also concerned with the *meanings* they attribute to their actions and the situations. So, when considering consumption in pubs it is important to recognize that consumption is both a material and a symbolic activity, expressive of identities, lifestyles and taste. It has been argued that modern societies have developed a **consumer culture** where individuals create and re-create their identities as much from their leisure activities and their activities as consumers, as they do from their work and employment. So, when individuals enter a particular pub they are purchasing far more than a material product, such as a drink or a meal. They are also purchasing an experience or ambience, which is associated with desire, and the creation and expression of identity and lifestyle. What is important is not so much the actual products that are consumed but the meanings attached to those products.

consumer society

Understanding this connection between consumption and expression of group or self identity brings an interesting perspective on the structural and organizational developments that have been taking place in the pub retailing sector over recent decades. As Brown and Patterson point out, 'the "traditional" English pub remained embedded in the national imagery, thanks in no small measure to The Rover's Return, The Queen Vic, The Woolpack and The Bull [in] Ambridge' (2000, p.653). But, as we shall see, the image of the pub as an 'icon of the everyday' obscured significant changes that were taking place in the pub retail sector as a whole.

We noted earlier that class, gender, family-centredness, pub layout and age were all factors influencing the social and cultural changes taking place in pubs. One response by pub retailers to the growing potential for female customers and family groups has been to implement a process of the domestication and feminization of pubs. Pubs are no longer private, hidden, virtually exclusively male, functional drinking activity spaces as observed by Mass-Observation (see Figure 5.7a). For example, if you examine the plan of the Admiral Nelson (Figure 5.7b) you will see a more recent example of that same traditional layout, with its inevitable consequences for segregation of people and activities. This is in sharp contrast to the now much more common open-plan layout of pubs, such as that of the Majestic Hotel (see Figure 5.7c), which facilitates easier access and a more flexible mixing of social groups. With the 'opening up' of the geography of pub space, the pub has become, paradoxically, both more anonymous yet more open and welcoming, easier to assess visually and to access physically, and less 'excluding' of wider groups of people. Pubs have become carpeted and furnished. There are soft furnishings and household artefacts, magazines

Figure 5.7 *Changes in the social role of the pub have been reflected in their changing spatial layouts*
(a) Typical medium-sized pub as described in Mass-Observation, pre-WW2
(b) Elevation and plan of the Admiral Nelson Inn, 1960
(c) Elevation and plan of the proposed Majestic Hotel, 1965

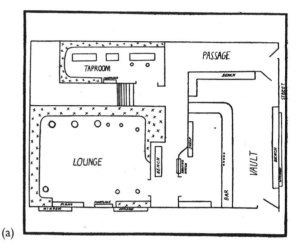

(a)

(b)

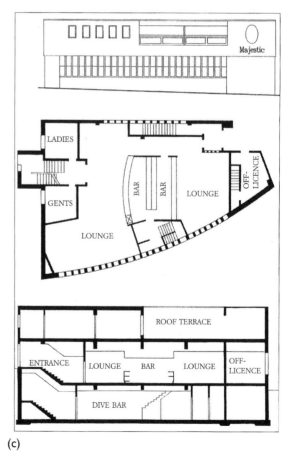

(c)

and newspapers, children's areas and tiled washrooms, all replicating, on a grander scale, elements of home and family life. Pubs are now major providers of meals eaten out, encouraging people who would not normally go to a restaurant to eat out on a more regular basis (Warde and Martens, 2000, pp.23–6), and they continue to provide music, TV, games and entertainment. The pub has become a mirror image of home, a home from home in a different sense, expressive of certain lifestyles and values.

However, it is evident that not all pubs are the same and that the same customers do not always want to 'consume' the same experience in the same pub. As we have noted, pubs have ambiences and customers are consuming more than the product on sale. They are places where people can create and recreate social identities. There are Irish pubs and Australian pubs, young pubs and gay pubs, pubs for professional men and women, pubs with a whole mix of ages and social groups, pubs that welcome families and pubs that do not. At the beginning of the 1990s less than 5 per cent of the 65,000–70,000 pubs nationally could be said to have a 'brand identity', such as 'Toby', 'Beefeater', 'Brewers Fayre' or 'Berni'. The assumption in the business at that time was that customers 'were not consumers: they were locals in their local'. They were individuals who 'wanted a "personal relationship" with the landlord, to be treated as individuals and to be welcomed by a "friendly host"' (Preece *et al.*, 1999, p.18). But potential customers were not necessarily locals in their locality and they did not necessarily want to engage with the landlord at the bar.

Growing numbers of pubs, however, are no longer owned or tenanted by the 'landlord'; they are increasingly 'managed houses', particularly in the large, branded organizations, and they are more likely to have managers who are young and female than was ever historically the case with the publican (Mutch, 2000). Some customers may, of course, be local and for them their 'local' may still persist. But, for others, consumption was increasingly founded less on economic and social location and more on fluid and flexible individual tastes and preferences. Where 'market research previously segmented the population into sets of recognizable consistent typologies of customers' it increasingly needs to recognize that 'individuals do not remain true to type' (Williams, 1998, p.222). Consequently, for pubs to adapt and appeal to the individual's expression of lifestyle and identity through their choice of consumption of product and services, a change of direction was needed. One marketing solution to this problem has been an explosion in the 'themed environment' or the 'concept' pub. For example, the 'Irish' theme pub, such as O'Neill's or Scruffy Murphy's, works by offering the consumer a particular experience which is not an 'authentic' representation of Ireland today but an 'attempted evocation of the way things were' in the past (Brown and Patterson, 2000, p.656). They allow individuals to identify with an image or brand, which expresses lifestyle and identity. Similarly, the proliferation of new spirit-based mixer drinks and 'designer' beers, intended to be drunk from the bottle, are as much about fashion and status as they are about the drink itself. Take the drink out of the bottle and people no longer know what you like, what you can afford and how you like to express yourself.

4.3 Work in leisure: leisure in work

So far we have concentrated on the pub as a site of leisure and pleasure but for many people the pub is also their workplace. Remember the landlords of The Hare and Hounds, Tom and Joan? For them the pub is not only their workplace but it is also the place where they live. It is their 'home'. Tom and Joan have a problem in that it is difficult for them to draw the boundaries between their work and leisure and between their home and their place of work. As Joan says, 'Managing a pub is more a way of life than a job'. And, as Marshall has argued, 'bar work, though clearly not a leisure pursuit, is nevertheless different from "real work" such as is undertaken elsewhere, for example in industry. Neither work nor leisure it is, in fact, a whole way of life' (1986, p.33). For Tom and Joan the public world of their working lives and the private world of their home and family are difficult to separate, with the world of work often invading their private lives. They have had to develop rules and strategies to protect themselves from the pressures of work and to clearly demarcate their work and leisure spheres. So, as Tom says, 'Well, I was pretty tired and emotional that day, I must admit. Joan and I had been working flat out over Christmas and New Year ... and I broke my rule about not drinking whilst working and, frankly, we were both getting close to deciding to leave the pub trade altogether.'

Some of the stresses and pressures that Tom and Joan experience as landlords arise in part from their role in providing a 'service' to the customer. As Tom says, 'it's part of the job to smile at the punters, whatever you might actually think of them or what they are saying'. But public house employees in general feel these kinds of stresses and pressures as they go about their day-to-day tasks. In her influential study of service workers in the airline industry, Hochschild (1983) identified those occupations which had a significant amount of what she called **'emotional labour'**: bar tenders, food and counter workers and waiters were included in her categories. Emotional labour requires the worker 'to display publicly an emotion that they may not necessarily feel privately' (Wharton, 1996, p.92). For, not only do feelings and emotion 'shape and lubricate social transactions' (Fineman, 1993), but the work which one does also has significant implications for the ways in which we see ourselves and others see us. It has implications for our sense of self and for our identities. Pub work is 'service work', which involves a whole range of emotional 'performances', a feature of many routine face-to-face jobs.

emotional labour

As a sociologist I, too, am interested in pubs as the site of everyday experience, leisure and work, and have, with a fellow researcher, been involved in an ethnography of a small business enterprise, one that owns and operates a number of pubs. This has required a lengthy period of observation, accompanying the managing director on business, going with directors and other staff on their travels, visiting the bank and the accountant and observing activities and interactions in pubs and meeting-rooms. Directors' board meetings, managers' meetings, training days, brewery visits, visits to pubs, attendance at court, trips to builders' yards, electricians and retail parks, have all been part of the project so far. We have become part of the 'human furniture' of the business and people seem to trust us. However, before our formal interviewing started it was decided that the observational work should be supplemented with some participant observation; this would give some depth of insight into the experience of pub work that only such a method could provide. Research work of this kind is indeed 'work' in every sense of the word. One is simultaneously collecting research information, doing some initial analysis, maintaining one's research access, making new research contacts and – of course – doing the normal tasks of a bar worker.

You should now read Reading 5.4, 'Learning the ropes in a dipsomaniac's paradise', which is a set of research notes based on a short period of participant observation undertaken by the author.

1   What can you infer from this account about the difficulties facing a 'participant observer'?

2   What can you infer about issues of power and control?

3   Are there any ethical issues that you think might arise for this researcher?

4   In what way does this record move beyond description to conceptualization?

What is immediately obvious from this account is that conflict arises from simultaneously participating and observing. For the researcher it is important to gain an understanding of the everyday events which are taking place. This involves both observing and describing what people are doing and a process of making inferences and interpretations. And this is all in addition to 'learning the ropes', coming to terms with an unfamiliar organizational setting and a new group of people, which, because of the difficulties of the task, is in danger of distracting the researcher completely. Obviously, everything that is observed or inferred has to be remembered until the researcher can find time and privacy to make notes. It is a very complex activity and one which is full of pitfalls, notably that things will be missed, misinterpreted and mis-remembered.

Whilst these notes are written from the researcher's point of view there is clearly a process of inference going on which involves attempting to view the situation from the point of view of the customer. Note the observation that, surprisingly, customers are 'nervous and awkward' and the advice to the barworker is that they need to inspire confidence if the 'service encounter' is going to work properly. So, the worker has to learn to 'pull off a performance' (Goffman, 1959) and convince the customer that they know what they are doing, even if they do not. Understanding this is a vital part of 'learning the ropes' and it is only too clear from this account what can go wrong if that performance fails. The worker is either treated as inexperienced, therefore unable to perform a successful service encounter, or treated publicly and visibly as the 'novice' who, from then on, can do nothing right in the eyes of the customer. Some service encounters are complicated by the fact that some of the customers have a special relationship with the pub. They are treated differently from other customers and are compromised when the new bar worker innocently attempts to treat them according to standard service encounter 'rules'.

Fundamental to this notion of the service encounter is an understanding that relationships are unequal. The bar worker is obliged to engage in 'emotional labour' but the customer has no obligation to reciprocate. If the worker doesn't know the ropes, or understand the rules, then the performance is flawed and power shifts in the direction of the customer. These power relationships are also gendered. The researcher is a woman and this is likely to influence the encounter, depending upon whether the customer is male or female. Here, the worker is in no doubt that she is an incompetent novice, even when the male customer is generously offering a drink. There are established rules of engagement and the worker doesn't know them. This also places the worker in an unequal power relationship with other workers and this could have negative implications for the ability to learn the ropes. Fortunately, this is not the case here.

Ethical issues are raised by any participant observation but especially if the people don't know that they are being observed. It is often necessary for such research to be done covertly to be successful, but here the other bar workers are fully apprised of the situation and are supportive. Is this how it really is for new workers learning the ropes? On the other hand, the customers are not party to the situation and may feel abused in some way if they discover later that the researcher is not a bone fide bar worker at all and was watching them with a different set of concerns in mind. These are ethical matters, which have to be carefully considered beforehand if the research is not to be compromised. Similarly, the other workers will need to be certain that the researcher will not betray any confidences concerning training practices and health and safety issues. The researcher has to behave 'as if' they are a bar worker working to the same rules as everyone else.

This is one very small piece of material in the context of the wider research project and it indicates how much work will need to be undertaken to do 'an ethnography' of this business. More importantly, it illustrates for us how such self-evident, routine, habitual and mundane descriptions can be analysed sociologically to generate, or apply, concepts such as 'learning the ropes', 'pulling off a performance', 'emotional labour' and gender and power inequalities. It highlights the capacity for the study of 'everyday life' to connect the individual with the social as well as to deliver sociological understandings of social interrelationships and large-scale social, economic and cultural processes.

SUMMARY OF SECTION 4

In this section change as opposed to continuity has been emphasized. Factors influencing drinking habits have been explored and the pub has been placed firmly in its economic and cultural context, showing how:

1   There has been a cultural shift from active and communal forms of leisure to more passive and individualized forms and the 'consumer society' has provided many other forms of leisure to compete with the public house.

2   Pubs have adapted and been 'opened up' both physically and socially. Social taboos have been relaxed and the pub has become a 'home from home' for new groups of people, especially women and families. The geography of social space within the pub has broken down social barriers and created a more accessible and open environment.

3   Pubs are expressive of lifestyle and identities. Sociologically the shift from observing what people *do* to attempting to understand the *meanings* that they attribute to their actions has been significant. Consumption is a symbolic as well as a material activity.

4   Pubs are sites of work as well as leisure. Studying the 'service encounter' gives insight into the concept of emotional labour. We have examined a set of research notes derived from participation observation, exploring ethical issues and the ways in which the sociologist can use observations to move beyond description to conceptualization.

5 Conclusion

In this chapter we have analysed the pub as a site of everyday life, as an 'icon of the everyday' and as key social institution. Our focus on everyday life has told us something about social relationships and societal processes, about culture, gender, class, power, regulated space and consumption. And by placing the pub in its social and historical context we have identified historical continuities and contemporary changes. We have examined the process of 'doing sociology', beginning with an example of 'fiction science' and ending with participant observation, exploring observation and ethnography in between.

In our analysis of the pub and everyday life it has been argued that, although the notion of the 'traditional English pub' has continued to remain embedded in national imagery, the pub as a social institution has changed in many significant ways. However, the fact that the pub has adapted in response to changing social and cultural conditions does not necessarily mean the social processes taking place in the pub can also be assumed to have necessarily changed in fundamental ways. Despite changes in norms and expectations, the presence of women in public houses, particularly when unaccompanied by men, is often seen as problematic. So, for example, in the late 1980s Hey argued that, despite the increasing domestication and feminization of pubs, women were still not really welcome in them. During the same period, Fiske *et al.* suggested that, in spite of real increases in the number of women frequenting pubs, their presence should still be understood as 'exceptions whose significance is still read off from the (male) dominant model' (1987, p.4). And in the early twenty-first century a leading female writer for the *Good Beer Guide 2001* has argued that, while increasing numbers of women are going to pubs, 'the local is still perceived as a predominantly male domain' (*The Guardian*, 18 September 2000).

There are further continuities beyond issues of gender, as Gary Younge illustrates in this description:

> Walk into a pub in this small Somerset village, even when Euro 2000 is on the big screen, and there will be that same momentary silence you will hear in just about any rural bar in Britain as you single-handedly integrate a social space. A tiny stretch of time when the dart seems to hover at the dartboard and beer remains suspended between tap and glass – just long enough so that everyone notices, but short enough that anyone could claim you were imagining it. Not hostile stares, for good-natured conversation soon follows, but the over-long glances from people not used to strangers and for whom a non-white face denotes not just ethnicity but geography. It means 'you are not from here'.
>
> (*The Guardian*, 19 June 2000)

In this article Younge is talking particularly about 'race' and ethnicity. But the issues go wider than that. They encompass locality, class, rural environment, community, gender and the notion of 'stranger'. The moment he captures will resonate with the experience of anyone who has found themselves in any pub where they are 'strangers' and are seen by the locals to be 'not from here'.

Pubs are many and varied and the physical changes that have taken place within them are amenable to observation and description. But understanding the dynamics of the social processes and relationships that take place within them requires a form of sociological analysis that is able to give insight into processes, meanings and interpretations. The study of everyday life has the potential to illuminate the dynamics of these social processes. They are the things with which the sociology of everyday life should be concerned.

References

Brake, M. (1980) *The Sociology of Youth Culture and Youth Subcultures*, London, Routledge and Kegan Paul.

Brown, S. and Patterson, A. (2000) 'Knick-Knack Paddy-Whack give a pub a theme', *Journal of Marketing Management,* no.16, pp.647–62.

Clark, P. (1983) *The English Alehouse: A Social History 1200–1850*, London, Longman.

Felski, R. (1999–2000) 'The invention of everyday life', *New Formations,* no.39, pp.15–31.

Fineman, S. (1993) *Emotion in Organization*, London, Sage.

Fiske, J., Hodge, B. and Turner, G. (1987) *Myths of Oz: Reading Australian Popular Culture*, London, Allen & Unwin.

Glover, B. (1995) *Brewing for Victory: Brewers, Beer and Pubs in World War II*, Cambridge, The Lutterworth Press.

Goffman, E. (1959) *The Presentation of Self in Everyday Life*, Garden City, NY, Doubleday Anchor.

Gurney, P. (1988) *Bolton Working Class Life in the 1930s: A Mass-Observation Anthology*, Brighton, University of Sussex Library.

Hammersley, M. and Atkinson, P. (1990) *Ethnography: Principles and Practice*, London, Tavistock.

Harrisson, T. (1942) 'Preface' to Mass-Observation (1987/1943) *op. cit.*.

Hey, V. (1986) *Patriarchy and Pub Culture,* London, Tavistock.

Hochschild, A. (1983) *The Managed Heart*, Berkeley, CA, University of California Press.

Jennings, P. (1995) *The Public House in Bradford, 1770–1970*, Keele, Keele University Press.

Jennings, H. and Madge, C. (eds) (1987) *May the Twelfth: Mass-Observation Day-surveys, 1937, by over two hundred observers*, London, Faber.

Junker, B.H. (1960) *Field Work: An Introduction to the Social Sciences*, Chicago, IL, University of Chicago Press.

Marshall, G. (1986) 'The workplace culture of a licensed restaurant', *Theory, Culture and Society,* vol.3, no.1, pp.33–47.

Mass-Observation (1987) *The Pub and the People: A Worktown Study*, London, The Cresset Library. First published in 1943.

Mintel (2000) *Pub Visiting*, Mintel International Group Limited.

Mutch, A. (2000) 'Trends and tensions in UK public house management', *International Journal of Hospitality Management,* vol.19, no.4.

Preece, D., Steven, G. and Steven, V. (1999) *Work, Change and Competition: Managing for Bass*, London, Routledge.

Schutz, A. and Luckmann, T. (1974) *The Structures of the Life-world,* London, Heinemann Educational Books.

Warde, A. and Martens, L. (2000) *Eating Out: Social Differentiation, Consumption and Pleasure*, Cambridge, Cambridge University Press.

Watson, D.H. (2001) 'Learning the ropes in a dipsomaniac's paradise', unpublished field notes.

Watson, T.J. (2000) 'Ethnographic fiction science: making sense of managerial work and organisational research processes with Caroline and Terry', *Organisation*, vol.7, no.3, pp.489–510.

Wharton, A. (1996) 'Service with a smile: understanding the consequences of emotional labor' in Macdonald, C.L. and Sirianni, C. (eds) *Working in the Service Society,* Philadelphia, PA, Temple University Press.

Whitehead, A. (1976) 'Sexual antagonism in Herefordshire' in Barker, D.L. and Allen, S. (eds) *Dependence and Exploitation in Work and Marriage*, London, Longman.

Williams, A. (1998) 'The postmodern consumer and hyperreal pubs', *International Journal of Hospitality Management*, vol.17, pp. 221–32.

Younge, G. (2000) 'Strangers at the gate', *The Guardian*, 19 June.

Readings

5.1 Mass-Observation, Preface to *The Pub and the People* (1943)

The structure of Mass-Observation remains very much as it was at the beginning – a team of whole-time paid investigators, observing others objectively; and a nation-wide system of voluntary observers providing information about themselves and their everyday lives. … The trained investigators operate from London (82, Ladbroke Road, W.11) though of course they are at any one moment distributed around the country on different studies. But for three years this team concentrated its whole attention on one town in the North, 'Worktown'.

We have called it 'Worktown', not because we take it as a typical town or as a special town, but because it is just a town that exists and persists on the basis of industrial work, an anonymous one in the long list of British towns where most of our people now earn and spend. For three years in Worktown we lived as part of the place. For the first two years we were practically unnoticed, and investigators penetrated every part of local life, joined political, religious and cultural organizations of all sorts, worked in a wide range of jobs and made a great circle of friends and acquaintances at every level of the town structure from the leading family through the Town Council to the permanently unemployed and the floating population of the Irish dosshouse dwellers.

The original team of investigators came in simply because they were enthusiastic for the idea of making an anthropological survey of ourselves. …

…

One of the basic institutions in British work life is the public house. Many books have been written about it; they are referred to and listed in this volume. But there has been little attempt to make an objective, unbiased appraisal of the pub, and especially of how the pub works in *human* terms of everyday and everynight life, among the hundreds of thousands of people who find in it one of their principal life interests. Mass-Observation has no interest in either proving pubs are good or pubs are bad.

We do not suppose, of course, that Worktown pubs are 'typical', any more than Professor Malinowski considers the Trobriand Islands typical. The object of our studies in Worktown was to take the whole structure of the place and analyse it out. This cannot be done in more than one town at once, and the interrelationships *within* the town, irrespective of relationship to other towns, were the broad basis of our study problem. The obsession for the typical, the representative, the 'statistical sample', has exercised a serious limitation on the British approach to human problems and is largely responsible for generally admitted backwardness of social science in this country. The real issues of sociology can only be faced if the sociologist is prepared to plunge deeply under the surface of British life and become directly acquainted with the mass of people who left school before they were 15, and who are the larger subject-matter of British social science. The issues cannot be fully viewed by statistical interviewing, the formal questionnaire, and the compilation of data on the library level. That, at least, is Mass-Observation's view, the incentive of our particular line of approach. There is room for every sort of sociology in this country, because there is so little of any one sort. There is no need to criticize other sorts; but it is necessary to stress that at present the social sciences are still rather one-sided and rather more academic than the subject itself requires and deserves.

The reader will notice that in this volume there is not, for instance, any attempt to make a statistical sample of interviews. There is not one single direct *interview* in the whole book, though there are many reported conversations with informants of all sorts. There are plenty of statistics; they are nearly all statistics of *observation*. Mass-Observation, as its name implies, considers that one of the clues to development in the social sciences is the actual observation of human behaviour in everyday surroundings. We cannot afford to devote ourselves exclusively to people's verbal reactions to questions asked them by a stranger (the interviewer) in the street, without running a grave risk of reaching misleading conclusions. What people say is only one part – sometimes a not very important part – of the whole pattern of human thought and behaviour.

Main stages in the Worktown survey were thus:

(a) Public house reconnaissance and description; preliminary penetration. 3 months.

(b) Penetration by observers into all parts of Worktown pub life. 2 months.

(c) Observation without being observed. 10 months.

(d) Work conducted more openly; active co-operation with all sorts of people in all spheres of local life. The study of individuals, letters, diaries, documents. 3 months.

(e) Data from important people. 2 months.

(f) Studies of statistics, organizations and published sources. 3 months.

...

The picture ends with the war. The book stands, with trivial modification, as completed in 1939. No attempt has been made to cover the wartime period which is bringing many significant new developments. The consumption of beer has increased very considerably in Worktown since the war, and the social structure of the pub is subject to great new pressures. The last [i.e. 1914–18] war transformed pub-life. There were drastic restrictions upon the hours during which pubs could be open, drastic increases in the price of drink (between 1914 and 1921 duty on each barrel of beer rose from 7s. 9d. to 100s.), a considerable weakening of beer's alcoholic content, a considerable decrease in the amount of beer drunk, and a 600 per cent fall in the number of convictions for drunkenness. These changes, brought about by the war, remained. They became accepted as pub normality. Numerous local and other restrictions (such as the 'no-treating' rule which was an attempt to alter the basic pattern of pub life) were temporary, and produced no post-war effects. A competent and well documented account of these restrictions is to be found in Arthur Shadwell's *Drink in 1914–1922*. Further changes are now afoot.

Even for those of us who took part in the investigation, there is something strange and remote about reading the results again now. Will the highly technical cult of pigeon-racing ever reappear? Shall we see again the esoteric rites of the Buffaloes? And the strange way they play dominoes in Worktown? And the elaborate class structure of the pub, which changes every week-end? Swiggling, standing rounds,

the spittoon, the complex system of bookmakers' runners, the annual booze-up on Trinity Sunday, the 'Diddlum Clubs', the trend towards bottled beer – what of all these things now? Already it is probable that much that is described here is part of history, the past. If so, we shall indeed have done one of the principal jobs which we set out to do five years ago, when we determined to attempt to describe and record history as it was made. ...

...

For guidance as regards techniques of investigation, we have turned principally, when puzzled ourselves, to field work that has been done in America, where sociology is so much in advance of anything yet seen in Europe. Here we should like to acknowledge our indebtedness particularly to Professor E.W. Burgess and the Faculty of Sociology in the University of Chicago, which has published several fundamental studies in this field; also to the work of Dr Dollard, Dr Elton Mayo and their associates. We were fortunate, in the later stages of our Worktown study, to be visited by several American sociologists who were most helpful and we should particularly like to thank Professor H. C. Brearley of South Carolina.

Finally, we owe more than we can ever show – more indeed, than we can ever know – to the people of Worktown. I think I speak for most of the 80 people who came especially to Worktown to help in these studies, when I say that we found an almost unfailing pleasure, honour, hospitality, among the hundred thousand people of this great, smoky, anonymous industrial town. Whatever we thought of the pubs individually, all of us found there friendliness and the company of British working life. There are many other sides to Worktown's story not dealt with in this study of the pub though fully analysed in the other studies in the series. Whatever these people's limitations, and whatever our own, there emerges unmistakable through this research a basic goodness of heart in the individual, confused with an indecision of purpose and function in the community, which provide the ground both for hope and for concern about a future which can and surely must be based on the satisfying of the normal, social, psychological and physical needs and hopes and dreams of the ordinary people who drink and laugh, occasionally fight, cry and die in the pages that follow.

Source: Mass-Observation, 1987/1943, pp.xiv, xv–xvii, xix–xx

5.2 Mass-Observation, 'The pub' (1943)

It is no more true to say that people go to public houses to drink than it is to say they go to private houses to eat and sleep. These are the things that people do in pubs:

SIT and/or STAND

DRINK

TALK   about   betting
                 sport

THINK   work
                 people

SMOKE   drinking
                 weather

SPIT   politics
                 dirt

Many PLAY GAMES

cards
dominoes
darts
quoits

Many BET

receive and
pay out losings and winnings

PEOPLE SING AND LISTEN TO SINGING: PLAY THE PIANO AND LISTEN TO IT BEING PLAYED.

THESE THINGS ARE OFTEN CONNECTED WITH PUBS ...

...   weddings and funerals.
quarrels and fights.
bowls, fishing and picnics.
trade unions.
secret societies. Oddfellows. Buffs.
religious processions.
sex.
getting jobs.
crime and prostitution.
dog shows.
pigeon flying.

PEOPLE SELL AND BUY

bootlaces, hot pies, black puddings, embrocation.

Also

LOTTERIES AND SWEEPSTAKES happen.
PREJUDICES gather.

All these things don't happen on the same evenings, or in the same pubs. But an ordinary evening in an ordinary pub will contain a lot of them.

Here is a characteristic record of such an evening:

> This pub is at the corner of a block of brickfronted houses, whose front doors open directly on to the pavement. The road is cobbled; the bare, flat façades of the houses are all tinted to the same tone by the continual rain of soot from the chimneys of the mill opposite and the chimneys of all the other mills that stand in all the other streets like this.
>
> The pub isn't much different from the other houses in the block except for the sign with its name and that of the brewing firm that owns it, but its lower windows are larger than those of the others, and enclosed with stucco fake columns that go down to the ground; and the door, on the corner, is set at an angle; it is old-looking, worn, brown; in the top half is a frosted-glass window with VAULT engraved on it in handwriting flourishes; at the edges of the main pane are smaller ones of red and blue glass.
>
> The door opens with a brass latch, disclosing a worn and scrubbed wooden floor, straight bar counter brown-painted with thick yellow imitation graining on the front panelling; at its base is a scattered fringe of sawdust, spit-littered, and strewn with match-ends and crumpled cigarette packets. Facing the bar a brown-painted wooden bench runs the length of the room.
>
> Four yellowish white china handles, shiny brass on top, stand up from the bar counter. This is important, it is the beer engine, nerve-centre of the pub. Behind the bar, on shelves, reflecting themselves against the mirrors at the back of their shelves, are rows of glasses and bottles, also stacked matches and Woodbine packets. Beer advertising cards and a notice against betting are fixed to the smoke-darkened yellowish wallpaper; and

on the wall, beside the door, is a square of black glass, framed in walnut, that has painted on it, in gilt, a clock face with roman numerals, and the letters NO TICK. (The clock can't tick, it has no works; but if you are a regular the landlord will give you credit.)

Five men, in caps, stand or sit, three at the bar, two on the bench. They all have pint mugs of mild.

From the back parlour can be heard the sound of a man singing a sentimental song. In here they are discussing crime, manslaughter and murder. A small, thin man (whose name subsequently turns out to be X) appears to be a little drunk, and is talking very loudly, almost shouting. Another chap, called Y, also has a lot to say.

x (to y): 'If a man says you're a jailbird he's no right to say it – if he *is* a man.'

Another man: 'He can have you oop for defamation.'

Y: 'I've seen cases in the paper where a man's been found guilty and it's a bloody shame.'

x (very slowly): 'I'll tell you a bloody case, I'm telling you …'

Y: 'Awright.'

x: 'There were two navvies — '

Another man, who has been quiet up to now, suddenly says, in indignant sounding tones, 'No, they weren't navvies', to which X simply replies 'Ah'm sober enough' and goes on, apparently irrelevant – 'There isn't a law made but what there's a loop'ole in it. Marshall Hall said that afore 'e was made a Sir – some big trial it were, for murder, an' it lasted a week, he'd strangled 'er wi' a necklace, it were that Yarmouth murder. He 'a won t' case, too, but for that courtin' couple, they were passing and they 'eard 'er screamin' and they thought they were only, you know, 'avin' a bit. Instead o' that 'e were stranglin' 'er. D'you know why there's a loophole in these 'ere laws. Well, them there M.P.s – 'ave you ever noticed there's always some lawyer puts up. Now the reason for that — '. He looks up and sees, through the serving hatch at the back

of the bar, a man going into the parlour and shouts out 'Eh, Dick, lend us two an' six. We're skint'. Dick shouts back something inaudible and goes on into the parlour.

X stands silent for a moment, beerswallowing. One of the men on the bench says to him 'Are you workin'?'

x: 'I'll never work no more. I've an independent fortune every week.

Questioner turns to the barmaid, who has now come in from the parlour, and says 'Molly, you don't know Mr X, do you?' (Meaning that she knows him pretty well.) She laughs and replies: 'No, I don't know him.'

x: 'None of that, Mr X. I call 'er Molly, not Mrs …'. He trails off, not knowing her surname.

The chaps begin to talk about swimming. X, irrepressible, knowing everything, chips in 'I'll tell you 'oo were a good lad – Bob Robbins'.

The singer in the parlour, who has been steadily working through three verses, now finishes with a prolonged and loud note, and there is the sound of some clapping.

The talkers have now divided into two groups, one around X, the other around an old man who is arguing about the age of the swimming baths. He keeps on saying 'I remember it being built', to which another chap replies, disagreeing, 'My father works there.'

x: 'That lad could fly through t' water like a bloody fish.'

Y: 'Bill Howard, that's 'is name.'

x: 'Goes into water like a bloody fish.'

OLD MAN (loud): 'I remember it being built.'

x: I'll tell you what 'e could do – you know when you're walking along the towing path, you an' me walking along the towing path, 'e'd keep up wi' you, you an' me, walking decent tha knows, 'e'll keep up wi' you.'

x stops, drinks, and the old man can be heard stubbornly reiterating: 'I remember it being built.'

x: 'I'll tell you the hardest feat that was ever known – for a man to fall off the top of the bath and not go to the bottom and not go to the top, as long as 'e can 'old 'is breath – I've seen (name inaudible) do that. 'e could do a 'undred yards in eleven seconds – wi'out any training. What could 'e do wi' training? I'm telling you, he could stay in t' water, not go to the top and not go to the bottom – an' I'll tell you 'ow 'e did it.'

Y (interrupting): ' 'ave another.'

x: 'Aye.'

While he is getting his drink a chap stands up, and says 'I swim that road', demonstrating convulsive sidestroke movements with his arms.

The old man looks up from his argument and remarks 'I go left 'and first'. And returns to the swimming bath discussion.

x, now with another beer, carries on: 'He'd drop into the water and neether go to the bottom or go to the top ...'

In the parlour they are singing the chorus of a jazz song, which the barmaid hums loudly.

It is now half past eight, and more people are coming in. Two old men arrive; both have gaps in their front teeth; wearing clogs, dark scarves knotted round pink wrinkled necks, white hair raggedly protrudes from behind their old caps; their coats, trousers, and waistcoats are all different yet appearing alike to be made of a shapeless greasy grey-blue cloth. They sit together, talking in undertones. Their beermugs are placed on the edge of the bar counter, and they have to reach forward, half standing up, to get at them. They both smoke pipes, from which drift the ropey smell of cheap twist. At regular intervals they shoot tidy gobs of spittle across into the sawdust. They reach for their mugs together, and drink the same amount at each swig. The mugs stand untouched for several minutes, with a last inch of beer in them; then one of the men stands up, drains his mug, and bangs it on the counter:

The barmaid has gone out, and the landlord takes her place. (He is large, redfaced, clear blue eyes, about 45, wears a clean dark-grey suit, no coat, clean white shirt, sleeve rolled up, no collar or tie.) He draws off two halfpint glasses from one of the middle taps; the old man pays him, and

the two empty the glasses into their mugs. During this transaction no one has said anything. Both men, standing, take a long, simultaneous swig, and sit down. One remarks, suddenly loud 'Well, of all the bloody good things at Ascot t'other week anyone following Aga Khan t'other week would 'ave 'ad a bloody picnic'.

X bawls across at him 'What dost tha know about bloody horses. I'll bet thee a bloody shilling and gie thee two thousand pound start an' I'll 'ave bloody Lawson agen 'im. Why 'e's seven bloody winners at meeting, you bloody crawpit.' The old man says nothing.

A group of four men has gathered round the table, and is playing dominoes. Each has a pint mug at his elbow. At the end of the round they turn the dominoes face downwards and stir them noisily. They play with a lot of loud talking and joking.

One says ' 'oo went down then?'

'Jimmy.'

'Oh, Jimmy went down.'

'I did.'

'My down – one an' one.'

'If we're down we're down, that's all. What's the use of worrying.'

'Come on, man, don't go to bloody sleep. Th'art like a bloody hen suppin' tea; when th'art winnin' it's awreet, but when th'art losin' it's all bloody wrong.'

They talk about the holidays, which begin next week.

'I'm not savin' oop twelve bloody months for t' sake a gooing away fer a week. Wife's always asking what I do wi' me overtime, and I towd 'er – why, I bloody well spend it, what dost think – and she says – Tha owt t' 'ave more bloody sense.'

So on, until, at about 10.20, they leave; standing for from one to three minutes outside, and calling 'Good night' as they walk, at about two miles an hour, to their private houses, which are seldom more than three minutes' walk away.

Source: Mass-Observation, 1987/1943, pp.19–25

5.3 Ann Whitehead, 'Sexual antagonism in Herefordshire' (1976)

In a rural parish in England where I did fieldwork in 1967 the worlds of men and women are segregated and opposed, as are gender stereotypes in which women are held in contempt. This cleavage affects the interpersonal relations of men and women with members of their own sex, and with each other in marriage. My observations suggest that men are both overtly and covertly hostile in their behaviour towards women, that the social control of all women and of particular wives is a burning issue and that some husbands and wives quarrel frequently and violently. Values of masculinity and virility, in which women are objectified, are cultural counters of male competition. This creates difficulties in establishing the personal bond between a man and a woman, which remains hesitantly and differentially held as a (submerged?) ideal in marriage.

...

This paper focuses not merely on marital roles, but on the context of the wider relations between men and women within which marital roles are set. In particular it discusses the consciousness of sexuality as a dominant aspect of the behaviour of men and women. It also emphasizes the use made of women as a differentiated category to symbolize, express and maintain both solidarity and ambivalent rivalry between men. My material emphasizes that the complexity of social relations between men and women cannot be reduced to 'shopping lists' of who washes up, hits the children or baths the baby, nor of where men and women are in the labour force and how much they get paid. The content of marital roles may be changing. Gender stereotypes and the ideological use of gender differentiation remain.

This paper also implies that studying the family as itself a system of production, and studying the relation between the form of the family and the major mode of production within which it is embedded, while they are essential, are unlikely to be the entire key to understanding relations between the sexes and sexual antagonisms. Gender stereotyping, sexual antagonisms and their symbolic uses appear to be universal; the nuclear family and capitalism are (or were) not. An implicit question throughout this paper then is, what is the significance of the frequent use to which ideologies of gender differentiation and the symbolism of sexual relations are put, to express solidarity, submissiveness, inequality and control? And what is the link between this and the relations of production in which men and women engage?

Readers familiar with a major published debate in recent writings on women, that between radical feminists (e.g. Firestone, 1971) and the rest (who did not like to call themselves feminists a few months back) will recognize this impasse. I find myself quite unable to deal with the implications of this at this time, but I offer instead this ethnographic romp to add to the complexity.

'Women suffer from petty jealousies'

The community I am discussing is a small parish (total population about 550) in the north-west of Herefordshire, about 6 miles from the Welsh border.

...

When men and women normally only meet in defined situations, in which they stand in relatively formalized specific role relationships, what happens when they meet in more undefined and informal situations is extremely interesting. In general, in Herefordshire, these situations are characterized by joking and teasing.

Some leisure activities are specifically designed to promote such cross-gender contact as is required to choose a marriage partner and make the joint decision which marriage in this culture does demand. Most adults met their spouses at a dance, at church or chapel, or at the Young Farmers' Club. The most popular form of Saturday evening entertainment for the unmarried, as for their parents, was still dancing, and dances were attended at village halls over a wide area. Farmers' children tend to go and sit at these dances in mixed gender groups. Non-farmers' children almost invariably go out in single gender groups. Girls go dancing with their peers from the neighbourhood or from school and occasionally go to a pub, especially if it has a jukebox. Boys go drinking or to watch football with neighbours, friends from school or work. It is when they go together to dances that they are seriously looking for a girl. The teenagers sit in separate groups of boys and girls and the girls often dance together. The separate sets tease and flirt with each other. Boys and girls at first go home separately. Any relationship between an individual boy and girl begins and proceeds through the joking and flirting of the groups. The joking and teasing are about personal attributes and allegedly emotional intentions, about attractions and presumed likings. Boys and girls appear to have equal resources and skills in playing the verbal games. A boy and girl will eventually seek each other out from these groups, and in doing so bear the brunt of teasing from their friends. Even then, when they go out alone there seems to be little direct communication between them. Instead close friends are used to relay information about intentions and feelings and the boy and the girl use this information and indirect signs and clues to interpret each other's behaviour and actions. When they are together in public they still joke and tease. The total number of boy-friends and girl-friends which any girl or boy has is usually quite small, and few relationships are experienced where a couple are alone together for any length of time.

Boys and men do not give up the old patter of going out with their mates when they are courting, but often reserve special nights – Friday and Saturday – for their girl-friends. They spend the other evenings drinking with their peers, but once married they do not even reserve Friday and Saturday for their wives.

The licensed familiarity of the pub

Drinking in pubs was both ideally and in practice a man's privilege. Men, as we shall see, took care that it remained so. Nevertheless a few women could occasionally be found in pubs in the parish, or more often drinking in pubs outside it. For some men and women these dramatic encounters are some of their main experience of non-family, informal cross-gender contact; and I should like to describe them in some detail.

…

The young married men who drank at The Waggoner rarely brought their wives to the pub. As I shall describe below, their husbands' involvement in the pub was a bitter source of complaint for their wives, and the social visibility of events in the pub and in the marriages of its regular drinkers affected events in both arenas.

The response of some wives to their husbands' drinking was never to enter The Wagonner at all. One evening, when a particularly good and boisterous time was being had, with everyone still drinking at 2.00 a.m., a thunderous knocking was heard at the back door. Here the landlady was greeted by a wife, who, remaining firmly outside, wanted to know whether her husband was coming home that night, as one of his children was ill. This wife never set foot inside the pub even when she had to make odd purchases there. Other drinkers' wives … drink with each other outside the parish. Their husbands occasionally

brought them to a special evening at The Wagonner, such as the annual pheasant supper, or over Christmas. When they did so the husband and wife dressed in their best clothes and drank in the top bar. When I was staying in the home of one of the drinkers he took me and his wife to a darts match in the pub. His responsibility for us two women prevented him from engaging in the normal jokes and banter with his male friends, and the experiment was never repeated.

…

'We come here to have a good time'

The bottom bar of The Wagonner … was a special arena of social affairs in a number of senses. Situated in the centre of the parish, The Wagonner drew most of its customers from the immediate locality, and was the pub with the least number of ephemeral or unconnected visitors, although some of its core customers were from outside the parish. All its customers rank lowest on the parish's status and prestige dimensions. Some regulars are gardeners, timber workers, lorry drivers and labourers; a number of men work irregularly on timber work or casual jobs; of the three prominent farmers who drank regularly there are two bachelors who work for brothers; the farmers with smaller acreage are the least successful, or have retired early.

The links between the customers outside the pub are complex and dense. Some of them work together in their ordinary jobs, many of them are neighbours, a few of them are distant kin or affines, some of them spend much of their spare time together. There is a high degree of overlap in these separate links, so for the set of men at the pub there is little spatial or temporal segregation of separate segments of activity and relationship from each other. Work and non-work life are intimately intertwined. The links often reach into other areas of men's lives, especially their homes and marriages, so that all the drinkers have problems of information management. The pub also functions as a clearing house for various forms of casual labour, bringing together men who are seeking casual work and men who seek labour. Many married men who drank at The Wagonner spent much of the time outside their regular employment in these jobs. Men meet to go off to jobs from the pub, and return to it after they have finished. 'Working' at the weekend or in the evening is thus synonymous with spending it drinking.

A day in The Wagonner was a long round of coming and going, with scant attention paid to licensing hours. The first drink of the day was often dispensed at 7.30 a.m. and the last not until midnight or later. The drinkers positively defined the situation as one of gregariousness. No one drank alone. The chairs, tables and benches were arranged in such a way as to encourage conversation between all. The customers and landlady thought of it as a friendly pub where you come to have ' a good time'. Men who wanted to talk privately did so outside – either publicly or covertly by going outside to the men's lavatory together. Business matters and matters of conflict were not discussed. The drinking was largely reciprocal exchange between equals. There were only two customers – both farmers who frequented the bottom bar – who did not interact with the others in terms of defined broad equality ('Boss' and 'Uncle').

In the pub men were brought together into focused interaction (Goffman, 1961), in a situation of defined equality in which drinking sustained and made possible a whole set of other activities. Certain personal psychological and social characteristics were left behind on entering and a premium was placed on other kinds of behaviour and activity (cf. Szwed, 1966). Within the pub, activity might be focused on darts, or quoits or on a card game, but the primary activity was verbal. This provided other rewards than simply those of companionship and the stimulus and pleasure of drinking. The pub was a place where men gathered, passed on, appraised and assessed news and information about events and the people they all knew. The customers also took a great interest, disguised and undisguised, in the affairs of other drinkers. Frequently, however, the conversation developed into a highly characteristic set of exchanges in which joking and humour were uppermost. The joking, teasing and humour might be subtle or crude, but it was all pervading, continuous and almost impossible to convey. No opportunity was lost of making a witty remark, no statement went unchallenged which could form the subject of a joke, no suggestive remark or obscene interpretation escaped, no action or comment went unseen or unheard. At these times the pub was an unparalleled situation of social drama. It was a circle of recreation and entertainment in which the conversation proceeded by allusion and innuendo, brimmed over with laughter and jokes and was full of banter, obscenities and long competitive exchanges.

I must stress that not only was there more joking and teasing than in any other social situation in the parish, it was unlike that, for example, at the other pub, in that it was not joking of an anecdotal or archetypal kind involving the use of universal humorous situations. The joking depended for its humour on reference to matters which were internal to the set of men in the pub. The dynamic of the exchange involved finding a point of vulnerability in another customer (either present, just left or about to) and pointing to it by a remark which made everyone laugh. Even ribald exchange and obscenities were funny because they were applied to the people present. A ready subject for joking was stereotyped references to the characteristics associated with certain statuses – farmers, older batchelors, young men without sexual experiences. Some of this joking among other things serves to demarcate statuses and reaffirms the importance of these status differences . A brief and pointed repartee may also serve to remind people of uncomfortable transgressions, or to signify that the general company was aware of other events.

One evening in the pub, for example, the young, well-dressed and slightly reprobate son of the wealthy owner of the former estate in a nearby parish had been standing at the bar where he had had a boasting conversation with the landlord. As he left he bought a 'Babycham'. Whereupon one of the other customers said, 'What's that, a peace offering?' and another added 'Only one?'. He replied, 'If one won't do the trick, it's no good taking two', and walked out to yells of laughter.

The dynamics of this briefest of exchanges are complex. He was married but had a girl-friend. The state of his marriage was of interest, and the original question was a joking attempt to get a reaction. The intervention of a second speaker directed the episode against him for it referred to the fact that he had a girl-friend and a wife; but the victim triumphed for he managed a joke with sexual overtones and walked out.

The only response to joking was to joke about the weakness and vulnerabilities of your opponent. Men only scored in such joking, however, if they pointed to roughly comparable vulnerabilities. It is only prestigious to compete and verbally overcome someone if he was of equal status to yourself, and if you did not exploit weaknesses over which he had no control. When a low status timber worker, who was a little pompous, and had a discrepant status position due to his marriage to a farmer's daughter, joked at the expense of a half-witted man visiting from a neighbouring parish, although there was laughter, it was not considered very funny and the joke was not considered in good taste. Quite a lot of this joking is relatively innocent and light-hearted in purpose; much of it is barbed and pointed and constitutes a guise under which men say outrageous things to each other.

Much could be said about the source of the ambivalence which is being expressed in joking (see Whitehead, 1971). Here I want to concentrate on the use made of women as counters in joking currency. Within the pub, men's standing in general was associated with their ability to joke successfully, and importantly, not to get into a victim situation. In joking situations the joker and the victim are at least momentarily opponents, and the joker is united with the audience. Success at joking is a complex matter (cf. Kapferer and Handleman, 1972), but at least in part it depends on the willingness of the audience to force defeat on the victim. Men would joke against men with who they had relatively few direct relationships, and, as I have pointed out, joking was often about ascribed statuses. Some joking was thus indulged in for the sake of the rewards being successfully brought, rather than as an expression of a particular relationship. In joking sequences of this kind the choice of victim often changed frequently and an overall balance between the drinkers was maintained. Stereotypes about women and relations between men and women in general could be an important weapon in the battery of items used. Men who were status equals often engaged in prolonged and competitive joking and teasing in which there was mock abuse and the belittling of an opponent. It was not a big step from joking exchanges of these kinds between status equals to prolonged hostile joking and teasing about much more serious matters. The hostility is recognized for what it is. 'They teased my husband blind yesterday at the pub. They've been on to him at work as well. It's his own fault – he's a terrible teaser himself.' '[My husband] came home early last night – saying "the buggers will have me walking barefoot yet".'

The major content of teasing of this kind was the degree of control that a married man exerted over his wife's behaviour. The men acted as if a married man should be able to do just what he liked after marriage. He should be able to come to the pub every day; to stay all evening after 'calling in' on the way home from work, and to stay out as long as he liked. He could and must row with his wife, hit her or lay down the law. Rows and quarrels in which he had the upper hand brought a man esteem, but if his wife rowed with him, locked him out of the house or refused to cook for him, he lost esteem. If he babysat while his wife went out he lost face.

For many months the pub was taken up with what was going on in some of the men's marriages. Men were always subject to ribbing when their wives had been known to have gone out drinking. Attitudes towards the amount of freedom a young wife could have were changing and in general husbands could not expect to exercise the same amount of authority as their fathers. The young couples whose quarrels were most socially visible were wives who were either trying to establish rights to go out by themselves, or to have more of their husband's company. The social visibility of quarrelling may be part of the wives' tactics. The husbands of wives who simply did not go out, did not seem to stay at home much more (apart from one or two with very low wages). The drinkers who were not at risk (either because they did not have wives, or whose children were grown up) took a great delight in promoting difficult situations for the younger married men. The landlady arranged a series of friendly darts matches that 'coincidentally' occurred on the same night as bingo. Husbands appear to have been made extremely insecure about their control over their wives' sexuality: when a husband picked a quarrel with his wife, back from bingo twenty minutes later than expected, she said 'He thinks I went behind a hedge with someone – in weather like this.' (It was early February.)

Although control of sexuality is at the core of a husband's dislike of his wife going out, the key assessment which is often being made in the exchanges in the pub is which of the partners is in control. This may be articulated through the symbolism of threatened loss of sexual control. The other major piece of a wife's behaviour which invariably, although often indirectly, sparked off joking and teasing, was her evening at bingo. Bingo evenings had not been run very long in the parish, and almost every week there would be a conflict in one of the marriages of the drinkers around which of the couple should go out and which babysit. (…[T]here is a constraint on the use of parents as babysitters for some of these couples.) One evening a week when a husband could not go the pub seems rather little to the wives, but, because of its repercussions when they get into the pub situation, men were loth to allow even this. Thus after a particularly bad and protracted quarrel lasting a couple of days (during which the husband twice locked his wife out of the house), the couple agreed that she should not go to bingo any more, and that he should drink shandy at the pub. (Note *she* must not go out; *he* must moderate his drinking. This latter condition indicates the extent of nonunderstanding of the man's world at the pub. Shandy?) That marital power was partly the problematic thing is also shown in that when it has become known outside the pub that wives have done such things as lock husbands out, or not cooked a hot dinner all week, these two spark off joking in which the husband is bound to fail.

There is running through what I have said a distinction to be drawn between teasing and joking. Teasing is about real things that have happened. Joking is not about such real things, but the joking often has a sexual content. I have not been able to establish the circumstances under which men would be teased about real events in their marriages, and the circumstances in which the real events were only the initiation point for becoming a victim of joking which did not overtly refer to these events.

What goes on in the pub is obviously rewarding and exciting, but it is a finely balanced game. If men can gain temporary esteem through successful joking, they can easily lose it. Men are made vulnerable by their wives, but the agents of their vulnerability are often their closest male friends. The drinking situation is an arena of public confrontation in which men come together and engage in verbal competition. The content of the exchanges is such that information about the personal lives of other drinkers is at a premium. It is close friends who often have most inside knowledge, and who may eventually use this knowledge to be successful within the joking situation. As the teasing and joking ebb and flow, so too does the men's relation to the pub and its other customers become closer or more strained as they are subjected to, or become the protagonists in, the most extreme forms of teasing. Investment in the encounter situation of the pub makes for ambivalence in relations between men. Eventually men lose such face that they have temporarily to leave the pub and withdraw from close contact with other drinkers. Thus friendships blow hot and cold and men who have been constant companions for some weeks will avoid each other. (See Whitehead (1971) for detailed accounts.)

The Wagonner then is major locale for verbal games whose performance brings considerable psychological rewards for the members of the male clique. Women appear in these exchanges in at least three ways. Much of the language is obscene and vulgar; it is concerned, that is, with sex and sexual relations. The everyday use of obscenity in our culture presupposes, I would assert, a certain attitude towards women and their role in sexual relations. In addition, much of the exchange uses an ideology of gender differentiation as a source of humour in which stereotypes of women are, at their worst, contemptuous and degrading. Finally, control over the behaviour of specific wives is one counter in the apparently perpetual competition for male standing.

References

Firestone, S. (1971) *The Dialectic of Sex*, London, Jonathan Cape.

Goffman, E. (1961) *Encounters: Two Studies in the Sociology of Interactions*, Indianapolis, IN, Bobbs-Merrill.

Kapferer, B. and Handleman, D. (1972) 'Forms of joking activity: a comparative approach', *American Anthropologist*, vol.74.

Szwed, J.F. (1966) *Private Cultures and Public Imagery*, Newfoundland, Social and Economic Studies, no.2.

Whitehead, A. (1971) *Social Fields and Social Networks in an English Rural Area*, unpublished PhD thesis, University of Wales.

Source: Whitehead, 1976, pp.169,170,174–5,177,190–95

5.4 Diane Watson, 'Learning the ropes in a dipsomaniac's paradise' (2001)

I arrive at the pub with a sense of trepidation. I am thinking of what I have read in those occupational sociology studies about the struggle people have in 'learning the ropes' when starting a new kind of work. But soon I am taking up my position for the first time behind the bar. And Alex, the pub manager, watches as I pull my first pint. I do this remarkably easily and apparently very well. I later learn that this is the best first pint that Alex has every seen pulled! The skill, I realize, lies in going slowly and not being rushed by anyone. Lager is a different technique but again, I find, it is not too difficult. The point with the beer is to try to spill as little as possible whilst giving the customer a full pint with a good head. Some customers will ask for a flat pint and then the tap is taken off. This is also the case with shandy.

So, things aren't going too badly. But Alex then begins a run down of all the other drinks in the cabinets and in the optics. I need to know the prices of all these. I feel overwhelmed. I'll never remember all this information. The price of ales and lagers are on the pumps but a lot of them are not readable. Alex cleans them up and writes them in for me. But there are no prices on the bottles in the fridges and there seems to be quite a variation. How am I going to cope with all of this? The tills are manual and therefore a lot of adding up has to be done in the head. Alex points out that it is important that the bar worker makes customers confident about their ability to charge the correct price and to add up correctly. It is unlikely they will notice if I get it wrong, apparently. But they'll soon want to avoid me if I don't appear to know what I am doing.

However busy the bar gets I shouldn't allow the customers to hurry me, I'm told. That is when I'll begin to make mistakes. Alex shows me how to prioritize tasks in a busy bar. This is outlined in the pub company's new staff induction document. As part of my research I have managed to get hold of a copy of this. But Alex tells me he doesn't really use it. I should deal with the customers first, he says. I should then collect glasses and put them through the glass-washer, stacking the clean ones when I can. Cleaning the tables and the ashtrays comes last. I should always try to indicate that I have seen the next customer who is waiting to be served so that they know that I will be coming to them next.

The 11 am opening time is fast approaching but before the hands on the clock behind the bar reach 11, a couple come in and ask for coffee. Someone else, to my relief, serves them. But the hour strikes and I am on my own to face my first customer. I feel pretty anxious, telling myself that all sorts of other people do this so there is no reason why I shouldn't. But this doesn't help me very much. Customers begin to come in. Joe, one of the bar staff, is very reassuring and offers to give me help, should I need it. He helps me most, in fact, by taking the first couple of customers. But this is only a temporary respite.

Facing my first customer makes me feel awful. It is very embarrassing. But I make myself go forward and nervously greet the next one to approach the bar. I imagine that they somehow know how stupid I feel. But of course they cannot. And, indeed, my first pint goes well. In fact I am soon finding the pulling of pints physically very satisfying. And, to my relief, I am coping well with adding up the rounds. The problems come when people begin to order all the 'silly drinks' from the cabinets and I find I can't keep a track on the total as I fumble around for these odd concoctions. I keep a notepad by the till for emergencies but I am amazed how people are prepared to hand over their money even when I haven't yet come up with a total. Before long, though, I start to get confused and nearly overcharge a couple of women. They soon put me straight on the total, though. This means that I end up with an 'over-ring' and I have to start again. In my confusion I even try to hand the money back to them. They look at me blankly. I apologize and explain that I am new today. They are fine.

I carry on pulling pints and find myself thinking how easy it would be if it were all like this. However, I then notice that the Pedigree is very flat and I can't get a satisfactory head on it. I don't like giving it to the customers like this so I experiment with doing a top up. This works but I feel guilty about the beer I am wasting. Then I get totally confused when a customer offers me a drink. Alex hasn't briefed me on this. I try to decline the offer but the customer insists. I am rescued by Alex who tells me about the staff drinks book, pointing out that I can put the drink 'by' for later or another day and don't have to drink at work. I regain my composure and continue to pull the pints, relieved that it is simple pints that most people want.

I pour a pineapple juice for a young woman who points out that it is not mixed. I feel totally stupid, realizing that the jugs have enclosed tops and that I should have shaken the jug before serving. Why do I seem to lose my common sense in this situation? My worst moment comes, however, when an obviously romantically involved couple arrives. The man asks for a Martini and lemonade but I can't even find the Martini, never mind serve it. When I do find the drink I notice that there is no price on it. And the optic won't work for me either. It is a type of optic I haven't seen before and clearly the training doesn't extend to experimenting with spirits. I am lost but explain that I am under training and that I need to wait for the expert to come and show me. Alex helps out but I am now 'set up' with this customer, exactly as Alex warned might happen. I am now a novice, publicly and visibly, and for this 'pushy' customer nothing is going to be right. He soon decides that his glass in the wrong size. He also announces that the draught cider I poured earlier has gone flat. Alex goes to check the barrel but there is nothing wrong with it. And, as I thought, draught cider is pretty flat anyway. However, this illustrates to me that confidence in the bar staff is crucial to successful service. I am learning the ropes.

An interesting thing that I begin to notice is just how nervous and awkward so many customers are. Out of the corner of my eye I catch sight of a strange and unusual looking man. He looks to be in his sixties and he is wearing a grey suit. His skin is very brown and he has a long grey ponytail. He drinks a pint or two before ambling over to look at the range of our beers. I ask if I can help and he ponders on what he might want. 'I just need to browse for a while', he explains, 'it's a dipsomaniac's dream in here.' This makes my day.

On my second day I arrive at 10 am and use what I learned on the previous occasion to get the bar ready for serving. I'm feeling pretty confident now about finding my way around the bars and knowing what needs to be done. I'm still afraid of the coffee machine, however, and dread the arrival of the first customers. I spend some time writing up the prices of drinks in my notebook so that I can try to learn them before the customers start coming. I leave this by the till as an aide-mémoire. I wonder whether it will work. The sun is out and it is Friday. This means it is likely to get busy. Today I am working with Suzanne who is doing a languages degree and Dan in the kitchen is a maths graduate who is thinking of doing a PhD. They are all interested in my academic background and Nigel is very keen to be interviewed by me.

It is quiet until about 12.30. Someone then comes in and asks me if she has enough money for an orange and soda. Unfortunately she hasn't and she is very 'put out' by me. I am tempted to give it to her anyway but realize that I can't. I give her a glass of iced water instead. Only afterwards do I realize that she works at the theatre to which the pub is attached and that, with discount, she could have had the drink. Nigel says she is always grumpy anyway so not to worry. She comes back later for another drink of water and I apologize for not knowing who she was. She is very friendly and introduces herself to me and asks my name. All of a sudden, at that point however, customers begin to come in thick and fast. Some are regulars and talk to each other as they order the rounds. This makes it hard to remember what they want and even harder to add up the bill. Others come in large crowds and have huge orders. The theatre press officer comes in with a client. She knows that I am new and introduces herself to me. She has an account but I don't know anything about how it works. I just serve her and make a note of her bill to sort it out with Nigel afterwards.

I'm not yet sinking in this flood of customers but I do have a problem remembering all the prices. I feel really bad if I have to interrupt a colleague to ask a price, especially if they have been adding up a large round themselves and find themselves losing it because of me. Nevertheless I have learnt a lot from yesterday and don't make the same mistakes I made then. Rushing back and forth between the bars I worry about someone slipping on the kitchen floor. There is spilt mayonnaise and I skid in it. No one seems to have time or be concerned, so I decide to stop to mop it up with napkins and cover the dangerous spot on the floor. Coincidentally, I pick up on a conversation between the staff in the other bar about the floor in the main bar.

'This slippery floor is dangerous for our customers.'

'I know. We have a responsibility to protect our customers from injury and someone will slip on this.'

'Well, I have told Alex and he is in charge so the buck stops with him.'

'Yes, but we are all responsible if something happens, aren't we?'

It is now extremely busy and the pace of orders in the kitchen is frantic. There is no soup. It hasn't defrosted. This doesn't go down well with the serving staff. We have to remember to delete items from the board as they are sold out and we are not popular if we forget to let people know when the last cob of a particular filling has been sold. I am not making a very good job of my order dockets, largely because I don't think I have worked out what is done with these after the order has been placed. I give out ticket numbers but Suzanne has failed to give one to all the people she has served. Outside is a sea of faces and you just can't remember who ordered what, however hard you try. A woman complains that she has been waiting ages for her baguette and she hasn't got a ticket number. She wasn't given one. We work out that her order is in the queue and Mary says that her baguette is next. About half an hour later the same women apprehends me as I am delivering an order, reminding me that her order is next. I know this order I am carrying is designated for someone else but can't pass her over again. I feel awful for her so I give her one of the baguettes thinking I'll deal with the problem in a moment. This then causes consternation in the kitchen but miraculously we find a matching order and everyone is then happy. This confusion wasn't my fault but, being new, I am sure people thought it was. Anyway, I think that some of the subsequent confusions that arise are down to me. I make a mental note always to give out a ticket number and always to put the order on the spike so they know in the kitchen what they have sold. I know I have lost some tickets and that means that they won't have a record in the kitchen of what has been sold. I remember a conversation with Nigel about the importance of good stock control and I will lose a lot of sleep that night thinking about whether I have messed anything up.

It is clear that training really ought to go right back to essentials. In my case things have been assumed which shouldn't have been. But I will know next time how to handle it. It has been so busy that I have not been able to collect glasses and am really worried that we will run out. We don't. As the pace slackens off I start to collect glasses and clean things up. Amazingly, I am all cleared up before 3 pm. I have survived the rush of a busy Friday lunchtime.

It seems that I have done quite well. It is readily agreed that I should experience a busy Friday night soon. Nigel tells Tony, when Tony arrives to collect me, that I have been a great help. He assures Tony that he is not just being polite. I really have done well.

I am so pleased with myself. And later that week Magnus, who organised my participant observation access, says, 'You will be gratified to know that Alex Porter is very pleased with his new member of staff. You have fitted in really well. It seems that you worked really hard and that the job is yours any time you want it.' Phew!

Source: Watson, 2001

Community, everyday and space

Tim Jordan

Contents

1 Community and the everyday

At the end of the previous chapter, Gary Younge gave an account of being black and entering a pub that was, in an everyday sense, a white-only place. He finished with the phrase 'It means "you are not from here"', which could have easily been written 'you are not part of our community'. In a similar experience, US record producer Marshall Jefferson visited the UK dance club, Shoom, and said later, 'I thought Danny Rampling was the greatest DJ I'd ever seen in my life. … I was surprised because he was white, and I'd never heard a white DJ play like that' (Garratt, 1998, p.116). Seeing a white man playing music where you expected someone who was black, and being black where you are expected to be white, are different experiences, but together they demonstrate a disruption of the everyday and reveal the community each everyday is based on. Younge's presence makes evident the fact that the community based in many pubs is, possibly unconsciously, bounded by ethnicity, as does Jefferson's assumption about the nature of nightclub communities.

The everyday and community are closely linked. We find further evidence of this if we reflect briefly on discussions of the everyday in previous chapters. In Chapter 3 we looked at the street and came across groups that created common lives in public, in communities of gangs, for example; in Chapter 2 the characteristic approaches to romance of what might be called a 'community' of boys were explored. These examples point us to the connection between 'everyday' and 'community'. In this chapter we will extend our discussions of the everyday by exploring this link in detail. The link is strong enough that, at times, we will see that our sense of the everyday is based on the community with which we identify and in whose spaces we live, work and play. Similarly, our communities all involve and are built on a shared sense of what is and what is not everyday.

As you read in section 1 of Chapter 1, Felski (1999–2000) defined the everyday as consisting of three related forms: *routine, habits* and *home*. It can be argued that all three of these can shift depending on a shift in situation. For example, when Gary Younge entered a pub or when Marshall Jefferson entered a UK nightclub, a sense of the 'everyday' was ruptured. For Younge, the presence of a black man in what was, in the everyday sense, a white-only place, produced that pause or moment when the everyday lifted to reveal assumptions it normally obscures. Similarly, Jefferson's preconceptions about what sort of person he expected to create music in a club were revealed. It was the residents of the pub that Younge entered who had their everyday punctured; for Younge, it is clearly not uncommon to be treated suspiciously because he is black: this type of treatment is part of *his* everyday as a part of racist cultures. In both cases, we can see that beneath the everyday lie assumptions about who experiences an everyday as routine, habitual and home-like.

ACTIVITY I

Look up community in a dictionary (preferably a dictionary of sociology) and then look back at Chapters 1 on the home and 4 on work and economic life.

- Pick out at least two examples of community from each of Chapters 1 and 4.

- Think about why you have chosen these examples.

A sociology dictionary definition might suggest that community can be understood, in part, as an expression of **identity**. Identity can be broadly defined as the different ways people recognize in each other something common or shared between them. Those in the pub Younge entered registered the commonality of being 'white'. Put another way, part of the identity of visitors to that pub was being white and anyone entering who did not conform to that identity upset their everyday. In this way we can see the links between the everyday and the community: in this microcosm of everyday life, we can see that what is routine and habitual is only so for certain people because they identify with each other. Think of some other examples. If you are on a football terrace and can immediately pick up the right songs and chants then you confirm your identity as a fan like others. If you know what a study guide is and how it relates to textbooks, like those called *Understanding Everyday Life* or *Social Divisions and Differences*, then you may well be an Open University student. Then, if you saw someone on a train reading an Open University study guide, you might identify with that person. In all these and many other everyday actions we begin to see that what is routine, home-like or habitual is only so for certain people who share certain characteristics. This is most clearly demonstrated when the everyday is breached and implicit notions of identity and community are brought to the surface. We must also be careful about using identity in this context as it may imply too strong a sense of 'sameness'. Identities allow people to see each other as the same or as being like each other, but this does not mean that communities are entirely homogeneous, rather it means members of a community have a number of different ways of seeing others as like themselves. For example, you may talk to another Open University student and find they are a science rather than social science student. Different experiences of being an OU student may then emerge, demonstrating both identity and diversity within the OU student community.

identity

ACTIVITY 2

- Divide a piece of paper into three columns and put a heading on one column of 'community' and on one of 'everyday' (ignore the third column at present). In the community column write down all the communities you can think of that you are a part of. Remember, these can be drinking, sporting, familial or some other.

- In the 'everyday' column, write down what might be the everyday activities you undertake that correspond to each community.

- Keep the paper for Activity 3!

There are many possible answers for all of us as to what we might fill in under columns entitled 'community' and 'everyday'. Of course, there are no right answers here and the activity should simply help you to continue exploration of these two terms. It will have started you thinking about what we commonly understand as community and how this is expressed in everyday life. What we are doing here is providing a first – tentative – understanding of '**community**'. It could be said that communities are made up of people who identify with each other, and where those identities are created through everyday activities.

identity

Identities provide notions of sameness and difference that bind people into their communities. The everyday is involved as it is made up of the many different activities through which people build and maintain their identities and communities. We can see such processes of the everyday, identity and community in Watson's pub scenario from the previous chapter. Activities 1 and 2 and our discussion of identity and community will have started you thinking about 'common-sense' and dictionary definitions of community and how these might relate to everyday life.

**Toennies,
Ferdinand
Gemeinschaft
Geselleschaft**

Community has a long history within sociology, one that has already been introduced in the discussion of **Ferdinand Toennies** in Chapter 3. It is particularly Toennies' concepts of **Gemeinschaft** (community) and **Gesellschaft** (association) that have been important. The opposition between the two concepts was often understood as one between the community that existed in small villages and the anonymous, threatening, individualized life of city-dwellers. As you saw in Chapter 3, much sociological debate on community has focused on whether industrialization and its associated urbanization in the nineteenth and twentieth centuries led to a shift from small, personally based communities to large, anonymous collections of individuals in cities. Michael Young and Peter Willmott's now classic study of the East End of London (which you will look at in detail in section 2) registered this in its introduction from 1957:

> The wider family of the past has, according to many sociologists, shrunk in modern times to a smaller body. The ancient family consisted not only of parents and their children but also of uncles and aunts, nephews and nieces, cousins and grandparents. Kindred were bound together throughout their lives in a comprehensive system of mutual rights and duties, which were almost as binding in the agricultural society of our own past as in some of the surviving primitive societies studied by anthropologists. But as a result of the social changes set in motion by the Industrial Revolution, relatives have, we are told, become separated from each other. In urban, if not in rural, areas, children remain with their own parents only while they are still dependent.
>
> (Young and Willmott, 1957, pp.11–12)

This opposition between rural and urban was undermined when studies began to show that not only were there 'true' communities in cities, but that rural communities were often riven by economic and status divisions. The quote above from Young and Willmott continues, 'We were surprised to discover that the wider family, far from having disappeared, was still very much alive in the middle of London' (Young and Willmott, 1957, p.12). However, even with such criticisms, Toennies' distinction has had a powerful effect that echoes to the present day. In the wake of studies that found communities in urban areas and a lack of community in some rural areas, Toennies' conception became detached from a rural/urban opposition and has been recast more abstractly as a place/placeless opposition. David Morley's work on the home (which you met in Chapter 1) echoes the work of Toennies:

> In the traditional vision of things, cultures were understood as being rooted both in time and space, embodying genealogies of 'blood property and frontiers' and thus cultures 'rooted societies and their members: organisations which developed lived and died in particular places'. By contrast, the contemporary

world as a world of movement and … mobility (both physical and imaginative) is central to our conceptualisation of modernity.

(Morley, 2000, p.9)

Morley contrasts rootedness with mobility and we can imagine that being a regular in a pub provides a certain grounding (remember from Chapter 4 the 'regular of regulars' whose pint and peanuts are waiting for him). Morley also points out that there is an implied premise of space as part of that community. In many explorations of the nature of community, the notion of some particular spatial form or boundary is a crucial component. Toennies, for instance, was often seen as developing a contrast between being close to both nature and other humans in pre-industrial rural spaces and being denatured and divided from other humans in industrialized cities. This can lead us to recognize an opposition between 'real' or authentic communities that are rooted and have a defined space and 'failed' or inauthentic communities that are dispersed and in which people are mobile.

There are, then, two ideas we have identified that will structure our exploration of community. First, we have analysed the relationship between the everyday and community by showing how they overlap on issues of identity and how community seems to envelop the everyday. Second, we have introduced a key conceptual division from the history of thinking about community. This is the division between authentic and inauthentic communities and it rests largely on whether or not a community has a space of its own. Keep these two key ideas in mind as you work through this chapter as we examine a number of specific communities.

In section 2 we look at Michael Young and Peter Willmott's study, *Family and Kinship in East London*. Here, you will follow closely the everyday activities of Londoners in the 1950s and how they related to their community. You will also get the chance to explore what effect shifts in spatial location made to this community by following the move of some residents from inner urban East London to newly built suburbs.

In section 3 we will examine two – arguably placeless – communities: the community of the dance-floor and the virtual community of hackers. We will explore the particular community of the dance-floor created in the UK in the late 1980s by examining the ways in which common identities are created within it. Here we will investigate how such a transient, fleeting and imaginary place as the dance-floor might, or might not, be home to a community. We will then move on to look at a community that is linked by the electronic world of the internet – the 'virtual' community of computer hackers. By exploring how such a community of physically separated individuals might form boundaries and create an 'everyday', we will continue to refine and build our conceptions of community, the everyday and space.

The aims of this chapter are:

1   To provide an understanding of 'community' and how it relates to the everyday.

2   To examine how the notion of identity contributes to the sense of belonging to a community.

3   To examine relations between everyday activities, such as shopping, and the creation of a community.

4   To consider the ways in which communities involve a type of space that helps to form its boundaries.

5   To show interrelations between the everyday and community, particularly how a community defines what can be assumed to be everyday and how that everyday constitutes a community.

6   To show that space is an important component of the everyday and community, but that communities do not have to share the same physical location.

2 Communities in space

2.1 Kinship and community in 1950s' urban London

In 1957 Young and Willmott published their now classic study of community, *Family and Kinship in East London*. In it, they explored the nature of family and kinship in Bethnal Green, a working-class area of East London, and then followed residents who moved to newly built suburbs in an area they gave the fictional name of Greenleigh. We will follow them in looking at the nature of community in inner-city London and then in looking at how that sense of community changes when it shifts to the suburbs. We need to keep in mind, as we read, that Young and Willmott were themselves examining the nature of community, and examining the relationship between space and community. Here, we concentrate on:

■   how that community is affected by changes to its space;

■   how the everyday works to form a community, through the three concepts of routine, home and habit.

We can see the community found in Bethnal Green in action by following local resident, Mrs Landon, on a shopping trip. Mrs Landon was asked to comment on everyone she met.

1   MARY COLLINS. 'She's a sister of Sally who I worked with at the button place before I got married. My Mum knew her Mum, but I sort of lost touch until one day I found myself sitting next to her in Meath Gardens. We both had the babies with us and so we got talking again. I see quite a lot of Mary now.'

2   ARTHUR JENSEN. 'Yes, I knew him before I was married. He worked at our place with his sister and mother. He's married now.'

3   MAVIS BOOT. 'That lady there, I know her. She lives down our turning [streets are known as 'turnings'],' said Mrs Landon, as she caught sight in the butcher's of the back view of a large woman carrying the usual flat cloth bag. 'She's the daughter of one of Mum's old friends. When she died Mum promised to keep an eye on Mavis. She pops in at Mum's every day.'

4   JOAN BATES is serving behind the counter at the baker's. 'She used to be a Simpson. She lives in the same street as my sister. My Mum knows her better than me.'

5   SYBIL COOK. 'That's a girl I knew at school called Sybil.'

6   KATIE SIMMONS. 'She's from the turning. Mum nursed her Mum when she was having Katie.'

7   BETTY SALMON AND HER MOTHER. 'They live in the next turning to ours. Betty says she's had nothing but trouble with her daughter since she went to school.'

8   RICHARD FINBURGH. 'That man over there at the corner. He's a sort of relative. He's a brother of my sister's husband. He lives near them.'

9   PATRICK COLLIS. This was a man in an old car parked by the shops. 'His mother lives in the turning.'

10   AMY JACOBS is an old and bent woman who turns out to be Mrs Landon's godmother. 'Usually it's only when I'm with Mum that we talk.'

11   SADIE LITTLE. This time there was not even a nod. The two women walked straight past each other. 'She's quarrelled with my sister so we don't talk to each other.'

12   ALFRED CROSLAND. He is the father of the Katie seen a few minutes before.

13   VIOLET BELCHER, a tall, thin lady talking to another at the street corner, is an 'acquaintance of Mum's. She's got trouble with her insides.'

14   EMMA FRANCE. This was an elderly very jolly woman with grey hair and a loud laugh. She engaged Mrs Landon in conversation.

   'How's that other sister of yours?'

   'Lily?'

   'Yes, your Mum told me. She's gone to live in Bow, hasn't she?'

   'She's got a place with her mother-in-law there.'

   'She don't like it? No! It never did work and I don't suppose it ever will.'

They both collapsed in laughter at this. Afterwards Mrs Landon explained that Mrs France had been her landlady in the first rooms her Mum had got for her.

(Young and Willmott, 1957, pp.106–7)

Young and Willmott note dryly that this 'was just one unexceptional shopping trip', underlining that this trip is routine in the Bethnal Green community (*ibid.*, p.107). A number of aspects of this community can be immediately drawn out. First, there is the centrality of family relations. 'Mum' is clearly a major focus,

Figure 6.1 *A street in Bethnal Green: daily contact with family and friends*

but sisters and more distant relatives pepper the trip. The family here is both the close-knit family unit of mother, father and children as well as a kinship network that includes 'sort of' relatives. Second, relations extend beyond the family into wider networks such as school, common interests or life-situations, such as child-rearing. This is evidence of a wider community beyond family. A third aspect we might note is the predominance of women among the people that Mrs Landon meets, but as this was a day-time trip, many of the men would have been at work outside the home.

What is evident is that there is a structure to this community in the kinship 'rings' that can be seen to radiate out from married couples. Discussing the plan of their book, Young and Willmott described it as following the nature of Bethnal Green's community:

> We … move successively outwards from the married couple to the extended family, from the extended family to the kinship network, and from there to certain of the relations between the family and the outside world.
>
> (Young and Willmott, 1957, p.104)

You probably recognized that the main research technique used by Young and Willmott was qualitative interviewing. As you learned in Chapter 2, this is when a relevant and representative group of people is identified and then interviewed, one by one. A common set of questions is used in each interview, whose results are collated to be analysed. Young and Willmott's study conducted two different sets of interviews, one of 933 people and one of 45 married couples. The latter was done to explore in detail some of the results obtained in the first set of interviews. This allowed the researchers to produce not only a series of quotes from interviewees but a number of statistics as well. With these methods in mind, we can turn back to the results of the study.

Young and Willmott use the married couple as their starting-point and it quickly becomes obvious that the couple is important because it defines which two extended families are relevant to each household. The married couple links two sets of grandparents, children, uncles, aunts and cousins. A simple measure of the strength of the parent–child relationship is offered in the following table.

Table 6.1 Contacts of married men and women with parents

| | Fathers | Mothers | | |
	Number with father alive	Percentage of those with father alive who saw him in previous twenty-four hours	Number with mother alive	Percentage of those with mother alive who saw her in previous twenty-four hours
Men	116	30	163	31
Women	100	48	155	55

Source: Young and Willmott, 1957, p.46

Here, Young and Willmott quantify for us the routines out of which the everyday is constructed. At the very least, one-third of those living in Bethnal Green saw their parents every day and over half of mothers and daughters saw each other every day. These figures show that women were more likely to maintain family contacts and suggest they were the principal force in maintaining community. These contacts occur in many different ways; here are accounts by married daughters of their meetings with their mothers:

> 'My mum comes around at 3.15 – she comes round regularly at that time to spend the afternoon'; 'Mum's always popping in here – twelve times a day I should say'; 'Then my Mum and I collect Stephen from the school and go back to her place for tea'; 'We usually have dinner around at her place'; 'She's always popping in here'; 'We've got four keys – one for each of us, one for Mum and one for Mary. That's so they can come in any time they like'; 'Popping in' for a chat and a cup of tea is the routine of normal life.
>
> (Young and Willmott, 1957, p.47)

The everyday emerges as the cornerstone of community. The routine, repeated and home-based activity of 'popping in' creates close bonds between families. Young and Willmott note that homes are not closed to each other but are in some ways merged beyond the physical boundaries of walls, doors and windows. A lock on the door is no barrier to a mother who has a key and is expected to drop in regularly and whenever she feels like it. Another married daughter notes that 'any time during the day, if I want a bit of salt or something like that I go round to Mum to get it and have a bit of a chat while I'm there' (*ibid.*, p.44)

Figure 6.2 *Tea with the family – three generations*

For this sort of routine to be maintained, the physical fabric of the area must be conducive to easily popping around and Bethnal Green's characteristic working-class terraced housing meant that houses were closely packed together. Of course, there are also accounts of families that no longer get on. You may have noted that Mrs Landon's shopping diary shows that she passes Sadie Little without 'even a nod' and though this was not an internal family conflict, similar problems are found within families in Bethnal Green. However, it is clear these are in the minority and, though important to the individuals involved, did not define the nature of community in 1950s' Bethnal Green.

We shall now look more closely at the next 'ring' – what we call the kinship network. The first thing to look at is the proximity of relatives to each other.

Table 6.2 Numbers of relatives other than parents living in Bethnal Green

	Number of relatives, excluding parents, in Bethnal Green					
	None	**1–4**	**5–9**	**10–19**	**20–29**	**30 and over**
Number of couples	4	8	12	9	7	5

Notes: marriage sample = 45 couples with 1,691 relatives (relatives include siblings, siblings' spouses, uncles and aunts, nephews and nieces, and grandparents, but not cousins or more remote kin).

Source: Young and Willmott, 1957, p.87

What Table 6.2 measures is the relatives of each married couple, and allows us to gauge the links between two families and assess whether these links are contained within Bethnal Green. This containment means, in Young and Willmott's phrase, that geography and genealogy go together in forming everyday relations in Bethnal Green. And these kinship relations are very much like those found in core family relations. Here are reports of this wider kinship network:

> 'One of my mother's sisters lives just up the street. We don't visit, but we bang into each other nearly every day.'
>
> 'My aunts and uncles all live round here so I often see them. I usually stop for a chin-wag.'
>
> 'I see my aunt up the market sometimes and tell her how Mum's getting on.'
>
> 'I've got a lot of cousins and second cousins living around Hanley Street, and I'm always seeing them round the Green.'
>
> (Young and Willmott, 1957, pp.86–7)

Having explored the family and then the wider kinship network, we can see the community completed by non-family connections that are based on proximity within Bethnal Green. Returning to Mrs Landon's 14 contacts, we recall Sybil Cook who was at school with Mrs Landon. The key fact underlying the extension of family contacts into the wider community is that people live locally. Fifty-three per cent of people in the large sample had been born in Bethnal Green and of those not born locally more than half had lived there more than 15 years (*ibid.*, p.104). This high proportion of people who had lived in the local area either all their lives or for a long time provides a basis for wide community networks; play-mates from the street, school-friends, pub-companions and work-mates are all likely to live in local areas and to be 'bumped into' on a daily basis. For example, one 'sub-community' within the wider community is the 'turning':

> The residents of the turning, who usually make up a sort of 'village' of 100 to 200 people, have their own places to meet, where few outsiders ever come – …practically every turning has its one or two pubs, its two or three shops, and its 'bookie's runner'. They organize their own parties: nearly every turning had its committee and celebration …for the Coronation of 1953. Some turnings have little war memorials built into walls of houses with inscriptions …Pots and flowers are fixed in a half-circle to the wall; they are renewed regularly by the women of the turning, who make a street collection every Armistice Day.
>
> (Young and Willmott, 1957, pp.109–10)

The community found by Young and Willmott is now laid out before us, with all its routines, habits and home-lives. All these confirm that this community and its everyday patterns are intimately related. The community appears as something like a container for the wide range of everyday activities, all of which are marked as being part of Bethnal Green by the structures of family and relations. As has already been noted, the physical structure of the area is crucial. Pubs are local and frequent; sons and daughters are able to find housing locally, even if this is not always easy. Jobs are often local, adding to the community because work-mates are likely to live near-by.

Does space have to include place to form a community? Proximity and kinship – or what we might term geography and genealogy – are two prime structuring factors in the creation and maintenance of this community. But are they necessary? Is it necessary to live in close proximity to form a community?

Wilmott and Young test this connection by looking at what happens when geography changes, because this description of Bethnal Green was captured at the very time when many people were beginning to move away from inner urban areas to newly built suburbs in outer London.

SUMMARY OF SECTION 2.1

Communities in Bethnal Green are constructed out of:

1   'rings' radiating out from the married couple to the family to the kinship network to non-family friends and neighbours;

2   repeated contacts between family members and those connected through these 'rings';

3   certain forms of space that allow frequent contacts between people; and

4   Bethnal Green's everyday and its space.

2.2 Kinship and community in 1950s' suburban London

READING 6.1

Please read the first extract from Young and Willmott, which is reprinted as Reading 6.1.

As you read, consider the following questions:

1   What reasons are given for people making the move from Bethnal Green to Greenleigh?

2   What value is placed by residents on 'community' when discussing the shift?

3   What aspects of people's lives have become apparent in the move that were not apparent when they lived in Bethnal Green?

The first reading from Young and Willmott gives a flavour of the different type of geography that residents find when they move from Bethnal Green to Greenleigh. This shift is felt in many ways. A Mrs Sandeman said, 'When I first came ... I cried for weeks, it was so lonely. It was a shock to see such a deep hill going up to the shops' (Young and Willmott, 1957, p.122). It is clear that a different type of space opens up in Greenleigh: this is mainly defined by there being simply more space. Flats are larger (with more rooms); there is greater space between shops, houses, and pubs. For instance, there is one pub for every 400 people in Bethnal Green but one for every 5,000 in Greenleigh. Likewise, there is one shop for every 44 people in Bethnal Green but one for every 300 in Greenleigh. For those moving from Bethnal Green, however, the nature of the basic institutions of their community suddenly change by virtue of being fewer and farther apart.

READING 6.2

Now read Reading 6.2 which is a second extract from Young and Willmott.

As you read, keep the following questions in mind:

1   What changes, good and bad, to the everyday (routine, home and habit) occur in the shift from Bethnal Green to Greenleigh?

2   With such changes in the everyday, how has the nature of community changed?

3   What differences in space can you identify between Bethnal Green and Greenleigh? Do you think any of these differences in space affect the nature of community in the two places?

What is registered in much of Young and Willmott's evidence in this reading is the 'friction of distance'. Relatives are seen less often; trips outside the home result in fewer chance encounters; and home becomes a more welcoming but also more imprisoning place. This latter point reflects a significant difference between men and women's experience of space in Greenleigh and shows us how space is interwoven with their everyday lives. The central bond around which Bethnal Green's community revolved – that of mother and daughter – is stretched if not broken in the shift to the suburbs. This left women crying, as several say 'for weeks on end', as they tried to come to terms with an isolation that was a new experience. Men still travel to Bethnal Green (or areas near it) to work and in the process maintain some of their old communal ways. You will recall the example of the man who regularly visited relatives for a cup of tea to avoid the rush-hour and another who avoided the 'dryer' culture of Greenleigh by having his Friday night pint in Bethnal Green.

Figure 6.3 *Valence Circus, Becontree estate, Dagenham, 1945 – or Greenleigh. This is typical of the estates built by London County Council in the suburbs to rehouse people from the overcrowded slums of the East End*

All the everyday activities that had underpinned the Bethnal Green community change in Greenleigh. Shopping is no longer the communal experience that Mrs Landon's diary indicated. Pubs are rare and men tend to stay at home in the evenings. Men who have some contact outside the home through work tend to feel the advantages of Greenleigh more strongly than women who find themselves isolated. Schools are thought to be better, as are the facilities of home and the general environment for children. Children begin to assume the Greenleigh routine as their everyday. The everyday that is deeply undermined for parents by the different spaces and lives of Greenleigh begins to submerge again into assumed habits and routines that do not need to be thought about by their children. Here are some reports from parents of how their children have begun to assume Greenleigh as their everyday: 'When we go back to Bethnal Green – to see the relations – the children hang about and say "Come on Mum, when are we going home[?]"'; 'Sometimes we ask the children to torment them if they'll go back to London' (Young and Willmott, 1957, p.165).

In Greenleigh, we see that a different everyday emerges. This is centred on the home as a unit in its own right and less on homes that are merged into kinship networks. It is a suburban community with many of the features of suburban life that are experienced in countries across the world. For example, Morley suggests that television is a 'suburban medium' and we can see this already at work in 1950s' Greenleigh, which is early in both processes of suburbanization and the introduction of television. This classic statement of a father could be as true of television-watching now as it was a novel claim in 1957: 'The tellie keeps the family together. None of us ever have to go out now' (*ibid.*, p.143).

The everyday of suburban Greenleigh is of individualized family homes that are closed in on themselves. In suburban life, the home becomes a key site of the everyday, whereas in Bethnal Green the everyday constantly opened the home out to wider networks. In suburbia, the car becomes a central component of life because public transport cannot meet all the needs of dispersed communities. Women become more isolated, unable to find and create the links that sustained inner urban daily life, while at the same time finding increased resources for home-life. Men must commute to work and this is costly and tiring, but also offers a life outside the home (though it could be argued that the importance of this is over-emphasized by Young and Willmott when we consider that Greenleigh is new and little local employment has emerged).

ACTIVITY 3

Find the piece of paper you filled out for Activity 2 that is split between community and everyday.

1   Head the blank third column 'space'.

2   List any spatial characteristics you think are related to the everydays and communities you have previously listed.

3   Reflect on the interrelations between space, everyday and community in your own life that this might bring to light. Make sure you link at least one community to both an everyday and a space.

4   Keep this piece of paper for later (for after you have studied Reading 6.5).

We can see in Young and Willmott's case study how the three concepts of community, space and the everyday interlink. Activity 3 will also help you to explore this, and by now you may well have found one piece of paper divided into three columns seems too small for all your communities, everydays and spaces. We can see why it is both hard to disentangle the three and how they are often assumed in each other. This is because a typical space engages certain sorts of everyday actions that, when taken together, define the type of community at stake: close-knit kinship networks in which households are rarely closed to each other or individual family homes turned inward and opening out only rarely. The value of pursuing this classic sociological study in detail is that it provides us with a view of some people and their lives in a way that we can connect it to concepts of the everyday, space and community. However, we should also be aware that while we have emphasized this relationship between space and community in Young and Willmott, they were themselves critical of any assumption of space's ability to determine community.

Figure 6.4 *Breakfast with the family in the suburbs*

We do not have the room to bring our understanding of family life in the East End or in the London suburbs up-to-date here, nor do we need to have such a current understanding for Young and Willmott's study to introduce us to conceptions of community and the everyday. Of course, much has changed. London suburbs like Greenleigh have become 'normal' rather than newly built, with much newer housing developments on their outskirts. Bethnal Green has also changed, with its once homogeneous, white, working-class community expanding to include both gentrified middle-class and multi-ethnic components (Butler, 1996; Eade, 1996). Similarly, the presumption in Young and Willmott of the centrality of the nuclear family to community life has been overtaken by the development of varied family types: single-parent families, rates of divorce and of re-marriage, gay and lesbian families and other family types would now have to be taken into account by any modern-day Young and Willmott (Silva and Smart, 1999).

There is also a danger in looking closely at only one study: how can we be sure that Bethnal Green/Greenleigh and Young and Willmott's views of these two communities offer general conclusions? How can we be sure this study helps us to understand what community means outside of British, 1950s', urban and suburban lives? Are the links between everyday, community and space as strong as Young and Willmott's study suggest? Rather than pursuing the theme of suburbia, as it may be one that particularly privileges relations between space and community, it is time to turn to some different examples. To stretch the notion of community and explore whether the links between the three terms we have examined really hold or not, we now turn to two examples in the community of the dance-floor and the virtual community of hackers.

SUMMARY OF SECTION 2.2

Communities in Greenleigh are marked by:

1 greater availability of space both within and outside the home than in Bethnal Green;

2 emphasis on individual homes that are turned inward rather than opened out onto other homes;

3 advantages and disadvantages compared to Bethnal Green, but where the advantages are felt by both men and women but the disadvantages are most keenly felt by women.

---

3 Communities out of space: dancing and hacking

Can we really call people who meet occasionally on the dance-floor a community? Can people who have never physically met, and may have only ever communicated through text displayed on a computer screen, be thought to have common habits and routines? We are now going to stretch our understanding of communities as constituted by everyday actions that are played out in particular physically defined spaces around certain identities, by challenging it with communities that at first sight do not fit this understanding.

3.1 The chemical generation

There have undoubtedly been times when certain types of music, clothes, beliefs and drugs have come together to form something that looks like, and seems to those within it to be, a community or movement. In the late 1960s social and personal revolution became closely related to certain rock-music styles, a liking for LSD and long hair, and is now referred to as the hippie movement. At the same time, mods and rockers could be found in seaside resorts on bank holidays, each identifiable to themselves and each other through dress, hairstyles and choice of transport. The 1970s brought the shock of punk in the UK and new wave in the USA, and the 1980s brought the profoundly influential emergence of hip hop. Each of these movements, and others not mentioned, closely associated particular musical styles with a range of other markers, such as type of clothes, fashion or **ideologies**, to create the sense that a new **subculture** was being formed. What seem to be the momentary or fleeting pleasures of a Saturday night at the disco become transformed into a series of defining moments of, for some, social change. This section will briefly take up one of the more recent such subcultures, often called rave culture. In looking at rave, we will only briefly pass over its history to provide a context for the investigation of its rather spectacular notion of the everyday.

    Rave has several sources, and its arrival in 1987–8 in the UK came from a creative combustion that occurred when these sources clashed and came together. (The following account is drawn together from a number of sources: see Collin and Godfrey (1997), Garratt (1998) and Reynolds (1998).) The three main sources were: gay dance cultures; developments in music and discos within African-American cultures; and the arrival of British clubbers in the discos of the Balearic islands in Ibiza. By the late 1970s and early 1980s, a type of ecstatic disco had been created within gay cultures that were themselves 'coming out'. Certain types of high-energy and disco music were brought together with lavish and inventive club surroundings, various experience-enhancing drugs and a strong sense of community derived from being in openly gay surroundings. This particular type of nightlife cross-pollinated with a number of night-clubs based largely in African-American cultures in New York and Chicago: a number of African-American DJs (some also gay) pioneered ways of 'cutting' different records into each other using multiple turntables, and creating moods and music that generated a similar ecstatic feeling to that found in gay clubs. African-American musicians were already developing new sounds in 'hip-hop' and a number of DJs and musical experimenters mixed hip-hop, disco and soul music with electronic or techno music coming out of Europe. These two influences came together and met with the type of music and dance found particularly in Ibiza. By the mid-1980s a number of young Britons were travelling Europe taking with them experiences of UK clubs and of British-based but Jamaican-inspired sound systems. In Britain, the experience became associated with the drug now called 'E' or Ecstasy. The three sources of rave continued their own way but out of their cross-over emerged what we now call rave culture. What was experienced in Ibiza, and was to form the core of a rave culture that would be explored across the UK in the early 1990s, was a common experience on the dance-floor that opened up wider beliefs about a community.

ideologies
subculture

READING 6.3

You are now going to read an account of early rave. Although it does not explicitly use the concepts of everyday, community and space, you should see these concepts at work. After this reading, we will explore the interrelations of these concepts in the context of rave in more detail. Now read the extract from Reynolds' book, *Energy Flash: A Journey through Rave Music and Dance Culture* in Reading 6.3.

When you have read it, consider the following questions:

1   What elements might be thought to make a 'rave'?

2   What sense, if any, of the everyday is present?

3   Do you think the sense of community, and even of revolution, is naïve?

4   Do any of the communities, everydays and spaces you wrote down for Activity 3 involve a 'buzz'?

This activity may have had you both stretching your imagination to understand Reynolds' explorations of revolution and 'buzz' and trying to bring those terms home to your own experience. To continue this exploration we need to consider delineating rave more clearly.

Rave culture is a constellation of music, drugs, youth, dancing, fashion and money. At a rave-event thousands of people dance all night to a specific form of music, in a venue fitted with a lightshow and with many people taking drugs, usually E (Ecstasy). E's effect is that of a mild hallucinogenic combined with a physical lift. The key elements of raving are dance, lights, drugs, clothes, music and time and the possible combinations of these elements in a particular rave-event create a collective delirium so that people shift out of their everyday world. What can be hypothesized as the unifying or defining element of raving is an ongoing inducement into this state of something like rapture. This experience is a collective delirium produced by thousands of people jointly making the connections of drugs to dance, music to dance, dance to drugs, drugs to time, time to music and so on, and thereby gradually constructing the state of raving. As Hillegonda Rietveld noted, 'Egos melt in the sweltering, frenzied heat of the mass of sweating bodies' (Rietveld, 1993, p.63). 'Ravers' may no longer notice

Figure 6.5 *On the dancefloor at Shoom, April 1988*

the lights, the other ravers or the music as separate elements but feel them as an overall intense experience. This is clear in the descriptions of the club Shoom in Reading 6.3, where the billowing pink clouds alternately hid people from each other, leaving them dancing alone, and then opened out showing people all the others with whom they might identify.

This core experience of rave was produced in different ways over the ten years and more after 1987–8. In the late 1980s, police crack-downs and tabloid hysteria drove rave out of whatever legitimate venues had been set up and into a night-time world of chasing the secret event. Huge raves were held where thousands of people had to follow directions given from phone-lines only hours before the rave began. These illegal (or barely legal) events continued over several years before police activity began to close them down. Government alarm led to legislation in the Criminal Justice and Public Order Act 1994 that, among many other provisions, sought to define and criminalize music associated with rave. The experience did not disappear, however, leading police to reassess their strategies and begin to support legal venues (some of these obtained some of the first all-night licences granted in England).

By the mid-1990s rave cultures were fragmenting into various strands, including the emergence of 'Jungle' or 'Drum'n'Bass' as major new musical and clubbing forms. Rave found passionate homes across the world: in Blackburn, San Francisco, Manchester, Goa, Glasgow and elsewhere. Hand in hand with the euphoria that raving could produce, nevertheless, were times when the 'dream' met with mass markets, unsafe drugs and ignorance that led to deaths or increasing numbers of 'clubbers' being admitted to hospital in emergencies. Criminal gangs could be found moving in to control the lucrative drug trade. It could be argued that it was these and other events that sometimes led to disillusionment, risk and the end of the fleeting vision of revolution from the dance-floor.

We will not pursue rave in all its manifestations here (see Reynolds (1998) and Garratt (1998) for a more complete picture); instead we have already met and defined the common core of raving. It is the rave-event that forms what can be called the everyday of rave. Here we meet something of a paradox: we are describing an experience that involves thousands of others, lasts all night, means (probably) taking illegal, powerful and potentially dangerous drugs, has specific dress-codes, includes loud, repetitive, almost hypnotic music and, taken all together, produces a euphoric state. So, how can this be called everyday? Indeed, the experience is partially formed *against* the everyday, as a means of transcending and escaping the everyday. (You also met this in Chapter 2, where Peter Redman noted that romance can occupy the same role.) Yet, it also became the everyday that each rave-event sought to construct for as long as it could be made to last. Here we see a desire to take on what had been a carnival and make it into something experienced every day:

> [When one clubber] left her Filofax in a cab one night, with all her work contacts in it, she found herself wondering if it wasn't a sign that she should quit her job in PR and give herself up to the feeling completely. So many others felt the same that at one point the Ramplings [who ran the club Shoom] had to add a note in the hand-written newsletter they sent out to members pleading with them not to give up their day jobs.
>
> (Garratt, 1998, p.116)

Furthermore, the sense of there being a 'rave community' is underpinned by everyday moments. Read the beginning of Sheryl Garratt's acknowledgements in her book-length account of rave:

> So a big shout to all those who have driven me round the country, blagged me in at the door, queued for the loo with me, talked crap in the corner with me, had me back to their place, or piled back to mine. All those who have bought drinks and plane tickets, shared cubicles and hotel rooms, and offered lifts of all kinds.
>
> (Garratt, 1998, p.ix)

Rave demonstrates to us an extraordinary everyday, that some want to live within forever and others want to live within alongside their 'ordinary' everyday of day-jobs. Here is the everyday of rave and its community. It is an everyday that is constructed at each event on each dance-floor, whether that dance-floor is a farm in Kent, a beach in California or a club in an urban centre. It builds a community because it re-creates certain routine pleasures through which members of the rave community can identify each other and themselves as ravers. It is everyday because the myriad small experiences come to be recognized as routine and habitual. However extraordinary rave may seem, it is based on the creation of routine, home-like and habitual activities, such as those noted in Garratt's thanks.

Examining rave also has destabilizing effects on the concept of space that was employed when looking at Bethnal Green and Greenleigh:

> On Friday night I went to a night club in London and the next day, Saturday, I went to a gig in Bristol but the amazing thing was that they were the *same place* :-) I recognised it not only as the same place but they were also the *same time* … In any conventional fashion, the two dance-floors could not be in the same place at the same time but it was more that the place that the *trance* took me *was the same*. Both times I was transported through trance-dance.
>
> ('Andy', 1994, p.4)

Figure 6.6
Rave, Zurich, 1999

What 'Andy' refers to as the 'trance' is the core euphoria in rave and, when it was created, physical space no longer seemed relevant in understanding his experiences. Rave becomes routine when seen from within its own community and within that everyday space can no longer be understood as just physical. We could perhaps speculate that rave creates the same 'place' across numerous different spaces. Such a shift from talking about spaces to that of places attempts to register the disconnection of space from what has been its most powerful component – specific physical characteristics. We have seen this understanding in the conception of space that emerged when discussing community and the everyday in East London. There, space was easily and unthinkingly understood as physical. Put crudely, in Bethnal Green people were close together and in Greenleigh they were further apart and this difference marked both communities. Of course, notions of physicality should remain as part of a concept of space but, in the light of rave, they can no longer be assumed to determine the nature of space. To develop these arguments around extraordinary everydays and space, physicality and community, we can now turn to a community that lives nowhere.

SUMMARY OF SECTION 3.1

In this section we have seen how communities can be created out of extraordinary events like rave. We see how in the rave community:

1   the creation of a repeated experience of euphoria forms the basis for people to identify with each other;

2   'spaces' are created in which the core experience is repeated; but

3   'spaces' move and are created afresh and that communities are not fixed in a particular locality.

3.2 Hacking

ACTIVITY 4

Next time you make a phone call, think about the following questions:

- Where are you?

- Where is the person you are talking to?

- Where is the 'call' taking place?

So, where were you? Is the conversation in your home, in the other person's home or somewhere in the middle? In a similar way, imagine you were able to leave messages on any topic that interested you that could be picked up by many different people who then answered, leaving messages that you and others could pick up to examine and, in turn, reply to. This may seem confusing but if we take this description and instead of people's voices we imagine all these possible exchanges taking place with text appearing on computer screens, then we begin to get a sense of what everyday exchanges might be in virtual communities. These virtual communities are the result of worldwide networks of computers, particularly the internet (or the 'net').

We need to keep in mind two things when discussing the nature of community on the net. First, the internet allows the global exchange of information to anyone who connects to it. The information can be a computer program, text-message, video or sound. As long as something can be digitized (made into a file a computer can recognize), it can be passed around the internet. Second, the internet offers many opportunities for people to access information, such as documents, pictures, shopping and so on. For many users, the internet is like a vast combination of shopping mall and library. However, the internet is also a communications medium that allows people to correspond with each other. Moreover, this communication can be carried out in ways not usually available to us in non-electronic life because it can operate from many people to many people (or 'many-to-many'). For example, virtual communities are often based on bulletin board or newsgroup systems that allow users to post a message on topics. The message simply sits there waiting for anyone to come along and read it and either reply or not. In this way, communities develop with hundreds of topics pursued by groups of people. Communication can be sequential (or asynchronous), as in bulletin board systems, or may continue like a conversation with each line of text appearing simultaneously on the screens of everyone who is involved. This is what is usually called a chat-room. People can connect from around the world to such communities and develop ongoing conversations with other people who also visit regularly, just as they might when becoming a 'regular' in a pub.

What we need to understand is that there is more to the internet than online shops: it also allows communication through which people can meet and discuss all manner of things with each other. What we are asking here is: do communities mediated by these forms of communication exist? This would offer a sense of an everyday and of space located in the place that Activity 4 asked you to explore – the place between two connected telephones. However, with the internet the one-to-one phone space becomes the place between millions of connected computers or, as it is now often called, cyberspace.

READING 6.4

Now turn to Reading 6.4, which is the first of two extracts from an article on 'The sociology of hackers'. When you have read it, attempt to answer the following questions:

1   Do you think the distinction between 'hacking as computer intrusion' and 'hacking as novel use of technologies' is valid?

2   What is the difference between these two understandings of hacking?

3   In most countries, hacking is a crime. What type of crime do you think it most approximates?

You may have came up with crimes such as trespass or burglary, and for now, we should begin from the understanding that one of the longest existing virtual communities is that of hackers.

The question we can now look at is, given that communication and certain types of action are possible in cyberspace and that hackers are one of the longest standing groups to have inhabited cyberspace, in what ways can we understand hackers to be a community? Here we will rely on our understandings of the everyday and community already developed through this chapter and the book as a whole. We will first examine the ways in which hackers identify with each other. These are the topics of everyday interchanges between hackers through which the identity of a hacker is negotiated and developed. We will then turn to the ways in which hackers identify themselves against other communities, the way they form a boundary. This account of hackers is drawn essentially from a series of interviews conducted by Paul Taylor with hackers and computer-security industry staff (Taylor, 1998; Jordan and Taylor, 1998). There are a number of recurring themes that structure a hacker's identity: technology; secrecy and anonymity; changing membership; male dominance and motivations. We shall briefly look at each in turn.

Hackers have a particular relationship to technology. Hackers believe technology should be explored to reveal novel, unanticipated uses. Dutch hacker Ralph exemplifies this attitude: 'If you haven't got a kettle to boil water with and you use your coffee machine to boil water with, then that in my mind is a hack, because you are using technology in a way that it's not supposed to be used' (Taylor, 1998, p.16).

Hackers have an ambivalent relationship to secrecy and anonymity. Many hacks are illegal, and this of course necessitates the need for secrecy. However, a hacker receives no recognition of their hacking skills from other hackers unless their hack is both publicized and 'signed'. One example of this is the hack of the Labour Party website mentioned in Reading 6.4. In this case, a hacker managed to have their hack appear on the front page of UK national newspapers and be interviewed while keeping their identity secret. Signing a hack often means leaving some text on a computer containing a pseudonym or taking 'trophies' that might be files or documents that could only have come from the targeted computer.

Hackers believe that membership of their community changes quickly because hacking expertise develops quickly. Hacker Mike comments, 'If you stop, if you don't do it for one week then things change, the network always changes' (Jordan and Taylor, 1998, p.766). It is not so much the actual turnover of members that structures hackers' identities but their constant preoccupation with the possibility that they will drift away from their community unless they continually improve their expertise.

Hacking is overwhelmingly male and many hackers demonstrate ambivalent if not hostile attitudes to women. Hacker Johnson notes that 'most men see a problem or a puzzle as a direct challenge. They keep attacking it until it's solved, and then brag about it. Women will fuss with a problem for a little while, decide it's too hard, and will drop it' (Taylor, 1998, p.35). Even less misogynist male hackers, who acknowledge women's ability to hack, portray women as having 'separate spheres' of expertise in which they would rather give birth to systems than explore them.

Finally, hackers spend much time justifying and explaining to each other their motivations for activities that can amount to obsessions. One of the most famous hackers of all, Kevin Mitnick, portrayed his motivations this way: 'My motivation behind hacking activity in the past … was just from the gain of knowledge and the thrill of adventure, nothing that was well and truly sinister as trying to get any type of monetary gain or anything' (Jordan and Taylor, 1998, p.769; Shimomura, 1996; Littman, 1996). Motivations such as curiosity, power, addiction, boredom, politics and more, all circulate between hackers as means of mutually recognizing in each other the 'we' that creates the hacking community. These five concepts summarize the everyday of hackers. Nevertheless, hackers also form boundaries around this identity and in doing so complicate and build that identity further.

Having worked through all the activities, you should now have a thorough understanding of community, everyday and space in relation to your own communities, everydays and spaces. Your piece of paper with three columns might be a bit tattered by now, but perhaps you can review it thinking also of analogies, identities, boundaries and the like to gain a complex view of your social world. (To make an analogy involves arguing by comparison. For example, referring to hacking as 'burglary' argues that hacks are comparable to burglary and that they are crimes.)

READING 6.5

Now read the second extract on hackers, Reading 6.5. When you have done so, answer the following questions:

1   Does it seem possible that analogies can construct boundaries between communities?

2   Think back to the communities of Bethnal Green, Greenleigh and rave culture and see if any analogies are at work in those communities?

3   Examine the outline of your own communities, everydays and spaces created in Activities 2 and 3 and see if you can identify any 'internal' means of creating those communities.

We are now in a position to see hackers as a community, even though they are afloat in the non-physical reaches of cyberspace. From interview material and accounts of the exploits of hackers, Jordan and Taylor's work identifies just how we might conceive of a community even when the links between the members of the community are as free of physical space as it is possible to be. As with rave cultures we see powerful mechanisms at work through which identities can be created and maintained. Again we see an everyday that bears little resemblance to the 'ordinary' everyday we have previously examined, but is still recognizably an everyday. With hackers we have also seen how spaces of communication can support a community, even when physicality is nearly entirely absent. Though hackers, their computers and the wires that connect computers must exist physically, the interchanges that create the community exist somewhere in between the physical bodies of all the separated hackers, just as happens in phone conversations. Hackers do in fact meet, they are well known as the only criminal community that holds open, widely advertised and public conferences to discuss their criminal activities, but it is clear that the everyday of the hacking community goes on in cyberspace.

Hacking communities are marked by:

1   the construction of common identities through a communications medium that allows many-to-many communication but does not require face-to-face meetings;

2   identities that are constructed through discussions around five themes of technology, secrecy and anonymity, changing membership, male dominance and motivations; and,

3   boundaries around the community that are created out of differing metaphors for the activity of hacking.

4 When is the everyday 'everyday'?

We began by introducing two ideas that provided an initial definition of community. On the one hand, communities are formed when people are able to construct a 'we' or common identity out of the routines, home-lifes and habits of the everyday. In all four of our communities – Bethnal Green, Greenleigh, dance-floor and cyberspace – we have seen various, but very different, processes at work through which people come to understand that some other people are, in some way, 'like them' and this enables them to identify as members of a community. At first, we were able to employ a simple notion of space based on physical location. Bethnal Green and Greenleigh could be seen to be different communities, in part because of the difference between crowded, closely built inner-urban spaces and spread-out, individualized, suburban spaces. However, this notion of space did not survive exploration of the dance-floor and cyberspace. In these cases, there was some notion of boundary formation through the creation of particular non-physically defined spaces. Taken together, all four examples of community show that space is an important component of communities, even though space cannot be determined by physical location or physical characteristics. The three linked terms of everyday, community and space all participate in the construction of life. In conclusion, it will be useful to return to the question implied in the very first paragraph of this chapter because we can now ask: when is the everyday 'everyday'?

A conclusion we can now reach is that the everyday is only routine, home-like and habitual when individuals are part of the same community. Put another way, when people are engaged in everyday activities they only appear as everyday when people are from a community. Taking illegal drugs, dancing till morning and chasing a party around the countryside become routine and habitual only from within the community of ravers. Sitting for hours in front of a computer screen, chatting through typed text to others who are similarly seated at computer screens that could be anywhere in the world, is only everyday to those who are part of a virtual community. And, seeing your mother every day is only everyday if you are part of a community like Bethnal Green. Put differently, what is everyday can quickly become extraordinary. We can imagine that for many people seeing their mother and other relatives would hardly be everyday. Most obviously, we can think of immigrants for whom seeing a relative on the street might be completely unusual and surprising and not part of their everyday life.

These comments should not be understood as meaning that absolutely everything is everyday. Each of the communities we have examined defines some things as everyday and some as not. For many of us, the everyday routines of 1950s' Bethnal Green would be entirely extraordinary and confusing. Or the everyday of Greenleigh of a family sitting around the television might not be everyday for ravers or hackers, who have rather different ideas about what it is 'normal' to do. What is being developed here is not a refutation of the concept of the everyday, in the sense that the conclusion might be drawn that if raving and hacking have 'everydays' then anything can be everyday, but rather is a development of the concept of everyday. This development points out that the everyday is not the same for everyone but must be understood in relation to a community or space in which certain things are understood as being everyday.

Communities enclose and frame the everyday, allowing individuals to take certain routine and habitual actions for granted because all the individuals involved are members of the same community. How many of us have commented on the different everyday habits we encounter when overseas, such as failure to respect the British habit of queuing? This point can be reinforced by returning to Bethnal Green and asking of this community: how do all these relatives manage to live so closely together? The answer, explored by Young and Willmott, is that local estate agents are pressured to offer housing to local people and any housing that members of the community control is passed on to local people. Such a 'sons and daughters' policy, so named because sons and daughters of local people overwhelmingly receive local housing, is maintained through various means, such as bribing local estate agents and informal, communal pressures. Here is the report of Mr and Mrs Meadows who were allowed by one agent to move into the house next door to Mr Meadows' parents:

> 'He [the agent] said "You can have it, but there are lots of others in the street who want rooms and if I were you I'd let the top half to avoid animosity." There were quite a lot of daughters and sons in the street wanting a place, so that's what we did. We let the upstairs to a girl who'd just got married and whose mother lives at 39. When they got the upstairs and we got the downstairs, there wasn't any bad feeling – not that I know of, anyway – because the place had been taken over by two families who'd lived here for years.'
>
> (Young and Willmott, 1957, p.41)

The obvious possibility of 'bad feeling' is evidence of the local community's efforts to maintain their everyday lives by replicating the community as new generations emerge. Greenleigh, by contrast, was controlled largely by the then London County Council who allocated places according to need rather than to 'sons and daughters'. This leads to questions on difference and diversity: creating identities is as much about excluding some people as including others. For example, in the mid-1950s Bethnal Green was going through a period of full employment, which meant dirty and poorly paid jobs with the local council were not attractive to locals. This led to the following comment about council workers: 'Things have got so bad that they recently started about a dozen black men. They've got the rough and rebel from everywhere' (cited in Young and Willmott, 1957, p.96). The whiteness of Bethnal Green in the mid-1950s is assumed – it is everyday – until circumstances bring black workers into the area. Of course, Bethnal Green has changed a great deal since the 1950s, and this quote registers the beginning of one shift in the fracturing of an assumed, everyday racial homogeneity. We have now arrived back with Gary Younge entering a pub and by his presence unpicking the everyday.

Communities have boundaries. Communities have ways of defining who is 'one of us' and who is not. Communities are created out of processes of identification, through which individuals recognize similarities between each other. The everyday only remains everyday when there are identities between people. This is our first conclusion about community and the everyday, for the two are closely connected. Our second conclusion is that space plays an important role in the creation of communities and their everyday, but we cannot assume that space is defined by physical location. The physical may be a key component of a community's space, as it was in Bethnal Green and Greenleigh. However, a community's space may also be created in a range of different physical or non-physical locations, as with raving and hacking. What this chapter has established is that beyond the everyday there are a number of important sociological ideas that need to be connected to each other. The community and space need to be explored for us to begin to broaden our understanding of what the everyday means.

References

'Andy' (1994) *Rave: The Spiritual Dimension*, Liphook, Kaos Ltd.

Butler, T. (1996) *Rising in the East*, London, Lawrence and Wishart.

Collin, M. and Godfrey, J. (1997) *Altered States: the Story of Ecstasy Culture and Acid House*, London, Serpents Tail.

Eade, J. (1996) *Living the Global City*, London, Routledge.

Garratt, S. (1998) *Adventures in Wonderland: A Decade in Club Culture*, London, Headline.

Jordan, T. and Taylor, P. (1998) 'A sociology of hackers', *Sociological Review*, vol.46, no.4, pp.757–80.

Littman, J. (1996) *The Fugitive Game: Online with Kevin Mitnick, the Inside Story of the Great Cyberchase*, Boston, MA, Little, Brown and Co.

Morley, D. (2000) *Home Territories: Media, Mobility and Identity*, London, Routledge.

Redhead, S. (ed.) (1993) *Rave Off: Politics and Deviance in Contemporary Youth Culture*, Aldershot, Avebury.

Reynolds, S. (1998) *Energy Flash: A Journey Through Rave Music and Dance Culture*, London, Picador.

Rietveld, H. (1993) 'Living the dream' in Redhead, S. (ed.) *op. cit.*, pp.41–78.

Shimomura, T. (1996) *Takedown: The Pursuit and Capture of Kevin Mitnick, The World's Most Notorious Cybercriminal – by the Man who Did It* (with John Markoff), London, Secker and Warburg.

Silva, E. and Smart, C. (eds) (1999) *The 'New' Family?*, London, Sage.

Taylor, P. (1998) *Hackers: Crime in the Digital Sublime*, London, Routledge.

Young, M. and Willmott, P. (1957) *Family and Kinship in East London*, Harmondsworth, Penguin Books.

Readings

6.1 Michael Young and Peter Willmott, 'From Bethnal Green to Greenleigh' (1957)

Less than twenty miles away from Bethnal Green, the automatic doors of the tube train open on to the new land of Greenleigh. On one side of the railway are cows at pasture. On the other, the new housing estate. Instead of the shops of Bethnal Green there is the shopping centre at the Parade; instead of the street barrows piled high with fruit, fish, and dresses, instead of the cries of the costermongers from Spitalfields to Old Ford, there are orderly self-service stores in the marble halls of the great combines. In place of the gaunt buildings rising above narrow streets of narrow houses, there are up-to-date semi-detached residences. Bethnal Green encases the history of three hundred years. Cottages built for the descendants of Huguenot refugees, with their wide weavers' windows and peeling plaster, stand next to Victorian red-brick on one side and massive blocks of Edwardian charity on the other. Greenleigh belongs firmly to the aesthetics of this mid-century. Built since the war to a single plan, it is all of one piece. Though the Council has mixed different types of houses, row upon row look practically identical, each beside a concrete road, each enclosed by a fence, each with its little patch of flower garden at front and larger patch of vegetable garden at back, each with expansive front windows covered over with net curtains; all built, owned, and guarded by a single responsible landlord.

Instead of the hundred fussy, fading little pubs of the borough, there are just the neon lights and armchairs of the Merchant Venturer and the Yeoman Arms. Instead of the barrel organ in Bethnal Green Road there is an electrically amplified musical box in a mechanical ice-cream van. In place of tiny workshops squeezed into a thousand back-yards rise the first few glass and concrete factories which will soon give work to Greenleigh's children. Instead of the sociable squash of people and houses, workshops and lorries, there are the drawn-out roads and spacious open ground of the usual low-density estate. Instead of the flat land of East London, the gentle hills of Essex.

'When I first came,' said Mrs Sandeman, 'I cried for weeks, it was so lonely. It was a shock to see such a deep hill going up to the shops.'

We chose this estate for our inquiry because Greenleigh is, in the view of LCC [London City Council] officials, fairly typical of the estates to which Bethnal Greeners have been moved. We should issue two warnings. Our informants were only from Bethnal Green and their experience may be different from that of other residents on the estate. Secondly, our sample was very small – we interviewed forty-seven out of a sample of fifty couples in 1953, and of these only forty-one were available for a second interview two years later in 1955. ...

...

Greenleigh is only one of several terminal points for the great migration from the city. Relatively few houses have been built since the war inside London. ...

...

The population of Bethnal Green has fallen sharply. From 108,000 in 1931 it dropped to 90,130 in 1939, and was then almost halved, after the first waves of air raids, to 47,330 in 1941. It recovered to 60,580 in 1948 when some of the evacuees had returned; and from that date the borough has again lost population to the housing estates, retaining only 53,860 in 1955. Between 1931 and 1955 nearly 11,000 families, containing over 40,000 people were rehoused from Bethnal Green on LCC estates, many of them outside the county.[1]

The migration has left its mark on Bethnal Green. It is common to hear shopkeepers and publicans say they are losing business as the exodus to Essex goes on. School teachers complain they will soon have no pupils, clergymen that their parishes are emptying. At annual meetings of the local Labour Party there is the familiar lament: 'Once again many of our active members have moved out during the year.' The housing estates are no longer Siberias to which other, unknown people are banished; they are real places, at the end of the tube line, where one's own relatives have made their home. More than half the people in the Bethnal Green marriage sample had relatives on one or other of the six scattered LCC estates in Essex.

When they visit relatives on the estates or stay with them, the experience widens their horizons and raises their aspirations. They see a new house, also a new way of life. When a woman who has lived all her life in 'buildings' or in three cramped rooms in a grubby terraced cottage, is proudly shown round 'my sister's lovely new house with a garden out at Hainault', it is small wonder that admiration is sometimes tinged with envy or that 'dear old Bethnal Green' seems shabbier when she gets back to it. One Bethnal Green informant actually dislikes visiting her sisters because 'it gives me the needle afterwards with my dark place'; another because 'it disheartens you to see them nice places and come back to this dump'. If municipal housing within Bethnal Green has been a catalyst of social change, how much more so – for those who stay as well as for those who go – are the new estates 'out in the country'. In recent times the biggest change in Bethnal Green is Greenleigh.

Motives for migration

A migration such as this gathers its own momentum, people who have moved persuading others by their example. Some of our Greenleigh families followed in the train of kin. Mrs Mallows explained she used to live in a Council flat in Bethnal Green.

'I came out here to see my three sisters who've moved out here, and when I saw them all in their houses, I wanted to move out too, so we put an advert in a shop.'

Others took relatives with them or were joined by them after arrival. Mr Trent was one of those who had acted 'pathfinder' to his parents and his brother. There had been a big change for him between the two interviews of 1953 and 1955.

'My Mum's moved to Greenleigh since you were here before. She used to live in flats in Bethnal Green. Iris (Mr Trent's thirteen-year-old daughter) does for her. She goes in twice a week; she clears the place out and runs errands. All the children go round there and help. And I help with the gardening and I decorated her house. My father came down too, and my brother Tom has moved to Greenleigh as well. He wants it for the children. It's a mutual exchange.'

Although we found that a third of the Greenleigh couples had relatives on the estate in 1955 – nine out of forty-one had parent or sibling on the husband's side or the wife's, and a further five had more remote relatives living there. Once one member of a family has made the move, he is a magnet for the others.

It was easy enough to understand the people who already had relatives on the estate: they moved partly so that they could be near them. But what about the others? We have shown in the first part of this book how embracing kinship can be in Bethnal Green. People's lives are of a piece with their relatives; they gain evident advantage, as they see it, from the companionship and help of the family circle. Why then should they be ready to move away from their kin and the neighbours they know? One possible explanation was that the migrants might have had weaker family ties anyway. If so, they would neither have been so attached to the society of Bethnal Green, nor liable to suffer so much loss by leaving it.

To test this possibility, we asked the wives in the Greenleigh sample how much they saw their mothers before they left the borough, and drew a comparison with the ones in the Bethnal Green sample. There was no appreciable difference between them. Both sets of wives, those on the estate as well as those still in the borough, saw their mothers about four times a week; and the husbands in the two places were similarly alike in the extent to which they saw *their* mothers.

Frequency of contact is, of course, not necessarily a measure of affection, and in fact two of the wives admitted to relief at escaping from the coils of kinship. 'I don't mind about relatives,' Mrs Morrow said. 'You can't always be with relatives. The further away, the better you are – there's no jealousy amongst family or anything then.' Mrs Young said about her brothers and sisters – 'I don't mind not seeing much of them. I'm better off not so near to them. You don't get on each other's nerves.'

Mrs Morrow and Mrs Young were exceptional. Most of the Greenleigh wives not only had seen their mothers a good deal, as much as other dutiful daughters, but also seemed sorry to leave them. We therefore return to the question: If the migrants did not have weaker kinship attachments than other people, why did they come? The main reason is quite simple. The attraction is the house. Our couples left two or three damp rooms built in the last century for the 'industrious classes', and were suddenly transported to a spacious modern home. Instead of the tap in the backyard, there was a bathroom with hot and cold water. Instead of the gas stove on the landing, a real kitchen with a sink and a larder. Instead of the narrow living room with stained wallpaper and shaky floorboards, a newly painted lounge heated by a modern solid-fuel grate. And instead of the street for their children to play in, fields and trees and open country.

...

Who can wonder that people crowded into one or two poky rooms, carrying water up three flights of stairs, sharing a w.c. with other families, fighting against damp and grime and poor sanitation, should feel their hearts lift at the thought of a sparkling new house with a garden? 'When we first came we were thrilled,' said Mrs Lowie, explaining that their home in Bethnal Green had been so small that meals had to be eaten in relays. 'Back in Bethnal Green we had mice in two rooms,' said Mrs Sandeman. 'After that this seemed like paradise.' When Mrs Young and her husband and two children were living in two rooms, there was 'one toilet between five families' and the sink Mrs Young had to use was 'on the next floor up'. Mrs Windle was the same – 'We were very overcrowded – we had only two rooms. We had to go up and down stairs for every drop of water – to the wash-house outside.' All but a few of the families we saw had a similar tale to tell of their former homes.

Better for the kiddies

The house is not the only attraction. Greenleigh, being 'in the country' has, for some of the residents, other advantages over Bethnal Green. 'Everything seems quieter here, more calmer,' said Mrs Vince. 'The fresh air hits you when you come out of the station.' Many people value the air and fields even more for their children than for themselves. Greenleigh is generally thought 'better for the kiddies'.

So even where they left their kin with regret, the people were not deserting family so much as acting for it, on behalf of the younger rather than the older generation. The couples were at a stage of life when they were facing both ways, having responsibilities towards their children as well as towards their parents. Faced with the choice, they felt they had to put the one before the other. Mrs Ames, for example, said, 'We came to Greenleigh for Bill's sake. He was very ill with diphtheria. He got it by drinking the drain water from the sinks of the two families living above us. On top of that he was born bronchial. It has done the boy good to be out here.' 'I would go back if it weren't for the children,' said another mother. 'The children's health comes first – we're here to study them.'

...

Mrs Sandeman neatly posed the issue as she saw it – a conflict between kinship and the interests of the children – when, explaining that 'money was getting tighter,' she said:

I don't even go to my Mum now. I haven't got the fare money. But you've got to put up with things if you want a place for your children. Your children come first, I say.

...

This issue is one which every couple had to face for themselves before they came, and did not necessarily resolve after they had arrived. Many migrants in fact decided that they had made the wrong decision, and left the estate, most of them to return to the East End. Altogether, from the opening of the Greenleigh estate until March, 1956, 26 per cent of the tenants who had come there moved away again. But the rate of removals has been gradually falling in recent years: the numbers leaving in any year, as a proportion of all tenants living on the estate at that March, rose to 7 per cent in 1951–2 and then began to fall again, reaching 5 per cent in 1955–6.[2] Those who remain are the ones who have decided that, on balance, the advantages of the estate outweigh its disadvantaged.

To move or not to move – it is seldom an easy decision. Greenleigh has its attraction, but so too has Bethnal Green. The choice is such a difficult one because to leave the borough is usually to leave the relatives behind as well. What this means for new residents is the subject of the next [reading].

Notes

1 *London Housing Statistics, 1954–55*, p.93.
2 The information was supplied by the LCC Housing Department. The annual removal figures are lower than for similar LCC estates before the war, presumably as a result of full employment which makes it easier for people to pay higher rents. On the Dagenham estate the annual rate of removal in 1932 and 1933 was between 10 per cent and 12 per cent (Young, 1934, p.240). On the Watling estate the average annual rate was more than 10 per cent between 1927 and 1936 (Durant, 1939, p.16).

References

Durant, R. (1939) *Watling: A Survey of Social Life on a New Housing Estate*, London, P.S. King.

London County Council (1955) *London Housing Statistics, 1954–55*, October, London County Council.

Young, T. (1934) *Becontree and Dagenham*, London, Becontree Social Survey Committee.

Source: Young and Willmott, 1957, pp.121–30

Michael Young and Peter Willmott, 'The family at Greenleigh' (1957)

Once the family moves to the housing estate, the question of how they came to be there has for them an academic flavour, and for us the question now is the difference migration has made to them. Table 1 compares contacts with relatives before leaving Bethnal Green with those in 1953 and 1955. It records the *total* contacts of husbands and wives with parents and siblings on both sides: before he moved, the average husband, for example, saw one or other of his relatives on fifteen occasions in a week.

As one would expect, people saw very much less of relatives after moving to the estate. Some relatives, of course, if they already lived on the estate, were seen more often, but the general effect of this was slight, since under one-twentieth of all parents and siblings (18 out of 382) were on the estate even by 1955. Most relatives were seen less after the move. To reveal what difference this made we must rely on the accounts given in the interviews. Mr and Mrs Harper were one of the couples. Before their move, they led the kind of life we have described in the first part of this book. The contrast between old and new has been sharp.

Mrs Harper, a stout, red-faced woman in her late thirties, had, like her husband, always lived in the same part of Bethnal Green before she went to Greenleigh in 1948. She came from a large family – six girls and two boys – and she grew up amidst brothers and sisters, uncles and aunts and cousins. When she married at eighteen, she went on living with her parents, and her first child was brought up more by her mother than by herself. As the family grew, they moved out to three rooms on the ground floor of a house in the next street. Their life was still that of the extended family. 'All my family lived round Denby Street,' said Mrs Harper, 'and we were always in and out of each other's houses.' When she went to the shops she called in on her mother 'to see if she wanted any errands'. Every day she dropped in on one sister or another and saw a niece or an aunt at the market or the corner shop. Her many longstanding acquaintanceships were constantly being renewed. People were always dropping in on Mrs Harper. 'I used to have them all in,' she told us, 'relations and friends as well.' At her confinements, 'all my sisters and the neighbours used to help. My sisters used to come in and make a cup of tea and that.' And every Saturday and Sunday night there was a family party at Mrs Harper's mother's place: 'We all used to meet there week-ends. We always took the kiddies along.'

That busy sociable life is now a memory. Shopping in the mornings amidst the chromium and tiles of the Parade is a lonely business compared with the familiar faces and sights of the old street market. The evenings are quieter too: 'It's the television most nights and the garden in the summer.' Mrs Harper knew no one when she arrived at Greenleigh, and her efforts to make friends have not been very successful: 'I tried getting friendly with the woman next door but one,' she explained, 'but it didn't work.' It is the loneliness she dislikes most – and the 'quietness' which she thinks will in time 'send people off their heads'.

Her husband is of a different mind. 'It's not bad here,' he says. 'Anyway, we've got a decent house with a garden, that's the main thing – and it's made all the difference to the children. I don't let the other people here get me down.' He still works in Bethnal Green – there are no jobs for upholsterers at Greenleigh. This has its drawbacks, especially the fares and the time spent travelling, but it means he is able to look in on his parents once a week and call about once a month on his wife's father and eldest sister – Mrs Harper's mother having died, 'the old man lives with Fanny'.

Mrs Harper herself seldom sees her relatives any more. She goes to Bethnal Green only five or six times a year, when one of her elder sisters organizes a family party 'for Dad'. 'It costs so much to travel up there,'

Table 1 Changes in weekly contacts with relatives after migration
(Greenleigh sample – 39 husbands and 41 wives)

	Average number of contacts per week with own and spouse's parents and siblings		
	Before leaving Bethnal Green	**Greenleigh 1953**	**Greenleigh 1955**
Husbands	15.0	3.8	3.3
Wives	17.2	3.0	2.4

she said, 'that I don't recognize some of the children, they're growing so fast.' Tired of mooching around an empty house all day, waiting for her husband and children to return, with no one to talk to and with the neighbours 'snobbish' and 'spiteful', Mrs Harper has taken a part-time job. 'If I didn't go to work, I'd get melancholic.' Her verdict on Greenleigh – 'It's like being in a box to die out here.'

Mrs Harper's story shows how great can be the change for a woman who moves from a place where the family is linked to relatives, neighbours, and friends in a web of intimate relationships to a place where she may talk to no one, apart from the children, from the moment her husband leaves for work in the morning until he comes home again, tired out by the journey, at seven or eight at night. It is not just that she sees less of relatives than before: as a day-to-day affair, as something around which her domestic economy is organized, her life arranged, the extended family has ceased to exist. Other women remarked on their sense of loss. 'When I first came I felt I had done a crime,' said Mrs Prince, 'it was so bare. I felt terrible and I used to pop back to see Mum two or three times a week.' 'It's your family, that's what you miss. If you're with your family, you've always got someone to help you. I do miss my family,' 'We do miss the relatives out here,' 'I miss my Mum,' others told us in similar vein.

The loss was not so keen for all. One took her mother with her, another her husband's mother, two had sisters on the estate. But for most of the women the move meant a sharp break with the full life they had previously shared with others. For example, when they lived in Bethnal Green, twenty-four of the forty-one wives had seen one or more women relatives daily: at Greenleigh in 1955 only three did so.

…

On the one hand, by 1955 some families saw more than they had done two years before of relatives who had since joined them on the estate. An example is Mrs Trent. Her parents-in-law moved to Greenleigh between the two phases of interviewing, and she saw her mother-in-law three times a week instead of once in three months.

On the other hand, some women had 'settled down' at Greenleigh in the two years and had loosened their ties with their old homes. One thing we noticed in 1953 was that six of the women were still continuing to shop in Bethnal Green as often as once a week. Food was still rationed then and they had not broken their registrations with the shops they knew so well in Bethnal Green. If they went to Bethnal Green to shop, they could see relatives at the same time. By 1955 only one of the wives was going up to

Bethnal Green on a regular weekly shopping expedition, though others went occasionally to get clothing and other things cheaper there. 'I don't go up there for shopping now,' said Mrs Clive, 'not now we've got our own shopping centre here.' The effect this can have on meetings with kin was voiced by Mrs Rawson – 'I haven't seen my Aunt Ada for a long time. We used to be rationed in Bethnal Green and then I used to see her occasionally in the market, but not now.'

…

One link has not been broken by time – many of the husbands have continued to work in London. At Greenleigh there are local jobs in only a limited number of trades. There are few openings for tailors, cabinet makers, french polishers, dockers, or lorry drivers. In 1953, thirteen of the forty-seven husbands were working in the East End and a further nine in other parts of the County of London; by 1955 some individuals had changed one way or the other, and there were by then fifteen out of thirty-nine working in the East End and eight elsewhere in London. From the estate as a whole, more people were travelling to the East End in 1955 than in 1953.[1]

Since many men have to travel to the East End for their work, their contacts with relatives have in general fallen less since they moved to the estate than their wives'. The husband has to meet his fares out of an income already strained by the higher rent. But if he has to pay his fares anyway, he can not only get to work on the one ticket but to his relatives also, and in some ways their very presence at the other end of the line may relieve his daily journey. Mr Mallows finishes his work in Bethnal Green at five. At that time 'the guards are forcing people into those trains every night', so he goes to his father's, to have a cup of tea. When he has finished that and had a chat, the rush-hour is over; there is even a chance of getting a seat. Mr Parker used to go home every day for his dinner before he moved to Greenleigh. He cannot get used to the sandwiches which he takes instead, so he often has a hot meal at home with his mother. He has to pay her but at least that is cheaper than any other way of getting a hot dinner. Other men still make a point, as they did in Bethnal Green, of calling each week on their mothers, or they see their fathers and brothers at work, or just 'bang into' uncles and aunts and cousins on their walk from tube station to workplace, or in their dinner break.

They do not keep up with their own relatives alone; they do so with their in-laws also. Mr Ellis, who works in Bow, visits his wife's mother regularly once a month. Mr Lowie works in Bethnal Green as a cabinet maker and has his midday meal every day with his wife's sister. Other husbands call regularly to pay into family clubs, more often run by their wives' relatives than their own. Mr and Mrs Adams belong to a Public House Loan Club, and Mr Adams 'calls in on a Friday to give my sister our Club money. She takes it and pays it in for us.'

In 1955, six of the forty-one wives were working in London also. Mr Marsh had been working in a shop in Bethnal Green in 1953 and had kept in touch with the relatives, particularly his own mother; by 1955 he had got a job in a shop at Greenleigh instead, but now his wife was working for London Transport. 'Being on the buses,' he pointed out, 'the wife sees her mother and my mother more than I do now.'

It is not so much the distance that makes visiting difficult for the other women as the cost. Time and again, wives lamented that they were so short of money that they could not afford to visit Bethnal Green as often as they would like. 'If the fares were cheaper you could afford to go more often and it wouldn't be so bad,' was Mrs Adams's verdict. 'The fares put the damper on visiting relations more than anything else.'

…

Care in illness

Even those Greenleigh wives whose homes had not been visited by sickness had considered the prospect with misgiving. If husbands were away from work their families had to make do on a small sickness benefit, sometimes paid tardily at that.

> 'Last year my husband was off work and the health money took ages to come down. I told the rent collector and he said "That's no excuse." "Well, what am I to do," says I, "the health money's not come down. You know how long it always takes out here." Then on top of it all if I didn't have a saucy letter from them saying I'd missed a week's rent. It's above the limit, isn't it?'

Families with savings exhausted them. Families without had to borrow from relatives.

…

When the husband was ill, his wife looked after him. When the wife was ill, who looked after her? We asked wives at Greenleigh, as in Bethnal Green, who was the main person helping them with the home and children when they were last ill in bed. At Greenleigh there was, of course, less help from relatives. …

…

In Bethnal Green, people with relatives close by seldom go short of money in a crisis like this. If they do not belong to a family club from which they can draw a loan, some relative will lend them money. Borrowing from relatives is often more difficult at Greenleigh. 'You notice the difference out here,' said Mr Tonks, 'when you fall on hard times. Up there you were where you were born. You could always get helped by your family. You didn't even have to ask them – they'd help you out of trouble straight away. Down here you've had it.' 'That's why families stick together,' said a Bethnal Green husband. 'If you're short of money you can always go round your Mum and get helped out.'

…

Lack of places to go

One reason people have so little to do with neighbours is the absence of places to meet them. In Bethnal Green there is one pub for every 400 people, and one shop for every 44 (or one for every 14 households). At Greenleigh there is one pub for 5,000 people, and one shop for 300. Some services are not there at all. Cinemas, for instance – the nearest one is at Barnhurst,[2] several miles away, so far that the fares are 6d. each way. 'Then on top of that there's the ice in the picture palace and a quarter of sweets – makes it half a quid before you're through.'

So at Greenleigh practically no one goes out at night, except the small number of hardy people who attend meetings at the 'community centre', and the adolescents who can find nothing to do on the estate and spend the evening in East London before catching the last tube back. All the others stay at home, and a good many of them watch the television. The spread of television sets at Greenleigh and Bethnal Green is shown in Table 2.

Table 2 Television at Bethnal Green and Greenleigh

	Bethnal Green		Greenleigh	
	1953	**1955**	**1953**	**1955**
Television sets per 100 households	21	32	39	65

Note: The GPO Radio and Accommodation Department kindly supplied this information.

Not only is there a bigger proportion of sets on the estate; the increase between 1953 and 1955 was at a faster rate at Greenleigh than Bethnal Green.

The growth of television compensates for the absence of amenities outside the home, and serves to support the family in its isolation. Instead of going out to the cinema or the pub, the family sits night by night around the magic screen in its place of honour in the parlour. In one household the parents and five children of all ages were paraded around it in a half circle at 9 p.m. when one of us called; the two-month-old baby was stationed in its pram in front of the set. The scene had the air of a strange ritual. The father said proudly:

> 'The tellie keeps the family together. None
> of us ever have to go out now.'

…

We have in this chapter, to conclude, given a sketch of what happens when people move to the housing estate. We have discussed in turn the two sides of what is really a single change. When they leave the East End the people also leave their relatives behind them, and, although few of them cut the threads which connect them to their former homes, they can no longer see their old companions every day or even every week. In emergency, they can no longer so easily send word round to Mum's. When they arrive at Greenleigh, being deprived of relatives, they have to make do as best they can, sometimes with the aid of neighbours, but usually by their own devices. Children do more. Husbands do more. The family is more self-contained in bad times and in good.

Greenleigh, like anywhere else, has advantages as well as disadvantages, and, as always, human adaptability shows its power to find a compensation. There is the pleasure of washing baby in a bath with running hot water instead of a tub filled from kettles. There is the delight of a flower-garden on a hot summer's evening. There is the pride of showing the relatives the cupboards in the kitchen and the back-boiler which heats water as it heats space. There is variety and football on the tellie. There is the satisfaction of knowing that, even if they are making a sacrifice, it is for the good of their children, who are growing up in the country and attending fine schools which are the only public buildings on which money and ingenuity have been lavished. There is, above all, the possibility, even inside their own little home, of making good some of the loss of social life. Husband and wife are together and a closer partnership here can make isolation bearable. He is now the one who leads the active life of society, not only on the job but, sometimes too, on his round of the relatives after work is done. He is the messenger who brings back to Cambridge Avenue the news from the larger world of work and the smaller world of kinship. She is more dependent on him, for news and for the financial sacrifice which will sustain their domestic economy. If, now that he does not have to share her with so many others, he plays well his roles of messenger, earner, and companion, the strains of the new life are not without compensation.

Notes

1 This information was provided by the London Transport Executive.

2 This, like Greenleigh, and for the same reason, is a fictitious name.

Source: Young and Willmott, 1957, pp.131–40,142–3,145–6

6.3 Simon Reynolds, 'Energy flash: a journey through rave music and dance culture' (1998)

Living a dream: acid house and UK rave, 1988–89

…

Around this time – November 1987 – Danny Rampling and his wife Jenni started Shoom, a tiny club located in a Southwark gym called the Fitness Centre, just a few hundred yards south of the Thames. Although Danny supplied the club's musical vision (pure Balearic), the power-house behind Shoom is generally reputed to be Jenni Rampling. A formidable figure who'd previously been the manageress of the Bond Street branch of the shoe shop Pied À Terre, Jenni maintained the club's membership scheme and newsletter, kept the press at arm's length and controlled the door with a ruthlessness that became infamous.

'We used to say that Jenni had the Battle of Britain spirit,' recalls Mark Moore, 'There was this kind of naïve pioneering spirit.'

'The Ramplings were a very ordinary, upwardly mobile working class couple from Bermondsey,' remembers journalist Louise Gray, an early Shoom convert. 'Suddenly they were thrown into this fantastically trendy set where they had luminaries pounding on their doors, and they were being taken up by people like Fat Tony and Boy George – very queeny, nightlife sophisticates.'

The first time Gray actually managed to get inside Shoom, 'we arrived terribly early, about 10.30, and we couldn't really figure out what the fuss was about. There was about twenty people, dancing wildly. I was sitting talking, and then this girl just appeared absolutely out of nowhere, plonked herself down on my knee, grabbed the corners of my mouth and pulled them up into a smile. She said "Be Happy!" and then jumped off. I was completely nonplussed – I'd never experienced behaviour like that, and thought it quite crazed.'

Suddenly the club filled up very fast – not just with people, but with 'peasouper, strawberry-flavoured smoke, lit only by strobes. If you went on to the dancefloor, you could only see a few inches ahead. It was just exciting, there was a real contact high. I didn't have any drugs that night, but that was when I realized that drugs had something to do with it.' Drugs had everything to do with it: the name 'Shoom' was freshly-coined slang for rushing, for the surging, heart-in-mouth sensation of coming up on Ecstasy. The imagery on the flyers, membership cards and newsletters was blatantly druggy: pills with Smiley faces on them, exhortations to 'Get Right On One, Matey!!!'

Unlike your typical West End club, the Shoom scene was not about being seen, but about losing it – your cool, your self-consciousness, your *self*. Quoting T.S. Eliot, Gray describes the fruit-flavoured smoke as 'the fog that both connects and separates. You'd have these faces looming at you out of the fog. It was like a sea of connected alienation.'

Says Mark Moore: 'Often it was so chaotic, you couldn't really see in front of you, you couldn't really talk to anyone. So a lot of the time you just spent on your own dancing … You'd have people in their own world, doing that mad trance dancing, oblivious to everything else. But then you also had blokes coming up who were, like, "yeah, all right mate!! Smile! Smile!" And hugging you.'

Coming from the arty end of the gay scene, Moore was used to this kind of demonstrativeness. But at Shoom he encountered 'this whole new mentality … It was all these suburbanites who – without wishing to sound élitist – it was as if they'd taken this Ecstasy and they were releasing themselves, *for the first time*. It was like they'd suddenly been let out of this box

they'd been kept inside and they were just beginning to come to terms with the idea that, y'know, "I'm a man but I can hug my mate," stuff like that.' Gay behavioural codes and modes of expressivity were entering the body-consciousness of straight working-class boys, via Ecstasy.

Oriented around communal frenzy rather than posing, Shoom was the chrysalis for rave culture, in so far as *the rave* in its pure populist form is the antithesis of *the club*. At the same time, Shoom *was* a club, more so than most Soho nightspots in fact, because it had a membership scheme.

…

Revolution in progress

The democratic promise of the Balearic ethos could not be kept the preserve of the chosen few for long. In the spring of 1988, Oakenfold took it to the next level when he launched Spectrum as a Monday night club in the 2000 capacity Heaven, round the corner from where The Future had taken place. 'Everyone said to us, you can't do a club on a Monday. But we did a deal with Heaven so that as long as we broke even, it was okay. After two weeks, we owed twelve grand. The third week, they were all set to close us down, but we broke even. And from then on, it just got bigger and bigger.'

Spectrum's subtitle was 'Theatre of Madness', and this was no idle boast. 'I was quite shocked, almost appalled, actually,' remembers Nick Philip, a hip hop fan who was intrigued enough to check out Spectrum at its height. 'Just the hedonism, and how out of line everyone was getting. Back in the late eighties, the club scene was quite uptight, you had to wear exactly the right clothes to get in, and you might see the odd person there who was really out of it, but it was not the general rule. But at Spectrum, everyone looked like they were from fucking Mars. Drenched in sweat, wearing baggy shit, and all just looking at the DJ with their arms in the air, like it was some really weird religious ceremony. I was quite freaked out by it.'

The atmosphere was even more deranged at The Trip, a club started by Nicky Holloway in June 1988. Instead of the laid-back, sunkissed Balearic vibe, the music was full-on acid house. The location – The Astoria, in the heart of London's West End – signalled the scene's emergence into the full glare of public consciousness. When The Trip closed at 3 a.m., the punters would pour out into Charing Cross Road, stopping the traffic and partying in the street. 'Then the police would come,' remembers Mark Moore, 'and the sirens would get turned on. Everyone would crowd around the police van and chant "acieed!" –

the war cry of 1988 – "and dance to the siren". The police didn't know what to make of it, it was like, "what the fuck is going on?!?'" Then everyone would troop en masse to the municipal multi-storey car park near the YMCA in Bedford Street, where they'd dance around their vehicles to house music pumping out of the car stereos.

Because of Britain's antiquated club licensing laws, the night's mayhem ended prematurely. One result was the chill-out scene. 'The chill out was good, 'cos that's when you'd invite complete strangers back to your place and that's when you'd make new friends,' remembers Moore. If you wanted to carry on dancing through the night, you had to turn to the illegal warehouse parties of after-hours, unlicensed clubs like the legendary RIP at Clink Street.

...

Absolute beginners

Ecstasy had been available in London since the early eighties, but the supply was highly restricted. You had to know someone who brought it over from America, where it was legal until 1985. There was something of an Ecstasy scene at Taboo, Leigh Bowery's club for fashion freaks, but nobody had discovered its application as a trance-dance drug. Instead, small groups of friends were using it for private bonding sessions.

In 1988, Ecstasy became much easier to get hold of, though it was still rather pricey at around £20 a tab. In the spring of that year, Louise Gray had her first Ecstasy experience at a Hedonism warehouse party in West London. 'I remember at one point feeling immensely hot and claustrophobic, having to go outside and lie down, and thinking that I might throw up. People figured out pretty soon that Ecstasy did something to your stomach, during the initial rush. Some people had to shoot off immediately to the loo, 'cos they were going to get the runs; others were sick. After Hedonism, I remember being put in a taxi by my friend, and lying on the floor of this cab at five in the morning, telling this cabbie my life story!'

Nobody really knew much about Ecstasy, about how it worked or what was the best way to take it. People quickly worked out that alcohol dulled the E buzz; at Shoom, Lucozade became the beverage of choice, partly because it replenished energy and partly because it was the only drink available at the Fitness Centre. Myths sprang up around the new drug, like the notion that vitamin C killed the buzz, which ruled out orange juice. There was also considerable confusion over Ecstasy's legal status, and nobody knew if it was an addictive substance or not. The other big Ecstasy myth concerned the drug's aphrodisiac powers. 'All these strange reports were coming through that it turned you into a sex fiend,' says Gray. 'But if anything it was the complete opposite. Very little sex happened that year. People were very cuddly, and that was very nice: you could be cuddled by complete strangers in a very non-threatening way, 'cos you knew nothing was going to happen. If you got upset about something, this crowd of strangers' hands would descend on you. It was touchy feely, an amorphous sensuality – but it wasn't a *sexuality*.

'That's one of the reasons the Ecstasy scene was so docile – the libido had actually been sublimated into a completely different form. People weren't going out to pull. You might meet someone there who was nice and then you'd see them and then sex would happen at some other stage. I think that was one of the reasons why you could have such an extraordinary mix of people – male gays, but also working-class boys who hadn't had any contact with the trendy culture, and maybe in another life they might have gone queer-bashing or Paki-bashing. Suddenly they were thrown into this environment where everyone was kissy-kissy, but it didn't matter, they weren't threatened in any way.'

...

Mantra for a state of mind

...

Because of Ecstasy and the mingling and fraternization it incited, the living death of the eighties – characterized by social atomization and the Thatcher inculcated work ethic – seemed to be coming to an abrupt end. 'Everyone was vitilized,' says Gray. And yet, for all the self-conscious counterculture echoes, acid house was a curiously apolitical phenomenon, at least in the sense of activism and protest. While the tenor of the peace-and-unity rhetoric ran against the Thatcherite grain, in other respects – the rampant hedonism, the fact that Ecstasy was priced out of the range of the unemployed – acid house's pleasure-principled euphoria was very much a product of the eighties: a kind of *spiritual materialism*, a greed for intense experiences.

...

By autumn 1988, it was possible to virtually live in this parallel universe, full time. There was a party every night. Fridays, there was The Mud Club and then A Transmission at Clink Street. Saturdays, the raver faced a dilemma – Shoom or The Trip – followed by RIP at Clink Street right through till dawn. Sunday night offered the mellow, coming-down-from-the-night-before vibe of Confusion, Nicky Harwood's club in Soho. Monday was Spectrum; Tuesday, you could go to the gay club Daisy Chain, at The Fridge in Brixton. Wednesday, the Pyramid at Heaven; Thursday, a new Heaven night called Rage. If this regime of bliss wasn't enough, there was a host of other acid nights around town like Babylon, Love,

Loud Noise, Enter the Dragon, Elysium and even the tacky old Camden Palace; at the weekends, there were also the one-off warehouse parties. Back then, remembers Barry Ashworth, 'You was *arseholed* four, five nights a week.'

Source: Reynolds, 1998, pp.38–48

6.4 Tim Jordan and Paul Taylor, 'A sociology of hackers I' (1998)

Introduction[1]

The growth of a world-wide computer network and its increasing use both for the construction of online communities and for the reconstruction of existing societies means that unauthorised computer intrusion, or hacking, has wide significance. The 1996 report of a computer raid on Citibank that netted around $10 million indicates the potential seriousness of computer intrusion. Other, perhaps more whimsical, examples are the attacks on the CIA world-wide web site in which its title was changed from Central Intelligence Agency to Central Stupidity Agency, or the attack on the British Labour Party's web site, in which titles like 'Road to the Manifesto' were changed to 'Road to Nowhere'. These hacks indicate the vulnerability of increasingly important computer networks and the anarchistic, or perhaps destructive, world-view of computer intruders (Miller, 1996, p.1; Gow and Norton-Taylor, 1996). It is correct to talk of a world-view because computer intrusions come not from random, obsessed individuals but from a community that offers networks and support, such as the long running magazines *Phrack* and *2600*. At present there is no detailed sociological investigation of this community, despite a growing number of racy accounts of hacker adventures.[2] To delineate a sociology of hackers, an introduction is needed to the nature of computer-mediated communication and of the act of computer intrusion, the hack. Following this the hacking community will be explored in three sections: first, a profile of the number of hackers and hacks; second, an outline of its culture through the discussion of six different aspects of the hacking community; third, an exploration of the community's construction of a boundary, albeit fluid, between itself and its other, the computer security industry.[3] Finally, a conclusion that briefly considers the significance of our analysis will be offered.

In the early 1970s, technologies that allowed people to use decentred, distributed networks of computers to communicate with each other globally were developed.[4] By the early 1990s a new means of organising and accessing information contained on computer networks was developed that utilised multi-media 'point and click' methods, the World-Wide Web. The Web made using computer networks intuitive and underpinned their entry into mass use. The size of this global community of computer communications is difficult to measure[5] but in January 1998 there were at least 40 million (Hafner and Lyons, 1996; Quaterman, 1990; Jordan, 1998; Rickard, 1995; Quaterman, 1993). Computer communication has also become key to many industries, not just through the Internet but also through private networks, such as those that underpin automated teller services. The financial industry is the clearest example of this, as John Perry Barlow says 'cyberspace is where your money is'. Taken together, all the different computer networks that currently exist control and tie together vital institutions of modern societies; including telecommunications, finance, globally distributed production and the media (Castells, 1996; Jordan, 1998). Analysis of the community which attempts to illicitly use these networks can begin with a definition of the 'hack'.

Means of gaining unauthorised access to computer networks include guessing, randomly generating or stealing a password. For example in the Prestel hack, which resulted in the Duke of Edinburgh's mail-box becoming vulnerable, the hacker simply guessed an all too obvious password (222222 1234) (Schifreen, hacker, interview). Alternatively, some computers and software programmes have known flaws that can be exploited. One of the most complex of these is 'IP spoofing' in which a computer connected to the Internet can be tricked about the identity of another computer during the process of receiving data from that computer (Felten *et al.*, 1996; Shimomura, 1996; Littman, 1996). Perhaps most important of all is the ability to 'social engineer'. This can be as simple as talking people into giving out their passwords by impersonating someone, stealing garbage in the hope of gaining illicit information (trashing) or looking over someone's shoulder as they use their password (shoulder surfing). However, what makes an intrusion a hack or an intruder a hacker is not the fact of gaining illegitimate access to computers by any of these means but a set of principles about the nature of such intrusions. Turkle identifies three tenets that define a good hack: simplicity, the act has to be simple but impressive; mastery, however simple it is the act must derive from a sophisticated technical expertise; and illicit, the act much be against some legal, institutional or even just perceived rules (Turkle, 1984, p.232).[6] Dutch hacker Ralph used the example of stealing free telephone time to explain the hack:

> It depends on how you do it, the thing is that you've got your guys that think up these things, they consider the technological elements of the phone-booth and they think, 'hey wait a minute, if I do this, this could work', so as an experiment, they cut the wire and it works, now *they're hackers*. Okay, so it's been published, so Joe Bloggs reads this and says 'hey, great, I have to phone my folks up in Australia', so he goes out, cuts the wire, makes phone calls, He's a stupid ignoramus, yeah?

> (Ralph, hacker, interview)

A second example would be the Citibank hack. In this hack, the expertise to gain unauthorised control of a bank was developed by a group of Russian hackers who were uninterested in taking financial advantage. The hacker ethic to these intruders was one of exploration and not robbery. But, drunk and depressed, one of the hackers sold the secret for $100 and two bottles of vodka, allowing organised criminals to gain the expertise to steal £10 million (Gow and Norton-Taylor, 1996). Here the difference between hacking and criminality lay in the communally held ethic that glorified being able to hack Citibank but stigmatised using that knowledge to steal. A hack is an event that has an original moment and, though it can be copied, it loses its status as a hack the more it is copied. Further, the good hack is the object in itself that hackers desire, not the result of the hack (Cornwall, 1985, p.7).

Notes

1   Thanks to Sally Wyatt, Alan White, Ian Taylor and two anonymous referees for comments on this piece.

2   Meyer and Thomas (1989) and Sterling (1992) provide useful outlines of the computer underground, while Rosteck (1994) provides an interesting interpretation of hackers as a social movement. Previous accounts lack detailed survey work.

3   This analysis draws on extensive fieldwork consisting of both a quantitative questionnaire (200 respondents) that outlines the extent and nature of hacking and 80 semi-structured interviews with hackers (30), computer security professionals (30) and other interested parties (20). A full methodology and list of interviewees is available in Taylor (1993). All notes of the following form (Shifreen, hacker, interview) indicate that Shifreen was a hacker interviewed for this project.

4   It is of course impossible to provide an adequate history of computer networking here and would distract from the main purpose of present arguments.

5   See Jordan (1998) for a full description of methodologies for counting internet users.

6   The concept of a 'hacker' has had several manifestations, with at least four other possibilities than a computer intruder. This paper is concerned solely with hacker in the sense of a computer intruder, though see Taylor (1993) for further discussion (Levy, 1984; Coupland, 1995). It should also be noted that hacking makes most sense within a society in which knowledge has become extensively commodified and is subject to a process in which it can be extensively copied (Mosco and Wasco, 1988).

References

Castells, M. (1996) *The Rise of the Network Society: Vol. I, The Information Age*, Oxford, Blackwell.

Cornwall, H. (1985) *The Hacker's Handbook*, London, Century Communications.

Coupland, D. (1995) *Microserfs*, London, HarperCollins.

Felten, E., Balfranz, D., Dean, D. and Wallack, D. (1996) 'Web-spoofing: an internet con game', *Technical Report 540–96*, Department of Computer Science, Princeton, NJ, Princeton University, also at http://www.cs.princeton.edu/sip.

Gow, D. and Norton-Taylor, R. (1996) 'Surfing superhighwaymen', *The Guardian*, 7 December, p.28.

Hafner, K. and Lyons, M. (1996) *Where Wizards Stay Up Late: The Origins of the Internet*, New York, Simon and Schuster.

Jordan, T. (1998) *Cyberpower: A Sociology and Politics of Cyberspace and the Internet*, London, Routledge.

Levy, S. (1984) *Hackers: Heroes of the Computer Revolution*, Harmondsworth, Penguin Books.

Littman, J. (1996) *The Fugitive Game: Online with Kevin Mitnick, The Inside Story of the Great Cyberchase*, Boston, MA, Little, Brown and Co.

Meyer, G. and Thomas, J. (1989) 'The baudy world of the byte: a post-modernist interpretation of the computer underground', paper presented at the American Society of Criminology annual meeting, Reno, Nevada, November 1989.

Miller, S. (1996) 'Hacker takes over Labour's cyberspace', *The Guardian*, 10 December.

Mosco, V. and Wasco, M. (eds) (1988) *The Political Economy of Information*, Madison, WI, University of Wisconsin Press.

Quaterman, J. (1990) *The Matrix: Computer Networks and Conferencing Systems Worldwide*, Bedford, Digital Press.

Quaterman, J. (1993) 'The global matrix of minds' in Harasim, L. (ed.) *Global Networks: Computers and International Communication*, Cambridge, MIT Press, pp.35–6.

Rickard, J. (1995) 'The internet by the numbers: 9.1 million users can't be wrong', *Boardwatch*, vol.9, no.12, also available at http://www.boardwatch.com

Rosteck, T. (1994) 'Computer hackers: rebels with a cause', honours thesis, Sociology and Anthropology, Concordia University, Montreal, also at http://www.geocites.com/CapeCanaveral/3498

Shimomura, R. with Markoff, J. (1996) *Takedown: The Pursuit and Capture of Kevin Mitnick, The World's Most Notorious Cybercriminal – by the Man who Did it*, London, Secker and Warburg.

Sterling, B. (1992) *The Hacker Crackdown: Law and Disorder on the Electronic Frontier*, London, Viking.

Taylor, P. (1993) 'Hackers: a case study of the social shaping of computing', unpublished PhD dissertation, University of Edinburgh.

Turkle, S. (1984) *The Second Self: Computers and the Human Spirit*, London, Granada.

Source: Jordan and Taylor, 1988, pp.757–60

 ## Tim Jordan and Paul Taylor, 'A sociology of hackers II' (1998)

External factors: the boundary between computer underground and the computer security industry

Hackers negotiate a boundary around their community by relating to other social groups. For example, hackers have an often spectacular relationship to the media. Undoubtedly the most important relationship to another community or group is their intimate and antagonistic bond to the computer security industry (CSI). This relationship is constitutive of the hacking community in a way that no other is. Put another way, there is no other social group whose existence is necessary to the existence of the hacking community. Here is a sample of views of hackers from members of the CSI.

> Hackers are like kids putting a 10 pence piece on a railway line to see if the train can bend it, not realising that they risk derailing the whole train.
>
> (Mike Jones, security awareness division, Department of Trade and Industry, UK, interview)

> Electronic vandalism.
>
> (Warman, London Business School, interview)

> Somewhere near vermin.
>
> (Zmudsinski, system engineer/manager, USA, interview)

Naturally, hackers often voice a similar appreciation of members of CSI. For example, while admitting psychotic tendencies exist in the hacking community Mofo notes:

> My experience has shown me that the actions of 'those in charge' of computer systems and networks have similar 'power trips' which need to be fulfilled. Whether this psychotic need is developed or entrenched before one's association with computers is irrelevant.
>
> (Mofo, hacker, interview)

However, the boundary between these two communities is not as clear as such attitudes might suggest. This can be seen in relation to membership of the communities and the actions members take.

Hackers often suggest the dream that their skills should be used by CSI to explore security faults, thereby giving hackers jobs and legitimacy to pursue the hack by making them members of the CSI. The example of a leading member of one of the most famous hacker groups, the Legion of Doom, is instructive, Eric Bloodaxe, aka Chris Goggans, became a leading member of the hacking community before helping to set up a computer security firm, Comsec, and later moving to become senior network security engineer for WheelGroup a network security company (Quittner and Slatalla, 1995, pp.145–7,160). On the CSI side, there have been fierce debates over whether hackers might be useful because they identify security problems (Spafford, 1990; Denning, 1990). Most striking, a number of CSI agencies conduct hacking attacks to test security. IBM employ a group of hackers who can be hired to attack computer systems and the UK government has asked 'intelligence agents' to hack its secure email system for government ministers (Hencke, 1998).[1] In the IBM case, an attempt at differentiating the hired hackers from criminal hackers is made by hiring only hackers without criminal records (a practice akin to turning criminals who have not been caught into police). Both sides try to assure themselves of radical differences because they undertake similar actions. For example, Bernie Cosell was a USA commercial computer systems manager and one of the most vehement anti-hackers encountered in this study, yet he admitted he hacked

> … once or twice over the years. I recall one incident where I was working over the weekend and the master source hierarchy was left read-protected, and I really needed to look at it to finish what I was doing, and this on a system where I was not a privileged user, so I 'broke into' the system enough to give myself enough privileges to be able to override the file protections and get done what I needed … at which point I put it all back and told the systems administrator about the security hole.
>
> (Cosell, USA systems manager, interview)

…

Cosell's analogy continues to draw on real world or physically based images of buildings being entered but tries to come closer to the reality of how hackers operate. However, the ethical component of the analogy has been weakened because the damage hackers cause becomes implied, where is the bomb?[2] Cosell cannot claim there will definitely be a bomb, only that it is possible. If all possible illegal actions were prohibited then many things would become illegal, such as driving because it is possible to speed and then hurt someone in an accident. The analogy of breaking and entering is now strong on implied dangers but weak on the certainty of danger. The analogies CSI professionals use continue to change if they try to be accurate. 'My analogy is walking into

an office building, asking a secretary which way it is to the records room and making some Xerox copies of them. Far different than breaking and entering someone's home' (Cohen, CSI, interview). Clearly there is some ethical content here, some notion of theft of information, but it is ethically far muddier than the analogy burglar offers. At this point, the analogy breaks down entirely because the ethical content can be reversed to one that supports hackers as 'whistle-blowers' of secret abuses everyone should know about.

> The concept of privacy is something that is very important to a hacker. This is so because hackers know how fragile privacy is in today's world … In 1984 hackers were instrumental in showing the world how TRW kept credit files on millions of Americans. Most people had not even heard of a credit file until this happened … More recently, hackers found that MCI's 'Friends and Family' programme allowed anybody to call an 800 number and find out the numbers of everyone in a customer's 'calling circle'. As a bonus, you could also find out how these numbers were related to the customer … In both the TRW and MCI cases, hackers were ironically accused of being the ones to invade privacy. What they really did was help educate the American consumer.
>
> (Goldstein, 1993)

The central analogy of CSI has now lost its ethical content. Goldstein reverses the good and the bad to argue that the correct principled action is to broadcast hidden information. If there is some greater social good to be served by broadcasting secrets, the perhaps hackers are no longer robbers and burglars but socially responsible whistle blowers. In the face of such complexities, CSI professionals sometimes abandon the analogy of breaking and entering altogether; 'it is no more a valid justification to attack systems because they are vulnerable than it is valid to beat up babies because they can't defend themselves' (Cohen, CSI, interview). Here many people's instinctive reaction would be to side with the babies, but a moment's thought reveals that in substance Cohen's analogy changes little. A computer system is not human and if information in it is needed by wider society, perhaps it should be attacked.

The twists and turns of these analogies show that CSI professionals use them not so much to clearly define hacking and its problems, but to establish clear ethical differences between themselves and hackers. The analogies of baby-bashing and robbery all try to establish hacking as wrong. The key point is that while these analogies work in an ethical and community building sense, they do not work in clearly grasping the nature of hacking because analogies between real and virtual space cannot be made as simply as CSI professionals would like to assume.

> Physical (and biological) analogies are often misleading as they appeal to an understanding from an area in which different laws hold ... Many users (and even 'experts') think of a password as a 'key' despite the fact that you can easily guess the password, while it is difficult to do the equivalent for a key.
> (Brunnstein, academic, Hamburg University, interview)

The process of boundary formation between the hacking and CSI communities occurs in the creation of analogies by CSI professionals to establish ethical differences between the communities and their reinterpretation by hackers. However, this does not exclude hackers from making their own analogies.

> Computer security is like a chess-game, and all these people that say breaking into my computer system is like breaking into my house: bull-shit, because securing your house is a very simple thing, you just put locks on the doors and bars on the windows and then only brute force can get into your house, like smashing a window. But a computer has a hundred thousand intricate ways to get in, and it's a chess game with the people that secure a computer.
> (Gongrijp, Dutch hacker, interview)

Other hackers offer similar analogies that stress hacking is an intellectual pursuit. 'I was bored if I didn't do anything ... I mean why do people do crosswords? It's the same thing with hackers (J.C. van Winkel, hacker, interview). Gongrijp and van Winkel also form boundaries through ethical analogy. Of course, it is an odd game of chess or crossword that results in the winner receiving thousands of people's credit records or access to their letters. Hackers' elision of the fact that a game of chess has no result but a winner and a loser at a game of chess whereas hacking often results in access to privileged information, means their analogies are both inaccurate and present hacking as a harmless, intellectual pursuit. It is on the basis of such analogies and discussions that the famed 'hacker ethic' is often invoked by hackers. Rather than hackers learning tenets of the hacker ethic, as

seminally defined by Steven Levy, they negotiate a common understanding of the meaning of hacking of which the hacker ethic provides a ready articulation.[3] Many see the hacker ethic as a foundation of the hacker community, whereas we see the hacker ethic as the result of the complex construction of a collective identity.

The social process here is the use of analogies to physical space by CSI and hackers to establish a clear distinction between the two groups. In these processes can be seen the construction by both sides of boundaries between communities that are based on different ethical interpretations of computer intrusion, in a situation where other boundaries, such as typical actions or membership, are highly fluid.

Notes

1 Our research also leads us to believe that CSI uses teams of hackers to test security far more often than CSI professionals publicly admit.

2 Other CSI professionals offered similar analogies, such as finding someone looking at a car or aeroplane engine.

3 Steven Levy distilled a hacker ethic from the early, non-computer intruder, hackers. This ethic is often invoked by all types of hackers and Levy defines the tenets as: all information should be free; mistrust authority, promote decentralisation; hackers should be judged by their hacking, not by bogus criteria such as degrees, age, race or position; you can create art and beauty on a computer; and, computers can change your life for the better (Levy, 1984, pp.40–45).

References

Denning, P. (1990) *Computers Under Attack: Intruders, Worms and Viruses*, New York, Addison-Wesley.

Goldstein, E. (1993) 'Hacker testimony to House Subcommittee largely unheard', *Computer Underground Digest*, vol.5, no.43.

Hencke, D. (1998) 'Whitehall attempts to foil net hackers', *Guardian Weekly*, 26 April 1998, p.8.

Levy, S. (1984) *Hackers: Heroes of the Computer Revolution*, Harmondsworth, Penguin Books, pp.40–5.

Quittner, J. and Slatalla, M. (1995) *Masters of Deception: The Gang that Ruled Cyberspace*, London, Vintage.

Spafford, E. (1990) 'Are computer hacker break-ins ethical?', *Princeton University Technical Report*, CSD-TR-994, Princeton, NJ, Princeton University.

Source: Jordan and Taylor, 1998, pp.770–5

Accounting for the everyday

Sue Hemmings, Elizabeth B. Silva
and Kenneth Thompson

Contents

1 Introduction

As you will recall from the Introduction to this book, sociological enquiry into the everyday has proceeded from a number of different starting-points and been informed by a range of theoretical concerns. The democratic and industrial revolutions of the eighteenth and nineteenth centuries gave rise to an increasing concern with the ordering of ordinary people's everyday lives, not just as citizens and workers, but also with regard to aspects of their private or domestic lives. The rise of sociology in the nineteenth century was partly due to concern among the middle and upper classes about the threat to social order posed by political and industrial revolutions, as well as reformist desires to improve the lives of the lower classes. Initially, sociological attention was focused on the 'big picture' – the macro-social structures that seemed to hold the key to explaining how the **macro-sociology** social order was maintained or changed. **Macro-sociological** approaches to the everyday have considered how it is structured and determined by social relations and processes, such as those of class, gender, 'race' and ethnicity. In this view, the everyday is seen as occurring within an overarching framework of power that shapes the conduct of all aspects of social life.

micro-sociology **Micro-sociological** approaches, however, start from a very different viewpoint: their focus of study is on the finer detail of face-to-face interaction and the ways in which social life is made possible through the creation and maintenance of shared meanings, understandings and unwritten rules of behaviour. In today's sociology, the rigid distinction between micro and macro levels has been eroded. An emphasis on the detailed ethnographic study of ways of life has illuminated the rich texture of the everyday and the ways in which it is in small-scale everyday practices that power and inequalities are lived through and reproduced. This is not just an academic concern. These processes involve the exercise of power and consequently have also been the focus of social movements. Feminism, for example, has posed political questions about the forms of power involved in the relationships of gender that inform and organize the practices of everyday life – where 'the personal is political'.

It is worth recapitulating on some of the characteristics that have been associated with the concept of everyday life. We shall then move on to consider how these have featured or been modified in recent studies. A useful reminder of these characteristics is given in Rita Felski's definition:

> ... everyday life is grounded in three key facets: time, space and modality. The temporality of everyday ... is that of repetition, the spatial ordering of the everyday is anchored in a sense of home and the characteristic mode of experiencing the everyday is that of habit.
>
> (Felski, 1999–2000, p.18)

When we begin to look at how these factors operate in different situations and examine how this affects the lives of particular groups, it becomes clear that these mundane characteristics of everyday life have great significance. Ethnographic studies have called attention to the distinctive temporal and spatial arrangements that characterize the organization of everyday life.

In this chapter we focus on the ways in which time and space are not external factors impinging upon the everyday but produced within it. In section 2 we return briefly to Lefebvre's (1991a/1947) approach to the everyday and question whether subsequent contributions and debates have modified some of the assumptions underlying his account. (He published the first volume of his three-volume work, *Critique of Everyday Life*, in 1947, and the first two volumes were not available in English until 1991.) He was writing in the context of debates within post-war Marxism and he considered the concept of the everyday to be his major contribution to sociology. For Lefebvre, writing within the revolutionary tradition – not just Marxist, but also dating from the French Revolution – the everyday sphere was a brake on progress and had to be transformed. In 1968 Lefebvre was to reflect on the circumstances in which the book was written – in the heady days after the French Liberation in 1946 – and he noted how it bore the marks of that time of reconstruction, when many people believed that they were building a new society, although in retrospect 'all they were really doing was to re-establish the old order in a slightly modified form' (Lefebvre, 1984/ 1968, p.30). At the same time, other approaches to the everyday were being developed within British and American sociology. Whereas Lefebvre's discussion rested on a set of polarized distinctions – between genders, between habit and resistance, between imposed power and forms of opposition – there has emerged a more complex and varied understanding of the everyday.

In section 3 we explore some of the complexities of the everyday as they relate to two of the characteristics touched on by Lefebvre – time and routine. We discuss contexts of everyday life situations, of paid and unpaid work, clock-time, lived experiences and other ways of marking time. In addition, we explore the context of home life through an ethnographic study, bringing out important differences with respect to gender and the role of children in everyday routines.

In section 4 our attention turns to another key facet of the everyday – that of space. Turning again to Lefebvre, we consider the processes by which each society establishes spatial relationships between, for example, home and work, the public and the private. Relationships of space, from a global to an intimate scale, are woven into the very fabric of the everyday. We look in more detail at these arguments by examining the ways in which modern gender and sexual identities have been constructed in and through the spatial relationships of the modern world.

Finally, in section 5, we return to look at the social and political implications of various accounts of the everyday. Is the everyday a routinized and reactionary sphere, opposed to modern developments, or is it caught up in those developments?

AIMS

The aims of this chapter are:

1   To review the main themes of this book: the everyday as a distinctive set of relations to time and space, and as a characteristic mode of experience, and to place approaches to these themes in the context of broader debates.

2   To review how our understanding of the everyday has been modified and made more complex and varied in the context of the debates that have occurred within and between sociology, feminism and cultural studies.

3   To review different approaches to the relations between power, politics and the everyday.

2 Understanding the everyday: from simplicity to complexity

It sometimes takes a dramatic occurrence to make us aware of the taken-for-granted assumptions, routines and practices of everyday life, and their social and political significance. The French Revolution was such an event. In fact, it resulted in an effort to completely reorganize the way time was structured. Unsurprisingly, this met with a great deal of resistance, and much of everyday life in France continued to follow its accustomed patterns. However, the dramatic effort to revolutionize time itself illustrates the social significance of the way basic aspects of everyday life are structured.

ACTIVITY I

Read the following extract from the *Encyclopaedia Britannica* on 'The French republican calendar'.

After you have read it, note down answers to the following questions:

- What was the political objective in instituting this new calendar?

- What factors would have limited its impact?

- How would your own consciousness of time and its organization be affected if such a scheme were instituted by government edict?

THE FRENCH REPUBLICAN CALENDAR

In late eighteenth-century France, with the approach of the French Revolution, demands began to be made for a radical change in the civil calendar that would divorce it completely from any ecclesiastical connections. The first attacks on the Gregorian calendar and proposals for reform came in 1785 and 1788, the changes being primarily designed to divest the calendar of all its Christian associations. After the storming of the Bastille in July 1789, demands became more vociferous, and a new calendar, to start from 'the first year of liberty', was widely spoken about. In 1793 the National Convention appointed Charles-Gilbert Romme, President of the Committee of Public Instruction, to take charge of the reform. Technical matters were entrusted to the mathematicians Joseph-Louis Lagrange and Gaspard Monge and the renaming of the months to the Paris deputy to the convention, Philippe Fabre d'Églantine. The results of their deliberations were submitted to the convention in September of the same year and were immediately accepted, it being promulgated that the new calendar should become law on October 5 1793. The French republican calendar, as the reformed system came to be known, was taken to have begun on September 22, 1792, the day of the proclamation of the Republic and, in that year, the date also of the autumnal equinox. The total number of days in the year was fixed at 365, the same as in the Julian and Gregorian calendars, and this was divided into 12 months of 30 days each, the remaining five days at year's end being devoted to festivals and vacations. These were to fall between September 17 and 22 and were specified, in order, to be festivals in honour of virtue, genius, labour, opinion, and rewards.

Figure 7.1 *Calendar from the time of the French Revolution: front page of Fabre d'Églantine's calendar, 1794*

In a leap year an extra festival was to be added – the festival of the Revolution. Leap years were retained at the same frequency as in the Gregorian calendar, but it was enacted that the first leap year should be year 3, not year 4 as it would have been if the Gregorian calendar had been followed precisely in this respect. Each four-year period was to be known as a Franciade. The seven-day week was abandoned, and each 30-day month was divided into three periods of 10 days called décades, the last day of a décade being a rest day. It was also agreed that each day should be divided into decimal parts, but this was not popular in practice and was allowed to fall into disuse. The months themselves were renamed so that all previous associations should be lost, and Fabre d'Églantine chose descriptive names as follows (the descriptive nature and corresponding Gregorian calendar dates for years 1, 2, 3, 5, 6, and 7 are given in parentheses): *Vendémiaire* ('vintage', September 22 to October 21), *Brumaire* ('mist', October 22 to November 20), *Frimaire* ('frost', November 21 to December 20), *Nivôse* ('snow', December 21 to January 19), *Pluviôse* ('rain', January 20 to February 18), *Ventôse* ('wind', February 19 to March 20), *Germinal* ('seedtime', March 21 to April 19), *Floréal* ('blossom', April 20 to May 19), *Prairial* ('meadow', May 20 to June 18), *Messidor* ('harvest', June 19 to July 18), *Thermidor* ('heat', July 19 to August 17), and *Fructidor* ('fruits', August 18 to September 16). The French republican calendar was short-lived, for while it was satisfactory enough internally, it clearly made for difficulties in communication abroad because its months continually changed their relationship to dates in the Gregorian calendar. In September 1805, under the Napoleonic regime, the calendar was virtually abandoned, and on January 1, 1806, it was replaced by the Gregorian calendar.

(Source: *Encyclopaedia Britannica*)

According to the historian Simon Schama (1989, pp.771–7), the attempt to reconstruct time and create a new 'empire of images' had the political aim of detaching republican citizens from the superstitions, religious traditions and authority that were embodied in the Gregorian calendar. The new calendar would replace religious images with those of the cult of nature, and with festivals that celebrated secular virtues, culminating every four years in a great festival occasion of patriotic games on the 'day of the Revolution' (10 August). The reconstruction of calendar time can be seen to be part of a revolutionary project that had the secularization of everyday life at its core. The factors that limited its impact can be easily imagined. Schama comments that it is unlikely the peasants appreciated the replacement of Sunday and 'Saint Monday' (the tradition of taking a second day of rest), with one day off every ten days. The fact that other countries kept to the Gregorian calendar also meant that 'revolution in one country' was shown to be difficult to maintain in the modern world of increasing international travel and commerce.

If we are to speculate on our possible reactions were such a scheme to be instituted by government (or the European Union) today, we might draw on the lessons from the French Revolution and predict considerable resistance. Of course, it is possible to point to some contemporary economic trends – such as pressures on workers to work at weekends – as having a similar disturbing effect on traditional calendar time-patterns. This is one reason why Sunday is no longer a 'sacred day of rest'; another reason is that in an increasingly multicultural society, it may not be the appropriate day.

The fact that the proponents of revolutionary modernization in France thought it necessary to attempt to reorganize time itself tells us something about how fundamental this mundane, taken-for-granted, aspect of everyday life is to the ordering of society. The relatively short-lived nature of the experiment also tells us something about how there can be resistance to change in patterns of everyday life. To attempt to change the social order at this fundamental level really was a politically revolutionary act.

It was the political relevance of everyday life that drew Lefebvre (1984/ 1968) to make it a renewed focus of study in the mid-twentieth century. According to Lefebvre, everyday life was above all a temporal term, conveying the fact of repetition – cyclical rhythms of habitual living that happen day after day. Such repetition and habit were found to be particularly strongly embedded in the domestic social space, which he saw as the realm of women. In his view, repetition was a problem, or a 'riddle', because it was fundamentally at odds with the modern drive towards progress and accumulation. It was as if everyday life lagged behind the historical possibilities of modernity. He saw women's association with the routines of cyclical time as a sign of their close connection to nature, with its biological and seasonal rhythms. Lefebvre chose to emphasize the negative view of women's association with the everyday life, but others, especially some feminists (Smith, 1987), have taken a different and more positive view.

Everyday life has been described in both negative and positive terms as either the basis for tactical resistance to the strategies of the powerful (de Certeau, 1984) or as the dull sphere of repetition and routine wherein relationships of power are conserved (Lefebvre, 1984/1968). The Canadian sociologist, **Erving Goffman**, in *The Presentation of Self in Everyday Life* (1959), took what might be described as a 'democratic' view, adopting a 'dramaturgical' framework. He quoted Shakespeare's line that all the world is a stage and we are all players. Everyday life was to be investigated in terms of social actors' performances and their tactics for managing impressions and getting by in social interactions. Until recently, the primary sociological focus on everyday life has been on the micro-social dimensions of social life in all their specificity and detail:

Goffman, Erving

> In its heyday 'everyday life' served as a rubric through which to assert the sociological significance of the structures and practices of micro-social settings from streets of lounge rooms and bars to backyards.
>
> (Crook, 1998, p.539)

This was the contribution made by American sociology's ethnographic studies of aspects of everyday life, such as the Chicago School studies of inner-city communities (as you saw in Chapter 3) and by post-war British community studies like that of the break-up of the working-class community of Bethnal Green (Young and Willmott, 1957) (which you met in Chapter 6). Subsequently, for a time in British sociology the concept of community was criticized heavily on the grounds that it encouraged a romanticized view of the everyday life of certain local areas, especially the old working-class areas and rural villages. Critics suggested that sociologists should treat all localities as simply local social systems that were not separate from larger social systems. One result of **community studies** becoming unfashionable was a loss of focus upon this dimension of everyday life.

More recently, sociologists who have written about everyday life processes have attempted to link the micro- and macro-social levels. In doing this, they have given more emphasis to the dimensions of time and space in everyday life settings. Gender differences feature prominently in such studies, although not always in quite the ways assumed by Lefebvre.

3 Time and routine

You are aware by now that a key idea of previous chapters is that time is a crucial component of everyday experiences. Time, however, forms an aspect of our daily lives that many of us rarely reflect on. The chores, routines and decisions, the co-ordination of actions, and so on, that comprise the everyday are frequently seen as mundane and beneath analysis. This section will review:

1   the shifting nature of social time, including what counts in different times; and

2   the gendered aspects of everyday routines.

3.1 Using/spending/counting/running out of time

Urban modernity runs on clock-time. Time has been speeded up and broken into ever-smaller pieces. How is time spent? How are hours and minutes and days used? Time passes us by: often the feeling is of a flow of movement external to one's self. Time is counted and measured everywhere: clocks tell you the time – from the top of corporate buildings and towers to displays on cookers. Computer screens have digital clocks and even eggs have sell-by dates on their shells. Before the industrial revolution, time-counting as we now know it was little used. Nowadays, fast food, fast travel, 'quality time' are just some of the few ways time has currently been marked up in the West. Time seems to be at a premium like never before. It is to be protected, managed, not wasted, because it is a resource. We never have enough of it.

However, time can be measured and felt in many different ways. The clock is only one way of experiencing and measuring time. To ask 'How old are you?', the Guarani-Kaiowa Indians in Brazil ask, 'How many times has the Guavira flowered in your lifetime?' (Griffiths, 1999, p.7). Small children on a journey commonly ask, 'When are we going to be there?', as they learn to experience time in the same way as adult members of their society. For people who are terminally ill, and for those around them, temporal experiences reach beyond the realm of everyday time and bring to the fore many different times. This is how forty-nine-year-old Dominique, teacher, mother of two children and married to Brian, describes her perception of time:

> I feel squashed by time: time running out and time lasting too long. There is Brian's illness and everyone around me dying: close members of my family, neighbours, my dog. There is so little time to accomplish things while

simultaneously time is dragging on – waiting for death. I am cornered, squeezed between the two. I can only just cope with the routines of daily living while for me personally time is standing still.

(Adam, 1995, p.56)

Temporality is an integral element of the individual self and all social relationships. This is something you can test for yourself in the next activity.

ACTIVITY 2

How do you use (or spend) your time in a typical day? What time do you get up? How does the day go by?

On a sheet of paper, write down your daily routine. Make three columns for:

1   the clock hours from the time you get up until when you go to bed;

2   the main time changes of activities (and the nature of the activity) in your day; and

3   the main places or spaces where each activity takes place.

Note down your typical daily pattern of routines in columns 2 and 3.

Investigate the daily routines of any two other people by using the same kind of data-recording instrument and asking them a similar set of questions. (You should note also their gender and age.)

Observe the temporal structures of your daily pattern and those of each of the two other people. What are the similarities and the differences? How would you explain the patterns found?

You might find it useful to compare your own findings here with the ways in which the relations between time and everyday life have been discussed in previous chapters. In the discussion of the home and everyday life in Chapter 1, Tony Bennett remarks on the links between repetition and habit with the temporality of the everyday as crucially anchored in the home. In this case, the gendering of time and the contested separation of public and private time are relevant. In Chapter 2, Peter Redman discusses the tension of romance as, on the one hand, an escape from the entanglements of everyday life and, on the other, as a part of the routine of the everyday. Both extraordinary and ordinary times are important in this context. The analysis of the street in Chapter 3 by Peter Hamilton is connected to a concern with historical time, marking changes from agrarian to industrial society, the emergence of life in cities, and the advent of 'modernity'. Celia Lury's Chapter 4 remarks that the temporalities of everyday life are configured in bounded spaces and categories, such as home and work, private and public, women and men, and that profound historical transformations have affected the social organization of time within these spaces and categories. This movement is exemplified in Chapter 5 where Diane Watson shows that the gendered and generational segregation of pubs has changed over time, as newer identifications between leisure time and home have emerged. In Chapter 6, Tim Jordan remarks on the varied lived experiences of time and space that different groups have in their everyday lives.

The sociological analysis of time also raises many questions about what matters in temporal analysis: How is the counting done? What is the value of time? Whose time counts and is valued? For instance, we can measure our time spent in particular activities, as you did in Activity 2. This has been an important method for analysis of time-use both in the industrial sector and in activities of social reproduction. In the 1920s, the advent of the **Fordist** assembly-line was accompanied by time-and-motion studies to organize the flows of production. During the 1980s, the Japanese 'just-in-time' method advocated the promptness of supply and delivery as part of a more efficient production process. **Flexibilization** in forms of production came to replace the old Fordist methods, which had been based on standardization and rigid tasks and work functions. In other areas of life, such as the home, and in investigations of the expenditure of social time in the activities of **social reproduction**, time-use diaries have been widely employed. The methodologies of time-use budgets (based on collections of diary data) have been criticized because of their misconceptions and lack of accuracy, particularly as they generally assume rigid gender roles, discrete activities and distinct spatial divisions. Lately, they have become more sophisticated as a means of ascertaining changes in behaviour and attitudes. A brief consideration of time-shifts in both industrial production and in social reproduction will illustrate some of the difficulties associated with the analysis of time-use.

Fordism

flexible specialization

social reproduction

3.2 Time-shifts

Work time has been the subject of extensive study in sociology and labour history. The labour and economic historian, E.P. Thompson (1967), wrote one of the best-known essays on the establishment of industrial capitalism, 'Time, work-discipline and industrial capitalism'. In it, he charts the transition from task-oriented to clock-oriented work. We noted above that time-and-motion studies were developed at the beginning of the twentieth century. In Chapter 4 Celia Lury showed that in the work of Marx and Weber a connection is made between the production of commodities, the Protestant ethic and time-thrift. Building on this framework, Thompson drew attention to how time became an instrument of power, and was used by employers to discipline, subordinate and control workers. A consequence of the prevalence of clock time, and of the consolidation of the historical separation between home and work, was that the new distinction between work and 'life' also involved a distinction between work-time – seen as belonging to employers – and 'own-time' or free-time. Thompson's work is important, but his work has been criticized because of the gendered nature of his analysis. The experiences of male industrial workers, which inform Thompson's analysis, have been found not to have much in common with women's experiences. The sociologist Miriam Glucksmann (1990, 2000) remarks that for women workers the distinction between task- and clock-orientated time does not appear so absolute. Also, home and work are not completely separate in women's everyday lives: much domestic management, social networking for domestic support, and even tasks associated with home life, get intermeshed in women's working routines. It is similarly difficult to trace the boundaries between work and leisure in the everyday lives of women and to draw distinction between tasks:

Take the case of a woman doing the ironing. At the same time she is watching television. A load of washing went into the washing machine about half an hour ago and will soon be ready to be transferred to the dryer. So she is keeping an ear open for the washing machine, and also an eye on the oven where a meal, prepared earlier, is now cooking. And all this is being done not in her own house but in the home of her elderly aunt, and they are chatting together the while. Clearly our friend is undertaking many different activities at the same time, productive and reproductive labour in the case of cooking, washing and ironing. She is also caring; watching television could count as leisure though it might more appropriately be considered as a medium for caring and emotion work. But none of these activities is differentiated from each other in reality. What is most significant about them is temporal integration of the multiplicity of tasks, an issue posing problems which time study budgets are now taking on board.

(Glucksmann, 2000, p.114)

We will return to this issue of gendered time after considering another important historical change in social temporality in modern western societies. If marked shifts in social time have resulted from the transition from agrarian to industrial societies, another important time shift is marked by the development of the service sector and its growing importance. Jonathan Gershuny (2000) makes the point that in our work time we gather the means for consuming the products of someone else's work during our non-work time. Three categories of time-use are present in these instances: paid work; unpaid work; and consumption. Yet these are, he argues, very fluid and changing distinctions:

Take all that work we do that is *not in* the national accounts. This problem, and the economic category, was dismissed years ago as the 'housekeeper paradox'. *So* the widowed clergyman marries his housekeeper, and what was waged labour and inside the national accounts, now becomes unpaid labour and the National Product is diminished.

...

Take the transport industry: half a million people, in mid-twentieth-century Britain, working on trains and buses to move 50 million people across the landscape. In little more than a quarter of a century, nine-tenths of that work disappeared. Where did it go to? Did we stop moving? What happened, of course, was that the technology changed, and instead of buying 'final transport services' – and employing all those transport workers – we now buy goods (cars), and materials (petrol), and intermediate services (running repairs and 'services'), and then we produce the transport services ourselves, by driving the cars. So while that particular activity, the provision of final transport services, may have disappeared from the national accounts, it has gone somewhere else: into the time budgets of private households. ... [I]n the lives of those busy people who, in the absence of a substantial public transport system must devote a substantial part of their weekend to transporting children and elderly relatives across the landscape.

...

[W]ho is it, exactly, that does these new things that appear in the household's time budgets? When the laundry service disappeared, and we bought a washing machine, who had to work that machine at home?...

(Gershuny, 2000, pp.2–3)

Gershuny's examples demonstrate the social invisibility of various issues of time that create pressures, stress and unhappiness, and increase inequalities, not just by gender, but also between different social groups. Different relationships between paid work time, unpaid work (caring included), leisure or consumption time, and sleep reveal ways of living that link the everyday with broader social movements. Until very recently, these issues of time were virtually invisible within academic social scientific analyses.

3.3 Routine matters

The greatest post-war change in the use of time in the western industrialized world has been the increase in female labour-market participation.

> In 1971, 91 per cent of men of working age, compared with 57 per cent of women, were economically active in Great Britain. ... Women's activity rates generally increased from the early 1970s to reach 72 per cent by Spring 1997, but men's activity rates slowly declined in the 1980s and 1990s to 85 per cent in 1997. It is projected that the gender gap will narrow further over the next decade and, if these long-term trends continue, by 2011 there will only be a six percentage point difference between female and male activity rates.
>
> (Equal Opportunities Commission, 1998)

Let's look first at a couple of definitions:

> *Economically active*: this refers to people who are employees, self-employed, participants in government employment and training programmes, doing unpaid family work, and those who are unemployed on the International Labour Organization's (ILO) definition.
>
> *Economically inactive*: refers to people who are neither in employment nor unemployed, according to the definition of the ILO. For example, those looking after a home or retired or those permanently unable to work.

What are the consequences of such increases in female economic activity rates for the use and structures of time in society? And in people's daily lives?

The woman in the household that acquired the washing-machine, in Gershuny's example mentioned above, is now more likely to have a job than she was in the mid-century, when she could have called on the laundry service. Jobs (paid and unpaid) accumulate on women. Man of these jobs, however, and the dynamic of activities between them, like the fragmentation in the use of time of the woman doing the ironing, in Glucksmann's example above, are issues of time that require detailed investigation. Taken from research carried out by one of us (Silva, forthcoming 2002), Figure 7.2 depicts the patterns of routines in the everyday lives of nine people in five households in contemporary Britain. These are graphic representations of the temporal cycle of the waking days of particular individuals. In the study, Silva notes that routines are located in culture, history and personal biographies. The manner in which data about routines were collected was similar to the task you undertook for Activity 2. People were asked to detail how a 'normal' weekday would go by from the time they woke up until they went to bed:

The manners in which people kept track of their everyday narratives were … quite diverse. Some lost themselves in side-tracked accounts of events triggered by a recollection of some occurrence in the everyday. Normally men were either very brief or concentrated on events at the workplace. Because I was interested in what happened in the home I encouraged people (most often I saw myself encouraging men) to tell me what happened in the home. … I also encouraged accounts of people's perceptions of their partners' and children's routines. Again, for men this had to be prompted more often than for women. Women's routines appeared more generally imbricated with those of their children, in particular, but also with those of their partners.

Because some people's daily lives have different set patterns for different days of the week, we would normally talk about these differences. Time, space,

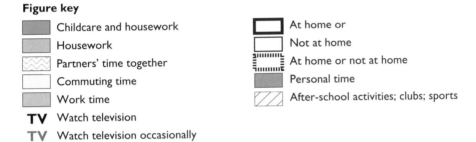

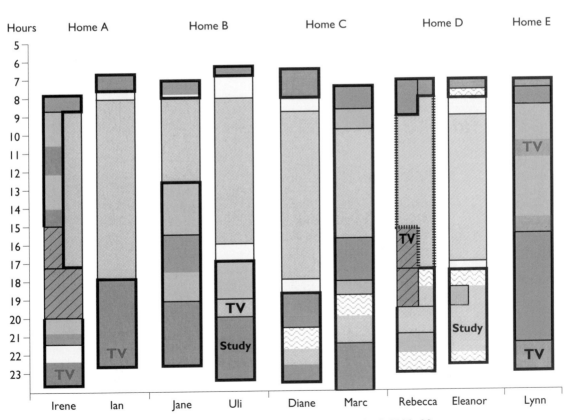

Figure 7.2 *Space, activity and time of everyday life: women and men in England, 1998–99*

activity and persons appeared as recurrent elements in the narratives of routines. Time routines were constructed around activities done in particular spaces, involving specific persons. The common ingredients of 'normal' routine included getting up, washing, having breakfast, giving children breakfast, taking children to school, doing childcare, setting off to work, commuting, doing housework (cleaning, cooking, washing, ironing), working, having personal time, engaging in relational time, and watching television. The activities most permeated with other concomitant activity (or activities) were childcare, housework, watching television, having personal time or engaging in relational time. Work was the most preserved single activity done in isolation.

(Silva, forthcoming 2002, p.7)

As you can see from Figure 7.2, only two people, Marc, in Home C, and Lynn, in Home E, spend the day at home. However, their experiences of home life differ dramatically. Marc shares a home with Diane. His normal routine involves: early childcare and housework, working from home between 10 a.m. and 4 p.m., and also from 8 p.m. to 9.30 p.m., after an interval between about 4 p.m. and 7 p.m., when he is again involved in childcare and housework. Between 7 and 8 p.m. he spends time with Diane. (We can see that in Diane's account, however, that she says that she spends time with Marc in the evening between about 8.30 p.m. and 9.30 p.m.) Between 9.30 p.m. and nearly midnight Marc has some personal time.

In contrast to Marc, Lynn does not have a partner in the home. We can see from her account that she starts her day with some personal time, then does childcare until about 9 a.m. and housework until 11 a.m. She has some more personal time, when she also watches television between 11 a.m. and 1 p.m., does some more housework until 2 p.m. and has some personal time until 3.30 p.m. She is then involved in childcare until 9 p.m., from which time she has personal time, watching television until after 11 p.m. when she goes to bed.

In accounting for the routines of 37 people in 20 households, Silva (forthcoming 2002) notes that time spent in the home is very significant for most people. Nevertheless, there are important variations between the women's and men's patterns. What is more relevant, however, is that there are various new experiences of everyday routines that related to different ways of living, away from traditional models of a male breadwinner and a female homemaker. For instance, if you look again at Figure 7.2, you will note that whereas both men in Homes A and B spend most of their waking hours out of the home, only Ian (Home A) presents a pattern of traditional provider. This does not match, however, with a traditional full-time homemaker role for his wife Irene – she has a part-time job. She also carries out all the responsibilities for childcare and housework. Home, for Ian, is an uncontested place of personal time and replenishment. What is interesting is that Ian's experience is exceptional. All the women in Figure 7.2 have some paid work, with the exception of Lynn, who is a lone mother of four children and living on social benefit.

The time problems in everyday life is usually different for women and men, but patterns of routine have a close relation with care activities in the home. Although the gendered pattern found in households tend to be conventional, sometimes it is reflexively negotiated to conform to changing life circumstances. In general, men tend to do more when women are not present. Men's time tends to be less fragmented and more exclusively relational even when doing childcare. An element of inequality is revealed in this because: 'Time is a resource, and being in charge of one's own time and of the time of others signifies having individual and social power' (Silva, forthcoming 2002, p.18).

Although women have generally less power than men in heterosexual family life, inequalities may be less marked where both adults operate in a balanced way in their 'caring routines'.

READING 7.1

You should now read Reading 7.1, 'Gender and routines in narratives of everyday life in families', by Elizabeth B. Silva.

While you are reading, keep the following questions in mind and, when you have finished, write down your answers:

1   Do you agree that gendered experiences of time are relevant? Why? If not, why not?

2   What are the structural constraints in social time that most strongly impinge on the everyday routines of the people studied by Silva?

3   Looking back at your own data collected for Activity 2, can you identify any particular issue of everyday routine that Silva has not analysed?

SUMMARY OF SECTION 3

We have discussed the significance of experiences of time in the everyday and remarked on a few key aspects:

1   Diverse cultural constructions of time exist, and these are linked to different historical periods, groups of people and to different places.

2   Different chronological and internal, emotional experiences of time often co-exist within the self and in relationships.

3   Gendered temporal structures relate to the constructions of boundaries between work and leisure.

4   Time has been explicitly visible, measured and valued only when it carries a price value. This has devalued particular social groups and increased inequalities.

5   Contemporary western post-industrial societies are experiencing great changes in the patterns of time-use, due mainly to increased female labour-market participation. This has important bearings upon how individuals organize their everyday life routines.

4 Space and the everyday

As the preceding section shows, 'time' – the ways in which the temporal is conceptualized, compartmentalized and lived through – is a key element in theorizing 'the everyday'. Felski argues, however, that time and space operate very differently from one another in the construction of the everyday: 'While everyday life expresses a specific sense of time, it does not convey a particular sense of space. In fact, everyday life is usually distinguished by an absence of boundaries, and thus a lack of clear spatial differentiation.' (Felski, 1999–2000, p.22).

There is not, then, a single characteristic of space which epitomizes the everyday. Yet if we look back through the earlier chapters of this book we can see that the social organization of space, the relationships between homes, streets, pubs, workplaces and communities, is an integral element of the everyday.

The sociological importance of these spaces lies in:

- the social practices by which abstract space becomes a series of specific spaces which are sites of particular kinds of social action;

- the cultural practices through which spaces are imbued with shared social meanings that enable members of a society to know what actions are appropriate in this or that space and to understand the actions of others;

- the relationships between specific spaces as nodal points within the flow of power through social space.

4.1 The production of social space

'Space' can be seen as something outside of the social realm, as either a neutral backdrop to social life or as a series of fixed and essential attributes of landscape and physical geography that contain and shape social life. Every society, however, produces its own social space. As a Marxist theorist, Lefebvre emphasizes that social space incorporates and allocates appropriate places to two sets of relationships: those of reproduction (relationships of sexuality, biological reproduction, child-rearing, family) and those of production (the ways in which economic life and particularly labour are organized). In advanced capitalist societies, he argues, a third set of relationships is also necessary: those that ensure the reproduction of the society as a whole.

Lefebvre (1991b) illustrates his argument by comparing medieval and modern space. Medieval society (with feudal economic organization) produced a social space characterized by manors, monasteries and cathedrals. These acted as anchoring points in a network of lanes and roads which ran through a landscape transformed by farming and other productive practices of peasant communities. Some of these buildings remain in European landscapes today, although they are largely transformed from the economic, political and spiritual hubs that they were. Lefebvre asserts that today capitalism has produced space as an abstraction. Modern space is characterized by a vast network of banks, business centres and productive enterprises linked by motorways, airports and the new communication technologies. In the social space of advanced capitalism the manor becomes a country hotel or conference centre, the cathedral a venue for classical concerts and site of tourism and both can be visited through their web-pages.

Lefebvre introduces three interlinked concepts to develop his analysis of social space:

- *spatial practice*: this embraces the ways in which each society, with its own form of economic and political as well as social organization, creates particular spatial relationships between production and reproduction and thus particular places for these activities characteristic of each society.

- *representations of space*: these are the formal images of space developed in advanced capitalism by planners and other professional groups.

- *representational spaces*: these are the commonsense, everyday ways in which space is understood, experienced and 'lived'. These symbols and images about space emerge through practice and are far from formal systems of thought, often containing contradictions.

Lefebvre's three interlinked concepts of space allow us to consider processes that are in constant interaction with each other and also to link macro-sociological concerns of social structure with small-scale social interactions. One way of thinking about this model is to take a concrete example. As you saw in Chapter 6, in 1950s' Britain, many major housing projects were undertaken. These included the construction of thirteen 'New Towns' designated in the 1940s, one of which was Harlow in Essex. Like other new towns, Harlow continues to develop but the discussion here builds on a study by Judy Attfield (1989) which considers the earlier years of the new town, from 1951 to 1961. Lefebvre's assertion that every society produces its own social space can be used as a starting-point for the spatial analysis of social life.

Spatial practice

In the years following the Second World War a new political and economic settlement was being achieved in Britain and across the rest of the western world. Following the demobilization of the wartime economy, governments used the newly available economic tools of Keynesianism (state investment, as advocated by the economist, John Maynard Keynes) to intervene in the management of the capitalist economy. This saw the emergence of the welfare state in Britain within which housing policy was to occupy an important position. Post-war governments were haunted by the failure of inter-war governments to deliver the 'homes fit for heroes' promised after the First World War; furthermore, there was also a high level of housing shortage following the war-time destruction of major cities. The role of cities themselves was changing in the post-war world: the small-scale production of the inner-city workshop was being supplanted by the mass production of large factories built on the outskirts of towns and cities alongside the newly emergent road network. It was the development of social housing for rent in the post-war world that made possible for many young couples the separation of home from both the world of employment and the broader extended family. The creation of new towns was in part the result of a particular ordering of space linked to these economic relationships established between classes and genders in the years following the Second World War.

Representations of space

New towns were also the creations of a growing band of professionals that included architects, designers and town and country planners. A romantic longing for the supposed simplicity and community of pre-industrial life was linked to Victorian ideologies of women's domesticity. Unlike the pre-industrial village, home and work were firmly separated and women were placed in the home. To protect this vision, Harlow Development Corporation initially turned down planning applications from firms that would seek to employ large numbers of women. Alongside these ideas sat the more progressive ideas of modernist architects and designers, who believed that good functional design would not only improve the living conditions of people but also somehow improve the people themselves. In 1959, *Design*, the magazine produced by the Council of Industrial Design urged designers to:

> Focus on space, a key word, space that gives freedom. Destroy the distinction between rooms. The home is subservient to life in the home. Banish the cold formality of front parlours that attempt to impress callers – then stand unused, to collect dust … Push back the wall, bring the kitchen in, dissolve divisions that separate life into compartments … Allow freedom to change and space to move.

> (quoted in Attfield, 1989, p.219)

Representational spaces

The people who moved to Harlow took with them knowledge about space as they had habitually used it in their old homes and communities. Many found it difficult to come to grips with a town still under construction and lacking many of the recognizable landmarks of a town centre. Domestic labour, discounted by male planners, continued to be a source of pride for women, many of whom entered paid employment to buy the new 'labour-saving' tools of the housewife's trade of the home. Architects' attempts to modernize the use of space in the home were resisted as the lived meaning of the space for its inhabitants overtook the meaning of planners. Open-plan houses, advocated by architects, for instance, had disrupted the spatial organization of the home and for some time created a sense of disorientation among their inhabitants. The parlour stands as a symbol for this. In the eyes of the modernist planners the parlour (locked from Sunday to Sunday) was a cluttered dust-trap, a waste of usable space and a pointless 'status symbol' through which a wife demonstrated her husband's ability to provide for the family. For the housewife, however, the parlour represented a space that she could claim as her own – an island of peace and tidiness among the continually messy use made by the family of the rest of the house. Amid the open-plan structures, heavy furniture and drapes could be used to create smaller and more familiar spaces. Experts (modernist architects and designers) would point out where residents had in their view got it wrong:

> They fight shy of open-plan living … there is a strong tendency to shelter behind net curtains. Large windows are obscured by elaborate drapes and heavy pelmets, by dressing table mirrors and large settees … By careful arranging and draping, the open plan houses are being closed up again, light rooms are darkened and a feeling of spaciousness is reduced to cosy clutter … in achieving

cosiness they are completely at variance with the architects' achievements in giving them light and space.

(*Design*, quoted in Attfield, 1989, p.219)

ACTIVITY 4

Think about some of the places you have lived:

- When were they built?

- What social and economic conditions surrounded their construction?

- What sort of people were they built to house?

- Did you use them in the way their designers intended?

Domestic space and residential areas as we know them have been produced by large-scale social processes like industrialization, deindustrialization, urbanization and suburbanization as well as by the assumptions of planners and developers about what people want and need. When considering your own experiences, you may have thought of any country, of rural or urban areas, of an apartment converted from industrial spaces, high-rise public housing, a Victorian terrace or possibly a new housing estate. You may have thought of 'a family home', communal living arrangement or one-person household. A bedroom may have been converted to a bathroom or used as a dining-room or study. It is through everyday practices located in social space that we influence and are influenced by broader social conditions.

We have shown how Lefebvre's claim that every society produces its own social space can be used as a starting-point for a spatial analysis of social life. The new towns of the 1950s were chosen as an example here because they were brought into being through clear political and professional agendas at a time when the relationships of production and reproduction were in a state of post-war flux. All places exist for a variety of economic, political and social reasons. In the case of older settlements these are often overwritten such that traces of the past continue on into the present, even if their place within social space has been changed radically: new towns, developed on green-field sites, would seem to present a clean sheet for analysis. Yet, even a new town is already located in a global web of political and economic relationships, and the role of representation in the construction of social space shows how older ideas can remain potent forces.

4.2 Space and the production of gender

We saw in the previous section that women and men are positioned differently within social space, that space has a **gender** dimension and that gender is spatially organized. Gender is a socially produced and maintained phenomenon: differences which appear to be fixed, natural and of the very essence of women and men are the result of complex social and political conditions, of the ways in which we organize and understand the world and our own place within it.

gender

Connell (1995) considers the four-hundred-year history of the production of what he calls 'the modern gender order'. He identifies four historical trends that have been particularly important in its formation, each of which has a clear spatial dimension:

1 the growth of individualism and the ethical primacy of the heterosexual household following the Protestant Reformation;

2 the creation by European Atlantic powers of overseas empires;

3 the growth of cities as trading centres;

4 the creation of strong centralized states as a result of European territorial wars.

These dimensions link the creation of gender from the modern experience of ourselves as individuals, in intimate relationships and in the public realm, to the global order. The power relations of Empire created masculinities of conqueror and conquered, of the colonial bureaucrat and the slave trader. Centralized states created bureaucrats and administrators. They also created soldiers, who maintained the spatial order of Empire both at home and in the colonies. The development of the city as a trading-centre created new workplace identities as the businessman emerged in the counting-house, the warehouse and the exchange. The movement of peasants from country to city created the conditions for the emergence of the urban working class. The relative anonymity of the city offered the individual more autonomy than was possible in closed feudal society. At the same time, however, law, medicine and other professions closely regulated that individual.

The modern gender order has located the dominant image of men as out in the world as soldiers, politicians, bureaucrats, businessmen, workers and autonomous individuals. Where are the women in this account? The list of historical trends above identifies only one place for women, and that is within the heterosexual home. This creation of a separation between women and men and the maintenance of the boundaries between feminine and masculine are expressed spatially:

> Boundaries between the public and private, the political and social, the productive and reproductive, and justice and family were established, and justified by women's absence in the first and presence in the second.
>
> (Schirmer, 1994, p.88)

The public/private divide has been used both to explain and to justify women's subordinate position in society (Davidoff, 1998). The notions of public and private are very difficult to pin down: their meaning shifts in different theoretical approaches and the boundaries between the two in the social world are constantly contested. In political theory, the public is associated with the general good and the private with specific and individual needs. The state – in the sphere of politics – is the realm of the public but when people come together on the basis of self-interest, for example in market relationships, we find the realm of the private. This distinction was initially drawn to describe the experiences of men and presupposes a prior division between the realm of the domestic and the realm of public, civil and economic life.

It is this second distinction that feminists usually mean by the public/private divide, where the private is defined as the realm of the domestic, reproduction and family and the public as all broader aspects of social life including employment, political activity and the membership of groups within civil society.

As Don Slater notes: 'Public and private are seen as different realms of experience and value, spatially and temporally separated and epitomized by different sorts of people and roles' (Slater 1998, p.144).

Women and children were represented as physically and emotionally weak, in the grip of natural impulses, as less than whole individuals and located within the private realm, spatially segregated into the home. For men, home became the 'haven in the heartless world', particularly valorised by those at the far reaches of the Empire as a place to defend and to return to. Men could act in the world as apparently disinterested social agents precisely because the responsibility for meeting their particular needs devolved to women in the domestic realm.

These views today may sound like distant voices from a Victorian past. Yet as the basis of the modern gender order, their traces can be found in debates about the appropriate public role of women and in the social institutions and spatial organization of everyday life:

> [D]espite their instability and mutability, public and private are concepts which also have had powerful material and experiential consequences in terms of formal institutions, organizational forms, financial systems, familial and kinship patterns, as well as language. In short they have become part of the way our whole social and psychic worlds are ordered, but an order that is constantly shifting, being made and remade.
>
> (Davidoff, 1998, p.165)

The extent to which these boundaries are, and have always been, contested cannot be stressed too strongly. Women were active throughout the nineteenth century in campaigns outside of the home: from the abolition of the slave trade, temperance leagues, social-purity campaigns, to the suffrage campaign itself.

"HER MOTHER'S VOICE."

Figure 7.3 'Her Mother's Voice', Harold Bird, Anti-Suffrage Review, January 1912. Anti-suffrage literature drew on a repertoire of images of home-life destroyed by the mother's unwomanly participation in politics outside of the home.

Figure 7.4 *'Mrs How-Martyn Makes Jam': postcard in a series of 'Suffragettes at Home' published in* The Vote *and independently by the Women's Freedom League. Some pro-suffrage material sought to show that suffragettes were 'proper women' by repositioning them in the home.*

In pursuit of a place in public life women transgressed the spatial organization which had located them in the private and the home. This was resisted by the anti-suffrage forces through the re-assertion of those other binaries that shape the gender order. As a result, in anti-suffrage propaganda we find the linked ideas that women's participation in political life would necessarily lead to the destruction of home and family life; that women who were active in public space were 'unwomanly' and hysterical, ugly or lesbian (Tickner, 1987): see Figures 7.3 and 7.4.

Politically active women have challenged the boundary between public and private in many ways. Like the suffragettes, organized groups of women have periodically occupied public space as a form of political protest. In doing so, not only are they transgressing the spatial organization of social life which would place women in the domestic realm, they are doubly transgressing by introducing 'private' issues into the public arena and hence denying the validity of the public/private dichotomy. The United Kingdom in the 1980s saw a long-running campaign by groups of women against the deployment of US cruise missiles at Greenham Common. One protest strategy was the placing of baby clothes and children's toys around the perimeter fence of the base – a very visible challenge to the boundaries of the public and private: see Figure 7.5.

A second feminist challenge to the separation of the public and private was to demonstrate that the public is constituted only because of the private and is thus contingent upon it. One feminist campaign demanded 'wages for housework' to demonstrate that what went on unpaid in the home was not only physical labour but also economically important. A more academic dimension to these debates came from Marxist feminist economists (Rowbotham, 1973) who sought to incorporate the value of the domestic labour carried out by women into the Marxist understanding of the relationship between the (male) worker and the employer. Feminists were criticized by some black and working-class

Figure 7.5 *Greenham Common Peace Protest, 1984: the boundaries of the public and private graphically challenged.*

women for using a white and middle-class model of domestic and family life in these debates. Far from being wholly oppressive, the 'privacy' of the home could provide a haven for black women in racist societies. Equally, the separation of the domestic from the productive economy was a middle-class ideal that was rarely realized within the working classes where the private sphere of the home was often used as a source of income, and where production as well as reproduction occurred (low-paid homeworking). Working-class women had also always had direct as well as mediated relationships with the world of paid employment. Whilst middle-class women struggled for the right to participate in employment, for working-class women participation was not the issue, the terms and conditions of that participation were.

In a comparison of four areas in late Victorian England, Doreen Massey (1994) found different working-class masculinities and femininities emerging within the broader development of capitalism. The Durham coalfield, for example, was characterized by a rigid sexual division of labour with a muscular masculinity and housebound femininity. Cooking, washing and caring for husbands and sons working in coal-mines was heavy work, but conducted within the home and outside of wage labour; it therfore did not challenge the notion of women's labour as reproductive and left individual women economically dependent. In Hackney, on the other hand, it was imperative for women to find paid employment as male wages were low; there was also opportunity as the city location generated a market for clothing. Work took the form of sweated labour within the home. Although this placed women within the economic relationships of production, it contained them within domestic space and thereby posed no threat to the existing gender order. In the Fens of East Anglia, women found seasonal employment in agriculture, and worked alongside men in labouring gangs. This work did challenge the ideal of feminine weakness and also located women in paid employment in public. The social conditions of the Fens, nevertheless, ensured that the work was conducted under the watchful eye of the whole rural community. The situation was very different in the Lancashire cotton towns (the first area of the country to industrialize). Here, women found waged employment, economic independence and participated in political organization. All four groups of women were engaged in heavy physical work, three of them received wages for their efforts, but it was only the 'factory girls' around whom public concern was raised. The boundary being challenged was both social and spatial as these women experienced freedom in the public sphere outside of the control of men.

4.3 Space and the production of sexuality

The sociological study of gender has led to the topic of sexuality. You read how responses to suffragettes as 'not proper women' illustrated a perceived mutually constitutive relationship between notions of gender-appropriate behaviour and sexuality. Similarly, many of the concerns voiced about 'factory girls' revolved around fears of their supposed heterosexual promiscuity. Dominant notions of both femininity and masculinity encode an assumed heterosexuality and, increasingly, sociologists have come to view sexuality not as a property of the individual but as a series of institutionalized relationships; and sexual identity not as the expression of the truth of the inner self but sustained through its **sexualities** habitual and repetitive performance. The performativity of **sexuality** is, it could be argued, like other aspects of the everyday produced by habit and repetition. But how is it constituted spatially?

The organization of space informs the organization of sexualities: Peter Redman showed in Chapter 2 how the romance narratives of young men are about heterosexual identities and a heterosexual use of space. In the heterosexual romance narrative, eyes can meet across crowded rooms, hands can be held and kisses stolen as lovers walk down the street. Imagine, however, these events if the lovers are of the *same* sex. The unwritten rules of everyday life concerning the public expression of affection and sexual attraction are different for heterosexual and homosexual couples. Public space both assumes and provides opportunities for the performance of heterosexuality. You saw in Chapter 4 that the workplace is a key site for boundary work. Cockburn (1991) has documented the many ways in which the workplace assumes heterosexuality – from everyday conversations about life outside work to the display of family photographs on workers' desks. Adkins' (1995) study of workers in leisure industries showed the extent to which being a barmaid involves the performance of a sexualized and flirtatious heterosexuality. It could be argued that private space, too, assumes a normative heterosexuality in its implicit notion of the family home.

The use of spatial strategies in the management of sexual identities is widely experienced among gay men, lesbians and other sexual minority groups. The social assumption of heterosexuality makes the management of identity across time and space a daily achievement:

> To avoid a rupture of their 'identity' many lesbians use time–space strategies to segregate their audiences. These include establishing geographical boundaries between past and present identities, separating different activity spheres and hence identities in space, expressing a lesbian identity only in formal 'gay

spaces', confining their 'gay' socializing to homes or informal 'gay spaces', expressing their lesbian identity only in public places at specific times, and altering the layout and decoration of private spaces to conceal clues about their sexual identity from specific people.

(Bell and Valentine, 1995, p.147)

It can be asserted, then, that everyday space is heterosexual space. Within gay and lesbian movements in the West, the claiming and creation of specifically 'gay' and/or 'lesbian' space has been an important feature in the creation of modern gay and lesbian identities. Most major cities contain areas of 'gay space', created through and for the performance of gay identities. These are usually the institutions of the commercial 'gay scene' – pubs, clubs and bars, and sometimes gyms, bookshops and advice centres. The relationship between 'gay' (male) space and lesbian space is a far from straightforward one and the two can be found separately and together. These 'gay spaces' have been described as 'colossal closets' (Hindle, 1994) in that they enable a public expression of a gay identity but within strict spatial constraints. Equally, recent years have seen erosion of the boundaries of gay space: in areas such as Manchester's 'gay village' and the 'gay capital of Europe' (which Amsterdam has been marketed as), heterosexual tourism makes the venues mixed and the space, as a consequence, a performative parody of gay space.

READING 7.2

Please now turn to Reading 7.2, 'Wherever I lay my girlfriend, that's my home' by Lynda Johnston and Gill Valentine This extract will draw your attention to the ways in which spatiality and sexual identity are linked:

■ When you are next in a public place make a point of noting the everyday interactions around you which reproduce space as heterosexual.

■ Consider your own home: in what ways does it enable some sexualities and constrain others?

SUMMARY OF SECTION 4

1 Everyday life takes place within socially produced space.

2 Social space is constituted through the relationships between production and reproduction; representation and everyday practices.

3 The modern gender order developed from a set of global spatial relationships between imperial states and colonies, urban centres and the countryside, the private and the public realm.

4 Spatial boundaries are not fixed: they must be maintained through repetition and are challenged constantly.

5 Sexualities, like gender identities, are spatially reproduced and contested.

5 Relations to the everyday and the politics of everyday life

5.1 Sociological views on the everyday

In this section we want to look in more detail at some of the contributions to the study of everyday life that have come from recent sociological approaches, and from feminism and cultural studies. We shall then consider their implications for the politics of everyday life. First, however, it might be useful to look again at our starting-point – Lefebvre's concern about the conservative characteristics of the everyday – and see whether our discussion of studies of time and space has already begun to raise questions about that characterization.

ACTIVITY 5

Look back on what you have learned in sections 3 and 4, and in earlier chapters, such as those on the home (Chapter 1) and community (Chapter 6). How do you think these discussions of time and space in the everyday life situations of homes and communities might alter the kind of view presented by Lefebvre in the following passage?

> Common denominator of activities, locus and milieu of human functions, the everyday can also be analysed as the uniform aspect of the major sectors of social life: work, family, private life, leisure. These sectors, though distinct as forms, are imposed upon in their practice by a structure allowing us to discover what they share: organized passivity. This means, in leisure activities, the passivity of the spectator faced with images and landscapes; in the workplace, it means passivity when faced with decisions in which the worker takes no part; in private life, it means the opposition of consumption, since the available choices are directed and the needs of the consumer created by advertising and market studies. This generalized passivity is moreover distributed unequally. It weighs more heavily on women, who are sentenced to everyday life, on the working class, on employees who are not technocrats, on youth, in short on the majority of people – yet never in the same way, at the same time, never all at once.
>
> (Lefebvre, 1987, p.10)

Lefebvre's piece seems to stress passivity as a uniform aspect of the everyday milieu. This is held to be particularly the fate of women, workers and youth. Consumers are also portrayed as passive: subjected to the imposition of restricted choices and wants that are created by advertising. In the concluding sentence, nevertheless, Lefebvre seems to row back a little from this assertion of uniform passivity: it never occurs 'in the same way, at the same time, never all at once'. Elsewhere, he mentions the potential within the everyday for change. Therefore, what subsequent approaches to studying everyday life might ask is: how, when and why is there scope for variation and less passivity in what might be called the 'politics of everyday'? We have already seen, in the discussion of studies of time, that post-industrial societies are experiencing great changes and variations in patterns of time-use due to increasing female labour-market participation, which has a knock-on effect on other everyday life routines. Changes in gender relations and sexualities are also sources of variation and contestation with regard to spatial relations, perceptions and boundaries. Studies of consumption, including television-viewing and other activities, raise further questions about the variable degree of passivity and imposition involved. (Although, on the question of the effects of market research and branding in integrating consumption and production, you should refer back to Celia Lury's discussion in Chapter 4.)

In contrast to early accounts of the everyday, whether of a Marxist such as Lefebvre, or sociologists of community, it is clear that the recent revival of interest in the everyday has produced a more complex and dynamic view of the connections between the micro- and macro-social levels. This more recent work has 'done some good, focusing attention on the micro-politics of conformity and resistance, re-asserting the connectedness of the micro- and macro-social, and problematizing the production and management of experience' (Crook, 1998, p.539).

This interconnectedness is also discussed by sociologist Anthony Giddens (1992), who looks at the interplay between expert systems of knowledge and the reflexive consciousness of 'ordinary' people in their everyday lives. He noted that expert knowledge is even part of intimacy in modernity, as shown by the contents of magazines and television programmes that provide technical information about 'relationships'. However, he does not agree with **Jürgen Habermas** and Lefebvre in seeing this as a one-way process in which the private 'life-world' is colonized by abstract systems emanating from powerful public institutions. Giddens viewed it as more of a two-way process and placed his emphasis on the active choices made by individuals: **Habermas, Jürgen**

> The self today is for everyone a reflexive project – a more or less continuous interrogation of past, present and future. It is a project carried on amid a profusion of reflexive resources: therapy and self-help manuals of all kinds, television programmes and magazine articles.
>
> (Giddens, 1992, p.30)

Although no-one can become an expert in many specialized systems of knowledge, most people pick up bits and pieces of expert knowledge as they interact with these systems, and routinely apply them in their day-to-day activities. In other words, they re-appropriate what they need from these expert knowledges and adapt them to their needs. Giddens' view is politically more optimistic than that of Habermas or of Lefebvre. Building on Goffman, he emphasizes that all social interaction involves 'reflexivity' – monitoring one's behaviour in relation to that of others. Mostly, in everyday life, we depend on a 'practical consciousness' of 'knowing how to go on', made up of a wealth of taken-for-granted mutual knowledge about the routine requirements of the diverse contexts of activity. If pressed, we may be able to give reasons and offer an account of how our actions make sense; we may even draw on smatterings of expert knowledge. Mostly, our accounts, nonetheless, tend to be situationally specific rather than expressed in terms of abstract principles.

5.2 Ethnomethodological and ethnographic research

ethnomethodology   We find the influence of **ethnomethodology** in Anthony Giddens' (1990) work. This was an approach developed by Harold Garfinkel at the University of California in the late 1960s. The term means the 'methods' that people use on a daily basis to accomplish their everyday lives. Ethnomethodologists maintain that sociology needs to study the ways in which social order is an ongoing practical accomplishment. Ethnomethodology is the study of:

> ... the body of common-sense knowledge and the range of procedures and considerations by means of which the ordinary members of society make sense of, and find their way about in, and act on the circumstances in which they find themselves.
>
> (Heritage, 1984, p.4)

As social actors, we are able to give accounts of our actions. These may be accepted or rejected by others. It is these 'accounting practices', especially in the form of conversations, that ethnomethodologists are keen to study. The significance of the ethnomethodologists' approach lies in their methods of research and in their success in revealing how everyday social reality is constructed in various settings, ranging from the home to major institutions. Whereas macro-sociological studies might have looked at the effects of political and industrial revolutions on social order, ethnomethodologists focus on disturbances at the micro-social level. As you saw in Chapter 3, some early ethnomethodological research took the form of 'breaching experiments', in which normal everyday practices were violated in order to shed light on the methods by which people construct social reality. One of the most famous was when Garfinkel asked his students to spend periods in their homes acting as if they were boarders:

> They were instructed to conduct themselves in a circumspect and polite fashion. They were to avoid getting personal, to use formal address, to speak only when spoken to.
>
> (Garfinkel, 1967, p.47)

They then returned to relate the reactions of other family members. 'Reports were filled with accounts of astonishment, bewilderment, shock, anxiety, embarrassment, and anger, and with charges by various members that the student was mean, inconsiderate, selfish, nasty, or impolite' (*ibid.*). Family members demanded that they account for their behaviour, asking such questions as:

> 'Did you get fired?'
>
> 'Are you sick?'
>
> 'Are you out of your mind or are you just stupid?'
>
> (Garfinkel, 1967, p.47)

ethnography   Garfinkel's conclusion was that members of a society use their 'common-sense' knowledge of appropriate rules of behaviour to avoid acting inappropriately. Few sociologists today would be prepared to conduct breaching experiments that deliberately disrupted a home situation. Studies of everyday life in the home adopt a more naturalistic approach more akin to **ethnography** than ethnomethodology. As we have seen, these provide fascinating information about the ways in which time and space are organized in domestic settings, and of how people account for those practices. Elizabeth B. Silva's ethnographic research, which we discussed in section 3, provides a good example of the complex and varied picture of everyday life routines that emerges when a sociologist allows people to talk at length about a 'normal' weekday. Some feminists (see Felski, 1999–2000; Young, 1997) had criticized male sociologists such as Lefebvre, who generalized about women and their attachment to everyday routines. He considered this to be a hindrance to modern political progress. To feminists, this view takes no account of the actual work done by women in the home. According to Dorothy Smith, the everyday activities of women may look as though they consist simply of taken-for-granted routines, but they are also sophisticated and problem-solving exercises, such as 'holding in place the simultaneous and divergent schedules and activities of a family' (Smith, 1987, p.66). Similarly, feminists have been critical of the patronizing views of post-war urban planners who took it upon themselves to design new towns in ways that assumed women should remain at home and not go out to work (as we discussed in section 4).

5.3 Cultural studies and the everyday

The contribution of feminism to the recent study of everyday life has also been evident in research in the field of cultural studies. In the post-Second World War era, cultural studies had a distinctly masculine standpoint: in France, as we have noted, Lefebvre was generalizing about everyday life in ways that suggested women's mental horizons were so hemmed in by the pressures of domestic life as to make them incapable of critical thought. In Britain, as the book introduction outlined, the key figures in the development of cultural studies were **Richard Hoggart, Raymond Williams** and E.P. Thompson. Although they provided a valuable stimulus for empirical studies of popular culture, their works betrayed a distinct fondness for traditional working-class male forms of social solidarity, with less awareness of the negative consequences of these for women. Richard Hoggart, in his largely autobiographical book, *The Uses of Literacy* (1957), wrote from the standpoint of a working-class grammar-school boy – occupying an 'in-between space', neither still working-class nor yet middle-class. Here, he describes doing his homework in a space cleared on the kitchen table among piles of ironing and cups of tea, in the presence of 'uncomprehending' women:

**Hoggart, Richard
Williams, Raymond**

> With one ear he hears the women discussing their worries and ailments and hopes, and he tells them at intervals about his school and the work and what the master said. He usually receives boundless uncomprehending sympathy; he knows they do not understand, but still he tells them; he would like to link the two environments.
>
> (Hoggart, 1957, p.296)

Both Hoggart and Williams saw themselves as occupying a standpoint on the margins, outside the social and cultural mainstream, although they both went on to occupy prestigious positions. In so far as their cultural studies had a concern with issues of power, it was with the possibilities for resisting the deleterious effects of mass media culture. This interest in the power of resistance to cultural domination was to become a central concern of the Birmingham Centre for

Hall, Stuart
subculture
youth culture

Contemporary Cultural Studies (CCCS) – founded by Hoggart in 1964 and subsequently directed by **Stuart Hall** – as is evident in Hall and Jefferson's study of **subcultures** and **youth cultures**, *Resistance through Rituals: Youth Subcultures in Post-War Britain* (Hall and Jefferson, 1976). Although the standpoint of the researchers into youth subcultures was much more sympathetic towards the new forms of popular culture and how youth used them to create distinctive styles, it was still mainly masculine in its focus. This partial perspective was noted by a number of women researchers (Women's Studies Group, 1978) and subsequently much more attention was given to women's subcultures, the cultural construction of femininities, and women's cultural practices.

moral panics

Another missing standpoint in early cultural studies was that of racial or ethnic minorities. It was not that 'race' issues had been completely neglected. One of the most important studies produced by CCCS in the 1970s was *Policing the Crisis* (Hall *et al.*, 1978), which analysed how a '**moral panic**' arose as a result of sensationalist press reports of an alleged increase in the street crime of mugging. However, this was studied from the standpoint of revealing how ideology functioned to divert attention from a crisis of capitalism and the state. A different focus began to emerge in the 1980s. In *The Empire Strikes Back* (CCCS, 1982. p.8), Paul Gilroy and colleagues stated that their study was 'conceived as a corrective to the narrowness of the English left' whose studies had neglected the role of blacks and black struggles. In Gilroy's later works, such as *There Ain't No Black in the Union Jack* (1987), issues of 'race' and ethnicity are placed at centre-stage.

This problem of reconciling or negotiating the various cultural forms and representations that constitute everyday life is one that presents itself particularly acutely to members of minority ethnic groups in modern societies. Ethnographic studies of such groups often focus on the ways in which different cultural elements are combined in everyday lives, creating a hybrid 'diasporic' culture – one which neither corresponds to that of a distant country of origin nor to that of the dominant culture in the society of domicile. Michel de Certeau's accounts of North Africans living in low-income housing developments in France show that they manage to insinuate their own ways of living into the system imposed on them by a tactical use of the constraining order and of elements drawn from North African culture (de Certeau, 1984, p.30). Recent ethnographies have studied the everyday practices by which members of minority ethnic groups negotiate selectively between various cultural resources ranging from traditional religious practices to television, videos and the internet (Cottle, 2000). If all of modern life bears witness to the compression of time and space, minority ethnic groups experience its effects more than others. Their everyday is closely bound into transnational networks or diasporas. The efforts of minority ethnic groups to make coherent sense of the many and varied cultural representations and practices that constitute their everyday lives provide a graphic illustration of the fact that culture always involves power, because it is both a constraint and a resource.

Bourdieu, Pierre

Lefebvre's writings on everyday life were constantly seeking to understand this relationship of culture and power – the notion that everyday life culture is both a constraint and a resource. His successors have continued this quest for understanding: **Pierre Bourdieu** (1984), for instance, has been concerned with inequalities in the distribution of 'cultural capital' (cultural resources) between classes, as revealed by indicators such as rates of museum-visiting for different classes. De Certeau (1984) focuses on the tactics and ruses that ordinary people employ in their cultural practices, such as viewing television. Resistance was also a major theme in the studies carried out by Stuart Hall and his colleagues at Birmingham CCCS. Subsequently, studies have added a greater appreciation of the dual nature of everyday cultures as not only constraining but also enabling. This has been particularly evident in studies carried out from the standpoint of women (Smith, 1987) and minority ethnic groups (Cottle, 2000). In part, these are a reaction against what critics have seen as a rather patriarchal attitude in earlier writings, where these groups were viewed as 'victims' or passive objects to be worked on by culture, rather than as creative and knowledgeable users of cultural resources.

SUMMARY OF SECTION 5

1   We began by examining Lefebvre's comments about passivity in the everyday in the light of some sociological approaches that have explored the micro-social and macro-social aspects of everyday life.

2   We considered some of the contributions coming from cultural studies, particularly concerning culture and power.

3   Giddens talks about the penetration of the micro-social sphere of the home by expert systems of knowledge. But he adopts a more sanguine view than Habermas, who is concerned about the colonization of the life-world by the abstract systems of public institutions.

4   We showed how ethnomethodologists represent an interesting example of attempts in US sociology to expose the everyday practices by which people construct social reality and account for it. The ethomethodological approach is particularly interesting because it set out to reveal people's own practices for making 'normal' sense of their activities, as well as using unusual research methods such as 'breaching experiments'.

5   Ethnographic studies of home life by sociologists and feminists were shown to have built up a complex picture of everyday routines, especially with regard to the gendered division of labour and leisure activities.

6   Cultural studies have evolved from a concern with resistance to mass culture and its ideology to approaches which attribute more scope to the creative power of active consumers of cultural products such as television, whilst locating these in the constraining context of other elements of everyday life.

7   Studies of ethnic minorities' cultural practices can reveal problems that face all of us in making coherent sense of the cultural resources and representations that constrain and empower us in the construction of modern everyday life.

6 Conclusion

The emphasis of this book on the everyday in contemporary sociology, feminism, and cultural studies may seem like a step back from the more momentous concerns of the social sciences of earlier periods – such as the concern with the transition to modernity, the class divisions produced by capitalism, gender divisions, or the operation of major social institutions. However, as we found when returning to the perceptions of theorists of the everyday, this basic layer of social life is the very stuff of which these large-scale social phenomena are made. Studying the everyday provides a way to link the micro-sociological analysis of small-scale social interaction with the broader processes of social reproduction and social change.

The analysis of the social world takes place from within that world. It is not surprising, then, that some of the theorists we have considered reproduce within their work widely held social assumptions about gender and ethnicity. Equally, we have looked at work generated from within feminism and cultural studies that challenges these assumptions in the academic as well as the broader social realm. Sociology itself is one of the expert systems which for Giddens characterize the modern world.

Everyday life is like the air we breathe or the ground on which we build: it is the foundation of social life. In learning to make strange the taken-for-granted realities within which we live our lives, we take a major step towards adopting a sociological imagination and towards the analysis of the traditional sociological concerns of social order and social change.

References

Adam, B. (1995) *Timewatch: The Social Analysis of Time*, Cambridge, Polity Press.

Adkins, L. (1995) *Gendered Work: Sexuality, Family and the Labour Market,* Buckingham, Open University Press.

Attfield, J. (1989) 'Inside Pram Town: a case study of Harlow house interiors, 1951–61' in Attfield, J. and Kirkham, P. (eds) *A View From the Interior: Women and Design,* London, The Women's Press.

Bell, D. and Valentine, G. (1995) 'The sexed self – strategies of performance and sites of resistance' in Pile, S. and Thrift, N. (eds) *Mapping the Subject: Geographies of Cultural Transformation,* London, Routledge.

Bourdieu, P. (1984) *Distinction: A Social Critique of the Judgement of Taste*, London, Routledge and Kegan Paul.

Centre for Contemporary Cultural Studies (CCCS) (1982) *The Empire Strikes Back*, London, Hutchinson.

Certeau, M. de (1984) *The Practice of Everyday Life* (trans. S.F. Rendall), Berkeley, CA, University of California Press.

Connell, R.W. (1995) *Masculinities*, Cambridge, Polity Press.

Cockburn, C. (1991) *In the Way of Women,* London, Macmillan.

Cottle, S. (ed.) (2000) *Ethnic Minorities and the Media: Changing Cultural Boundaries,* Buckingham, Open University Press.

Crook, S. (1998) 'Minotaurs and other monsters: "Everyday Life" in recent social theory', *Sociology*, vol.32, no.3, pp.523–40.

Davidoff, L. (1998) 'Regarding some "Old Husbands' Tales": public and private in feminist history' in Landes, J.B. (ed.) *Feminism, the Public and the Private*, Oxford, Oxford University Press.

Equal Opportunities Commission (1998) *Social Focus on Women and Men*, ONS, London, The Stationery Office.

Felski, R. (1999–2000) 'The invention of everyday life', *New Formations*, no.39, pp.15–31.

Garfinkel, H. (1967) *Studies in Ethnomethodology*, Englewood Cliffs, NJ, Prentice-Hall.

Gershuny, J. (2000) *Changing Times: Work and Leisure in Postindustrial Society*, Oxford, Oxford University Press.

Giddens, A. (1990) *The Consequences of Modernity*, Cambridge, Polity Press.

Giddens, A. (1992) *The Transformation of Intimacy: Sexuality, Love and Eroticism in Modern Societies*, Cambridge, Polity Press.

Gilroy, P. (1987) *There Ain't No Black in the Union Jack*, London, Hutchinson.

Glucksmann, M. (1990) *Women Assemble: Women Workers and the New Industries in Inter-War Britain,* London, Routledge.

Glucksmann, M. (2000) *Cottons and Casuals: The Gendered Organization of Labour in Time and Space,* Durham, The Sociology Press.

Goffman, E. (1959) *The Presentation of Self in Everyday Life*, Garden City, NY, Doubleday Anchor

Griffiths, J. (1999) *Pip Pip: A Sideways Look at Time*, London, Flamingo.

Habermas, J. (1987) *The Theory of Communicative Action*, Cambridge, MA, MIT Press.

Hall, S., Critcher, C., Jefferson, T., Clarke, J. and Roberts, B. (1978) *Policing the Crisis,* London, Macmillan.

Hall, S. and Jefferson, T. (eds) (1976) *Resistance Through Rituals*, London, Hutchinson.

Heritage, J. (1984) *Garfinkel and Ethnomethodology*, Cambridge, Polity Press.

Hindle, P. (1994) 'Gay communities and gay space in the city' in Whittle, S. (ed.) *The Margins of the City: Gay Men's Urban Lives,* Aldershot, Arena.

Hoggart, R. (1957) *The Uses of Literacy*, London, Chatto & Windus.

Johnston, L. and Valentine, G. (1995) 'Wherever I lay my girlfriend, that's my home: the performance and surveillance of lesbian identities in domestic environments' in Bell, D. and Valentine, G. (eds) *Mapping Desire: Geographies of Sexualities*, London, Routledge.

Lefebvre, H. (1984) *Everyday Life in the Modern World*, London, Allen Lane, The Penguin Press/New York, Transaction Press. First published in France in 1968.

Lefebvre, H. (1987) 'The everyday and everydayness', *Yale French Studies*, Special Issue, pp.7–11.

Lefebvre, H. (1991a) *The Critique of Everyday Life*, Volume 1, London, Verso. First publsihed in France in 1947.

Lefebvre, H. (1991b) *The Production of Space* (trans. D. Nicholson-Smith), Oxford, Blackwell.

Massey, D. (1994) *Space, Place and Gender*, Cambridge, Polity Press.

Rowbotham, S. (1973) *Women's Consciousness, Man's World*, Harmondsworth, Penguin Books.

Schama, S. (1989) *Citizens*, New York, Knopf.

Schirmer, J. (1994) 'The claiming of space and the body politic within national-security states' in Boyarin, J. (ed.) *Remapping Memory: the Politics of Timespace*, Minneapolis, MN, University of Minnesota Press.

Silva, E.B. (forthcoming 2002) 'Routine matters: narratives of everyday life in families' in Crow, G. and Heath, S. (eds) *Times in the Making*, Basingstoke, Macmillan/Palgrave.

Slater, D. (1998) 'Public/Private' in Jenks, C. (ed.) *Core Sociological Dichotomies*, London, Sage.

Smith, D. (1987) *The Everyday World as Problematic*, Milton Keynes, Open University Press.

Thompson, E.P. (1967) 'Time, work-discipline and industrial capitalism', *Past and Present*, vol.38, pp.56–97.

Tickner, L. (1987) *The Spectacle of Women: Imagery of the Suffrage Campaign 1907–14*, London, Chatto & Windus.

Women's Studies Group (1978) *Women Take Issue*, London, Hutchinson.

Young, I.W. (1997) 'House and home: feminist variations on a theme' in *Intersecting Voices: Dilemmas of Gender, Political Philosophy and Policy*, Princeton, NJ, Princeton University Press.

Young, M. and Wilmott, P. (1957) *Family and Kinship in East London*, London, Routledge and Kegan Paul.

Readings

7.1 Elizabeth B. Silva, 'Gender and routines in narratives of everyday life in families' (2002)

Feminists have challenged the idea of linear time arguing that it is incompatible with women's everyday temporal experiences (Davies, 1990). These challenges have brought about an awareness of the gendered notion of time. However, Odih (1999) argues that epistemological dualistic frameworks are often employed in analyses of gendered time, creating a belief that it is possible to concretely oppose male and female times. The alleged boundary between masculine and feminine needs to be addressed. The definition of women's time as circular, repetitive and never-ending draws attention to the embodied aspects of daily life. Male time is defined as linear, purposeful and achieving. Yet, when one acknowledges that gender identities are potentially multiple, unstable and contingent, the dualist opposition between a female time and a male time is dissolved (Odih, 1999). However, the argument that women and men use time differently because of their distinct life situations is powerful and has real grounding. Gender is significant to variations of time insofar as women's subordinate economic and social positions result from practices of power that constrain women's abilities to make decisions about their time and that of others. However, the opposition of largely undifferentiated categories of powerful men and powerless women needs to be qualified. As with men, female experiences are not homogeneous, despite particular forms of masculinity and femininity prevailing at different historical periods. Gendered times are constructed in relations between women and men and they also change along the lifecourse. The construction of gendered routines is related to the gendered location.

In my study, how far do the everyday routines of women and men who live with school-age children differ? Is it possible to talk of a gendered routine pattern? How is this pattern constituted?

The 37 personal narratives of routine show that time spent at home was very significant for most people. Only sixteen individuals spent equal or longer time away from home than in the home. They were thirteen men and three women. Thus, more women spent longer hours in the home than men. This echoes a relatively traditional gender pattern, but variations within this trend were also interesting and not straightforwardly gendered. For instance, four men did not go out to work and three women had their everyday routines mostly away from home. The 37 accounts include nine people who were at home all day long: five women and four men. This nearly equal gender split of the 'home-bound' group, however, contained different gendered home-life experiences. All of these men worked from home, while the women did not – with one exception. The routines of women who stayed at home all day were concentrated on childcare, personal time and housework. The woman who worked from home had a routine pattern similar to the men who also worked from home. All those five people working from home had their routines more fragmented than either their male counterparts who worked out of the home, or the women who were full-time home-based.

These patterns show a combination of gender and routine not simply split along male and female lines but along lines of involvement with homely activities, mainly centred around the care of children. Activities for adults, male or female, were generally organized around the needs of children and normally only one adult was involved. Where the man cared for children he also did housework (but rarely the laundry), though no woman was present. Whenever a woman was present it was she who did the care of children, although a man may have helped, particularly in the evening routines (with homework, tea, play and bedtime rituals).

Mothering and caring for dependants are activities where the self gets the most subordinated to the needs of others. Women's ascribed domestic roles and subordinate position has meant that they generally have more experience of relational time. In the home, time is rarely demarcated between work, leisure and personal (Adam, 1995; Sullivan, 1997). When men do 'mothering' their time becomes more 'relational' and the home tends to be gendered differently.

In my study there was plurality and difference between households. Looking at each individual and their household patterns, there was very little sense of a normative gendered pattern setting everyday routines overall. This is not to say that gender was unimportant. On the contrary, it is significant that only four men appeared to break out of the traditional mode of male routine in the home, and that four women remained in the traditional mode of female routine. It is, however, more important that sixteen women did not operate within traditional female routine patterns of full-time housewifery, while thirteen men did still model their everyday life according to the 'provider', 'sole-breadwinner' model of the family. Out of these men, five had no involvement with the care of children or housework in a normal weekday, and four had some involvement in the evenings only.

These patterns were established in relation to concrete situations of the labour market and in interaction between partners. Although this interactive process does not indicate consensus about the outcomes, there was little sense of complaint or resentment about these routine patterns in the narrative accounts. However, current conflicts in the home between women and men are often conflicts over time (Silva, 1999). Some men use professional commitments as an argument against women's demands that they take on more work in the home (Hochschild, 1997). This may be a conscious strategy they are not ashamed to confess:

ELIZABETH: '… so you are at home by eight-ish?'

GABRIEL: 'yeah, usually home for eight or if I choose to, I'll… just after seven.'

ELIZABETH: '…do you tend to see your kids before they go to bed or not?'

GABRIEL: 'It goes through periods… I tend, I tend to see them…. But – … to be quite frank, I deliberately avoid getting back… – I tend to, to not rush back.'

ELIZABETH: 'Is Tracy conscious of that?'

GABRIEL: 'I think she probably is, yeah. I certainly am.'

ELIZABETH: [Talking about Frances serving her husband Robert a meal at 9 p.m. everyday] 'Do you think you should do more?'

ROBERT: 'Eh?'

ELIZABETH: 'Do you feel you should do more?'

ROBERT: 'I don't feel guilty, put it that way!'

ELIZABETH: 'Why not?'

ROBERT: 'Don't see any reason why I should! No, I think it's just, I don't know really, I suppose it's just habit.'

Frances worked part time (job share) in a bank. Robert's work time went from midday to 8 p.m. It is notable that in Frances' narrative of everyday routine serving Robert a meal at 9 p.m. was a very matter-of-fact activity: uncontentious, taken-for-granted, very much in the same manner as Robert saw it.

Frances says:

> Robert works every day …he finishes work at half past eight and gets home about nine o'clock at night so when he comes in at night, I then make a bite to eat for him, and I have a bite with him, and then we settle down to watch television at that point.

For Tracy, who worked full time from home, Gabriel's pattern also appeared uncontroversial. She says: [The kids are in bed about 7.30 p.m.].

> When they're in bed – I usually have supper with Gabriel when he's back and – maybe about half past eight, quarter to nine, I will go and do another two or three hours' work if I need to.

Intersubjective negotiations appeared very relevant for the gendered locations of these individuals. These may have been related to more conventional patterns of gender relations, as seemed to be the case with Frances and Robert, or they may have resulted from modern reflexive choices to fit everyday life issues to life-stage circumstances, more in line with Beck-Gernsheim's (1998) argument.

Gabriel recounts:

> [W]hen they [the kids] were younger, things were quite different then because – I worked from home for two days a week, Tracy was lecturing at the college and I used the technology to move my hours around it. So I could take the kids to school and collect the kids from school … I'd work on a computer in the middle of the day and late in the evening and I'd still do a full day's work but I'd be looking after the kids as well. So – from that point of view, the technology enabled me to enable Tracy to, to, to do her teaching. I wouldn't have been able to do it any other way …

Doing housework *per se* did not figure strongly in the routine narratives of either women or men, although it was more present in the women's accounts. Childcare was a much more visible activity. Only two women did as much housework as childcare: Brenda and Rosanne. Housework occupied some daily time for Wendy, Rena, Chris, Phil, Jane, and Marc. Housework also took place mostly during childcare hours, with all those who had paid jobs, and also cared for children, doing their paid work mostly during school hours. Only two women did not have any paid work: Rosanne and Lynn, the first a convinced housewife, the second a lone mother of four children with very low labour-market skills.

The involvement of men in feeding children and themselves (for example, Phil, Ray and Marc) and the not-a-big-issue approach to feeding husbands in the evening, illustrated by the quotes from Tracy and Frances above, indicate that the effort in these activities was not to be remarked. The easiness of tasks and the ability to combine managing home and children with working for pay was achieved by, on the one hand, the availability of technological aids for everyday living, and, on the other, by established patterns of daily routine. These set routine patterns of dealing with housework, and the technical artefacts in the home, usually involved a negotiated gender division of labour (in the less traditional homes), the help of older children, and also the help of other adults. Some of the better-off households bought some form of domestic time as they paid for cleaners, babysitters and childminders. All of these were women. Some poorer and well-off families also enrolled the help of grandparents (more often grandmothers) in childcare, particularly with the school runs and after-school care.

Marc and Diane (household 16) had deeply egalitarian gender principles, which they applied to home management. Marc was an academic researcher and writer working from home. Diane was a senior civil servant who worked long hours. Marc's everyday routines involved being up by 7.30 a.m., getting his children (two girls, 9 and 11, and one boy, 15) breakfast, making his wife's sandwiches, taking the girls to school, tidying the house up, doing his own work from home (he was writing a book and working on consultancies), being home for when the children got back from school, checking homework, having chats, cooking dinner. He cooked three evening meals a week, his son two. After meals the son tidied up and the daughters rotated at various jobs: unloading the dishwasher, sorting out drawers. Marc and Diana had coffee in their private room, talked for about one hour, going then back to finish bits of their respective

work and going to bed at about 11.30pm. Wednesdays also involved Marc doing the laundry and changing bed clothes. (He was one of two men in my study who did some laundry work).

At Brenda's (household 3), very clear work rotas were set for the children. They had four children: a girl aged 11, and three boys, 13 years, 10 years and 11 months. Because of the baby, Brenda was working only three mornings a week. Her husband Colin, a self-employed builder, did nothing in the home. His routine involved getting up at 5.30/6.00 a.m. to be at work by 6.30 a.m. At work he did 'what is to be done'. By 6.30 p.m. he got back home, 'I have my tea, sit down and relax.' The only bit of housework he would involve himself with was 'sticking things in the dishwasher'. 'But no, I don't do the washing up. Brenda does that. It's her bit.' Brenda managed home with her children. Daniella, 11, said about washing-up:

> It is done in the dishwasher. The dishwasher does all apart from what doesn't fit in. On night times we have a day each: Charlie, myself, Eric, mum. We load, wash-up, wipe the worktops, empty bags in bin, the boys fight, they moan but get on.

About the laundry:

> It is mostly mum who does it. I do some to help her out, on Saturday. I get the washing and put it in the washer, then I change it over to the dryer, then put it on the basket. Mum does most of the ironing. I sometimes do some.'

Chris (household 13) worked as a 'lollipop lady', school playground supervisor, and as a hairdresser. Phil was an actor and a writer. Chris also gave the children certain jobs to do, mostly on Saturdays. 'It's a cleaning-day ritual'. Greg, 13, did dusting and vacuuming. Georgia, 11, polished and sometimes 'hoovered'. Josh, 8, and Joseph, 6, did the windows, polished the pictures, tidied up their bedrooms and made their beds.

I have remarked elsewhere (Silva, 1999) that in advertisements for household appliances in the 1930s up to the 1970s women were invited to conceal their efforts in doing housework tasks behind a carefully projected image of a cheerful and happy housewife and mother. I also noted that by the 1990s there were changes to this advertised prescription and women who did not enjoy cooking or cleaning, who were no good at it, or had no time to get involved and be cheerful about it, were also appearing in advertisements of technologies for housework. These were changes reflecting different associations between care, women and work in the house. Changes have happened not only in marketing, but also in the design and manufacturing of appliances, which have increasingly, although slowly, come to suit more flexible styles of living. Expert knowledge, or dedication of longer hours, is no longer required. Moreover, of course, there are hardly any adult women available in the home to do full-time housework. In this study only Rosanne (household 6) was a full-time dependent housewife with no paid job.

These people's lives appeared to conform to a pattern marked by their own working lives and by the school life of their children. How did leisure in the home conform to their choices of living?

Only four partners mentioned the same getting-up time. While the morning routines were quite separate for partners living together, with each one going to their own affairs, the evening saw the appearance of the television in the narratives, mostly after the children went to bed. Daytime television watching figured very little in the routine accounts of women and men. Two exceptions were Nancy, who turned the telly on first thing in the morning, when coming into the kitchen, and left it on until she went to bed; and Phil, who worked from home and timed his lunch-break by the BBC *One O'Clock News*. Children in eight households watched television before going to school. The television served adults as a kind of 'electronic nanny'. However, the television was on for most of the day in a number of homes. During the research period, televisions were found on at different times of the day in nine households. These included all those homes that used morning television as 'nannies'. Having the television on did not mean that people were watching any programmes in particular. For many, the television was on as 'background noise' (Katie), 'for company' (Nancy), 'so I don't feel alone' (Lynn), or, as in Richard's account:

> I do bits and pieces of working or I'll watch some TV but – a lot of the times I just – I end up sitting in this state where I just literally drift over in my mind, so even if I'm watching TV a lot of the time I'm not really watching TV, it's just things drifting over in my mind.

Evening television-watching fitted this mode for most people. Television was placed within a personal time of relaxation or of relating with one's partner. This was the everyday pattern for 24 of the men and women. Occasional evening viewing was mentioned by three other people. It was often a 'time of one's own'. However, six women and four men did not account for a role of the television in their everyday lives. This does not mean they did not ever watch television. Households 1, 13, 16 and 17 were generally TV-free, although only those in household 16 had made a conscious decision not to have a television in the home. Diane (household 16) said:

> 'I experimented with a TV in my bedroom. It was not healthy for the relationship. – Not having a TV makes us go out. We spend evenings together, chatting. I talk on the phone to a friend. I don't want one. We don't, as a couple.'

There were particular characteristics about these four virtually TV-free households. In household 1 Tracy, an architect, was the only woman in this study who worked from home. She looked after two sons out of school hours. Gabriel was also an architect. They both caught up with work in the evenings. In household 13 Phil, an actor and writer, worked from home and was in charge of the daytime care of his four children. Chris's various jobs ('lollypop lady', school playground supervisor, hairdresser) meant that she came in and out of the house at various times of the day and evening. In the evening they both shared the care of the children and had some time together. In household 16 Marc worked from home and looked after the two younger children out of their school hours. Diane worked long hours and she did not get directly involved in the home's daily affairs. In household 17 Rebecca sometimes worked from home and Eleanor out of the home. Evening routines changed depending on whether Rebecca's daughter was there (usually half of the week), but time was mostly spent replenishing oneself or the relationship.

In my findings leisure in the home did not have great significance and the main 'gadget for leisure', the television, appeared as a minor 'event' in the daily routine. Television was not central to the construction of everyday routines in these households. If some families tuned in to breakfast TV, after-school children's television and evening broadcasting programmes, the media was by no means a relevant apparatus to the structuring of domestic time.[1] Perhaps this is a particularity of households with school-age children.

Despite the flexible arrangements of working hours and some variation in the gender of the carer for children, the rigidity of school hours and the education system calendar appeared to structure most family arrangements. Family time constructions appeared linked to dual-time schemes of workdays and holidays. For most people real family time happened at the weekend, mainly on Sundays. Interestingly this was the time that most of the women and men in my study spontaneously referred to as 'routine'. Sundays and other holidays were perceived as extraordinary because then time was in people's power. Personal needs and set routines were then less focused, and investment in the self and in relationships were at centre stage. The Sunday routine may have involved going to mass, or going on family walks, engaging in particular forms of leisure, but more often it meant eating together. In a few cases this meant a proper Sunday dinner. Often the meal was just a time when people living together were available for each other.

Certainly, children's affairs were prominent in the narratives of everyday routines. This is an empirical fact. But the analysis of time in home life, in particular the extent of 'choice' of routine patterns, is also a subject bound by complex explorations about the boundaries of the public and the private in people's lives, and in particular in family contexts.

Feminist writings on social time have identified a co-existence of public time, biological time, internal time, and so on, without a pre-established order. Sometimes these temporal orders are in conflict, and temporal priorities are also variable in the lifecourse. Temporal orders of reference in this study varied according to gender, labour-market participation and the presence of small children. Even when women were not in paid employment, paid work gave a general meaning to time, because of its overall social dominance. This happens even when time is 'contaminated' by emotions and affections. Thus, distinction of what is public and private is ambiguous, and the boundaries between them are fluid and changeable. Clearly, the choices of individuals and households showed fragmented and diverse patterns of everyday routines. The key setter of routine patterns for the women and men in my study was school hours. Secondly, it was paid-work hours, but these also varied. In the making-up of the household routine the negotiations of gender locations were crucial. The care of children was central, but the gender of the carer (still mostly female), and the ways caring activities were organized, varied within each household's particular arrangements.

Note

1 My findings differ from those by Silverstone (1993, p.293), who argued that broadcasting '[p]rogramme schedules provide a framework for the day's routines reinforcing, if not creating, a pattern of daily life already imposed around the demands of work'. I discuss the implications of these findings regarding theoretical approaches to studying family home life in Silva (2000).

References

Adam, B. (1995) *Timewatch: The Social Analysis of Time*, Cambridge, Polity Press.

Beck-Gernsheim, E. (1998) 'On the way to a post-familial family: from a community of need to elective affinities', *Theory, Culture and Society*, vol.15, nos 3–4, pp.53–70.

Davies, K. (1990) *Women and Time: The Weaving of the Strands of Everyday Life*, Aldershot, Avebury.

Hochschild, A.R. (1997) *The Time Bind*, New York, Metropolitan Books.

Odih, P. (1999) 'Gendered time in the age of deconstruction', *Time and Society*, vol.8, no.1, pp.9–38.

Silva, E.B. (1999) 'Transforming housewifery: dispositions, practices and technologies' in Silva, E.B. and Smart, C. (eds) *The 'New' Family?*, London, Sage, pp.46–65.

Silva, E.B. (2000) 'The material and the moral in everyday life', paper presented at the Inaugural Symposium of the National Everyday Cultures Programme, Milton Keynes, The Open University, May.

Silverstone, R. (1993) 'Time, information and communication technologies and the household', *Time and Society*, vol.2, pp.283–311.

Sullivan, O. (1997) 'Time waits for no (wo)man: an investigation of the gendered experience of domestic time', *Sociology*, vol.31, no.2, pp.221–39.

Source: Silva, forthcoming 2002

Lynda Johnston and Gill Valentine, 'Wherever I lay my girlfriend, that's my home' (1995)

The performance and surveillance of lesbian identities in domestic environments

Home is a word that positively drips with associations – according to various academic literatures it's a private, secure location, a sanctuary, a locus of identity and a place where inhabitants can escape the disciplinary practices that regulate our bodies in everyday life ... Above all the home is often presented as being synonymous with the heterosexual 'family' and the ideal of family life ... But not all homes are exclusively occupied by heterosexuals. 'Home' can take on very different and contradictory meanings for sexual dissidents who share a house with heterosexual family members ...

Being in a private space is at the heart of what it means to be 'at home' ... [The] ability 'to relax' and 'to be yourself' away from the gaze of others, was also identified as one of the most important meanings of home by participants in Peter Saunders' (1989) research ... he states: 'The home is where people are offstage, free from surveillance, in control of their immediate environment. It is their castle. It is where they feel they belong' (Saunders, 1989, p.184).

But although the home may be a more or less private place for 'the family' it doesn't necessarily guarantee freedom for individuals from the watchful gaze of other household members: 'the public world does not begin and end at the front door' (Allan and Crow, 1989, p.5). Rather, the ideology of 'the family' actually emphasizes a form of togetherness, intimacy and interest in each others' business that can actually deny this privacy. Linda McDowell (1983) is one of many authors to have argued that women have little access to private space within the family home. Likewise, children's space (usually a bedroom) is often subject to intrusion and violation by parents (Hunt and Frankenberg, 1981) and young people usually have less power than other members of the household to make decisions that determine the 'family lifestyle' (Madigan *et al.*, 1990). The privacy of a place is not therefore necessarily the same as having privacy in a place. In this sense the distinction between public and private is complex and hard to draw, being simultaneously articulated at a multiplicity of levels.

Lesbians living in (or returning to) the 'family' house, who haven't 'come out' to their parents, can find that a lack of privacy from the parental gaze constrains their freedom to perform a 'lesbian' identity 'at home'. Home is not for them the place where they can, in Peter Saunders' words, establish the 'core' (Saunders 1989, p.187) of their lives. ... Rather it is a location where their sexuality must often take a back seat. The most obvious expression of their identity – lesbian sex – is definitely off limits (at least when parents have them under surveillance) ... fear of being 'found out' or of giving themselves away drives many women to use time/space strategies to separate the performance of their lesbian identity from the performance of their identity as a daughter (Valentine, 1993b).

> My sister knows, my parents don't ... I moved away so there didn't seem any point in saying anything. I mean I got a job here away from them and they were back in Cardiff, so there was no need for them to find out. But now they've moved to Redcar [a few miles away] which is a source of irritation to me.
>
> (Sandra, English lesbian)

Unlike Janice and Sandra, Julie is 'out' to her family, but in practice it makes little difference to her experience of the asymmetrical family home, as her sexual activity is still policed by her vigilant parents.

> When I came out to my parents, my mother said 'there's only one stipulation, you can bring your girlfriends home but they can't sleep in the same room with you' ... That was it. When I have taken a lover home there she has just been really different. It's felt really uncomfortable.'
>
> (Julie, New Zealand lesbian)

Whilst some parents may also feel squeamish or prudish about their daughter having sex with a male partner under the family roof, within the discourse of heterosexism, a male partner is at least the established 'norm' and although 'sex' may be banned, kissing, holding hands and other expressions of (hetero)sexuality are usually accepted as part and parcel of 'normal' relationships. For many lesbian couples, the expression of anything beyond 'friendship' is tantamount to 'flaunting it' and so they modify their behaviour to such an extent that their relationship is virtually invisible.

...

... [S]emi-fixed domestic items, from curtains and wallpaper to pictures and books, are all supposed to help inhabitants to communicate an identity and outsiders to read it (Rapoport, 1981). Many asymmetrical family homes are impregnated with 'heterosexuality'. Its overwhelming presence seeps out of everything from photograph albums to record collections. But the love that dare not speak its name in the family house can hardly cover the walls and smile down from the picture frames. And so lesbians restrict the performance of their sexual identity in their own physical surroundings, hiding pictures of lesbian icon kd lang under the mattress and gay fiction behind the bookcase, ever cautious that the privacy of their bedroom may be subject to the gaze of brothers, sisters and parents.

...

... The home can therefore be a site of tension for women who identify as lesbians – a place where the ideal of the home as a place of security, freedom and control meets the reality of the home as a site where heterosexual family relations act on and restrict the performance of a lesbian identity. Rather than being 'where above all one feels "in place"'(Eyles, 1984, p.425), 'at home' is where many lesbians feel 'out of place' and that they don't belong or fit in. ...

But the heterosexual family home isn't only a site of oppression, but also a site of subversion – a place where a lesbian identity can sometimes be discreetly performed so that it is not read as such by other family members. For example, by dressing in a way that has lesbian meaning for them, ... or more subtly listening to the music of lesbian icons. ...

...

At home: making lesbian space

Housing in nineteenth- and twentieth-century Britain has been and is 'primarily designed, built, financed and intended for nuclear families – reinforcing a cultural norm of family life with heterosexuality and patriarchy high on the agenda' (Bell, 1991, p.325). As Louise Johnson argues:

> What is being offered to both women and men is a set of recognisable cultural symbols (chief of which is the suburban home and its ownership) ... [but housing] also allows the subversion of dominant social relations. For there is no reason why 'Bedroom 1' should not be occupied by children or a gay couple.
>
> (Johnson, 1992, p.44)

Lesbians occupying a home built on these traditional cultural symbols often do subvert them by making structural changes to the house to express a non-heterosexual identity or lifestyle, as this woman explains:

> I've made my room ... I've built a mezzanine bed, and I have lots of things of comfort around me in my room ... Things which reflect me and reflect the things that I've done in my life, or the people that are important to me and my lifestyle.
>
> (Mary, New Zealand lesbian)

... women also make more conscious efforts to produce a space within which they feel 'at home'. Posters depicting famous lesbians, pictures, personal photographs, music collections and colour schemes (and the compulsory cat and/or dog) are used to make the house a 'lesbian' space. ...

But our identities are not singular; they are multiple and often contradictory. Identities performed by lesbians in their homes may reduce discordant spaces and odd juxtapositions; on the one hand, spaces may resonate with lesbian identities, on the other hand they may resonate with childhood things that reflect the identities of the 'child', 'the daughter' and 'the biological family'. This interface of needs and desires between the lesbian home and the parental home is captured by this woman, who expresses a need to have artistic objects around her that remind her of her upbringing, and her attachment to her 'family' home:

> Pictures, colours and comfortable things from my family, like, my mum, my grandmother and my aunty all paint and they've always had paintings around them. That's been their hobby, and I pick up from that.
>
> (Elaine, New Zealand lesbian)

Tensions between parents and a daughter's lesbian identity can resurface even when she has fled the heterosexual nest. Having a home of one's own may allow a woman enough control over the space to express her sexuality in the physical environment but it doesn't necessarily guarantee freedom from the prying eyes of parents, relatives and neighbours. Discouraging people from popping in and trying to arrange planned rather than spontaneous visits can buy enough time for the home to be 'prepared' for visitors. Alternatively, visitors can be limited to one or two rooms that are 'produced' for public scrutiny to symbolize the whole home ...

...

'The home', particularly for those who are very wary about the personal and employment consequences of being 'outed', can therefore take on a vital role as a lesbian social venue and meeting place. Indeed, in many provincial towns and rural areas, informal networks of private homes fill the entertainment gap created by a complete absence of lesbian institutional spaces. And, in other places, homes become alternative focal points for groups of women alienated from gay bars and institutional spaces because of political or personality clashes.

> Most of the lesbian bit of my life is home-based I suppose, with supper parties and things.
>
> (Sara, English lesbian)

But this is not to suggest that the lesbian home is anymore the idyllic romanticized haven that the heterosexual nuclear family was before it fell from grace under the weight of feminist critiques of domestic violence and so on. Like the heterosexual home, the lesbian home is also a site of conflict and disagreement. It is a site where a lesbian identity must be performed, but it is also a site where this identity comes under surveillance from other lesbians. 'Political correctness', which has come to haunt the lesbian feminist landscape, or other 'orthodoxies', can be invoked by some women to regulate the performative aspects of others' lesbian identities within the domestic environment.

...

The privacy of the home is not always the same thing as privacy from the neighbours. Prying eyes over the garden fence, eavesdropping through badly soundproofed walls, and the efficiency of local gossip networks can expose the most 'closeted' of couples to neighbourhood surveillance. Usually, this evokes nothing more than a few snide or petty remarks but occasionally lesbian and gay homes can become the target of hate campaigns or vicious attempts to restore the 'respectability' of the neighbourhood by driving the occupants out of the street ...

...

We all have a multiplicity of subject positions and identities. 'Home' is one site where our identities are performed and come under surveillance and where we struggle to reconcile conflicting and contradictory performances of the self. 'Home' itself is also a term laden down with a baggage of multiple meanings: shelter, abode, hearth, heart, privacy, roots, paradise and so on. For women who identify as lesbians, the parental (or 'family') home is often a site where they have to manage the clash of their identity as a lesbian with their identity as 'daughter' from a heterosexual family. The struggle to control how their identity is read and received under the surveillance of vigilant parents can rob the parental home of its meaning as a place of 'privacy', 'roots' and 'paradise'. Whilst being a place of material and emotional comfort ('shelter', 'abode', 'hearth', and even 'heart') that can meet the needs and desires of the 'daughter', the parental home does not appear to meet the needs and desires of the 'lesbian'. It is a location where lesbianism and heterosexuality do battle. The heterosexuality of the home can inscribe the lesbian body by restricting the performative aspects of a lesbian identity but it can also be subverted itself by covert acts of resistance.

The 'lesbian home' is one site of lesbian identity construction and maintenance. Constituted to meet the needs and desires of lesbians, it appears to be a place of significance, of 'roots' and even 'paradise', for many women. But despite the greater freedom to perform lesbian identity within the boundaries of a 'lesbian home', it is still a location where this identity comes under the surveillance of others, especially close family, friends and neighbours. It is not necessarily a place of 'privacy'. In some cases the physical site of the home is actually altered depending on the relationship of the visitor to the occupants so that a lesbian identity is not performed in the physical environment to the 'wrong audience', thereby disguising the identity of the occupants. Alternatively, in an attempt to create the privacy necessary to conceal a lesbian relationship, couples can often withdraw from family, friends and the local neighbourhood and become isolated. This isolation can become stiflingly claustrophobic, smothering relationships and enabling abusive domestic situations to develop unnoticed under this cloak of privacy. Thus a lesbian home is not necessarily a place of emotional and physical well-being ('hearth' and 'heart'). Neither is it always a stable 'shelter' or 'abode' – domestic conflicts between women and their children and the usual ebb and flow of sexual relationships can all contribute to a fluidity in the membership and constitution of lesbian households.

The meaning of 'home' to the lesbians involved in this research are numerous and beset with contradictions. They are perhaps most neatly summed up by Massey when she writes about the home (in a different context): 'each home-place is itself ... a complex product of the ever-shifting geography of social relations present and past' (Massey, 1992, p.15).

References

Allan, G. and Crow, G. (eds) (1989) *Home and Family: Creating the Domestic Sphere*, Basingstoke, Macmillan.

Bell, D. (1991) 'Insignificant others: lesbian and gay geographies', *Area*, no.23, pp.323–9.

Eyles, J. (1984) *Senses of Place*, Warrington, Silverbrook Press.

Hunt, P. and Frankenberg, R. (1981) 'Home: castle or cage?' in *An Introduction to Sociology*, Milton Keynes, Open University Press.

Johnson, L. (1992) 'Housing desire: a feminist geography of suburban housing', *Refractory Girl: A Feminist Journal*, no.42, pp.40–7.

McDowell, L. (1983) 'City and home: urban housing and the sexual division of space' in Evans, M. and Ungerson, M. (eds) *Sexual Divisions: Patterns and Processes*, London, Tavistock.

Madigan, R., Munro, M. and Smith, S.J. (1990) 'Gender and the meaning of home', *International Journal of Urban and Regional Research*, no.14, pp.625–47.

Massey, D. (1992) 'A place called home?', *New Formations*, no.17, pp.3–15.

Rapoport, A. (1981) 'Identity and environment: a cross-cultural perspective' in Duncan, J.S. (ed.) *Housing and Identity*, London, Croom Helm.

Saunders, P. (1989) 'The meaning of "home" in contemporary English culture', *Housing Studies*, no.4, pp.177–92.

Valentine, G. (1993) 'Negotiating and managing multiple sexual identities: lesbian time-space strategies', *Transactions of the Institute of British Geographers*, NS18, pp.237–48.

Source: Johnston and Valentine, 1995, pp.99–113

Readings in sociology and everyday life

Contents

Henri Lefebvre:
'Everyday life in the modern world' (1968)

What we want to demonstrate is the fallacy of judging a society according to its own standards, because its categories are part of its publicity – pawns in a game of strategy and neither unbiased nor disinterested; they serve a dual practical and ideological purpose. A century ago individualism provided philosophers and scholars (historians, economists, etc.) with categories and images, and it was necessary to raise this veil in order to catch a glimpse of reality and thence of possibility; today ideologies have changed and they bear names such as functionalism, formalism, structuralism, operationalism or scientism; they parade as 'non-ideologies' in order to merge more readily with the imagination; they disguise the basic fact – or factual basis – that everything stems from everyday life which in turn reveals everything, or, in other words, that the critical analysis of everyday life reveals 'everything' because it takes 'everything' into account.

To sum up:

(a) Is the quotidian definable? Can it serve as the starting point for a definition of contemporary society (modernity), so that the inquiry avoids the ironic slant, the identification of a fragmentary or partial sphere, and encompasses its essence and its unity?

(b) Does this method lead to a coherent non-contradictory theory of the contradictions and conflicts in social 'reality', to a conception of the real and the possible?

To these questions, formulated in the most scientific way possible, our reply is a condensation of the previous assertions. Everyday life is not a discarded space–time complex nor a clear field left to individual freedom, reason and resourcefulness; it is no longer the place where human suffering and heroism are enacted, the site of the human condition. It has ceased to be a rationally exploited colonial province of society, because it is not a province and rational exploitation has availed itself of more refined methods than heretofore. Everyday life has become an object of consideration and is the province of organization; the space–time of voluntary programmed self-regulation, because when properly organized it provides a closed circuit (production–consumption–production), where demands are foreseen because they are induced and desires are run to earth; this method replaces the spontaneous self-regulation of the competitive era. Thus everyday life must shortly become the one perfect system obscured by the other systems that aim at systematizing thought and structuralizing action, and as such it would be the main product of the so-called 'organized' society of controlled consumption and of its setting, modernity. If the circuit is not completely closed it is not for want of purpose or strategical intent but only because 'something' irreducible intervenes, 'something' that is perhaps Desire, or Reason (dialectics) or even the City. ... The only way to stop the circuit from closing is to conquer the quotidian, attack it and transform it by making use of another form of strategy. Time alone will reveal whether it will be possible for those who are willing to recapture in this way the lost harmony of language and reality, of significant actions and learning.

This coherent logical theory is also conducive to practical action, but it presupposes a preliminary action or thought-action; certain conditions are required for a conception of the quotidian and a theory of quotidianness, the first being that one must live or have lived in it; it is also essential not to take it for granted but to see it in critical perspective. Short of these two conditions understanding becomes impossible and our words will fall on deaf ears – and none are so deaf as those who refuse to hear.

Everyday life weighs heaviest on women. It is highly probable that they also get something out of it by reversing the situation, but the weight is none the less on their shoulders. Some are bogged down by its peculiar cloying substance, others escape into make-believe, close their eyes to their surroundings, to the bog into which they are sinking and simply ignore it; they have their substitutes and they are substitutes; they complain – about men, the human condition, life, God and the gods – but they are always beside the point; they are the subject of everyday life and its victims or objects and substitutes (beauty, femininity, fashion, etc.) and it is at their cost that substitutes thrive. Likewise they are both buyers and consumers of commodities and symbols for commodities (in advertisements, as nudes and smiles). Because of their ambiguous position in everyday life – which is specifically part of everyday life and modernity – they are incapable of understanding it. Robotization probably succeeds so well with women because of the things that matter to them (fashions, the house and the home, etc.), notwithstanding – or on account of – their 'spontaneity'. For adolescents and students the situation is reversed, since they have never known everyday life; they would like to take part in it but are afraid of being caught up in it, and all they know about it is through their parents, a vague potentiality in black and white. There exists an ideology or mythology of maturity for their personal use that belongs to parents, connects paternity and maternity, culture and submission.

What of the intellectual? He is in it all right! Intellectuals have careers, wives, children, time-tables, private lives, working lives, leisure, dwellings in one place or another, etc.; they are in it, but in a slightly marginal position so that they think of themselves as being outside and elsewhere. They have a number of successful means of evasion, and all the substitutes are at their disposal – dreams, make-believe, art, culture, education, history and many more besides. They frequently even accept the system of methods by which social experience and everyday life are submitted to compulsion, conditioning, 'structuring' and programming, calling it 'social science', 'urban science' or 'organizational science'; intellectual honesty in such 'operationalism' is not imperative. The more serious specimens of this breed of theoreticians elaborate sub-systems and specific codes to organize a society, that in turn organizes everyday life in approximate categories such as environment, dwellings, furnishings, horoscopes, tourism, cookery, fashions – all the specialized activities that provide subject-matter for pamphlets, theses, catalogues, guide books. These honest theoreticians impose their own limits to their endeavours and refuse to question invisible patterns, ignore the significant absence of a general code. Scientism and positivism provide excellent subjects for discussion and perfect substitutes which oppose and imply each other: pragmatism, functionalism, operationalism on the one hand, and on the other problems tactfully left to the experts. Criticism, protests, objections or any attempt to seek an opening 'elsewhere' are dismissed as utopia by these ideologists; and how right they are! They are supported by a special brand of reason and restricted rationality (their own).

Source: Henri Lefebvre, *Everyday Life in the Modern World* (trans. S.Rabinovitch), London, Allen Lane The Penguin Press, 1971 (from Ch. 2 'The bureaucratic society of controlled consumption', pp.71–4). First published in France in 1968.

Jim McGuigan:
'Culture and the public sphere' (1996)

And yet, as Habermas (1990, p.19) remarks, to use a quotation ... that I am rather fond of, 'Everyday communication makes possible a kind of understanding that is based on claims to validity and thus furnishes the only real alternative to exerting influence on one another in more or less coercive ways.' To appreciate the faith and hope that Habermas places in everyday communication, it is important to grasp his distinction between 'system' and 'lifeworld'.

For Habermas (1987), 'system' is represented by economy and bureaucracy with their respective steering mechanisms of money and power. Modern society is systemically very complex, functioning above and beyond most of our everyday understandings. These systems work according to an instrumental rationality which suspends questions of human value and meaning. Such questions are consigned, instead, to the lifeworld, where our sense of self and the situations we live in day-to-day are circumscribed. Modernisation, in effect, argues Habermas (1987, p.155), brings about an 'uncoupling of system and lifeworld'. The point is that the lifeworld, under modern conditions, continues to operate according to principles of communicative rationality whereas instrumental rationality animates systemic processes. The medium of communicative rationality is language, which facilitates the shared orientation to mutual understanding: the media of instrumental rationality are money and power, systems of reward and punishment, the carrot and the stick.

In addition to the 'uncoupling' of lifeworld and system there is also the chronic problem, identified by Habermas, of the 'colonization' of the lifeworld by system imperatives. Strange as it may seem in the postmodern world, once upon a time there was a political project dedicated to attacking these systems of domination head-on that had a certain historical credibility. It imagined the possibility of abolishing capitalism and even the 'withering away' of state bureaucracies. This has become an implausible imaginary, according to Habermas (1992, p.444). The best we can hope for now, under present conditions, is to defend and extend the communicative rationality of 'the lifeworld' against the instrumentalist encroachments of 'the system'. With this diagnosis, Habermas (1987, p.392) is a keen supporter of what he calls 'the new politics', which in its various forms, including green politics and popular cultural and social movements in general, is concerned with 'the quality of life'.

References

Habermas, J. (1987) *The Theory of Communicative Action, Volume 2: The Critique of Functionalist Reason*, Cambridge, Polity Press.

Habermas, J. (1990) *Moral Consciousness and Communicative Action*, Cambridge, Polity Press.

Habermas, J. (1992) 'Further reflections on the public sphere' in Calhoun, C. (ed.) *Habermas and the Public Sphere*, Cambridge, MA, MIT Press.

Source: Jim McGuigan, *Culture and the Public Sphere*, London, Routledge, 1996 (p.179).

Alfred Schutz:
'The reality of the world of daily life' (1944)

The natural attitude of daily life and its pragmatic motive

We begin with an analysis of the world of daily life which the wide-awake, grown-up man who acts in it and upon it amidst his fellow-men experiences within the natural attitude as a reality.

'World of daily life' shall mean the intersubjective world which existed long before our birth, experienced and interpreted by Others, our predecessors, as an organized world. Now it is given to our experience and interpretation. All interpretation of this world is based upon a stock of previous experiences of it, our own experiences and those handed down to us by our parents and teachers, which in the form of 'knowledge at hand' function as a scheme of reference.

To this stock of experiences at hand belongs our knowledge that the world we live in is a world of well circumscribed objects with definite qualities, objects among which we move, which resist us and upon which we may act. To the natural attitude the world is not and never has been a mere aggregate of colored spots, incoherent noises, centers of warmth and cold. Philosophical or psychological analysis of the constitution of our experiences may afterwards, retrospectively, describe how elements of this world affect our senses, how we passively perceive them in an indistinct and confused way, how by active apperception our mind singles out certain features from the perceptional field, conceiving them as well delineated things which stand out over against a more or less unarticulated background or horizon. The natural attitude does not know these problems. To it the world is from the outset not the private world of the single individual but an intersubjective world, common to all of us, in which we have not a theoretical but an eminently practical interest. The world of everyday life is the scene and also the object of our actions and interactions. We have to dominate it and we have to change it in order to realize the purposes which we pursue within it among our fellow-men. We work and operate not only within but upon the world. Our bodily movements – kinaesthetic, locomotive, operative – gear, so to speak, into the world, modifying or changing its objects and their mutual relationships. On the other hand, these objects offer resistance to our acts which we have either to overcome or to which we have to yield. Thus, it may be correctly said that a pragmatic motive governs our natural attitude toward the world of daily life. World, in this sense, is something that we have to modify by our actions or that modifies our actions.

Source: Alfred Schutz, *Collected Papers, Vol. 1: The Problem of Social Reality* (edited and introduced by M. Natanson), The Hague, Martinus Nijhoff, 1967 (pp.208–9).

Don H. Zimmerman and Melvin Pollner:
'The attitude of everyday life' (1970)

According to Schutz,[1] the world, as it presents itself to the member operating under the jurisdiction of the attitude of everyday life, is a historical, already organized world. It did not appear with the member's birth; it will not perish with his death. From the beginning, the world is experienced *pretheoretically* as the prevailing and persistent condition of all the members' projects. It furnishes the resistant 'objective structures', which must be reckoned with in a practically adequate fashion if projects of action are to be effected successfully.

The attitude of everyday life sustains particular doubts, but never global doubts. Indeed, that the existence of the world is never brought into question is an essential requirement for any particular doubt. That is, from the perspective of the attitude of everyday life, the world and its objective constitution are taken for granted from the outset. Not only is the global existence of the world taken for granted, the thesis that the world presents itself to alter essentially as it does to ego – with due allowance for different temporal, spatial, and biographical perspectives – is also merely assumed. The world is *experienced* as an intersubjective world, known or knowable in common with others.

The member takes for granted that the social world and, more specifically, the aspect of it relevant to his interest at hand, is actually or potentially assembled or assembleable by rule or by recipe. That is, he may know, or take it that he could determine by inquiry, the rules or recipes whereby he and others might gear into or understand some activity. Put another way, the member assumes that such structures are actually or potentially locatable and determinable in their features by recourse to such practices as asking for or giving instruction concerning a given matter. Everyday activities and their perceived connected features present themselves with the promise that they may be understood and acted upon in practically sufficient ways by competent employment of appropriate proverbs, paradigms, motives, organizational charts, and the like.

Under the attitude of everyday life, the features of this known in common world are addressed with pragmatic motive. What is known or knowable about its organization awaits recognition or discovery precipitated by the occurrence of particular projects [whose] execution depends on coming to terms with more or less circumscribed features relevant to the anticipated action. Accordingly, under the auspices of members' practical interests in the workings of the everyday world, the member's knowledge of the world is more or less ad hoc, more or less general, more or less fuzzy around the periphery. The member finds out what he needs to know; what he needs to know is relative to the practical requirements of his problem. His criteria of adequacy, rules of procedure, and strategies for achieving desired ends are for him only as good as they need to be.

The social structures that present themselves under the attitude of everyday life are for the member only minutely of his doing. They are encountered as resistive to his wish and whim, and they transcend their particular appearances. As omniprevalent and pervasive conditions and objects of members' projects, the world is available for practically adequate investigation and description. From the standpoint of the member, the world and its exhibited properties are not constituted by virtue of their having been addressed. For the member operating under the attitude of everyday life, the world offers itself as an a priori resistive, recalcitrant, and massively organized structure into which he must gear himself.

Note

1   Most of Schutz's work was devoted to articulating the formal properties of the 'attitude of everyday life'. An overview of that work may be found in Maurice Natanson's and Aron Gurwitsch's introductions to Schutz (1962, 1966).

References

Schutz, A. (1962) *Collected Papers I: The Problem of Social Reality* (ed. M. Natanson), The Hague, Martinus Nijhoff.

Schutz, A. (1966) *Collected Papers III: Studies in Phenomenological Philosophy* (ed. I. Schutz), The Hague, Martinus Nijhoff.

Source: Don H. Zimmerman and Melvin Pollner, 'The everyday world as a phenomenon' in Douglas, J.D. (ed.)*Understanding Everyday Life: Toward the Reconstruction of Sociological Knowledge*, London, Routledge and Kegan Paul, 1970 (pp.84–6).

Agnes Heller:
'The heterogeneity of everyday life' (1970)

Everyday and non-everyday thinking

Like everyday life, everyday thinking too is heterogeneous. The thought processes evinced in the various forms of everyday activity have this in common – they all arise from the facticity of the everyday. They arise, on the one hand, from the fact that heterogeneous forms of activity have to be co-ordinated and carried out in a relatively short time; and, on the other hand, from the fact that at different times, in different societies and in different classes these heterogeneous activities vary in kind, which means that the knowledge required for the appropriation and performance of these activities is also a variant. From the first of these twin facts arises the general structure of everyday thinking, from the second is derived the concrete content of everyday thought. Of course, not every form of knowledge can be made 'everyday'; not every form of knowledge can be fitted into the structural system of everyday thinking. Any form of knowledge which cannot be so accommodated remains professional knowledge and is not a necessary condition for the reproduction of a particular person born into a given society.

Everyday thinking as a function of everyday living can be considered as an invariant. Its structure, however, and its contents are variables, highly disparate in their rate of change. The structure of everyday thinking changes very slowly, and it contains completely stagnant aspects. Its contents change relatively quickly. But even these contents are prone to conservatism, inertia, if we compare everyday thinking with scientific thinking.

The inertia inherent in the content of everyday thought is dual in character. The duality arises from its close ties with the structure of everyday thought. Since the contents of everyday thought – as we shall see in due course – are embedded in a very largely pragmatic and economic structure, they are by definition inert *vis-à-vis* the products of thought which transcend the purely pragmatic. This transcending of the pragmatic may possibly come about in the *intentio obliqua* of science (philosophy), in the discovery of problem complexes the cognitive understanding of which runs contrary to the anthropocentric experience gained in the pragmatic approach and the needs or interests of the everyday 'person', whether particular or individual.

In so far as the institutionalized or other objectivations which go beyond the everyday have been alienated, the pragmatism of everyday thinking appears *vis-à-vis* these objectivations as 'natural common sense', as the yardstick of normality. In so far, however, as these objectivations represent a deeper connection with the generic, the contents of everyday thinking appear as a system of prejudices; and 'common sense' acquires a negative evaluative imprint.

...

Everyday life and social structure

We may start with a question: is it possible to read off, to discern from its everyday life and thinking, the social structure of a given period and, secondly, the stage which that structure represents in the generic development of the human race?

The social division of labour means that people lead very different everyday lives in a given society, their differentiation turning upon such factors as class, stratum, community, order, etc.; and this in turn means that from the everyday life of any one man, indeed of any one class, we cannot learn everything about the structure of the given society. The everyday life of the serf cannot fully express the structure of feudalism, any more than can the everyday life of the knight.

So, for the moment at least, the answer to our question must be in the negative; not only because of the division of labour but also because of the fact that a particular society is to be identified by its aggregate of objectivations and the relationships between them. The level of production and distribution, the degree of excellence reached in the arts and sciences, the structure of the society's various institutions and the types of human activity performed in them – from such data we can effectively read off what sort of society we have to do with, what it has to give mankind and what it may, on the other hand, take from us. It is clear that there neither is nor can be a society in which the generic objectivations are represented by nothing more than the aggregate of everyday lives.

On closer inspection, however, our initial 'no' turns out to require some qualification.

Persons are born into a given world, and it is the conditions imposed by this given world – at least in so far as their immediate environment is concerned – that they must appropriate and make their own if they are to survive. The production and distribution system that is internalized in their everyday life, the moral precepts and practices which become its inseparable paraphernalia, the role played in it by art and science, the nature of the art and science called upon to play this role – all of this tells us much about the structure of a given society.

Source: Agnes Heller, *Everyday Life* (trans. G.L. Campbell), Part II The Everyday and the Non-everyday, Ch. 4 'The heterogeneity of everyday life', London, Routledge and Kegan Paul (1984) (pp.49–50, 53–4). First published in Hungary in 1970.

Michel de Certeau:
'The practice of everyday life: "making do" – uses and tactics' (1984)

… I resort to a distinction between *tactics* and *strategies*.

I call a 'strategy' the calculus of force-relationships which becomes possible when a subject of will and power (a proprietor, an enterprise, a city, a scientific institution) can be isolated from an 'environment.' A strategy assumes a place that can be circumscribed as *proper (propre)* and thus serve as the basis for generating relations with an exterior distinct from it (competitors, adversaries, 'clientèles', 'targets', or 'objects' of research). Political, economic, and scientific rationality has been constructed on this strategic model.

I call a 'tactic', on the other hand, a calculus which cannot count on a 'proper' (a spatial or institutional localization), nor thus on a borderline distinguishing the other as a visible totality. The place of a tactic belongs to the other. A tactic insinuates itself into the other's place, fragmentarily, without taking it over in its entirety, without being able to keep it at a distance. It has at its disposal no base where it can capitalize on its advantages, prepare its expansions, and secure independence with respect to circumstances. The 'proper' is a victory of space over time. On the contrary, because it does not have a place, a tactic depends on time – it is always on the watch for opportunities that must be seized 'on the wing'. Whatever it wins, it does not keep. It must constantly manipulate events in order to turn them into 'opportunities'. The weak must continually turn to their own ends forces alien to them. This is achieved in the propitious moments when they are able to combine heterogeneous elements (thus, in the supermarket, the housewife confronts heterogeneous and mobile data – what she has in the refrigerator, the tastes, appetites, and moods of her guests, the best buys and their possible combinations with what she already has on hand at home, etc.); the intellectual synthesis of these given elements takes the form, however, not of a discourse, but of the decision itself, the act and manner in which the opportunity is 'seized'.

Many everyday practices (talking, reading, moving about, shopping, cooking, etc.) are tactical in character. And so are, more generally, many 'ways of operating': victories of the 'weak' over the 'strong' (whether the strength be that of powerful people or the violence of things or of an imposed order, etc.), clever tricks, knowing how to get away with things, 'hunter's cunning', maneuvers, polymorphic simulations, joyful discoveries, poetic as well as warlike. The Greeks called these 'ways of operating' *mētis* (Détienne and Vernant, 1974). But they go much further back, to the immemorial intelligence displayed in the tricks and imitations of plants and fishes. From the depths of the ocean to the streets of modern megalopolises, there is a continuity and permanence in these tactics.

…

A distinction between *strategies* and *tactics* appears to provide a more adequate initial schema. I call a *strategy* the calculation (or manipulation) of power relationships that becomes possible as soon as a subject with will and power (a business, an army, a city, a scientific institution) can be isolated. It postulates a *place* that can be delimited as its *own* and serve as the base from which relations with an *exteriority* composed of targets or threats (customers or competitors, enemies, the country surrounding the city, objectives and objects of research, etc.) can be managed. As in management, every 'strategic' rationalization seeks first of all to distinguish its 'own' place, that is, the place of its own power and will, from an 'environment'. A Cartesian attitude, if you wish: it is an effort to delimit one's own place in a world bewitched by the invisible powers of the Other. It is also the typical attitude of modern science, politics, and military strategy.

The establishment of a break between a place appropriated as one's own and its other is accompanied by important effects, some of which we must immediately note:

1   The 'proper' is *a triumph of place over time*. It allows one to capitalize acquired advantages, to prepare future expansions, and thus to give oneself a certain independence with respect to the variability of circumstances. It is a mastery of time through the foundation of an autonomous place.

2   It is also a mastery of places through sight. The division of space makes possible a *panoptic practice* proceeding from a place whence the eye can transform foreign forces into objects that can be observed and measured, and thus control and 'include' them within its scope of vision. To be able to see (far into the distance) is also to be able to predict, to run ahead of time by reading a space.

3   It would be legitimate to define the *power of knowledge* by this ability to transform the uncertainties of history into readable spaces. But it would be more correct to recognize in these 'strategies' a specific type of knowledge, one sustained and determined by the power to provide oneself with one's own place. Thus military or scientific strategies have always been inaugurated through the constitution of their 'own' areas (autonomous cities, 'neutral' or 'independent' institutions, laboratories pursuing 'disinterested' research, etc.). In other words, *a certain power is the precondition of this knowledge* and not merely its effect or its attribute. It makes this knowledge possible and at the same time determines its characteristics. It produces itself in and through this knowledge.

By contrast with a strategy (whose successive shapes introduce a certain play into this formal schema and whose link with a particular historical configuration of rationality should also be clarified), a *tactic* is a calculated action determined by the absence of a proper locus. No delimitation of an exteriority, then, provides it with the condition necessary for autonomy. The space of a tactic is the space of the other. Thus it must play on and with a terrain imposed on it and organized by the law of a foreign power. It does not have the means to *keep to itself*, at a distance, in a position of withdrawal, foresight, and self-collection: it is a maneuver 'within the enemy's field of vision', as von Bülow put it,[1] and within enemy territory. It does not, therefore, have the options of planning general strategy and viewing the adversary as a whole within a distinct, visible, and objectifiable space. It operates in isolated actions, blow by blow. It takes advantage of 'opportunities' and depends on them, being without any base where it could stockpile its winnings, build up its own position, and plan raids. What it wins it cannot keep. This nowhere gives a tactic mobility, to be sure, but a mobility that must accept the chance offerings of the moment, and seize on the wing the possibilities that offer themselves at any given moment. It must vigilantly make use of the cracks that particular conjunctions open in the surveillance of the proprietary powers. It poaches in them. It creates surprises in them. It can be where it is least expected. It is a guileful ruse.

In short, a tactic is an art of the weak. Clausewitz noted this fact in discussing deception in his treatise *On War*. The more a power grows, the less it can allow itself to mobilize part of its means in the service of deception: it is dangerous to deploy large forces for the sake of appearances; this sort of 'demonstration' is generally useless and 'the gravity of bitter necessity makes direct action so urgent that it leaves no room for this sort of game.' One deploys his forces, one does not take chances with feints. Power is bound by its very visibility. In contrast, trickery is possible for the weak, and often it is his only possibility, as a 'last resort': 'The weaker the forces at the disposition of the strategist, the more the strategist will be able to use deception' (Clausewitz, 1955, pp.212–13). I translate: the more the strategy is transformed into tactics.

Clausewitz also compares trickery to wit: 'Just as wit involves a certain legerdemain relative to ideas and concepts, trickery is a sort of legerdemain relative to acts' (*ibid.*, p.212). This indicates the mode in which a tactic, which is indeed a form of legerdemain, takes an order by surprise. The art of 'pulling tricks' involves a sense of the opportunities afforded by a particular occasion. Through procedures that Freud (1960) makes explicit with reference to wit, a tactic boldly juxtaposes diverse elements in order suddenly to produce a flash shedding a different light on the language of a place and to strike the hearer. Cross-cuts, fragments, cracks and lucky hits in the framework of a system, consumers' ways of operating are the practical equivalents of wit.

Lacking its own place, lacking a view of the whole, limited by the blindness (which may lead to perspicacity) resulting from combat at close quarters, limited by the possibilities of the moment, a tactic is determined by the *absence of power* just as a strategy is organized by the postulation of power. From this point of view, the dialectic of a tactic may be illuminated by the ancient art of sophistic. As the author of a great 'strategic' system, Aristotle was already very interested in the procedures of this enemy which perverted, as he saw it, the order of truth. He quotes a formula of this protean, quick, and surprising adversary that, by making explicit the basis of sophistic, can also serve finally to define a tactic as I understand the term here: it is a matter, Corax said, of 'making the worse argument seem the better.' In its paradoxical concision, this formula delineates the relationship of forces that is the starting point for an intellectual creativity as persistent as it is subtle, tireless, ready for every opportunity, scattered over the terrain of the dominant order and foreign to the rules laid down and imposed by a rationality founded on established rights and property.

In sum, strategies are actions which, thanks to the establishment of a place of power (the property of a proper), elaborate theoretical places (systems and totalizing discourses) capable of articulating an ensemble of physical places in which forces are distributed. They combine these three types of places and seek to master each by means of the others. They thus privilege spatial relationships. At the very least they attempt to reduce temporal relations to spatial ones through the analytical attribution of a proper place to each particular element and through the combinatory organization of the movements specific to units or groups of units. The model was military before it became 'scientific'. Tactics are procedures that gain validity in relation to the pertinence they lend to time – to the circumstances which the precise instant of an intervention transforms into a favorable situation, to the rapidity of the movements that change the organization of a space, to the relations among successive moments in an action, to the possible intersections of durations and heterogeneous rhythms, etc. In this respect, the difference corresponds to two historical options regarding action and security (options that moreover have more to do with constraints than with possibilities): strategies pin their hopes on the resistance that the *establishment of a place* offers to the erosion of time; tactics on a clever *utilization of time*, of the opportunities it presents and also of the play that it introduces into the foundations of power. Even if the methods practiced by the everyday art of war never present themselves in such a clear form, it nevertheless remains the case that the two ways of acting can be distinguished according to whether they bet on place or on time.

Note

1   'Strategy is the science of military movements outside of the enemy's field of vision; tactics, within it' (von Bülow).

References

Clausewitz, K. von (1955) *De la guerre*, Paris, Minuit. (*On War* (trans. M. Howard and P. Paret), Princeton, NJ, Princeton University Press, 1976.)

Détienne, M. and Vernant, J.-P. (1974) *Les Ruses de l'intelligence: La mètis des Grecs*, Paris, Flammarion.

Freud, S. (1960) *Jokes and their Relation to the Unconscious* (trans. J. Strachey), London, The Hogarth Press and the Institute of Psychoanalysis.

Source: Michel de Certeau, *The Practice of Everyday Life* (trans. S.F. Rendall), extracted from 'General introduction' and Part I: A Very Ordinary Culture, Ch. III ' "Making do": uses and tactics', Berkeley and Los Angeles, CA, University of California Press, 1984 (pp.xix–xx, 35–9).

John Fiske:
'Cultural studies and the culture of everyday life' (1992)

Brett Williams (1988) gives a good example of both living in a mainly black, working class culture, and providing an academic account of it. She moves between the two habituses in a way I believe to be exemplary.

Her study details some of the key features of a habitus whose culture is of the material density of embodied practices. One of these she calls 'texture.' By 'texture' she refers to dense, vivid, detailed interwoven narratives, relationships, and experiences. The materially constrained narrowness of the conditions of everyday life are compensated for and contradicted by the density and intensity of the experiences, practices, and objects packed into them. She finds this density as she follows a man down his neighborhood main street, when every store, every encounter, every piece of gossip exchanged is packed with concrete meanings in its minutiae. The density of apartment life is part of the conditions of oppression, yet it is also available to be turned by popular creativity and struggle, into a textured culture: 'The Manor's dense living, in combination with the poverty of its families is battering. Using a small space intensively, cleaning it defensively, and lacking the resources to expand or transform it, families need to work out ways to make that density bearable.'

Williams goes on to describe how Lucy and Robert, as typical renters, cope with their material conditions by 'texturing domestic density by weaving through it varied sights, sounds and rhythms' (p.102). To middle class taste their apartment would seem intolerably cluttered with knickknacks and decorations yet Robert still feels a need to fill what seems to him to be a glaringly empty space. It is as though a density which is chosen by Lucy and Robert becomes a way of negotiating and coping with a density that is imposed upon them: constructing a bottom-up density is a tactic of popular culture for 'turning' the constraints of a top-down density. It is an instance of the creative use of the conditions of constraint.

Television is used to increase, enrich and further densify the texture. It is typically left on all the time, adding color, sound and action to apartment life: it is used to frame and cause conversations, to fill gaps and silences. It can provide both a means of entering and intensifying this dense everyday culture and a way of escaping it, for it is also used to dilute 'the concentration of crowded families, whose members can tune into television, establish a well of privacy, and yet remain part of the domestic group' (pp.102–3).

Television not only enriches and enters the interwoven texture of everyday life, it re-presents it, too. Programs like *Dallas*, with its 'vivid historically interwoven concreteness' offered renters 'the same kind of texture that is so valued on the street'. The women in the apartments lived in and with *Dallas* over a number of years, growing to know each character in 'painstaking detail.' Williams concludes: 'As renters texture an already dense domestic situation by weaving in more density, shows like these favorites are appropriate vehicles' (Williams, 1988, p.106).

Leal (1990; Leal and Oliver, 1988) too, has shown how certain formations of the people (in her case first generation urbanized Brazilian peasants) weave a densely textured symbolic environment through which they live. She analyzes in detail one such environment, or rather a mini-environment *or 'entourage'* constructed from objects placed around the TV set. Around the TV set were plastic flowers, a religious picture, a false gold vase, family photographs, a broken laboratory glass and an old broken radio. Williams finds the culture in the density itself, but Leal interprets this texture. Her analysis shows how these people live meaningfully within the contradictions between the city and the country, urban sophistication and rural peasantry, science and magic, the future and the past. In the suburbs they are placed on the spatial boundary between the city and the country, as first generation migrants they are on the equivalent historical boundary between the past and the future.

Their use of photographs was an instance of this cultural process. On the TV set were large pictures of dead or absent family members, typically ones left behind in the country, and stuck into their frames were small I.D. photos of those who had moved to the city: the I.D. photos were not only signs of family, but also signs of modern, urban life. As Leal comments 'The social system that broke these kinship webs is reproduced in the symbolic system within the photograph frames' (p.23) and these lost kinship webs are reasserted, reformed through bricolage. So, too, the plastic flowers were considered more beautiful than natural ones because they bore meaning of the urban, the manufactured, the new; and also because they cost money. They were validated by their origins in the 'better' life the people hoped to find by their move to the city. Natural flowers, on the other hand, were from the life they were fleeing. Leal also shows how class specific these meanings are – in the middle-class homes, for instance, there was a reversal of values so that peasant art would be displayed as bearers of valid meanings of the country and an escape from the urban. In those homes, of course, plastic flowers would never raise their cheap, manufactured, urbanized heads. Her interpretation of this dense texture of objects continues, including the TV set which is seen as 'a vehicle of a knowledgeable and modern speech' (p.24). Her readings reveal a popular culture in process by which the people live within the larger social order not in a reactive, but a proactive way. The entourage of objects around the TV set comprises

> a symbolic system, including an ethos of modernity, that is itself part of a larger symbolic universe that has as its principal focus of significance the city and industry. This system of meanings seeks to 'conquer' the urban power space (that of capitalistic relations), while insistently trying to differentiate and delimit urban cultural space from the rural space that is still very close to the actors, by manipulating signs that are shared by their group as indicators of social prestige.
>
> (Leal, 1990, p.25)

Studies such as Leal's and Williams's show how the material, densely lived culture of everyday life is a contradictory mixture of creativity and constraint. This is a way of embodying and living the contradictory relations between the dominant social order and the variety of subaltern formations within it. Williams comments somewhat sardonically that 'A passion for texture is not always rewarded in American society, and more middle-class strategies for urban living aim at breadth instead' (1988, p.48). It is a comment that I wish to extend to cover academic theory as part of middle-class strategies for living.

The social order constrains and oppresses the people, but at the same time offers them resources to fight against those constraints. The constraints are, in the first instance, material, economic ones which determine in an oppressive, disempowering way, the limits of the social experience of the poor. Oppression is always economic. Yet the everyday culture of the oppressed takes the signs of that which oppresses them and uses them for its own purposes. The signs of money are taken out of the economic system of the dominant and inserted into the culture of the subaltern and their social force is thus complicated. The plastic flowers are for Leal's newly suburbanized peasant, deeply contradictory. They have a mystique because of the 'mystery' of their production (unlike natural flowers) – they are fetishes, syntheses of symbolic meanings, of modernity: but they are also commodity fetishes. They require money, another fetish, and transform that money into an object of cultural display. Real money is not an appropriate decoration or cultural object, but transformed money is; its transformation occurs not just in its form, coin to plastic flower, but in the social formation, theirs to ours. The commodity fetish is deeply conflicted: it bears the forces of both the power bloc and the people. It produces and reproduces the economic system, yet simultaneously can serve the symbolic interests of those subordinated by it. The plastic flowers, Leal argues, because they cannot be produced within the domestic space but must be bought, bring with them the 'social legitimacy, prestige and power' that, in an urban capitalist society can most readily be gained, in however transformed a manner, from the order of oppression.

References

Leal, O.F. (1990) 'Popular taste and erudite repertoire: the place and space of television in Brazil', *Cultural Studies*, vol.4, issue 1, pp.19–29.

Leal, O.F and Oliver, R. (1988) 'Class interpretations of a soap opera narrative: the case of the Brazilian novella *Summer Sun*', *Theory, Culture and Society*, vol.5, pp.81–9.

Williams, B. (1988) *Upscaling Downtown: Stalled Gentrification in Washington, DC*, Ithaca, NY, Cornell University Press.

Source: John Fiske, 'Cultural studies and the culture of everyday life' in Grossberg, L., Nelson, C. and Treichler, P.A. (eds) *Cultural Studies*, London, Routledge, 1992 (pp.155–7).

Erving Goffman:
'The presentation of self in everyday life' (1959)

When an individual enters the presence of others, they commonly seek to acquire information about him or to bring into play information about him already possessed. They will be interested in his general socio-economic status, his conception of self, his attitude towards them, his competence, his trustworthiness, etc. Although some of this information seems to be sought almost as an end in itself, there are usually quite practical reasons for acquiring it. Information about the individual helps to define the situation, enabling others to know in advance what he will expect of them and what they may expect of him. Informed in these ways, the others will know how best to act in order to call forth a desired response from him.

For those present, many sources of information become accessible and many carriers (or 'sign-vehicles') become available for conveying this information. If unacquainted with the individual, observers can glean clues from his conduct and appearance which allow them to apply their previous experience with individuals roughly similar to the one before them or, more important, to apply untested stereotypes to him. They can also assume from past experience that only individuals of a particular kind are likely to be found in a given social setting. They can rely on what the individual says about himself or on documentary evidence he provides as to who and what he is. If they know, or know of, the individual by virtue of experience prior to the interaction, they can rely on assumptions as to the persistence and generality of psychological traits as a means of predicting his present and future behaviour.

> ...

The expressiveness of the individual (and therefore his capacity to give impressions) appears to involve two radically different kinds of sign activity: the expression that he *gives*, and the expression that he *gives off*. The first involves verbal symbols or their substitutes which he uses admittedly and solely to convey the information that he and the others are known to attach to these symbols. This is communication in the traditional and narrow sense. The second involves a wide range of action that others can treat as symptomatic of the actor, the expectation being that the action was performed for reasons other than the information conveyed in this way. As we shall have to see, this distinction has an only initial validity. The individual does of course intentionally convey misinformation by means of both of these types of communication, the first involving deceit, the second feigning.

> ...

Let us now turn from the others to the point of view of the individual who presents himself before them. He may wish them to think highly of him, or to think that he thinks highly of them, or to perceive how in fact he feels towards them, or to obtain no clear-cut impression; he may wish to ensure sufficient harmony so that the interaction can be sustained, or to defraud, get rid of, confuse, mislead, antagonize, or insult them. Regardless of the particular objective which the individual has in mind and of his motive for having this objective, it will be in his interests to control the conduct of the others, especially their responsive treatment of him.[1] This control is achieved largely by influencing the definition of the situation which the others come to formulate, and he can influence this definition by expressing himself in such a way as to give them the kind of impression that will lead them to act voluntarily in accordance with his own plan. Thus, when an individual appears in the presence of others, there will usually be some reason for him to mobilize his activity so that it will convey an impression to others which it is in his interests to convey. ...

Of the two kinds of communication – expressions given and expressions given off – this report will be primarily concerned with the latter, with the more theatrical and contextual kind, the non-verbal, presumably unintentional kind, whether this communication be purposely engineered or not. ...

I have said that when an individual appears before others his actions will influence the definition of the situation which they come to have. Sometimes the individual will act in a thoroughly calculating manner, expressing himself in a given way solely in order to give the kind of impression to others that is likely to evoke from them a specific response he is concerned to obtain. Sometimes the individual will be calculating in his activity but be relatively unaware that this is the case. Sometimes he will intentionally and consciously express himself in a particular way, but chiefly because the tradition of his group or social status require this kind of expression and not because of any particular response (other than vague acceptance or approval) that is likely to be evoked from those impressed by the expression. Sometimes the traditions of an individual's role will lead him to give a well-designed impression of a particular kind and yet he may be neither consciously nor unconsciously disposed to create such an impression. The others, in their turn, may be suitably impressed by the individual's efforts to convey something, or may misunderstand the situation and come to conclusions that are warranted neither by the individual's intent nor by the facts. In any case, in so far as the others act *as if* the individual had conveyed a particular impression, we may take a functional or pragmatic view and say that the individual has 'effectively' projected a given definition of the situation and 'effectively' fostered the understanding that a given state of affairs obtains.

There is one aspect of the others' response that bears special comment here. Knowing that the individual is likely to present himself in a light that is favourable to him, the others may divide what they witness into two parts: a part that is relatively easy for the individual to manipulate at will, being chiefly his verbal assertions, and a part in regard to which he seems to have little concern or control, being chiefly derived from the expressions he gives off. The others may then use what are considered to be the ungovernable aspects of his expressive behaviour as a check upon the validity of what is conveyed by the governable aspects. In this a fundamental asymmetry is demonstrated in the communication process, the individual presumably being aware of only one stream of his communication, the witnesses of this stream and one other. ...

Now given the fact that others are likely to check up on the more controllable aspects of behaviour by means of the less controllable, one can expect that sometimes the individual will try to exploit this very possibility, guiding the impression he makes through behaviour felt to be reliably informing.[2] For example, in gaining admission to a tight social circle, the participant observer may not only wear an accepting look while listening to an informant, but may also be careful to wear the same look when observing the informant talking to others; observers of the observer will then not as easily discover where he actually stands. A specific illustration may be cited from Shetland Isle. When a neighbour dropped in to have a cup of tea, he would ordinarily wear at least a hint of an expectant warm smile as he passed through the door into the cottage. Since lack of physical obstructions outside the cottage and lack of light within it usually made it possible to observe the visitor unobserved as he approached the house, islanders sometimes took pleasure in watching the visitor drop whatever expression he was manifesting and replace it with a sociable one just before reaching the door. However, some visitors, in appreciating that this examination was occurring, would blindly adopt a social face a long distance from the house, thus ensuring the projection of a constant image.

This kind of control upon the part of the individual reinstates the symmetry of the communication process, and sets the stage for a kind of information game – a potentially infinite cycle of concealment, discovery, false revelation, and rediscovery. It should be added that since the others are likely to be relatively unsuspicious of the presumably unguided aspect of the individual's conduct, he can gain much by controlling it. The others of course may sense that the individual is manipulating the presumably spontaneous aspects of his behaviour, and seek in this very act of manipulation some shading of conduct that the individual has not managed to control. This again provides a check upon the individual's behaviour, this time his presumably uncalculated behaviour, thus re-establishing the asymmetry of the communication process. Here I would like only to add the suggestion that the arts of piercing an individual's effort at calculated unintentionality seem better developed than our capacity to manipulate our own behaviour, so that regardless of how many steps have occurred in the information game, the witness is likely to have the advantage over the actor, and the initial asymmetry of the communication process is likely to be retained.

When we allow that the individual projects a definition of the situation when he appears before others, we must also see that the others, however passive their role may seem to be, will themselves effectively project a definition of the situation by virtue of their response to the individual and by virtue of any lines of action they initiate to him. Ordinarily the definitions of the situation projected by the several different participants are sufficiently attuned to one another, so that open contraction will not occur. I do not mean that there will be the kind of consensus that arises when each individual present candidly expresses what he really feels and honestly agrees with the expressed feelings of the others present. This kind of harmony is an optimistic ideal and in any case not necessary for the smooth working of society. Rather, each participant is expected to suppress his immediate heartfelt feelings, conveying a view of the situation which he feels the others will be able to find at least temporarily acceptable. The maintenance of this surface of agreement, this veneer of consensus, is facilitated by each participant concealing his own wants behind statements which assert values to which everyone present feels obliged to give lip service.

Notes

1   Here I owe much to an unpublished paper by Tom Burns of the University of Edinburgh. He presents the argument that in all interaction a basic underlying theme is the desire of each participant to guide and control the responses made by the others present. A similar argument has been advanced by Jay Haley in a recent unpublished paper, but in regard to a special kind of control, that having to do with defining the nature of the relationship of those involved in the interaction.

2   The widely read and rather sound writings of Stephen Potter [e.g. *Lifemanship, One-Upmanship*] are concerned in part with signs that can be engineered to give a shrewd observer the apparently incidental cues he needs to discover concealed virtues the gamesman does not in fact possess.

Source: Erving Goffman, *The Presentation of Self in Everyday Life*, 'Introduction', Harmondsworth, Penguin Books, 1971 (pp.13,14,15,16,17–18,19–21). First published in the USA in 1959.

Harold Garfinkel:
'Studies of the routine grounds of everyday activities' (1967)

Making commonplace scenes visible

In accounting for the stable features of everyday activities sociologists commonly select familiar settings such as familial households or work places and ask for the variables that contribute to their stable features. Just as commonly, one set of considerations are unexamined: the socially standardized and standardizing, 'seen but unnoticed', expected, background features of everyday scenes. The member of the society uses background expectancies as a scheme of interpretation. With their use actual appearances are for him recognizable and intelligible as the appearances-of-familiar-events. Demonstrably he is responsive to this background, while at the same time he is at a loss to tell us specifically of what the expectancies consist. When we ask him about them he has little or nothing to say.

For these background expectancies to come into view one must either be a stranger to the 'life as usual' character of everyday scenes, or become estranged from them. As Alfred Schutz pointed out, a 'special motive' is required to make them problematic. In the sociologists' case this 'special motive' consists in the programmatic task of treating a societal member's practical circumstances, which include from the member's point of view the morally necessary character of many of its background features, as matters of theoretic interest. The seen but unnoticed backgrounds of everyday activities are made visible and are described from a perspective in which persons live out the lives they do, have the children they do, feel the feelings, think the thoughts, enter the relationships they do, all in order to permit the sociologist to solve his theoretical problems.

Almost alone among sociological theorists, the late Alfred Schutz, in a series of classical studies[1] of the constitutive phenomenology of the world of everyday life, described many of these seen but unnoticed background expectancies. He called them the 'attitude of daily life'. He referred to their scenic attributions as the 'world known in common and taken for granted'. Schutz' fundamental work makes it possible to pursue further the tasks of clarifying their nature and operation, of relating them to the processes of concerted actions, and assigning them their place in an empirically imaginable society.

The studies reported in this paper attempt to detect some expectancies that lend commonplace scenes their familiar, life-as-usual character, and to relate these to the stable social structures of everyday activities. Procedurally it is my preference to start with familiar scenes and ask what can be done to make trouble. The operations that one would have to perform in order to multiply the senseless features of perceived environments; to produce and sustain bewilderment, consternation, and confusion; to produce the socially structured affects of anxiety, shame, guilt, and indignation; and to produce disorganized interaction should tell us something about how the structures of everyday activities are ordinarily and routinely produced and maintained.[2]

…

Background understandings and 'adequate' recognition of commonplace events

What kinds of expectancies make up a 'seen but unnoticed' background of common understandings, and how are they related to persons' recognition of stable courses of interpersonal transactions? …

Undergraduate students were assigned the task of spending from fifteen minutes to an hour in their homes viewing its activities while assuming that they were boarders in the household. They were instructed not to act out the assumption. Thirty-three students reported their experiences.

…

Students reported that this way of looking was difficult to sustain. Familiar objects – persons obviously, but furniture and room arrangements as well – resisted students' efforts to think of themselves as strangers. Many became uncomfortably aware of how habitual movements were being made; of *how* one was handling the silverware, or *how* one opened a door or greeted another member. Many reported that the attitude was difficult to sustain because with it quarreling, bickering, and hostile motivations became discomfitingly visible. Frequently an account that recited newly visible troubles was accompanied by the student's assertion that his account of family problems was not a 'true' picture; the family was *really* a very happy one. Several students reported a mildly oppressive feeling of 'conforming to a part'. Several students attempted to formulate the 'real me' as activities governed by rules of conduct but gave it up as a bad job. They found it more convincing to think of themselves in 'usual' circumstances as 'being one's real self'. Nevertheless one student was intrigued with how deliberately and successfully he could predict the other's responses to his actions. He was not troubled by this feeling.

Many accounts reported a variation on the theme: 'I was glad when the hour was up and I could return to the real me.'

…

In another procedure students were asked to spend from fifteen minutes to an hour in their homes imagining that they were boarders and acting out this assumption. They were instructed to conduct themselves in a circumspect and polite fashion. They were to avoid getting personal, to use formal address, to speak only when spoken to.

…

… [F]amily members were stupefied. They vigorously sought to make the strange actions intelligible and to restore the situation to normal appearances. Reports were filled with accounts of astonishment, bewilderment, shock, anxiety, embarrassment, and anger, and with charges by various family members that the student was mean, inconsiderate, selfish, nasty, or impolite. Family members demanded explanations: What's the matter? What's gotten into you? Did you get fired? Are you sick? What are you being so superior about? Why are you mad? Are you out of your mind or are you just stupid? One student acutely embarrassed his mother in front of her friends by asking if she minded if he had a snack from the refrigerator. 'Mind if you have a little snack? You've been eating little snacks around here for years without asking me. What's gotten into you?' One mother, infuriated when her daughter spoke to her only when she was spoken to, began to shriek in angry denunciation of the daughter for her disrespect and insubordination and refused to be calmed by the student's sister. A father berated his daughter for being insufficiently concerned for the welfare of others and of acting like a spoiled child.

Occasionally family members would first treat the student's action as a cue for a joint comedy routine which was soon replaced by irritation and exasperated anger at the student for not knowing when enough was enough. Family members mocked the 'politeness' of the students – 'Certainly Mr. Herzberg!' – or charged the student with acting like a wise guy and generally reproved the 'politeness' with sarcasm.

Explanations were sought in previous, understandable motives of the student: the student was 'working too hard' in school; the student was 'ill'; there had been 'another fight' with a fiancee. When offered explanations by family members went unacknowledged, there followed withdrawal by the offended member, attempted isolation of the culprit, retaliation, and denunciation. 'Don't bother with him, he's in one of his moods again'; 'Pay no attention but just wait until he asks me for something'; 'You're cutting me, okay I'll cut you and then some'; 'Why must you always create friction in our family harmony?' Many accounts reported versions of the following confrontation. A father followed his son into the bedroom. 'Your Mother is right. You don't look well and you're not talking sense. You had better get another job that doesn't require such late hours.' To this the student replied that he appreciated the consideration, but that he felt fine and only wanted a little privacy. The father responded in a high rage, 'I don't want any more of *that* out of *you* and if you can't treat your mother decently you'd better move out!'

There were no cases in which the situation was not restorable upon the student's explanation. Nevertheless, for the most part family members were not amused and only rarely did they find the experience instructive as the student argued that it was supposed to have been. After hearing the explanation a sister replied coldly on behalf of a family of four, 'Please, no more of these experiments. We're not rats, you know.' Occasionally an explanation was accepted but still it added offence. In several cases students reported that the explanations left them, their families, or both wondering how much of what the student had said was 'in character' and how much the student 'really meant'.

Notes

1   Alfred Schutz, *Der Sinnhafte Aufbau Der Sozialen Welt* (Wein, Verlag von Julius Springer, 1932); *Collected Papers I: The Problem of Social Reality*, ed. Maurice Natanson (The Hague, Martinus Nijhoff, 1962); *Collected Papers II: Studies in Social Theory*, ed. Arvid Broderson (The Hague, Martinus Nijhoff, 1964); *Collected Papers III: Studies in Phenomenological Philosophy*, ed. I. Schutz (The Hague, Martinus Nijhoff, 1966).

2   Obversely, a knowledge of how the structures of everyday activities are
    routinely produced should permit us to tell how we might proceed for the
    effective production of desired disturbances.

Source: Harold Garfinkel, *Studies in Ethnomethodology*, Ch. 2 'Studies of the routine
grounds of everyday activities', Englewood Cliffs, NJ, Prentice-Hall, 1967 (pp.36–8,
44–5, 46–9).

Christena E. Nippert-Eng:
'Transitional acts as rituals' (1996)

Just before leaving work in the evening, a number of Lab employees have made it a practice to call home. They have ritualized this act to the point where it is now an important part of their transition from work to home. Hellos and good-byes, drinking, eating, clothes-changing and appearance alterations, music listening, and napping all may assume a ritualized, highly predictable role in commuting transformations. At given points in our trips, we rely on these more or less heavily and more or less consciously. They remind us where we are, where we're going, who we must become, and who we must leave behind.

In *The Elementary Forms of the Religious Life* (1965/1912), Emile Durkheim offers a remarkable collection of insights on the transformational importance of ritual. He describes a 'negative cult' of behaviors that separate the profane and sacred realms of social life. These behaviors stem from a variety of taboos and dictums about mixing the objects and classes of people who belong to these different, mutually exclusive and antagonistic realms. We follow these principles to segregate realm-specific elements into distinct spaces and times,[1] creating a mental, behavioral, and spatio-temporal 'abyss' between worlds. This chasm maintains realm integrity by combating the 'polluting' (Douglas 1984/1966), intermingling of their elements.

Rituals, argues Durkheim, function to help people mentally transcend this boundary between sacred and profane ways of thinking and being. Through our actions and focus on the symbolic value of artifacts, we shed a given, realm-specific mentality and embrace another. Rituals, as 'regularly repeated acts,' are absolutely essential for us to 'place ourselves within [a] sphere of action.' Through their repetition, we renew the effects of being in either the sacred or profane states of mind, re-embracing our distanced selves. In other words, rituals help us make the transformations between everyday, profane selves and their special, sacred counterparts.

The segmentation of home and work leads us along a process with amazing parallels to the creation and maintenance of Durkheim's sacred and profane worlds. The boundary work of home and work creates and maintains these more or less distinct, everyday experiential realms just as religious rituals demarcate profane and sacred realms of being. For this reason, we also require visible, tangible, repeated actions to invoke and maintain either the home or work ways of being.

Commuting routines, for instance, bridge home and work. They allow us to leave one cognitive territory and enter another, transforming from oneself to another. These often ritualized actions function as mental bridges between the mentalities that they help trigger and preserve.

In this sense, getting dressed in the morning and changing after work, or consuming certain beverages and foods at different times, are examples of highly significant boundary work. Their appearance during the liminal space and time of the commute is a logical manifestation of our transitional demands. Like the purifying rituals of Durkheim's priests and followers, these acts preserve the integrity of each realm, each territory of the self while allowing us to transcend them. As such, they play a significant role in solving the self-transformation problems posed by life in a highly segmentist culture. Their frequently ritualized enactment indicates just how important and useful these transformational acts can be, which is why we repeat them over and over again.

My primary concern in this work is with personal, ritual*ized*, or ritualistic, actions. These may or may not have the shared, collective meaning traditionally associated with the concept of 'rituals'. Nonetheless, I very much view ritualized action of this nature from the Durkheimian perspective.

Not only do I see such ritualized action as 'a type of critical juncture wherein some pair of opposing social or cultural forces comes together' (Bell, 1992, p.16), but I specifically see it as a place where an *individual's* disparate social forces/realms of action come together and are made sensible. Moreover, a transitional, ritualized action accommodates the mental continuities *and* discontinuities of realms as we cross physical realm borders. It allows us to maintain a certain stability of these categories and self-juxtapositions even as it may help us create new ones.

(Routine behavior, for instance, is particularly important, for it triggers mentalities and reinforces well-established concepts, frameworks, and identities. New, spontaneous behavior, however, challenges understandings/categories/boundaries/selves. If it is repeated, conceptual boundaries may change, along with our understandings of these categories and selves. If a boundary-challenging behavior is immediately abandoned, however, realms and their relationship may remain intact, confirmed and strengthened by this behavioral test.)

Through symbolic activity, then, the combination of mental understandings and physical behavior becomes so much more powerful than either manifestation alone. Ritualized, transitional acts are a synergy of what is mental and physical, symbolic and practical. In fact, for me, any practical, physical, or physiological import these actions possess is superseded by (and is less interesting than) the mental, transcendent function they fulfil. Ritualized, transitional acts are one of the essential forms of boundary work, then, fusing what is cultural and personal, invisible and visible, as we create and maintain the realms of 'home' and 'work'.

Notes

1 See Eviatar Zerubavel's elaboration on the temporal dimension of separating the sacred from the profane in *Hidden Rhythms* (1981).

References

Bell, C. (1992) *Ritual Theory, Ritual Practice*, New York, Oxford University Press.

Douglas, M. (1984) *Purity and Danger: An Analysis of the Concepts of Pollution and Taboo*, London, ARK. First published by Routledge and Kegan Paul, 1966.

Durkheim, E. (1965) *The Elementary Forms of the Religious Life*, New York, The Free Press. First published in 1912.

Zerubavel, E. (1981) *Hidden Rhythms: Schedules and Calendars in Social Life*, Berkeley, CA, University of California Press.

Source: Christena E. Nippert-Eng, *Home and Work: Negotiating Boundaries through Everyday Life*, Ch. 2 'Cognitive engineering: bridging time, space and self', Chicago, IL, The University of Chicago Press, 1996 (pp.145–8).

Richard Hoggart:
'The immediate, the present, the cheerful: fate and luck' (1957)

...

There are many thrifty working-class people today, as there have always been. But in general the immediate and present nature of working-class life puts a premium on the taking of pleasures now, discourages planning for some future goal, or in the light of some ideal. 'Life is no bed of roses', they assume; but 'tomorrow will take care of itself': on this side the working classes have been cheerful existentialists for ages. Even of those who spend a more than usual amount of time worrying about how things are going to 'pan out', it is true to say that their life is one of the immediate present to a degree not often found among other classes.

Wives will still 'slip out' with their purses at 4.30 on many a day to get something for tea. There is little on the shelf and that is for special occasions. But this is not necessarily the living from hand to mouth which indicates poverty; it is not altogether indolence and forgetfulness: it is part of the climate of life; one moves generally from item to item. Wage-packets come in weekly and go out weekly. There are no stocks, shares, bonds, securities, property, trade assets. Someone left a few hundreds as a lump sum will still be called 'rich'. The little payment-books cluttered behind an ornament are marked by the week too, and are usually for 'paying-off'; e.g. for paying-off a debt already incurred – a clothing-check spent, last week's rent. Forms of saving or paying in advance are traditionally for specific purposes, as in the insurances against death or illness; or are usually for short-term if recurrent purposes, as with the payings-in for Christmas or holidays. A mistrust of a more general kind of saving is still quite common; you might 'get knocked down tomorrow', and then what would all the 'scratting and misery' of saving have done for you? And within that remark can be seen the real grounds for mistrust and for the resulting emphasis on making use of the money now. If people wasted nothing and lived with carefully calculated economy, they might be able to save a modest amount. They might, but it is not certain; and the discipline required would be more than most people would think worth while. It would mean a bare, oatmealy sort of life, for very little at the end; life 'wouldn't be worth living'.

This helps to explain two features in the spending of money which members of other classes find particularly difficult to appreciate. First, the way in which working-class people, once their immediate dues have been met, will spend much of the remainder on 'extravagances'. This will often happen even though there may be more money in the house than there has been for years, or than there well may be in a few months more. Second, of habits with money which exasperate or puzzle outsiders, is the order of priority into which working-class people will range the items between which they have to divide their income.

Thus, the replacement of necessary household equipment is likely to rank lower in the scale than it would among the middle classes; sheets are often badly worn and much mended, and towels inadequate in number. This may not be due simply to a shortage of money; the shillings which bought a rather elaborate frame for a photograph on the dresser or a new ornament would have bought an extra pair of towels. And 'keeping a good table' usually means providing meals well-supplied with meat, especially for the man at the head of the house. This is still a common assumption, whether the husband is on heavy or light work. I know many working-class men who would be 'dashed' if they came home and found only one, not two, chops ready for them; or, if there were cold boiled ham, they would expect a quarter of a pound. 'Pleasure' – smoking and drinking, for example – is given a similarly high priority. Pleasures are a central part of life, not something perhaps to be allowed after a great number of other commitments have been met. The importance of each item in this rough financial pattern will vary from family to family; those who reverse the pattern itself are unusual.

Life goes on from day to day and from week to week: the seasons turn over, marked by the great festivals regarded as holidays or beanfeasts, and by an occasional special event – a wedding in the family, a charabanc trip, a funeral, a cup-tie. There is bound to be some planning; a twelve-week Christmas club for presents and extras, perhaps a club for Whitsuntide clothes paid in advance, and, after that, saving for a holiday in some cases. But in general the striking feature is the unplanned nature of life, the moment-to-moment meeting of troubles or taking of pleasure; schemes are mostly short-term.

Socially, also, each day and each week is almost unplanned. There is no diary, no book of engagements, and few letters are sent or received. If a member of the family is away, a weekly letter is somewhat painfully put together on Sunday. Relatives or very close friends who have gone to live away are likely to be communicated with only by Christmas card, unless there is a special family event. But if they come back to live in the area the relationship will be taken up as though it had never been interrupted. And if one-time near neighbours meet by chance in town there will be a good gossip, one which seems just a continuation of its predecessors.

No dates are likely to be made for those few visitors who are on 'dropping-in' terms. A very frequent visitor may say on leaving that he might see them on Tuesday, but this is not regarded as an engagement to visit them, but rather as an indication that until then he will not be able to look in. The appearances of most other people who are on 'dropping-in' terms are likely to be as predictable as the planets.

All these things contribute to a view of life among working-class people which can from some angles look like a kind of hedonism, which finds life largely acceptable so long as the big worries (debt, drink, sickness) keep away, and so long as there is adequate scope for 'having a good time'. But it is a mild hedonism, one informed by a more deeply rooted sense – that the big and long-distanced rewards are not for them. At a first hearing, 'why worry?' may seem to suggest a trivial attitude; but only those who expect to have to worry a lot would coin such a phrase and use it so frequently. And so with all the other phrases of this type – 'Always look on the bright side', 'keep smiling', 'a little of what y'fancy does y'good', 'life i'n't worth living without a bit of fun', 'make the most of each day', 'we 'av'n't much money but we do see life'. Conversely, there is the dislike of meanness and tight-fistedness – 'Ah '*ate* mean fowks', and ''E's as mean as muck'.

Source: Richard Hoggart, *The Uses of Literacy: Aspects of Working-class Life with Special Reference to Publications and Entertainments*, Ch. 5 'The full rich life', Harmondsworth, Penguin Books, 1958 (first published by Chatto & Windus, 1957) (pp.132–6).

Dorothy E. Smith:
'The everyday world as problematic: the standpoint of women' (1988)

The standpoint of women therefore directs us to an 'embodied' subject located in a particular actual local historical setting. Her world presents itself to her in its full particularity – the books on her shelves, the Cowichan sweaters she has bought for her sons' birthdays, the Rainforest chair she bought three years ago in a sale, the portable computer she is using to write on, the eighteenth-century chair, made of long-since-exhausted Caribbean mahogany, one of a set of four given her by her mother years ago – each is particularized by insertion into her biography and projects as well as by its immediacy in the now in which she writes. The abstracted constructions of discourse or bureaucracy are accomplishments in and of her everyday world. Her reading and writing are done in actual locations at actual times and under definite material conditions. Though discourse, bureaucracy, and the exchange of money for commodities create forms of social relations that transcend the local and particular, they are constituted, created, and practiced always *within* the local and particular. It is the special magic of the ubiquity of text and its capacity to manifest itself as the same in diverse multiple settings that provide for the local practices of transcendence.

A standpoint in the everyday world is the fundamental grounding of modes of knowing developed in a ruling apparatus. The ruling apparatus is that familiar complex of management, government administration, professions, and intelligentsia, as well as the textually mediated discourses that coordinate and interpenetrate it. Its special capacity is the organization of particular actual places, persons, and events into generalized and abstracted modes vested in categorial systems, rules, laws, and conceptual practices. The former thereby become subject to an abstracted and universalized system of ruling mediated by texts. A mode of ruling has been created that transcends local particularities but at the same time exists only in them. The ruling apparatus of this loosely coordinated collection of varied sites of power has been largely if not exclusively the sphere of men. From within its textual modes the embodied subject and the everyday world as its site are present only as object and never as subject's standpoint. But from the standpoint of women whose work has served to complete the invisibility of the actual as the locus of the subject, from the standpoint of she who stands at the beginning of her work, the grounding of an abstracted conceptual organization of ruling comes into view as a product in and of the everyday world.

Sociology is part of the ruling apparatus. Its relevances and subtending organization are given by the relation of the ruling apparatus to the social world it governs. The institutional forms of ruling constitute its major topics – the sociology of organizations, of education, of health, of work, of mental illness, of deviance, of law, of knowledge, and the like. The organization of sociological thinking and knowledge is articulated to this institutional structure. It pioneers methods of thinking and the systematics of articulating particular actualities to a generalized conceptual order that serves it. To a significant extent, sociology has been busy clarifying, organizing, mapping, and extending the relations of the institutional forms of ruling to the actualities of their domains.

Women's lives have been outside or subordinate to the ruling apparatus. Its conceptual practices do not work for us in the development of a sociological consciousness of our own. The grid of political sociology, the sociology of the family, of organizations, of mental illness, of education, and so forth, does not map the unknown that extends before us as what is to be discovered and explored; it does not fit when we ask how we should organize a sociology beginning from the standpoint of women. We start, as we must, with women's experience (for what other resource do we have?); the available concepts and frameworks do not work because they have already posited a subject situated outside a local and actual experience, a particularized knowledge of the world. Women are readily made the objects of sociological study precisely because they have not been its subjects. Beneath the apparent gender neutrality of the impersonal or absent subject of an objective sociology is the reality of the masculine author of the texts of its tradition and his membership in the circle of men participating in the division of the labor of ruling. The problem confronted here is how to do a sociology that is for women and that takes women as its subjects and its knowers when the methods of thinking, which we have learned as sociologists as the methods of producing recognizable sociological texts, reconstruct us as objects.

If we begin where people are actually located in that independently existing world outside texts, we begin in the particularities of an actual everyday world. As a first step in entering that standpoint into a textually mediated discourse, we constitute the everyday world as our problematic. We do so by interesting ourselves in its opacity for we cannot understand how it is organized or comes about by remaining within it. The concept of problematic transfers this opacity to the level of discourse. It directs attention to a possible set of questions that have yet to be posed or of puzzles that are not yet formulated as such but are 'latent' in the actualities of our experienced worlds. The problematic of the everyday world is an explicit discursive formulation of an actual property of the organization of the everyday world. I am talking about a reality as it arises for those who live it – the reality, for example, that effects arise that do not originate in it. Yet *I am talking* (or rather writing) about it. I am entering it into discourse. The term 'problematic' enters an actual aspect of the organization of the everyday world (as it is ongoingly produced by actual individuals) into a systematic inquiry. It responds to our practical ignorance of the determinations of our local worlds so long as we look for them within their limits. In this sense the puzzle or puzzles are really there. Hence an inquiry defined by such a problematic addresses a problem of how we are related to the worlds we live in. We may not experience our ignorance as such, but we are nonetheless ignorant.

The problematic, located by our ignorance of how our everyday worlds are shaped and determined by relation and forces external to them, must not be taken to imply that we are dopes or dupes. Within our everyday worlds, we are expert practitioners of their quiddity, of the way they are just the way they are. Our everyday worlds are in part our own accomplishments, and our special and expert knowledge is continually demonstrated in their ordinary familiarity and unsurprising ongoing presence. But how they are knitted into the extended social relations of a contemporary capitalist economy and society is not discoverable with them. The relations among multiple everyday worlds and the accomplishment of those relations within them create a dynamic organization that, in the context of contemporary capitalism, continually feeds change through to our local experience. In the research context this means that so far as their everyday worlds are concerned, we rely entirely on what women tell us, what people tell us, about what they do and what happens. But we cannot rely upon them for an understanding of the relations that shape and determine the everyday. Here then is our business as social scientists for the investigation of these relations and the exploration of the ways they are present in the everyday are and must be a specialized enterprise, a work, the work of a social scientist.

Source: Dorothy E. Smith, *The Everyday World as Problematic: A Feminist Sociology*, Pt 2 Finding and Writing a Sociology for Women, Ch. 3 'The everyday world as problematic: a feminist methodology', Milton Keynes, Open University Press, 1988 (pp.108–10).

Rita Felski:
'The invention of everyday life' (1999–2000)

Habit

The temporality of everyday life and its spatial anchoring are closely connected. Both repetition and home address an essential feature of everyday life: its familiarity. The everyday is synonymous with habit, sameness, routine; it epitomises both the comfort and boredom of the ordinary. Lefebvre writes: 'The modern … stands for what is novel, brilliant, paradoxical … it is (apparently) daring, and transitory', whereas 'the quotidian is what is humble and solid, what is taken for granted … undated and (apparently) insignificant' (Lefebvre, 1984, p.24).

The idea of habit crystallises this experience of dailiness. Habit describes not simply an action but an attitude: habits are often carried out in a semi-automatic, distracted, or involuntary manner. Certain forms of behaviour are inscribed upon the body, part of a deeply ingrained somatic memory. We drive to work, buy groceries, or type a routine letter in a semi-conscious, often dream-like state. Our bodies go through the motions while our minds are elsewhere. Particular habits may be intentionally cultivated or may build up imperceptibly over time. In either case, they often acquire a life of their own, shaping us as much as we shape them.

…

Phenomenological studies of everyday life are, by contrast, much less censorious of habit. Indeed, they suggest that everyday life is self-evident and that this is necessary rather than unfortunate. Everyday life simply *is* the routine act of conducting one's day-to-day existence without making it an object of conscious attention. 'The reality of everyday life is taken-for-granted *as* reality. It does not require additional verification over and beyond its simple presence. It is simply *there*, as self-evident and compelling facticity. I *know* that it is real. While I am capable of engaging in doubts about its reality, I am obliged to suspend such doubt as I routinely exist in everyday life' (Berger and Luckmann, 1967, p.37).

In other words, everyday life is the sphere of what Schutz calls the natural attitude. This does not mean that the forms of everyday life are inevitable or unchanging. Long before the current interest in gender as performance, ethnographers such as Goffman were describing the performance of self in daily life and noting the socially constructed and conventional nature of our identities. The point is, however, that such performances are for the most part automatic, conducted with a constant, but semi-conscious vigilance. Unless a specific problem emerges to demand our attention, we rarely pause to reflect upon the mundane ritualised practices around which much of our everyday life is organised. As Schutz and Luckmann point out, 'our natural attitude of daily life is pervasively determined by a *pragmatic motive*' (Schutz and Luckmann, 1983, p.6).

...

... [H]abit is not something we can ever hope to transcend. Rather it constitutes an essential part of our embeddedness in everyday life and our existence as social beings. For example, the contemporary city may constitute a chaotic labyrinth of infinite possibilities, yet in our daily travels we often choose to carve out a familiar path, managing space and time by tracing out the same route again and again. Furthermore, habit is not opposed to individuality but intermeshed with it; our identity is formed out of a distinctive blend of behavioural and emotional patterns, repeated over time. To be suddenly deprived of the rhythm of one's personal routines, as often happens to those admitted to hospitals, prisons, retirement homes or other large institutions, can be a source of profound disorientation and distress. Furthermore, even the most esoteric and elevated of activities contain routinised elements. Lefebvre notes that no cultural practice escapes the everyday: science, war, affairs of state, philosophy all contain a mundane dimension (Lefebvre, 1961, p.61).

...

Making peace with the everyday

In conclusion I want to draw together the various threads of my argument and to elaborate on its implications. How useful is the idea of everyday life? What exactly does it mean? How should it be applied? While much of my paper has focused on the contrasting definitions of everyday life in sociology and cultural studies, I now want to make more explicit connections to feminist scholarship.

Feminism has, of course, traditionally conceived itself as a politics of everyday life. In practice, this has meant very different things. On the one hand feminists have deployed a hermeneutics of suspicion vis-à-vis the everyday, showing how the most mundane, taken-for-granted activities – conversation, housework, body language, styles of dress – serve to reinforce patriarchal norms. The feminist gaze reveals the everyday world as problematic, in Dorothy Smith's (1988) phrase; it is here, above all, that gender hierarchy is reproduced, invisibly, pervasively and over time. This sensitivity to the power dynamics of everyday life has been heightened by the impact of poststructuralist thought, with its suspicion of any form of fixity. As a result, much current feminist scholarship is involved in a persistent questioning of the commonsensical, taken-for-granted and mundane.

On the other hand, everyday life has also been hailed as a distinctively female sphere and hence as a source of value. The fact that women traditionally cook, clean, change diapers, raise children and do much of the routine work of family reproduction is perceived by some feminists as a source of strength. Because of this grounding in the mundane, it is argued, women have a more realistic sense of how the world actually operates and are less estranged from their bodies and from the messy, chaotic, embodied realities of life. Thus, from the perspective of feminist standpoint theory, women's connection to daily life is something to be celebrated. Here everyday life is not a ruse of patriarchy but rather a sign of women's grounding in the practical world.

My discussion has shown, I hope, that this ambivalence has a history, that everyday life has long been subject to intense and conflicting emotional investments. Without wishing to deny the new insights generated by feminism, I would suggest that it also continues a tradition of thought that has viewed the everyday as both the most authentic and the most inauthentic of spheres. It is in this context that one can speak of the invention of everyday life. In one sense the phrase sounds paradoxical, precisely because daily life refers to the most mundane, routine, overlooked aspects of human experience – those seemingly beyond the reach of invention, abstraction and theory. Yet I have tried to show that everyday life is not simply a neutral label for a pre-existing reality, but is freighted down with layers of meanings and associations.

One of these associations is, of course, gender. I have explored some of the ways in which everyday life has been connected to women, without simply endorsing the view that women represent daily life. The problem with this view, as the work of Lefebvre makes particularly clear, is that it presents a romantic view of both everyday life and women by associating them with the natural, authentic and primitive. This nostalgia feeds into a long chain of dichotomies – society versus community, modernity versus tradition, public versus private – which do not help us to understand the social organisation of gender and which deny women's contemporaneity, self-consciousness and agency. Furthermore, to affirm women's special grounding in everyday life is to take at face value a mythic ideal of heroic male transcendence and to ignore the fact that men are also embodied, embedded subjects, who live, for the most part, repetitive, familiar and ordinary lives.

What I have found helpful in the phenomenological scholarship is that it takes seriously the ordinariness of everyday life without idealising or demonising it. Within cultural studies, everyday life is often made to carry enormous symbolic weight. Either it is rhapsodically affirmed and painted in glowing colours or it is excoriated as the realm of ultimate alienation and dehumanisation. Yet if the everyday is an indispensable aspect of all human lives, as I have argued, it becomes harder to endow it with an intrinsic political content. The everyday is robbed of much of its portentous symbolic meaning.

Thus it makes more sense to think of the everyday as a way of experiencing the world rather than as a circumscribed set of activities within the world. Everyday life simply is the process of becoming acclimatised to assumptions, behaviours and practices which come to seem self-evident and taken for granted. In other words, everydayness is not an intrinsic quality that magically adheres to particular actions or persons (women, the working class). Rather, it is a lived process of routinisation that all individuals experience. ...

Such routinisation may be politically problematic or even dangerous in some contexts, but it is surely a mistake to see habit as such as intrinsically reactionary. The work of Heller and Schutz is valuable in affirming the pragmatic need for repetition, familiarity and taken-for-grantedness in everyday life, as a necessary precondition for human survival. As Susan Bordo [1990] points out in another context, it is an intellectual delusion to think that we can simply abandon our habits, blindspots and assumptions and embrace an infinitely shifting, self-undermining multiplicity of perspectives. This belief is a delusion because such habits form the very basis of who we are. Influenced by modernist ideals of innovation and irony, contemporary theorists have tended either to excoriate the everyday for its routine, mundane qualities, or to celebrate the everyday while pretending that such qualities do not exist. It is time, perhaps, to make peace with the ordinariness of daily life.

References

Berger, P. and Luckmann, T. (1967) *The Social Construction of Reality: A Treatise in the Sociology of Knowledge*, Harmondsworth, Penguin Books.

Bordo, S. (1990) 'Feminism, postmodernism and gender-skepticism' in Nicholson, L. (ed.) *Feminism/Postmodernism*, New York, Routledge.

Lefebvre, H. (1961) *Critique de la vie quotidienne, vol. 2*, Paris, L'Arche.

Lefebvre, H. (1984) *Everyday Life in the Modern World*, New York, Transaction.

Schutz, A. and Luckmann, T. (1983) *The Structures of the Life-World*, vol. 1, Evanston, IL, Northwestern University Press.

Smith, D.E. (1988) *The Everyday World as Problematic: A Feminist Sociology*, Milton Keynes, Open University Press.

Source: Rita Felski 'The invention of everyday life', *New Formations*, no.39 'Cool Moves', Winter 1999–2000 (pp.15,26,27,28,30–31).

Roger Silverstone:
'Television, ontology and the transitional object: routines, rituals, traditions, myths' (1994)

> If the subject cannot be grasped save through the reflexive constitution of daily activities in social practices, we cannot understand the mechanics of personality apart from the routines of day-to-day life … Routine is integral both to the continuity of the personality of the agent, as he or she moves along the paths of daily activities, and to the institution of society, which *are* such only through their continued reproduction.
>
> (Giddens, 1984, p.60)

Routines, rituals, traditions, myths, these are the stuff of social order and everyday life. Within the familiar and taken for granted, as well as through the heightened and the dramatic, our lives take shape and within those shapes, spatially and temporally grounded and signified, we attempt to go about our business, avoiding or managing, for the most part, the traumas and the catastrophes that threaten to disturb our peace and our sanity. It is not always easy. Not only are we faced with the persistent contradictions and irresolvable challenges of daily life – problems of death, identity, morality – but the bases on which our security is grounded shift with each twist of the modern or post-modern screw; with industrialisation and post-industrialisation, with shifts in population, social structure, technology and cultural values. These shifts and their ontological effects have been much discussed in recent years (Lasch, 1977; Berger *et al.,* 1974; Ignatieff, 1984). Significant among prime causes are, it is often argued, the media, above all television (Postman, 1987; Mander, 1978).

But, for most of us most of the time, everyday life does go on, and it is sustained through the ordered continuities of language, routine, habit, the taken for granted but essential structures that, in all their contradictions, sustain the grounds for our security in our daily lives. These comments may seem jejune. They are nevertheless central to our understanding of the place of the media, not just as disturbers (their most common characterisation), but also as sustainers, of social reality. …

Ontological security is sustained through the familiar and the predictable. Our commonsense attitudes and beliefs express and sustain our practical understandings of the world, without which life would quickly become intolerable. Common sense is sustained by practical knowledge and expressed and supported by a whole range of symbols and symbolic formations. The symbols of daily life: the everyday sights and sounds of natural language and familiar culture; the publicly broadcast media texts on billboards, in newspapers, on television; the highly charged and intense private and public rituals in domestic or national rites of passage or international celebrations; all these symbols, in their continuity, their drama and their ambiguity, are also bids for control (see Martin, 1981, p.70, on working-class culture). Defensive or offensive, they are our attempts, as social beings, to manage nature, to manage others, and to manage ourselves. They have their roots in the individual's experience of the basic contradictions of social life; the independence–dependence, identity–difference problem which Winnicott analyses; and they also have their roots in the collective experience of sociality, in the demands of co-presence or face-to-face interaction (Goffman, 1969), in the emotional charge of the sacred (Durkheim, 1971) and in the demands of and for structure expressed in all our cultural forms, prototypically in myth (Lévi-Strauss, 1968) and ritual (Turner, 1969).

...

The routines and rhythms of everyday life are multiply structured in time and space. The daily patterns of work and leisure, of getting up and going to bed, of housework and homework: the clock times, free and indentured, are themselves embedded in the times of biography and the life-cycle, and in the times of institutions and of societies themselves – the *longue durée,* slow and glacial (Scannell, 1988, p.15). Everyday life is the product of all these temporalities, but it is in the first, in the experienced routines and rhythms of the day, that time is felt, lived and secured. And time is secured in the equally differentiated and ordered spaces of everyday life: the public and the private spaces; the front-stages and the back-stages; the spaces of gender and generation, domesticity and community.

References

Berger, P., Berger, B. and Kellner, H. (1974) *The Homeless Mind: Modernization and Consciousness*, Harmondsworth, Penguin Books.

Durkheim, E. (1971) *The Elementary Forms of the Religious Life*, London, George Allen & Unwin.

Giddens, A. (1984) *The Constitution of Society*, Cambridge, Polity Press.

Goffman, E. (1969) *The Presentation of Self in Everyday Life*, Harmondsworth, Penguin Books.

Ignatieff, M. (1984) *The Needs of Strangers*, London, Chatto and Windus.

Lasch, C. (1977) *Haven in Heartless World*, New York, Basic Books.

Lévi-Strauss, C. (1968) *Structural Anthropology*, Harmondsworth, Penguin Books.

Mander, J. (1978) *Four Arguments for the Elimination of Television*, Brighton, Harvester.

Martin, B. (1981) *A Sociology of Contemporary Cultural Change*, Oxford, Blackwell.

Postman, N. (1987) *Amusing Ourselves to Death*, London, Methuen.

Scannell, P. (1988) 'Radio times: the temporal arrangements of broadcasting in the modern world' in Drummond, P. and Paterson, R. (eds) *Television and its Audience: International Research Perspectives*, London, British Film Institute.

Turner, V.W. (1969) *The Ritual Process*, London, Routledge and Kegan Paul.

Source: Roger Silverstone, *Television and Everyday Life*, , Ch. 1 'Television, ontology and the transitional object', London, Routledge, 1994 (pp.18–19,20).

Pierre Bourdieu:
'Class tastes and lifestyles: the choice of the necessary' (1979)

The principle of the most important differences in the order of lifestyle and, even more, of the 'stylization of life' lies in the variations in objective and subjective distance from the world, with its material constraints and temporal urgencies. Like the aesthetic disposition which is one dimension of it, the distant, detached or casual disposition towards the world or other people, a disposition which can scarcely be called subjective since it is objectively internalized, can only be constituted in conditions of existence that are relatively freed from urgency. The submission to necessity which inclines working-class people to a pragmatic, functionalist 'aesthetic', refusing the gratuity and futility of formal exercises and of every form of art for art's sake, is also the principle of all the choices of daily existence and of an art of living which rejects specifically aesthetic intentions as aberrations.[1]

Thus manual workers say more often than all the other classes that they like interiors that are clean and tidy and easy to maintain,[2] or the 'value for money' clothes which economic necessity assigns to them in any case. The doubly prudent choice of a garment that is both 'simple' ('versatile', 'all-purpose'), i.e., as little marked and as unrisky as possible ('no-nonsense', 'practical'), and 'good value for money', i.e., cheap and long-lasting, no doubt presents itself as the most reasonable strategy, given, on the one hand, the economic and cultural capital (not to mention time) that can be invested in buying clothes and, on the other hand, the symbolic profits that can be expected from such an investment (at least at work – unlike clerical workers, for example).

...

Thus, although working-class practices may seem to be deduced directly from their economic conditions, since they ensure a saving of money, time and effort that would in any case be of low profitability, they stem from a choice of the necessary ('That's not for us'), both in the sense of what is technically necessary, 'practical' (or, as others would say, functional), i.e., needed in order to 'get by', to do 'the proper thing and no more', and of what is imposed by an economic and social necessity condemning 'simple', 'modest' people to 'simple', 'modest' tastes. The adjustment to the objective chances which is inscribed in the dispositions constituting the habitus is the source of all the realistic choices which, based on the renunciation of symbolic profits that are in any case inaccessible, reduce practices or objects to their technical function, a 'short back-and-sides' or 'quick trim-up' at the barber's, 'a simple little dress', 'solid' furniture etc. Thus nothing is more alien to working-class women than the typically bourgeois idea of making each object in the home the occasion for an aesthetic choice, of extending the intention of harmony or beauty even into the bathroom or kitchen, places strictly defined by their function, or of involving specifically aesthetic criteria in the choice of a saucepan or cupboard. Festive meals and 'Sunday best' clothes are opposed to everyday meals and clothes by the arbitrariness of a conventional division – 'doing things properly' – just as the rooms socially designated for 'decoration', the sitting room, the dining room or living room, are opposed to everyday places, that is, by an antithesis which is more or less that of the 'decorative' and the 'practical', and they are decorated in accordance with established conventions, with knick-knacks on the mantelpiece, a forest scene over the sideboard, flowers on the table, without any of these obligatory choices implying decisions or a search for effect.

This conventionalism, which is also that of popular photography, concerned to fix conventional poses in the conventional compositions (see Bourdieu *et al.*, 1965, pp.54–64), is the opposite of bourgeois formalism and of all the forms of art for art's sake recommended by manuals of graceful living and women's magazines, the art of entertaining, the art of the table, the art of motherhood. In addition to providing a form of basic security in a world in which there can be hardly any assurance, the choice of 'doing the proper thing' or 'the done thing' (the vendors of domestic goods understand the power of 'It's the done thing' over working-class insecurity) has a natural place in an economy of practices based on the search for the 'practical' and the refusal of 'frills' and 'fancy nonsense' (see Delsaut, 1975).

Even the choices which, from the standpoint of the dominant norms, appear as the most 'irrational' are grounded in the taste of necessity – plus, of course, the entirely negative effect of the absence of information and specific competence which results from the lack of cultural capital. For example, the taste for the trinkets and knick-knacks which adorn mantelpiece and hallways is inspired by an intention unknown to economists and ordinary aesthetes, that of obtaining maximum 'effect' ('It'll make a terrific effect') at minimum cost, a formula which for bourgeois taste is the very definition of vulgarity (one of the intentions of distinction being to suggest with the fewest 'effects' possible the greatest expenditure of time, money and ingenuity). What is the 'gaudy' and the 'tawdry', if not that which creates a big effect for a small price, the 'follies' that are only permissible so long as you can say to yourself, 'They were almost given away'? Street hawkers and sales-promotion specialists know that they must release the brakes and censorships which forbid 'extravagances' by presenting the forbidden goods as 'bargains' – the unfashionable settee which, if you can forget the colour and just think of the price, is exactly the one you had always wanted 'to go in front of the TV', or the unwearable nylon dress you ended up buying because it was reduced in the sale, though you had 'sworn you would never again wear nylon.'

And if it still needed to be proved that resignation to necessity is the basis of the taste of necessity, one only has to consider the waste of time and energy resulting from the refusal to subject the daily management of domestic life to the constraints of rational calculation and formal life-principles ('a place for everything', 'everything in its time' etc.), which only apparently contradicts the refusal to devote time and care to health ('molly-coddling yourself') or beauty ('getting dolled up'). In fact, in these two features of their life-style, working-class women, doubly dominated, show that they do not set sufficient value on their trouble and their time, the only things they can spend (and give) without counting, to be concerned about sparing and saving them, or, to put it another way, that they do not value themselves sufficiently (and they do indeed have a low value on the labour market, unlike bourgeois women with their skilled labour-power and cultivated bodies) to grant themselves a care and attention which always imply a certain indulgence and to devote to their bodies the incessant care, concern and attention that are needed to achieve and maintain health, slimness and beauty.[3]

Notes

1   It is no doubt the same 'realism' which excludes from political or union action everything which might give it a purely symbolic air as regards the means used (in contrast to the exhibitionism of student demonstrations) and especially the goals pursued.

2   The members of the working classes, like the members of dominated ethnic groups, may make it a point of honour to belie the image that the dominant have of their class. Thus the working-class cult of cleanness or honesty ('poor but honest'), like some forms of conspicuous sobriety, no doubt owes something to the concern to belie bourgeois prejudice. The same intention of rehabilitation underlies the discourse designed to persuade oneself that 'all we lack is money' (and not taste) and that 'if we had the wherewithal, we'd know what to buy' (or 'how to dress properly').

3   This would explain the image that working-class women have of feminist demands.

References

Bourdieu, P. *et al.* (1965) *Un art moyen: sur les usages sociaux de la photographie*, Paris, Minuit.

Delsaut, Y. (1975) 'L'économie du langage populaire', *Actes*, 4, pp.33–40.

Source: Pierre Bourdieu, *Distinction: A Social Critique of the Judgement of Taste* (trans. R. Nice), Part III: Class Tastes and Life-Styles, London, Routledge and Kegan Paul, 1984 (pp.376–80). First published in France in 1979.

Acknowledgements

Grateful acknowledgement is made to the following sources for permission to reproduce material in this book:

Text

Reading 1.1: Hareven, T.K. (1993) Chapter 5 'The home and the family in historical perspective', *Home: A Place in the World*, Arien Mack (ed.), New York University Press; *Reading 1.2:* Dolores Hayden (ed.), *The Grand Domestic Revolution: A History of Feminist Designs for American Homes, Neighborhoods and Cities*, 'Domestic evolution or domestic revolution?' (MIT Press, 1982); *Reading 1.3:* Bennett, T. *et al.* (1999) Chapter 2 'Cultural choice and the home', *Accounting for Tastes: Australian Everyday Cultures*, Cambridge University Press; *Reading 1.4:* Morley, D. (2000) Chapter 2 'Heimat, modernity and exile: at home in the Heimat', *Home Territories: Media, Mobility and Identity*, Taylor & Francis/Routledge. Reproduced by permission of Taylor & Francis, Inc./ Routledge, Inc; *Reading 1.5:* Felski, R. (1999) 'The invention of everyday life', *New Formations*, Cool Moves, Lawrence and Wishart, London; *Reading 2.1:* Pearce, L. and Stacey, L. (eds) (1995) 'The heart of the matter: feminists revisit romance', in *Romance Revisited*, Lawrence & Wishart, London; *Reading 2.2:* Reprinted by permission of Sage Publications Ltd from Lindholm, C. (1999) 'Love and structure', in Featherstone, M. (ed.) *Love and Eroticism.* Copyright © Theory, Culture & Society 1999; *Reading 2.3:* Beck, U. and Beck-Gernsheim, E. (1995) *The Normal Chaos of Love*, translated by Mark Ritter and Jane Wiebel, Polity Press, © Suhrkamp Verlag Frankfurt am Main 1990; *Reading 3.1:* Reprinted with the permission of The Free Press, a Division of Simon & Schuster, Inc., from *The Sociology of Georg Simmel*, translated and edited by Kurt H. Wolff. Copyright © 1950, copyright renewed 1978 by The Free Press; *Reading 3.2:* Whyte, W.F. (1981) Extracts from 'The gang and the individual – 1943', *Street Corner Society: The Social Structure of an Italian Slum*, 3rd edn, University of Chicago Press; *Reading 3.3:* Watt, P. and Stenson, K. (1998) Extracts from 'The street: "It's a bit dodgy around there"', *Cool Places: Geographies of Youth Cultures*, Skelton, T. and Valentine, G. (eds) Taylor & Francis/Routledge, Reproduced by permission of Taylor & Francis, Inc./Routledge, Inc.; *Reading 3.4:* Anderson, E. (1990) Extracts from 'Street etiquette and street wisdom', *Streetwise: Race, Class, and Change in an Urban Community*, University of Chicago Press; *Reading 3.5:* Donald, J. (1999) Extracts from 'Rationality and enchantment: Paris', *Imagining the Modern City*, The Athlone Press Limited; *Reading 4.1:* Lefebvre, H. (1971) in trans. Rabinovitch, S. 'An inquiry and some discoveries', *Everyday Life in the Modern World*, Allen Lane The Penguin Press/Editions Gallimard. © Sacha Rabinovitch, 1971; *Reading 4.2:* Sweet, M. (2000) 'Chucked out your chintz?',

The Independent Magazine. 2 September 2000. Independent Newspapers Limited; *Reading 4.3:* de Certeau, M. *et.al.* (1998) 'Gesture sequences', in Giard, L. (ed.) and Tomasik, T.J. (trans.), *Practice of Everyday Life,* Vol.2, University of Minnesota Press. Copyright 1998 by the Regents of the University of Minnesota; *Reading 4.4:* Baudrillard, J. (1996) 'Credit', in Benedict, J. (trans.), *The System of Objects.* Verso; *Reading 4.5:* Lunt, P. and Livingstone, S. (1992) 'Saving and borrowing', *Mass Consumption and Personal Identity: Everyday Economic Experience,* Open University Press; *Readings 5.1 and 5.2:* Mass-Observation (1943), extract from *The Pub and the People: A Worktown Study by Mass-Observation,* Reproduced with permission of Curtis Brown Group Ltd, London on behalf of the Trustees of the Mass-Observation Archive, Copyright © The Mass Observation Archive; *Reading 5.3:* Whitehead, A. (1976) Extracts from 'Sexual antagonism in Herefordshire', *Dependence and Exploitation in Work and Marriage,* Diana Leonard Barker and Sheila Allen (eds), The British Sociological Association; *Reading 6.1:* Young, M. and Willmott, P. (1957) Chapter 8, 'From Bethnal Green to Greenleigh', *Family and Kinship in East London,* Reproduced by permission of Taylor & Francis, Inc./Routledge, Inc.; *Reading 6.2:* Young, M. and Willmott, P. (1957) Chapter 9, 'The family at Greenleigh', *Family and Kinship in East London,* Reproduced by permission of Taylor & Francis, Inc./Routledge, Inc.; *Reading 6.3:* Reynolds, S. (1998) 'Living a dream: acid house and UK rave, 1988–89', *Energy Flash: A Journey through Rave Music and Dance Culture,* Macmillan, London, UK; *Readings 6.4 and 6.5:* Jordan, T. and Taylor, P. (1998) 'A sociology of hackers 1', vol. 46, Blackwell Publishers Limited; *Reading 7.1:* Silva, E.B. (2001) 'Routine methods in narratives of everyday life in families', G. Crow and S. Heath (eds), *Times in the Making,* Palgrave Publishing Ltd; *Reading 7.2:* Johnson, L. and Valentine, G. (1995) 'Wherever I lay my girlfriend, that's my home – the performance and surveillance of lesbian identities in domestic environments', David Bell and Gill Valentine (eds), *Mapping Desire: Geographies of Sexualities,* International Thomson Publishing Services Limited; *Reading A:* Lefebvre, H. (1968) *Everyday Life in the Modern World,* translated by Sacha Rabinovitch (1971), Allen Lane The Penguin Press, published in French as *La vie quotidienne dans le monde moderne* by Éditions Gallimard; *Reading B:* McGuigan, J. (1996) *Culture and the Public Sphere,* Routledge; *Reading C:* Schutz, A. (1944) 'The reality of the world of daily life' in *Collected Papers 1, The Problem of Social Reality,* Martinus Nijhoff, 1967; *Reading D:* Zimmerman, D.H. and Pollner, M. (1970) 'The everyday world as a phenomenon' in Douglas J.D. (ed.) *Understanding Everyday Life: Toward the reconstruction of sociological knowledge,* Routledge & Kegan Paul; *Reading E:* Heller, A. (1970) 'The heterogeneity of everyday life' in *Everyday Life,* translated by G. L. Campbell, Routledge & Kegan Paul, first published in Hungarian as *A mindennapi élat* © Akadémai Kiado; *Reading F:* de Certeau, M. (1984) *The Practice of Everyday Life,* translated by Steven F. Rendell, University of California Press; *Reading G:* Fiske, J. (1992) 'Cultural studies and the culture of everyday life' in Grossberg, L., Nelson, C. and Treichler, P.A. (eds) *Cultural Studies,* Routledge; *Reading H:* Goffman. E. (1959) *The Presentation of Self in Everyday Life,* Penguin Books Ltd; *Reading I:* Garfinkel, H. (1967) *Studies in Ethnomethodology,* Prentice-Hall, Inc; *Reading J:* Nippert-Eng, C.E. (1996) *Home and Work: Negotiating Boundaries through Everyday Life,* The University of Chicago Press; *Reading K:* Hoggart, R. (1957) *The Uses of Literacy,* Penguin Books in association with Chatto & Windus; *Reading L:* Smith, D.E. (1988) *The*

Everyday World as Problematic: A Feminist Sociology, Open University Press; *Reading M:* Felski, R. (1999–2000) 'The invention of everyday life', *New Formations, Cool Moves,* No. 39, Winter 1999–2000, Lawrence & Wishart; *Reading N:* Silverstone, R. (1994) *Television and Everyday Life,* Routledge; *Reading O:* Bourdieu, P. (1979) *Distinction: A Social Critique of the Judgement of Taste,* translated by Richard Nice, Routledge & Kegan Paul, first published in French as *La Distinction: Critique sociale du jugement* by Les Editions de Minuit.

Figures

Figure 1.1: BBC TV Stills Library, Courtesy of Caroline Aherne; *Figure 1.2:* Oil painting by Pieter de Hooch, (1663) *Woman Peeling Apples,* Reproduced by permission of the Wallace Collection, London; *Figure 1.3:* Benjamin Spiers, *Away from the world and its Toils and its Cares,* 1855 Courtesy of Christopher Wood Gallery, London; *Figure 1.5:* From *History of the Machine,* Nordbok International, AB., Gothenburg, 19, p.159; *Figure 1.6:* George Smith, *Into the Cold World,* 1876. Private Collection. Reproduced by kind permission. Photo: Christopher Wood Gallery, London; *Figures 1.7:* From Dolores Hayden, *Seven American Utopias:* The Architecture of Communitarian Socialism (MIT Press, 1976); *Figure 2.1:* (a) Still from *Neighbours,* 1985, Photo: © Pearson Television Limited; (b) Photo: The Advertising Archives; (c) Photo: PA Photos Limited; *Figure 2.2:* Still from *Brief Encounter,* 1945, Photo: Cineguild/Rank (Courtesy Kobal); *Figure 2.3:* Still from *Beautiful Thing,* 1996, Photo: World Productions/Channel Four (Courtesy Kobal); *Figure 3.1:* Roger Mayne; *Figure 3.2:* Les Wilson; *Figure 3.3:* Humphrey Spender; *Figure 3.4:* Martin Parr/Magnum Photos; *Figures 3.5 and 3.10:* Willy Ronis/Rapho/Network; *Figure 3.6:* Photo: Garry Winogrand. Courtesy Fraenkel Gallery, San Francisco; © 1984, The Estate of Garry Winogrand. All rights reserved. Used with permission. The Museum of Modern Art, Photographic Library, New York; *Figure 3.7:* 'Paris Street: Rainy Day', 1876/77. © Charles H. and Mary F. S. Worcester Collection, The Art Institute of Chicago; *Figure 3.8:* Photograph by Umbo (Otto Umbehr) 1902–1980. © Galerie Rudolf Kichen, Cologne. The Metropolitan Museum of Art, Photographic Library, New York; *Figure 3.9:* Photograph by Eugene Atget (1857–1927). Collection Bibliothèque Historique de la Ville de Paris; *Figures 4.1 and 4.2:* Nineteenth-century advertisements for Pears Soap. From: A. McLintock, *Imperial Leather,* 1995, Figs. 5.1 and 8.1. With kind permission of Lever Fabergé; *pp.171–3: The Independent Magazine,* 2 September 2000, pp.11,13,14 and 17. Photographs © Jim Naughten; *p.185:* Drawing by Emily Watson; *Figures 5.1 and 5.2:* Photographs by Humphrey Spender, © Bolton Museum and Art Gallery, from *The Pub and the People: A Worktown Study by Mass-Observation,* 1987, The Cresset Library; *Figures 5.3, 5.5 (both), 5.6 (all):* Photographs courtesy of Tony Watson; *Figure 5.4:* Photograph by Shirley Baker, from Shirley Baker, *Street Photographs: Manchester & Salford,* 1989, Bloodaxe Books, Newcastle upon Tyne; *Figure 5.7:* (a) From *The Pub and the People: A Worktown Study by Mass-Observation,* 1987, The Cresset Library, Reproduced with permission of Curtis Brown Group Limited, London on behalf of the Trustees of the Mass-Observation Archive, © The Mass-Observation Archive; (b) and (c): From Paul Jennings, *The Public House in Bradford, 1770–1970,* Edinburgh University Press, 1996, Figs 10.1, 10.2; *Figure 6.1:* 'Women in Bethnal Green Road, chatting by the market stalls.' Photo: Mary Evans Picture Library; *Figure 6.2:* Photo: Hulton Archive; *Figure 6.3:* Photo: reproduced by permission of Library Services, London Borough of Barking and Dagenham; *Figure 6.4:* Photo: Topham Picturepoint; *Figure 6.5:* From: Sheryl Garratt, *'Adventures in Wonderland: A Decade of Club Culture*, 1998, Headline, London. Photo: © David Swindells; *Figure 6.6:* 'Rave Party, Zurich, 7/8/1999.' Photo: European Press Agency/PA Photos; *Figure 7.1:* Front page of Fabre d'Eglantine's Calendar, 1794. Drawing by Debucourt. © Bibliothèque National de France; *Figure 7.3:* Cartoon by Harold Bird from: *Anti-Suffrage Review*, January 1912 in L. Tickner, *The Spectacle of Women*, Chatto & Windus (1987) © The Women's Library, London Guildhall University; *Figure 7.4:* Published by the Women's Freedom League from the series Sufragettes at Home (**3**), in L. Tickner, *The Spectacle of Women*, Chatto & Windus (1987) © The Museum of London Picture Library; *Figure 7.5:* Photo: Maggie Murray/Format Photographers.

Tables

Tables 4.1 and 4.2: Lunt, P. and Livingstone, S. (1992) 'Saving and borrowing', *Mass Consumption and Personal Identity: Everyday Economic Experience.* Open University Press; *Tables 6.1 and 6.2:* Young, M. and Willmott, P. (1957) Chapter 9, 'The family at Greenleigh', *Family and Kinship in East London*, Reproduced by permission of Taylor & Francis, Inc./Routledge, Inc..

Cover photographs

Front cover, top right, courtesy the Ferns family (photograph by Mike Levers); back cover, top, photograph by Tony Watson. All other photographs © United National Photographers (UNP): clubbing – Martin Pope, curry kitchen – Nigel Hillier, arcade and espresso bar – Matt Griggs, pub – Charles Knight, 'Barbie Street' (back cover) – Mike Poloway.

Every effort has been made to trace all the copyright owners, but if any has been inadvertently overlooked, the publishers will be pleased to make the necessary arrangements at the first opportunity.

Index